CINEMA, THE MAGIC VEHICLE:

A Guide to Its Achievement

by

ADAM GARBICZ

and

JACEK KLINOWSKI

Journey Two:

The Cinema in the Fifties

The Scarecrow Press, Inc.

Metuchen, N.J., & London

1979

ACKNOWLEDGMENTS

The authors wish to thank the film archives and libraries in many countries for their assistance. Much of the research for the book was done at the Information Department, British Film Institute. Special thanks are due to Mr. Akira Shimizu, General Secretary of the Japan Film Library Council, for supplying information on a number of Japanese pictures. We are also grateful to Dr. Timothy Burstein for reading the final manuscript.

Most of the stills in the book were provided by the Stills Library of the National Film Archive, London. We wish to thank Film Polski, Warsaw, for supplying stills for Kanal and Ashes and Diamonds.

FRONTISPIECE

Ikiru: Watanabe sitting on the swing in the playground singing his beloved song on the last evening of his life.

Library of Congress Cataloging in Publication Data (Revised)

Garbicz, Adam.
Cinema, the magic vehicle.

Includes indexes.
CONTENTS: journey 1. The cinema through 1949. --journey 2. The cinema in the fifties.
1. Moving-pictures--Plots, themes, etc. I. Klinowski, Jacek, joint author. II. Title.
PN1997. 8. G35 791. 43'09 75-2183
ISBN 0-8108-0801-3 (v. 1)
ISBN 0-8108-1241-X (v. 2)

Printed in the United States of America

CONTENTS

LIST OF FILMS DISCUSSED*

*This list is divided, by symbols, into three categories that in the opinion of the authors reflect the relative standards of the films discussed: † indicates a film of the first rank; + indicates one of the second rank; no symbol denotes a work of the third rank.

La Strada

PREFACE

The purpose of this book is to give a panoramic view of the achievement of the cinema through the "film-by-film" approach. It is not meant as a history of the cinema, but rather a description of its lasting achievements. We don't deal only with cult-movies or the so-called milestones--there are enough books which analyze these in great detail. While not actually trying to make obscure discoveries we feel that people interested in the cinema need a broad yet detailed description of movies which are good and exciting to watch, especially if relatively little known. The book discusses pictures from all over the world which in our opinion are of interest to a serious student of the cinema.

A need for a radical revision of critical scales and values involved in judging classical movies has been felt for some years. Opinions have originally been established without a perspective, on the spur of the moment, often wrongly. The judgments of many older cinema histories now often seem almost ridiculous, apart from being accompanied by factual errors. This book suggests such a revision. We have looked at the past cinema as it stands today and selected films which appear to us outstanding.

To choose outstanding films is a difficult and controversial task. Often films are assessed from the point of view of the development of cinema in the country of origin and their local importance, by measuring them against the local scale of difficulty. In fact, this point of view is obligatory for a film historian, who without it cannot explain the specific features of the development of the cinema in countries big and small. Global criteria would be something abstract in that context, since the importance of a picture for the country of origin is not always proportional to its artistic quality. And yet there exists something which can be called the "world" standard of a picture. The critics sense this and use it without justifying themselves.

We have applied aesthetic and stylistic criteria to films made all over the world in the course of the 50's. What makes the films of Bergman or Buñuel works of art? What elements of style and film technique are involved? What are the vital components of their personal vision? How do their films compare with the work of other film-makers?

It seemed to us that the most logical way to answer such questions would be to discuss pictures individually, in the form of mini-essays. We have tried not to assume any previous knowledge of the cinema on the part of the reader. This is why a short introduction-synopsis of the most important events in cinema history is included. The text of the critiques always tries to set each film in its historical context and to outline the relevant trends and styles.

We are aware that we will be criticized mainly because of what we have omitted rather than because of what we have included. In our defense we quote the sheer size of our choice (317 pictures discussed for the 50's alone) and also wish to stress the coherence of the choice. The films defend themselves together, as a group chosen using a given set of critical criteria.

The subject matter of the book is feature cinema, i.e., "fiction" films almost always over 60 minutes in projection time. Because of sheer numbers involved we could not include documentaries with no fictional element.

The arrangement of the material in the book is chronological. Titles of films are given according to the year production was completed, which is more relevant than the sometimes much later release date. This arrangement makes it easier to give a coherent account of the development of schools and trends: to show that no work of art is isolated but must always be treated as a product of its time and to draw attention to the exchange of ideas and the interaction of film-makers from different countries. When read together, the essays dealing with the films of any director should give an account of his line of development. Similarly the critiques of westerns, for instance, are so written as to reflect the development of the genre.

The order in which individual pictures are discussed within a given year, although subjective, is in our intention an indication of their relative quality. It is often difficult to justify in so many words aesthetic visual judgments. To give an example, the plot of Stroheim's The Wedding March is to say the least banal while the formal aspect of the film gives strong hints of dilettantism. The greatness of this captivating picture seems to be derived from the difficult to describe, obsessive precision of detail and the compelling, realistic mise en scêne. To quote from this volume, another example of a great film based on a second-rate, melodramatic plot is Becker's Casque d'or.

Each entry is composed of three parts: screen credits, the outline of the plot (except for Shakespearean films and those which are made from massive epic novels and not particularly distinguished --for example Gerasimov's The Quiet Don), and finally a discussion.

The relevance of screen credits is rarely appreciated by authors of film books. What is more, they are seldom given correctly. One feels that the standard of research in cinema studies does not match that for studies in the fields of literature, theatre and music. Yet screen credits can often give more idea of a film than scores of words, and are for this reason of special interest to students of the cinema. We know some who collect them straight from the screen (alas, even there there are mistakes--we have recently seen a film which incorrectly gives the name of a famous French actor appearing in an episodic part). Finally, there is the reference value of film credits, seriously threatened by years of copying from book to book. We have taken great pains to give credits correctly, to check each of them individually against primary sources (often even with the person involved), to check the spelling of foreign words and the uniformity of transcriptions from Cyrillic, Bengali and Japanese, and to check the titles of literary originals. Quite simply, this book provides the most correct list of film credits anywhere to be found.

TECHNICAL NOTES

Screen Credits. The discussion of each film is preceded by its screen credits. These include the names of all the people creatively involved in the making of the film: director, scriptwriter, music composer, art director, editor, producer and the actors. In animated pictures the names of animators are given, and in ballet films the name of the choreographer. If something in the picture which is normally done routinely is of particularly high standard, we give the name of the person responsible. For instance, one must quote Saul Bass as the designer of the credit sequence in Carmen Jones.

In the case of films based on literary works the original title of the book is given in order to make it easier to find, should the reader so wish.

For wide-screen pictures we give the type of wide-screen system (CinemaScope, VistaVision etc.) and for color films the type of color system.

The Spelling of Names. Although the silent film director Victor Sjöström did make several films in America under the name of Seastrom, he was a Swedish director and must be treated as such. Accordingly, the preceding volume quoted only his real name. This practice actually removes ambiguities: the Sjöström who in 1928 directed The Wind in America is clearly the same person who appeared in 1957 as Professor Borg in Bergman's Wild Strawberries in Sweden. Other examples of people who simplified their names while working abroad are: the cinematographer Eugen Schüfftan, the director Max Ophüls, the actor Adolf Wohlbrück and the actress Anna Maria Pierangeli. On the other hand, there are film-makers who lived away from the countries where they were born for most of their creative lives. It is therefore only right to talk about Douglas Sirk and not use the director's real name, Dietlef Sierck. The same applies to the permanently assumed names of film actors: one would not say Norma Jean Mortenson but Marilyn Monroe. When, however, pseudonyms were created whimsically for use in one film only, it is preferable to refer to the person's real name.

Running Times. Films discussed in this volume are, as are most made after 1929, sound films. They must be shown (because of the soundtrack) at a uniform speed of 24 frames per second, corresponding to 90 feet per minute of running time. If a sound film is shown on television the rate of projection is, for purely technical reasons, 25 frames per second. This difference is too slight to be heard on the soundtrack, but in terms of projection time television films run 4 percent faster than in the cinema. This difference must be taken into account when applying the running times quoted in the book to films seen on television.

Many pictures these days (for instance Renoir's The Testament of Dr. Cordelier) are made specifically for television. The table giving length (in feet and meters) together with the corresponding running times (in minutes) for the speeds of 24 and 25 frames per second (used in cinema and television projection, respectively) follows.

References to Titles. Film titles quoted anywhere in the text without the production date in brackets are discussed elsewhere in the book and can be located through the index. Films followed by dates are only mentioned in passing and are generally not enlarged upon. Film titles are underscored and are listed under the names by which they are most commonly known in English-speaking countries. Titles of books are in quotation marks. Sometimes, usually in the case of French productions, only the original title of a film is ever used. Finally, since the original title of every picture is given both in the text and in the index (and thus the problem of mistaken identity does not arise) the book sometimes takes no account of the numerous English language titles which some films have acquired over the years.

COMPARISON OF LENGTH AND RUNNING TIMES
FOR PROJECTION IN CINEMA AND ON TELEVISION

	Cinema		Television	
Mins	Meters	Feet	Meters	Feet
40	1097	3600	1142	3749
41	1124	3690	1171	3843
42	1152	3780	1200	3937
43	1179	3870	1228	4031
44	1207	3960	1257	4124
45	1234	4050	1285	4218
46	1261	4140	1314	4312
47	1289	4230	1343	4406
48	1316	4320	1371	4500
49	1344	4410	1400	4593
50	1371	4500	1428	4687
51	1399	4590	1457	4781
52	1426	4680	1485	4875
53	1453	4770	1514	4968
54	1481	4860	1543	5062
55	1508	4950	1571	5156
56	1536	5040	1600	5250
57	1563	5130	1628	5343
58	1591	5220	1657	5437
59	1618	5310	1685	5531
60	1645	5400	1714	5625
61	1673	5490	1743	5718
62	1700	5580	1771	5812
63	1728	5670	1800	5906
64	1755	5760	1828	6000
65	1783	5850	1857	6093
66	1810	5940	1885	6187
67	1837	6030	1914	6281
68	1865	6120	1943	6375
69	1892	6210	1971	6468
70	1920	6300	2000	6562
71	1947	6390	2028	6656
72	1975	6480	2057	6749
73	2002	6570	2085	6843
74	2029	6660	2114	6937
75	2057	6750	2143	7031
76	2084	6840	2171	7124
77	2112	6930	2200	7218

Mins	Cinema Meters	Cinema Feet	Television Meters	Television Feet
78	2139	7020	2228	7312
79	2167	7110	2257	7406
80	2194	7200	2285	7499
81	2221	7290	2314	7593
82	2249	7380	2343	7687
83	2276	7470	2371	7781
84	2304	7560	2400	7874
85	2331	7650	2428	7968
86	2359	7740	2457	8062
87	2386	7830	2486	8156
88	2414	7920	2514	8249
89	2441	8010	2543	8343
90	2468	8100	2571	8437
91	2496	8190	2600	8531
92	2523	8280	2628	8625
93	2551	8370	2657	8718
94	2578	8460	2686	8812
95	2606	8550	2714	8906
96	2633	8640	2743	9000
97	2660	8730	2771	9093
98	2688	8820	2800	9187
99	2715	8910	2828	9281
100	2743	9000	2857	9375
101	2770	9090	2886	9468
102	2798	9180	2914	9562
103	2825	9270	2943	9656
104	2852	9360	2971	9750
105	2880	9450	3000	9843
106	2907	9540	3028	9937
107	2935	9630	3057	10031
108	2962	9720	3086	10125
109	2990	9810	3114	10218
110	3017	9900	3143	10312
111	3044	9990	3171	10406
112	3072	10080	3200	10500
113	3099	10170	3228	10593
114	3127	10260	3257	10687
115	3154	10350	3286	10781
116	3182	10440	3314	10875
117	3209	10530	3343	10968
118	3236	10620	3371	11062
119	3264	10710	3400	11156
120	3291	10800	3428	11250
121	3319	10890	3457	11343
122	3346	10980	3486	11437
123	3374	11070	3514	11531
124	3401	11160	3543	11625
125	3428	11250	3571	11718
126	3456	11340	3600	11812
127	3483	11430	3629	11906

Mins	Cinema Meters	Cinema Feet	Television Meters	Television Feet
128	3511	11520	3657	12000
129	3538	11610	3686	12093
130	3566	11700	3714	12187
131	3593	11790	3743	12281
132	3621	11880	3771	12375
133	3648	11970	3800	12468
134	3675	12060	3829	12562
135	3703	12150	3857	12656
136	3730	12240	3886	12750
137	3758	12330	3914	12843
138	3785	12420	3943	12937
139	3813	12510	3971	13031
140	3840	12600	4000	13124
141	3867	12690	4029	13218
142	3895	12780	4057	13312
143	3922	12870	4086	13406
144	3950	12960	4114	13499
145	3977	13050	4143	13593
146	4005	13140	4171	13687
147	4032	13230	4200	13781
148	4059	13320	4229	13874
149	4087	13410	4257	13968
150	4114	13500	4286	14062
151	4142	13590	4314	14156
152	4169	13680	4343	14249
153	4197	13770	4371	14343
154	4224	13860	4400	14437
155	4251	13950	4429	14531
156	4279	14040	4457	14624
157	4306	14130	4486	14718
158	4334	14220	4514	14812
159	4361	14310	4543	14906
160	4389	14400	4571	14999
161	4416	14490	4600	15093
162	4443	14580	4629	15187
163	4471	14670	4657	15281
164	4498	14760	4686	15374
165	4526	14850	4714	15468
166	4553	14940	4743	15562
167	4581	15030	4772	15656
168	4608	15120	4800	15749
169	4636	15210	4829	15843
170	4663	15300	4857	15937
171	4690	15390	4886	16031
172	4718	15480	4914	16124
173	4745	15570	4943	16218
174	4773	15660	4972	16312
175	4800	15750	5000	16406
176	4828	15840	5029	16499
177	4855	15930	5057	16593

Mins	Cinema Meters	Cinema Feet	Television Meters	Television Feet
178	4882	16020	5086	16687
179	4910	16110	5114	16781
180	4937	16200	5143	16874
181	4965	16290	5172	16968
182	4992	16380	5200	17062
183	5020	16470	5229	17156
184	5047	16560	5257	17250
185	5074	16650	5286	17343
186	5102	16740	5314	17437
187	5129	16830	5343	17531
188	5157	16920	5372	17625
189	5184	17010	5400	17718
190	5212	17100	5429	17812
191	5239	17190	5457	17906
192	5266	17280	5486	18000
193	5294	17370	5514	18093
194	5321	17460	5543	18187
195	5349	17550	5572	18281
196	5376	17640	5600	18375
197	5404	17730	5629	18468
198	5431	17820	5657	18562
199	5458	17910	5686	18656
200	5486	18000	5714	18750
201	5513	18090	5743	18843
202	5541	18180	5772	18937
203	5568	18270	5800	19031
204	5596	18360	5829	19125
205	5623	18450	5857	19218
206	5650	18540	5886	19312
207	5678	18630	5915	19406
208	5705	18720	5943	19500
209	5733	18810	5972	19593
210	5760	18900	6000	19687
211	5788	18990	6029	19781
212	5815	19080	6057	19875
213	5843	19170	6086	19968
214	5870	19260	6115	20062
215	5897	19350	6143	20156
216	5925	19440	6172	20250
217	5952	19530	6200	20343
218	5980	19620	6229	20437
219	6007	19710	6257	20531
220	6035	19800	6386	20625
221	6062	19890	6315	20718
222	6089	19980	6343	20812
223	6117	20070	6372	20906
224	6144	20160	6400	21000
225	6172	20250	6429	21093
226	6199	20340	6457	21187
227	6227	20430	6486	21281

	Cinema		Television	
Mins	Meters	Feet	Meters	Feet
228	6254	20520	6515	21375
229	6281	20610	6543	21468
230	6309	20700	6572	21562
231	6336	20790	6600	21656
232	6364	20880	6629	21750
233	6391	20970	6657	21843
234	6419	21060	6686	21937
235	6446	21150	6715	22031
236	6473	21240	6743	22125
237	6501	21330	6772	22218
238	6528	21420	6800	22312
239	6556	21510	6829	22406
240	6583	21600	6857	22500

OUTLINE OF THE MAIN EVENTS IN CINEMA HISTORY IN THE FIFTIES

GENERAL COMMENTS. The year 1950 found cinema both stylistically and technically mature. The era of the wide screen began a little later with the giant costumer The Robe (1953), although CinemaScope had been invented way back in 1927 in France by Claude Autant-Lara. Near-perfect color systems were at hand, although the cinema was forced into making almost exclusively color pictures only in the late 60's by the introduction of color television. The feverish work on developing various fanciful cinematographic techniques such as 3-D cinema and even "smell cinema" came in the late 50's, but none of these caught on with the sole exception of the Todd-AO system which employs a 65mm Eastman Colour negative printed onto 70mm wide print stock.

As concerns the language of the cinema, there were available in 1950 sophisticated models of screen expression based on editing (the films of D. W. Griffith, Sergei Eisenstein and Vsevolod Pudovkin) and on fluid description with the camera (the works of Alfred Hitchcock and Jean Renoir). Theories advocating direct reflection of reality (Robert Flaherty, Jean Epstein, the Italian Neorealists) and theories recommending profound visual transformation of reality (the works of Expressionism and Impressionism) were known, as were all the elements of cinematic punctuation, editing and almost the entire aesthetic code of the screen narrative. Cinema had thus at its disposal a sufficient fund of means of expression--and yet by the close of the decade had not become the medium which expresses reality fullest both intellectually and artistically. There were two reasons for this. The first was the strained international situation, particularly in the early 50's, which harmed objectivity and freedom of expression in many countries. The second, much more important reason, was cinema's hereditary complaint--its fairground pedigree. Film-makers tried very hard to prove that cinema was a proper art form; this finally became something of a habit which persisted for long after it ceased to be necessary and drove many serious pictures into stilted academicism. On the other hand, the aesthetic awareness of the general public was not yet such as to encourage film-makers to make individual and nonconformist cinematic statements. The spectator was generally led by the hand, the narrative technique pandered to his idle habits while the more serious cinema often exploited his snobbery for its own aims. It is very interesting to see that the elaborate narrative techniques of the 50's were almost totally forgotten twenty years later.

The majority of the cinema of the 50's was thus smooth, dramatically polished, often dull and superficial--psychologically, pictorially, situationally. It was a cinema which decked itself in the plumes of an art form, which willingly took refuge in historical subjects and in more or less abstract disputes on the interior of man. In the final effect it was a cinema of lonely masters followed by a guild of skillful and well-meaning, if often eclectic, craftsmen. Still, the elite was composed of major directors and thus the 50's brought many brilliant films. All the same, it is true to say that there were no perspectives of development along the existing thematic and stylistic patterns. The cinema of the 50's was a colossus on legs of clay which had either to collapse, or to be replaced by a more sophisticated creation, firmly rooted in current reality.

This state of affairs persisted almost until the close of the decade, when currents of thematic and formal reform in France, England, the U. S. S. R. and Poland began to wash away the foundations of the respectable edifice of Art Cinema.

JAPAN. Only the Japanese cinema did not conform to the above description. The 50's saw the second renaissance of the Japanese film industry, much grander than the first, way back in the 30's, and brought a number of outstanding pictures, firmly rooted in the national cultural tradition and proving their makers' ability to observe the human being. The leading Japanese directors in the 50's were Kurosawa, Ozu, Mizoguchi and Ichikawa, followed by Kinoshita, Naruse, Gosho, Yamamura, Shindo and Imai.

Akira Kurosawa is an admirer of European culture, and his films are fruits of his fascination with the psychological novels of Dostoyevsky (The Idiot), the plays of Shakespeare (The Throne of Blood inspired by "Macbeth") and Gorky (The Lower Depths). Kurosawa is considered the least "Japanese" of the above list of directors. All the same, his work frequently refers to the national cultural tradition and history (as in Rashomon, Seven Samurai and The Hidden Fortress). Kurosawa's towering talent, his humanism and sensitivity (Ikiru) made him a major universal artist.

Yasujiro Ozu was a patient observer of traditional Japanese family life. His films, Tokyo Story, Early Spring and Floating Weeds, are filled with the sense of nostalgic beauty and a resigned reflection on the constantly changing stream of life. Ozu's work, described as a series of haiku, miniature poetic observations of isolated, fleeting events, is characterized by unusual formal restraint and great narrative economy.

Kenji Mizoguchi's work is the highest expression of the traditional jidai-geki genre (period films set before 1868). His realism combined with a painter's eye and the extraordinary sense of atmosphere seen in all his works brought him acclaim in the west. His style is conventional (equating a scene and a shot) and his main theme is the situation of the woman in Japanese society. Mizoguchi's works in the 50's were: The Lady of Musashino, The Life of Oharu, Ugetsu Monogatari, Sansho the Bailiff, A Story from Chikamatsu, The Woman of Rumour, The Empress Yang Kwei-Fei, New Tales of the Taira Clan and Street of Shame.

Kon Ichikawa's sensitivity and his acute aesthetic sense made him find melancholy beauty where it is least expected (The Heart, The Burmese Harp, Punishment Room, The Flame of Torment, Odd Obsessions and Fires on the Plain).

SATYAJIT RAY. The 50's saw the emergence of Satyajit Ray as a major director. In 1950 he bought screen rights to the novel "Pather Panchali" and in 1955 transferred it to the screen using his own money for the purpose. With Pather Panchali and the remaining parts of the "Apu Trilogy," namely Aparajito and The World of Apu, and also with The Music Room Ray showed himself as a gentle humanist, portraying the sensitivity of the Bengalis, their customs and tradition. A very talented director (which is seen, for instance, in the narrative structure of Pather Panchali) Ray added new tones to the scale of expression of the cinema.

FRANCE. In France, the most outstanding director of the 50's was Robert Bresson, whose work such as Diary of a Country Priest, A Man Escaped and Pickpocket is characterized by psychological and moral gravity and pure, ascetic style. Albert Lamorisse was the poet of the French cinema and his films, Crin Blanc and The Red Balloon can be compared with the writings of Saint-Exupéry ("The Little Prince"). Jacques Tati, a Gallic joker, was the most original comedian in the whole of the French cinema. He started from clowning, more primitive even than Mack Sennett's silent grotesques, and his early films, L'Ecole des facteurs (1947) and Jour de fête, were based not so much on the kinetics of movement as on somewhat unsophisticated laughter at human defects. But Tati soon began to follow the tracks of Buster Keaton on the soil of the sound cinema. In Mr. Hulot's Holiday and Mon oncle he achieved interesting results in looking at the absurdities of bourgeois existence and created a comic universe of his own.

There were two more directors in France who are exempt from the criticism applicable to the rest of the French cinema by the originality and integrity of their style. Jacques Becker was an excellent painter of the milieu (sometimes a very specific one), a very good psychologist and a fine craftsman: Casque d'or, Touchez pas au grisbi, Le Trou. But he was enclosed in a world of his own, very much like Max Ophüls in fact--refined and elegant if very far from current reality (La Ronde, Le Plaisir, Lola Montès).

René Clair's films in the 50's dealt with psychological reality rather than everyday reality: Les Belles de nuit is a subtle and charming story about beautiful dreams of a certain music teacher, and Les Grandes manoeuvres a refined love story. In Porte des

Lilas, his best film of the decade, Clair went far beyond the populist convention and demonstrated the traditional values of French culture: warmth towards those who are motivated by love, friendship and striving towards freedom.

By contrast, the remaining major French directors of the earlier period became fossilized and lost touch with contemporary reality (Carné with Les Tricheurs), and even if they dealt with things that are worthwhile and beautiful, this was in the framework of a theatre of shadows, rather than tangible things. Their pictures developed a characteristic anecdotal quality. This is true, for instance of Jean Renoir's Eléna et les hommes, Le Déjeuner sur l'herbe and The Testament of Dr. Cordelier. This is apart from the actual artistic quality of these films; it is the type of cinema which is at issue. Duvivier made La Fête à Henriette--interesting if completely marginal. Christian-Jaque apart from the picaresque Fanfan-la-Tulipe threw in Race for Life, a well-meaning picture about international efforts to save the lives of a crew of a ship who are suffering from food poisoning. Autant-Lara, a pillar of the French cinéma de qualité, was ambitious in his social satires, such as The Red Inn and Scarlet and Black, but as time went by evolved towards libertine pamphlets, while something more radical was called for--for instance his erstwhile Le Diable au corps. Le Chanois was also committed but much too sentimental and referred to individual rather than general problems (Address Unknown). A special place is taken by Clément, a master of film-making, if a director without an individual style. Clément directed such fine pictures as The Secret Game and Gervaise, while the appearance of Knave of Hearts and Plein soleil gave rise to animated controversy on the problem of cynicism.

Perhaps not so far from Clément, but antipodean to the rest, was the French film noir, which can be described as the screen version of Existentialism. Clouzot, a radical anti-bourgeois worn out by illness and by being persecuted for The Crow, portrayed man in dark and pessimistic colors. The Wages of Fear, with its message that only the strong survive in a cruel and hostile world, fits this description very well. This film and Les Diaboliques are characterized by naturalistic style and a great flair for suspense. Other French directors of the film noir were Ciampi (The Heroes Are Tired) and Yves Allégret (The Proud Ones).

The only French director with a social problem and constructive criticism to offer was André Cayatte. At first lawyer, journalist and writer, he regarded cinema as a didactic medium. He was mainly preoccupied with the problems of justice (Let Justice Be Done, We Are All Murderers, An Eye for an Eye); Before the Deluge deals with human consequences of the war scare in France. Cayatte's crusading cinema uses excellent film-making craft and is an example of classical screen rhetoric.

BERGMAN. In Sweden Ingmar Bergman emerged as a director of major stature. After being preoccupied in the late 40's by the problem of adolescence (a period closed with Summer with Monika) Bergman became interested with grave existential problems which he discussed on the screen in a powerful and imaginative way in The Naked Night, The Seventh Seal and Wild Strawberries. A Lesson in Love and Smiles of a Summer Night are bitter-sweet comedies concerned with Scandinavian eroticism, while Brink of Life tells about three women who meet at a maternity clinic.

ITALY. In Italy, the 50's brought several brilliant films from Federico Fellini. Fellini grew up, as it were, on the ashes of Neorealism, the trend which became extinct at the beginning of the decade because of political pressures and the improvement of the economic situation in Italy. Neorealism advocated social reform and its appeal was mostly emotional; it lacked adequate intellectual backing which would enable its ideas to survive in the changed conditions. Still, Neorealism gave the world cinema an awareness of the power of the medium in portraying acute social realities. Fellini is often incorrectly considered a descendant of Neorealism. In fact, he was writing scripts for Neorealist films (such as Rome, Open City) as a scriptwriter-craftsman and before he was able to express freely his temperament and real artistic personality on the screen he did not do anything remarkable--Variety Lights (1950) and

The White Sheik (1952). Fellini's break came with I vitelloni. However, the dominant characteristics of his work (a glittering panopticon being in essence the n-th power of local color and the specific Italian attitude to life) have no more in common with Neorealism than with the whole of Italian art--sensuality and an idealistic search for dignity and goodness in man. This is evident in all of Fellini's films from 1953 onwards: in I vitelloni, La strada, Il bidone, Le notti di Cabiria, right to the celebrated La dolce vita at the close of the decade.

The "rosy Neorealism" combined a Neorealist attention to custom with an optimistic attitude to life. This trend dealt mainly with the problems of young couples in love. Sometimes the films of "rosy Neorealism" had a black ring around them, like in the tragic ending of Dreams in the Drawer. Post-Neorealism, the other remnant of the main trend, did not really contain a social aspect and was telling stories about the troubles of everyday existence, in a mood close to the Japanese shomin-geki genre. A typical post-Neorealist picture is The Railroad Man.

Michelangelo Antonioni began his work in the feature cinema with Cronaca di un amore (1950) and I vinti (1953) but both these pictures were formally imperfect. From 1955 onward, with The Girl Friends and Il grido, Antonioni was able to convince the spectator as to his observations. He had a lot of new things to say about inter-human relationships, and his best works were made in the 60's.

BARDEM. Juan Antonio Bardem seemed for a time a Spanish equivalent of Antonioni. His early films, Grand' Rue and Death of a Cyclist, instantly brought him the acclaim owed to a major director. However, his inventiveness burnt out quite unexpectedly, something which cannot be explained merely by his difficulties with the Spanish censorship. The difference in quality between Bardem's Grand' Rue and any of his films of the 60's is like the gulf between the first and second part of his Sonatas (1959): the first, permeated by the national Spanish spirit, is close to masterpiece, while the second is a complete failure.

BUÑUEL. In 1950 Luis Buñuel emerged, in Mexico, after many years of obscurity. Anarchistic Surrealist of the late 20's and 30's, he challenged the fossilized conventions of the bourgeoisie in the name of respect for nature and the vital forces of man. After 1932 he ceased independent creative work for a lengthy period, returning to it only at the close of the 40's. After two insignificant melodramas he made *Los olvidados.* His next film of note was *Adventures of Robinson Crusoe.* In 1958 he made *Nazarin,* considered by many his finest work.

THE UNITED STATES. Partly under the influence of television, the American cinema became interested in the man in the crowd. This is especially evident in the films of Delbert Mann and his scriptwriter Paddy Chayefsky: *Marty,* *The Bachelor Party* and *Middle of the Night.*

Elia Kazan, in the 50's in his peak period, made a series of fine films which said a lot about man, although not always in relation to current reality: *Panic in the Streets,* *A Streetcar Named Desire,* *Viva Zapata!,* *On the Waterfront,* *East of Eden,* *Baby Doll,* *A Face in the Crowd.* Another important American director was Nicholas Ray with *In a Lonely Place,* *The Lusty Men,* *Johnny Guitar,* *Rebel Without a Cause,* *Bigger Than Life* and *Bitter Victory.* Lumet's *Twelve Angry Men* and Logan's *Picnic* were also influential. Notable American film-makers were Aldrich, Preminger and the socially-conscious directors such as Wise (*I Want to Live*), Brooks (*Blackboard Jungle*), Kramer (*The Defiant Ones*) and Kubrick (*Paths of Glory*). A number of critical pictures (including the last-named) revised the accepted attitudes towards the army and war.

Because of constant production difficulties Orson Welles did not in the 50's have a chance to realize fully his great talent. He was mainly preoccupied with the problems of evil (*Othello,* *Touch of Evil*).

HITCHCOCK. By contrast to Welles, the 50's were the best period in the work of Alfred Hitchcock, who supplemented the mastery of suspense, black humor and dynamic imagery by a maturity of themes and thoughts. Yet he did not cease to provide high-standard screen entertainment or abandon humor, but while entertaining the audience touched upon serious moral and existential problems. This is all the more remarkable, since he seemed to do it as if in passing, or even simply unintentionally. From Strangers on a Train, a film which continues his Nietzschean interests, through The Wrong Man (1957) and Vertigo, pictures which demonstrate how easily human existence can be put into question--Hitchcock proceeded to make The Birds, an allegory on the fragility of mankind's status. Rear Window, To Catch a Thief, The Man Who Knew Too Much and North by Northwest are sustained in a much lighter mood. A situation which recurred throughout Hitchcock's work in the 50's was a lonely man's encounter with unexpected danger; there was also the escalation of a catastrophic mood of fear which would culminate in Psycho. Stylistically Hitchcock came to prefer a slower narrative rhythm than before, although he gradually tempered the use of very long takes on which were based Rope and Under Capricorn. He finally left the studio and showed he could make good use of natural locations. Briefly--Hitchcock created the prototype of the intelligent modern thriller.

THE WESTERN. The genre underwent considerable evolution during the decade. The era of the "superwestern" (to use André Bazin's description of the evolved genre) opened in 1952 with Zinnemann's High Noon. So far the western was interested in pioneering legends, adventure, and generic anecdote spiced with a sense of humor. Now description was replaced by analysis and the characters were judged in the light of their motivation, while many pictures sounded an allegorical tone. Other fine superwesterns to follow High Noon were Delmer Daves's 3:10 to Yuma, John Sturges's The Last Train from Gun Hill and Anthony Mann's The Naked Spur, The Man from Laramie, The Tin Star and Man of the West. All these pictures contain precise characterization of an obstinate protagonist who overcomes mental stress and physical suffering, and give psychological complexity to the negative characters. They often evoke the sense of a lurking, aggressive and powerful evil. Other outstanding westerns were Boetticher's Seven Men from Now and Delmer Daves's

The Last Wagon and Cowboy which reconstructed the 19th-century West as it was. In general, the western attempted to reconsider various psychological, moral and sociological aspects of the 19th-century West, to interpret real events and to give a moral dimension to the choices people then were forced to make.

THE MUSICAL. The musical underwent very dynamic development in the early 50's, moving on from the traditional formula whereby the development of the plot was combined with singing-dancing interludes to the integration of the story, ballet and song. The most advanced attempt at doing this was Gene Kelly's Invitation to the Dance, a feature-length screen ballet; other interesting works were An American in Paris and Singin' in the Rain.

THE SOVIET UNION. After the political upheaval of 1956 important changes took place in the Soviet cinema. The chilling Stalinist period came to an end and more authentic characters began to appear on the screen. The directors who were first to inject a dose of truth into Soviet cinema were Chukhrai with The Forty-First and Kalatozov with The Cranes Are Flying. They were soon followed by other film-makers, mainly young. Soviet cinema began to revise, for the time being only partially, traditional attitudes towards the Revolution, the Second World War (Ballad of a Soldier, Destiny of a Man) and towards contemporary reality.

THE POLISH SCHOOL. Almost simultaneously, and also following a political change, a trend known as the Polish School came into being. Its central concern was also to revise attitudes towards the past. It turned out to be a very thorough revision--on the one hand giving justice to the contribution of non-leftist Poles to the liberation of the country from the Nazi occupation and on the other hand questioning the positive and the negative aspects of national Polish attitudes. The Polish School was very monothematic, but at the same time extremely varied stylistically and intellectually. Each of its leading directors (Wajda with his trilogy consisting of A Generation, Kanal and his masterpiece, Ashes and Diamonds; Munk with Eroica and Cross-Eyed Luck; Kawalerowicz with Baltic Express; Kutz with The Cross of Valour) represented a different creative attitude.

ENGLAND. The "angry young men" posed a bold challenge to stagnating British arts. Particularly in the theatre (John Osborne) and the cinema, where the "Free Cinema" movement led by directors such as Lindsay Anderson, Tony Richardson and Karel Reisz set out to make committed films which took interest in the individual and stressed the significance of everyday life. Free Cinema was referring to the tradition of the British documentary. The revival of British cinema started in the late 50's with Clayton's Room at the Top and Richardson's Look Back in Anger and had its peak in the early 60's.

THE NOUVELLE VAGUE. But the most important and far-reaching changes in world cinema were brought about by the French Nouvelle Vague, the movement which was an expression of rebellion of the young against the old, of middle-class intellectuals against the complacent, comfortable bourgeois flattered by le cinéma de papa ("dad's cinema") as they contemptuously called the contemporary French productions. The film-makers of the Nouvelle Vague developed under the wings of André Bazin, the enormously influential critic and theorist. Bazin was the founder and co-editor (until his premature death in 1958) of "Cahiers du Cinéma," a journal which was at the focus of the movement. Another influence was the American films shown by Henri Langlois at the Cinémathèque Française. The origins of the Nouvelle Vague can be traced back to Alexandre Astruc's celebrated 1948 article introducing the concept of caméra-stylo ("camera-pen") which demanded that film become a completely independent form of expression, formed directly through the camera and not secondary to the verbal ideas of the scriptwriter. Astruc wrote his article while under the impression of Leenhardt's Les Dernières vacances; this film and Astruc's own Le Rideau cramoisi (1952) were precursors of the Nouvelle Vague. The principal tenet of the movement was spontaneous representation of life on the screen, which culminated later in cinéma-vérité ("candid camera"), the trend professing directorial non-interference in reality. From the economic point of view the idea was cheapness (Chabrol, one of the group, made his first film on inherited money). Film technique of the Nouvelle Vague was characterized by a highly mobile camera, long takes, the use of subjective narrative, stressed poetic atmosphere and often perverse irony, a certain free-thinking irreverence. Stylistically the Nouvelle Vague was very varied, although ideologically it was entirely inscribed in the liberal sphere of ideas, the common denominator being hatred of the bourgeoisie. However, the importance of the movement rests not in its ideology but in its destruction of old stereotypes, in liberating expression, demonstrating that the audience is willing to see on the screen problems of current reality and to discuss them. In the beginning the movement did not have a program; it was only in May 1959, during the Cannes Film Festival, that a group of young film-makers signed the "Manifesto of the Nouvelle Vague." Between 1959 and 1960 some sixty-seven directors made their debut in France. The most important were: Chabrol with Le Beau Serge and Les Cousins, Godard with A bout de souffle, Franju with La Tête contre les murs and Eyes Without a Face, Truffaut with Les Quatre cents coups, Rohmer with Le Signe du lion. Malle, who debuted a year earlier with Lift to the Scaffold, joined the movement with Les Amants.

Opinions vary as to the membership of the Nouvelle Vague; the fact remains that Alain Resnais, the most important director to debut in feature film in 1959 (with his very influential Hiroshima mon amour) was not among the signatories of the Manifesto. Resnais was stylistically different from Bazin's followers in that he based his narrative on editing (which according to Bazin "disrupts reality") instead on long fluid takes. Throughout his work Resnais's main preoccupation was with memory, its whims and resources and its relationship to the present.

Despite leaving behind only a handful of really outstanding directors (essentially the ones mentioned above), the Nouvelle Vague allowed the cinema to be itself--liberating it from pomposity and academicism, and transforming it into a living art form.

1950

RASHOMON (Rashō-mon) Akira Kurosawa

Script: Shinobu Hashimoto and Kurosawa, after two stories, "Yabu-no naka" (In a Brushwood) and "Rashō-mon" (Rashō Gate), by Ryunosuke Akutagawa. Photography: Kazuo Miyagawa. Music: Fumio Hayasaka. Art Direction: So Matsuyama. Cast: Toshiro Mifune (Tajomaru), Masayuki Mori (Takehiro), Machiko Kyo (Masago), Takashi Shimura (Woodcutter), Minoru Chiaki (Priest), Kichijiro Ueda (Commoner), Daisuke Kato (Policeman), Fumiko Homma (Medium).

Masaichi Nagata for Daiei, Japan. 7894 ft., 88 mins.

Medieval Japan; a time of famine and civil turmoil. Three men, a woodcutter, a commoner and a Buddhist priest, shelter from the rain under the gate to the city of Kyoto. The woodcutter describes how he found the body of a nobleman in the wood. We are given four different versions of what had happened. Tajomaru, the notorious bandit, was arrested and confessed to the murder of the man and the rape of his wife. He tells how he met them in the forest, was inflamed by the wife's beauty and raped her having first tied up her husband. Afterwards the woman insisted that she could not bear the thought of two men being alive who had witnessed her shame. In the ensuing duel Tajomaru killed the husband. The wife's story is different. After Tajomaru raped her, she freed her husband. When he treated her with contempt, she killed him and then fainted. The dead samurai conveys his evidence through a medium. After the rape the wife begged Tajomaru to kill the husband. The bandit left her, disgusted. She ran away while the nobleman killed himself with a dagger. Finally, the woodcutter tells

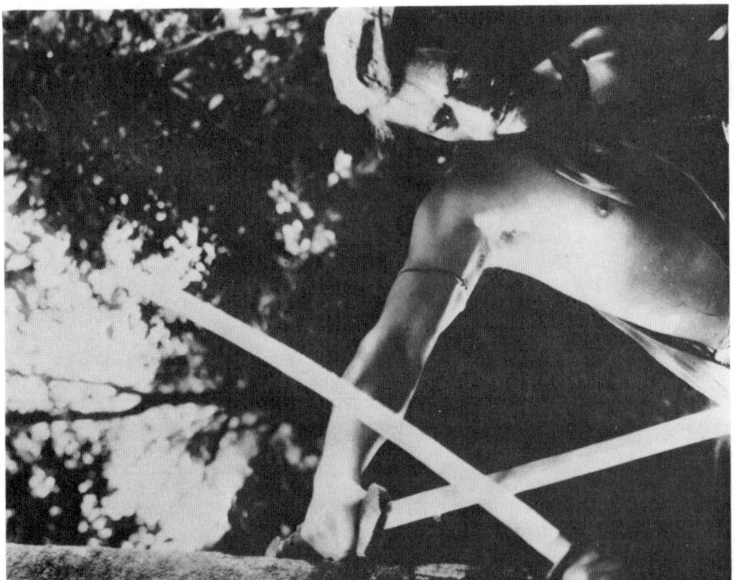

Rashomon

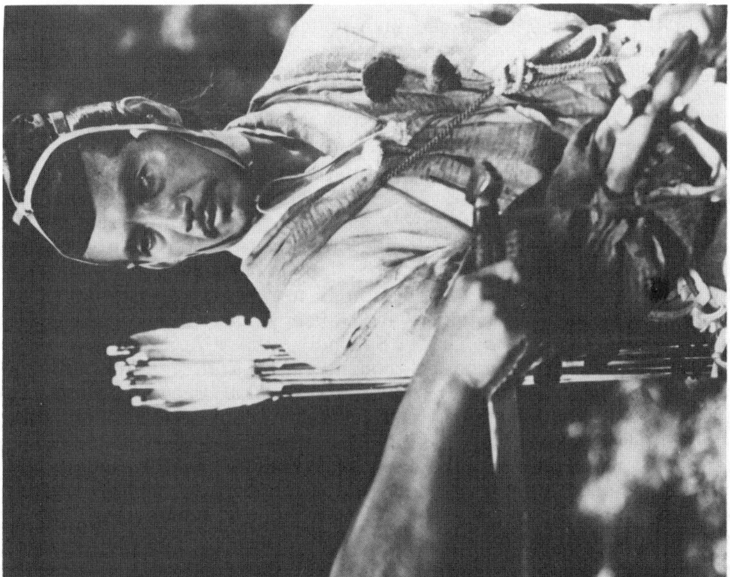

Rashomon

his story. The husband was a coward, and the wife goaded the two men to a fight in which he met his death. It becomes clear that the woodcutter stole the wife's dagger.

In the epilogue the three men under the gate hear the cry of an abandoned baby. The commoner tries to steal the baby's clothes, but the woodcutter offers to take care of it, thus restoring the priest's dwindling faith in mankind.

Rashomon was received as a revelation at the 1951 Venice Film Festival. It won the Golden Lion and virtually introduced the Japanese cinema to the west. The film continues to exert peculiar fascination over audiences all over the world. The Japanese themselves, who do not seem to rate the film particularly highly, do not understand why it caused such a stir. In fact there are very good reasons for this. Firstly, Rashomon is a superb allegory about failings and weaknesses of mankind--and such universal parables easily overcome their national setting. Secondly, the film coincides with certain developments in modern thought. The 20th-century philosophers, particularly Bertrand Russell and Gottlob Frege, probed the complex problems surrounding truth and falsehood and studied their relationship with observable reality; the physicists discovered the "uncertainty principle" and the laws of relativity, while modern art took an increased interest in exploring the notorious misfit between illusion and reality. As a result, it suddenly became clear that reality is less well defined than was once thought. Rashomon reflects these profound intellectual problems in mature yet accessible artistic form. The film's fascination relies partly on posing questions of which people are deeply aware, even if they are not able to formulate them. What is reality? What is the basis of human experience? What is the real truth in this story of rape and murder? Kurosawa, whose primary concern was not to tantalize people with existential puzzles, answers that there is no "real" truth about the events, and the film demonstrates that one's particular "kind of truth" depends on one's station in life and vested interests. Donald Richie remarked: "Kurosawa does not question truth. He questions reality."

This message is communicated through the film's rich symbolism and the main visual metaphors: sun shines directly into the camera lens as the woodcutter journeys through the forest, the dagger thrown by the wife falls point first and quivers, sunlight is reflected by the blade of a sword. The forest itself serves as a symbol of the complexity of reality. The great photographer Miyagawa created many impressionistic, poetic images: the cool breeze which wakes the bandit, the whirling sleeves of the medium, the wife idly moving her hand in the stream, the desperate fight between the two men. The photography impresses with masterly use of visual contrasts and great pictorial economy. There are violent camera movements, fast cutting (the film has 420 separate shots) and the use of wipe, the director's favorite tool of cinematic punctuation.

In contrast to Kurosawa's earlier films, social angle is virtually absent. Everyone is seen as having a fixed station in life, which is not questioned but used as an element in an intellectual dispute. But Rashomon ends on an unmistakable humanist note. The film is outstandingly acted by its small cast: Machiko Kyo, beautiful, elusive and mysterious, epitomizes oriental inscrutability; Toshiro Mifune is the brutish and savage Tajomaru; Masayuki Mori --the proud samurai; Takashi Shimura--the devious but kind-hearted woodcutter; while Fumiko Homma makes a great impression as the medium. A work of passion, power and beauty, Rashomon is one of the masterpieces of modern cinema.

DIARY OF A COUNTRY PRIEST (Journal d'un curé de campagne)
Robert Bresson

Script: Bresson, from the novel by Georges Bernanos. Photography: Léonce-Henry Burel. Music: Jean-Jacques Grünenwald. Art Direction: Pierre Charbonnier. Cast: Claude Laydu (Curé d'Ambricourt), Marie-Monique Arkell (Countess), André Guibert (Curé de Torcy), Jean Riveyre (Count), Nicole Ladmiral (Chantal), Nicole Maurey (Louise), Martine Lemaire (Séraphita), Serge Bento (Mitonnet), Jean Danet (Olivier), Antoine Balpêtré (Dr. Delbende), Léon Arvel (Fabregard), Yvette Etiévant (Housekeeper), Gaston Séverin (Canon), Bernard Hubrenne (Dufréty), Germaine Stainval (Café owner), Gilberte Terbois (Mlle Dumouchal).

Léon Carre for Union Générale Cinématographique, France. 10,800 ft., 120 mins.

There are only a handful of films which penetrate to the very foundations of the Christian faith as does Bresson's Diary of a Country Priest--perhaps only Rossellini's Francis, God's Jester (made by coincidence in the same year but so completely different in tone) and Dreyer's The Word. Bresson makes films in his own time, but what he does he does well: in the fifteen years following Les Dames du Bois de Boulogne he made only three pictures, and they are all great. He now abandons the polished elegance of that society melodrama for the severe style which became his hallmark.

The young parish priest meets with hostility and distrust from the inhabitants of the grim village of Ambricourt. Lonely and tormented by stomach pains, he is comforted only by the genial Vicar of Torcy. He tries to intervene in the deep conflicts at the local château. The Count is having an affair with his daughter's governess, the Countess still mourns over the death of her infant son many years ago, while the daughter, disenchanted and angry, contemplates suicide. The priest helps the Countess to rediscover her faith; she

Diary of a Country Priest

dies in peace the same night. He is blamed for the death but refuses to come to his own defense by producing the Countess's letter. He goes to consult a doctor at Lille who diagnoses advanced cancer of the stomach. The priest dies in an attic inhabited by an old friend, an unfrocked priest and his mistress. His dying words are: "All is Grace."

Bresson's aim was maximum fidelity to the famous novel by Georges Bernanos. Every line of dialogue comes from the book, whose text is never condensed, but cut. Minor characters are eliminated. Bresson interviewed over 100 candidates for the main part (non-believers were ruled out) before finally choosing 24-year-old Claude Laydu. He then prepared the actor for the part by talking to him about it every Sunday for a year. Laydu totally identified with the character he portrayed. Reportedly he starved himself during shooting to get the appearance of a sick man. Even the clothes he wore were borrowed from actual priests.

The way the novel is used inspires fundamental questions on the relationship between literature and the cinema. The film is arranged as a series of episodes which start with shots of a diary's pages. This sets the monotone mood. Often text is set over the image, which creates a fascinating effect. André Bazin commented: "Bresson disposes once and for all of that commonplace of criticism according to which image and sound should never duplicate one another. The most moving moments in the film are those in which text and image are saying the same thing, each however in its own way. The sound never serves simply to fill out what we see."

He was not a perfect parish priest: he was too proud, perhaps too severe with himself; he did not have the strength, the experience or the genial temperament of the Vicar of Torcy. He may have had momentary doubts. But he staked everything on his faith. The priest's last words are the key to the film's message: faith as the ultimate reality. Death is merely a deliverance. Bresson's interests are not in the psychology, but in the soul. Thus psychological analysis is abandoned, and the inner conflicts are never outwardly revealed, there is no development of character (although the Vicar of Torcy with his common sense does provide an alternative attitude towards priesthood), and no symbolism at all. Diary of a Country Priest was shot entirely on location. The visual key to the film is greyness, and the grim landscapes, bare trees and overcast skies above the desolate parish are shown in delicate monotone photography.

The last image of the film is now famous: a 90-second shot of a plain cross, slightly out-of-focus, which dominates the screen while the voice of the Vicar of Torcy describes his friend's death. A great, unforgettable elliptic image of the ultimate sacrifice. Thus the spiritual has taken over from the physical. Bazin again: "At the point which Bresson has reached, the image can become more eloquent only by disappearing altogether. The spectator has been led, step by step, towards that night of the senses of which the only expression is a light on a blank screen.... Just as the blank page of Mallarmé and the silence of Rimbaud is language at its highest state, the screen--free of images and handed back to literature, is the triumph of cinematographic realism."

Only perhaps the overly emotional, effusive music is a flaw in this austere film. The words of Bernanos, the grey vistas of provincial France, Laydu's expressive face combine to create an image of unassailable dignity, a supreme example of the cinema of the interior of man.

MIRACLE IN MILAN (Miracolo a Milano) Vittorio De Sica

Script: Cesare Zavattini, De Sica, Suso Cecchi D'Amico, Mario Chiari and Adolfo Franci, from the novel, "Totò il Buono," by Zavattini. Photography: Aldo Graziati. Music: Alessandro Cicognini. Art Direction: Guido Fiorini. Cast: Francesco Golisano (Totò), Brunella Bovo (Edvige), Paolo Stoppa (Rappi), Guglielmo Barnabò (Mobbi), Emma Gramatica (Lolotta), Anna Carena (Marta), Alba Arnova (Statue), Flora Cambi (Unhappy Girl in Love), Virgilio Riento (Sergeant), Arturo Bragaglia (Alfredo), Erminio Spalla (Gaetano), Riccardo Bertazzolo (Athlete), Angelo Prioli (Commandant), Francesco Rissone (Second Commandant).

Societá Produzioni De Sica/ENIC, Italy. 8983 ft., 100 mins.

Miracle in Milan is a present-day fairytale, in which a child's naive vision of the world collides with the stark facts of life and the imperfections of human nature. De Sica has turned one of Zavattini's most personal scripts into a rich, kaleidoscopic panorama of the problems facing Italy in the crucial period of the early 50's. *Miracle in Milan* is a poetic comment on the social tensions in Italy, a summing up of the style and achievement of Neorealism and an attempt to go beyond the basic factographic principles of the movement, a meditation on the effectiveness of remedying the ills of a political system by art and, finally, a semi-philosophical attempt to consider the prospects of man within modern civilization. It is a work of spiritual dilemma, a work on the crossroads.

Totò the Good, the hero of the film, is a foundling who was taken care of by a kindly old lady and brought up to be kind and gentle. Evangelically pure, unaware of the rules of struggle for survival, Totò is confronted with ruthless striving for gain. Like an apostle of virtue he goes among the Milan poor, to become their leader and benefactor. He creates a happy microcosm of freedom and peace, and initiates the building of a housing estate. But happiness is unattainable: in the crowd of beggars who were all equal when at the bottom, class divisions soon begin to appear. The settlement itself is brutally attacked by big capital when oil is struck there. Totò exchanges humility for struggle, but in vain. He and his comrades are doomed to failure: all that remains for them to do is to fly away on broomsticks to a better land, a land without social divisions and barriers of property, where "good morning" really means good morning.

How is one to interpret the ending? It sounds like a whisper of despair. De Sica himself would not acknowledge this, but still, for the sake of truth, he preserves it within the picture, closing his eyes in a gesture of the now merely irrational hope. A realist, he knows that his teaching of goodness is a utopian concept. It is utopian even among the poor. Yes, the system is wrong, but so is man himself when isolated from it. Thus despite all the radicalism of the picture reaching a climax in the finale, De Sica, who was because of Miracle in Milan sharply attacked by the Italian Right, stops short of declaring himself a Communist.

The style of Miracle in Milan makes it one of the most original works in the history of cinema: the sharp realist view of the world is here combined with a fairytale quality of a naive painting; social detail--with a fine if somewhat over-smart symbolism; a calm and nostalgic mood of the Milan suburbs--with a venomous jibe at the bourgeoisie; intellect with simple-heartedness; grandiloquence with lyricism. Of course, some ingredients of less than prime quality must have stolen into this fanciful layer-cake. Such as almost the entire satirical content of the film, jarring in its mixture of sharpness and sterility. But that which is decisive for the deeply moving overall effect surely belongs to the pure world of poetry, and a number of episodes (the funeral of Totò's adoptive mother, the beggars watching the sunrise, the aria of a suicide) are the quintessence of screen beauty. It was achieved with the help of one of the greatest cameramen of the Italian cinema--the prematurely deceased Aldo Graziati, known as G. R. Aldo.

FRANCIS, GOD'S JESTER (Francesco, giullare di Dio)
Roberto Rossellini

Script: Rossellini, Federico Fellini, Felix Morlion and Antonio Lisandro, inspired by "I fioretti" (Little Flowers), a collection of stories and legends about St. Francis of Assisi (San Francesco d'Assisi, or rather St. Giovanni Francesco Bernardone, 1181?-1226) and the Franciscan monks, completed in the 14th century. Photography: Otello Martelli. Music: Renzo Rossellini. Art Direction: Virgilio Marchi. Cast: Brother Nazario (Francesco Bernardone), Aldo Fabrizi (Tivanno Nicolaio), Arabelle Lemaître (Chiara), and the monks of Nocere Inferiore Monastery.

Francis, God's Jester

Angelo Rizzoli, Italy. 93 mins.

Italy in the early 13th century. Violent conflicts between individual cities tore the country apart, leading to famine and pestilence. Only the powerful abbeys resisted the upheaval, protected by their haughty spiritual immunity. At the same time, corruption and greed were rife among the clergy. A need for change was felt within the Church: the ideals of life according to Christ's teaching, in humility, purity and evangelic poverty were seen to be lost. The many religious sects which appeared as a result were ferociously persecuted by Rome. And then, when everything was enveloped in chaos--St. Francis of Assisi came. He did not come to fight heresies or to defend dogmas. He did not have theological erudition. He brought no more than a great and warm heart, and a message of love and joy which was to triumph over despair and discontent. Franciscan monks told the story of the remarkable life of their founder in the delightful book called "Little Flowers," and Rossellini, aware of the modern relevance of the Franciscan message, transferred the story to the screen, retaining its episodic structure and the fairytale quality.

Francesco comes back together with other friars to Santa Maria degli Angeli from Rome through the rain; Brother Ginepro gives his habit to a poor traveller and returns naked; Giovanni the Simple, wishing to be like Francesco, joins the community; Sister Chiara (St. Clare) visits the monks; Brother Ginepro cuts the foot off a pig to feed a sick brother; Francesco meets a leper and kisses him; Brother Ginepro goes off to preach and through his humility overcomes the cruelty of Nicolaio, the tyrant of Viterbo; Francesco tells Brother Leone that bearing injuries in silence is an example of perfect joy and sends his brothers out to preach far and wide. He spins them round on a crossroads until they all fall down; each sets off down the road in the direction in which he has fallen.

"This is a film about harmony. There is perfect accord between Man and Nature, between heaven and earth. The earth, the fire and the water are no longer man's enemies ... but are his allies and accomplices." In such words José Luis Guarner described Francis, God's Jester. It is a tender and lyrical film--yet never sentimental. Rossellini succeeded in rendering ideally the very spirit of the Franciscan teaching, with its disarming, angelic simplicity and perfect charity. Ginepro wants to give his own foot to "brother pig" in return for the one he has cut off to feed a sick companion. Seraphic and childlike and yet made of flesh and blood, St. Francis himself is both a man of God and an Italian with the attendant characteristic spontaneity and ostentation of feelings. The recurrent motif of juggling refers to the monks' basic naivety, their childish joys as God's simpletons.

Francis, God's Jester is also a fascinating piece of historical cinema--if by the adjective "historical" one means "true to the spirit and mentality of a bygone epoch." The intellectual and emotional climate of medieval Italy, with its violence and brutality, is captured perfectly. Consider only the episode, both humorous and frightening, of Brother Ginepro's encounter with the tyrant Nicolaio, encased in armor so heavy that he cannot move. It is interesting that Rossellini does this without the use of the décor of the time; architecture is symbolized rather than shown--while the clothes, the monks' habits, are essentially timeless. Strangely, Rossellini found it easier to evoke the spirit of the 13th century than that of the Second World War in The General della Rovere. He was to make use of his sense for the essence of history in the films he made for Italian television in the 60's and 70's.

An amazingly modern picture, Francis, God's Jester was not appreciated at the time of its release. Now it appears as a great movie.

SUNSET BOULEVARD Billy Wilder

Script: Charles Brackett, Wilder and D. M. Marshman Jr., based on the story "A Can of Beans," by Brackett and Wilder. Photography: John F. Seitz. Music: Franz Waxman; also Richard Strauss ("Dance of the Seven Veils" from "Salome"). Art Direction: Hans Dreier and John Meehan. Cast: William Holden (Joe Gillis), Gloria Swanson (Norma Desmond), Erich von Stroheim (Max von Mayerling), Nancy Olson (Betty Schaefer), Fred Clark (Sheldrake), Jack Webb (Artie Green), Lloyd Gough (Morino), Franklyn Farnum (Undertaker), Cecil B. De Mille, Hedda Hopper, Buster Keaton, H. B. Warner, Ray Evans, Anna Q. Nilsson, Jay Livingston (Themselves), Larry Blake (First Finance Man), Charles Dayton (Second Finance Man).

Charles Brackett for Paramount, U.S.A. 9881 ft., 110 mins.

Sunset Boulevard, Hollywood. Norma Desmond, a once-famous queen of the silent screen, lives in an eerie, brooding mansion attended only by Max von Mayerling, once her director and now her butler. Everyone thinks she has been dead for years. Yet she lives--refusing to acknowledge the fact that her fame died with the coming of the sound cinema, and spinning fantastic dreams of a comeback. She says wistfully: "I am big, it's the pictures that have got small. We didn't need dialogue. We had faces then," and her illusions are sustained by the butler who secretly writes letters which she believes come from her fans. While escaping creditors a struggling young scriptwriter dodges the car he cannot pay for into the drive of Norma's house. She employs Joe to work on a dreadful script which she had been writing for years. The script has her cast as Salome. Joe accepts, partly out of curiosity, partly because he needs money. But Norma becomes more and more dependent on him, showers him with presents and, with an attempted suicide, forces him back when he wants to leave. But Joe sneaks out at night to work on a script of his own and falls in love with a girl. When he eventually decides to leave Norma for good he tells her the truth about her planned comeback. She kills him for shattering her dream. Then, having lost her mind, she majestically descends the grand staircase to meet the news cameramen and the police; she believes they are applauding her return to the screen.

Wilder's pictures examined various aspects of American mythology; but Sunset Boulevard tackles the greatest myth of all. Told in a flashback by a dead man floating at dawn in a lighted swimming pool, the picture offers a devastating vision of Hollywood, a haunting, claustrophobic, sinister and unforgiving reassessment of its past glories. Wilder and Brackett set out to dissect the "star system" which Hollywood built so assiduously for whole decades. The peculiar fascination of their film is in great part based on the fact that real people play themselves. Norma, played by Gloria Swanson, a real diva of the silent screen, visits the real Cecil B. De Mille on the set of a real picture--Samson and Delilah (1949), a ridiculous and elaborate spectacular. When the butler projects her famous film--it is Queen Kelly, in which Gloria Swanson really starred, and which was really directed by Erich von Stroheim who plays the butler. Buster Keaton, the great comic of the silent cinema gives a vignette appearance as a player in a mournful game of bridge with a group of other aging stars. He is described in the dialogues as "a wax figure" and says in the whole film just one, highly significant word--"pass." These scenes of Sunset Boulevard have a curious déjà vu quality.

The film derives much of its power from the formal principle of contrast: between the glorious, larger-than-life past and the sober present; between fantasy and reality. In juxtaposing a banal and cynical young writer and a half-crazy aging diva, Wilder criticizes both the casual vulgarity of today and the ostentatious poses of the past. Norma's mansion is full of relics of her great days: a 1932 model car upholstered in leopard skin, a bed in the shape of a gondola, an enormous organ in the drawing room. Norma's pet chimpanzee is buried in a coffin lined with red satin. Gloria Swanson managed in Sunset Boulevard just the feat her heroine was dreaming of: she survived, spanning the past of Hollywood with its present and showing herself as a versatile, accomplished actress. The scene of Norma's being recognized by the old employees of the studio is so oddly touching because it could very well have been real. Other remarkable moments of Sunset Boulevard include her impersonating Charlie Chaplin; the scene in which she sits, transfixed, watching her past self on the screen, and of course the mesmerizing final scene of an entrée which is also an exit. Pathetic and grandiose, an epitome of the madness and mythology of a past era, Swanson gave a captivating performance with which she later became identified in popular memory. Billy Wilder made a remarkable journey in time; Sunset Boulevard is not only his most important and independent work, but also the most ambitious film ever made about Hollywood.

LET JUSTICE BE DONE (Justice est faite) André Cayatte

Script: Cayatte and Charles Spaak. Photography: Jean Bourgoin. Music: Raymond Legrand. Art Direction: Jacques Colombier. Cast: Claude Nollier (Elsa Lundestein, the accused), Antoine Balpêtré (Presiding Judge), Valentine Tessier (Mme. Micoulin), Raymond Bussières (Félix Noblet), Jacques Castelot (Gilbert de Montesson), Jean Debucourt (Michel Caudron), J.-P. Grenier (Jean-Luc Flavier), Noël Roquevert (Théodore Andrieux), Michel Auclair (Serge Kremer), Marcel Pérès (Evariste-Nicolas Malagré), Agnès Delahaie (Nicole Vaudremont).

Silver Films, France. 9603 ft., 107 mins.

Let Justice Be Done is the first film of the famous courthouse series in which André Cayatte, a former lawyer and journalist, subjects the mechanism of the judicial system to moral scrutiny. Cayatte did not immediately touch upon the dilemmas inherent in his previous profession; in his early films, during the eight years since his directorial debut, his work was commercial and second-rate. But now, his cinematic craft mature, Cayatte institutes his own proceedings against Official Justice and the society which uses it as an excuse to shirk moral responsibility for individuals in collision with the law. Let Justice Be Done deals with the problems of euthanasia. A woman doctor is accused of the murder of her incurably ill lover--she finally agreed to his pleas to be given a fatal dose of morphine. There is, however, some doubt as to her real motives, as the dead man left her all his money, and because she was at the same time involved with another man. Her guilt is to be decided by the jury, in theory the most democratic part of the judicial system. And yet this impartiality is but an illusion, says Cayatte. The jury's verdict is no more than the resultant of the views of a group of people; all are unbiased in theory, but in fact each of them enters the courthouse with the burden of personal experiences and views. An individual cannot be absolutely impartial in his judgment, and neither can a randomly assembled group of people. The accused is finally sent to prison, but the verdict is the result of chance: the five-year sentence would have given way to "not guilty" if one of the jurors had been through a personal tragedy (and a subsequent change of mind) a mere one day earlier. The argument put forward by the director is deeply moving in its matter-of-factness, the functionality of the realistic narrative, the emotional involvement. The fact that Cayatte goes too far in his eloquence, criticizing the system in force without suggesting alternative solutions, does not lessen the humanist value of his protest. This is because the main strength of the film lies not in the reiteration of the old truth that absolute justice is unattainable, but in the appeal to consciences, an exhortation to cherish moral sensitivity when faced with each individual situation, to relentless observance of the spirit of the law and not its letter.

LOS OLVIDADOS (The Young and the Damned) Luis Buñuel

Script: Buñuel and Luis Alcoriza. Photography: Gabriel Figueroa. Music: Rodolfo Halffter, from themes by Gustavo Pittaluga. Art Direction: Edward Fitzgerald. Editing: Carlos Savage. Cast: Alfonso Mejía (Pedro), Roberto Cobo ("El Jaibo"), Estela Inda (Marta, Pedro's mother), Miguel Inclán (Don Carmelo, the blind man), Mario Ramírez ("Ojitos"-"Big Eyes"), Alma Delia Fuentes (Meche), Efraín Arauz ("Cacarizo"-"Pockface"), Javier Amezcua (Julián), Francisco Jambrina (Farm School Director), Jesús García Navarro (Julián's father), Jorge Pérez ("Pelón").

Oscar Dancigers for Ultramar Films, Mexico. 8020 ft., 88 mins.

This film was included in the first volume, but we have now established that it was made in 1950 (shooting was between February 6 and March 9, 1950; the Mexican premiere was on November 9 of the same year). Revised credits for Los olvidados are given above; discussion of the film can be found in "Journey One" on pages 506-7.

MISS JULIE (Fröken Julie) Alf Sjöberg

Script: Sjöberg, from the play by August Strindberg. Photography: Göran Strindberg. Music: Dag Wirén. Art Direction: Bibi Lindström. Cast: Anita Björk (Miss Julie), Ulf Palme (Jean), Märta Dorff (Kristin), Anders Henrikson (Count), Lissi Alandh (Berta), Inger Norberg (Julie as a child), Jan Hagerman (Jean as a child), Ake Fridell (Robert), Inga Gill (Viola), Ake Claesson (Doctor), Kurt-Olof Sundström(Fiancé), Max von Sydow (Groom).

Rune Waldekranz for Sandrew Bauman, Sweden, 90 mins.

In adapting August Strindberg's 1888 stage play, Sjöberg tried to achieve much more than a perfectly cinematic version of the Swedish classic of world literature. To quote his own words, he wanted to X-ray the human soul, to enter the jungle of complexes, inhibitions and contradictory emotions in order to determine the

Miss Julie

psychological present by way of examining the past. The result is remarkable: Strindberg's drama is framed in a rich visual form, overwhelming with its sensual, hallucinatory, catastrophic climate and the impressively consistent psychological portrayal of the heroine.

The play itself was, of course, very fine starting material from this point of view. Strindberg's Miss Julie is one of the fullest female characters in the whole of 19th century literature. This beautiful aristocrat, intelligent and full of life, carries on her shoulders an unbearable onus of puritan upbringing which stifles her natural human instincts. To boot, she carries the heritage of the frustration of her mother, whose futile attempts at breaking out of the limitations of her station in life and at achieving understanding with her husband ended in madness and setting fire to the family residence. Julie rebels in a similar way, again in vain. The action of the film takes place on Midsummer Eve at a country estate. The Count has gone away and the folk of the manor are celebrating the festival. Julie, the Count's daughter, is bored. She humiliates her fiancé and begins to flirt with her father's valet, Jean. Jean tells her how he has been fascinated by her since he was a child. Finally Julie gives herself to him. She tells Jean of her unhappy life. A few minutes after her father's return Julie kills herself, unable to bear the disgrace and humiliation. Like a moth she perishes in the flame of freedom which fascinated her so much.

The film preserves nearly all the original dialogue; it has to since the play runs for only about 50 minutes (and involves only three characters: Julie, Jean the valet and Kristin the cook). Miss Julie is the peak of Sjöberg's achievement as a director: he developed the drama using purely cinematic means, saturated it with brutal poetry and spiritual anxiety, brought out its psychological undertones not only via the composition of the frame, visual metaphors, feverish movements of the camera and dissolves, but also by the very character of the staging of many situations. The most distinct example of this is the bold manner of handling flashbacks, materialized as the background of current events. A similar device had already been employed by Duvivier in Un Carnet de bal and by Lean in Brief Encounter, but Sjöberg used it with full consistency. Actually, not only flashbacks but also the heroine's thoughts (in the conditional mood) are represented visually in this way. Göran Strindberg, the cameraman (and August's grandson) responded excellently to the director's requirements and equipped the film with wonderful photography employing a wide range of light and shade--equally ravishing in expressing the breath of Nature in the locations and in the dark interiors used as background for the luminous silhouette of the heroine. And if one of the finest Swedish films of the pre-Bergman era does not achieve the fullness of expression, the author of the play is more to blame than the director of the film. Sjöberg was not able to break completely through Strindberg's fatalistic coolness, and the excellent, vivid roles of Anita Björk and Ulf Palme could not change the fact that the film is somewhat lacking in human warmth.

IN A LONELY PLACE Nicholas Ray

Script: Andrew Solt, based on a novel by Dorothy B. Hughes and an adaptation by Edmund H. North. Producer: Robert Lord. Photography: Burnett Guffey. Music: George Antheil. Art Direction: Robert Peterson. Cast: Humphrey Bogart (Dixon Steel), Gloria Grahame (Laurel Gray), Frank Lovejoy (Brub Nicolai), Carl Benton Reid (Captain Lochner), Art Smith (Mel Lippman), Jeff Donnell (Sylvia Nicolai), Martha Stewart (Mildred Atkinson), Robert Warwick (Charlie Waterman), Ruth Gillette (Martha), Morris Ankrum (Lloyd Barnes), William Ching (Ted Barton), Steven Geray (Paul), Alice Talton (Frances Randolph), Jack Reynolds (Henry Kesler), Ruth Warren (Effie), Guy Beach (Swan).

Robert Lord for Santana, U.S.A. 8375 ft., 93 mins.

Even those of Nicholas Ray's films which suffer from lack of logical balance and excessively emphatic handling of the theme usually manage to come into their own, often thanks to the director's exceptional sense for the absorbing and the topical and almost always thanks to the fascinating multi-dimensional personalities of the leading characters. Admittedly, this richness often resides in the neighborhood of psychological deviations which makes Ray hover on the brink of Hollywood psychopathological kitsch, but his directorial bravura allows him to escape the pitfalls. In In a Lonely Place Humphrey Bogart and Gloria Grahame form what is probably the most interesting acting team in any Ray picture. Bogart is an embittered and frustrated scriptwriter suspected of murdering a hat-check girl; Grahame is a pretty neighbor with whom he falls in love. The continuing suspicions of the police cast a shadow on the affair; by the time the real murderer confesses it is too late: the relationship is shattered.

However, neither the surprisingly untypical hero, impulsive, undisciplined and violent-tempered, nor the enigmatic heroine were used to the full. The penetrating analysis of the characters is clearly more interesting than the adventures in which the script seeks to involve them; the sparkling dialogue, visual richness and tense atmosphere rise considerably above the level of the story content of the picture. Notwithstanding its faults In a Lonely Place must be considered one of the most interesting films of its kind in the 50's.

THE ASPHALT JUNGLE John Huston

Script: Ben Maddow and Huston, from the novel by William Riley Burnett. Photography: Harold Rosson. Music: Miklós Rózsa. Art Direction: Cedric Gibbons and Randall Duell. Cast: Sterling Hayden (Dix Handley), Louis Calhern (Alonzo D. Emmerich), Jean Hagen (Doll Conovan), James Whitmore (Gus Minissi), Sam Jaffe ("Doc" Erwin Riedenschneider), John McIntire (Police Commissioner Hardy), Marc Lawrence (Cobby), Barry Kelley (Lt. Dietrich), Anthony Caruso (Louis Ciavelli), Teresa Celli (Maria Ciavelli), Marilyn Monroe (Angela Phinlay), William Davis (Timmons), Dorothy Tree (May Emmerich), Brad Dexter (Bob Brannon), John Maxwell (Dr. Swanson).

Arthur Hornblow Jr. for MGM, U. S. A. 10,072 ft., 112 mins.

At the crossing of the returning wave of 30's gangster films and the contemporary tendencies of the "police documentary" à la Hathaway (Call Northside 777) Huston gives his own vision of the underworld, a vision tinged with a sweet-and-sour tone of understanding for the criminals. They are, after all, searching for happiness, just like anyone else. Being a gangster is simply a profession which follows from human enterprise, only channelled in the wrong direction--such is the film's message; it would later find its fullest expression in Dassin's famous Rififi. As is usual in Huston's cinema, he who challenges fate suffers defeat. Riedenschneider, a clever criminal, plans a million dollar jewel store robbery while serving a prison sentence. He recruits a crooked lawyer, Emmerich, to provide the backing, a fast-shooting killer, Dix, and three other people. After the robbery, Emmerich tries to double-cross his associates and get hold of the jewels; Dix kills his partner and goes into hiding. The police close in; Emmerich commits suicide, Riedenschneider is arrested. Dix and his girl set off for his old country home; he reaches it only to die from his wounds. The price of life had to be paid by everyone concerned--the conclusion is similar to that in hundreds of films of this kind, but in The Asphalt Jungle it completes something which is more than just a verbatim display of dramatic events. The narrative is rough in texture and, with the profusion of dialogue and the prevalence of close shots, amounts to the future "television" narrative. The value of this film rests in its searching observation of failed people. The ordinariness of the characters is stressed. Huston is concerned with man and the ways of his life--thus the defeat of people who were doomed to failure because they tried to materialize their dreams acquires the dimensions of a genuine tragedy. The poetic story of a young gangster who needed the money to buy back his family's old farm and who dies among his home Kentucky fields remains a memorable finale.

ADDRESS UNKNOWN (Sans laisser d'adresse) Jean-Paul Le Chanois

Script: Le Chanois and Alex Joffe. Photography: Marc Fossard. Music: Joseph Kosma. Art Direction: Max Douy. Cast: Bernard Blier (Emile Gauthier), Danièle Delorme (Thérèse Ravenaz), Pierre Trabaud (Gaston), Julien Carette (Upholsterer), Gérard Oury, Juliette Gréco, Arlette Marchal, Pierre Mondy, Sophie Leclair.

Raoul Ploquin/Hoche Productions/Silver-Films, France. 90 mins.

A young girl from the provinces wanders helplessly through Paris in search of the father or her newly-born child. The man who seduced her is a yellow press journalist, a petty bourgeois pseudointellectual; all the same, finding him seems Thérèse's last chance, since she cannot return home alone. She does not know the man's address, and her fruitless peregrinations would probably end in suicide--if it were not for the help of a Paris taxi driver who has just become a father himself. Sympathetic towards the girl's plight and determined to stand against injustice, he gives her courage and strength.

The synopsis of Le Chanois's film would seem to indicate a melodrama; but appearances are deceptive. Instead of lamenting the unjust wrong, the film, sustained in the spirit of the republican traditions of the French Revolution of 1789, offers emotions of a different kind. It talks about human solidarity, in the tones of a ballad inspiring confidence in the moral sense of the working classes and combines tragic accents with warmth and humor. In *Address Unknown*, the culmination of the populist current in the French cinema, everything relies on delicate simplicity, a scrupulous observation of the everyday Paris off the tourist routes. The realist tissue of the film allows one to forgive a certain obtrusiveness in some situations; the precision with which the various milieux the heros come across in search of the culprit overshadows the unimportant story. Thus René Clair's pre-war traditions blend in France with the social tendencies in post-war cinema: perhaps all this is not too ambitious, but it is surely unpretentious. And human, too: the film of Le Chanois is a pleasant touch of optimism.

ALL ABOUT EVE Joseph L. Mankiewicz

Script: Mankiewicz and Mary Orr, from a short story "The Wisdom of Eve," and a radio play by Orr. Photography: Milton Krasner.

Music: Alfred Newman. Art Direction: Lyle Wheeler and George W. Davis. Cast: Bette Davis (Margo Channing), Anne Baxter (Eve Harrington), George Sanders (Addison De Witt), Gary Merrill (Bill Sampson), Celeste Holm (Karen Richards), Hugh Marlowe (Lloyd Richards), Thelma Ritter (Birdie), Marilyn Monroe (Miss Caswell), Gregory Ratoff (Max Fabian), Barbara Bates (Phoebe).

Darryl F. Zanuck for 20th Century-Fox, U. S. A. 12,428 ft., 138 mins.

A shy provincial girl comes to the dressing room of a famous actress. Full of admiration for her favorite heroine, and dreaming of going on the stage, she asks for help and advice in making the first steps. Disarmed by the girl's directness and simplicity, the actress allows Eve to become her assistant. She is pleased to find that the girl is talented and tolerates even a certain importunity on the part of her pupil who begins to interfere with her private life. It soon turns out that all this is only an innocent overture to something far less pleasant: Eve zealously exploits an opportunity and takes the star's position by storm. But now in the dressing room of the new queen of the theatre a young stage-struck admirer appears....

As Sunset Boulevard, made in the same year, explodes the myths of Hollywood, All About Eve does the same to Broadway. In fact Mankiewicz had wider ambitions; he was concerned not only with the rules of the game in the theatrical world, but wanted to make a vitriolic comment on the ruthless struggle for fame and position in all professional enclaves and also some misogynic observations on the hypocrisy and malice of women. Fortunately, the latter element is kept at bay by the excellent performance from Bette Davis: at once theatrical and natural, wearing an actor's mask and yet simply human. The great actress gives the film a somewhat different tone than that intended by the director: her presence turns All About Eve above all into a drama of transience, the passing away into oblivion of a woman who is losing both her youth and the applause of the audience. It is in fact largely because of Bette Davis that one ranks the picture so highly. Mankiewicz, one of the most original and most nonconformist Hollywood scriptwriters, a sharp observer and an excellent psychologist, was known to be led by his noble intentions to results as dreadful as The Barefoot Contessa (1954). His intelligence and ambitious intentions too often collided with an astonishing lack of subtlety and aesthetic judgment. In All About Eve, decidedly his best work, he is, however, an effective and unobtrusive director and precise and penetrating scriptwriter. Bette Davis, George Sanders and Anne Baxter who give the three outstanding performances had at their disposal closely-knit, dramatically accomplished material and a dialogue which, although profuse and sometimes resorting to clichés, is firm and effective.

THE ROAD TO HOPE (Il cammino della speranza) Pietro Germi

Script: Federico Fellini, Tullio Pinelli and Germi, from the novel "Cuori negli abissi" (Hearts in the Abyss) by Nino Di Maria. Photography: Leonida Barboni. Music: Carlo Rustichelli. Cast: Raf Vallone (Saro), Elena Varzi (Barbara), Saro Urzí (Ciccio, the guide), Franco Navarra (Vanni), Liliana Lattanzi (Rosa), Mirella Ciotti (Lorenza), Saro Arcidiacono (Accountant), Chicco Coluzzi (Buda), Luciana Coluzzi (Luciana), Angelina Scaldaferi (Diodata), Carmela Trovato (Cirmena), Assunta Radico (Beatificata), Francesca Russella (Grandmother), Francesco Tomolillo (Misciú), Angelo Grasso (Antonio), Giuseppe Priolo (Luca), Paolo Reale (Brasi), Renato Terra (Mommino).

Luigi Rovere for Lux Film, Italy. 9977 ft., 111 mins.

Italian Neorealism, a movement which in the first post-war years had been characterized by spontaneity and sincerity but also by an aesthetic imbalance and exaggeration in the story content, reached maturity towards the turn of the decade in the films of such masters as De Sica and Visconti. In their works vehemence is replaced by restraint, passionate argument by matter-of-fact description, where drama resides in facts rather than gestures. In The Road to Hope Pietro Germi follows the example of De Sica's Bicycle Thieves and builds the film on his own experience aided by newspaper reports.

A group of Sicilians are forced by the closure of the local sulphur mine to emigrate in search of a living. The man supposed to arrange their passage to France turns out to be a crook and vanishes on the way. The party includes Saro, a young widower with three children and Barbara, mistress of a bandit called Vanni. They travel across the country on foot taking casual jobs. Before long Vanni disappears. After they help with harvesting at a farm and are declared blacklegs, part of the group turn back. Finally the remainder reach the French frontier. Vanni, jealous of Saro and Barbara, waits for them and Saro kills him in a fight. The group try to steal across the border surreptitiously, but are apprehended. Everything seems lost--but the impoverished appearance of the migrants wins compassion from the French border guards who allow them, in a gesture of understanding, to proceed to their El Dorado.

A noble ending, but in fact doubly false--as a touch of optimism without justification in real conditions in France at the time, and as a mark of avoidance of a clear social conclusion. The latter was in fact typical of the Neorealist movement. As a matter of fact it is not only the finale which is at fault, but practically the entire second part of the film, in which Germi too often resorts to clichéd, tabloid situations. On the other hand, the early part of the film maintains good pace and suggestive atmosphere. In the final effect, however, The Road to Hope is not unimportant reflection of the social conditions in post-war Italy (even if Germi's approach to them is superficial), and a work with a carefully considered formal aspect. Subcutaneous drama is here blended with muted suggestiveness, and the opening sequence of the sit-in strike in the mine, full of classical visual dignity, swollen with ominous silence and a sense of impending doom, belongs to the best in the Neorealist cinema.

PANIC IN THE STREETS Elia Kazan

Script: Richard Murphy, from a story "Quarantine, and Some Like 'em Cold" by Edna and Edward Anhalt, adapted by Daniel Fuchs. Photography: Joseph MacDonald. Music: Alfred Newman. Art Direction: Lyle R. Wheeler and Maurice Ransford. Cast: Richard Widmark (Dr. Clinton Reed), Paul Douglas (Police Captain Warren), Barbara Bel Geddes (Nancy Reed), Jack Palance (Blackie), Zero Mostel (Fitch), Dan Riss (Neff), Alexis Minotis (John Mefaris), Guy Thomajan (Poldi), Tommy Cook (Vince), Edward Kennedy (Jordan), H. T. Tsiang (Cook), Lewis Charles (Kochak), Raymond Muller (Dubin), Tommy Rettig (Tommy Reed), Lenka Peterson (Jeanette), Pat Walshe (Pat), Paul Hostetler (Dr. Paul Gafney), George Ehmig (Kleber), John Schilleci (Lee), Waldo Pitkin (Ben), Leo Zinser (Sergeant Phelps), Beverly C. Brown (Dr. Mackey), William A. Dean (Cortelyou), H. Waller Fowler Jr. (Murray), Red Moad (Wynant), Irvine Vidacovich (Johnston), Val Winter (Comissioner Dan Quinn), Wilson Bourg Jr. (Charlie), Mary Liswood (Angie Fitch), Aline Stevens (Rita Mefaris).

Sol C. Siegel for 20th Century-Fox, U. S. A. 8545 ft., 95 mins.

The body of a murdered man found on the New Orleans waterfront turns out to be infected with bubonic plague. Dr. Reed of the Public Health Service and Captain Warren of the Homicide Squad are called in to investigate. The doctor insists that to avoid panic no mention of the disease must be made in the press, the victim and the murderer must be identified, and anyone who might have come into contact with them isolated. Warren is skeptical about Reed's attitudes, and the doctor goes to investigate on his own. He traces the disease to a rat-infested ship which has had a case of plague on board, then to a quayside Armenian café, whose frightened proprietor denies all knowledge of the victim--until the next day, when his wife dies from plague. The murderer is finally caught after a chase along the waterfront warehouses.

The problem in Panic in the Streets is twofold: is one entitled to withhold a news item from the media in the public interest? Should the public's cooperation with the authorities be absolute in such cases? Kazan's answer to both these questions is "yes" and one is bound to agree. He does not moralize; perhaps only his Dr. Reed takes his duties a tiny bit too seriously. Although the final sequence of the chase is very impressive and very well staged in the real location of the New Orleans waterfront (using local people in smaller parts) the treatment of the story is not unduly sensational. Panic in the Streets is an involving and extremely competent "police documentary" in the style of the films made in the 40's by Hathaway-De Rochemont. It is in fact on a par with their best achievements, The House on 92nd Street and Call Northside 777, and is much superior to their Kiss of Death. Richard Widmark is memorable as the underpaid doctor; his part is given extra depth by the convincing domestic scenes with Barbara Bel Geddes as his patient wife.

LA RONDE Max Ophüls

Script: Jacques Natanson and Ophüls, based on the play "Reigen" (The Round Dance) by Arthur Schnitzler. Photography: Christian Matras. Music: Oscar Straus and Joë Hajos. Art Direction: Jean d'Eaubonne. Cast: Adolf Wohlbrück [Anton Walbrook] (The Narrator), Simone Signoret (Léocardie, the whore), Serge Reggiani (Franz, the soldier), Simone Simon (Marie, the chambermaid), Daniel Gélin (Alfred, the son of a good family), Danielle Darrieux (Emma Breitkopf, the married woman), Fernand Gravey (Charles, the husband), Odette Joyeux (Anna, the grisette), Jean-Louis Barrault (Robert Kühlenkampf, the poet), Isa Miranda (Charlotte, the actress), Gérard Philipe (The lieutenant), Jean Clarieux (Brigadier), Robert Vattier (Professor Schüller), Marcel Mérovée (Toni), Charles Vissière (Concierge).

Sacha Gordine, France. 8730 ft., 97 mins.

The years Ophüls spent in the U. S. A. were creatively not a great success. Having arrived in 1941, he was involved in several abortive projects and did not complete a film until 1947. In all he directed four pictures, of which only Letter from an Unknown Woman is really outstanding, although Caught (1948) and The Reckless Moment (1949) are also of interest. In 1950 he returned to France where he had worked in the years 1934-40.

As did Liebelei and Letter from an Unknown Woman, the stylish La Ronde brings to life Imperial Vienna at the turn of the century. Like Liebelei, it is made from a play by Arthur

Schnitzler. A member of a group of Austrian writers (which included Hugo von Hofmannsthal) Schnitzler was largely preoccupied with portraying the emotional agony, despair and nervous tension concealed under the smooth surface of elegant society. The group referred to their work as Nervenkunst ("the art of the nerves") and used an allegoric, Impressionistic style which was in sharp contrast with the verbatim realism of the older generation of writers. In fine arts their work was paralleled by the "Vienna Secession." Such is "Reigen," a bitter-sweet comment on the illusions and disappointments of love.

As indicated by the title, La Ronde is based on the motif of a circle. The film is composed of ten episodes. The ironic Master of Ceremonies sets in motion the symbolic merry-go-round in a Vienna square. The wheel of Fate begins to turn: a prostitute gives herself to a soldier who leaves her for a maid servant; she in turn allows herself to be seduced by her young master who then goes off to pursue a married woman; she breaks off the affair to return to her husband unaware that he is deceiving her with a shop-girl; she in turn is a victim of a poet who soon resumes his affair with a middle-aged actress; the actress leaves him for a wealthy young officer; after a drunken evening the officer wakes up in the bed of the prostitute of the first episode; on his way out he meets the soldier coming in. Thus the circle is closed.

An enchanting and sophisticated picture, La Ronde relies on the juxtaposition of Ophüls's romantic directorial style with the stark world of hedonism and betrayal which he portrays: the film is at once cynical and tender, wistful and cutting, romantic and ruthless, nostalgic and tragic. The best scenes are those between the young wife (Danielle Darrieux) and her sanctimonious husband, but Ophüls's dazzling technical virtuosity is present throughout: the magically fluid movement of the camera constantly circling in elaborate traveling shots, the fine editing, the brilliant dialogues. Last but not least, there is the unforgettable, haunting waltz by Oscar Straus.

SKIPPER NEXT TO GOD (Maître après Dieu) Louis Daquin

Script: Jean de Hartog, from his own play. Photography: Louis Page. Music: Jean Wiener. Cast: Pierre Brasseur (Captain of the "Jeune Nelly"), Jean-Pierre Grenier (Le Bosco), Loleh Bellon (Hélène), Jean Mercure (Rabbi), Abel Jacquin (American officer), Pierre Latour (Second officer), Jacques François (Doctor), Louis Seigner (Pastor), Albert Rémy.

Coopérative Générale du Cinéma Français/Silver Films, France. 92 mins.

Humanism as a challenge to Fascism; the collapse of Christian order in the time of the Brown Shirts--these are the controlling ideas in Daquin's optimistic picture about the self-purification of man's spirit in an encounter with evil. The hero of the title, the skipper of a Dutch cargo ship equipped for carrying cattle, is prepared to take on board the devil himself if only the reward is high enough. Hamburg, Germany, 1938: the captain takes as passengers 150 German Jews heading for a refuge in Egypt. To him these people are like any other cargo; but as it turns out he will have to take an active interest in their affairs. To the refugees' despair their visas are forged, and the skipper has to determine the port of destination. The verbatim interpretation of the Bible on which he has so far based his morals has not equiped him either to strike an understanding with the strangers from Nazi Germany or to find a solution to their plight. The captain (brilliantly portrayed by Pierre Brasseur) must face up to the most difficult test. This brute pickled in sea water can find the strength needed for taking the heroic decision only within himself. He deliberately sinks his ship: now the refugees _have_ to be allowed ashore.

A triumph for basic humanitarian principles: insofar as God is to be found in love of other human beings, this morality play made by a leftist director is very close to Ingmar Bergman's film _In a Glass Darkly_ made 11 years later, in spite of the different basic situations and the style of film-making of both pictures. Daquin's film relies almost exclusively on simple execution, the use of limited cinematic space and the dramatic employment of silence.

NO PEACE AMONG THE OLIVES (Non c'è pace tra gli ulivi)
Giuseppe De Santis

Script: De Santis, Libero De Libero, Carlo Lizzani and Gianni Puccini, from a story by De Santis and Puccini. _Photography_: Piero Portalupi. _Music_: Goffredo Petrassi. _Cast_: Raf Vallone (Francesco Dominici), Lucia Bosè (Laura), Folco Lulli (Bonfiglio), Maria Grazia Francia (Maria Grazia), Dante Maggio (Salvatore), Michele Riccardini (Police Sergeant), Vincenzo Talarico (Lawyer).

Domenico Forges Davanzati for Lux, Italy. 107 mins.

Making _No Peace Among the Olives_ De Santis did not wish to abandon the vehemence of his earlier _Bitter Rice_, but resolved to give it more outward dignity. So strip-cartoon style was replaced by ponderous classical leanings; the ambivalence of a _film noir_ gave way to the grave tones of a morality play. But the director's interests and method remained unchanged: _No Peace Among the Olives_ is still basically a sensational picture with social undertones.

The antagonists are Francesco, a young shepherd from the Abruzzi region of Italy and the racketeer Bonfiglio, a wealthy local man who has stolen Francesco's flock while the owner was in the war. The victim recovers his property during the night; he is arrested, charged with theft and sent to prison. Afraid of Bonfiglio, the neighbors do not dare to tell the truth in court. Neither does Laura, Francesco's girl, whom her family plan to marry off to Bonfiglio. This particular danger is averted: just before the wedding Francesco's sister confesses to having been raped by Bonfiglio who must thus marry her instead. But justice must be found by the hero himself. Francesco escapes from prison, hides in the mountains with the help of the local shepherds and finally challenges the villain. Bonfiglio flees in panic; betrayed by the stolen sheep who follow his tracks, he throws himself over the cliff. Truth finally triumphs: Francesco surrenders to the law, is cleared and reunited with Laura.

In the arrangement of the plot, characterization, stylization of the actors' movements and finally the photography, the picture is close to the style of the Mexican films of Fernández and Figueroa. No Peace Among the Olives cannot however be accused of lack of authenticity. Its faults, the same as a matter of fact as in the case of the above-mentioned Mexican film-makers (self-consciously aesthetic, high-contrast photography; two-dimensional, tabloid characters; a certain lack of originality in the plot) are compensated by the directorial bravura and the inner tension of the story. Raf Vallone and Lucia Bosè, the leading actors, also do quite well. Bosè, Miss Italy 1947, began here her film career in a part originally designed for Silvana Mangano, who was unable to appear.

THE MEN Fred Zinnemann

Script: Carl Foreman. Photography: Robert De Grasse. Music: Dimitri Tiomkin. Cast: Marlon Brando (Ken), Teresa Wright (Ellen), Everett Sloane (Dr. Brock), Jack Webb (Norm), Richard Erdman (Leo), Arthur Jurado (Angel), Virginia Farmer (Nurse Robbins), Dorothy Tree (Ellen's mother), Howard St. John (Ellen's father), Nita Hunter (Dolores), Patricia Joiner (Laverne), John Miller (Doolin), Cliff Clark (Dr. Kameran).

Stanley Kramer, U. S. A. 7871 ft., 87 mins.

How should somebody live who used to be a sportsman but is now deprived of the use of his legs and virtually reduced to half his former self by a war wound and passes his days in a hospital, among other paraplegics? One can find relief only in another human being. Zinnemann reliably transferred to the screen a very interesting script, although he did not really impress his individual stylistic seal. In this simple and quiet film he portrayed the relationship between a man whose physical condition has brought him close to suicide, and a girl who provides inner strength for both.

Ken is paralyzed from the waist down. He is bitter and resentful; at first he even refuses to see his ex-fiancée, Ellen. However, weeks in the hospital are a powerful influence. Ken sees that other paraplegics were able to overcome their physical incapacity and even make jokes about it. He marries Ellen despite the opposition from her parents and the doctor's warning that he will almost certainly be impotent. A few hours after the wedding the hidden fears and insecurities build up into an emotional outburst. Ken returns to the hospital, but his former companions do not sympathize with his rejection of Ellen. Finally the two face life together.

The Men is made with vividness and truth and one instantly recognizes in the film the creative stamp of Carl Foreman, the scriptwriter and the interests of Stanley Kramer, the ambitious producer. Although there is no conventional happy ending, the disabled man does return to society. It is a pity though that the film's attention is totally concentrated on Ken's problems and diverted from those of Ellen, although they are equally formidable. Despite the considerable difficulty of the part of the half-paralyzed hero, Marlon Brando reveals a great acting talent. The Men deserves additional acclaim for discovering this brilliant actor for the cinema.

WAGON MASTER John Ford

Script: Frank S. Nugent and Patrick Ford. Photography: Bert Glennon and Archie Stout. Music: Richard Hageman. Art Direction: James Basevi. Songs: Stan Jones. Cast: Ben Johnson (Travis Blue), Harry Carey Jr. (Sandy), Joanne Dru (Denver), Ward Bond (Wiggs), Charles Kemper (Shiloh Clegg), Alan Mowbray (Dr. A. Locksley Hall), Jane Darwell (Sister Ledyard), Ruth Clifford (Fleuretty Phyffe), Russell Simpson (Adam Perkins), Kathleen O'Malley (Prudence Perkins), James Arness (Floyd Clegg), Fred Libby (Reese Clegg), Hank Worden (Luke Clegg), Mickey Simpson (Jesse Clegg), Francis Ford (Peachtree).

John Ford and Merian C. Cooper for Argosy Pictures, U. S. A.
7691 ft., 86 mins.

The classical purity of Wagon Master is the reason why this modest film has been acclaimed as a masterpiece of the western genre. John Ford himself considered the picture to be particularly close to the ideal he wanted to achieve. Indeed, for all its uncomplicated story the film is directed with a classic mastery: already the prologue perfectly describes the characters, enucleates the plots, establishes the dramatic mood and provides a touch of light relief. The narrative is continued according to the principal rules of the western. The axis of the plot, set in 1870, is the westward journey of a Mormon wagon train to establish new settlements on the Utah-Arizona border. The travelers, led by the hot-tempered Brother Wiggs, encounter first an itinerant medicine show and then a group of mysterious "hunters" who turn out to be vicious outlaws. During the journey across the vast expanse of desert and the mountains the outlaws take over the caravan, but are defeated just as the fertile plains are reached.

The story of Wagon Master is entirely contained within the "western trail" pattern, one of the seven classical types of western. The film is a reiteration of many constant Ford motifs and characters. For instance, Dr. Locksley Hall, a drunken quack who clings to the vestige of his professional dignity comes straight from My Darling Clementine; so do the bad men led by their sinister "uncle." The ornaments of Wagon Master are the sequences of the Mormons' departure on their trek, the tribal dances round the Indian campfire and also the dynamic scenes of the exposition, the passage through rocky highlands and the culminating fight with the outlaws.

THE GUNFIGHTER Henry King

Script: William Bowers and William Sellers, from a story by Bowers and André de Toth. Photography: Arthur Miller. Music: Alfred Newman. Art Direction: Lyle Wheeler and Richard Irvine. Cast: Gregory Peck (Jimmie Ringo), Helen Westcott (Peggy Walsh), Millard Mitchell (Sheriff Mark Strett), Jean Parker (Molly), Karl Malden (Mac), Skip Homeier (Hunt Bromley), Anthony Ross (Charlie), Verna Felton (Mrs. Pennyfeather), Ellen Corby (Mrs. Devlin), Mae Marsh (Mrs. O'Brien), Richard Jaeckel (Eddie), B. G. Norman (Jimmie).

Nunnally Johnson for 20th Century-Fox, U. S. A. 7595 ft., 84 mins.

Jimmie Ringo, a professional gunman past his prime, returns to the town of Cheyenne after an absence of years. Tired and anxious to settle down, he has come to take his wife and son to a new peaceful life. But he finds it impossible to live down his myth as the best gun in the west: three avengers are on his trail and many young men want to try their skills against him, while children hope to catch a glimpse of the famous gunman through the saloon window. The Marshal, a former member of his gang, orders him away and his wife is reluctant to follow; she only relents on condition that he first serves a year as a trial period. As Ringo rides off he is shot in the back by a young assassin--who finds that it is his turn to be a wanted man.

Many consider The Gunfighter the first psychological western. Set in the 1880's, the plot remains within the traditional confines of the genre--for instance in using the classical motif of the outlaw weary of killing and constant flight but finding it impossible to stop. But the tone is different than before: traditional open landscapes give way to a brick-walled, chair-less saloon, and the erstwhile romantic convention is replaced by the aura of authenticity strongly reminiscent of actual photographs of the 19th-century West. Terse and economical, nostalgic rather than melodramatic, dispensing with music (apart from the credit sequence), the film concentrates on the analysis of social rejection, on its likeable anti-hero--outstandingly well played by Gregory Peck. Good, atmospheric camera work makes dramatic use of the contrast between sunlit streets and the darkness of the saloon. Closely following the trauma of McCarthyism, The Gunfighter was on its release received as an allegory about a society which thrives on violence.

1951

UMBERTO D. Vittorio De Sica

Script: Cesare Zavattini and De Sica, from a story by Zavattini. Photography: Aldo Graziati. Music: Alessandro Cicognini. Art Direction: Virgilio Marchi. Cast: Carlo Battisti (Umberto Domenico Ferrari), Maria Pia Casilio (Maria, the maid), Lina Gennari (Mrs. Belloni, the landlady), Memmo Carotenuto (Neighbor in hospital), Alberto Albani Barbieri (Landlady's lover).

DEAR-Film (De Sica-Amato-Rizzoli), Italy. 8043 ft., 89 mins.

A picture which must be considered the leading work of Neorealism, Umberto D. lacks many of the usual attributes of the movement. It is completely devoid of dynamic action, social panorama is beyond the camera's field of vision, and the hero, a retired clerk, seems a rather peripheral character who would normally be of no interest to the cinema of the period. But the makers of the film felt differently: De Sica's father was a modest bank clerk and his first name was Umberto. Even though the director and the scriptwriter never discussed it, Umberto D. was on Zavattini's part a gesture of reciprocity after his cherished Miracle in Milan had been made: a script which would be as personal to De Sica as that film was to himself. The origins of this lucid, simple chamber drama about a lonely old age pensioner predestined the film's greatness.

Umberto Domenico Ferrari has no family, few friends and a dog as his only companion. His pension is inadequate and he cannot find the 15,000 lire which he owes in rent. In his absence his landlady uses his room (which he has occupied for 30 years) as a meeting place for lovers and anyway intends to evict him as she will need the room when she gets married. When repeated attempts to obtain the money fail, Umberto D. decides to commit suicide. He is prevented from taking his life by his dog. So he is alive, but the situation has not changed and there is no hope of a better tomorrow--a conclusion more bitter than in earlier films of the team De Sica-Zavattini. Umberto D. strongly attacks the social structure of post-war Italy. It is precisely because of the director's affectionate attitude towards the title character that the quiet film about a private tragedy, a matter which others acknowledge only with reluctance, is more resounding and expressive than many works which accuse society with emphasis and dramatic tension. It is remarkable how far De Sica is from maudlin sentimentality and from the temptation to idealize the hero. Umberto D., typically for the Neorealist cinema played (very accurately) by a non-professional, in private life a university professor, is like any ordinary man of his age. What became then of the didacticism on which De Sica relied so much in Bicycle Thieves and Miracle in Milan? It might seem to have given way completely to a helpless statement of facts. Yet some of it remained--in the film's final plea for human kindness, for understanding and help for those humiliated and forgotten, in the manner of showing the old man's struggle to preserve his dignity.

For all its simplicity of construction Umberto D. is a very remarkable proof of the narrative scope of the cinema: in no other Neorealist film can one find so many examples of the use of what may be described as "thinking camera." Particularly notable are such scenes as the zoom from behind the hero's head towards the pavement below which suggests suicidal thoughts; his anxiety when, having decided to beg he turns his hand at the last minute pretending he was trying to see whether it was raining; the aerial shots of the confrontation between the demonstrators and the police which in a few seconds tell the spectator a lot about the feelings among the community of old age pensioners: the way the reasons for Umberto's final decision are revealed by showing the behavior of the dog; and finally the description, with camera pans and a few lines of dialogue, of the life of a young servant girl, who is in many ways akin to the protagonist. Few works of the screen succeeded in communicating the intentions of the makers so movingly, with such naturalness and directness. In fact with too much directness: the uncompromising Umberto D., made at a time when the papers reported suicides of elderly people every day, was a resounding box-office failure.

THE IDIOT (Hakuchi) Akira Kurosawa

Script: Eijiro Hisaita and Kurosawa, based on the novel "Idiot" by Fyodor Dostoyevsky. Photography: Toshio Ubukata. Music: Fumio Hayasaka. Art Direction: So Matsuyama. Cast: Masayuki Mori (Kinji Kameda), Toshiro Mifune (Denkichi Akama), Setsuko Hara (Taeko

The Idiot

Nasu), Takashi Shimura (Ono), Yoshiko Kuga (Ayako Ono), Chieko Higashiyama (Satoki Ono), Minoru Chiaki (Mutsuo Kayama), Chiyoko Fumiya (Noriko), Kokuten Kodo (Jyunpei), Eiko Miyoshi (Kayama's mother), Notiko Sengoku (Takako), Daisuke Inoue (Kaoru), Eijiro Yanagi (Tohata), Bokuzen Hidari (Karube), Mitsuyo Akashi (Akama's mother).

Sojiro Motoki for Shochiku, Japan. Originally 265 mins., reduced to 14,907 ft., 166 mins. The original version does not exist.

A director interested in the basic tenets of human existence, Kurosawa always had a great admiration for Russian literature, especially for Dostoyevsky and Gorky. "The Idiot" is his favorite Dostoyevsky novel and Prince Myshkin his favorite literary character. It has been Kurosawa's cherished project to transfer it to the screen, and he expended more effort on The Idiot than on any other of his pictures. Following is an attempt at synopsizing the complex plot.

On a train to Hokkaido, Akama (the equivalent of the book's Rogozhin) becomes involved in a conversation with Kameda (Prince Myshkin) who has just left a hospital in Okinawa and suffers from dementia epilepsia. Akama is about to take over the inheritance after the death of his father, who had previously thrown him out for embezzling money in order to buy a diamond for Taeko (Nastasya), the woman Akama loves. Kameda is captivated by Taeko's beauty. His relative, Ono, is arranging for Taeko, who is the mistress of a rich man, to marry his secretary, Kayama. Kayama is in fact in love with Ono's own daughter, Ayaka. Also Taeko is fascinated by Kameda who offers to take care of her, penniless, and cut the bargaining. She finally goes with Akama, though she cannot forget Kameda and his child-like sincerity. Ayaka, also in love with Kameda, in vain tries to win him over. She runs away and Kameda goes to look for her. He returns to find that Akama has killed Taeko in a fit of rage and jealousy. Kameda and Akama go mad together.

Having received terrible reviews after its Japanese release and also in the U.S.A. where it was shown in 1963, The Idiot was until quite recently considered the one unmitigated Kurosawa failure. It is in fact nothing of the sort--this is Kurosawa at his best. The novel, set in 19th-century St. Petersburg, is transposed to modern times, to the snowy country of Hokkaido, the northern-most island of Japan, the region closest to Russia in climate and custom. The style of clothing and the furniture are European. Kurosawa tried to stress the universal character of the story not by transforming it bodily into Japanese history and custom (as he later did in The Throne of Blood) but by suspending it in a curious time-space vacuum. The film seems set neither in Japan nor in Europe, but in that "country of the soul" where all Dostoyevsky's stories are set. It is simply the novel's spiritual equivalent. For all his pains Kurosawa was criticized for making an "un-Japanese" picture. Indeed, the essence of Dostoyevsky and the feel of St. Petersburg are captured wonderfully--with constantly falling snow, heavily clad human figures scurrying along chilly streets and open fires inside homes. As Delannoy did in La Symphonie pastorale, Kurosawa uses snow as

The Idiot

the visual key to the story--to create a mood of spiritual exaltation, purity and a sense of isolation of characters.

Kurosawa had to reduce the number of secondary characters and generally to compress the events of the vast novel; the result of his efforts was still further cut by the studio. This gave rise to a certain sketchiness of the narrative, particularly in the beginning. More importantly, Kurosawa dispensed with the book's main points. Much of it would hardly apply anyway, since the story has been updated. Thus from a complex psychological discourse with strong social overtones he retained simply a story of passion, love and innocence.

The Idiot is the most contemplative of his works, its acting trance-like and stylized. One can discover here in embryo many episodes from his later films. Among the most memorable is the mesmeric moment as Kameda and Akama, having just got off the train, look at the photograph of Taeko in a shop window; the scene of the ice festival with masked figures converging on Kameda, and the magical closing sequence as the two men huddle together after Taeko's murder. An interesting stylistic device is the use of wipe when the type of story would make one expect dissolves. To quote Tom Milne's perceptive comment, The Idiot "... manages to convey the interlocking despair of human relationships, quite magnificently, through a simple stylistic device: the triangular grouping in which, usually in monologue, one person explains, one listens intently, and a third, marginally excluded, is baffled by the spellbinding emotional waves he cannot quite grasp...."

TERESA Fred Zinnemann

Script: Stewart Stern, from a story by Alfred Hayes and Stern. Photography: William J. Miller. Music: Louis Applebaum. Art Direction: Leo Kerz. Cast: Anna Maria Pierangeli [Pier Angeli] (Teresa), John Ericson (Philip Quas), Patricia Collinge (Philip's mother), Richard Bishop (Philip's father), Peggy Ann Garner (Susan), Ralph Meeker (Sergeant Dobbs), Bill Mauldin (Grissom), Ave Ninchi (Teresa's mother), Franco Interlenghi (Mario), Edward Binns (Sergeant Brown), Rod Steiger (Frank).

Arthur M. Loew--Fred Zinnemann for MGM, U.S.A. 9186 ft., 102 mins.

While Zinnemann did not generally impress with the stylistic qualities of his films (apart from High Noon, excellently constructed and narrated with classical nobility), he usually displayed an excellent sense for the intrinsic values of the script. Teresa is an extreme example of this: neither the photography nor the acting contribute anything to the film and considered in isolation from the whole appear mediocre. On the other hand the problem and the story are so interesting in themselves as to elevate the rank of the picture. Under the surface of a run-of-the-mill plot about an American soldier who marries the young daughter of an Italian family with whom he is billeted and brings her home to New York, the film provocatively juxtaposes two female mentalities--European and American. To use Philip Wylie's terminology--mommism, a matriarchal family structure based on a strong interaction between mother and son. At the same time there is in the film a disguised, but not unintentional, attack on the brutal struggle for survival which often destroys weaker individuals (the story is told by Philip, in a long flashback, to a veterans' administration psychiatrist). To Zinnemann a social system which forces man into compulsory economic situations, which makes him lose individuality, is antihumanist. Teresa is to a certain extent a continuation of The Men in its discussion of the readjustment to the society of veteran soldiers. All these problems are seen in the film through the eyes of a young Italian peasant girl who, like the Austrian-born Zinnemann, looks at America as an outsider. It is thanks to this female character, directed by Zinnemann with tenderness (which sometimes quite unnecessarily gravitates towards sentimentality) that the drama becomes genuinely moving, and the film's reflections on the problems of the alienation of the individual are very far in tone from stiff journalism. It is an interesting coincidence that the leading part in the picture is played by the youthful Anna Maria Pierangeli who had just arrived in America from Italy where she had already acquired a considerable reputation as an actress in her part of Mirella in Leonide Moguy's Domani è troppo tardi (1950). By a wry coincidence, the future life of the actress (involved for a while with James Dean) had a lot in common with the story of the heroine of Teresa.

STRANGERS ON A TRAIN Alfred Hitchcock

Script: Raymond Chandler and Czenzi Ormonde, from the novel by Patricia Highsmith adapted by Whitfield Cook. Photography: Robert Burks. Music: Dimitri Tiomkin. Art Direction: Ted Haworth and George James Hopkins. Cast: Farley Granger (Guy Haines), Robert Walker (Bruno Anthony), Ruth Roman (Anne Morton), Leo G. Carroll (Senator Morton), Patricia Hitchcock (Barbara Morton), Laura Elliott (Miriam), Marion Lorne (Mrs. Anthony), Jonathan Hale (Mr. Anthony), Norma Varden (Mrs. Cunningham), Howard St. John (Captain Turley), John Brown (Professor Collins).

Alfred Hitchcock for Warner Bros., U.S.A. 9072 ft., 101 mins.

The idea of "murder by proxy" is the starting point of one

of the most brilliant Hitchcock films. Two men meet on a train apparently by chance, while traveling to New York. Guy, a tennis champion, wants to divorce his small-town wife in order to marry a senator's daughter; Bruno, obviously familiar with Guy's private life, confesses that he, on his part, hates his father and suggests a murder pact with the exchange of victims--impossible to detect, he says, as there would be two very good alibis and no apparent motive. Guy laughs the idea off, but Bruno goes ahead with his part of the "deal" and kills Guy's wife. He then demands that Guy fulfill his part of the bargain; first he tries persuasion, but later....

Hitchcock clearly demonstrates that propensity for evil is lying dormant in everybody. Bruno becomes the executor of Guy's unconscious desires, which is essentially the "Dr. Jekyll and Mr. Hyde" motif. Hitchcock commented: "whether it's Guy or Bruno, it's obviously a single personality split in two." The picture frequently uses Freudian symbols (there are hints that for Bruno crime is compensation for sexual failure), underlining them by contrasts of light and darkness. However, the main strength of Strangers on a Train is not its philosophy, but its excellent film-making and the most precise observation of detail and behavior: in the opening sequence the director introduces the protagonists with marvelous economy by showing the shoes of passengers boarding the train; further remarkable scenes include the macabre joke as Bruno demonstrates murder methods to an elderly rich woman at the senator's house; the killing of Guy's wife at a fun-fair shown reflected in the lens of her fallen spectacles; Guy's tennis match intercut with Bruno's desperate attempts to retrieve the lighter which he has dropped down a drain and which he needs to frame Guy; and finally the famous shot at the match when Bruno is the only spectator in a crowd whose head does not follow the ball. Hitchcock's jugglery with the feelings of the audience is here brought to perfection, while his wide use of parallel editing resulted in a highly economic handling of cinematic time. Granger is miscast and uninspiring as Guy; Walker very good as the sinister Bruno (one must remember, however, that a psychopath is always a more attractive part); Lorne excellent in the small part of Bruno's doting and completely crazy mother. If only it wasn't for the film's logical flaw at the end--why on earth does Bruno jump onto the moving merry-go-round?

THE RED BADGE OF COURAGE John Huston

Script: Huston, from the novel by Stephen Crane, adapted by Albert Band. Photography: Harold Rosson. Music: Bronislau Kaper. Art Direction: Cedric Gibbons and Hans Peters. Editing: Ben Lewis, supervised by Margaret Booth. Cast: Audie Murphy (Henry Fleming), Bill Mauldin (Tom Wilson), John Dierkes (Jim Conklin), Royal Dano (Tattered Soldier), Arthur Hunnicutt (Bill Porter), Tim

Durant (General), Douglas Dick (Lieutenant), Andy Devine (Talkative Soldier), Robert Easton Burke (Thompson).

John Huston for MGM, U. S. A. Originally 78 mins., cut to 6203 ft., 69 mins. in released version.

The question of what The Red Badge of Courage could have been like if Huston had been allowed to realize his plans is one of the great movie mysteries, as intriguing as what ¡ Que Viva Mexico! would have been if Eisenstein had been allowed to finish it. Sadly, we shall never know the answer to either. Huston, who was working on a picture which questions the validity of war as a way of solving conflicts at the unfortunate time when the Korean war raged and McCarthyism was spreading to Hollywood, found it impossible to conform to the "patriotic" requirements of MGM. His film was after all starring Audie Murphy, the most decorated American soldier in the Second World War. In an attempt to make it more acceptable (and more commercial) the studio frantically edited and re-edited the film until finally releasing it in a version running a mere 69 minutes. The result was that Huston renounced the film which he thought his best work to date. The wheelings and dealings surrounding The Red Badge of Courage, one of the legends of Hollywood, are the subject of the bestselling book "Picture" by Lillian Ross, which probably attracted more attention than the film it is about.

Stephen Crane's 1895 novel uses war merely as a pretext for a psychological study of a young recruit, and its horrors are shown via his dramatic experiences. Everything in the book is seen through the eyes of a greenhorn, a private who does not understand the rationale of war. To stress the general applicability of the story, Crane purposely does not use surnames or mention place names. Huston preserved this in the film. He tried to demonstrate that to his protagonist bravery and cowardice are no more than two extreme states of the emotional spectrum, and that the borderline between them is often ambiguous. It is interesting that this problem reappeared a few years later in Chukhrai's Ballad of a Soldier. Huston said that he did not want the war as shown in his film to be understood only as the war between the North and the South, but a war which shows the uselessness of the courage of the protagonist--who in the film's finale storms a piece of crumbling wall. This was seen as a blasphemy against the history of the United States: MGM re-edited the material so as to show how a soldier can defeat fear and become a hero. As a study of the human element of warfare The Red Badge of Courage is thus related to the earlier Twelve O'Clock High, although it is set in the past.

In the film as it appears on the screen, a young Northern recruit is being tested in battle during the closing stages of the Civil War. It is a story of his first experience of active combat. Afraid, he flees from the battlefield, joins retreating wounded troops and strikes a friendship with the Tattered Soldier. They witness the death of the brave Tall Soldier, the boy's confidant. While returning

The Red Badge of Courage

to the unit the recruit goes through his baptism of fire, receives "the red badge of courage"--a wound from the butt of a rifle. This is a turning point: his doubts are resolved and he joins in the fighting with newly-found courage. He returns to the unit and becomes a hero in a victorious charge.

The film is striking despite its mutilation. Formally, it is far ahead of its time. The narrative is terse and extraordinarily clear. Huston was always anxious to render the times and their atmosphere faithfully on the screen, particularly in the 50's when he was making period films, other examples being Moulin Rouge and Moby Dick. The visual style of The Red Badge of Courage is influenced by Brady's famous photographs of the Civil War. The atmosphere is brilliantly created with images: wonderfully poetic in the moments of stillness, with sun shining through the trees, but dynamic and dramatic in action scenes, suggestive of fear and confused emotions. Harold Rosson's camera is almost constantly involved in fast movements and long panning shots. The acting is excellent, particularly Royal Dano's powerful part of the Tattered Soldier.

ONE SUMMER OF HAPPINESS (Hon dansade en sommar)
Arne Mattsson

Script: Wolodja Semitjov, from the novel, "Sommardansen" (Summer Dances), by Per Olof Ekström. Photography: Göran Strindberg. Music: Sven Sköld. Cast: Folke Sundquist (Göran Stendal), Ulla Jacobsson (Kerstin Frederiksson), Edvin Adolphson (Anders Persson), Irma Christenson (Sigrid), Gösta Gustavsson (Berndt Larsson), John Elfström (Clergyman), Erik Hell (Torsten), Berta Hall (Anna), Nils Hallberg (Nisse), Sten Maltsson (Olle), Arne Källerud (Viberg), Gunvor Pontén (Sylvia), Sten Lindgren (Göran's father).

Lennart Landheim for Nordisk Tonefilm, Sweden. 93 mins.

The renaissance of the Swedish cinema begun in the early 40's with Sjöberg's The Road to Heaven and several other films which were indissolubly linked with the Scandinavian landscape and stressed man's bonds with Nature, was very short-lived. It came to an end with Mattsson's One Summer of Happiness and with Summer with Monika made one year later by Ingmar Bergman, the man who would soon become one of the world's leading film directors. Both these films made a strong impression and became widely known; they are not only fine but thematically important. One Summer of Happiness is based on a well-known novel which was considered by the young Swedes as the best reflection of the problems of young people after the war. The picture comes to the defense of love and accuses the backward puritan morality. During the summer holidays a student meets and falls in love with a 17-year-old old country girl, thereby rebelling against his parents who plan for him a wife from a good middle-class family. Göran loses his Kerstin in a road accident which seems literally obtained through prayer by the local pastor who with blind hatred observed the sinful union of the young couple. The story, unsophisticated, and in parts even doubtful, has nonetheless great charm on the screen. It is not that Mattsson displayed some particular directorial brilliance; he never succeeded in becoming a leading film-maker even on the scale of his native Sweden. But in this film he showed a wonderful intuition and with a few excellent strokes took the film way above its second-rate literary origin. Such a stroke was for instance the idea of showing the whole story in flashback within the framework of the funeral of the ill-fated heroine, a device which gives the story of young lovers an elegiac flavor. The scenery is likewise very well chosen and its bonds with the characters give the film an unexpectedly strong feel of authenticity: the narrative is crisp and points are at times made quite inventively (the pans of the camera looking into the faces of mourners during the funeral), but resolute and spontaneous--which results in a harmonious proportion between the film's lyricism and social criticism. The responsibility for the photography, music and acting was in good hands. From among the cast one must single out Ulla Jacobsson. One Summer of Happiness marks the beginning of her distinguished acting career.

TWO PENNYWORTH OF HOPE (Due soldi di speranza) Renato Castellani

---

Script: Castellani and Titina De Filippo, from a story by Castellani and E. Margadonna. Photography: Arturo Gallea. Music: Alessandro Cicognini. Cast: Vincenzo Musolino (Antonio), Maria Fiore (Carmela), Filomena Russo (Antonio's mother), Luigi Astarita (Pasquale Artu, Carmela's father), Luigi Barone (Priest), Carmela Cirillo (Giulia), Felicia Lettieri (Carmela's mother), Gina Mascetti (Flora Angelini), Alfonso Del Sorbo (Sacristan), Tommaso Balzano (Luigi Bellomo), Anna Raiola (Mrs. Bellomo).

Sandro Ghenzi for Universalcine, Italy. 8820 ft., 98 mins.

The cardinal intention of the Neorealists during the classical period of the movement was to arouse protest; at first against the war, later against social injustice and the selfishness of the rich. Castellani, who at the time of his debut in the early 40's was involved with the old and formalist "calligraphist" cinema, declared his accession to Neorealism on a different basis: he did not start from a thesis and subsequently prove it as did De Sica and De Santis, but from behavioral observation. He had already used this method in Sotto il sole di Roma (1948). Castellani did not want to arouse anger but optimism, which he felt was more needed. Apart from the question whether or not he was right, his screen comedies, vibrant with human temperaments, perfectly exemplify the situation of Neorealism at the time when the immediate post-war poverty was beginning to give way to the "economic miracle" of the mid-50's. "Things are going to improve, and a smile helps in building the future prosperity"--this attitude, formed as a matter of fact under the influence of government policies, resulted in practice in a shift of the Italian cinema towards the optimistic, populist "rosy realism" and was accepted, temporarily or permanently, by a majority of Italian directors including De Sica in his L'oro di Napoli (1954). It would be a mistake however to identify these tendencies with compromise; at least in the early instance of Two Pennyworth of Hope where the destitute hero declares in the final scene: "if Providence or someone else does not give me happiness and enough money for normal living, I will put things right and get these things myself."

Two Pennyworth of Hope would later be considered by other Italian film-makers to be the best description of the plight of Italian peasants. One might add that the picture is addressed to a wide public and reflects its mentality, living problems and way of life. The heroes of the story, filmed in the village of Boscotrecase on the slopes of Mt. Vesuvius (in the film the village is called Cusano), are Carmela, the daughter of the local fireworks manufacturer, relatively affluent in comparison with the general poverty of the neighbors, and Antonio, a young man who has to support a mother and five sisters of which two are of marriageable age, but without a dowry. Antonio has just returned from the army and takes odd jobs in the village; for a while he works in the local church during the day and as a Communist agitator at night. Carmela, resolute and temperamental, wants him to marry her, but Antonio is too preoccupied with his family to think about personal problems. When he finally decides to embark on a romance and is treated contemptuously by Carmela's father, he must find a dowry for his sister before he can get married himself. This turns out to be very difficult: the jealous Carmela loses him several jobs; he cannot earn much in the nearby Naples, either. Antonio comes into his own as a result of dramatic events: Carmela's father throws her out of the house virtually naked. Antonio clothes her on credit at a friendly stall-keeper's and with the support of everyone in the village decides to embark on married life virtually from square one.

This final scene is in fact the quintessence of the whole film--elemental, exuberant, but never trivial. This is a very suitable ambience for the actors (non-professional apart from the leading man). The Italians, buoyant and ostentatious in many real-life situations, come out well as amateur film actors, especially in dialect-spoken folkloristic comedy. With a well-written script at his disposal Castellani had in fact little to worry about. It was enough to put together the individual situations, extract from them interesting social comment (for instance on the Italians' preoccupation with personal dignity or on the formation of their later very common oscillation between the Roman Catholic Church and the Communist Party) and to leave the rest to the actors. Castellani said that the inhabitants of Boscotrecase who really lived in poverty gave him a lesson in optimism and humor and that he tried to make use of it in the film. It was a great pity that other Italian film-makers, encouraged by Castellani's success, interpreted this lesson too superficially. The host of comedies made later in a similar vein was simply a collection of paler and paler imitations of Two Pennyworth of Hope.

THE BROWNING VERSION Anthony Asquith

Script: Terence Rattigan, adapted from his own play. Photography: Desmond Dickinson. Art Direction: Carmen Dillon. Cast: Michael Redgrave (Andrew Crocker-Harris), Jean Kent (Millie Crocker-Harris), Nigel Patrick (Frank Hunter), Brian Smith (Taplow), Wilfrid Hyde White (Frobisher, headmaster), Bill Travers (Fletcher), Ronald Howard (Gilbert), Paul Medland (Wilson), Ivan Sampson (Lord Baxter), Josephine Middleton (Mrs. Frobisher).

Teddy Baird for Javelin, G. B. 8136 ft., 90 mins.

Andrew Crocker-Harris, a classics master in a well-known English public school, is about to retire prematurely because of bad health. His life has been a complete failure: his unsympathetic wife is having an affair with another teacher, his colleagues treat him with malice, his pupils dislike him as a petty classroom tyrant, the headmaster tells him with glee that he will not be given a pension. To compensate for his failures and complexes Crocker-Harris has developed a cold, forbidding manner. But the protective shell he has built around himself cracks when one of his pupils, Taplow, gives him the Browning version of Agamemnon. When his wife suggests maliciously that the boy did it to avoid punishment, her lover leaves her shocked at her callousness and Crocker-Harris decides to part from her. Finally, in defiance of the headmaster, he makes a speech to the school telling the boys about the failure of his life. The applause he receives will enable him to face the future with more courage.

Apart from the ending, The Browning Version is a faithful and accurate screen adaptation of the play by Terence Rattigan. Ironically, it is precisely the ending, rather cheap in its forced optimism and out of step with the rest of the story (apart from being psychologically improbable) that is the film's main weakness. Its strength on the other hand is the distinguished part from Michael Redgrave--commanding, dignified, resigned and sympathetic. In fact, the film relies almost entirely on him and the parts of the wife and the headmaster (who tends to be comical) are somewhat short of successful. Only concentrated film-making and a profound psychological scrutiny of the protagonist could bring about a picture like this--seemingly grey and yet so rich in meanings. Restrained, unobtrusive, free from grandiloquence, very ordinary and yet subtle--The Browning Version is a lesson of dignity and honesty.

THE AFRICAN QUEEN John Huston

Script: James Agee and Huston, from the novel by Cecil Scott Forester. Photography: Jack Cardiff. Music: Allan Gray. Art Direction: Wilfred Shingleton. Editing: Ralph Kemplen. Cast: Katharine Hepburn (Rose Sayer), Humphrey Bogart (Charlie Allnutt), Robert Morley (Brother Samuel Sayer), Peter Bull (Captain of "Luisa"), Theodore Bikel (First officer of "Luisa"), Walter Gotell (Second officer of "Luisa"), Gerald Onn (Petty officer of "Luisa"), Peter Swanwick (First officer of "Shona"), Richard Marner (Second officer of "Shona").

S. P. Eagle (Sam Spiegel) for Romulus/Horizon Films, G. B. / U. S. A. 9270 ft., 103 mins. Technicolor.

Adventure in Huston's cinema turns out not to be always of the tragic variety after all. The African Queen reveals another facet of the old myth--fate sometimes smiles on those who were ennobled through persistent struggle towards a goal. Rightly so: if Adventure polarizes human characters, why should it not also reward those who emerge victorious?

The time is 1914. Brother Samuel Sayer and his sister Rose, a puritanical old maid, run a British mission in the Congo. When the First World War breaks out, the Germans who rule the roost there destroy the mission; Brother Samuel dies. The devout woman acquires new energy; she sees the fight with the enemy as her moral obligation. Charlie Allnutt, a down-and-out, gin-soaked Canadian captain of "The African Queen" persuades Rose to escape with him. After surmounting a variety of obstacles such as dangerous rapids, a dead branch of the river, crocodiles, leeches and bombardment from the enemy fortress, the two find they are in love. They are arrested by the Germans and sentenced to death but manage to escape at the last moment and safely reach British territory.

The story, no doubt colorful but also somewhat strip-cartoon in style, probably would not seem very authentic on the screen (not to mention being as likeable as it is) were it not for Huston's sureness of hand, Cardiff's splendid location photography and above all Katharine Hepburn and Humphrey Bogart who are so excellently truthful in their parts. Huston intended The African Queen to be much more serious in tone, but the couple of leading actors reacted to the series of unexpected events on the set with such a sense of humor that many scenes came out nearly Chaplinesque. What director would resist the temptation to make use of such effects? Certainly not Huston: was he to throw away what Fate brought him in the course of the Adventure of the making of The African Queen?

THE LAVENDER HILL MOB Charles Crichton

Script: T. E. B. Clarke. Photography: Douglas Slocombe. Music: Georges Auric. Editing: Seth Holt. Art Direction: William Kellner. Cast: Alec Guinness (Holland), Stanley Holloway (Pendlebury), Sidney James (Lackery), Alfie Bass (Shorty), Marjorie Fielding (Mrs. Chalk), Edie Martin (Miss Evesham), John Gregson (Farrow), Arthur Hambling (Wallis), Gibb McLaughlin (Godwin), John Salew (Parkin), Ronald Adam (Turner), Sidney Tafler (Clayton), Clive Morton (Station Sergeant), Frederick Piper (Café Proprietor), Peter Bull (Joe the Gab), Patric Doonan (Craggs), Audrey Hepburn (Chiquita).

Michael Balcon for Ealing Studios, G. B. 7043 ft., 78 mins.

A sparkling crime comedy, The Lavender Hill Mob combines a profusion of situational gags with an ironic, self-critical attitude to the British way of life; a brisk pace with a skillful musical illustration, the rock'n'roll mobility of the camera with the bravura editing. Alec Guinness, who presides over all this, further justifies his reputation as a splendid character actor. Here he plays Mr. Holland, a respectable and trusted employee of the Bank of England, whose job is to supervise deliveries of bullion from the gold refinery to the bank's vaults. But he would like a £1,000,000 part of it for himself, and has conceived a clever plan for the actual robbery. When he meets Mr. Pendlebury, a manufacturer of metal souvenirs, he gets the brilliant idea of melting the gold down and taking it out of the country in the form of Eiffel Tower paperweights. They coopt two professional thieves. The operation is a success and the perpetrators are soon in Paris. If it were not for a silly misunderstanding caused by the difference of the French and English pronunciation, everything would have gone fine. Several paperweights are mistakenly sold to a party of English schoolgirls. So Holland and Pendlebury have to go back to England where they are awaited by the police who, in spite of having made many mistakes, are still the British Police and know how to do a good job.

While poking fun at the police, T. E. B. Clarke at the same time acknowledges their skill; while endowing the leader of the gang with brilliant intelligence he does not omit stressing the English inflexibility of thinking. Fully developed characters and situational originality of the logically watertight script (awarded an Oscar in 1951) are the starting points for the success of this intelligent comedy.

THE LADY OF MUSASHINO (Musashino Fujin) Kenji Mizoguchi

Script: Yoshikata Yoda and Tsuneari Fukuda, based on the novel by Shohei Ooka. Photography: Masao Tamai. Music: Fumio Hayasaka. Art Direction: Takashi Matsuyama. Editing: Ryoji Bando. Cast: Kinuyo Tanaka (Michiko Akiyama, "The Lady of Musashino"), Masayuki Mori (Tadao Akiyama, her husband), So Yamamura (Eiji Ono, Michiko's cousin), Yukiko Todoroki (Tomiko, Ono's wife), Minako Nakamura (Yukiko Ono), Akihiko Tatayama (Tsutomu Miyaji, Michiko's cousin), Eitaro Shindo (Shinzaburo Miyaji, Tsutomu's father), Kiyoko Hirai (Tamiko Miyaji), Noriko Sengoku (Ono family's maid).

Hideo Koi for Toho, Japan. 8294 ft., 92 mins.

The Lady of Musashino is the story of a gentle and sensitive woman who lost her parents in the war. Anxious to protect the estate left to her, Michiko lives on Musashino Field, a piece of waterlogged land, with her husband Akiyama, a successful translator of Stendhal. Her cousin Tsutomu is repatriated after the war and falls in love with her, while Akiyama is involved in an affair with Tomiko, the coquettish wife of a relative living nearby. A man of cheaply "modernist" ideas ("to me adultery is an expression of free spirit") Akiyama connives at his wife's friendship with Tsutomu. When a storm breaks out and prevents Michiko and Tsutomu from returning home from a walk, they pledge eternal love to each other. But Tsutomu leaves, finding the situation insufferable. Tomiko runs away with Akiyama (who took the title to the house with him) but abandons him as soon as he runs out of money. On his return home Akiyama finds his wife dead. The note she left reads: "My dear Tsutomu, I cannot make you happy unless I kill myself."

A highly complex and openly melodramatic story. Mizoguchi admitted that the film "didn't quite work." He tried to handle too much at once; several themes (the love story, Michiko's anxiety to protect the Musashino Field, social changes in postwar Japan, the invasion of Western civilization (a bar in the city is called "La vie est belle"), the life of students in town). The several sub-plots (Akiyama-Michiko, Michiko-Tsutomu, Tsutomu-the girl student he lives with) do not quite come together. The result is that the picture lacks the power and intensity of Mizoguchi's great films.

The value of The Lady of Musashino rests in the fine evocation of atmosphere--right from the opening shot of water flowing over reeds, from which the camera moves, in a huge crane shot, to outline the area and introduce the characters living in neighboring houses. This is a film of sensual visual description obtained through luminous photography and lush camera movements. The lyrical images, some of them recalling Renoir's Partie de campagne, include Tsutomu's return from the war, Michiko and Tsutomu's walk to the "Pond of Love," and the storm. There is also fine acting, particularly from Kinuyo Tanaka. Mizoguchi's favorite actress, she was to shine in his next picture, the famous The Life of Oharu.

A PLACE IN THE SUN George Stevens

Script: Michael Wilson and Harry Brown, based on the novel "An American Tragedy" by Theodore Dreiser and the play, adapted from the novel, by Patrick Kearney. Photography: William C. Mellor. Art Direction: Hans Dreier and Walter Tyler. Music: Franz Waxman. Cast: Montgomery Clift (George Eastman), Shelley Winters (Alice Tripp), Elizabeth Taylor (Angela Vickers), Herbert Heyes (Charles Eastman), Raymond Burr (Marlowe), Keefe Brasselle (Earl Eastman), Anne Revere (Hannah Eastman), Fred Clark (Bellows), Shepperd Strudwick (Anthony Vickers), Frieda Inescort (Mrs. Vickers), Lois Chartrand (Marsha), Kathryn Givney (Louise Eastman), Ted de Corsia (Judge), Walter Sande (Jansen), John Ridgely (Coroner), William R. Murphy (Whiting), Douglas Spencer (Boatkeeper), Charles Dayton (Kelly), Paul Frees (Morrison), John Reed (Joe Parker), Marilyn Dialon (Frances Brand), Ian Wolf (Dr. Wyeland).

George Stevens for Paramount, U. S. A. 10,990 ft., 122 mins.

The screen rights to "An American Tragedy," Dreiser's celebrated novel had a long history. First, Sergei Eisenstein, the great Soviet director planned to make it into a film during his stay in America, but Paramount rejected his script. After several other futile attempts by various directors, the story did reach the screen in 1931 in a film directed by Josef von Sternberg. The film gave rise to the famous court case, whereby the author accused the producers of mutilating the novel. Twenty years later Paramount decided to try again, this time entrusting the direction to George Stevens. The title was changed to A Place in the Sun and the hero renamed (in the novel he is called Clyde Griffiths).

A runaway from the poverty and severity of the religious mission run by his mother, George Eastman by chance meets a rich uncle who gives him a job in his factory. George seduces Alice Tripp, a fellow worker. When his rich relations, who have so far been ignoring him take him up again, George is promoted at work and invited to society parties. There he meets the rich and beautiful Angela Vickers. In the meantime Alice finds herself pregnant. The search for an abortionist proves fruitless, and she insists that George marry her. But by now he has become obsessed by the urge for social advancement, and sees Alice as the only obstacle to an exciting, prosperous future with Angela. He decides to murder Alice during a boat trip. Although in the event he is unable to go through with his plan, the girl accidentally drowns. George is arrested, brought to trial and sentenced to death for murder. After conversations with his mother and the prison chaplain he comes to realize that his intention to kill Alice and his failure to save her are tantamount to murder.

Dreiser saw the source of the tragedy in the protagonist's ambitions, in his being consumed by the desire to turn the American Dream into reality, and in the damage done to him by a puritan upbringing. The book emanates a profound sense of futility and loss and squarely accuses society which has destroyed his sense of values.

While von Sternberg's An American Tragedy, basically a study of frustrated aspirations, largely disregarded the social implications of the novel and concentrated instead on psychological realism, A Place in the Sun centers on the love story between George and Angela and on George's illusions and uncertainties. It offers no challenge to the American society and, just as the first version, largely abandons social comment. George is not at all confused as the hero was in the novel, but merely unfortunate; the film only briefly dwells on his adolescence. Angela is romanticized, which would have been justified if the film was a subjective vision, as seen through the eyes of an infatuated man. Karel Reisz comments in his review that Angela's visit to George in the condemned cell, during which she declares undying love for him "makes ... the precise opposite to Dreiser's point. In the novel, Angela refuses to see George from the moment he is accused; the suspicion of guilt and the revelation of his affair with a working girl are as socially undesirable as the murder itself." A Place in the Sun is thus essentially a glamorous "boy meets girl" picture, in which only the plot remains from the novel. This may not necessarily have been a bad thing, since the book now seems long-winded and stolid. In effect therefore neither film version is really "An American Tragedy," if for different reasons.

This way or the other, the novel's intensity wins now as it won before and A Place in the Sun succeeds in establishing a mood of its own. In his first socially critical film Stevens does in the end achieve the fatalism of Dreiser's novel. This is largely due to the very good film-making. The narrative style is more muscular than is usual in his pictures: The story is told slowly, but not heavily. Stevens often resorts to big close-ups (mainly in scenes between George and Alice) and slow, lingering dissolves. Particularly well handled are the scenes of the boat trip on a remote lake. Montgomery Clift, diffident and charming, gives an excellent performance as a social climber come to grief; he is accompanied by

Elizabeth Taylor as a spoilt rich man's daughter, and by Shelley Winters as a solid working-class girl.

THE RED INN (L'Auberge rouge) Claude Autant-Lara

Script: Jean Aurenche, based on the folk story "L'Auberge sanglante de Peyrebelle". Dialogues: Aurenche and Pierre Bost. Photography: André Bac. Music: René Cloërec. Art Direction: Max Douy. Cast: Fernandel (Monk), Julien Carette (Martin, the innkeeper), Françoise Rosay (Marie Martin), Marie-Claire Olivia (Mathilde), Didier d'Yd (Janou), Lud Germain (Fetiche), Nane Germon (Elisa), Gregoire Aslan (Barbeuf), Jean-Roger Caussimon (Darwin), Jacques Charron (Rodolphe), A. Vialla (Marchioness), Dalibert (Woodcutter). Sung Commentary: Yves Montand.

Simon Schiffrin for Memnon Films, France. 8550 ft., 95 mins.

The Red Inn is virtually a summary of the formula which dominated world cinema during the 8-year period in the 50's between the end of Neorealism and the arrival of the French Nouvelle Vague and was characterized by the literary nature of the narrative, the thematic turning towards the past and was addressing itself to the popular audience. These features, which can hardly be considered positive, appeared particularly clearly in France, where the work of leading directors sounded a loud empty tone. Claude Autant-Lara, doubtless an intelligent director sincerely engaged in caricaturing the bourgeoisie found objects for satire not in the streets of 1951 Paris but in 19th-century drawing rooms from the novels of Stendhal, as in Scarlet and Black, or in snowbound back-of-the-beyond at the time of Restoration, as in The Red Inn. What is more, Autant-Lara did not deal with real-life conflicts, but with somewhat varnished plots, colorful rather than engulfing. He came closer to modern times later in the 50's, in La Traversée de Paris (1956) set in wartime France and in En cas de malheur (1958). Still, both these films were stale cinema, ambiguously reconciled with commercial interests. The Red Inn is an old wife's tale about horrible crimes in suspicious places and begins with a ballad sung by Yves Montand while the camera shows a vista as if from a puppet show--paper landscape under cotton wool snow. Perhaps what is to follow will be for real. Not a chance. The whole film is dominated by stiff and theatrical settings, stiff photography and also some of the acting. In fact all this would be unacceptable if Autant-Lara, assisted by Fernandel (who gives a really good performance as a monk) did not touch the film with the magic wand of bravura direction. This changed everything: artificiality was concealed under magic atmosphere, vigorous and intelligent humor, and the film turned out to be sufficiently intriguing to be forgiven for its faults.

It is true, the script was a sound basis for the success of this perverse, macabre tale. Inn-keeper Martin and his wife Marie murder their customers for money. They are overjoyed when a coach breaks down and the passengers arrive at the inn for the night. Marie confesses to the monk who is also staying at the inn of their past crimes and tells him about the one they plan to commit the next day. The monk is in some difficulty: he cannot reveal the secret of the confession, but still feels he must warn the prospective victims. He does this using a very clever trick. In vain: although the murderous hoteliers are arrested before they have time to carry out their evil plans, the coach crashes into a precipice, the bridge over which had had its pillars sawn away by a servant. So what was to be, is, despite the derisive words of the ballad proclaiming that happiness is exclusively for the virtuous.

THE UNDERDOG (Der Untertan) Wolfgang Staudte

Script: Fritz Staudte and Wolfgang Staudte, from the novel by Heinrich Mann. Photography: Robert Baberske. Music: Horst-Hanns Sieber. Art Direction: Erich Zander and Karl Schneider. Cast: Werner Peters (Diederich Hessling), Erich Nadler (Father Hessling), Gertrud Bergmann (Mother Hessling), Carola Braunbock (Emmi Hessling), Emmi Burg (Magda Hessling), Eduard von Winterstein (Buck, magistrate and liberal leader), Paul Esser (von Wulkow, government representative), Raimund Schelcher (Wolfgang Buck, defense counsel), Ernst Legal (Pastor Zillich), Wolfgang Kühne (Dr. Mennicke, public prosecutor), Friedrich Maurer (Herr Göpel), Fridel Nowak (Frau Göpel), Sabine Thalbach (Agnes Göpel), Hans-Georg Laubenthal (Mahlmann), Renate Fischer (Gusti Daimchen), Paul Mederow (Dr. Heuteufel), Fritz Staudte (Kuhlemann), Friedrich Gnass (Napoleon Fischer, Hessling's chief mechanic).

DEFA, East Germany. 9721 ft., 108 mins.

One very rarely encounters a note of national self-criticism as strong as in The Underdog. Following Heinrich Mann's novel, Staudte picks to pieces the Germanic myths of strength, subservience to authority, unthinking obedience to discipline and fear of those in power. It is true, this exercise in total satire talks ostensibly about Imperial Germany, but the final commentary adds what Mann merely suggested: as the main character behaved in the Kaiser's day, many others did later. The results one can see for oneself on the screen: ruins of a German town destroyed in the last war shown against the statue of Wilhelm II.

The Underdog is the life story of the only son of a provincial paper mill owner, from his birth in 1885 until he becomes an overlord of his native Netzig and the owner of his father's mill which manufactures toilet paper "World Glory" with the Kaiser's aphorisms printed on it. Childhood, university, membership of the New Teutonia Corps, doctorate in chemistry, army service, directorship of the mill: at every stage immorality, stupidity, the show of strength. Diederich seduces a young girl; when her father demands that he marry her, he threatens him with violence. He then goes on to marry an heiress.

Staudte achieved his aims with impressive accuracy; it is a pity though that, in spite of the generally good pace and no lack of ideas, the very vehemence of the attack on Kaiser-worship resulted in a certain stylistic heaviness. The director and the title character are separated by an abyss both intellectually and in their awareness of history, but their very different rationales give off a similar sound. So, verbatim narrative dominates in the film and is reinforced by the commentary which generally merely supports the image and does not of itself initiate any new ideas. And if from time to time there is in the film an occasional departure towards the ironic or towards Expressionist metaphor, these passages are as a rule weaker than the rest which is realist and somewhat didactic in tone. Despite these faults and the rather dull touch of filmed literature (which is something typical of the cinema of the early 50's) one cannot deny The Underdog merit. In the very difficult field of screen satire Staudte's film is actually among the more interesting efforts.

DEATH OF A SALESMAN Laslo Benedek

Script: Stanley Roberts, based on the play by Arthur Miller. Photography: Franz F. Planer. Music: Alex North. Art Direction: Cary Odell. Cast: Fredric March (Willy Loman), Mildred Dunnock (Linda Loman), Kevin McCarthy (Biff), Cameron Mitchell (Happy), Howard Smith (Charley), Royal Beal (Ben), Don Keefer (Bernard), Jesse White (Stanley), Claire Carleton (Miss Francis), David Alpert (Howard Wagner), Elizabeth Fraser (Miss Forsythe), Patricia Walker (Letta).

Stanley Kramer, U. S. A. 10,054 ft., 112 mins.

Willy Loman, a middle-aged traveling salesman, interrupts a business trip and returns home to contemplate the stages of his progressive decline. He tries to grasp the reasons for the failure of his business and of his family life. Memories and fantasies crowd his mind. He feels a sense of guilt towards his wife and is mortified to see his failure reflected in his sons. Willy remembers how he tried to find an office job when his earnings as a salesman began to dwindle, and how he tried, in vain, to persuade his elder son Biff to do the same. He remembers how his son lost respect for him when he found him in a sleazy hotel bedroom with a prostitute. Bewildered and desperate, Willy kills himself.

For the theme of his first important picture Benedek reached for Arthur Miller's celebrated play which Elia Kazan had directed on stage in New York and London. It is said that the play's associative style is the result of Miller's experience as a radio writer. This is a very faithful screen adaptation, enacted, as on the stage, on two dramatic levels: the prosaic present and the idealized memories of the protagonist. The interesting thing is that both levels are often combined within a single take. In other words, that which is normally shown as a flashback and dealt with in cuts and dissolves, serves as background for current events. This device of stage provenance had already shown itself to be cinematically effective in Duvivier's Un Carnet de bal and Sjöberg's Miss Julie. In Death of a Salesman it is enough for Willy to go through a door to find himself in the past. Imaginatively used, the method gives very powerful results by following the logic of the workings of the hero's mind; as Will talks to his wife, he remembers another room he shared with a prostitute--this is shown directly in the background through the open door.

Fredric March is very effective as the demented salesman, and the parts of his wife and sons are also well played. Death of a Salesman is a forceful study of a man at the end of his tether, and a deeply tragic demonstration of the human price paid for the cult of success.

THE YOUNG CHOPIN (Młodość Chopina) Aleksander Ford

Script: Ford, inspired by short stories by Jerzy Broszkiewicz, Stanisław Hadyna, Gustaw Bachner and Jan Korngold. Dialogues: Leon Kruczkowski. Photography: Jaroslav Tuzar. Music: Fryderyk Chopin, Johann Sebastian Bach, Wolfgang Amadeus Mozart, Nicolo Paganini, Joseph Franz Karl Lanner, Josef Slavík and Kazimierz Serocki, arranged by the latter. Art Direction: Roman Mann, Cast: Czesław Wołłejko (Fryderyk Chopin), Aleksandra Śląska (Konstancja Gładkowska), Jan Kurnakowicz (Professor Jan Elsner), Igor Smiałowski (Tytus Wojciechowski), Justyna Kreczmarowa (Zuzka), Leon Pietraszkiewicz (Senator Novosiltsov), Gustaw Buszyński (Prince Adam Czartoryski), Seweryn Butrym (Prince Franciszek Drucki-Lubecki), Jerzy Duszyński (Stefan Witwicki), Jerzy Kaliszewski (Maurycy Mochnacki), Zbigniew Łobodziński (Seweryn Goszczyński), Tadeusz Białoszczyński (Joachim Lelewel).

Wytwórnia Filmów Fabularnych Nr 1 w Łodzi, Poland. 9440 ft., 105 mins.

An experiment in the field of screen biography, The Young Chopin claims as many virtues as it has striking faults which badly date the film. This is perhaps the most characteristic Aleksander Ford work, at once spontaneous and artificial, innovatory and academic. The idea was to show the life of Chopin in the five year period from the start of his musical studies until the November Rising in Poland against the Russian rule (1830-31) and at the same time to explore the sources of the composer's inner development as expressed in his work. This was the period of fiery Romanticism, a trend particularly close to the Polish national temperament. Therefore Ford inscribed the film in the Romantic aesthetic framework--with a lack of structural self-control; but with dynamism, lyrical grandiloquence, and visual metaphors which refer to 19th-century painting. This is what gave The Young Chopin the mark of originality, although it carried with it pictorialist falseness and outworn symbolism. The atmosphere, the very painstaking designs and the outstanding acting from Wołłejko as Chopin, even though the historical background inspired by the Socialist Realism is stiff and bookish, made Chopin true and convincing as a man and artist. The film portrays his music, against the background of the period, in all its splendor. The early parts of the picture which describe the political situation in Poland under the rule of the Tsarist governor Novosiltsov are quite lamentable--with obtrusive, loaded dialogues and heavy-handed portrayal of characters. But the sequence of a country wedding which immediately follows is a true masterpiece of editing, visual composition, cinematic rhythm and camera work. From this sequence onwards the film, dull so far, has nothing for which to apologize until the finale in which Ford again slips into rhetoric and "artistic" allegories. In the meantime however he manages to show with great skill, using very little dialogue, the links between the great artist and the folklore which inspired his work. Ford conveys the poetry of the Polish landscape very well and for the first time in the cinema creates a convincing atmosphere of artistic creativity in the field of music. The autonomous richness of expression of these scenes mean that in Ford's Chopin "bio-pic" the scales are tipped towards the positive.

REPAST (Meshi) Mikio Naruse

Script: Sumie Tanaka and Toshiro Ide, from the novel by Fumiko Hayashi. Script Supervision: Yasunari Kawabata. Photography: Masao Tamai. Music: Fumio Hayasaka. Art Direction: Satoru Chuko. Cast: Ken Uehara (Hatsunosuke Okamoto, a young salaried man), Setsuko Hara (Michiyo, his wife), Yukiko Shimazaki (Satoko Okamoto, his niece), Kan Nihonyanagi (Kazuo Takenaka, Michiyo's cousin), Hisako Takibana (Sumi Takenaka, Kazuo's mother), Eitaro Shindo (Yuzo Takenaka, Kazuo's father), Haruko Sugimura (Matsu Murata), Yoko Sugi (Mitsuko Murata), Keiju Kobayashi (Shinzo Murata),

Ranko Hanai (Koyoshi Dohya), Akiko Kazami (Seiko Tomiyasu), Mitsue Tachibana (Katsuko Suzuki), Chieko Nakakita (Keiko Yamakita).

Toho, Japan. 8711 ft., 97 mins.

Naruse gained international recognition with Mother and in fact outside Japan he is known only by this one film. In his own country however Mother is recognized as only a small part of his achievement and together with Ozu and Mizoguchi, Naruse is considered there one of the greatest Japanese film-makers. While Ozu was interested in relations between different generations within a family and Mizoguchi portrayed lonely women in his films, Naruse, particularly after 1950, combines as it were both these interests. He deals with women within marriage. In a long series of very closely related films Repast is probably the one which reflects Naruse's attitudes with greatest clarity. The main preoccupation of the heroine--the preparation of meals--is determined already in the film's title. Such is the scale within which she is permitted to realize and express her personality. Well, it had been like this for centuries--and not only in Japan, although there the discrimination against women was particularly glaring. A moment comes when Michiyo realizes that such a good and quiet life does not satisfy her. She wants her worth to be recognized--so she resigns her position as barely noticed servant of her dull husband and leaves the household.

The narrative of Naruse's films is sustained in specific, traditionally Japanese moods, mono-no-aware and kanashimi, which can be described as the beauty of sadness, the understanding of the contradictions of existence, a melancholy acceptance of the unavoidability of fate combined with a deep love of life. The climate of the works of Ozu and Mizoguchi is very similar, but Naruse commanded neither the power of Ozu's psychological observation nor Mizoguchi's vehement tragic sense. The result is that the contents of Naruse's films are often made less than real by these moods: when poeticizing blurs social reality and the sharpness of events, ersatz sentimentality steals onto the screen. This weakness, of which the Japanese are aware, explains the disparity between the director's reputation at home and abroad. But Naruse's cinema contains more than a sometimes artificial subtlety. The director left behind a number of outstanding pictures, such as the intelligently ambiguous pre-war Wife, Be Like a Rose; Mother which with its contemplation of detail recalls the works of Ozu; Floating Clouds with its piercing pessimism; and finally Repast in which a muslin subtlety of characterization does not disagree with psychological intimacy but supports it symbiotically.

A STREETCAR NAMED DESIRE Elia Kazan

Script: Tennessee Williams, from his own play adapted by Oscar

Saul. Photography: Harry Stradling. Music: Alex North. Art Direction: Richard Day. Cast: Vivien Leigh (Blanche DuBois), Marlon Brando (Stanley Kowalski), Kim Hunter (Stella Kowalski), Karl Malden (Mitch), Rudy Bond (Steve Hubbell), Nick Dennis (Pablo Gonzales), Peg Hillias (Eunice Hubbell), Wright King (Young collector), Richard Garrick (Doctor), Ann Dere (Strange woman), Edna Thomas (Mexican woman), Mickey Kuhn (Sailor), Chester Jones (Street vendor), Marietta Canty (Negro woman).

Charles K. Feldman--Elia Kazan for Warner Bros., U. S. A. 122 mins.

Blanche DuBois arrives penniless in New Orleans to stay with her sister Stella and the sister's husband Stanley. She reaches their seedy tenement house apartment in a streetcar called "Desire." A southern belle past her prime, she has nothing to her name apart from a refined upbringing, a bad reputation as a neurotic nymphomaniac and the memories of a genteel youth. She is desperate to escape soiled reality. Stanley ruthlessly shatters Blanche's illusions. He discovers her past and reveals it to her middle-aged suitor. As Stella is having a baby in a hospital, Stanley rapes Blanche thus finally disturbing her precarious mental balance. The only refuge remaining for her is madness.

The play, dense and evocative, relies for its impact on the clash between beautiful fantasy and seedy reality and on the oppressive, claustrophobic climate of the South, which Williams always renders so well. The picture follows the play's plot closely; the trouble is that it is very difficult to break through the essentially theatrical character of Williams's writing. Kazan did not even try ("Of all my films, Streetcar is one which is most like theatre ... a beautiful play that I shot without softening or deepening it, filming it as it was because there was nothing to change..."). Part of the blame can be assigned to the leading actress: Vivien Leigh had previously appeared in the play in England, directed by Laurence Olivier, and Kazan complained of her acting being false and theatrical in the first part of the film. Yet he is not without blame himself. It is simply that the narrative virtuosity of the story was dampened by the profuse theatrical dialogues, especially since Kazan staged the film in a theatrical fashion (the recurrent symbolic figure of a blind Mexican flower-seller completely misfires), almost entirely in the interiors, and allowed the actors too much dramatic amplitude in expressing feelings. This criticism applies mainly to Vivien Leigh's histrionic portrayal of Blanche, but even in part to the celebrated "method" performance from Marlon Brando, whose Stanley Kowalski, a mumbling, primitive, sweaty, vulgar but tender "Polack" made him an international star. In fact only Kim Hunter as Stella gives a truly cinematic performance. Kazan did not really succeed in conveying the mood of the South--with its heat, its madness, its sexual tension.

Still, there are compensations. The excellent use of the soundtrack (in evoking, for instance, the voices from the past which haunt Blanche) is an example of how a director can tone down theatricality, if not actually remove it. Similar comment can be made about the dreamlike music (by Alex North, whose scores had often been rather heavy). On the other hand, the photography is unadventurous: the camera is used to relate a story and to pace dramatic tension, but does not create independent values of its own--apart from isolated instances, like the scene of Stanley's rape of Blanche, concluded with a shot of a shattered mirror reflecting Blanche's bent head.

A Streetcar Named Desire is simply a well told psychological drama, fortunately handled without directorial hysteria--an interesting film, if essentially a superficial one. It is a far cry from such Kazan works as East of Eden or Baby Doll.

ALICE IN WONDERLAND Clyde Geronimi, Hamilton Luske and Wilfred Jackson

---

Script: Winston Hibler, Bill Peet, Joe Rinaldi, Bill Cottrell, Joe Grant, Del Connell, Ted Sears, Erdman Penner, Milt Banta, Dick Kelsey, Dick Huemer, Tom Oreb and John Walkridge, from the books "Alice's Adventures in Wonderland" and "Through the Looking-Glass and What Alice Found There" by Lewis Carroll. Visual Inspiration: John Tenniel's drawings for first editions of Lewis Carroll's books. Designs and Animation: Milt Kahl, Ward Kimball, Franklin Thomas, Eric Larson, John Lounsbery, Oliver Johnston Jr., Wolfgang Reitherman, Marc Davis, Les Clark and Norman Ferguson (Animating directors); Hal King, Judge Whitaker, Hal Ambro, Bill Justice, Phil Duncan, Bob Carlson, Don Lusk, Cliff Nordberg, Harvey Toombs, Fred Moore, Marvin Woodward, Hugh Fraser and Charles Nichols (Character animators); Joshua Meador, Dan MacManus, George Rowley and Blaine Gibson (Effects animation). Music: Oliver Wallace. Songs: "Very Good Advice," "In a World of My Own," "All in a Golden Afternoon," "Alice in Wonderland," "The Walrus and the Carpenter," "The Caucus Race," "I'm Late," "Painting the Roses Red" and "March of the Cards" by Bob Hilliard and Sammy Fain; " 'Twas Brillig" by Don Raye and Gene DePaul; "A Very Merry Un-birthday" by Mack David, Al Hoffman and Jerry Livingston; "We'll Smoke the Blighter Out," "Old Father William" and "A E I O U" by Oliver Wallace and Ted Sears. Voices: Kathryn Beaumont (Alice), Ed Wynn (Mad Hatter), Richard Haydn (Caterpillar), Sterling Holloway (Cheshire Cat), Jerry Colonna (March Hare), Verna Felton (Queen of Hearts), Pat O'Malley (Walrus/Carpenter/Tweedledee/Tweedledum), Bill Thompson (White Rabbit/Dodo), Heather Angel (Alice's sister), Joseph Kearns (Doorknob), Larry Grey (Bill), Queenie Leonard (Bird in the Tree), Dink Trout (King of Hearts), Doris Lloyd (The Rose), James Macdonald (Dormouse), The Mello Men (Card Painters), Don Barclay.

Walt Disney Productions, U. S. A. 6772 ft., 75 mins. Technicolor.

The Alice books were written, under the pen-name of Lewis Carroll, by the Oxford mathematician, Charles Lutwidge Dodgson for Alice Liddell, the little daughter of a friend. For their charm, wit, political satire and the sometimes savage caricature of real Oxford dons and people from the public arena, they soon achieved tremendous popularity not only among the young. The story goes that Queen Victoria, enchanted by Carroll's account of Alice's adventures, ordered all his writings to be brought to her. She was most surprised when they all turned out to be about mathematics!

Made only two years after Cinderella, Alice in Wonderland amounts to considerable progress in the originality of Disney's design. It seems that much of the merit for this is owed to Lewis Carroll and his wonderful imagination. This time Disney really had things to draw! He could not claim merit in the past for modernizing or developing the run-of-the-mill didacticism of such age-old fairy tales as "Cinderella," but when it came to "Alice in Wonderland," this classic of children's literature, he transplanted it to the screen beyond reproach. Although of course many political references must have got lost in the process, the film is as rich in ideas as the book, and is maintained in the same spirit of a perhaps cool, but imaginative Surrealist romp. Take for example the Cheshire Cat character, or such scenes as the game of croquet or the Mad Hatter's tea party. Alice in Wonderland revives the burlesque of the silent cinema, something done only once before, by Jacques Tati in Jour de fête. The inner logic of Lewis Carroll's fantasies, their philosophical undertones and his splendid ability of observing the regularities inherent in human actions are all closely related to what had come out spontaneously of man's collisions with the surrounding world in the screen comedies of the 20's, particularly in those of Buster Keaton.

LE PLAISIR Max Ophüls

Script: Jacques Natanson and Ophüls, based on the stories "Le Masque," "La Maison Tellier" and "Le Modèle" by Guy de Maupassant [A fourth sketch for the film, to be called "La Femme de Paul" was abandoned for lack of money.] Music: Joë Hajos and Maurice Yvain, with themes from Jacques Offenbach. Art Direction: Jean d'Eaubonne. Costumes: Georges Annenkov.

LE MASQUE: Photography: Christian Matras. Cast: Claude Dauphin (Doctor), Janine Viénot (His friend), Jean Galland (Ambroise, the masked man), Gaby Morlay (Denise, his wife), Paul Azaïs (Director of the dance hall), Emile Genevois (Bellboy), Gaby Bruyere (Frimousse), Huguette Montréal and Liliane Yvernault (Dancers).

LA MAISON TELLIER: Photography: Christian Matras. Cast: Madeleine Renaud (Madame Tellier), Danielle Darrieux (Rosa), Ginette Leclerc (Flora), Mila Parély (Raphaële), Paulette Dubost (Fernande), Mathilde Casadesus (Louise), Jean Gabin (Joseph Rivet), Héléna Manson (Marie Rivet), Joëlle Jany (Constance Rivet), Pierre Brasseur (Julien Ledentu, a salesman), René Blancard (Mayor), Amédée (Waiter), Michel Vadet (Sailor), Joe Dest (The German), Claire Olivier (Mme. Tourneveau), Georges Vitray (The captain), Arthur Devère (Employee), Charles Vissière (Old man from Normandy), Zélie Yzelle (His wife), Antoine Balpêtré, Marcel Pérès, Louis Seigner, Robert Lombard, Henri Crémieux, Jean Mayer, Palau and Georges Baconnet (Clients of the Maison Tellier).

LE MODELE: Photography: Philippe Agostini. Cast: Daniel Gélin (Jean), Jean Servais (Narrator [Guy de Maupassant]), Simone Simon (Joséphine), Michel Vadet (Journalist), René Pascal, Marcel Reuzé.

Stera Films C. C. F. C., France. 8550 ft., 95 mins.

A comparison of de Maupassant's writing with Ophüls' baroque cinematic style, a confrontation of their fields of interest leads to one inescapable conclusion: Ophüls could hardly find himself a more suitable scriptwriter than de Maupassant. Of course, this argument works both ways: the master of literary miniature so precise in detail, atmosphere, subtle in the description of moods and feelings had a most worthy screen adapter in the maker of Liebelei.

Le Plaisir is composed of three stories. "The Mask" is a story of an old man who wants to retain his youth and who goes to the Palais de la Danse every night wearing a mask which makes him look young. "La Maison Tellier," the longest of the three parts, is about the Sunday excursion of Madame Tellier and the girls from her brothel to the first communion of a niece. Finally, "The Model," the last and the weakest story about a successful artist goading his pretty mistress into suicide. She jumps out of a window but survives as a cripple. Remorse makes the painter marry her.

The stories themselves offer the spectator little apart from dainty observations about human passions, illusions and sentiments--with the exception perhaps of the first where tension-filled frames erupt in the finale with a veritable drama of passing time. All the same, they are told, for all their respect for de Maupassant's behavioral and psychological observation, with lustre and vividness, intelligence, discreetness and Ophüls' characteristic flair in the use of the camera.

THE TALE OF GENJI (Genji Monogatari) Kozaburo Yoshimura

Script: Kaneto Shindo, from the novel by Murasaki Shikibu. Script Supervision: Junichiro Tanizaki. Photography: Kohei Sugiyama. Music: Akira Ifukube. Art Direction: Hiroshi Mizutani. Cast: Kazuo Hasegawa (Hikaru Genji), Michiyo Kogure (Fujitsubo), Machiko Kyo (Awaji), Nobuko Otowa (Murasaki), Mitsuko Mito (Aoi), Yuji Hori (Yoshinari), Denjiro Okochi (Harima Nyudo), Yumiko Hasegawa (Oborozukiyo), Eitaro Ozawa (Mikado), Chieko Higashiyama (Kokiden).

Masaichi Nagata for Daiei, Japan. 11,158 ft., 124 mins.

Yoshimura, who entered Shochiku way back in 1929 broke with the studio to form, in March 1950, together with Kaneto Shindo, the independent film company Kindai Eiga Kyokai (Association of Modern Art Cinema). Himself a director since 1951, Shindo wrote the scripts for Yoshimura's best films.

Yoshimura specializes in period films which often reflect modern problems, and is particularly interested in women. A very versatile director, he handled a great variety of themes and never lacked ideas or courage when it came to introducing technical innovations. For instance, he has been influenced by Pudovkin's ideas on editing which, together with the use of a very mobile camera (the critics once accused him of making the audience "seasick") give his films a greater dramatic economy and a faster pace than is usual in Japan. He was always able to offer a new interpretation to old and well-known things, and has a great gift for choosing a style appropriate for each theme. In short, in his eclecticism Yoshimura resembles the French director René Clément.

The Tale of Genji is a film version of what is simply the world's first novel--written in the 11th century by a lady-in-waiting at the Imperial Court. It had not been filmed before for a very simple reason: prior to 1945 it was forbidden to film dramas set inside the Court. The novel, published in English in two fat volumes, is very difficult to synopsize. Set in the Meian era (8th century), it concerns the search for the perfect woman by an illegitimate son of the Emperor. Genji is a sort of Japanese Don Juan, a man said to be more beautiful than any woman in the empire. It was considered a shame to dress him in man's clothing. After his mother dies, Genji grows up loved by his father, but detested by the father's new favorite and by a court minister. The minister's daughter loves him, but Genji marries Aoi and founds a clan. He falls in love with a favorite, Fujitsubo, and meets her niece Murasaki. He adopts Murasaki and gives her a gentle upbringing. After his wife's death Genji becomes involved in intrigues and has to take refuge with his uncle who plans to marry him to his daughter Awaji. Genji likes the girl but she is in love with a young man, Yoshinari. When the new Emperor summons Genji and makes him Prime Minister, Genji brings with him Murasaki (who loves him in secret), Awaji and Yoshinari. When Awaji tells him she is expecting a child by Yoshinari, the furious Genji attacks the young man and is brought back to reason by Murasaki. Finally Genji understands Murasaki's love and swears fidelity to her.

While tracing the tortuous story of love adventures, Yoshimura is at pains to reproduce richly the indolent life at the court, the manners and custom of the time, and to give delicate psychological portrayals of the characters. Murasaki's plight seems as real today as it was in the past.

THE LOST ONE (Der Verlorene) Peter Lorre

Script: Lorre, Benno Vigny and Axel Eggebrecht. Photography: Václav Vích. Music: Willi Schmidt-Gentner. Art Direction: Franz Schroedter and K. Weber. Editing: Karl Otto Bartning. Cast: Peter Lorre (Dr. Karl Rothe), Karl John (Hösch), Helmut Rudolph (Colonel Winkler), Renate Mannhardt (Inge Hermann), Johanna Hofer (Mrs. Hermann), Lotte Rausch (Helene), Gisela Trowe (Prostitute), Eva-Ingeborg Scholz (Ursula Weber), Kurt Meister (Preefke), Alexander Hunzinger (Drunkard), Hansi Wendler (Secretary), Josef Dahmen (Canteen manager), Anneliese Witt (Polish woman), Georg Siebert (Blaschek), Hans Fitze (Publican), Kurt Fuss (Bald man), Helmut Eichberg (Lt. Col. Bydersalm), Peter Ahrweiler (Lt. Col. Marquardt), Joachim Hess (Lieutenant), Frauke Stephan (Nurse), Hans Schmitz (Paschke).

Arnold Pressburger, West Germany. 98 mins.

It is a matter of regret that Peter Lorre's great performance as a child murderer in Fritz Lang's M, apart from establishing his reputation as the most unusual actor of his generation, made him type-cast as a sardonic psychopathic killer. Lorre, who left Germany soon after the Nazis came to power, appeared as such in character parts in Hitchcock's The Man Who Knew Too Much and Secret Agent in England, and in scores of Hollywood pictures of which the most notable were The Maltese Falcon, Casablanca and Arsenic and Old Lace. After the war Lorre briefly returned to Germany where he made The Lost One, his only film as director.

Dr. Karl Rothe, a physician in a refugee camp, encounters his former colleague, Hösch, in a new transport of refugees. During a nocturnal drinking session Rothe remembers past events. During the war he worked as a research biologist. When told that his fiancée was passing the secret results of his work on a new vaccine to London, he strangled her. With the help of Hösch who worked as a counter-intelligence agent, the murder was passed off as suicide. But it unleashed in Rothe a compulsion to kill women who reminded him of his dead fiancée. Declared dead in an air raid, he began work in the camp under the name of Neumeister. In the morning Rothe shoots Hösch with his own gun and then commits suicide by walking into an on-coming train.

Lorre's film noir is indirectly a comment on his reasons for having left Germany in 1933, and also throws much light on his entire acting career from M onwards--as psychopath-in-chief of the cinema of the 30's and 40's, as Anthony Perkins was (although admittedly in a different style) in the 60's and 70's. The Lost One is not however a conventional attack on the Nazi past, but rather a study of the pressures on an individual by a society in which human values ceased to count, the description of conditions which made Nazism possible and which turned Dr. Rothe into a pathological killer. He was not a victim of a pernicious philosophy or of orders which he had to carry out--but of an all-pervading atmosphere of evil. The mood of The Lost One is strange and dreamlike, an effect for which Vích's Expressionistic photography is greatly responsible. The critic Tony Rayns considers the film "Lorre's hommage to the work of his fellow Hollywood exile, Fritz Lang" and indeed there are here many images, motifs and stylistic devices of Lang's cinema including the structure of the story told, fatalistically, entirely in flashback (compare Lang's Destiny). One also wonders whether the motif of the railway line in the beginning and the end was not inspired by Tolstoy's "Anna Karenina."

AND YET WE LIVE (Dokkoi Ikiteru) Tadashi Imai

Script: Ujitoshi Iwasa, Kenzo Hirata and Imai. Photography: Yoshio Miyajima and Shunichiro Nakao. Music: Masao Oki. Art Direction: Kazuo Kubo. Cast: Chojuro Karawazaki (Shuzo Mori, a casual laborer), Shizue Karawazaki (Sato, his wife), Rosaku Karawazaki (Yuichi, their son), Yoshiko Machida (Tamiyo, their daughter), Kanemon Nakamura (Hanamura, a casual laborer), Isao Kimura (Mizuno), Hatae Kishi (Mizuno's wife), Shotaro Ichikawa (Mizuno's father), Izumi Imamura (Mizuno's sister), Katsuyuki Terada (Yoshi Mizuno), Ken Terada (Ken Mizuno), Choko Iida (Akiyama, an old woman), Kunitaro Karawazaki (Yamakawa Oya).

Shinsei Eiga/Zenshinza, Japan. 9203 ft., 102 mins.

After the period immediately following the war when leftist tendencies gained ground in Japan, big capital and right-wing forces began increasingly to regain their old influence. As a matter of fact, this state of affairs was convenient to the occupation forces. The deepening class struggle was evidenced by the famous 200-day (from spring to autumn 1948) strike at Toho, the largest film corporation in Japan. The local trade union stood up in defense of over 200 people who had been dismissed; the showdown ended in compromise, but a group of film-makers left Toho soon afterwards to form, in early 1950, an independent company called Shinsei Eiga. Among them was the communist Tadashi Imai, a director of some 11 years' standing, maker of the popular films Blue Mountains (1949) and Until the Day We Meet Again (1950), an anti-militarist story of a couple of lovers in wartime. Imai also directed the first film produced by the new company, And Yet We Live, a dramatic story of a four-strong working family which unemployment had deprived of livelihood. Casual collecting of scrap metal suffices only to feed the children, the attempt to steal meets with no success, the father's efforts to find work fail and finally the decision to commit suicide is reached. Although--like in Umberto D.--the sudden realization of the value of a close person's life (the drowning little son) provides salvation and the tragic decision is not fulfilled; the hero--again like in Umberto D.--only finds himself where he started from. Such is life: at that time in Japan there were cases of people advertising their lives for sale for 50,000 yen to be paid to the advertiser's family. This was only 1000 times as much as the price of a cinema ticket. Fifty thousand yen was also the price of one share in Imai's film, sold to the future audience on the co-operative principle.

While the "Neorealist" style of Kurosawa's One Wonderful Sunday and Drunken Angel was a spontaneous outcome of a creative program, Imai, fascinated by Shoeshine and Bicycle Thieves, consciously patterned his film on Neorealism. The parallels between And Yet We Live and Umberto D. are quite striking and go as far as the characteristic "circular" structure: in the finale of both films characters return to the starting point. In fact Imai did not want to copy the means of expression of the Neorealists but to use the same creative method. His aim was to create a proletarian cinema which would reflect social reality; such cinema did not exist in Japan. This is perhaps why And Yet We Live is as convincing and, for all its simplicity, as individual as the works of the Italian Neorealism. The subject matter was sufficiently important to make possible a work which, while dispensing with emphasis, moralizing and formal virtuosity, is one of the more interesting early post-war Japanese films.

AN AMERICAN IN PARIS Vincente Minnelli

Script: Alan Jay Lerner and Alan Lin. Photography: Alfred Gilks and John Alton (ballet sequence photography). Music: George Gershwin. Songs: Ira and George Gershwin (lyrics by E. Ray Goetz and B. G. DeSylva). Art Direction: Cedric Gibbons and Preston Ames. Choreography: Gene Kelly. Editing: Adrienne Fazan. Cast: Gene Kelly (Jerry Mulligan), Leslie Caron (Lise), Oscar Levant (Adam Cook), Georges Guetary (Henri Baurel), Nina Foch (Milo Roberts), Eugene Borden (Georges Mattieu), Martha Bamattre (Mathilde Mattieu), Ann Codee (Thérèse), George Davis (François), Hayden Rorke (Tommy Baldwin), Paul Maxey (John McDowd), Dick Wessel (Ben Macrow), Mary Young (Old Woman Flower Vendor).

Arthur Freed for MGM, U. S. A. 10,204 ft., 113 mins. Technicolor.

It is difficult to find anything particularly original in the plot of this story about an American painter resident in the capital of France, a rich lady compatriot who buys his paintings and wants to organize an exhibition of his work and a Paris shop girl who is his friend's girl. If one considers, however, that the scriptwriter's task was to prepare the groundwork for a fairy-like spectacle, the simplicity of the plot must be regarded as its strength and not as its weakness. The abandonment of the formula whereby colorful adventures of situational comedy are somewhat artificially seasoned with dancing interludes amounts to a new development in the genre. Kelly and Donen used a different formula in On the Town and Singin' in the Rain: they expanded the story and integrated it with dance. Minnelli on the other hand, who already in the 30's had a considerable reputation as a theatrical set designer and ballet director, places in An American in Paris the main stress on the visual aspect, and entrusts to the choreography even the solution of the plot. This 17-minute final spectacular is decisive for the quality of the film. From the formal viewpoint the film is a five-part illustration of Gershwin's music whose individual fragments (springtime in Paris, flower fair, a walk, the blues, the finale) are filmed with different color dominants and the set designs attempt to correspond to the style of the paintings of Dufy, Manet, Renoir, Utrillo, Rousseau, Degas and Toulouse-Lautrec. The imitation of Renoir, despite the stunning verve of the staging, irritates somewhat with its impudent copying of Impressionism with the aid of plastic sets--but the cascades of color and light, the narrative rhythm and the grace of the movements of the pair of leading actors (Kelly is at times even outdone by the debuting Leslie Caron who was, after the success of An American in Paris, whisked away to Hollywood) ensure for the picture a leading position in the annals of the genre. Many consider it the best of all.

ACE IN THE HOLE (THE BIG CARNIVAL) Billy Wilder

Script: Wilder, Lesser Samuels and Walter Newman. Photography: Charles Lang Jr. Music: Hugo Friedhofer. Art Direction: Hal

Pereira and Earl Hedrick. Cast: Kirk Douglas (Charles Tatum), Jan Sterling (Lorraine Minosa), Bob Arthur (Herbie Cook), Porter Hall (Jacob Q. Boot), Frank Cady (Federber), Richard Benedict (Leo Minosa), Ray Teal (Sheriff), Lewis Martin (McCardle), John Berkes (Papa Minosa), Frances Dominguez (Mama Minosa), Gene Evans (Deputy Sheriff), Frank Jaquet (Smollett), Harry Harvey (Dr. Hilton), Geraldine Hall (Mrs. Federber), Richard Gaines (Nagel), Bob Bumpas (Radio announcer).

Billy Wilder for Paramount, U. S. A. 10,007 ft., 111 mins.

Chuck Tatum, a hard-bitten, once successful reporter reduced to a local paper in Albuquerque, New Mexico, does not particularly enjoy the prospect of covering a rattle-snake hunt and waits for a big break which would take him back onto a big national newspaper. His chance comes when a man searching for Indian relics in a cave beneath the Mountain of the Seven Vultures is trapped by a stone fall. Tatum promptly bribes the local sheriff to give him exclusive coverage of the story and to slow down rescue operations so that they take at least six days (while in fact the job can be done in one) during which time he hopes, with the help of the man's estranged wife, to spin out the story and hit national headlines. The drama attracts thousands of sightseers who camp around the site in cars, tents and caravans and boost the local trade. Tatum whips up their interest with lurid news bulletins and songs about the trapped man played through loudspeakers. Soon a carnival arrives...

Made soon after Wilder's break with the scriptwriter Charles Brackett, Ace in the Hole dissects the sensation-mongering press as uncompromisingly as Sunset Boulevard dissected Hollywood. Perhaps with more courage, if one is to consider that in Sunset Boulevard Wilder was safely dealing with a relic of the past. His story of a ruthless news-hound who manipulates the masses for personal gain foreshadows Kazan's A Face in the Crowd. Primarily an action story which does not pretend to raise serious moral issues (there is never any doubt that Tatum's machinations are unadulterated wickedness) Ace in the Hole is notable for its convincing characterization and vigorous handling of situations (note the crowd scenes). Only the ending is a compromise: Tatum, somewhat unconvincingly conscience-stricken, tries in vain to save the trapped man at the last moment, and then turns against the man's sluttish wife who stabs him to death with a pair of scissors. One feels that the story should have been taken to its chilling logical conclusion. Kirk Douglas's excellent performance as the wiry, merciless, uncannily energetic reporter would only be bettered by his role of Colonel Dax in Kubrick's Paths of Glory.

DETECTIVE STORY William Wyler

Script: Philip Yordan and Wyler, based on the play by Sidney Kingsley. Photography: Lee Garmes. Art Direction: Hal Pereira and Earl Hedrick. Cast: Kirk Douglas (James McLeod), Eleanor Parker (Mary McLeod), William Bendix (Lou Brody), Cathy O'Donnell (Susan Carmichael), Lee Grant (Shoplifter), Horace McMahon (Lieutenant Monaghan), Bert Freed (Dakis), Frank Faylen (Gallagher), George MacReady (Karl Schneider), Michael Strong (Lewis Abbott), Joseph Wiseman (Charles Gennini), Craig Hill (Arthur Kindred), William Phillips (Callahan), Gerald Mohr (Tami Giacopetti), Grandon Rhodes (O'Brien), Luis Van Rooten (Joe Feinson), Warner Anderson (Endicott Sims), Gladys George (Miss Hatch).

William Wyler for Paramount, U.S.A. 9344 ft., 104 mins.

In the space of two years after Champion, the picture which gained him wide popularity, Kirk Douglas appeared in four films, the best known of which is Wilder's Ace in the Hole. His next outstanding appearance was in Wyler's Detective Story, a record of one night in a New York City precinct police station.

Douglas plays Detective Jim McLeod, a cop with a reputation for toughness, who regards his crusade against crime as a personal affair after his father, a criminal, drove his mother into a lunatic asylum. "I built my whole life on hating my father," he says. A pathetic shoplifter is brought in, then a young man who stole money from his employer to be able to take a girl out, then two cat burglars--and McLeod treats all with equal ruthlessness. The main episode concerns his attempt to put behind bars an abortionist doctor. Ignoring the pleas of the man's lawyer, McLeod beats up the suspect. Disturbed at the allegations of McLeod's personal motives for his vendetta against crime, the station's commanding officer discloses to him that his own wife went to the abortionist many years ago. McLeod is stunned. The wife, unable to bear his taunts, walks out on him. Soon afterwards he is shot dead while trying to prevent a prisoner from escaping.

Semi-documentary in tone (much along the lines of the Hathaway-De Rochemont "police documentary"), Detective Story is equipped with a tidy plot, is well edited, photographed and smoothly put together. It is also well acted--by Douglas himself, Eleanor Parker as his wife, William Bendix as his sympathetic partner and Lee Grant as the shoplifter. Perhaps only the explanation for the central character's obsession with crime is not really sufficient. Not too well received at the time of release, mainly because of its explicit portrayal of force, this absorbing study of a policeman being infected by the violence he is supposed to fight foreshadows the tough dramas of the late 60's and early 70's--such as Bullitt and Dirty Harry.

OUTCAST OF THE ISLANDS Carol Reed

Script: W. E. C. Fairchild, from the novel by Joseph Conrad. Photography: John Wilcox. Music: Brian Easdale. Cast: Trevor Howard (Peter Willems), Ralph Richardson (Captain Lingard), Kerima (Aissa), Robert Morley (Almayer), Wendy Hiller (Mrs. Almayer), George Colouris (Babalatchi), Frederick Valk (Hudig), Wilfrid Hyde White (Vinck), Betty Ann Davies (Mrs. Willems), Annabel Morley (Nina Almayer), A. V. Bramble (Badavi), Peter Illing (Alagappan), Dharma Emmanuel (Ali), James Kenney (Ramsey), Marne Maitland (Mate).

Carol Reed for London Films, G. B. 9225 ft., 102 mins.

The works of Joseph Conrad are notoriously difficult to transfer to the screen, and Outcast of the Islands is quite simply the most successful such attempt until Wajda's The Shadow Line in the 70's. The story of the novel (an early work, part of a trilogy of which the remaining parts are "Almayer's Folly" and "Aissa Saved") is extremely complex. Briefly: Willems is dismissed by a trading company operating in a Far Eastern port and turns for help to his old friend, Captain Lingard. They travel to Lingard's trading post in the islands, which is managed by Almayer, married to Lingard's adopted daughter. A conflict of characters develops between Willems and Almayer; a local politician schemes to use Willems with the help of the beautiful Aissa; Willems agrees to navigate the secret channel for an Arab trader, but he is abandoned by Almayer's men. Half-deranged, he retires with Aissa into sombre solitude, thus becoming the "outcast of the islands."

Conrad's eerie analyses of the dark forces in man hint that the prime human motivation is basically evil; the main problem is always the conflict of characters. Outcast of the Islands is in many ways reminiscent of White Shadows in the South Seas: a jaded picture of the East; squalid exploitation of the natives by greedy white traders. The complexity of the story does not allow Reed to develop the characters fully and the film functions mainly as a study of man's love-hate relationship with the object of his unescapable desire, relying on Trevor Howard's powerful performance as Willems, while Ralph Richardson is a very interesting Lingard. The designs and the camera work are very appropriate for the story.

1952

WE ARE ALL MURDERERS (Nous sommes tous des assassins)
André Cayatte

Script: Cayatte and Charles Spaak. Photography: Jean Bourgoin. Art Direction: Jacques Colombier. Cast: Marcel Mouloudji (René Le Guen), Raymond Pellegrin (Gino), Antoine Balpêtré (Dr. Albert Dutoit), Claude Laydu (Philippe Arnaud, a counsel), Paul Frankeur (Léon), Amedeo Nazzari (Dr. Albert Detouche), Georges Poujoly (Michel Le Guen), Julien Verdier (Marcel Bauchet), Louis Seigner (Abbé Roussard), André Reybaz (Father Simon), Juliette Faber (Mme. Sautier), Yvonne Pierreux (Yvonne Le Guen), Jérôme Goulven (Noblet), Charles Lemontier (Prosecutor), François Joux (Sautier), Henri Vilbert (Counsel Mousset), Line Noro (Louise Arnaud), Marcel Pérès (Malingre), Sylvie (Gino's mother), Renée Gardes (Le Guen's mother), Yvette Etievant (Bauchet's wife), Léonce Corne (Captain at the military court), Lucien Nat (Leading Counsel), Henri Crémieux (Bauchet's counsel), Jean-Paul Moulinot (Governor of the Santé prison), Jean-Marc Tennberg (Fred), Jacques Morel ("Gros" Charles), Anouk Ferjac (Agnès), Louis Arbessier (Deputy prosecutor), Guy Decomble (Police inspector), Charles Bouillaud (Policeman), Alexandre Rignault (Gendarme), Liliane Maigne (Rachel), Daniel Mendaille (Chief warden), René Lacourt (Balloon-seller).

François Carron for Union Générale Cinématographique/Jolly Film/Labor Films, France. 9977 ft., 111 mins.

We Are All Murderers is a picture as surprising as it is exceptional: there is no other picture of comparable stature and fervent humanist message, which is to the same extent a "filmed thesis" to use Cayatte's own description. The film is a protest against capital punishment and the thesis is contained in its title; the argument is conducted from an orthodox Christian standpoint: society has no right to take the life of an individual, particularly since it is ultimately responsible for his actions. While Let Justice Be Done demonstrated the imperfection of a verdict caused by the imperfections of the members of the jury, We Are All Murderers is about the imperfections of everybody. In his next film, Before the Deluge, Cayatte pushed the concept of the collective guilt of society still further--but the logical conclusion of this is helplessness which he cannot admit: if everybody is guilty, no one is. In We Are All Murderers the problem is presented in a much more balanced way. The argument is logically impeccable, even though one might call it somewhat one-sided. Cayatte, a lawyer by training, remains a lawyer in the cinema and uses the language of the film as if it were courtroom rhetoric. Perhaps even more subtly: he does not stoop to use an effect just for its own sake, even though he has mastered the cinematic tricks very well. In fact he plays down his film-making skills and uses the means of expression functionally--perhaps he tries to kill two birds with one stone by appealing both to the spectator's mind and to his feelings. In the last frames of the film the words "The End" are replaced by the question: "If you were the President of the Republic, would you condemn this man to die?"

In support of his argument Cayatte tells the stories of five men sentenced to death. Gino is a Corsican to whom family vengeance is an unavoidable duty established by centuries of tradition. Two rival bands have avenged the death of one chief by the assassination of another. Gino has been sentenced to death to put a stop to the vendetta--in other words, to stop Corsicans killing one another, Society is going to kill one of them.

Dr. Dutoit, entangled in a triangle between his wife and mistress, has been convicted, on circumstantial evidence, of poisoning the wife. He denies the charge even under the blade of the guillotine. He is to be executed to serve as a deterrent to other husbands.

The third case story is quite unusual--Bauchet, a simple peasant, tortured and killed his small daughter because the child's crying disturbed his sleep--he is clearly a sick man.

Malingre, the fourth, raped and murdered a little girl. Medical examination reveals that he suffers from a brain tumor. This is removed by Dr. Detouche whereupon Malingre has become a different person.

Yet to Cayatte these cases are only auxiliary. His main interest is the most typical murderer in judicial practice. Le Guen, a young gangster, was born and brought up in the slums. His sister was a prostitute; he first came across death as a teenager when he surreptitiously took away the body of a German soldier killed by his sister in a drunken brawl. This action brought Le Guen into contact with the Resistance Movement. It was during the occupation;

We Are All Murderers

We Are All Murderers

volunteers to fight the Nazis were needed. Le Guen was asked to join, he underwent training in using a gun, but never had an opportunity to learn how to use a pen. So he killed while knowing almost nothing about the world; in a drunken fit he did not hesitate to shoot even at his own superiors. When Liberation came, Le Guen kept his gun and went on using it without qualms for his own ends. When a woman rejected him because he was dirty he killed a balloon-seller to get the money for a bath and later a police inspector and the bath-house attendant. Apprehended and accused of multiple murder, he was defended by an inexperienced court-appointed lawyer, who became completely committed to the case and not only looked after the accused, but also saved his brother from the criminal environment. All the same he could not do very much for Le Guen, who in the meantime went through a complete metamorphosis, at last began to learn and came to understand the wrongness of his actions. Cayatte has no doubts that to execute Le Guen would be tantamount to judicial murder, cruel and useless in view of the prisoner's re-education. He rejects completely the deterrent action of capital punishment, arguing that in all five cases the knowledge of the penalty would not have affected the actions of the criminal.

One may consider the convicts in Cayatte's lawsuit against the judiciary as rather far removed from the statistical average. The case of the Corsican vendetta is certainly unusual while the sentencing to death on circumstantial evidence of the doctor raises the separate question of the inevitability of judicial errors. Incidentally, in the latter case the moral justification of the death penalty is the weakest. To this one may reply that the case histories described in We Are All Murderers could be easily replaced by real and more convincing ones. Take for instance the (later) notorious case of Caryl Chessman who in 1948 was found guilty on circumstantial evidence of kidnapping and rape and was finally executed in 1960 by which time he was a completely changed man--a highly qualified lawyer and the author of several books on the sociology of crime. Even if in these cases Cayatte made his argument too easy, in the story of Le Guen he certainly did not avoid negatives in portraying the main character and based his strongest arguments not on sentimentalizing him but on a solid elucidation of the circumstances which pushed him towards crime. In the final effect then Cayatte uses an intellectual rather than emotional argument when refusing any moral justification for the sending of human beings to the guillotine: in accordance with natural justice Le Guen is not guilty.

This conclusion is supported by images which constantly condense and augment all shades of tension. Take the silent battle of views of the two prison chaplains; the unforgettable scene of the doomed man being dragged along the corridor by the guards to the place of execution while the cells explode in unison with the accusation: "assassins! assassins!"; the final suspense when the defense lawyer waits for a telephone call from the President's office; the awesome sequence of the transport of a corpse hidden inside a barrel organ across Paris swarming with Nazi soldiers; the agony of the prisoners who listen intently at the cell door to know whether the guards are creeping in their socks to get their next victim; the dramatic moment when Le Guen is besieged in the bath-house. How distant are the organ tones of We Are All Murderers from the café-piano music of the rest of the contemporary French cinema; how different its raw texture seems from the psychological debates of mass-produced screen melodramas. Cayatte took a great task upon himself and proved that he could measure up to it. His voice in the defense of man's most valuable possession counts among cinema's best achievements and is well worthy of a motto from the poem written in the 17th century by John Donne from which Ernest Hemingway took the title of his famous novel:

> No man is an Iland, intire of it
> selfe; every man is a peece of the
> Continent, a part of the maine; if a
> Clod bee washed away by the Sea,
> Europe is the lesse, as well as if a
> Promontorie were, as well as if a
> Mannor of thy friends or of thine
> owne were; any mans death dimin-
> ishes me, because I am involved
> in Mankinde; And therefore never
> send to know for whom the bell
> tolls; It tolls for thee

ROME, ELEVEN O'CLOCK (Roma ore 11) Giuseppe De Santis

Script: Cesare Zavattini, De Santis, Rodolfo Sonego, Gianni Puccini, Elio Petri and Basilio Franchina, inspired by Petri's newspaper report. Photography: Otello Martelli. Music: Mario Nascimbene. Cast: Carla Del Poggio (Luciana), Lucia Bosè (Simona), Raf Vallone (Carlo), Massimo Girotti (Nando), Eva Vanicek (Gianna), Lea Padovani (Caterina), Elena Varzi (Adriana), Maria Grazia Francia (Cornelia), Delia Scala (Angelina), Irene Galter (Clara), Paolo Stoppa (Clara's father).

Paul Graetz/Transcontinental Films, Italy. 101 mins.

On January 15, 1951, a serious accident occurred in Rome. Over 200 girls turned up to be interviewed for a secretarial job advertised in a newspaper; the staircase collapsed under the weight of the applicants. The motif of tragedies brought about by unemployment was often used by the Neorealists to quote only De Sica's Bicycle Thieves, and Zavattini began work on the script immediately after reading about the disaster in a women's magazine. But the first version of the script lacked naturalness. In this situation the makers of the film did what was very much in the spirit of Neorealism: they inserted a similar job offer in a newspaper and began to look for material in the life stories of some of the many girls who replied to the advertisement; as a bonus they offered the girls work as extras on the film.

Such were the beginnings of the last classical masterpiece of Neorealism. The outcome may seem surprising if one considers that half of the film was shot in the studio, that the photography is not documentary in character and very careful compositionally and that the leading parts were taken by professional actors. Is this then a proof that it was not the manner of execution, but the character of the plot which was the most important for Neorealism? Not quite: Rome, Eleven O'Clock combines leftist interpretation of real and topical social problems with directorial skill relying on the reconstruction of facts with dramatic awareness.

The use of a number of sub-plots, which was one of the weaknesses of late Neorealism as it replaced the idea of reflecting the complexity of life by a collection of small generic observations, played in Rome, Eleven O'Clock a cementing role comparable to that in Griffith's Intolerance, although the majority of the sub-plots are not brought to traditional feature-film conclusions. The synthetic treatment of ideas in the fashion of Intolerance was further reinforced by the multi-layer quality of the mise en scène within almost every frame. The deep-focus photography, so vital to the Neorealists as the best cinematic representation of reality, especially in the exteriors, was here used to perfection. Also the sound-track is multi-layer in character, which is to reflect the hubbub of everyday life--with a few exceptions, that is, which only confirm the rule: key lines of the dialogue are stressed by lowering the level of background sounds.

Since De Santis used straight cuts as the only form of editing and only occasionally ended shots by having the frame dominated by dark accents, the narrative is even more fluid than if there was only a single plot. Otello Martelli took great care over the photography, but never departed from natural shots. Well used in the film are such powerful means of dramatic expression as the contrast of sound and silence like in the scene of Simona's silent return to Carlo, and the stressing of significant detail, a practice which originated in the silent cinema and which was prominently revived by Welles in Citizen Kane. The acting is fine, if not at all hieratic as it was in No Peace Among the Olives or ostentatious as in De Santis' earlier films. In Rome, Eleven O'Clock acting is, as everything else, subordinate to naturalness. De Santis did not lose any of his earlier dynamism but obtained it with finer means. He reached creative maturity; not by making reality appear more attractive but by recreating it more effectively, he achieved the fullness of social concern. Alas, this turned out to be his swan song: as a result of a variety of factors Italian Neorealism began to decline rapidly. None of De Santis' subsequent films reached a standard comparable with that of Rome, Eleven O'Clock.

HIGH NOON Fred Zinnemann

Script: Carl Foreman, based on the story "The Tin Star" by John W. Cunningham. Photography: Floyd Crosby. Music: Dimitri Tiomkin. Song "Do Not Forsake Me, oh My Darlin' ": Dimitri Tiomkin and Ned Washington. Art Direction: Rudolph Sternad. Cast: Gary Cooper (Will Kane), Thomas Mitchell (Jonas Henderson), Katy Jurado (Helen Ramirez), Grace Kelly (Amy Kane), Lloyd Bridges (Harvey Pell), Otto Kruger (Percy Mettrick), Henry Morgan (William Fuller), Lon Chaney Jr. (Martin Howe), Ian MacDonald (Frank Miller), Eve McVeagh (Mildred Fuller), Harry Shannon (Cooper), Lee Van Cleef (Jack Colby), Sheb Woolley (Ben Miller), Tom London (Sam), Robert Wilke (James Pierce).

Stanley Kramer, U. S. A. 7641 ft., 85 mins.

Thirteen years after Stagecoach, which elevated the classical western onto the Olympus of art cinema, High Noon, another crucial work for the genre was made. Until 1952 western situations revolved around pioneering legend, adventure, generic anecdote with its inseparable sense of humor and the judgment of the characters by subjecting them to a test in action and above all by observing their attitudes towards the law seen as an idealistic imperative. High Noon opens, as it were, new territories: description is replaced by analysis, people of the West are shown not from the outside but in the light of the moral motivation of actions. In his celebrated article ("Evolution du Western," Cahiers du Cinéma, No. 54 (1955) p. 23) André Bazin calls this new genre "le surwestern." We have adopted the term "superwestern." This new approach had to cause a revaluation of the mythologized stereotype and had to make human relations in the 19-century West appear more realistic on the screen--because Foreman, the scriptwriter, cast on the scenery of those times the social mechanisms which are known to operate in situations of this kind. The orthodox view of the western as a folk morality play may prompt one to ask whether the proposed revision of the convention is admissible and to question the precise affiliation of Zinnemann's film. The arrangement of the plot and a number of hints in the dialogue indicate clearly that the idea was to make High Noon into an allegory of America in the era of McCarthy and the Cold War, of the times when a frightened and (generally) silent majority helplessly looked on at the struggle of the few who professed the right to individual conscience. But if one is to realize that the essence of a western is the hero's search for a moral ideal, High Noon offers just that plus a reflection that this search is a tragic and often futile undertaking. Real life confirmed this reflection in a way: because of pressure from the House Un-American Activities Committee, Foreman left the U. S. A. soon after High Noon and settled in England.

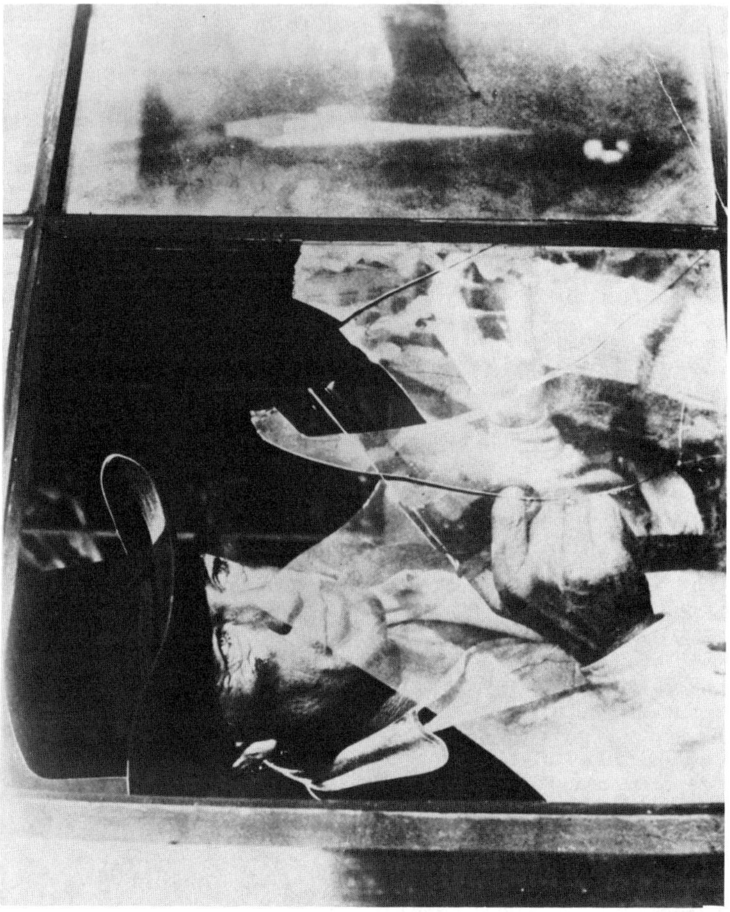

High Noon

In the morning of the day of his retirement as Marshal of a small town called Hadleyville, Will Kane marries Amy, a beautiful Quaker girl, and looks forward to the quiet existence of a farmer. Suddenly the news arrives that Frank Miller, a notorious criminal, is expected by train at noon; three of his confederates are already in town. Miller, whom Kane had arrested five years previously, had been sentenced to death; this was subsequently commuted to life imprisonment; now he has been pardoned. Miller threatened to take revenge on the man who arrested him; it is obvious he will do so on the day when there is officially no marshal in Hadleyville. Will Kane turns back from the road to a happy and peaceful life, in spite of the advice of friends and even despite estrangement from his wife. Why? He is not bound by duty. He explains that he does not want to live in fear for the rest of his life. But the real reason is the moral imperative: one must not leave evil an open road. He tries to persuade townspeople to help him. But the townspeople, although grateful to Kane for bringing order to Hadleyville, are not anxious to help and retreat when the Mayor asks: "Why does this man want to endanger himself, his wife and others?" As noon approaches, Kane remains alone. He faces the four criminals single-handed, only in the critical moment helped by his wife--the one whose religion forbids killing. He finally wins the struggle against evil, against the littleness of the townsfolk, against fear.

Every situation and almost every line of dialogue of High Noon are charged with metaphorical meaning, obtained with impressive intelligence and precision. The fluent sequence of dramatic events is supported by the logically faultless description of the characters and their motivation, which makes High Noon function at once as a psychological western, a sociological western, a political allegory and finally as a timeless morality play. Despite all this, Foreman's script is gripping, perfect in its dramatic construction (which invokes the classical unities of time, place and action) and--surprisingly--not at all artificial. The waiting Marshal learns about the arrival of the bandit by hearing the sound of breaking glass; this comes naturally to the spectator, just as natural as would seem the sight of a thief breaking a shop window in order to steal. However, the sound of breaking glass has a metaphorical meaning: evil is betrayed by its own arrogance. The Marshal was quite right: this is not his private affair, but a question of defending the life and property of others. When the Quaker girl shoots one of the bandits in the back at the crucial moment, her action is psychologically logical and at the same time clearly defines the philosophy of the makers of High Noon: one must resist Evil with all available means. At the same time the philosophy of the West is being redefined: what is decisive is not the idealistic rules of the game or the law as such, but the gun. When the judge who sentenced Miller to death learns of his return, he packs his belongings in panic. We see him fold up the American flag, the symbol of his office, just as he tries to justify his decision. But this very forceful metaphor does not sound a false note: anxious to save his face the judge explains himself with special eloquence.

It would have been sufficient for Zinnemann to transfer Foreman's script to the screen with his usual painstaking efficiency to safeguard a very good film. But this time the Muses awoke and the standard of direction matched the brilliance of the script. In the final sequence, made with less involvement, the classical western adventure dominates. This is a noble sequence, though not self-consciously brilliant. The raison d'être of all this was beyond the traditional western framework: the chamber character of the drama, the lack of open spaces and a greater reliance on dialogues, the observance of the three classical unities. Zinnemann makes this raison d'être legitimate and binding. By paring the frame down to simple visual accents he clearly determines the situation of the hero, builds up tension by means of excellent editing (with recurrent inserts of the face of the clock), and with high contrasts of light and shade lets the spectator sense the heat which pours down on the lonely marshal from a cloudless, deadpan and sinister sky. Zinnemann was at pains to imitate in the film the visual style of 19th-century photographs of the West, one of the characteristics of which was the lack of clouds which was caused by the quality of early photographic materials. The cloudless skies of High Noon, so different from the usual Hollywood practice, are an important component of the drama. By casting the splendid Gary Cooper in the leading part, and by the way he directed him, Zinnemann conveyed the weight of the drama already with the very physical predispositions of Marshal Kane. In all this there is a component of lucky intuition leading to such a fascinating final result. Also Tiomkin's ballad, fine and simple, confirms the rule. Its subsequent popularity brought the sophisticated picture closer to the spectator, made it part of everyone's experience to be kept in constant memory.

IKIRU (Living) Akira Kurosawa

Script: Shinobu Hashimoto, Hideo Oguni and Kurosawa. Photography: Asaichi Nakai. Music: Fumio Hayasaka. Art Direction: So Matsuyama. Cast: Takashi Shimura (Kanji Watanabe), Nobuo Kaneko (Mitsuo Watanabe), Kyoko Seki (Kazue Watanabe), Miki Odagiri (Toyo), Kamatari Fujiwara (Ono), Makoto Kobori (Kiichi Watanabe), Kumeko Urabe (Tatsu Watanabe), Yoshie Minami (Maid), Nobuo Nakamura (Deputy Mayor), Minosuke Yamada (Saito), Haruo Tanaka (Sakai), Bokuzen Hidari (Ohara), Minoru Chiaki (Noguchi), Shinichi Himori (Kimura), Kazuo Abe (City Assemblyman), Masao Shimizu (Doctor), Yunosuke Ito (Novelist), Ko Kimura (Intern), Atsushi Watanabe (Patient), Yatsuko Tanami (Hostess), Seiji Miyaguchi (Gang-boss), Daisuke Kato (Gang member), Ichiro Chiba (Policeman), Toranosuke Ogawa (Park Section chief), Akira Tani (Old man in bar).

Shojiro Motoki for Toho, Japan. 11,700 ft., 130 mins. Original running time 143 mins.

Old age, inevitability of death, recapitulation of one's life--these problems are, and by their very nature must be, among the most basic of human interests. Kurosawa did not intend to approach them with the gravity and intellectual commitment of a Thomas Mann or a Goethe and planned *Ikiru* as a modest film. Even in his own appraisal of his work Kurosawa does not rate this picture too highly. Yet this story of the last weeks of life of an elderly civil servant mortally ill with gastric cancer is among his finest and most penetrating works. It is such right from the prologue which simply shows an X-ray photograph--a concrete image, a statement of fact which makes the grumpy Watanabe realize that the end is near. He has spent thirty years applying his seal to piles of documents at the city office. Fragments of past memories (brilliantly interwoven both on the screen and on the soundtrack with the description of Watanabe's present activities) lead the hero to the conclusion that his life had been worth little to himself and virtually nothing to other people. This sets off a moral impulse to leave something behind: Watanabe finds a long-neglected petition and overcoming bureaucratic obstacles causes a sewage dump in a poor district of Tokyo to be turned into a children's playground. At this point the narrator simply informs us that five months later Watanabe died. At an all-night wake his colleagues discuss his life. The story emerges step by step and is told in a flashback. A policeman tells how he found Watanabe dead on a child's swing in the completed playground. He had died amid falling snow singing his beloved song:

> "Life is so short,
> Fall in love, dear maiden,
> While your lips are still red,
> And before you are cold,
> For there will be no tomorrow.
> Fall in love, dear maiden,
> While your hair is still black,
> And before your heart withers,
> For today will not come again."

The office workers discover Watanabe's greatness little by little after their superiors have left and sake has opened the gates to frankness. Watanabe's actions cause a wave of enthusiasm and his colleagues promise to continue his work and to live up to his memory. But it soon turns out that all this was caused by drink and not by a genuine change of heart: the resolution is soon forgotten, and the bureaucrats return to their offices and their seals. Was thus Watanabe's action in vain? No--for the playground remained. The moralist Kurosawa concludes that one must seek greatness within one's own self. This is an Existentialist conclusion: "A man *is* what he *does*." At the same time *Ikiru* seems the clearest assertion of Kurosawa's belief that progress *can* be achieved only through the actions of outstanding individuals.

One finds it difficult to agree with Kurosawa who considers *Ikiru* pretentious in comparison with the later *I Live in Fear*. True, at times the director allowed himself to be carried away on a wave of emotion--for instance in his constant invoking on the soundtrack of the song from Watanabe's childhood which others have forgotten. The novelist with whom Watanabe makes a night-club tour when he learns of his terminal illness does not seem a convincing character. Finally, snow in Tokyo is too much of a rarity to fall precisely at the hour of the hero's death. But on the other hand the sheer magnificence of this sequence on the swing, one of the most memorable in all cinema, could outweigh even much more serious criticisms.

Ikiru contains also a sequence which gave rise to much controversy--the enormously long sequence of the wake which takes up the whole second part of the film. Devoid of music, which Kurosawa did not feel able to reconcile with the ragged, arrhythmic narrative (so very different from the earlier parts of the film) this sequence is exceedingly static--perhaps not in comparison with the future films of Jacques Rivette, but certainly in comparison with the rest of the cinema of the 50's, also in Japan--and seems a denial of dramatic common sense. And yet it is this part of Ikiru which is crucial, as the intellectual summing up of the film and a source of most interesting comments about human actions. Neither would it be fair to hold against Kurosawa a certain technical awkwardness. For it is precisely in the sequence of the reminiscences about Watanabe, a tired sequence, losing fluency and concreteness in the vapors of alcohol, that Kurosawa showed with brilliant precision the fluctuations of people's moods and the vicissitudinous meanderings of their thoughts. Is one therefore entitled to conclude that Ikiru conforms to the rule (evident in I Live in Fear, further confirmed by Dodes'ka-den and partly by The Idiot) that it is those parts of Kurosawa's films which he cares most about that are the most doubtful? Not surprisingly this is a very touchy subject with Kurosawa. All one can say is that one of the world's greatest film directors can afford this to be true. Ikiru, grown from everyday life and steeped in the atmosphere of ordinariness and nevertheless achieving the dimensions of a great humanist morality play, is an ample proof.

THE SECRET GAME (Jeux interdits) René Clément

Script: Jean Aurenche, Pierre Bost, François Boyer and Clément, from the novel by Boyer. Photography: Robert Juillard. Music: Narciso Yepes. Art Direction: Paul Bertrand. Cast: Brigitte Fossey (Paulette), Georges Poujoly (Michel Dollé), Lucien Hubert (Michel's father), Suzanne Courtal (Michel's mother), Jacques Marin (Georges Dollé), Laurence Badie (Berthe Dollé), André Wasley (M. Gouard), Amedée (Francis Gouard), Denise Perronne (Jeanne Gouard), Louis Sainteve (Priest), Pierre Merovée (Raymond Dollé).

Robert Dorfmann for Silver Films, France. 102 mins.

June 1940: France is about to fall to the Nazis. Among refugees fleeing from Paris are the 5-year-old Paulette, her parents and her puppy. Only the girl survives an aerial attack on a congested bridge; having wandered into the countryside she is found by 11-year-old Michel, son of the peasant Dollé family who take in the delicate Parisian child. On the first evening she overhears comments about the dead refugees (including her parents) being buried "like dogs." To Paulette and Michel this is the beginning of the "forbidden games" of the film's original title. Too young to understand death, the children steal crosses from the local cemetery in order to put them on the graves of dead animals, starting with Paulette's puppy. This leads to a violent conflict with another family, whom Michel's parents suspect of the thefts. When the truth finally comes out, Michel is punished and Paulette handed over to the authorities. As we last see her she is looking for her parents, crying, in a throng of refugees at a Red Cross post.

Clément uses the plot to attack the religious hypocrisy and empty conventions of the adult world. The cross does not really mean anything to Michel's parents and death is considered an awesome taboo. In a scene as symbolic as it is macabre, two heads of families, engaged in a fight, fall into a freshly dug grave. Although cursory, the portrayal of the peasant family deserves special mention. Robust, even ribald, but short of becoming malicious, it is done in the style known as "La Jument verte" (Green Nag), from the title of a book by Marcel Aymé (1933). The adults' bigotry and their insensitivity towards children destroy Paulette's only chance to return to normal life. But the real cause of suffering is the war, and this heart-rending film is above all an imaginative plea for peace.

The ease with which Clément switches over from the brutally realistic description in the first minutes of the film to the idyllic treatment of the children's furtive games reflects the versatility (not to say "eclecticism") of his entire career. Clément is used to moving from one cinematic genre to another and to handling each of them differently: his previous two films were Les Maudits, an apocalyptic drama set aboard a submarine carrying a group of Nazi survivors to South America, and the quasi-Neorealist Le Mura di Malapaga; his chronologically next are Knave of Hearts, a social comedy set in London and Gervaise, a naturalistic tale of suffering taken from a novel by Zola. A mixed bag indeed. Although in The Secret Game Clément uses elements of pre-war screen poeticism which has by 1952 become somewhat anachronistic, he does it well, and his fascinating vision of the private world of children is one of very few such attempts to succeed in the cinema. The reason is that he does not succumb to the temptation to withdraw into that world himself, and tells the story objectively.

Both children play very well: Brigitte Fossey is a refined, reserved city child, Georges Poujoly--a matter-of-fact young peasant. The Secret Game won the Grand Prix at the 1952 Venice Film Festival and an Oscar for Best Foreign Film the following year. But what one remembers most vividly from this film will not be found on the screen--it is the wonderful, melancholy guitar tune by Narciso Yepes. It is impossible to forget.

THE LIFE OF OHARU (Saikaku Ichidai Onna) Kenji Mizoguchi

Script: Yoshikata Yoda and Mizoguchi, from the novel "Koshuku Ichidai Onna" (The Life of a Woman Who Loved Love) by Saikaku Ihara. Photography: Yoshimi Hirano. Music: Ichiro Saito. Art Direction: Hiroshi Mizutani. Editing: Toshio Goto. Cast: Kinuyo Tanaka (Oharu), Tsukie Matsura (Tomo, Oharu's mother), Ichiro Sugai (Shinzaemon, Oharu's father), Toshiro Mifune (Katsunosuke), Toshiaki Konoe (Lord Tokitaka Matsudaira), Hisako Yamane (Lady Matsudaira), Jukichi Uno (Yakichi Senya), Eitaro Shindo (Kohei Sasaya), Akira Oizumi (Fumikichi, Sasaya's friend), Masao Shimizu (Kikuno Koji), Daisuke Kato (Tasaburo Hishiya), Toranosuke Ogawa (Yataemon Isobei), Eijiro Yanagi (Daimo Enaka), Yuriko Hamada (Yoshioka), Hiroshi Oizumi (Manager Bunkichi), Haruo Ichikawa (Iwabashi), Kikue Mori (Myokai, the old nun), Chieko Hagashiyama, Sadako Sawamura.

Hideo Koi-Yoshikata Yoda-Kenji Mizoguchi-Hiroshi Mizutani for Shintoho, Japan. Originally 13,339 ft., 148 mins., cut to 11,970 ft., 133 mins.

The Silver Lion for The Life of Oharu at the 1952 Venice Film Festival finally won Mizoguchi an international reputation. High time indeed, if one considers that the great director, then 56, was near the end of his career.

The Life of Oharu chronicles the waning fortunes of the daughter of a rich merchant. We first meet Oharu, a 50-year-old prostitute, as she contemplates her past in a temple. In 1686 she was a beautiful girl and served at the Imperial Palace in Kyoto. When she fell in love with a man below her class, she and her parents were exiled from the capital and her lover beheaded for violating the social code. Taken as a concubine by Lord Matsudaira, she was sent back home as soon as she bore him an heir. Her father, deeply in debt, forced her to work as a courtesan in a geisha house. A client who wanted to buy her turned out to be a counterfeiter. Hired as a servant by a merchant, she was soon dismissed because of the jealousy of his wife and because her past was revealed. She was briefly happily married to a fan maker, but her husband was killed by thieves. She was preparing to enter a convent, but was dismissed on having been discovered with a former employer, whose advances she found impossible to reject. She escaped with a petty thief who was soon caught; Oharu was reduced to being a beggar and then a common prostitute. Her son, now head of the Matsudaira Clan, took interest in her, but she was immediately sent back to begging for "being a shame to the clan." Oharu leaves the temple and continues on her way through the countryside.

Mizoguchi not for the first time shows himself as a master of period cinema. The Life of Oharu is perhaps the fullest expression of his life-time interest in the victimization of woman in feudal Japan. The owner of the geisha house tells Oharu: "to us you are like a fish, to be disposed of as we want." Justice and humanity are unobtainable to someone who is treated like a material object, and the heroine can take refuge only in dreams and memories. This is a complete, balanced and assured vision of early 18th-century Japan, with its pyramid-like social system and the implacable rules of social advance and damnation. Once she broke the rules, Oharu's life has to follow an inevitable course, and Mizoguchi uses his heroine's descent of the social ladder to review the various social milieux of the period. The price to be paid for this survey is having every possible disaster befall the heroine--a melodramatic device, even if countered by a certain detachment in handling the story.

Equilibrium is the key to The Life of Oharu: equilibrium between various episodes, within individual sequences, between objects within a single frame. Also the acting is very carefully balanced. Kinuyo Tanaka, the outstanding actress who later became Japan's first woman film director, gives what is probably her best performance. The photography, served in long fluid takes, creates a painterly, atmospheric vision full of beautiful visual compositions. Also the use of the soundtrack, with its noises, songs, chanting and periods of silence, is outstanding. The film's most memorable scene, of Oharu being allowed to have a brief glimpse of her son surrounded by his suite, is accompanied by wonderful, startling music.

As Mizoguchi was making The Life of Oharu, his fortunes with the producers were rather low. He had to work, in very difficult conditions, in a disused armaments factory after Shintoho refused him its studios. He gave unusual attention to every detail and the result is minutely realistic. Mizoguchi commented on the famous literary work on which the script is based: "Among the works of Saikaku there are many others I would like to film because it would allow me to depict men and women as part of the social system of the time." He has certainly done it in The Life of Oharu; more--the heroine's suffering is universal and the film has great relevance to the present. It was applauded by feminists all over the world.

CRIN BLANC (The Wild Stallion) [White Mane] Albert Lamorisse

Script: Lamorisse. Photography: Edmond Séchan. Music: Maurice le Roux. Cast: Alain Eméry (Folco), Pascal Lamorisse (Folco's brother), Laurent Roche (Gardien of the Camargue).

Les Films Montsouris, France. 47 mins.

The Camargue is a wild area of the South of France, in the delta of the Rhône. Wild horses roam vast expanses of long grass, while babies are playing in the sand among tortoises and flamingos. Lamorisse's film is a story of a small boy's fascination with the proud and beautiful stallion at the head of the herd. Folco befriends Crin Blanc ("White Mane") but people who catch horses for money stand in the way of this friendship. The Gardiens of the Camargue repeatedly try to capture Crin Blanc, but he always escapes. Folco catches him, gives him shelter and heals his wounds. The Gardiens try to smoke the horse out. In a desperate bid to escape, the boy rides Crin Blanc through swamps to the seashore. There is no place for the two friends in the mercenary world. Together they disappear among the waves bound for "a wonderful country where horses and people are always friends."

Born in 1922, Lamorisse is usually described as "the poet of the French cinema." His films have something of the fairytale about them. His first short film was made in 1947 in Tunisia. Another, Bim le petit âne (1949) was about a little Arab boy and his donkey, with a commentary written--significantly--by Jacques Prévert. Lamorisse created his own inimitable style--tender and wistful, though never sentimental. Such is Crin Blanc, his first longer project. As the later The Red Balloon, this is an allegory about man's search for the beautiful and the unattainable. But Lamorisse's films would never again be so unredeemably tragic. The very imaginative photography makes good use of visual contrasts: between the langorous nostalgia of open spaces and the rapid movement (note the sequence of the fight of the horses); between the fierce stallion and a gentle little boy. Percussion music is very effectively used on the soundtrack.

Lamorisse had the misfortune to appear at a time when world cinema turned towards exploring the cruel and the violent, and away from the poetic. As a result critics were often unkind to him. The critic Jerzy Płażewski well formulated the case for the director's defense. He observed: "It is somehow felt that it is shameful to praise subtlety and purity of spirit. Why should Lamorisse be ashamed of these things at a time when film makers ceased to be ashamed of anything?"

CASQUE D'OR Jacques Becker

Script: Becker and Jacques Companéez. Photography: Robert Le Fèbvre. Music: Georges Van Parys. Art Direction: Jean d'Eaubonne. Cast: Simone Signoret (Marie), Serge Reggiani (Manda), Claude Dauphin (Félix Léca), Raymond Bussières (Raymond), Gaston Modot (Danard), Paul Barge (Inspector Juliani), Daniel Mendaille (Proprietor of riverside "guinguette"), Loleh Bellon (Léonie Danard), Dominique Davray (Julie), Odette Barencey (Eugénie), William Sabatier (Roland), Jean Clarieux (Paul), Fernand Trignol (Proprietor of "Ange Gabriel"), Claude Castaing (Fredo), Paul Azaïs (Ponsard).

Spéva-Films/Paris-Film, France. 96 mins.

In his earlier pictures, particularly in Goupi Mains Rouges and Antoine et Antoinette, Becker demonstrated his acute sense of the milieu. Casque d'or, his first period film, sees Becker's art of observation brought to absolute perfection. The story is set in the 1900's in Paris and centers around a beautiful gigolette nicknamed "Casque d'or" because of her head of golden hair.

Joinville is a popular destination for Sunday outings from Paris. Among people in a riverside dance hall are Marie, her apache lover Roland who is a member of a gang of cut-throats headed by Léca, and Manda, a young ex-convict who is now a carpenter. Manda and Marie are instantly drawn towards each other. A few days later Manda kills Roland, having been provoked to a fight. He flees with Marie to the country where they enjoy a few days' happiness. But Léca tricks Manda into giving himself up to the police by telling him that Raymond, his best friend, has been charged with the killing. Marie helps the two friends to make a break from custody during transfer to another prison. Manda kills Léca in revenge and again gives himself up. He is sentenced to death and guillotined. As Marie watches, from a window overlooking the prison courtyard, the knife of the guillotine plunging down, she relives her great love. The image dissolves into a shot of her dancing in Manda's arms.

Becker described the effect he was aiming at in Casque d'or as "something between the writing of Eugène Sue and the paintings of Auguste Renoir." What he meant was that he wanted this story of an amour fou, based on authentic judicial records, to combine the intense, almost lurid quality of Sue's novels with the sensual visuality of Renoir's pictures. Indeed, the plot is sheerest melodrama when considered on its own. But Becker approached it with seriousness and concentrated means of cinematic expression--and achieved a stylish result, a film which excellently captures the essence of the period and is full of penetrating observation. The for-

Casque d'or

mula of *Casque d'or* is not that of simple realism, but consists of conveying the feel of the period via its contemporary local mythology, from the popular, proletarian viewpoint: "Aren't the cops mean but the simple folk brave, just and strong? Their solidarity is real solidarity, their loyalty real loyalty and their love real love." The detail of the period and of the milieu is minutely reflected in costumes and behavior: the straw-hatted *apaches* cut bread with flick-knives, while craftsmen gird themselves with sashes. Everyone has his own sense of identity, style and dignity. Registered with very straightforward photography, this now seems even more striking than at the time of the film's release.

The film-making in *Casque d'or* is brilliant. The narrative is dense yet extremely economical, the style laconic with the short-cuts in the story very skillfully performed. But when an event requires time to develop Becker always knows how to fill the cinematic space thus created--he throws in a joke or an observation. Also the dialogues are very sparing and largely replaced by acting. It is interesting that the actors, while being perfectly credible, consciously maintain a certain distance from the characters they portray. This effect, very difficult to achieve in the cinema, must be based on first-rate acting. Simone Signoret as the sensuous Marie with her proud lingering gait, Serge Reggiani as Manda--intense and direct and Raymond Bussières as his friend provided just that. Becker's portrayal of his protagonists is sympathetic and romantic--but not even a bit sentimental.

It is significant that Becker is little concerned with the social implications of the story. Lindsay Anderson said in his review of the film: "While the outcome of the love between Marie and Manda lacks nothing in terror and pity, it provokes no protesting cry against society or destiny: the human responsibility is grimly accepted. This is an interesting contrast to the films of Carné and Prévert, and the impression is one of greater maturity. Manda is master of his fate as Gabin in *Quai des Brumes* and *Le Jour se lève* is not; and at his death there is no cutting away to ship's siren or to unheeded alarm clock."

MR. HULOT'S HOLIDAY (Les Vacances de M. Hulot) Jacques Tati

Script: Tati and Henri Marquet, with assistance from P. Aubert and Jacques Lagrange. *Photography*: Jacques Mercanton and Jean Mousselle. *Music*: Alain Romans. *Art Direction*: R. Briancourt and Henri Schmitt. *Cast*: Jacques Tati (Monsieur Hulot), Nathalie Pascaud (Martine), Michèle Rolla (Aunt), Louis Perrault (Fred), André Dubois (Commandant), Valentine Camax (Englishwoman), Lucien Frégis (Hotel proprietor), Raymond Carl (Waiter), René Lacourt (The Stroller), Marguerite Gérard (Stroller's wife), Suzy Willy

(Commandant's wife), Michèle Brabo (Holidaymaker), Georges Adlin (South American).

Cady-Films/Discina, France. 8200 ft., 91 mins.

Mr. Hulot's Holiday is made in the form of a vacation sketchbook of Jacques Tati's worthy autobiographic hero. Hulot--independent albeit searching for warm contact with people, a hunched and gawky pole-like fellow who constantly puffs at his pipe and moves in a somewhat bird-like fashion--would from now on be the leading character of all the films of Tati, the man who is to the French screen comedy what Buster Keaton had been for the American.

We first meet Hulot when he arrives at a seaside village near Caen in his antiquated car and, in the splendidly conveyed good-humored mood of a banal holiday, proceeds to make casual acquaintances with other holidaymakers. Amiable, full of cheer and good will, anxious to please, Hulot nonetheless always has the bad luck of incurring everybody's displeasure, even as he merely sneaks by in the background of the frame. He opens the door and a gale blows through the hotel. He takes two other people for a trip in his car; the car runs away onto someone's private property and the passengers are fired on by the furious owner; and so on. He leaves a veritable trail of disasters behind him. To boot, Hulot does not realize how disastrous his actions are; he does not see that he is different and that this compromises the ordered world of a town-dweller on holiday.

Tati, a perceptive observer of human behavior, draws a whole gallery of colorful screen characters just to be able to ridicule them mercilessly. In doing this he not only continues but actually develops the convention of the sound burlesque--his holidaymakers are fuller and more credible than the characters in the films of Keaton and Chaplin. What is more, Tati enriches the classical comic arsenal by a whole plethora of new gags based purely on the sound. These are his trump card. Characteristically, at the same time he avoids using dialogues and even, while poking fun at the quirks of technical inventions, actually ridicules spoken word on the screen. Tati's weak point is the lack of coherence of the comic situations: Mr. Hulot's Holiday, although far superior to Jour de fête as far as the plot is concerned, is still only an enumeration of gags and never reaches (with the exception perhaps of the scene in which Hulot, on the eve of his departure, accidently sets off a shed full of fireworks) the lightness and the fluency of comical scenes in the best silent burlesques. Another deficiency, both in Tati as a director and as an actor, is the lack of lightness of execution. The angularity of the hero's movements does not suffice to conceal the artificiality of many situations. But one must not complain too much. In 50 years sound cinema has not produced (apart from the episodic flash of Pierre Etaix's talent in Le Farceur) another genuine heir to the former excellence of the genre.

OTHELLO Orson Welles

Script: Welles, from the play "Othello, the Moor of Venice" by William Shakespeare. Photography: Anchise Brizzi, Aldo Graziati, Georges Fanto; also Obadan Troiani and Alberto Fusi. Music: Francesco Lavagnino and Alberto Barberis. Art Direction: Alexandre Trauner. Cast: Orson Welles (Othello), Micheál MacLiammóir (Iago), Susanne Cloutier (Desdemona), Robert Coote (Roderigo), Hilton Edwards (Brabantio), Michael Lawrence (Cassio), Fay Compton (Emilia), Nicholas Bruce (Lodovico), Jean Davis (Montano), Doris Dowling (Bianca), Joseph Cotten (Senator), Joan Fontaine (Page).

Mercury, Morocco. 8173 ft., 91 mins.

While the moral dilemmas of man have remained essentially the same, each historical period saw something different in Shakespeare's tragedy. Early 20th-century "Freudian" interpretations, for instance, regarded Othello as a tangle of hidden complexes. During the 30's a trend in the French theatre which included the playwrights Giradoux, Cocteau and Claudel, took interest in "modernizing" old tragedies by giving them a contemporary setting. Welles, for his part, provides what is undoubtedly a new look at Shakespeare's play. His concern was to find a modern, cinematic treatment suitable for the times in which drama is devalued by the tragic and violent events reported in the newspapers every day. What Welles comes up with can be described as a reporter's approach, employing the anxious, ubiquitous camera. Othello is not tragic and the murder seems above all else sad and useless, like so many deaths these days. Welles removed more than half the text, mixed up the sequence of some episodes and gave individual scenes different weight than in the play. It is clear that he tried very hard to be "modern" and original: some effects are used for their own sake, including the purely sound credits (read by Welles himself).

In his book "Put Money in Thy Purse" Micheál MacLiammóir gave an engaging description of the phone call in which Welles offered him the role of Iago: "I said I was very ill; he said the trip and the sight of him would cure me. Said I was very old; he said so was he (the actor was 50, Welles was 34). Said I'd never played Iago; he said he'd never played Othello. Said I had put on weight; he said so had he and that we'd be two Chubby Tragedians together.... Said I didn't see myself as villain; he said unmentionable word and that I was patently villainous in all eyes but my own...."

The filming of Othello took over three years, and was interrupted and re-started several times while Welles tried to raise money by acting in other people's films (among others in Reed's The Third Man). The shooting was done partly in Morocco, partly in Italy.

Othello

These circumstances are reflected in the final result: the jerky narrative leaves the overall impression of unevenness, the quality of the sound is terrible and the dialogues often difficult to understand. In short, Othello suffers from the same faults as Welles's previous Macbeth--and offers similar compensations. Despite its faults the film is as brilliant as it is powerful--a flamboyant work with a strange fascination. Even the Cannes Film Festival jury, usually so keen on technical perfection, saw this and gave Othello the Grand Prix in 1952.

Laurence Olivier once said that Othello is the most difficult part Shakespeare ever wrote, and one must agree--it is so difficult because it is so ambiguous. As in the later film by Yutkevich, Welles's Othello is Othello betrayed rather than Othello jealous. He is shown as a noble man who is a victim of Iago's evil machinations; there are suggestions of Iago's repressed homosexuality as a reason. Welles is fascinated by the Iago character and can congratulate himself at the outcome of that phone conversation: Othello's sinister alter ego, he is a figure of Byzantine intrigue, a personification of destructive ambition, of irrational evil. The picture's opening scene, of the funeral procession of Othello and Desdemona, is memorable: Iago is dragged past the cortège and thrown into a cage which is then hauled up the walls of the fortress.

Thus the theatrical origin of the story is eliminated by the superb images, dynamic camerawork and the sheer appeal of a barbaric spectacle. The style of imagery and editing (the film has more than 500 separate shots) is in sharp contrast to Welles's earlier films (in The Magnificent Ambersons he was using ten-minute-takes!). On the other hand, this "visuality," defying the old theatrical saying that "the eye takes from the ear," cooled down the Moor's drama somewhat. It is interesting that Welles as an actor did not help in this respect: proud and cold, the protagonist is shown as much less human than in Shakespeare. Othello is not among his best achievements as an actor.

MOTHER (Okā-san) Mikio Naruse

Script: Yoko Mizuki. Photography: Hiroshi Suzuki. Music: Ichiro Saito. Cast: Kinuyo Tanaka (Masako Fukuhara), Kyoko Kagawa (Toshiko), Eiji Okada (Shinjiro), Masao Mishima (Toshiko's father), Akihiko Katayama (Suzumi, Toshiko's brother), Daisuke Kato (Kimura), Chieko Nakakita (Aunt Noriko).

Ichiro Nagashima for Shintoho, Japan. 8809 ft., 98 mins.

Mother is based on the prize-winning essay in a girls' school competition on the theme "My Mother." One of the favorite specialities of Japanese cinema is shomin-geki, a middle-class psychological-generic family story, and making a film on the basis of a child's essay would be a quite natural attempt at adding authenticity to a popular genre in the same manner as practiced by the Italian Neorealists. But Naruse did not intend Mother to be a photograph of social conditions; he was interested exclusively in human feelings portrayed as simply as possible. The film is a quiet homage to material sacrifice. A poor washerwoman from the outskirts of Tokyo whose husband and eldest son died, finds her only source of happiness in the incessant caring for her remaining children.

The story is seen through the eyes of the eldest daughter, Toshiko. The film is consistently sustained in warm tonality. There are no dramatic tones in photography or the editing even in the scenes when first the son and then the husband die. The handful of events shown with a characteristic openness and marginal sub-plots were to be a slice of life--but life seen from a very special viewpoint. Poverty intimated, but not followed up dramatically looks in Mother like a convention, relations between social classes are abstract, and the film's wide spectrum of psychological nuances lacks amplitude. There is here no euphoria or dejection, and all is contained between little joy and little sadness. Even nature, traditionally a very important factor in Japanese cinema, here seems to lack vitality. The sky in Mother is always the same, light-grey and misty. Appropriately for a typical shomin-geki film the camera is immobile; the commendable richness of observation is achieved through the use of very frequent editing cuts, but even so all changes of angle are not accompanied by changes of emotional temperature of vision. The style of film-making is thus meant to generate the traditional Japanese mood shikata ga nai ("it can't be helped"): beauty resides in limitation, in placid acceptance of everyday events, in ardent submission to one's duty. Naruse's consistency, the intimacy and honesty with which he draws out his quarter-tones prevents Mother, one of the most famous haha-mono ("mother films"), from being challenged on sociological grounds. Even though it offers merely a conservative vision of Japanese mentality and way of life--it is a very faithful vision.

LES BELLES DE NUIT René Clair

Script: Clair. Photography: Armand Thirard; also Robert Juillard. Music: Georges Van Parys. Art Direction: Léon Barsacq. Cast: Gérard Philipe (Claude), Martine Carol (Edmée), Gina Lollobrigida (Cashier/Leila), Magali Vendeuil (Suzanne), Marylin Bufferd (Clerk/Mme. Bonacieux), Paolo Stoppa (Director of Opera House), Raymond Bussières (Roger), Bernard La Jarrige (Léon), Jean Parédès (Paul), Raymond Cordy (Gaston/Marquis), Albert Michel (Postman).

Franco-London Film/Angelo Rizzoli, France/Italy. 7830 ft., 87 mins.

After La Beauté du diable, which Clair himself described as an act of penance for his earlier disregard for the plot in his films, the director returns once more to formal gambols and cinematic finesse. Les Belles de nuit, the film whose sole aim is to amuse, is in a way a summing up of Clair's style and creative intentions. Clair has once said that "it is usual for each century to misunderstand itself and, in its ignorance of itself, to turn with regret towards the past." He has also said that the story of Les Belles de nuit (the name of the flower, known in English as "the Marvel of Peru," which blossoms at night) is as unnecessary as the tale of the nightingale and the rose.

A provincial music teacher is dissatisfied with his life and seeks refuge in dreams. If things are bad now, perhaps they were better in the past? So, Claude returns in his dreams to the fin-de-siècle, then the times of the conquest of Algeria, the French Revolution, the Musketeers of the preceding monarchy and finally right back to prehistory--only to find that it is best to live in the present, for every dog has his day and melancholy is soon turned into happiness. Claude's opera is accepted for performance and he falls in love with the garage proprietor's pretty daughter.

The peregrinations of the hero through the various historical periods are to Clair an excuse for his own journey through the styles of traditional cinema: the present-day sequences spring from a populist spirit, the Algerian episode harks back to exotic drama, while the old France is shown in the Rococco style. The charm with which Clair does all this, his skillful blending of sub-plots and moods, his warm treatment of screen characters makes full use of the magic of the cinema. The only thing which is lacking is a bit of seriousness. But, in the end, can one be sure that the nightingale and the rose are really of no use at all?

SUMMER WITH MONIKA (Sommaren med Monika) Ingmar Bergman

Script: Per-Anders Fogelström and Bergman, adapted from the novel by Fogelström. Photography: Gunnar Fischer. Music: Erik Nordgren. Art Direction: P. A. Lundgren and Nils Svenwall. Cast: Lars Ekborg (Harry), Harriet Andersson (Monika), John Harryson (Lelle), Georg Skarstedt (Harry's father), Åke Fridell (Monika's father), Naemi Briese (Monika's mother), Dagmar Ebbesen (Harry's aunt), Åke Grönberg (Foreman), Gösta Eriksson (Glass shop manager), Ivar Wahlgren (Villager), Renée Björling (Villager's wife), Catrin Westerlund (Villager's daughter).

Summer with Monika

Svensk Filmindustri, Sweden. 8700 ft., 97 mins.

This is the first important work of a director whose name was to become almost synonymous with Swedish cinema for three decades. Born in 1918, Bergman started his work in films with the script for Sjöberg's Frenzy in 1944. In the same year he debuted as a director on the professional stage, a career which he conducted in parallel with that of film director, which he became the following year. In his early films, which include It Rains on Our Love (1946), The Devil's Wanton (1948), To Joy (1949) and Summer Interlude (1950), Bergman was mainly interested in the conflict between life and death usually shown against a background of the problems of youth. These pictures were stylistically influenced by the French Poetic Realism.

Summer with Monika, Bergman's 12th film in seven years' work as a director, occupies a special place in his oeuvre. In almost every way it is in sharp contrast to both his earlier and later pictures: it has neither the romantic atmosphere of Music in Darkness (1947) nor the philosophical interests of The Naked Night and The Seventh Seal. The film's allegiances are with the Neo-national movement in the Swedish cinema begun ten years earlier with Sjöberg's The Road to Heaven--the movement which referred to the great days of the silent cinema in Sweden, and placed great stress on the links between man and splendidly shown Scandinavian nature.

Harry, an errand boy at a crockery warehouse meets by chance Monika, a girl who works in a nearby greengrocer's. He is attracted by Monika's openly sensual nature. Infatuation develops into a love affair, and after a quarrel with her father Monika goes off with Harry on a motor boat holiday to the archipelago outside Stockholm. At the end of the idyll Monika announces she is pregnant and Harry agrees to marry her. But she soon becomes frustrated by the monotony of married life and spending days in a shabby flat looking after the baby; on his return from a business trip Harry discovers that she has been sleeping with a former lover in his absence. After a row Monika leaves the flat. Harry is left with the baby, the memories of the summer and an uncertain future.

As in the films of Bergman's masters, Sjöström and Stiller, nature becomes almost a participant in the story. Love flourishes against the background of sunny landscapes, while quarrels and misunderstandings between Harry and Monika are accompanied by storm and rain (a dramatic device known as "pathetic fallacy"). Similarly when the lovers leave for their holiday, Stockholm is bright and exhilarating, but dark, rainy and depressing when they return. There is also the Midsummer Night which brings into the open hidden instincts and desires. Firmly rooted in the Scandinavian tradition, the Midsummer Night motif was used by Sjöberg in Miss Julie, and later by Bergman himself in Smiles of the Summer Night.

A realistic study of the disintegration of an immature

relationship between two young people, Summer with Monika has no "message" and no transcendental implications--it is only a melancholy observation on the transience of love. The narrative is stark and abrupt and the photography masterly. But the film's main strength is surely Harriet Andersson as Monika: sensuous, slovenly, animalistic, she gives a splendid portrayal of adolescent female sexuality.

MOULIN ROUGE John Huston

Script: Anthony Veiller and Huston, from the novel by Pierre La Mure. Photography: Oswald Morris. Music: Georges Auric. Art Direction: Paul Sheriff. Costumes: Marcel Vertès. Editing: Ralph Kemplin. Cast: José Ferrer (Henri de Toulouse-Lautrec/ Comte de Toulouse-Lautrec), Colette Marchand (Marie Charlet), Suzanne Flon (Myriamme Hayem), Zsa Zsa Gabor (Jane Avril), Claude Nollier (Countess de Toulouse-Lautrec), Katherine Kath (La Goulue), Muriel Smith (Aicha), Georges Lannes (Patou), Harold Gasket (Zidler), Walter Crisham (Valentin Déssossé), Mary Clare (Mme. Loubet), Rupert John (Chocolat), Lee Montague (Maurice Joyant), Jill Bennett (Sarah), Eric Pohlmann (Bar proprietor), Maureen Swanson (Denise), Jim Gérald (Cotelle), Tutti Lemkow (Aicha's partner).

John Huston for Romulus, G. B. 10,731 ft., 119 mins. Technicolor.

Huston has once commented that his primary interests are always in the human being. One may be permitted to add that this is always a human being pitted in a lonely struggle against fate, intense and determined. Such a man was without a doubt the great painter Henri de Toulouse-Lautrec, a crippled aristocrat rejected by his environment, the man who overcame physical handicaps with his extraordinary passion for life and art. Toulouse-Lautrec is therefore a typical Huston protagonist.

Moulin Rouge can surely be described as one of the finest screen biographies--with the qualification that it is more of a film about the interior of a man, than about the events of the life of an historical personality. For instance, Jane Avril was in reality a dancer, not a singer. Huston's adaptation of the novel (which is as well-known as it is second-rate) did not go in the direction of verifying events and details. On the contrary: the famous Impressionist painter is in the film outwardly even more of a character from a scandalizing novel and the Paris of the period as seen on the screen does not resemble the real one too much. But the interior of the hero is true--this is the truth of a lonely man's spasmodic search for feeling, of wisdom acquired through painful experience and arduous yet dignified struggle for a new art. If sometimes melodrama lurks from the screen, it is soon overshadowed by scenes as fine as for instance the one of the painter's unfulfilled suicide; if despite Ferrer's fine acting certain situations may seem unconvincing, a dense, authentic and fascinating mood is always there. As far as fidelity to the period is concerned, it is remarkable how much truer and convincing is the elemental scene of the dance in Moulin Rouge than its pretty-pretty counterpart in Renoir's empty French Cancan (1955).

But far from being all, this is not even the most important aspect of Huston's film. The photography of Moulin Rouge put an end to cinema's traditional coloristic scale. It is as revelatory as the intense Eastmancolour images in Kinugasa's contemporary (if shallow) Gate of Hell (1953) in Japan. Oswald Morris faithfully rendered the color tonality and texture of Impressionist paintings, those slightly blurred contours of objects, the tingling sensation of light within a pastel scale of tones. Morris made a careful study of Toulouse-Lautrec's work and of that of other Impressionists. In this respect Moulin Rouge was considerably ahead of its time: it is only in much later films, when color completely monopolized the movies, that one comes across comparably faithful replicas of a painter's use of light and color.

THE NAKED SPUR Anthony Mann

Script: Sam Rolfe and Harold Jack Bloom. Photography: William Mellor. Music: Bronislau Kaper. Cast: James Stewart (Howard Kemp), Robert Ryan (Ben Vandergroat), Janet Leigh (Lina Patch), Ralph Meeker (Roy Anderson), Millard Mitchell (Jesse Tate).

William H. Wright for MGM, U. S. A. 8180 ft. , 91 mins. Technicolor.

Anthony Mann became in the 50's the indisputable master of the superwestern, the genre created by Zinnemann and Foreman, the makers of High Noon. Although the western was not Mann's only interest (he began his career in sensational dramas and finally betrayed the western genre for the sake of gigantic spectaculars), the eleven westerns he directed in the period 1950-1960 are among the stylistically purest works of the genre. The characteristic features of Mann's psychological superwestern are: a precise characterization of protagonists who evolve towards inner maturity and obstinately strive towards their goals overcoming mental stress and physical suffering; a psychological complexity also of the negative characters; precise description of human motives and actions; the excellent use of open air locations stressing the links between man and nature; the combination of stillness and naturalistically (and credibly) shown violence; and finally the juxtaposition of open landscapes with the sense of a lurking, aggressive and powerful evil. All the same, it has been rightly said that Mann's westerns are grand style without grand content. Most of them have an exemplary dramatic construction built around plots which are really too insubstantial for a full-length feature film. Some of Mann's earlier westerns like Winchester '73 (1950) lose congruity and scope and degenerate into variations on traditional motifs. Only four, chronologically, The Naked Spur, The Man from Laramie, The Tin Star and Man of the West do justice to the fame of their director.

The Naked Spur is a story of five people. Howard Kemp has captured the outlaw Ben Vandergroat for the $5000 reward helped by an old prospector and a former cavalry officer who now demand a share in the money. The party includes Ben's girl companion, Lina. Ben is trying to break free; in the end only Lina and Kemp survive and set off to start a new life in California.

Magnificent mountain landscapes are a background for an excellent study of characters and a source of discreet lyricism with which Mann underscores the events in his films. James Stewart as Kemp strengthens his reputation as one of the most interesting actors in western movies.

VIVA ZAPATA! Elia Kazan

Script: John Steinbeck, based on the novel "Zapata the Unconquerable" by Edgcumb Pinchon. Photography: Joseph MacDonald. Music: Alex North. Art Direction: Lyle Wheeler and Leland Fuller. Editing: Barbara McLean. Cast: Marlon Brando (Emiliano Zapata), Jean Peters (Josefa Espejo), Anthony Quinn (Eufemio Zapata), Joseph Wiseman (Fernando Aguirre), Arnold Moss (Don Nacio), Lou Gilbert (Pablo), Harold Gordon (Francisco Madero), Alan Reed (Pancho Villa), Fay Roope (Porfirio Díaz), Florenz Ames (Señor Espejo), Mildred Dunnock (Señora Espejo), Frank Silvera (Gen. Huerta), Margo (Posadera), Nina Varela (Aunt), Bernie Gozier (Zapatista), Frank De Kova (Col. Jesús Guajardo), Joseph Granby (Gen. Fuentes), Will Kuluva (Lazaro), Harry Kingston (Don García), Pedro Regas (Innocente).

Darryl F. Zanuck for 20th Century-Fox, U. S. A. 10,160 ft., 113 mins.

Viva Zapata! is the story of the rise to power and the martyrdom of the Mexican revolutionary leader. From a tenant-farmer in south Mexico, Emiliano Zapata became a general in the civil wars of 1911-1919. The film charts Zapata's early struggles against the dictatorship of Porfirio Díaz who has been President for over 30 years; his leadership of the guerrilla struggle for land for the Indians; his marriage to the daughter of a rich landowner; his appointment to the presidency; his subsequent retirement to the mountains to teach the peasants to be afraid of no one; his betrayal by a friend and his death at the hands of the National Army. A fascinating man, Zapata was the only one of all the Mexican revolutionary leaders to identify himself totally with the cause and to take nothing for himself. His life has since become a legend.

Kazan had no part in Steinbeck's confusing script, and it is much to the director's credit that he was still able to create a powerful and authentic vision of Mexico, the film at moments reminiscent of Eisenstein's passionate ¡Que Viva Mexico! On the intellectual level the message that power corrupts may seem unoriginal, but Kazan was not concerned with a message. His aim was to give a cinematic portrayal of an extraordinary man, to convey his sense of destiny, his apostolic mission of giving land to the peasants. All the same, the process whereby revolution is eroded by private interests is very perceptively observed. Kazan's aim was to show how this occurs rather than why and consequently some of the characters (such as Zapata's shrewd brother played by Anthony Quinn, or the fanatical Fernando Aguirre who finally betrays the hero) are generalizations rather than proper screen characters. Thus the film contains a warning against abuse of power, equally applicable to the right as to the left.

Among the picture's several marvellous moments there is a scene which parallels one in Eisenstein's Alexander Nevsky. Soldiers are leading Zapata after he has been arrested; peasants begin to gather around the convoy; Zapata's brother starts to tap two pebbles against each other; everybody joins in the tapping using all kinds of objects; a procession begins to form; more and more groups of peasants appear from the forest along the road; a frightened officer asks what they want ("we are just making sure that he does not try to escape, because you may then shoot him"). Another memorable thing in the film is the motif of the white horse which Zapata once gave to a young boy and which he encounters at the end, at the hacienda to which he has been lured--to be shot at by an entire regiment. The horse senses the danger, begins to prance and gallops away before the start of the shooting. Zapata's men catch sight of the horse, the messenger of death, lonely on a hill. This is the film's last frame. The white horse is also a symbol of continuing struggle. According to Mexican ballads it still roams the mountains of Morelos.

Rebellious and obstinate, Zapata is a typical Kazan protagonist: spiritually related to Terry Malloy in On the Waterfront and Cal Trask in East of Eden. It is significant that it is with characters like him that Kazan's cinema functions best. Some scenes in Viva Zapata! instantly convey the hero's personality--like the one in which the illiterate Zapata is being taught to read by his bride on their wedding night. Much credit for this result is due to Marlon Brando's brilliant performance.

Yet Viva Zapata! is a very uneven film. It has excellent scenes, but also clear faults: incoherent narrative composed simply of a series of separate episodes from Zapata's life, uneven directorial involvement, but most of all poor characterization. Quite apart from the fact that some supporting characters are purposely poster-like, they are not convincing: Madera, for instance, is irritatingly naive, and the American too mentorial. It is interesting that A Streetcar Named Desire, Kazan's previous work, had very fine characterization to offer while being of little interest visually. With Viva Zapata! precisely the reverse applies. Despite its faults the film succeeded in striking a visionary chord, a curious tone of authority which continues to fascinate audiences.

A CITY ON TRIAL (Processo alla città) Luigi Zampa

Script: Suso Cecchi D'Amico, Ettore Giannini, Diego Fabbri, Turi Vasile and Zampa, from the story by Giannini and Franco Rossi. Photography: Enzo Serafin. Music: Enzo Masetti. Art Direction: Aldo Tommasini. Cast: Amedeo Nazzari (Judge Spicacci), Mariella Lotti (Elena Spicacci), Silvana Pampanini (Liliana), Paolo Stoppa (The Delegate Perrone), Franco Interlenghi (Luigi Esposito), Irene Galter (Nunziata), Eduardo Cianelli (Alfonso Navona), Dante Maggio, Turi Pandolfini, Bella Starace Sainati, Mariella Lotti, Gualtiero Tumaini, Titina De Filippo, Tina Pica.

Film Costellazione, Italy. 99 mins.

Naples at the beginning of the century. An investigating magistrate inquires into a certain double murder and encounters an elusive wall of silence and unfortunate coincidences. Finally he realizes that he is up against the Camorra, the local Mafia. An honest and conscientious man, Spicacci patiently edges forward towards truth. But the Camorra is all-powerful and ruthless and the magistrate's private life becomes entagled in the investigation. He is on the verge of surrender when the shock of the death of an innocent man finally prompts him to stand up to the evil and carry his work through to the end.

In his story about the by-products of expansive capitalism in the urban jungle Zampa does not match the inspiration and dramatic force of Vivere in pace, but instead offers what is probably the best film-making craft of his career, with intelligent generic observation, good characterization of the protagonists, skillful build-up of dramatic tension and a mood of isolation, climaxing situations and making good use of every minute of screen time to throw in new, well-drawn details. In his numerous films about contemporary life and in his strongly anti-fascist pictures about the times of Mussolini,

Zampa was too sarcastic and obtrusive in his social and behavioral criticism. In A City on Trial he had the good sense to leave social accents in the background--and achieved a much better result. The tale about the Camorra winding its black tentacles around the Naples of half a century earlier, found in the Italy of 1952 topicality equal perhaps to that of Germi's In the Name of the Law, a related work set in the present.

CHILDREN OF HIROSHIMA (Gembaku-no ko) Kaneto Shindo

Script: Shindo, based on the book of memories of children of Hiroshima, edited by Arata Osada. Photography: Takeo Ito. Music: Akira Ifukube. Art Direction: Takashi Marumo. Cast: Nobuko Otowa (Takako Ishikawa), Osamu Takizawa (Iwakichi), Takashi Ito (Taro), Niwa Saito (Natsue Morikawa), Taniye Kitabayashi (O-toyo), Yusaku Hanabusa (Kijima), Yiriko Hanabusa (Kijima's wife), Kennosuke Naruo (Sampei), Chikako Hosokawa (Takako's mother), Masao Shimizu (Takako's father), Fukuko Sayo (Woman in church).

Kindai Eiga Kyokai/Gekidan Mingei, Japan. 8809 ft., 98 mins.

Kaneto Shindo, born near Hiroshima, was among those filmmakers who in the years 1948-1952, a crucial period for the Japanese cinema, chose the path of creative independence. Shindo left Shochiku in 1950 together with Yoshimura, whose scriptwriter he had become, to establish an independent company, the Kindai Eiga Kyokai (Association of Modern Art Cinema). Shindo came to notice barely a year after his debut as a director in the new company--with Children of Hiroshima, his third picture. The film touches upon a most painful problem for the Japanese and is made with artistic responsibility, a characteristically Japanese subtlety and is sustained in the constructive Positivist spirit. As a matter of fact, this latter factor did not find favor with everybody--not even with the producers, the Japan Teachers Union. They considered Children of Hiroshima a travesty of "correct" attitudes and at once commissioned another director, Hideo Sekigawa, to make a counter-picture. His product, Hiroshima (1953), is cheaply drastic and scratched war wounds instead of trying to heal them.

It is worth noting that it had not been possible earlier to make films about the two atomic bombs dropped on Hiroshima and Nagasaki. The American forces maintained a total ban on all information concerning the explosions and their after-effects during the entire period of the occupation. In Shindo's film, however, the disaster which struck at 8:15 a.m. on August 5, 1945, occupies only a few minutes of the prologue. The story proper is set seven years later, in the summer of 1952. A young schoolteacher arrives in the ill-fated city to trace her friends and former pupils. Takako's encounters with these people are shown with quiet restraint, without emphasis or dramatic conflicts. The dialogues refer to details of everyday life. The story of Takako's wanderings through Hiroshima is told fluently with cut editing; and if taken out of context it would appear as a lyrical record of the return of a sensitive young girl to her memories. But behind the quiet present lurks a tragic past which, although already beginning to fade a little in people's memories, casts its black shadow onto the living. Thousands of people who survived the catastrophe spent the rest of their lives suffering from the effects of radioactivity. A girl is dying from radiation disease; another woman is unable to bear children. Takako meets an old beggar who had been blinded by the nuclear explosion and recognizes him as a servant in her home. There is in the film telling silence, interesting observations of people's reactions (for instance to the sound of aircraft engines) and the delicate optimism of the finale in which the heroine fulfills her decision to take care of an orphaned boy. This is all Shindo needed to make Children of Hiroshima. It is a lot. Like in the Polish The Last Stage, a film about another dreadful facet of the war, tragedy is expressed with greatest clarity not by showing the hecatomb of crowds, but by tracing the fate of individuals.

LIMELIGHT Charles Chaplin

Script: Chaplin. Photography: Karl Struss. Music: Chaplin. Art Direction: Eugène Lourié. Choreography: André Eglevsky, Melissa Hayden and Chaplin. Cast: Charles Chaplin (Calvero, a music-hall comedian), Claire Bloom (Terry, a ballet dancer), Sydney Chaplin Jr. (Neville, a composer), Nigel Bruce (Postant, an impresario), Norman Lloyd (Stage manager), Buster Keaton (Piano accompanist), André Eglevsky (Harlequin), Melissa Hayden (Columbine), Marjorie Bennett (Mrs. Alsop, the landlady), Snub Pollard (Street musician).

Charles Chaplin for Celebrated Films, U. S. A. Version released in England: 12,731 ft., 141 mins. Official registered length: 12,549 ft., 139 mins.

Charlie the Tramp is not here any more. His demise began with the coming of sound cinema and he appeared for the last time disguised as a Jewish barber in The Great Dictator. The Second World War prompted Chaplin to quit altogether joking in the garb of a sentimental tramp. Monsieur Verdoux was a bitter protest against the rules of modern civilization. The provocative tone of that film, its leftist message together with Chaplin's rather nonconformist private life brought about yet another campaign against him (this was the time of the Hollywood witch-hunts) which ended with Chaplin's return to his native England where he was very warmly received. In the course of less than two months, an extraordinarily short time by his standards, he made Limelight--an introspection, a kind of confession and his last important work. In the Calvero character one may find the spirit of the unforgettable bowler-hatted vagrant of yesteryear; the story of the ups and downs of Calvero's life is based on some events from Chaplin's biography and also from his father's. Beyond these references in the plot Chaplin offers a generalized comment on the ways of human life and a somewhat pantheist vision of the mission of an artist. Without these contexts Limelight is no more than a melodrama about an old music-hall comedian, destroyed by drink and the adversities of life, who has lost his ability to amuse the audience. One day he saves a young ballet-dancer who has tried to take her own life. He takes her into his flat, looks after her, and gives her spiritual strength, thus reviving in her the will to live and setting her on the right track.

But to Chaplin Limelight is much more than a story of the tragedy of an aging comedian in the world of London's turn-of-the-century music-halls. It is a testament, written at a time of crisis, long before the real onset of old age. This circumstance prompts one to disregard the many imperfections of Limelight: overloading with dialogue (just as in the case of Monsieur Verdoux), a few lengthy passages and a rather excessively metaphysical message. This is, above all, an affectionate, subtle and moving picture. Indeed, many scenes confirm Chaplin's reputation as an actor and director (of a fine acting team). Among them is the scene of the taming of a flea, Calvero's dream in which he imagines himself as a lion tamer, or his laughter therapy of the depressed Terry. In the final scene Calvero appears in a benefit show in an astonishing double act with Buster Keaton. This is a triumph, but his health cannot stand up to the strain. Calvero collapses into a huge drum in the orchestra pit. Shortly before he dies in the wings of the theatre, anxious not to stop amusing his audience, he offers a disturbing and perhaps significant line of dialogue: "Ladies and Gentlemen, I would like to say something, but I am stuck."

SINGIN' IN THE RAIN Gene Kelly and Stanley Donen

Script: Adolph Green and Betty Comden, suggested by the song "Singin' in the Rain" (lyrics by Arthur Freed, music by Nacio Herb Brown). Photography: Harold Rosson. Music: Nacio Herb Brown. Song lyrics: Arthur Freed. Choreography: Gene Kelly and Stanley Donen. Art Direction: Cedric Gibbons and Randall Duell. Editing: Adrienne Fazan. Cast: Gene Kelly (Don Lockwood), Donald O'Connor (Cosmo Brown), Debbie Reynolds (Kathy Selden), Jean Hagen

(Lina Lamont), Millard Mitchell (R. F. Simpson), Rita Moreno (Zelda Zanders), Douglas Fowley (Roscoe Dexter), Cyd Charisse (Dancer), Madge Blake (Dora Bailey), King Donovan (Rod), Kathleen Freeman (Phoebe Dinsmore, diction coach), Tommy Farrell (Sid Phillips).

Arthur Freed for MGM, U. S. A. 9238 ft., 103 mins. Technicolor.

Singin' in the Rain is the best-known work of the evolutionary musical, a trend which covered a long distance in the course of the 50's: from the loosely assembled plot with ballet interludes in On the Town to the unison of dance and socially-conscious vision of reality in West Side Story. The credit for leading the musical into new expanses goes to Gene Kelly and Stanley Donen. Their Singin' in the Rain reflects in a deforming mirror Hollywood at the time of the first talkies and follows the highly-polished pattern of American entertainment films while doing away with the earlier autonomy of the dancing and singing scenes.

Although much more substantial than in the films of Fred Astaire who had so far dominated the musical, the plot is still slight: a ridiculous costumer has been completed just as sound comes in and is being turned into a musical. The atrocious nasal voice of the blond star gives rise to many complications. But in the end Don, Cosmo and Kathy, three charming young people, make their reputation in the film world and also find personal happiness. Where are therefore the deserts of the makers? In their skill--the skill with which they blended the development of the plot with the impressive ballet sequences, the charm with which they combined allusive jokes with nostalgic reminiscences from the early days of the talkies, the ability to sustain a brisk pace. Finally, there are the fine performances from Gene Kelly and the rest of the cast. Singin' in the Rain is an excellent entertainment picture addressed to a wide audience. It is also, particularly in the first part, an example of intelligent entertainment. It is hardly surprising that its box-office success has been enormous.

THE CRUEL SEA Charles Frend

Script: Eric Ambler, from the novel by Nicholas Monsarrat. Photography: Gordon Dines. Music: Alan Rawsthorne. Art Direction: Jim Morahan. Editing: Peter Tanner. Cast: Jack Hawkins (Lieutenant Commander Ericson), Donald Sinden (Lieutenant Lockhart), John Stratton (Ferraby), Denholm Elliott (Lieutenant Morell), Stanley Baker (First Officer Bennett), John Warner (Baker), Bruce Seton (Petty Officer Tallow), Liam Redmond (Chief Engineer Watts), Virginia McKenna (Julie Hallam), Moira Lister (Elaine Morell), June Thorburn (Doris Ferraby), Megs Jenkins (Tallow's sister).

Leslie Norman for Ealing Studios, G. B. 11,359 ft., 126 mins.

The Cruel Sea is a screen adaptation of a bestselling novel partly based on its author's own experiences acquired during service in the Royal Navy in 1940-45. After the evacuation of Dunkirk, Monsarrat enlisted as a volunteer and served as a first officer on escort ships. Frend called on Monsarrat several days after the publication of the book to offer to make it into a film. This is not surprising if one realizes that the theme of The Cruel Sea is a logical continuation of Frend's earlier San Demetrio, London. The topic of both films, the painful wartime heroism, is the same. But now, from several years' perspective, this is seen not in the simple terms of discharging a duty to one's country, but as a complex and bitter reflection on human tragedies and the psychological damage caused by the war. While half of the novel is devoted to the personal affairs of the officers and men while on home leave, Ambler and Frend saw the film as an episodic chronicle of events at sea.

The story takes place during the Battle of the Atlantic and is concerned with two vessels: the "Compass Rose," a corvette escorting convoys to Gibraltar and the frigate "Saltash Castle" which took part in the northern convoys to Murmansk in Russia. The change of emphasis seems to have benefitted the film. While the private-life sub-plots, although treated with praiseworthy naturalness, are still a little common, the sea episodes, shot in authentic scenery (apart from the night scenes) appear much more expressive. Perhaps they lack constructional coherence and the ambition to go beyond faithful portrayal of typical situations--yet many dramatic episodes are staged very dynamically, with terse, factual dialogue and interesting use of soundtrack (with, among other things, sound flashbacks). It is worth mentioning such memorable moments as the saving of the shipwrecked sailors during the night alight with burning ships, the chase after a U-boat, the tense silence interrupted by the sound of tools while a shaft is being repaired, the sinking of the "Compass Rose," or the captain's tragic and yet right decision to detonate depth charges against a German submarine lurking in the deep below the shipwrecked British sailors who are waiting for help. Jack Hawkins, restrained and authentic, gives an excellent performance, very prominent against the background of a rather uneven acting team.

THE QUIET MAN John Ford

Script: Frank S. Nugent, from the novel by Maurice Walsh. Photography: Winton C. Hoch and Archie Stout. Music: Victor Young. Art Direction: Frank Hotaling. Editing: Jack Murray. Cast: John Wayne (Sean Thornton), Maureen O'Hara (Mary Kate Danaher), Barry Fitzgerald (Michaeleen Oge Flynn), Ward Bond (Father Peter Lonergan), Victor McLaglen ("Red" Will Danaher), Mildred Natwick (Sarah Tillane), Francis Ford (Dan Tobin), Arthur Shields (Rev. Cyril "Snuffy" Playfair), Eileen Crowe (Elizabeth Playfair), May Craig (Woman at railroad station), Charles FitzSimmons (Forbes), Sean McClory (Owen Glynn), Jack McGowran (Feeney), James Lilburn (Father Paul), Joseph O'Dea (Maloney), Ken Curtis (Dermot Fahy).

John Ford--Merian C. Cooper for Argosy/Republic, U.S.A. 11,632 ft., 129 mins. Technicolor.

With his protagonist, an American professional boxing champion, John Ford returns once more to Ireland, the country of his ancestors. After the drama of The Informer and the nostalgia of How Green Was My Valley the turn has come for a generic comedy.

After a successful career as a boxer, Sean Thornton returns to his native village in Galway to settle down quietly. Love for Mary Kate, an impulsive red-haired girl; an awkward courtship; objections from the girl's robust and narrow-minded brother; a spectacular final fight--in the course of the uncomplicated plot which unfolds at a leisurely pace we witness a succession of picturesque green landscapes and a host of equally picturesque Irish country folk. Ford does not (and probably did not intend to) reach artistic heights in The Quiet Man--but within its modest framework of a noisy plebeian spree the picture is a skillful visit to the Green Island. The film-making once more testifies to Ford's high class. Within exemplary structural frames the story develops at an excellently measured dramatic pace; the individual scenes are climaxed with great precision; the comedy inherent in situations and dialogues is always fully exploited. Barry Fitzgerald, Victor McLaglen and John Wayne make good use of their character parts while Victor Young's music tempers some images whose content might otherwise appear too unrefined.

THE SHEPHERDESS AND THE CHIMNEYSWEEP (La Bergère et le ramoneur) Paul Grimault

---

Script: Grimault and Jacques Prévert. Animation Direction: Grimault. Music: Joseph Kosma. Songs: Jacques Jansen, Eric Amado and Léo Noël. Voices: Pierre Brasseur (Wonderbird), Serge Reggiani (Chimneysweep), Anouk Aimée (Shepherdess).

Les Gémeaux/André Sarrut, France. 69 mins. Technicolor.

The kingdom of Tachycardie, an enormous palace-city ruled by a tyrant. Charles the Crosseyed ruthlessly maintains a social hierarchy similar to that in Fritz Lang's Metropolis: the submissive slaves who work "below" have no idea whatever what the royal apartments look like. But even cruel tyrants are powerless when love comes into play. The King loves a young dancer on a picture hanging on the wall in the palace, but the girl prefers the chimneysweep inhabiting the neighboring picture. As a result the sweethearts leave their respective pictures and try to get out of the palace to freedom. They would not be able to escape from the chase ordered by the furious King, were it not for the help of a cunning bird-anarchist. It is through his doings that a fearsome robot instead of capturing the fugitives devastates the palace, sends the King into space and finally destroys himself. The long-oppressed inhabitants of Tachycardie will now live in a new happy country.

The film, whose spirit is basically a quintessence of French republican traditions, is skillful in execution and original in its visual form. A fruit of more than six years' work, this first feature-length cartoon film from France is very different in design and mood from the streamlined efforts of Disney. Indeed, it is superior in many respects. Take, for instance, the designs--concrete in the description of objects, delicate in characterizing the couple of protagonists but grotesque in treatment of the negative characters. Disagreements with the producer who insisted on greater expressiveness at the expense of fleeting subtle poetry in the style of Jacques Prévert, prevented Grimault from making the film even better. This way or the other, although somewhat lacking in warmth, The Shepherdess and the Chimneysweep commands respect for its counterpoint handling of moods, the lightness of its wit, and the changing of the camera angles including the use, pioneering in a cartoon picture, of "freed camera" in the sequence of the breathtaking chase on the facade of the palace. Alas, Grimault was not destined to be Disney's competitor. The film was not a commercial success and for the next 15 years remained his only attempt in the field of full-length animated cartoon.

FANFAN-LA-TULIPE Christian-Jaque

Script: René Wheeler and René Fallet; also Christian-Jaque and Henri Jeanson, inspired by 18th-century French folk tales. Photography: Christian Matras. Music: Maurice Thiriet and Georges Van Parys. Art Direction: Robert Gys. Editing: Jacques Desagneaux. Cast: Gérard Philipe (Fanfan-la-Tulipe), Gina Lollobrigida (Adeline), Noël Roquevert (Fier-à-Bras), Oliver Hussenot (Tranche-Montagne), Marcel Herrand (King Louis XV), Jean-Marc Tennberg (Lebel), Jean Parédès (Captain de la Houlette), Nerio Bernardi (La Franchise), Henri Rollan (Field Marshal), Geneviève Page (Mme. de

Pompadour), Sylvie Pélayo (Henriette de France), Georgette Anys (Tranche-Montagne's wife).

Films Ariane/Filmsonor/Giuseppe Amato, France/Italy. 8820 ft., 98 mins.

The elegant wars of Louis XV seen through the lorgnette of a joker--and rather not from the point of view of the royal court, but from that of the people from among which the hero of the title comes.

During the Seven Years War Fanfan is recruited for the King's army by a sergeant whose beautiful daughter, Adeline, lures prospective soldiers with splendid prophecies. She tells Fanfan that he will marry the King's daughter; the film shows the hero in pursuit of his destiny. He rescues Princess Henriette from the bandits, then narrowly escapes the death sentence imposed by the King after Fanfan climbed to the castle to see her again, courts Adeline, saves her from the King's clutches and takes into captivity the entire enemy army. The prediction is finally fulfilled: the grateful King adopts Adeline and gives Fanfan her hand.

Fanfan-la-Tulipe is a French swashbuckler in the best tradition of Alexandre Dumas' adventure novels. The film's tongue-in-cheek tone is only an excuse for the fast narrated story of romance. Fanfan survives his incredible adventures unscathed (in the cloak-and-dagger genre this is usually reserved for those of noble birth) thanks to his remarkable fencing skills. The spoken commentary can hardly be considered a success, but the whole relies on the proverbial Gallic charm; in the first place on the personal charm of Gérard Philipe who, against the background of the rather sluggish extras and thanks to speeded-up photography, acquires the status of a first class swashbuckling hero. It is true that Christian-Jaque does not at times go beyond the level of a plebeian farce, but he conducts the whole with great lightness, and in the star scenes (like, for instance, the chase after a coach) can muster considerable directorial skills. Fanfan-la-Tulipe is in the cinema of the 50's the most skillfully done and the most popular period adventure in the light vein.

THE LUSTY MEN Nicholas Ray

Script: Horace McCoy and David Dortort, from a story by Claude Stanush. Photography: Lee Garmes. Music: Roy Webb. Editing: Ralph Dawson. Cast: Susan Hayward (Louise Merritt), Robert Mitchum (Jeff McCloud), Arthur Kennedy (Wes), Arthur Hunnicutt (Booker Davis), Frank Faylen (Al Dawson), Walter Coy (Buster Burgess), Carol Nugent (Rusty), Maria Hart (Rosemary Maddox), Lorna Thayer

(Grace Burgess), Burt Mustin (Jeremiah), Karen King (Ginny Logan), Jimmy Dodd (Red Logan), Eleanor Todd (Babs).

Jerry Wald--Norman Krasna, U. S. A. 112 mins.

Jeff McCloud, a former rodeo champion, returns to his native Oklahoma where he meets Wes Merritt, a young ranch hand, and his wife Louise. The Merritts are dreaming of a ranch of their own and need money to buy it. Wes asks Jeff to teach him rodeo technique and they go on a professional rodeo tour on a 50/50 basis. Louise tries to stop her husband from rodeo riding, but he is too intoxicated with success. Wes in turn becomes jealous of Jeff's attention to Louise and in a showdown with his partner tells him that he is pulling him along; to demonstrate that he is still a rodeo star, Jeff enters a competition and is killed. Wes sobers up, makes up with his wife and they leave together to buy a place of their own.

The milieu is well described--without hysteria or exaggeration (which with Ray is big praise) although the script provides a number of dramatic situations which might have attracted him in that direction. One may even describe the film as quiet and toned-down. It is the people who are characterized best: tough rodeo enthusiasts and their wives. The Lusty Men is in fact a nicely "American" film, a solid, atmospheric rodeo tale with good dialogues and the photography which makes one think of Hemingway. The situations are rather classical: but there is good acting, a note of poetry, a subtle reflection on the destiny of man--on the fate of such people as Jeff, Wes and Louise.

VACUUM ZONE (Shinkū Chitai) Satsuo Yamamoto

Script: Yusaku Yamagata, from the novel by Hiroshi Noma. Photography: Minoru Maeda. Music: Ikuma Dan. Art Direction: Yasuzo Kawashima. Cast: Takashi Kanda (Mine, a troop commander), Yoshi Kato (Lt. Hayashi), Eiji Okada (Sub-Lt. Okamoto), Yoichi Numata (Duty officer of the week), Koichi Nishimura (Sgt. Osumi), Isao Kimura (Kitani), Asao Sano (Ikeno), Isao Numazaki (Hikoza), Tsutomu Shimomura (Soda), Toshio Takahara (Some), Kiyoshi Nonomura (Uchimura), Kenji Susukita (Uchimura's father), Harue Tone (Harue).

Shinsei Eiga, Japan. 11,594 ft., 129 mins.

After And Yet We Live, Vacuum Zone is the second notable work of the independent left-wing cinema in Japan; a vehement accusation of militarism, particularly the inhuman conditions within the Imperial Army. Formerly a soldier in the forces occupying Manchuria, Yamamoto knew these problems well and was thus able to give Vacuum Zone a stamp of authenticity and conviction. Like Hideo Sekigawa's earlier Listen to the Roar of the Ocean (1950) and Imai's later The Tower of Lilies (1953), Yamamoto's anti-war picture had a considerable influence on the formation of pacifist sentiments in post-war Japanese society, probably because it argued with such directness and such force of persuasion: without the somewhat hysterical tone of the first and the melodramatism of the second of the above-mentioned pictures. Yamamoto offers perhaps the simplest and most traditional film-making of all leading Japanese directors, but in the framework of the social and political epic within which he moved, he knew how to exploit the logic of argumentation, the coherence of the execution and the emotional tension in the story. These features were lacking in the work of Kamei who came to grief on the rocks of cinematic rhythm and thus lost the power of his proletarian drama Woman Walking Alone on the Earth (1953); they were also lacking in most of Imai's work. Vacuum Zone, Yamamoto's first important picture, belongs together with Ichikawa's Fires on the Plain, Kobayashi's The Human Condition and Ieki's Brothers Born of Different Mothers to the most prominent pictures which reckon up with Japan's militaristic past.

MONKEY BUSINESS Howard Hawks

Script: Ben Hecht, Charles Lederer and I. A. L. Diamond, from a story by Harry Segall. Photography: Milton Krasner. Music: Leigh Harline. Art Direction: Lyle Wheeler and George Patrick. Editing: William B. Murphy. Cast: Cary Grant (Dr. Barnaby Fulton), Ginger Rogers (Edwina Fulton), Charles Coburn (Oliver Oxly), Marilyn Monroe (Lois Laurel), Hugh Marlowe (Harvey Entwhistle), Henri Letondal (Dr. Siegfried Kitzel), Robert Cornthwaite (Dr. Zoldeck), Larry Keating (G. J. Culverly), Douglas Spencer (Dr. Brunner), Esther Dale (Mrs. Rhinelander), George Winslow (Little Indian), Emmett Lynn (Jimmy).

Sol C. Siegel for 20th Century-Fox, U. S. A. 8709 ft., 97 mins.

Howard Hawks was never short of good spirits: one of the most universal thematically of the American film directors applied humor liberally not only in his comedies of various kinds--ranging from the crazy and near-Surrealistic Twentieth Century (1934) to the musicomedy Gentlemen Prefer Blondes (1953)--but also in adventure films and westerns (sometimes to excess, like in El Dorado). Together with His Girl Friday, Monkey Business is without a doubt Hawks's most successful comedy. Apart from some primitive jokes, the film contains many intelligent, ironic references and jibes at American snobberies and idiosyncrasies. One of them is the often irrational striving of the Americans to keep impeccable countenance in every situation.

The brash, hectic plot concerns a research chemist who works on a formula for the elixir of youth. What a scientist cannot achieve, a chimpanzee can: one of the lab monkeys breaks loose, mixes up chemicals lying about and dumps the concoction in the water container. The professor and his amiable, devoted wife drink from the container with quite unexpected consequences. They behave like schoolchildren, buy teenage clothes, sports cars, go to a skating rink, etc.

Hawks maintains fast pace throughout the film while the well-chosen acting team (led by Cary Grant and Ginger Rogers) cause cascades of laughter in the cinema and are easily forgiven for overdoing things occasionally. It was only Billy Wilder in Some Like It Hot (in cooperation with the same scriptwriter, I. A. L. Diamond) who managed successfully to let off such a firework of fun.

THE BIG SKY Howard Hawks

Script: Dudley Nichols, from the novel by A. B. Guthrie Jr. Photography: Russell Harlan. Music: Dimitri Tiomkin. Editing: Christian Nyby. Cast: Kirk Douglas (Jim Deakins), Dewey Martin (Boone Caudill), Elizabeth Threatt (Teal Eye), Arthur Hunnicutt (Zeb), Buddy Baer (Romaine), Steven Geray (Jourdonnais), Hank Worden (Poordevil), Jim Davis (Streak), Henri Letondal (Labadie), Robert Hunter (Chouquette), Booth Colman (Pascal), Paul Frees (McMasters), Frank de Kova (Moleface), Guy Wilkerson (Longface).

Howard Hawks for Winchester, U. S. A. 140 mins.

1830: Jim Deakins and Boone Caudill, two tough backwoodsmen, leave Kentucky and join a trading expedition from St. Louis up the Missouri, Platte and Cheyenne Rivers. They team up with a trapper, Zeb, and a whisky trader, Jourdonnais. They travel by boat to trade for beaver pelts with the Blackfoot Indians. Apart from natural hazards, the party have to struggle against a regular fur trading company, the Indians and the many complications caused by the presence aboard of a Blackfoot princess. There is also the theme of both Boone and Deakins' pursuit of the girl whom Hawks seems to identify with the primeval character of these territories.

The Big Sky is an epic western about the conquest of the unknown ennobled by dignified landscapes of the Missouri Valley; its theme is the interplay of attitudes, friendships and antagonisms within the group of pioneers. The film is impressive in its interesting intrigue, good dialogues and frequent change of mood. Still, it is a little on the heavy side (to quote Penelope Houston: "The Big Sky has the timeless, relentless quality of the long American historical novel, to which it is a screen equivalent"). It is impossible, however, not to recognize in it the sense of man's enthralling immersion in Nature, the pioneering spirit of last century discovery of new territories. The characters are less complex than in Red River, a film similar in type, but on the other hand seem more real, quite unlike the plot which approaches the fairy-tale towards the end. The Big Sky is an undisputed, if minor, classic of the traditional descriptive western.

LA FETE A HENRIETTE Julien Duvivier

Script: Duvivier and Henri Jeanson. Photography: Roger Hubert. Music: Georges Auric. Art Direction: Jean d'Eaubonne. Editing: Marthe Poncin. Cast: Dany Robin (Henriette), Michel Auclair (Maurice), Hildegard Kneff (Rita Solar), Michel Roux (Robert), Saturnin Fabre (Le Pochard), Julien Carette (Arthur), Henri Crémieux ("Sensation" scriptwriter), Louis Seigner ("Light-hearted" scriptwriter), Daniel Ivernel (Adrien), Micheline Francey (Script-girl), Odette Laure (Valentine), Jeannette Batti (Gisèle), Paulette Dubost (Mother), Alexandre Rignault (Father).

Regina/Filmsonor, France. 9334 ft., 104 mins.

The French Nouvelle Vague is not yet in existence--not even as a theoretical program; so there is still time left for light-hearted self-irony within the framework of the traditional cinema. Julien Duvivier, a classic at everything which would later be fervently condemned by the new cinema of the 60's, until he returns to grace in the times of Day for Night (1972), assumes an ironic distance from the arid run-of-the-mill productions of the contemporary cinema and offers the spectator some amusing variations on stereotyped commercial plots. In La Fête à Henriette two stock cinematic visions of reality are in contest: two tyro scriptwriters of whom one favors heavy drama and sex and the second prefers the more romantic stories are discussing a subject for a film. The two disagree vehemently and we are shown alternately the ideas of each of them. The story they finally evolve develops, like in Clair's Quatorze Juillet, on July 14, France's annual national holiday.

Robert, a reporter-photographer working for a Paris weekly promises his dressmaker fiancée to take her out on July 14, her birthday, while collecting material for his paper. Robert suddenly leaves Henriette at an open-air dance; the girl meets a handsome young crook and soon becomes entangled in a criminal affair. All this causes--how else--a lot of exquisite complications.

While pictures based on formulas similar to that in La Fête à Henriette are almost always rather vacuous, this time we have a film which is really light, intelligent and well constructed. Even the somewhat heavy charm of the two leading men is not too much of a drawback and is fully compensated for by the makers' visual imagination involving among other things, Duvivier's favorite tilted camera angles. One would have almost thought that the maker of Poil de carotte and Un Carnet de bal is still young. Not so: La Fête à Henriette is the last effort of any consequence by one of the veteran masters of the French cinema.

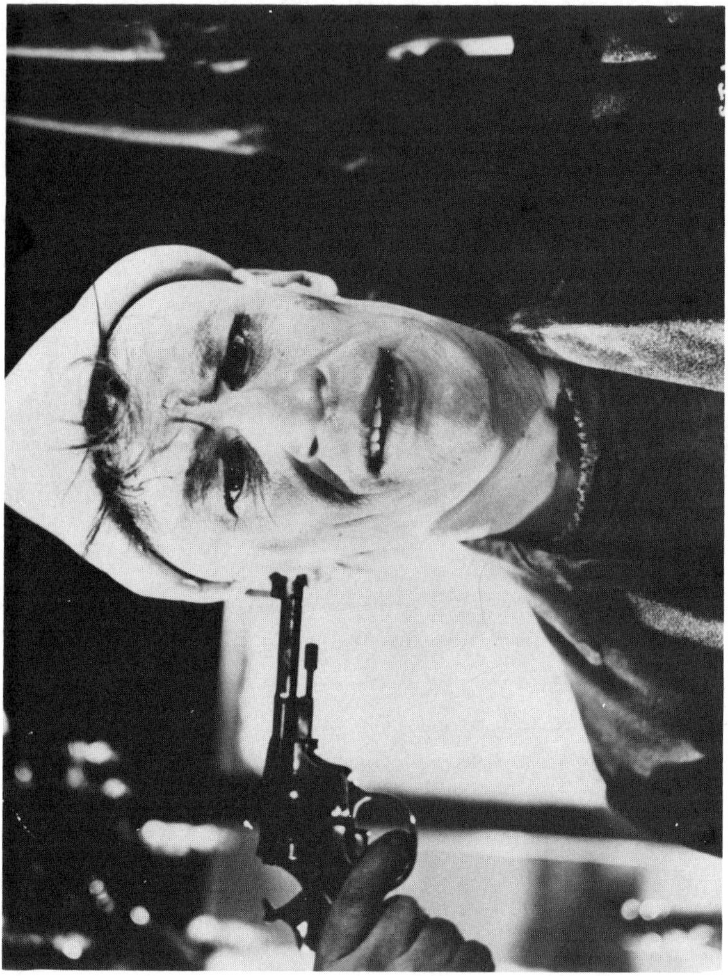

The Naked Night

1953

THE NAKED NIGHT (Gycklarnas afton) [Sawdust and Tinsel] Ingmar Bergman

---

Script: Bergman. Photography: Sven Nykvist and Hilding Bladh. Music: Karl-Birger Blomdahl. Art Direction: Bibi Lindström. Editing: Carl-Olov Skeppstedt. Cast: Åke Grönberg (Albert Johansson), Harriet Andersson (Anne), Hasse Ekman (Frans), Anders Ek (Teodor Frost), Gudrun Brost (Alma Frost), Annika Tretow (Agda Johansson), Gunnar Björnstrand (Sjuberg), Erik Strandmark (Jens), Åke Fridell (Officer).

Rune Waldekranz for Sandrews, Sweden. 8610 ft., 96 mins.

Prior to 1953 Ingmar Bergman had a reputation, to be sure, as an able scriptwriter and worthwhile director of pessimistic psychological dramas--but still seemed to be an imitator of Poetic Realism or a continuer of the post-war Existentialist trends rather than an independent creator of values. As a result Bergman's reputation was limited to his native Sweden. The Naked Night (also released as Sawdust and Tinsel) brought an unexpected qualitative leap to the work of the man who had already made 12 films. It is one of those pictures which are striking right from the very first frame and which proclaim the arrival of a truly outstanding director. It is true that a year earlier Bergman had made Summer with Monika, a picture of considerable interest. But that film, realistic and in its intentions close to crusading journalism, turned out to be an exception in Bergman's cinema, while The Naked Night has a quite different starting premise, content and style. Rather, with its pessimistic brooding about loneliness and humiliation in man's struggle

The Naked Night

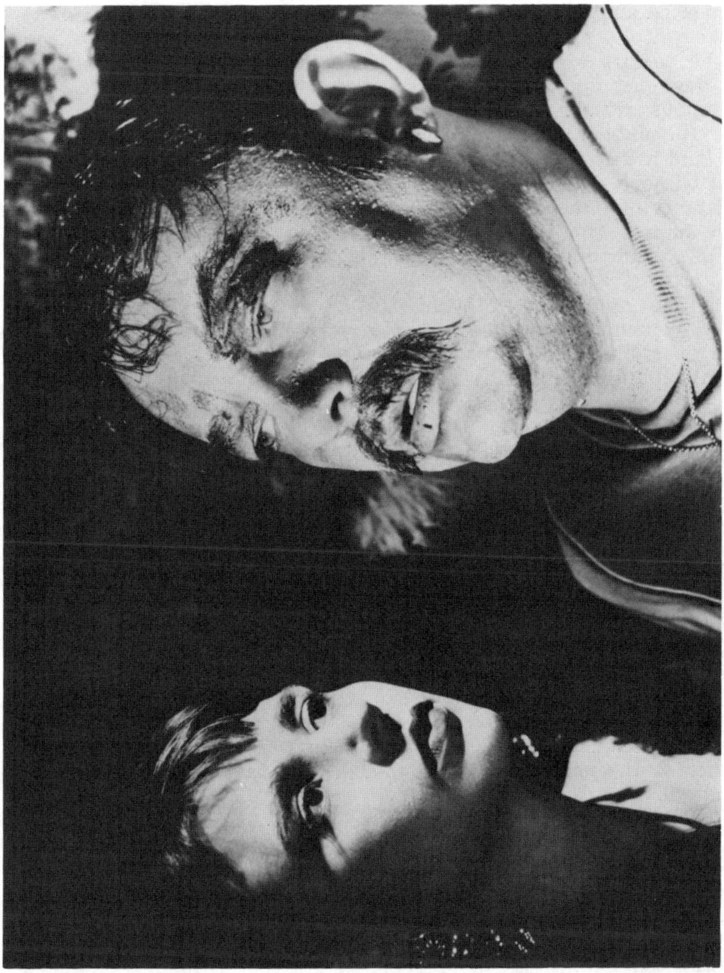

The Naked Night

for happiness, it directly refers to Bergman's earlier work--Port of Call (1948), The Devil's Wanton (1948) and Thirst (1949).

The story of The Naked Night is set in the late 19th century in a circus--a favorite location for debating the human condition in the theatre and the cinema. Life is said to reveal the best its wretchedness in the combination of the shoddy existence and the servile exhibitionism of circus performers. Life in the circus, now cheaply glorified, now used as a convenient excuse for pretentious dramas about defeated people, would seem to be a very uncertain material for ambitious artistic achievement. And yet Bergman (and a year later Fellini in La strada) managed just that, and did it without abandoning the usual thematic frames and a rather typical set of situations. The Naked Night is about people uncertain of the future, humiliated while fighting for the realization of their dreams, condemned to settle for things they despise.

The fascinating, nightmarish prologue, which uses a fadeout into white and is sustained in the style of the silent cinema, serves as an overture to the story proper. In the prologue a circus clown tells about the unfaithful aging wife who ran away with some artillery officers and bathed in the sea naked in front of the whole battalion, bringing humiliation upon her husband who tried to intervene to the accompaniment of cascades of the soldiers' laughter. This prologue introduces the drama of Albert, the corpulent owner of a shabby traveling circus and Anne, his beautiful equestrienne mistress. The circus stops for a one-night stand at a small provincial town. Both want to flee from their present existence--Anne into the embraces of a young actor from the local theatre; Albert into the four walls and a bourgeois happiness which his long-abandoned wife managed to achieve for herself. These attempts bring but humiliation to both. Albert is taunted by Anne's lover and is severely beaten. He tries to shoot himself; the gun misfires and, unable to muster up the courage to try a second time, Albert (in a heart-piercing scene) shoots the circus bear instead. Condemned to be with each other, Albert and Anne find the only solution in wearily moving off again together to the next town, even though they have in common only anguish and despair.

The motif of a human life reaching a point where hope ceases to exist, where--because of the conflict of the sexes, the impossibility of achieving spiritual contact or, to be more exact, because of the woman's doom-laden biologicality--the protagonists reach the lowest point of their existence, was present in Bergman's work from the very beginning, that is since he wrote the script for Sjöberg's Frenzy. As a matter of fact, this motif is already inherent in the traditional Swedish attitude of the struggle against loneliness motivated by metaphysical anguish. Bergman himself has once explained the origins of this national mood simply by invoking the bird's eye view of Sweden: a vast wilderness occasionally specked by solitary buildings. The Naked Night gives all this an excellent, moving and direct cinematic expression. The fine dramatic structure of the film is supplemented by the powerful mood, on achieving which Bergman expended much care, and which is often created, as in the prologue, by the first frames of a sequence. The images are dominated by ornamental, splendidly rich dusky frames. The director's skill is supported by the very evocative performances from Åke Grönberg and Harriet Andersson. The protagonists are faced with a very wide spectrum of situations, and in each of them the actors successfully combined authentic behavior with expressive conveyance of feelings. Blomdahl's score (which among other effects incorporates cannon shots into the music) interestingly partners the development of the plot and plays an important part in the film. In his quest for the sense of human existence Bergman did not find it easy to achieve again a comparable intellectual respectability, consistency of means of expression, pitch of emotional tension, and dramatic coherence. It is only in The Silence that he repeated all these qualities. The Naked Night, his first really outstanding film, remains to this day one of his best.

TOKYO STORY (Tōkyō Monogatari) Yasujiro Ozu

Script: Kogo Noda and Ozu. Photography: Yuharu Atsuta. Music: Takanori Saito. Art Direction: Tatsuo Hamada. Editing: Yoshiyasu Hamamura. Cast: Chishu Ryu (Shukishi Hirayama), Chiyeko Higashiyama (Tomi Hirayama), Setsuko Hara (Noriko), So Yamamura (Koichi), Haruko Sugimura (Shige), Kyoko Kagawa (Kyoko), Kuniko Miyake (Fumiko), Nobuo Nakamura (Kurazo Kaneko), Eijiro Tono (Numata), Hisao Toake (Hattori), Shiro Osaka (Keizo).

Takeshi Yamamoto for Shochiku, Japan. 12,509 ft., 139 mins.

Tokyo Story is the Ozu film most often shown abroad; until very recently his entire reputation in many countries relied on this one picture. One can only say that Ozu could have been less fortunate: Tokyo Story is one of his most accomplished and most universal works.

Shukishi and Tomi Hirayama, an elderly couple living in the town of Onomichi with their youngest daughter, decide to travel to Tokyo to see their married children. The visit is something of a disappointment. The son, who lives in a less attractive suburb than they have imagined, is a busy doctor, while the daughter runs a beauty salon. Both are too bound up in their daily routine to give much attention to their parents. They send them off to the hot-springs resort of Atami, ostensibly as a treat. But the Hirayamas feel ill at ease there and decide to return to Tokyo. The mother spends her last night in the capital with Noriko, widow of her son killed in the war, while the father gets drunk. On their way back they have to stop in Osaka, where their younger son lives, because Tomi falls

Tokyo Story

ill; she dies when they return home. The children rush back to Tokyo immediately after the funeral; only Noriko has the time to stay behind for a few days and to talk to the youngest daughter, Kyoko, who is a teacher. The father accepts his loneliness stoically and advises Noriko to get married again. He remains alone in the empty house, thinking of the years ahead of him.

Tokyo Story provides the clearest example of Ozu's mature style. The critic Marvin Zeman discovered that the key to the director's work is haiku, the miniature poetic form derived from the traditions of Zen Buddhism. The 18th-century poet Buson writes simply:

Before the white chrysanthemum
The scissors hesitate
A moment

A haiku has only three lines of text and almost always intimates the time of year (autumn in the above example), contemplating the contrast between that which lasts (the scissors) and that which passes (the chrysanthemum). The whole of Japanese art aims at a laconic isolation of a single volatile emotion, at creating in the mind of the reader a complete, albeit momentary, poetic image. Ozu's films are the screen equivalent of haiku--series of visual allegories about the world and about human life. To Ozu reality is composed of an infinity of simple events: fleeting, sad and recurrent. The existence of a gap between generations is not a new discovery; it is inevitable and Ozu simply records it with placid melancholy and with incomparable sensitivity. The awareness of the transience of everything worldly, steeped in the mood which is a mixture of grief and nostalgia, known in Japanese as mono no aware, is most marked in Ozu's late films. "Isn't life disappointing" asks Kyoko of Noriko, and Noriko agrees. She is the film's positive pole. But the other children are not condemned, as Ozu never condemns anybody. The inevitable has to be accepted stoically and this is intimated in the shot, so typical of Ozu, of the father sitting alone in the room contemplating what has passed and was loved. The whole of Tokyo Story is permeated by the sense of loss. Action would not change anything very much and this is the essence of the last image of the film: empty railway tracks as the noise of a train dies away.

Tokyo Story is made in Ozu's mature style: long-shots are only used at the beginning or end of a sequence to establish the setting, while the entire rest is shot in medium-shots. There are no tracking or panning shots, no zooms, fades, dissolves or wipes. The camera records the events from the eye-level of a Japanese sitting on a mat known as tatami and many scenes indeed take place around the table. Only once does the camera travel--inside a moving bus as the parents visit the sights of Tokyo. The editing is similarly restrained, almost austere, apart from the final mosaic of sound and picture in the last sequence. Ozu has assembled a wonderful team of actors. It includes Chishu Ryu who worked on almost all his films. Ozu kept even Setsuko Hara under control, with whose superstar attitudes Kurosawa found it difficult to cope. Tokyo Story is the best example of team acting in Ozu's cinema.

THE WAGES OF FEAR (Le Salaire de la peur) Henri-Georges Clouzot

---

Script: Clouzot; also Jérôme Géronimi, from the novel by Georges Arnaud. Photography: Armand Thirard. Music: Georges Auric. Art Direction: René Renoux. Editing: Madeleine Gug and Henri Rust. Cast: Yves Montand (Mario), Charles Vanel (Jo), Folco Lulli (Luigi), Peter Van Eyck (Bimba), Véra Clouzot (Linda), William Tubbs (O'Brien), Dario Moreno (Hernández, innkeeper), Jo Dest (Smerloff).

Filmsonor/C. I. C. C. /Véra Film/Fono Roma, France/Italy. 156 mins., later reduced to 12,995 ft., 144 mins.

The Wages of Fear, the finest achievement of the French film noir, is a brilliant adventure thriller which combines Existentialist contexts with social criticism.

Somewhere in Central America, in a small town which has grown around an American-run oilfield, there vegetates a group of foreign drop-outs. To get away from this country without hope is equivalent to finding the money for the air ticket. The opportunity comes when Southern Oil Company offers $2000 to volunteers who will drive two truck-loads of nitroglycerine, a high explosive, to a burning oil well several hundred miles away. Nitroglycerine is to be used to blow out the fire. The terrain is mountainous, the roads bad and the slightest jolt will set off an explosion. Two trucks embark on the suicidal expedition: the crew of one are two Frenchmen--Mario, an amiable Parisian and Jo, a middle-aged gangster; the second truck is driven by Luigi, a good-humored Italian bricklayer and Bimba, a mysterious Scandinavian. As they surmount the increasingly hazardous route the four men become besieged by fear, a stifling, overpowering fear which changes the attitudes of the desperadoes who can be blown up at any moment. Luigi and Bimba's truck does blow up; Jo is hurt in an accident and dies. Only Mario reaches the target. Yet he is not to escape destiny; intoxicated with triumph he drives recklessly on the way back and crashes his truck over a precipice.

The masterly build-up of tension is performed by Clouzot in the microcosm of four men and two trucks surrounded by distance and fear. The editing crescendos, the use of sound and the significant detail (which often takes on a symbolic meaning) play a very important part in the film. It is through the use of symbolic detail that the sensational plot of an illusory expedition for freedom is transformed into a tragedy about destiny, a metaphor about the irreversibility of human life. In vain Mario's talisman--a Paris underground ticket; in vain solidarity in the face of mortal danger; in vain love which almost telepathically binds Linda and Mario, the separated lovers. Men are condemned to fight a dramatic but futile struggle like the insects shown in the film's opening shot: a close-up of two beetles locked in combat; the camera reveals that they are tied to strings manipulated by a small boy. What then if not life, is to be won in the sombre The Wages of Fear? The answer rests in Existentialist philosophy--the heroic sense of being a human. During their Calvary the four drop-outs are given a chance to regain their self-respect and sense of dignity. Clouzot's very precise study of characters is no less worthy of attention than his narrative mastery. The diversity of the four leading characters may seem too ostentatious, but is justified by the final result: in the course of the inner metamorphosis by their characters, conducted by Clouzot with so much insight and logic, Vanel, Montand, Lulli and Van Eyck convey a lot about human beings in a crisis situation. This quality remains one of the most important in The Wages of Fear and on its own sufficiently compensates for what is questionable in the film--the pessimism of its intellectual premises.

I VITELLONI Federico Fellini

Script: Fellini, Ennio Flaiano and Tullio Pinelli. Photography: Otello Martelli, Luciano Trasatti and Carlo Carlini. Music: Nino Rota. Art Direction: Mario Chiari. Editing: Rolando Benedetti. Cast: Franco Interlenghi (Moraldo), Alberto Sordi (Alberto), Franco Fabrizi (Fausto), Leopoldo Trieste (Leopoldo), Riccardo Fellini (Riccardo), Leonora Ruffo (Sandra), Jean Brochard (Fausto's father), Carlo Romano (Signor Michele, an antiquary), Lida Baarova (Signora Giulia, his wife), Enrico Viarisio (Sandra's father), Paola Borboni (Sandra's mother), Claude Farère (Alberto's sister), Arlette Sauvage (Lady in the cinema), Achille Majeroni (Natale, the homosexual actor), Maja Nipora (Showgirl who goes to bed with Fausto), Silvio Bagolini (Giudizio, the simpleton who prays to the stolen statue), Vira Silenti (Leopoldo's "Chinese" date at the ball), Franco Gandolfi, Gondrano Trucchi, Guido Marturi, Milvia Chianelli.

Lorenzo Pegoraro for PEG Film/Cité Films, Italy/France. 9822 ft., 109 mins.

A major Italian director, Federico Fellini grew up, as it were, on the ashes of Neorealism, the movement which became extinct in the early 50's as a result of political pressures and the improvement of the economic situation in the country. Fellini is often incorrectly considered an heir to the Neorealist tradition. In fact, when he was writing scripts for Neorealist films (such as Rome, Open City) it was simply as a scriptwriter-craftsman. Until Fellini found himself able to express his directorial temperament and real artistic personality freely on the screen in I vitelloni, his films, comprising Variety Lights (1950) and The White Sheik (1952), were unremarkable. The principal features of Fellini's work, a glittering panopticon firmly rooted in local color and specific Italian attitude to life, have no more in common with Neorealism than with the rest of Italian art--sensuality and an idealistic belief in man's basic dignity and goodness.

Such is I vitelloni, a story of a group of young idlers in a small seaside town. The title translates as "big calves" and with the exception of Moraldo, Fellini treats the protagonists with a kind of contemptuous pity mixed with mock emotion. Sons of lower middle-class families, they feel they are too good for manual labor and live off their parents. So they do nothing, playing silly games, drifting aimlessly, engaging in nocturnal conversations in deserted streets, strolling along the beach in winter. They only perk up during the bathing season, and when it is over await the next for the whole year. Leopoldo is a would-be writer, Alberto a sentimental sissy. Fausto, a provincial Don Juan, is forced to marry Sandra, whom he made pregnant, and to take a job in an antique shop. Sandra leaves home with the baby when she discovers that he has been unfaithful. Fausto finds her at her father's house and the couple are reconciled--at least temporarily. After a masque ball, Alberto returns home to find his sister, who is supporting the family financially, about to leave with her lover. Still wearing woman's clothes from the ball, Fausto finds himself head of the family. Moraldo, Sandra's brother, is prompted by the events to leave for the big city.

The autobiographical aspect of I vitelloni has often been exaggerated. Although Fellini did spend his adolescence in the coastal resort of Rimini, he left for Florence at the age of eighteen, while his protagonists are in their late twenties. Soon after Fellini found himself in Rome working as a gagman and writer; at 21 he began working on a script which eventually became Rome, Open City. It is still true to say that I vitelloni, with its loose, episodic structure has the texture of a reminiscence and the logic of a personal diary, whereby the various characters are alternately brought to the forefront in a series of intertwined episodes.

As in Fellini's whole work, the principal value of I vitelloni is excellent observation of the milieu and the characters. The lethargy of an Italian backwater, fatal to individuals with a soft moral backbone is portrayed with feeling and brilliance. Very typical are the butterfly temperaments of the protagonists who alternate between diametrically opposed moods, easily passing from dejection to euphoria, from cynicism to plaintive helplessness. Their immaturity best comes to light during the masque ball, a scene at once comical and pathetic, in which the disguise hides not only faces but also a basic fear of reality, of making a serious choice in life, and provides an excuse to escape from the environment as well as from themselves. Fellini has no sympathy for his protagonists. The only affirmative accent in the film is Moraldo's final decision to leave the town. Thoughtful and sympathetic, Moraldo is the positive center of the picture, and clearly Fellini's spokesman. Perhaps in portraying the Moraldo character Fellini uses a few drops of awkward didacticism--but then he simply belongs to a different cinematic convention, warm and poetic, which is in sharp contrast with the malicious and caricatural treatment of his friends.

Thus I vitelloni is an analysis of immature mentality. The overpowering inertia of the province, the atmosphere of desolation and loss, the sense of futility and failure, these constant motifs in Fellini's cinema, are evoked via a wonderful cinematic imagery and the sensitive use of locations, such as the empty town square or the desolate beach at night. As Moraldo leaves, the camera in turn shows his friends, who have remained, asleep in their beds as if from a running train, and with the appropriate soundtrack. A powerful and memorable last touch on the director's part. This nostalgic and sensitive picture was very soon overshadowed by Fellini's subsequent work, which is without a doubt outwardly more impressive. Yet some hard-boiled connoisseurs of the cinema consider I vitelloni Fellini's best work.

THE LAST BRIDGE (Die letzte Brücke) Helmut Käutner

Assistant Director: Gustav Gavrin. Script: Käutner and Norbert Kunze. Photography: Elio Carniel; also Fred Kollhanek. Music: Carl de Groof. Cast: Maria Schell (Helga Reinbeck), Bernhard Wicki (Boro), Barbara Rütting (Milica), Karl Möhner (Sergeant Martin Berger), Horst Hächler (Lieutenant Scherer), Fritz Eckhardt (Haslinger), Robert Meyn (Rottsieber, German doctor), Pable Mincić (Momcilo, a mute), Tilla Durieux (Mara, an old peasant woman), Zvonko Zungul (Sava), Stevo Petrović (Ratko), Janez Vrchovec (Vlaho), Dragoslav Radolcić (English officer).

Cosmopol Film/UFUS, Austria/Yugoslavia. 104 mins.

It is something of a mystery why Helmut Käutner, who in Romance in the Minor Key (1943) proved to be one of the most talented German directors, has made so many failed films. Perhaps his somewhat feverish embarking on new projects was responsible. Seven films from the debut in 1939 to the above-mentioned adaptation of a story by de Maupassant; then after two more interesting wartime productions--again a run of second-rate efforts made in the years 1947-1952. But in 1954, when the critics have already concluded that the director has not lived up to his earlier promise, Käutner travels abroad and makes a film which is one of the finest anti-war films in the cinema.

The Last Bridge is a story of Helga, a German woman doctor, a patriot who is taken into captivity by Yugoslav partisans during the Second World War. At first she is reluctant when ordered to tend the sick and wounded; but the things she sees, coupled with a basic moral honesty make her change her views on the rationale of the opposing sides, and give help to the enemies of her country. Helga is hit by a stray bullet while crossing a bridge to deliver medical supplies to the partisans and dies in front of both fighting sides.

It is worth noting that Käutner's best film remains a one-off achievement in virtually all its aspects. This film could not be made twenty years later, in any case not in such form and not in such spirit of a compassionate statement on the scourge of war. However, many things in The Last Bridge which would later seem naive (in spite of being based on facts) or which would not escape a sober confrontation with the actual historical circumstances appeared way back in 1953, the time of the cold war, in a completely different light. The threat of a nuclear conflict united people of sometimes very different political orientations. Eight years had passed since the war and though people had not yet forgotten the ocean of common suffering, they are already beginning to admit the thought of forgiveness into their minds. But there was not enough time to consider fully the problems of historical rationale and political necessity. In this context The Last Bridge is a product of its time; but its message sounds sufficiently clear to resonate with the intentions of the peace movements in many countries. It had, of course, a special significance in post-war Germany. The fact that Käutner so very convincingly portrayed the inner metamorphosis of the heroine (incomparably played by Maria Schell); that, despite needlessly overcharging the film with dramatic climaxes and subplots, he preserved the balance between opposing arguments; that he did not abandon the concrete for the sake of the abstract--defend the message of the film, not only in the context of the time when it was made, but also in general. The Last Bridge is a manifestation of a certain attitude of mind which should not be shouted down by accusations of anachronism.

THE CRAB-CANNING SHIP (Kanikōsen) So Yamamura

Script: Yamamura, from the novel by Takiji Kobayashi. Photography: Yoshio Miyajima. Music: Akira Ifukube. Art Direction: Motoshi Kijima. Cast: So Yamamura (Matsuki), Masayuki Mori (Doctor), Akitake Kono ("Shibaura"), Kow Mihashi (Asakawa), Akira Tani (Suda), Mikizo Hirata (Foreman), Rosak Kawarazaki (Boy), Shin

Morinawa (Kurasa), Sumiko Hidaka (Whore), Sanaye Nakahara (Natsu), Haruye Wakahara (Dancer), Shisuye Yamagishi (Mother), Yasushi Mizura (Young man).

Tengo Yamada for Gendai-pro, Japan. 10,066 ft., 112 mins.

A resounding accusation of the inhuman exploitation in pre-war Japan, The Crab-Canning Ship is an epic fresco clearly inspired by the Soviet silent cinema. In 1926 a crab-canning vessel owned by a Japanese fishing enterprise carries out intensive fishing for crab in the North Pacific, off the Kamchatka Peninsula. The brutal treatment of the workers, the breaking of the sea code and above all the truly hell-like working conditions lead to a mutiny on board. The workers seize control of the vessel, but the rebellion is soon bloodily suppressed by a boarding party from an Imperial Navy warship.

These final scenes of the revolt are the best in the film, hysterically expressive, shown using fast, cut editing and in close rather than general shots. These scenes are a stylistically consistent culmination of the naturalistic trains of images of human degradation, played almost entirely on the highest note of expression, but defending themselves from the accusation of exaggeration with their matter-of-fact description of details and characters, the dramatic logic of events and their authentic mood of protest. The author of the literary original, a popular proletarian novel, was a leading activist of the Left and died in prison in 1933. Satoru (So) Yamamura, a well-known actor who in The Crab-Canning Ship debuts as a director, transferred the novel to the screen not only without the loss of its spirit, but also managed to combine concrete semi-documentary description with a generalizing vision of an acute social conflict within Japanese capitalism and to wrap up these contents in a dynamic, closely-knit visual form. The Crab-Canning Ship is one of the leading achievements of the militant independent cinema in Japan.

UGETSU MONOGATARI Kenji Mizoguchi

Script: Matsutaro Kawaguchi, from Yoshikata Yoda's adaptation of two stories, "Asaji ga yado" (The Inn at Asaji) and "Jasei-no in" (Serpent of Desire) from the classic collection of stories, "Ugetsu Monogatari" (Tales of the Pale and Mysterious Moon After the Rain) by Akinari Ueda (1768). Photography: Kazuo Miyagawa. Music: Fumio Hayasaka and Ichiro Saito. Art Direction: Kisaku Ito. Editing: Mitsuji Miyata. Cast: Masayuki Mori (Genjuro, the potter), Machiko Kyo (Princess Wakasa), Sakae Ozawa (Tobei), Mitsuko Mito (Ohama, Tobei's wife), Kinuyo Tanaka (Miyagi, Genjuro's wife), Sugisaku Aoyama (Old priest), Ryosuke Kagawa (Village chief), Mitsusaburo Ramon (Captain of Tamba soldiers), Kikue Mori (Ukan), Syozo Nanbu (Shinto priest), Ichisaburo Sawamura (Genichi).

Masaichi Nagata for Daiei, Japan. 8622 ft., 96 mins.

Outside Japan Ugetsu Monogatari is the most celebrated of Mizoguchi's films. It is considered his most perfect work and brought him the Silver Lion at the 1953 Venice Film Festival. The film is based on a 16th-century legend about two peasants who abandoned family happiness for the sake of illusions: fame, money, a woman-incarnation of beauty. The scene is a village on the shores of Lake Biwa at the time of the civil war at the end of the 16th century. The village, where Genjuro and his brother-in-law Tobei make their living as potters, is sacked by marauding soldiers. One can made a big profit on the already made pottery, but this involves danger. Genjuro wants to sell as much as possible, while Tobei decides to become a soldier. They set off together to the nearest town with a supply of pots. Tobei leaves behind his wife Ohama, who followed him to town, and fulfills his military plans. The wife is raped and finally becomes a prostitute. Genjuro meets a beautiful princess at the market-place; enchanted with her beauty he forgets his family and follows her to her castle; he lives with her until an itinerant monk reveals to him that the princess is but a ghost. The spell is broken; Genjuro returns home to his wife; but next morning a village elder explains that he must have seen an apparition, for his wife is dead and buried. Tobei and Ohama have also returned home. Genjuro is left with his memories and his experience.

Ugetsu Monogatari is a screen adaptation of the stories by the 18th-century writer considered to have been a Japanese equivalent of de Maupassant. If one considers that de Maupassant had always been Mizoguchi's favorite writer, one might be entitled to expect a film done with particular care. It was indeed: sophisticated in its delicate ethereal mood, refined pastel photography, harmony of the misty frames and an unfailing feel for the period. But Mizoguchi intended this film to be more than merely a remarkable formal exercise: Ugetsu Monogatari is also one of the fullest explications on the screen of the traditional Japanese mono no aware philosophy which professes acceptance of the inherent sadness of man's experience, the futility of his attempts to achieve a better lot in life and the sense of the beauty of existence. The film is also a praise of peaceful work and a protest against war which brings material destruction and the degeneration of human ambition. Finally, it is a poetic reflection on the ambivalence of values. So, Ugetsu Monogatari would seem to deserve nothing but praise.

However, this complex and multilayered work is short of being a masterpiece. Excessively lauded as an example of a faultless union of truth and fantasy, a quality so attractive to the French adherents of cinéma onirique, the film reveals precisely in that aspect a rather fundamental flaw between the multitude of subtle undertones of meaning and the certain coarseness with which it portrays reality. This is caused in equal parts by the deficiency in the acting and the awkwardness of the mise en scène (particularly felt in the more dynamic scenes)--all this despite Mizoguchi's stress on the authenticity of behavior, dialogues and designs. Akira Kurosawa, another great of the Japanese cinema said simply: "In Ugetsu when we get to the war scenes it just isn't war." The film's much-praised visual excellence is indisputable--but this is a cold and dead excellence, closer to traditional Japanese art than to the living visuality of the cinema. As a result the brittle aesthetic structure of the film is weakened by these flaws and in many places does not bear up to its role of a subtle medium for the director's message. Ugetsu Monogatari is thus a film of great intentions rather than great achievements. All the same, in this case even a partial result amounts to a lot: this poetic treatise about the aspirations of a man who abandons petty reality for the sake of grandiose dreams opened a window onto the spiritual panorama of Japan and remains one of the most original pictures in the cinema.

THERESE RAQUIN Marcel Carné

Script: Carné and Charles Spaak, inspired by the novel by Emile Zola. Photography: Roger Hubert. Music: Maurice Thiriet. Art Direction: Paul Bertrand. Editing: Henri Rust. Cast: Simone Signoret (Thérèse Raquin), Raf Vallone (Laurent), Sylvie (Madame Raquin), Jacques Duby (Camille Raquin), Roland Lesaffre (Blackmailer), Maria Pia Casilio (Georgette, the hotel maid), Marcel André (Michaud), Martial Rebé (Grivet), Nerio Bernardi (Doctor).

Robert and Raymond Hakim for Paris-Films/Lux-Film, France/Italy. 110 mins.

Les Portes de la nuit (1946), a tale of Destiny in post-liberation Paris, brought a resounding failure of Carné's imagery. Its feeble story seemed unconvincing when seen just two years after a grim and tragic war. It was sheerest kitsch, the result of a mishap which can befall any poet: an anachronism at odds with contemporary moods. Also unsuccessful, for rather similar reasons, were the director's two subsequent films, La Marie du port (1950) and Juliette ou la clé des songes (1951). For his next project Carné turned to one of the most interesting works of French naturalist literature, which had already been made into an outstanding film by Jacques Feyder in 1927. In Zola's novel Carné found some of his favorite motifs. Spaak, his scriptwriter, introduced rather substantial changes into the story, and updated it from Paris in the 1860's to contemporary Lyon.

Madame Raquin, her son Camille, whom she idolizes, and his wife Thérèse, live above their drapery shop. Camille befriends Laurent, an Italian truck driver who becomes a frequent visitor in the house. Thérèse and Laurent fall in love, but Thérèse is reluctant to leave her husband. On learning about the affair, Camille decides to remove Thérèse to the custody of his relatives in Paris, but is thrown off the train during a quarrel with Laurent. An inquest records a verdict of accident, but a man who traveled in the same compartment begins to blackmail the lovers. They decide to pay him off; but after collecting the money the blackmailer is accidentally killed by a truck and a letter to the police he left in case he fails to return is posted.

It is interesting to consider the changes Feyder and Spaak introduced to Zola's story, an arraignment of the false morality which brings about human tragedies and leads to crime. They saw it as a drama of Destiny and Fate. In the novel (and in Feyder's film which follows it closely) there was crime and remorse; the husband was deliberately drowned--here he is a victim of chance, of an accident during a scuffle on a moving train. (It is worth noting, on the other hand, that this change gets round the question of why the problem was not settled by a divorce). In the novel Thérèse is a calculating woman who counts on inheriting her husband's shop and money--here she is merely an unselfish victim of passion. In the novel Laurent is a vague cynic pretending to be an artist--here he is a decent proletarian. In the novel Thérèse and Laurent are victims of destructive sexuality and end up by taking poison (to illustrate Zola's thesis that there can be no love or happiness within bourgeois mentality)--here they try to live an ordinary life, but are victims of a blackmailer. In Carné there are no criminals and no agony of remorse; the blackmailer not only does not separate the lovers, but unites them. It is only through blind fate that he is killed and the police brought in.

The film is thus made somewhat in spite of the theme. But it succeeds all the same--because of the fascinating atmosphere it evokes. The excellent performance from Simone Signoret is largely responsible for this outcome--poisoned by the limited world of petty people, crestfallen, subdued, half-absent, shuddering under the pitiless stare of Madame Raquin, who became paralyzed after the death of her son. Thus the novel's protest against hypocrisy and false morality is preserved on the screen.

The story is told at slowed-down pace and dominated by a mood of greyness and depression, static scenes, long periods of silence while long takes reveal small gestures, an interplay of meaningful glances. One scene is particularly memorable: the close-up of the faces of Thérèse and Laurent in deep contrasts of light and shade just after Camille's death--a moment of suspense broken by the roar of a train on the next track.

SHANE George Stevens

Script: A. B. Guthrie Jr; also Jack Sher, from the novel by Jack Warner Schaefer. Photography: Loyal Griggs. Music: Victor Young. Art Direction: Hal Pereira and Walter Tyler. Editing: William Hornbeck; also Tom McAdoo. Cast: Alan Ladd (Shane), Jean Arthur (Marion Starrett), Van Heflin (Joe Starrett), Brandon De Wilde (Joey Starrett), Jack Palance (Wilson), Ben Johnson (Chris Calloway), Emile Meyer (Rufus Ryker), Edgar Buchanan (Lewis), Elisha Cook Jr. (Torrey), Douglas Spencer (Shipstead), John Dierkes (Morgan Ryker), Ellen Corby (Mrs. Torrey), Paul McVey (Grafton), John Miller (Atkey), Edith Evanson (Mrs. Shipstead), Leonard Strong (Wright), Ray Spiker (Johnson), Janice Carroll (Susan Lewis), Martin Mason (Howells), Nancy Kulp (Mrs. Howells), Howard J. Negley (Pete), Beverly Washburn (Ruth Lewis).

George Stevens--Ivan Moffat for Paramount, U. S. A. 118 mins. Technicolor.

A key picture in the development of the genre, Shane confronted the classical western with the contemporary development of the psychological western, and gave the result charm and popular appeal. At the roots of the film are two fundamental American myths: that of a man fighting on behalf of another man in the name of justice; and that of a stranger who brings a breath of adventure into a small, isolated community. The first myth is present in thousands of films; the second would soon be questioned in Picnic.

Turn-of-the-century Wyoming. Joe Starrett, his wife and young son farm peacefully. The neighborhood is terrorized by the Ryker gang, trying to keep the land for open-range grazing on behalf of a cattle baron. Shane, a fugitive from a gun-fighting past, arrives at the Starretts' house. Idolized by young Joey, he takes the homesteaders' side. The conflict is brought into the open when Ryker orders Wilson, a professional gunman, to kill Torrey, one of Starrett's friends. Shane prevents Starrett from fighting Wilson and himself kills both Wilson and Ryker. He then rides off.

Thus the film features a struggle between an ideal of good and the incarnation of evil. This is done on a very realistically and very convincingly shown period background. Shane is a structurally pure classical western, archetypal and mythological. Let us list the classical motifs which appear:

(1) the conflict between homesteaders and open-range farmers;
(2) the mysterious, noble stranger dressed in white. Having killed a man in the past he is doomed to wander forever;

Shane

(3) the hired black-garbed killer;
(4) the two culminations--the first with fists, the second with guns;
(5) the background of the action--a vast plain with mountains looming in the distance;
(6) the family--a robust and honest farmer, his gentle and beautiful wife and a young son.

Consider now how the classical western is confronted with the modern developments in the genre:

(1) the antagonistic arguments in the conflict between the open-range farmers and homesteaders are very truthfully shown from the historical point of view. At first cattle breeders use persuasion telling the newcomers: "It was us who conquered these lands. Many of us died in the process. Go away. We shall give you money." But they are up against the tide of history--for America was developed by the farmers. As the cattle breeders begin to lose the argument, they resort to violence--but this cannot avert their defeat;
(2) the noble knight is not really as spotless as he appears at first;
(3) the farmer breaks down under the pressure of events;
(4) the gentle and beautiful wife is not only a pretty face--she uses her brains. Also, she is in an emotional dilemma between Shane and her husband;
(5) the relationships in the triangle Shane-Starrett-Mrs. Starrett are complex and have psychological finesse;
(6) the baddies (the Ryker gang) are also differentiated in personality, and not just a mass;
(7) the death of Wilson, the gunman, is treated almost with sentiment: "it had to happen--but he was such a good shot."

Aesthetically, Shane makes sense only if the story is treated as seen through Joey's eyes. Despite the child's intercession, a certain "classicizing" gravity does make itself felt in the picture, especially since the film-making is a little heavy--which is a usual attribute of Stevens's style. Subtle things are not always shown subtly and the dialogues include many naive lines. Scenes which are executed faultlessly are the fights and the beautiful burial sequence. The film was made in pleasant color, with a good sense for the location, with feeling and lyricism--with an epic sense of western history, too. In the famous, nostalgic last scene young Joey runs after his idol shouting: "Shane, come back." But Shane will never return--the days of riders from nowhere and of private justice are over. Earlier in the film Shane was talking to the leader of the cattlemen. "Your days are over," says Shane. "Mine? What about yours, gunslinger?" asks the man. "The difference is, I know it" is the reply.

THE WILD ONE Laslo Benedek

Script: John Paxton, from the short story "The Cyclists' Raid" by Frank Rooney. Photography: Hal Mohr. Music: Leith Stevens. Art Direction: Walter Holscher. Editing: Al Clark. Cast: Marlon Brando (Johnny), Mary Murphy (Kathie), Robert Keith (Harry Bleeker), Lee Marvin (Chino), Jay C. Flippen (Sheriff Singer), Peggy Maley (Mildred), Hugh Sanders (Charlie Thomas), Ray Teal (Frank Bleeker), Will Wright (Art Kleiner), Yvonne Doughty (Britches), Gene Peterson (Crazy), Alvy Moore (Pigeon), John Brown (Bill Hannegan), Robert Osterloh (Ben), Robert Bice (Wilson), William Vedder (Simmy), Keith Clarke (Gringo), Gil Stratton Jr. (Mouse), Darren Dublin (Dinky), Johnny Tarangelo (Red), Jerry Paris (Dextro), Harry Landers (Go Go), Jim Connell (Boxer), Don Anderson (Stinger), Angela Stevens (Betty), Bruno VeSoto (Simmonds), Pat O'Malley (Sawyer), Eve March (Dorothy).

Stanley Kramer, U. S. A. 7114 ft., 79 mins.

After making Death of a Salesman, Benedek again showed talent in a classic leather-jacket-and-motorbike picture, a prototype of the bike films of the 60's and 70's, to mention only Corman's The Wild Angels and Hopper's Easy Rider. The interesting thing is that The Wild One foreshadows these not only in theme, but also in mood.

The Black Rebels motorcycle club led by Johnny arrive, riding in a military formation, at a race meeting. Before being told by the police to leave, they steal a statuette from among the prizes and give it to their leader. As they arrive in a small town, Johnny meets Kathie, a young waitress, and fights with Chico, leader of a rival gang. Tension mounts and is followed by trouble; when Kathie's father, a policeman, is seen to be lacking strength to intervene, the citizens band together against the gang. They capture and beat up Johnny assuming he tried to rape Kathie. A passer-by is killed by a bike which runs out of control as Johnny is knocked off it. Johnny is let off; before riding away he gives the statuette to Kathie.

Supposedly based on the actual story of cyclists taking over a small California town in the late 40's, this stylish and sober study of violence was refused a censor's certificate in Great Britain for over 14 years. The Wild One is a good example of what the censors consider subversive: the anarchistic tone of the film. The violence actually shown is inconsiderable, even by contemporary standards. The first half is particularly suggestive, with its direct, sharp observation, evocative photography of dark streets and the atmosphere of mounting unrest, the study of a situation which gets out of hand, a source of instinctive anarchy. Gang members come out into the streets from a hairdressing salon with hair dryers over their heads. The conclusion that violence breeds violence is a theme which came to be explored by the cinema during the following two decades, together with a number of motifs, such as the motif of an outsider, dressed in black leather, who ignores the law (an interesting reflection of the convention used by Stevens in Shane), the motif of a good girl attracted against her will by a villain, the motif of a bike as a sex symbol and the formalized, near-choreographic ride of the cyclists into town.

FOUR CHIMNEYS (Entotsu-no mieru basho) Heinosuke Gosho

Script: Hideo Oguni, from the novel "The Good People" by Rinzo Shiina. Photography: Mitsuo Miura. Music: Yasushi Akutagawa. Art Direction: Tomoo Shimogawara. Editing: Nobu Nagata. Cast: Ken Uehara (Ryukichi Ogata), Kinuyo Tanaka (Hiroko), Hiroshi Akutagawa (Kenzo Kubo), Hideko Takamine (Senko Azuma), Chieko Seki (Yukiko Ikeda), Ranki Hanai (Katsuko Ishibashi), Haruo Tanaka (Chuji Tsukahara).

Yoshishige Uchiyama for Eit-pro, Japan. 9678 ft., 108 mins.

Together with Ozu and Naruse, Heinosuke Gosho is the leading exponent of shomin-geki--a lower middle-class melodrama which is a specifically Japanese cinematic genre. Born in 1902, Gosho is one of the veterans of Japanese cinema. He made his first film as director in 1925 and also directed the first Japanese talkie, The Neighbour's Wife and Mine (1931), his best-known early work. Gosho, who never went beyond the shomin-geki genre, cares deeply for the common man and his problems. He believes that "all films, as all works of art, must touch the emotions of the audience and touch them deeply," and pursues this aim with pictures which mix humor and pathos, lyrical symbolism with realistic description and are often not free from sentimentality.

Four Chimneys, which won a prize at the 1954 Berlin Film Festival, fits this description perfectly. The central characters are Ryukichi and Hiroko, a childless couple who live in a poor industrial district of Tokyo. The area is dominated by four factory chimneys, but depending where one is they appear as one, two, three or four. The couple are unexpectedly left with a baby, the child of Hiroko's first husband and a woman he lives with. The baby's constant crying creates great tension in the household and leads Hiroko to attempt suicide. Kenzo and Senko, a tax collector and his girl rent two upstairs rooms. They also have their problems. Finally Ryukichi and Hiroko become used to the baby's presence, although they tried to get rid of it at first. One has to face life as it is, with its little joys and sorrows.

Such is Gosho's--and his characters'--attitude to life. Being oneself is always the most important thing, and life is what you make of it--the conclusion conveyed by the chimneys of the title, the film's central visual metaphor. A very appropriate metaphor in fact, much more original than the caged bird in Gosho's later Growing Up (1955), a visual comment on the fate of the heroine destined to a life of prostitution. The mood, known as nakiwarai, is one of laughter-through-tears, and is reminiscent of the films of Chaplin. With the multiplicity of shots, frequent use of close-ups and a highly mobile camera (what a contrast to Ozu, another shomin-geki director!) Gosho achieves precise characterization and a flowing rhythm; the mood is underlined with the use of jocular music.

FROM HERE TO ETERNITY Fred Zinnemann

Script: Daniel Taradash, from the novel by James Jones. Photography: Burnett Guffey. Music: George Dunning. Song "Re-enlistment Blues": James Jones, Fred Karger and Robert Wells. Art Direction: Cary Odell. Cast: Montgomery Clift (Robert E. Lee Prewitt), Burt Lancaster (Sgt. Milton Warden), Deborah Kerr (Karen Holmes), Donna Reed (Lorene), Frank Sinatra (Angelo Maggio), Philip Ober (Capt. Dana Holmes), Mickey Shaughnessy (Sgt. Leva), Harry Bellaver (Mazzioli), Ernest Borgnine (Sgt. "Fatso" Judson), Jack Warden (Corp. Buckley), John Dennis (Sgt. Ike Galovitch), Merle Travis (Sal Anderson), Tim Ryan (Sgt. Pete Karelsen), Arthur Keegan (Treadwell), Barbara Morrison (Mrs. Kipfer), Jean Willes (Annette).

Buddy Adler for Columbia, U. S. A. 118 mins.

From Here to Eternity has been described as the first major anti-war picture of the 50's. A tall claim, if one considers Huston's The Red Badge of Courage--but it is still a powerful picture. After Teresa and The Men, films which were concerned with the aftermath of the war, Zinnemann shows how corruption is brought about by the military mentality in peacetime.

Summer of 1941. Private Prewitt is transferred to Schofield Barracks, Honolulu. When, despite being an accomplished boxer, he refuses to join the boxing team (because he had once blinded a friend in the ring), Captain Holmes orders his sergeants to make Prewitt's life in the Army as difficult as possible. Prewitt finds consolation with Lorene, a hostess from the New Congress Club, while Sergeant Warden starts an affair with Holmes's wife, Karen, who tries to persuade him to become an officer so that she can marry him. Lorene, who longs for respectability ("when you are proper--you are safe") does not want to give up her job to marry Prewitt. Prewitt kills "Fatso" Judson, a savage sergeant who vengefully murdered his friend sent to "the stockade" and then hides in Lorene's apartment. War begins with the Pearl Harbor attack. Warden, who has ended the affair with Karen, goes off to the war. While trying to return to the barracks, Prewitt is challenged by a patrol and shot. Lorene and Karen meet for the first time on a boat bound for the United States.

From Here to Eternity is a laundered and diluted version of James Jones's novel. A brothel becomes a bar and a prostitute a dance hall hostess. The book describes the spiritual dichotomy of men who on the one hand hate the army machinery and on the other are motivated by a sense of loyalty. The film reduces this mostly to the officer/soldier conflict, revealing a deeply-set class structure and to the rebellion of army wives. But even here there is compromise: in the book Holmes won promotion, here he is put on trial. The film seems a little glib as a result and often hovers on the verge of melodrama. It starts slowly and takes a lot of time to explain the characters' motivation. Yet it largely retains the sour disenchanted mood of the original and includes several powerful scenes, such as Prewitt's trumpet solo in the bar. Montgomery Clift's refusal to join the boxing team is only a metaphor for opposition to the military, as long hair was fifteen years later, and the film attacks the essential brutality of the army machine with its disregard for the individual. The officers and men are bored and inactive; Holmes is more interested in the boxing championship than in the possibility of the outbreak of the war. The film never discusses the reasons for the war; its point is to demonstrate--via Prewitt's constant degradation in the army--the corruption and hypocrisy of the people who are there to fight it. The main character is a bit of a problem: those who read the book expected him to be a man of limited intelligence, and Montgomery Clift, while certainly stubborn and hard, seems much too refined for the part. From Here to Eternity was a big commercial success. It was quite something, even back in 1953, to award eight Oscars to a film not even in color. It is interesting that, possibly to demonstrate fairness towards the subject, the U. S. Army gave Zinnemann assistance during the production.

ROMAN HOLIDAY William Wyler

Script: Ian McLellan Hunter and John Dighton, from a story by the former. Photography: Franz F. Planer and Henri Alekan. Music: Georges Auric. Art Direction: Hal Pereira and Walter Tyler. Editing: Robert Swink. Cast: Audrey Hepburn (Princess Anne),

Gregory Peck (Joe Bradley), Eddie Albert (Irving Radovich), Hartley Power (Baird Hennessy), Laura Solari (Hennessy's secretary), Margaret Rawlings (Countess Vereberg), Harcourt Williams (Ambassador), Tullio Carminati (General Provno), Paolo Carlini (Mario Delani), Claudio Ermelli (Giovanni), Paola Borboni (Charwoman).

William Wyler for Paramount, U. S. A. 10,616 ft., 118 mins.

A teenage princess arrives in Rome on an official visit. She is received, how else, with suitable pomp and circumstance. But the princess is fed up with official ceremonies, the stiff harness of diplomatic protocol and dreams of living like an ordinary girl of her age. So she decides to play truant: she discovers Rome for herself and embarks on a romance with an American newspaperman who finds her asleep on a park bench. She sees the sights in his and his friend's company. Finally, to the relief of the worried officials, she ruefully returns to her public functions.

Such is the story of the most famous sentimental comedy of the 50's. The riches-to-rags idea (which reportedly Frank Capra intended to film at one time) was without a doubt material for a box-office hit, but hardly for something more ambitious. It was only the charm of Audrey Hepburn (given an Oscar for her first leading part) and the directorial precision of Wyler (who deserves merit both for discovering a new star and for devising a multitude of situational gags) that gave Roman Holiday wings. Not all situations are unpretentious and some are obtrusive; yet the absolute majority are examples of the reliable, traditional (in the best sense of the word) handling of movie situations--based on observation of behavior and mostly making do without dialogues. The most skillful in this respect is the sequence of Anne's visit to the reporter's flat. The tempo of the film leaves a little to be desired, but the fleeting mood of a carefree adventure is created faultlessly and is bound to disarm the malcontent. It is hardly surprising that the entertainment film of which all this can be said was very well received and became an example to many other directors to follow. But none of them could come up with a result which would match up to the original.

ESCAPE FROM FORT BRAVO John Sturges

Script: Frank Fenton, from a story by Philip Rock and Michael Pate. Photography: Robert Surtees. Music: Jeff Alexander. Art Direction: Cedric Gibbons and Malcolm Brown. Editing: George Boemler. Cast: William Holden (Captain Roper), Eleanor Parker (Carla Forester), John Forsythe (Captain John Marsh), William Demarest (Campbell), William Campbell (Cabot Young), John Lupton (Bailey), Richard Anderson (Lieutenant Beecher), Polly Bergen (Alice Owens), Carl Benton Reid (Colonel Owens).

Nicholas Nayfack for MGM, U.S.A. 8833 ft., 98 mins. Ansco Color.

Arizona during the Civil War. A large number of sullen Confederate prisoners are kept at Fort Bravo. Carla Forester arrives ostensibly to visit the commander's daughter, but really to help Captain Marsh, her lover, to escape. She meets Captain Roper at the Fort and falls in love with him--but still flees with Marsh and three other Confederate soldiers. Roper is sent in pursuit of the fugitives; he is rounding them up when the Indians attack. Marsh is wounded in the battle and dies. But the rescue party arrives in time and Carla and Roper return to safety and a new life together.

This western uses familiar situations and is very traditional with its moralizing intentions--idealistic, masculine, severe, optimistic in its attitude to man in action. The North-South division disappears to give way to common effort in the battle against the Indians. The Indians in Escape from Fort Bravo are shown very traditionally, as a threatening horde. The point of the film however is not their wickedness (despite the fact that the film does refer to the cruelty of the Mescalero Indians, although without showing it on the screen). They are simply seen as an "adversity"--and are used as an excuse for bringing out the common spirit of people portrayed as a group rather than separate individuals. The stress is on the sacrifice and community spirit of white Americans in a struggle against danger. It is less important what this danger is.

The dialogues are clever (almost too much so) and the action scenes well directed (the Indian attacks, the long final battle). On the other hand interior scenes are rather stereotyped while intimate scenes are sheer Hollywood confectionery. The Ansco color system is shown to be capable of very interesting results, and the locations are filmed particularly well. The film was shot in the Death Valley National Monument in Nevada.

WILD GEESE (Gan) Shiro Toyoda

Script: Masashige Narusawa, from the novel by Ogai Mori. Photography: Mitsuo Mimura. Music: Ikuma Dan. Art Direction: Takeo Kimura (supervision: Kisaku Ito). Cast: Hideko Takamine (Otama), Hiroshi Akutagawa (Okada, a student), Eijiro Tono (Suezo, Otama's patron), Jukichi Uno (Kimura, Okada's friend), Choko Iida (Osan), Eiza Tanaka (Zenso, Otama's father), Kumeko Urabe (Otsune, Suezo's wife), Miki Odagiri (Oume, Otama's maid), Kuniko Miyake (Osada, a seamstress).

Masaichi Nagata for Daiei, Japan. 9362 ft., 104 mins.

Wild Geese is a subtle tale of impossible love, set in the 1880's. The girl thinks she is the wife of a prosperous man, only to discover that he is a usurer and is already married; the boy, a poor and ambitious medical student, spins dreams of going to Europe. First encounter, several meetings as friends, then the parting when he leaves to study abroad. Confessions of love did not come, and the boy was not even aware of his feeling for the girl, while she did not reveal hers, aware of her impossible situation as a woman kept by a jealous moneylender. Only the wild geese which accompany their parting with sad wailing cries express the feelings of a lonely woman.

Such is the finale, so very Japanese in its reference to nature, of a picture which is very Japanese in its mood and philosophy. Toyoda, a film-maker respected for his thoughtful and careful direction of actors (or rather actresses, since most of his films are about women) creates in Wild Geese a delicate, lace-like setting for an intimate psychological study of the heroine played softly by Hideko Takamine. The most important part in achieving this result rests with the chiaroscuro texture of the photography, once described as having "a woodcut quality," and most impressive in the outdoor scenes.

THE PROUD ONES (Les Orgueilleux) Yves Allégret

Script: Jean Aurenche and Allégret, from Jean-Paul Sartre's scenario "Typhus," based on his own novel "L'Amour redempteur." Dialogues: Jean Clouzot, Pierre Bost and Aurenche. Photography: Alex Phillips. Music: Paul Misraki. Art Direction: Auguste Capelier and Gunther Gerzso. Editing: Claude Nicole. Cast: Michèle Morgan (Nellie), Gérard Philipe (Georges), Carlos Lopez Moctezuma (Doctor), Victor Manuel Mendoza (Don Rodrigo), Michèle Cordoue (Anna), André Toffel (Tom).

C. I. C. C. /Reforma/Chrysaor, France/Mexico. 105 mins.

The Proud Ones is the last interesting work by Yves Allégret who in the late 40's directed the pessimistic Une si jolie petite plage and Manèges. By 1953, after a succession of five poor pictures, Allégret's despondency was toned down if not compromised--and this is seen in The Proud Ones of which the first part is like the death throes of screen Existentialism, while the second part contains concessions towards a happy end. The latter circumstance prompted Jean-Paul Sartre, the pope of Existentialist philosophy, to disown the film based on his book whose title "Love, the Redeemer" was merely bitterly ironic.

While a young Frenchwoman, Nellie, is on a holiday in Mexico with her husband, the husband contracts cerebrospinal meningitis, a contagious disease, and dies. Nellie, penniless and unmoved by her sudden bereavement, meets a young French doctor, Georges, who has taken to drink after his wife died in childbirth. The two find that they are attracted to each other. Due to Nellie's influence Georges rediscovers in himself a will to live and ceases to drink. He gives her a spinal injection to prevent her becoming ill, and helps the many local victims of the disease. Nellie decides to stay on in Mexico and help Georges in his work.

Sartre was right: the happy end, moralizing and obtrusive, gives the whole film a melodramatic complexion. On the other hand he has partly himself to blame: a drunken foreign doctor in an exotic country is a stereotyped figure, after White Shadows in the South Seas. The Proud Ones is still a worthwhile picture because of the first part, where melodrama is kept at bay by the brutal realism in the film noir tradition, by the rich and precise psychological and social observation and by a fine sense for the locality--all of which combined to create an overwhelming, oppressive mood. Note in this context the scene of the doctor's weird, grotesque dance for the amusement of tourists in the local café at the beginning of the film and the grueling sequence of the spinal injection. The mood is well supported by the music and the loud and cheerful sounds and by the hard, clear photography. The camera observes the events, in tracking shots, like an impassive witness; its sudden stopping in front of an object creates a sense of depression and defeat. The exhausted Nellie rests in her room: silence; beads of perspiration on her skin; a cockroach comes out from hiding; the electric fan falters and fails. Finally, The Proud Ones greatly relies on the very good acting from Michèle Morgan and Gérard Philipe.

ADVENTURES OF ROBINSON CRUSOE (Robinsón Crusoe) Luis Buñuel

Script: Buñuel and Philip Roll, from the novel "The Life and Strange Surprizing Adventures of Robinson Crusoe, of York, Mariner," by Daniel Defoe. Photography: Alex Phillips. Music: Luis Hernández Bretón and Anthony Collins. Editing: Carlos Savage and Alberto Valenzuela. Art Direction: Edward Fitzgerald. Cast: Dan O'Herlihy (Robinsón Crusoe), Jaime Fernández (Viernes), Felipe de Alba (Captain Oberzo), Chel López (Bosun).

Oscar Dancigers--Henry F. Ehrlich for Ultramar Films, Mexico/U. S. A. 89 mins. Pathécolor.

When Buñuel tackled Daniel Defoe's famous novel, it was against a background of at least five earlier screen adaptations, all of them rather mediocre. He offered not only a fascinating poetic vision of a well-known story, but also a non-trivial comment on the functioning of society.

A 17th-century mariner is shipwrecked on a tropical island. He rescues from the wreck an Alsatian dog, a cat, several chests, some guns, a telescope, a Bible, some medical supplies, a handful of grain and a few gold coins. The island turns out to be uninhabited save for occasional visits by cannibals. Buñuel is essentially a moralist: "I didn't like the novel, but I did like the character. I accepted it because there is a certain purity about him." He used the film as an essay about the role of social convention in human behavior, a problem which fascinated him from the heady Surrealist days of the 20's until his virulent works in the 70's, such as The Discreet Charm of the Bourgeoisie.

The theme of the first half of Adventures of Robinson Crusoe is that of solitude. Robinson grows corn, learns to kindle fire, makes bread and pottery; thus he struggles year after year. He suffers badly from loneliness and talks to his animals and even cries out loud in the forest in order to hear his own voice. From a cheerful man he gradually turns into an eccentric recluse. This part of the film is almost documentary in style; simple everyday actions of the hero somehow appear captivating and important on the screen. Conventions seemingly cease to apply; Robinson slowly abandons values entrained by society and Buñuel studies this process intently.

The second half of the film, from the arrival of Viernes (Friday) centers on the theme of friendship, but also contains a few behavioral observations. For instance, it is fascinating how with the arrival of the noble savage Robinson instantaneously becomes a "civilized" man again. The tone changes, and the development of the slave-master relationship is observed in tones of gentle comedy, both touching and ironic. After a skirmish with the pirates Robinson and Viernes sail back to civilization and the film ends on a note of wistfulness and nostalgia.

Adventures of Robinson Crusoe was shot in the Manzanillo jungle, Mexico. Suffice it to say that Buñuel's use of nature here has rarely been equalled in cinema. Something funny happened to the color before the negative reached the laboratory (possibly because of the climate?) but, paradoxically, the resultant extravagant tonality only adds to the film's unusual appeal.

BEFORE THE DELUGE (Avant le déluge) André Cayatte

Script: Cayatte and Charles Spaak. Photography: Jean Bourgoin. Music: Georges Van Parys and Jean-Jacques Grünenwald. Art

Direction: Jacques Colombier. Editing: Paul Cayatte. Cast: Marina Vlady (Liliane Noblet), Clément Thierry (Philippe Boussard), Jacques Chabassol (Jean Arnaud), Roger Coggio (Daniel Epstein), Jacques Fayet (Richard Dutoit), Bernard Blier (Liliane's father), Antoine Balpêtré (Richard's father), Paul Frankeur (Philippe's father), Isa Miranda (Philippe's mother), Line Noro (Jean's mother), Jacques Castelot (Montesson), Delia Scala (Josette).

Union Générale Cinématographique/Documento Films, France-Italy. 128 mins.

Winter 1950. The Korean War is in full swing and there are fears that it might turn into a world conflict--the "deluge" of the title. France is in the grip of a war scare, and Cayatte's film describes the consequences.

Before the Deluge tells a story of five young people, all of them children of respectable middle-class families, and all under eighteen. Daniel, whose parents died in a Nazi concentration camp, is supported by an uncle who lives in America; Jean, an only child, is idolized by his mother; Richard, son of a musician whose wartime activities brought him prison and disgrace afterwards, is in love with Liliane, daughter of a professor; Philippe's father makes money while his mother is having an affair. All five are dreaming of going away, to a better world in a yacht given to Philippe by his mother. While listening to Hawaiian music, they devise a plan for raising the money for the trip. It is decided to burgle the flat of the lover of Philippe's mother. The scheme goes wrong and Jean kills a night watchman. The police suspect Daniel; threatened, the rest of the group submit him to a "test" during which he is strangled. They are caught and convicted. The parents are not punished: the suffering of their consciences will suffice.

In the earlier We Are All Murderers, a broadside against capital punishment, Cayatte accused society of killing the guilty. Now he goes further: we are all guilty, as the whole society bears the responsibility for the actions of individuals. A lawyer by profession, Cayatte constructs his films like a good attorney's speech--impeccably logical, if tendentious. In Before the Deluge the argument is reduced to absurdity: if everyone is guilty, no one is. He had gone too far; the logic of his reasoning is that any social system is superfluous.

While Before the Deluge is useless as a piece of social theory, it defends itself as a reasoned appeal to the public conscience. As Rebel Without a Cause, another document of the rebellion of the young in the 50's, the film did once have a topical journalistic value. This is now lost, but Cayatte's plea, inspired by the war fever of 1950, retains its value as a denunciation of psychoses of all kinds. Sensitive young people feel alienated and abandoned by their parents in a world which faces a danger--and this is shown to lead to a loss of moral instinct and finally to crime. War fever is well documented in the film and all the newspaper headlines and radio announcements referred to are authentic. The main strength of Before the Deluge is that it appeals to the intellect and not to the sentiment.

THE BIG HEAT Fritz Lang

Script: Sydney Boehm, based on the novel by William P. McGivern. Photography: Charles Lang Jr. Music: Daniele Amfitheatrof. Art Direction: Robert Peterson. Editing: Charles Nelson. Cast: Glenn Ford (Sergeant Dave Bannion), Gloria Grahame (Debby Marsh), Jocelyn Brando (Katie Bannion), Alexander Scourby (Mike Lagana), Lee Marvin (Vince Stone), Jeanette Nolan (Bertha Duncan), Peter Whitney (Tierney), Willis Bouchey (Lieutenant Ted Wilkes), Robert Burton (Gus Burke), Adam Williams (Larry Gordon), Howard Wendell (Commissioner Higgins), Cris Alcaide (George Rose), Michael Granger (Hugo), Dorothy Green (Lucy Chapman), Carolyn Jones (Doris), Ric Roman (Baldy), Dan Seymour (Atkins), Edith Evanson (Selma Parker).

Robert Arthur for Columbia, U. S. A. 8052 ft., 89 mins.

Dave Bannion, a police sergeant, tries to discover why another policeman committed suicide. A girl who could provide evidence is brutally murdered and Bannion's superiors order him off the case. Bannion picks up the trail of a gang headed by a racketeer posing as a respectable businessman; the gang reacts by killing Bannion's wife with a bomb intended for her husband. But the detective persists even after he is compelled to leave the force. It turns out that the dead policeman left a letter incriminating the racketeer. Finally the police join Bannion and the criminals are arrested.

The Big Heat is a classical film noir. The plot is based on Lang's constant motif of a loner locked in a lonely struggle; but this, and the post-Expressionist photography, are not the only analogies with the earlier works of the German master. With its mood and the theme of a man's obsessive quest for revenge, The Big Heat seems close to the police dramas of the early 70's. The loner is here more than a pawn at the mercy of fate; he is a man who achieves his aim thanks to intelligence, enterprise and the ruthless use of force. On the ruins of Lang's earlier inventive staging remain only his perfect cinematic craft and the escalation of violence (a gangster flings a pot of boiling coffee in a girl's face; she later retaliates in kind) in support of the doubtful logic of the script. While still Lang's best 50's picture, The Big Heat can be described as mere interest accrued to old investments.

STALAG 17 Billy Wilder

Script: Wilder and Edwin Blum, based on the play by Donald Bevan and Edmund Trzcinski. Photography: Ernest Laszlo. Music: Franz Waxman. Art Direction: Hal Pereira and Franz Bachelin. Editing: George Tomasini. Cast: William Holden (Sefton), Don Taylor (Lt. Dunbar), Robert Strauss (Stosh), Harvey Lembeck (Harry), Neville Brand (Duke), Richard Erdman (Hoffy), Otto Preminger Obersturmführer Von Scherbach), Peter Graves (Price), Gil Stratton Jr. (Cookie), Jay Lawrence (Bagradian), Sig Ruman (Schulz), Michael Moore (Manfredi), Peter Baldwin (Johnson), Robinson Stone (Joey), Robert Shawley (Blondie), William Pierson (Marko), Edmund Trzcinski (Triz).

Billy Wilder for Paramount, U. S. A. 10,846 ft., 121 mins.

In comparison with the bitter Ace in the Hole Wilder's subsequent picture, Stalag 17, brings a complete change of mood. In fact, the film has been accused of something exactly opposite: of treating serious things too lightly. Some said that the subject, a Nazi P. O. W. camp, was an altogether unsuitable theme for a comedy treatment.

After two American prisoners attempting to escape from Stalag 17 run straight into a German ambush, the prisoners in Barrack 4 realize that they have an informer in their midst. Their suspicions fall on Sefton, an unsociable and arrogant man who organizes gambling with cigarettes as prizes. When Dunbar, another prisoner, is arrested after revealing incriminating information during a conversation, the angry men beat Sefton up thinking it was he who passed the information to the Germans. To clear himself Sefton tracks down the real informer. Dunbar is rescued and, together with Sefton, successfully escapes from the camp as the informer is thrown out of the barrack to the Nazi machine guns to create a diversion.

The film was made from a Broadway hit and some of the actors actually repeat their stage performances. Suspense, melodrama and black humor are well mixed; the main source of comic situations is the confinement of men without women. Thus the P. O. W. 's spy on some Russian women prisoners in the next compound through a makeshift telescope (a scene considered outrageous in 1953); a fat prisoner sobs over a photograph of Betty Grable. Everybody plays practical jokes on the guard and the camp commandant (played with gusto by Otto Preminger, the film director).

But those who took Stalag 17 at its face value, as an irreverent farce, failed to appreciate the directorial intentions. The point is that Wilder challenges the notion, so far obligatory in Hollywood, that captivity in enemy hands brings out the virtues of solidarity and loyalty in the prisoners. Here they are shown in a different light: perhaps amusing--but quite unheroic. In fact, among the prisoners there is only one who complies with the old stereotype; ironically, it turns out to be him, the image of dignified uprightness, who is the Nazi spy! Thus Stalag 17 anticipated the satirical attitude to war which American cinema began to use in the late 60's. It is interesting to compare, for instance, the tone adopted by Wilder with that in Altman's M. A. S. H.

William Holden won an Oscar for the part of hard-bitten Sefton. Wilder himself was very pleased with the film: "There are five or six minutes, sometimes only thirty seconds, that I like in my pictures. Along with Sunset Boulevard, Stalag 17 is one of my favorites, perhaps because there were eight minutes that were any good."

BEAT THE DEVIL John Huston

Script: Anthony Veiller, Peter Viertel and Huston, from the novel by James Helvick. Dialogues: Truman Capote. Photography: Oswald Morris. Music: Franco Mannino; also Lambert Williamson. Art Direction: Wilfred Shingleton. Editing: Ralph Kemplen. Cast: Humphrey Bogart (Billy Dannreuther), Jennifer Jones (Gwendolen Chelm), Gina Lollobrigida (Maria Dannreuther), Robert Morley (Petersen), Peter Lorre (O'Hara), Edward Underdown (Harry Chelm), Ivor Barnard (Major Ross), Bernard Lee (C. I. D. Inspector), Marco Tulli (Ravello), Aldo Silvani (Charles), Saro Urzi (Captain).

John Huston--Humphrey Bogart--Jack Clayton for Romulus/Santana, G. B. 9000 ft., 100 mins.

Huston remains within his constant sphere of interest: Beat the Devil is another variation on the man-versus-fate theme. The very elaborate and somewhat extravagant story of intrigue and double-crosses opens in a Mediterranean port where a group of eight people wait for repairs to the ship which is to take them to Africa and concerns their pursuit of immeasurable wealth. This time it is in the form of vast uranium deposits. The story is evocative of The Treasure of the Sierra Madre; there are also resemblances to yet another Huston picture, The Maltese Falcon. Similar is the arrangement of conflicts and similar the ending in which those who challenge fate suffer moral defeat. Only this time the mood is different: Beat the Devil is a parody, an ironic satire on Huston's earlier films, ranging from subtle innuendos to mocking burlesque. Although the picture is at times tiresome, it finally wins the spectator with its originality. The comical Gina Lollobrigida goes somewhat counter to one's ideas about her acting abilities; there are also the sinister

Peter Lorre--and, of course, Humphrey Bogart. Beat the Devil was one of Bogart's favorite films.

TWO ACRES OF LAND (Do bigha zamin) Bimal Roy

Script: Salil Choudhury; also Hrishikesh Mukherjee and Paul Mahendra. Photography: Kamal Bose. Art Direction: Gonesh Basak. Music: Salil Choudhury. Editing: Hrishikesh Mukherjee. Cast: Balraj Sahni (Sambhu), Nirupa Roy (Paro), Rattan Kumar (Kanaya), Meena Kumari.

Bimal Roy, India. 12,000 ft., 133 mins.

The influence of Neorealism reaches as far as India: Bimal Roy, clearly inspired by the work of De Sica (particularly by Bicycle Thieves), makes a social drama which--while being deeply rooted in Bengal--in the method of execution and in many situations refers to the Italian cinema.

Sambhu, a peasant whose two-acre farm is situated within the estate of a rich landowner, is ordered to pay a debt of 200 rupees within three months, otherwise he will be expropriated, which his unscrupulous creditor very much desires, as he intends to build a factory on the land. In an effort to find the money, Sambhu sets off for Calcutta with his son Kanaya. The father gets work as a rickshaw coolie, while the son becomes a shoeshine boy. Alas, the defense of the land fails. The required sum is obtained too late and the whole family, now homeless, has to move to the city.

With this impressive, unromanticized vision of rural India Bimal Roy takes the Indian cinema out of its studio captivity. He was justly rewarded at two 1954 international film festivals (in Cannes and Karlovy Vary); but did not manage to change the unapproachable, hermetic character of the Indian cinema. Neither could Khwaja Ahmad Abbas do it some years previously. He was the director of Dharti ke lal (1944), a drama about the great famine in Bengal. While steadily producing several hundred pictures a year, the Indian film industry invariably continued with its formula of interminable historical reconstructions and song-and-dance films. Only Satyajit Ray became a triumphant exception to the rule.

A JAPANESE TRAGEDY (Nihon-no higeki) Keisuke Kinoshita

Script: Kinoshita. Photography: Hiroyuki Kusuta. Music: Chuji Kinoshita. Art Direction: Kimihiko Nakamura. Cast: Yuko Mochizuki (Haruko Inoue), Yoko Katsuragi (Haruko's daughter), Masami Taura (Haruko's son), Ken Uehara (Masayuki Akasaka).

Shochiku, Japan. 116 mins.

Japan's defeat in the Second World War had a traumatic effect on the whole country. The Emperor was no longer to be considered divine and on November 3, 1946, absolute power was transferred to an elected assembly. Many felt that the very fabric of Japanese society was put into question, including the oldest social customs. The country was pervaded by a mood of uncertainty and rent by rumors; one of them predicted that children would soon be free of the legal obligation to support their elderly parents.

Set in the seaside resort of Atami, A Japanese Tragedy is the story of a war widow who goes through hardship and sacrifice, including descending to prostitution, immediately after the war in order to bring up her son and daughter. Gradually rejected and then abandoned by her children, the mother commits suicide.

Kinoshita, whose work was always deeply rooted in tradition and was usually concerned with spiritual links between people (including members of a family, as in The Ballad of Narayama) was anxious to voice his concern at the apparent collapse of the traditional structure of the Japanese family brought about by the post-war upheavals and the advent of consumer society. Still, today the most interesting side of A Japanese Tragedy is not its story but its formal aspect, which employs the "stream of life" technique (Donald Richie compared the film to the novel "U. S. A." by John Dos Passos, that vast collage of America). To achieve a wider perspective, Kinoshita cast the narrative against the background of the political and social events in post-war Japan, using actual newsreel footage. The film starts with the heading "Life is not easy" and shows the war trials, strikes, riots and disasters which took place in that period. The time structure of the film is complex and the editing frequent. It would be almost impossible to guess, without the benefit of screen credits, that A Japanese Tragedy was made by the same man who directed the delicate She Was Like a Wild Chrysanthemum.

A HUSBAND FOR ANNA ZACCHEO (Un marito per Anna Zaccheo)
Giuseppe De Santis

Script: Cesare Zavattini, Salvatore Laurani, Alfredo Giannetti, Gianni Puccini, Elio Petri and De Santis. Photography: Otello Martelli. Music: Napolitan tunes in the arrangement of Tarchia and Alberto Continisio. Art Direction: Carlo Egidi. Editing: Gabriele Varriale. Cast: Silvana Pampanini (Anna Zaccheo), Massimo Girotti (Andrea), Amedeo Nazzari (Professor Illuminato), Umberto Spadaro (Don Antonio), Monica Clay (Signora Illuminato), Franco Bologna (Anna's brother), Carletto Sposito, Beniamino Maggio, Dora Scarpetta, Giovanni Bernardi, Anna Galasso, Nella Scolti.

Domenico Forges Davanzati, Italy. 94 mins.

With the gradual improvement of the economic situation in Italy and the weakening of the influence of the Left during the early 50's, the Neorealists abandoned film-protests made on behalf of whole social groups and moved towards small-scale dramas of private individuals. Thus the epic gave way to the more intimate.

Still, while De Sica's Umberto D. preserved the acuteness of Miracle in Milan, De Santis's A Husband for Anna Zaccheo is in this respect a far cry from his Rome, Eleven O'Clock of one year earlier. It is true that in this story about a girl too beautiful to find a suitable husband, too entangled in social imperatives to be able to think of real happiness, there is contained De Santis's old theme of the identity of love and freedom, as well as his practice (which originated in Bitter Rice) of attracting the spectator's attention to the film's problem via the beauty of the heroine. But this time the leading actress has something of the mannequin about her, and the film has the appearance of a commercial melodrama stylized after Neorealism and enacted within wooden sets, although in fact it is a real and piercing tragedy. De Santis abandoned his earlier stormy narrative style only to become insipid; relinquished the abrasive poster-like tone--and began to grow maudlin. And yet he touched upon the very important social problem of the acqusition of philistine attitudes by a significant part of the Italian working class who come to respect only position, official virtue and a full wallet.

The parents of Anna want her to marry a wealthy elderly man, while the girl herself is in love with a handsome sailor, Andrea. To provide herself with a dowry, Anna takes a job as a photographer's model and is seduced by the owner of the studio. Stricken by remorse, under pressure from her parents, she first attempts suicide and then breaks with Andrea. She still insists on not marrying her parents' choice. Perhaps tomorrow will bring better luck?

Anxious to address his social comment to the right audience, De Santis used sentimentality as an aid. One may accept excuses and take the director's intentions for what they are worth--but it is impossible to discover great cinema in A Husband for Anna Zaccheo. All that there is here is high narrative skill, watered-down versions of De Santis's earlier ideas--and the pitfalls of genericism looming in the background. Neorealism was forced into it by the growing anti-left strictures of the censors and the changed economic conditions. With the twilight of the trend came the end of De Santis's successes. A Husband for Anna Zaccheo is his last picture of any standard.

1954

SEVEN SAMURAI (Shichi-nin-no samurai) Akira Kurosawa

Script: Shinobu Hashimoto, Hideo Oguni and Kurosawa. Photography: Asaichi Nakai. Music: Fumio Hayasaka. Art Direction: So Matsuyama. Cast: Takashi Shimura (Kambei), Toshiro Mifune (Kikuchiyo), Yoshio Inaba (Gorobei), Seiji Miyaguchi (Kyuzo), Minoru Chiaki (Heihachi), Ko Kimura (Katsushiro), Daisuke Kato (Shichiroji), Keiko Tsushima (Shino), Kamatari Fujiwara (Manzo, Shino's father), Kuninori Kodo (Gisaku), Bokuzen Hidari (Yohei), Yoshio Tsuchiya (Rikichi), Yoshio Kosugi (Mosuke), Keiji Sakakida (Gosaku), Toranosuke Ogawa (Grandfather), Shimpei Takagi (Bandit chief), Yukiko Shimazaki (Rikichi's wife), Jiro Kumagai (Gisaku's son), Haruko Toyama (Gisaku's daughter-in-law), Gen Shimizu (Masterless samurai), Sojin Kamiyama (Minstrel-lute player).

Shojiro Motoki for Toho, Japan. Originally 17,980 ft., 200 mins., in reduced version 14,440 ft., 160 mins.

Kurosawa, who had long been planning to make a jidai-geki (period) picture, realizes this ambition in Seven Samurai, an evocation of the Sengoku era, a turbulent historical period--and one of his greatest cinematic accomplishments: entertaining, humanist, dynamic, moralist, heroic, compassionate and touching. The production difficulties have since become a legend; Seven Samurai was the most expensive Japanese film to date.

Sixteenth-century Japan: the proud and honorable knights errant, the samurai, have reached the end of their glory. A poor village is plundered annually by brigands. In despair the peasants decide to hire professional warriors to defend them from another

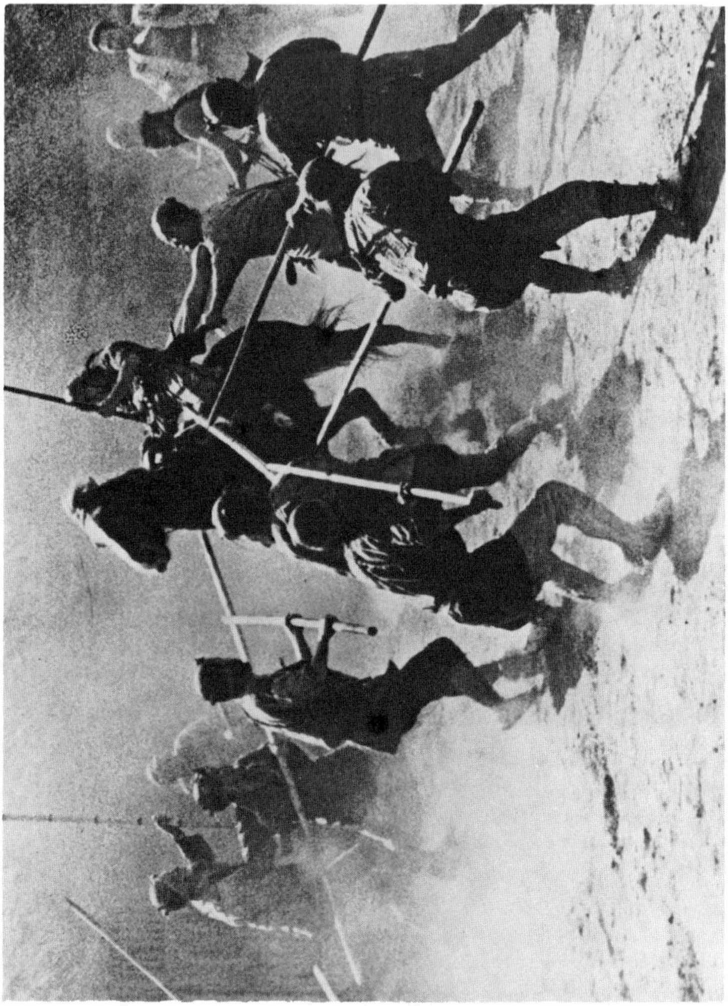

Seven Samurai

attack, bound to come when the crop ripens. They send a deputation to a nearby town which recruits a veteran samurai, Kambei, and later six more. The last is Kikuchiyo, a braggart of peasant stock who pretends to be a samurai. The seven are to fight in exchange for three meagre meals a day. They organize the defense of the village: train the peasants to fight and build the fortifications. Finally the bandits arrive. The samurai forestall an attack by storming the bandit fort and burning it. After a series of fierce battles the brigands are wiped out completely, but only three samurai survive. Watching the peasants planting rice for their next crop Kambei comments: "It is not we who have won... it is the peasants--they are the real winners."

Seven Samurai is one of the very rare movies which combine formal perfection with narrative clarity; intellectual content with entertainment value; scenes of fierce action with moments of lyricism; realism with allegory. Characterization of the protagonists is individual and complete; each samurai is given a differentiated personality, but the temptation to make them a cross-section of human attitudes is avoided. The interaction between the well observed characters provides the picture with an extra psychological level. The various motifs and sub-plots involving the samurai, the peasants and the bandits are very well balanced, with a different musical theme associated with each group.

Kurosawa prepared the film as a general prepares a battle. The topography of the village is clearly explained to the viewer, the strategy of its defenders described, the score of the dead kept. The narrative is conducted with clarity and economy. The pace and the overall balance of the picture is masterly. Kurosawa is always in full control of every scene: from the first frightening episode of the arrival, in full gallop, of the brigands, to the swiftly edited search for the samurai in town and the subsequent preparation by the villagers for the inevitable attack. But first and foremost Seven Samurai is a film of motion. Consider the scenes of desperate struggle in mud and rain, as the peasants let the bandits into the village in small groups and kill them: horses hooves, ferocious swordplay and the mounting death toll. These sequences are superb--powerful, epic, classic. Kurosawa's inspired use of the telephoto lens, rare at the time, creates a splendid sense of immediacy whereby one feels a participant in the events; slowed-down motion is very imaginatively used in scenes of death (for instance the killing of a child kidnapper in town); so are the frequent close-ups and deep-focus photography. In showing the youngest samurai falling in love with a peasant girl disguised as a boy by her mistrustful father the director introduces a tone of lyricism.

The film's message deserves special interest. Kurosawa's views seem to be that progress is possible either through the action of a lonely individual (as in the earlier Ikiru) or through the action of an elite (as in Seven Samurai). All the same the picture's symbolic ending has a definite Marxist ring around it. The samurai die out, but the peasants remain: thus the feudal past gives way to the future. Such is also the egalitarian message of the Kikuchiyo subplot: "every brave man can become a samurai."

LA STRADA Federico Fellini

Script: Fellini and Tullio Pinelli; also Ennio Flaiano. Photography: Otello Martelli. Music: Nino Rota. Art Direction: Mario Ravasco. Costumes: M. Marinari. Editing: Leo Catozzo. Cast: Giulietta Masina (Gelsomina), Anthony Quinn (Zampanò, the strongman), Richard Basehart (Tightrope walker known as "Il Matto"--"The Fool"), Aldo Silvani (Colombaioni, the circus owner), Marcella Rovena (Widow at the wedding who gives Zampanò her dead husband's suit), Livia Venturini (Young nun).

Dino De Laurentiis--Carlo Ponti, Italy. 9405 ft., 104 mins.

The cinema and the circus have a special place in Federico Fellini's artistic interests. He is even quoted as saying that he would have become a circus performer were it not for the invention of the art of moving images with which he became infatuated thanks to Roberto Rossellini while he worked as a scriptwriter and assistant director on Rome, Open City and Paisà. One may consider this confession of Fellini's as yet another of the easy myths about himself which the maker of La strada encourages, if not actually originates. Among them, for instance, is his alleged flight from home at the age of 12 to join an itinerant circus troupe. One way or another, the fact remains that the whole of Fellini's work is a consistent search for dazzling and magical means of expression. In his youth Fellini tried his hand at all sorts of fairground spectacles and he believes that the cinema augments and magnifies the essence of the circus. As a sensualist, he simply finds the movies a more sophisticated way of performing conjuring tricks; and as an artist serving society he sees it as a powerful medium for conveying the knowledge of life which he has found via the circus. The world under the big top is to Fellini a microcosm of society at large, and he considers it the mission of a circus artist to spread sublimation and love. It was not by accident that Fellini's script for Rossellini's Francis, God's Jester combined in its title a term from the world of circus gambols with the most sacred word of religion: Fellini sees the milieu of simple circus people, in close contact with Nature, as a more convincing source of ideas about the fellowship of man than the fossilized Catholic Church. Thus the conflicts between the director and the Church appear already in the early times when he is transferring to the screen things more substantial than the dazzling phantasmagoria of Fellini Roma, when the spirit has the upper hand over the matter in his films. The bone of contention was not his conflict with the teaching of the church but his Franciscan leanings. "If one is to understand Christianity as an attitude of love towards another human being, then all my films revolve around it. I show a world without love inhabited by people who exploit other people, but there is always among them some insignificant person who wants to give love and to live for the sake of love."

Such is the explication of La strada, a masterpiece in which there are portrayed two such people: Gelsomina, a half-witted life companion of a fairground athlete, and an acrobat known as The Fool, who is her spiritual teacher. Gelsomina, a simple peasant girl, has been hired by her mother to an itinerant strongman called Zampanò (a name derived from the Italian word for "claw"). They travel up and down the country. Brutish and taciturn, Zampanò trains Gelsomina to perform little antics to accompany his chain-breaking act. He seduces her, treats her like a slave and beats her up when she tries to run away. When they join a circus, Zampanò is imprisoned for attacking The Fool, a tightrope walker. Rejected, brutally treated and painfully aware of her loneliness in the cold of interhuman distances, Gelsomina suddenly finds the sense of existence when The Fool comforts her with a parable about a pebble which, although small and insignificant, does have a purpose in the world. Suddenly she grows pretty, brightens up with inner light: from now on she feels useful. It does not matter that Zampanò represents ignorant and primitive evil: for one can defeat evil with a humble sacrifice. Zampanò causes the death of both The Fool, whom he kills in a fit of irrational jealousy, and of Gelsomina, whom he abandons in illness. And yet even Zampanò eventually becomes capable of human emotion: some years later he learns of her death and on remembering her he cries, alone at a beach at night, for the first time in his life.

The Franciscan moral conclusion of La strada, considered by some a polemic with the Existentialist philosophy and by others as something related to Tolstoy's ideas of the attitude of passivity in the face of evil, might seem naively anachronistic--but one cannot deny its beauty, the same beauty that permeates all aspects of the film. And yet it is only the musical illustration with its four-theme score and the main motif played on a trumpet which is really pure and clear. The remaining components of this tale about provincial comedians are dominated by greyness: grey is the texture of the photography, drab and barren the landscape, grey and primitive is human life in this wind-chilled world. The dramatic structure and the mise en scène of the rather flimsy story are unimpressive: with long takes, generally dispensing with close-ups: rough editing and no attention paid to the unity of time, place and action and to the climaxing of conflicts. But everything is steeped in poetry, the poetry which can be obtained only with the magic touch of a great artist, a poetry so distant from current topicalities as to become timeless. Powerful through its spontaneity it brings down into ordinary life the metaphoric meaning of the film and makes real its character-symbols: Gelsomina-Love, Zampanò-Brutality, The Fool-Imagination. Poetry elevates the literal to the rank of extratemporal and unrepeatable.

EAST OF EDEN Elia Kazan

Script: Paul Osborn, from the novel by John Steinbeck. Photography: Ted McCord. Music: Leonard Rosenman. Art Direction: James Basevi and Malcolm Bert. Costumes: Anna Hill Johnstone. Editing: Owen Marks. Cast: James Dean (Caleb Trask), Julie Harris (Abra), Raymond Massey (Adam Trask), Richard Davalos (Aron Trask), Jo Van Fleet (Kate Trask), Burl Ives (Sheriff Sam Cooper), Harold Gordon (Gustav Albrecht), Albert Dekker (Will Hamilton), Lois Smith (Ann), Timothy Carey (Joe), Richard Garrick (Dr. Edwards), Mario Siletti (Piscora).

Elia Kazan for Warner Bros., U. S. A. 10,272 ft., 114 mins. CinemaScope. Warnercolor.

Together with Hemingway and Faulkner, John Steinbeck was the leading writer of the "heroic period" in modern American literature. Although not among his best novels, "East of Eden," published in 1952, is a document of important changes in American society brought about by the economic, political and social shock of the First World War--the collapse of puritanism and the increased influence of liberal attitudes. The era of action began, the cult of energy and enterprise, and the central conflict of Steinbeck's novel exemplifies the antagonism of two attitudes: the old-fashioned cult of hard work, honesty and thrift which was often accompanied by a lack of imagination, and the new, dynamic, expansive attitude whose future may have been uncertain, but the perspective always wide. Intentionally "universal," the book draws obvious biblical parallels: the names of characters are highly significant, and the Caleb-Aron relationship is suggestive of the story of Cain and Abel.

1913. Salinas Valley in California. Caleb, an uneasy adolescent, is a younger and less favored son of Adam Trask, a lettuce farmer near Monterey. Taciturn and rebellious, Cal is misunderstood by his austere and puritanical father, and is jealous of his brother Aron's happiness with his sweetheart Abra. Adam never speaks of his supposedly dead wife; Cal discovers that his mother in fact runs a brothel a few miles away. After a business venture fails, on which Adam staked almost all his money, Cal decides to help him. He borrows $5000 from his mother and invests it in pea farming; when war breaks out he makes a large profit on the crop. He then gives his father a gift of money on his birthday. But Adam accuses him of speculation and rejects the gift. Angry and desperate, Cal tells Aron about their mother. In shock and revulsion Aron enlists in the Army; Adam suffers a stroke. It is Abra's influence which reconciles the father and the son.

The theme of Kazan's film is not Steinbeck's theology but

modern alienation. Yet the picture is faithful to the novel in one important aspect--in its attitude to physical strength, its praise of the vital forces of nature which dictate a new moral code with a changed hierarchy of values. Gone is the America of dogmas which deprived man of free will. It is significant that Freud's ideas made such headway in America, becoming an important catalyst in the process of shaking off sexual complexes enforced by the strict Puritan upbringing which stifled natural human instincts. Cal feels oppressed by the atmosphere of his father's house. He epitomizes a whole generation choked by Puritanism.

On the other hand, owing to James Dean the film is a study of all rebel generations. Dean's gestures, his whole behavior, clearly do not belong to the times of the First World War--and this is why East of Eden has had such enormous resonance among the young. James Dean's specific psychological make-up was very suitable for a Kazan protagonist in general, and the part of Cal in particular. This is Dean's best film role and it is to the director's credit that he made full use of the actor's predispositions.

A lavish Hollywood production, East of Eden is Kazan's first film in color and on wide screen. His use of both is very original and the picture has exceptional visual suggestiveness. The excellent CinemaScope photography expertly guides the viewer's eye to the center of interest of the frame, there are constant panning and tracking shots, continually changing camera angles, deformation of perspective, impressive close-ups, suggestive editing. In dramatic scenes the frame is organized along diagonal lines; while lyrical scenes are photographed with pastel softness.

Kazan's interest in the themes of Steinbeck's novel sprang from deep inner conviction and personal idiosyncrasies--but it seems that recent experience also played a part. An ardent Anatolian, he had not long ago had much trouble with the House Un-American Activities Committee. His testimony had been the subject of much controversy--and it seems highly significant that East of Eden justifies instinctive decision-making, appropriate to circumstances. Through the Cal character Kazan shows action as an act of self-defense, a condition of spiritual survival. East of Eden is not a morality play, but a film about morality, about the concept of uncompromising, pragmatic action.

THE WORD (Ordet) Carl Theodor Dreyer

Script: Dreyer, from the play by Kaj Munk. Photography: Henning Bendtsen. Music: Poul Schierbeck. Art Direction: Erik Aaes. Editing: Edith Schlüssel. Cast: Henrik Malberg (Morten Borgen), Emil Hass Christensen (Mikkel Borgen), Preben Lerdorff Rye

The Word

Johannes Borgen), Cay Kristiansen (Anders Borgen), Birgitte Federspiel (Inger, Mikkel's wife), Ejner Federspiel (Peter Skraedder), Ove Rud (Pastor), Ann Elisabeth Rud (Maren Borgen, Mikkel's daughter), Susanne Rud (Lilleinger Borgen, Mikkel's daughter), Gerda Nielsen (Anne Skraedder), Sylvia Eckhausen (Kirstine Skraedder), Henry Skjaer (Doctor), Hanne Ågesen (Karen, servant at Borgen's farm), Edith Thrane (Mette Maren).

Erik Nielsen for A/S Film Centralen Palladium, Denmark. 11,286 ft., 125 mins.

One of the finest expressions of Christian faith on the screen, The Word is also the fullest manifestation of Dreyer's mystical philosophy. The theatre play written in 1932 by Kaj Munk, a Danish Lutheran pastor, tells the story of the supernatural return to life of a woman who died in childbirth. The theme of a miracle resulting from a profound spiritual bond with God, and perhaps even more the problem of the Resurrection (which Munk openly questions) had interested the maker of The Passion of Joan of Arc since the 30's. The first film version of the play was made in 1943 in Sweden by Gustav Molander, from a script by Rune Lindström. This did not stop Dreyer from planning his own screen version, especially since Molander's was not entirely faithful to the original. Dreyer directed the film with inspiration and great strength of conviction. It is a lucid and deeply humanist work about the need for and the beauty of, faith.

The events of The Word take place in a strict, God-fearing community on the west coast of Sweden. Morten Borgen, an adherent of the "divine grace" sect is involved in a feud with the followers of much stricter religious views. One of his sons, Mikkel, far from being excessively religious, shows himself as a light-hearted skeptic. Another son, Johannes, who has gone mad from overwork when studying Kierkegaard's pre-Existentialist philosophy, proclaims himself Jesus Christ and roams about the countryside, is a man of unyielding faith. Nobody takes him seriously until the family are stricken with disaster: Mikkel's wife, Inger, dies in childbirth. This event is a turning point for all. Johannes returns to sanity and, visited by the Holy Ghost, brings the dead woman to life on the day of her funeral; Mikkel returns to the faith; the third brother, Anders, marries Peter the Tailor's daughter in spite of religious differences between the parents.

With its majestic rhythm, its severity, the abandonment of close shots and the lack of dramatic editing, The Word stylistically tends to remain within earshot of the stage original. Dreyer shot the film in his native Jutland and used the open, wind-swept landscape and the ascetic architecture of the farm buildings quite literally, without attempting a visual transformation or even subjective vision. Even the key scene of the miracle, one of the most astonishing in all cinema, is quite deliberately filmed with ascetic directness. In the case of The Word simplicity is identical with dignity.

The first part of the film seems a little too static, but in the second part Dreyer's noble conviction, his precision in conducting the story, the almost-crystalline mood, result in a fascinating, high emotional pitch. The theme, in which any false note would be a disaster, Dreyer handles faultlessly; his direction is classical and yet vivid. Such perfect conveyance of the Christian message commands respect for The Word, despite the extremity of the film's philosophy. The message (God as the only mainstay for the weak and the helpless faced with the fear of existence and man's imperfection) was given a pure and mature artistic form. Independently from its message, in portraying the family relationship of Mikkel, Inger and their children, The Word is a touching praise of love.

SANSHO THE BAILIFF (Sanshō Dayu) Kenji Mizoguchi

Script: Yoshikata Yoda and Yahiro Fuji, based on the novel by Ogai Mori. Photography: Kazuo Miyagawa. Music: Fumio Hayasaka, Kanahichi Odera and Tamekichi Mochizuki. Art Direction: Kisaku Ito. Editing: Mitsuji Miyata. Cast: Yoshiaki Hanayaki (Zushio), Kyoko Kagawa (Anju), Kinuyo Tanaka (Tamaki, their mother), Eitaro Shindo (Sansho), Akitake Kono (Taro, his son), Masao Shimizu (Masauji Taira), Ken Mitsuda (Prime Minister Morozane Fujiwara), Chieko Naniwa (Woman servant), Kazukimi Okuni (Norimura), Yoko Kosono (Kohagi), Kimiko Tachibana (Namiji), Ichiro Sugai (Minister of Justice), Masashiko Tsugawa (Zushio as a boy), Naoki Fujiwara (Zushio as an infant), Keiko Enami (Anju as a girl), Ryosuke Kagawa (Ritsushi Kumotake), Kanji Koshiba (Kaikudo Naiko), Shinobu Araki (Sadaya), Reiko Kongo (Shiono), Shozo Nambu (Masasue Taira), Ryonosuke Azuma (Manager of a brothel), Teruko Omi (The other Nakagimi).

Masaichi Nagata for Daiei, Japan. 11,070 ft., 123 mins.

A timeless story of suffering and self-sacrifice, Sansho the Bailiff is the highest point in Mizoguchi's cinema--a work of great power and extraordinary visual beauty.

Eleventh-century Japan. Manors belonging to noblemen, spread throughout the country, are under control of ruthless bailiffs who rely on slave labor to work the land. The governor of the Tairo Province is banished for challenging feudal corruption; while traveling to join him in a remote region, his wife Tamaki, son Zushio and daughter Anju, are kidnapped. The mother is taken into prostitution, while the children are sold into slavery under Sansho, the brutal bailiff of the estate belonging to the Minister of Justice. Ten years pass. The young man has become brutalized by the barbaric violence at the manor, and his sister reminds him of their father's words: "a man without mercy is like a wild beast." Brother and sister hear a childhood song and learn that their mother is alive. Anju helps Zushio escape from the estate and drowns herself to avoid reprisals. Zushio reaches Kyoto, successfully petitions the Prime Minister for justice and is given the post of governor of Tairo in recognition of his father's services. He abolishes slavery in the province, arrests and banishes Sansho. Freed slaves burn the manor. Zushio later resigns his post and goes in search of his mother. He finally finds her, blind, on a seashore.

Tangible and immediate, Sansho the Bailiff handles action scenes with as much assurance as the scenes of contemplation. The film is a reflection on the workings of history, an attack against the baseness and cruelty of man, a praise of loyalty and sacrifice. Only through sacrifice can catharsis be achieved. Mizoguchi does not abandon his constant theme of women's suffering, although he does not give it the usual prominence. It is present in the motif of the mother's tragedy and in that of Anju, who is her brother's spiritual light and who sacrifices herself for the family. The picture's purposeful combination of an extremely refined, delicate visual form with scenes of barbaric violence is both a dramatic device and a message: the cruelty of man can only be countered, and purged, with the world of beauty. This is probably Mizoguchi's most formally perfect picture: grand, painterly and dynamic. Slow dissolves, sparing use of close-ups and the magic, translucent photography create a haunting, elegiac atmosphere. Nature is used more prominently here than perhaps in any other Japanese film: consider the unforgettable scenes of the abduction of the children and their separation from their mother, the flight through the forest, or the finale as Zushio finds his mother again. The gentle, almost fragile images in the opening scenes as the mother and the children are traveling to join their exiled father are a visual metaphor for the brittleness of human life and of family happiness.

JOHNNY GUITAR Nicholas Ray

Script: Philip Yordan, from the novel by Roy Chanslor. Photography: Harry Stradling. Music: Victor Young. Song "Johnny Guitar" by Peggy Lee and Victor Young. Art Direction: James Sullivan. Editing: Richard L. Van Enger. Cast: Joan Crawford (Vienna), Sterling Hayden (Johnny Guitar), Scott Brady (Dancin' Kid), Mercedes McCambridge (Emma Small), Ward Bond (John McIvers), Ben Cooper (Turkey Ralston), John Carradine (Old Tom), Royal Dano (Corey), Ernest Borgnine (Bart Lonergan), Frank Ferguson (Marshal Williams), Paul Fix (Eddie), Rhys Williams (Andrews), Ian MacDonald (Pete).

Herbert J. Yates--Nicholas Ray for Republic, U. S. A. 110 mins. Trucolor.

Johnny Guitar

The liberation of women started in Arizona in the post-Civil War period or we have all been deceived by Johnny Guitar. To use more moderate language, this is the first picture to show women as truly active participants in the events of the West.

The ex-dancehall girl, Vienna is now an ambitious squatter who wears breeches and carries a gun. She builds a gambling saloon and turns it into a successful business, and stakes a claim to the surrounding land, knowing she will be handsomely paid off when a railroad is eventually built through it. The neighbors, particularly the sour Emma Small, are jealous of Vienna's prosperity. Vienna is engaged in a love affair with an outlaw called The Dancin' Kid, who Emma imagines killed her brother in a stage hold-up. When Vienna refuses to give incriminating evidence against him, Emma persuades the Marshal to give her an order to quit. Vienna dismisses her staff and resolves to stay on and fight with the help of her ex-lover Johnny Guitar, a gunman anxious to settle down. Emma arouses the citizens to run Vienna out of town. The posse burn the saloon to the ground and attempt to lynch the owner. Vienna is saved by Johnny. She kills Emma during a fierce gunfight and finally finds peace in Johnny's arms.

Badly received on its release both in the U. S. A. and in England (where a reviewer ridiculed "its general effect of fascinating, portentous lunacy") Johnny Guitar was always highly regarded in Europe. French directors like to make references to it in their films: the maid in Godard's Pierrot le Fou saw it three times in one week; François Truffaut said that it bore more importance for his own life than it did for Nicholas Ray's. While Johnny Guitar is very well directed and contains effective dialogue, the reasons for this cult are purely stylistic. Although the western is not Ray's usual province, it is precisely in this story of a "rude primadonna of the west" that his tendency to exaggeration for once produced an effect of astonishing intensity. Johnny Guitar is lyrical, giddy, baroque, histrionic, theatrical, impassioned and flamboyant. The overall effect of this unusual psychological western is augmented by passionate use of the garish color technique ("Trucolor by Consolidated").

DEATH OF A CYCLIST (Muerte de un ciclista) Juan Antonio Bardem

---

Script: Luis F. de Igoa and Bardem. Photography: Alfredo Fraile. Music: Isidro B. Maiztegui. Art Direction: Enrique Alarcón. Editing: Margarita Ochoa. Cast: Lucia Bosè (María José), Alberto Closas (Juan Fernández Solé), Otello Toso (Miguel), Carlos Casaravilla (Rafa), Bruna Corrá (Matilde), Julia Delgado Caro (Doña María, Juan's mother), Matilde Muñoz Sampedro (Neighbor), Alicia Romay (Carmina), Mercedes Albert (Cristina), Emilio Alonso (Jorge).

Death of a Cyclist

Guion/Suevia/Cesáreo González/Trionfalcine, Spain/Italy. Originally 8220 ft., 91 mins., cut by the Spanish censors to 88 mins.

A university professor and the wife of an industrialist drive home after a secret meeting. The car is involved in an accident: a worker is knocked off his bicycle and dies. María José and Juan have been in love since youth. Now they are an integral part of the Franco establishment in Spain and both take advantage of all that opportunism can bring; she values a comfortable life most of all, he owes his position to influential friends. To report the accident to the police would mean the end to all that. But after a while Juan begins to hesitate. He is uneasy about his dependence on his brother-in-law, and he suffers a shock when a few days later, he is unfair to a girl student at an exam and this leads to riots at the university. Contacts with students and with the family of the dead cyclist bring back memories of youth; he grows disgusted with his present life and finally decides to resign from the university and to give himself up. María José is different: determined to defend her privileges she goes as far as to kill Juan, only to die, while speeding home, in an accident which is a mirror image of the first. But this time it is the cyclist involved who survives--and does not escape but goes to the police.

Within such a symbolic structure Bardem contains his comments on social relationships in Franco's Spain. Despite the film's pyramid of situational and pictorial metaphors, despite the guise of a sensational melodrama, the message of Death of a Cyclist was transparent enough to bring the director into serious trouble with the authorities. Yet the film was finally released in Spain and went on to win the Fipresci prize at the 1955 Cannes Film Festival, which put the seal on the critics' discovery of Bardem as one of the leading directors in the cinema of the 50's.

Bardem was not the only original film-maker in Spain: for several years he had been collaborating with Luis G. Berlanga, a social caricaturist and another reformer of the colorless Spanish cinema, who became known owing to the comedy Welcome, Mr. Marshall (1952) and went on to make The Executioner. Having to struggle continually with the censors, both directors had a limited scope of action and this caused the lameness of many of their films. It seems, however, that to Bardem this restraint was not of decisive importance, since he was at his best just when he expressed himself through a system of innuendos and symbols and a complex, baroque composition of the frame, as seen in his later Sonatas (1959). The first part of that film is a magnificent Spanish baroque poem pervaded with a dense atmosphere and the deep-purple tonality of the photography, while the second part, modeled after Eisenstein's film about Mexico, is a complete failure and makes one see reason in Truffaut's opinion of Bardem as basically an imitator. Certainly, Bardem can be eclectic, as proved by Death of a Cyclist, whose Expressionist inserts are somewhat jarring and the style of the film as a whole far less mature and pure than in the later Grand' Rue.

But the masterly execution, the intelligent visual suggestions and the pictorial intensity combining basic compositional values with metaphorical meaning (good examples of this are the two scenes of Juan's conversations with the girl student: in the first they are separated by empty space, and in the second by wire netting) and finally the dramatic cut editing which introduces the sense of anxiety and subcutaneous vehemence, give this first important Spanish film originality and class.

ON THE WATERFRONT Elia Kazan

Script: Budd Schulberg, suggested by a series of articles by Malcolm Johnson. Photography: Boris Kaufman. Music: Leonard Bernstein. Art Direction: Richard Day. Editing: Gene Milford. Cast: Marlon Brando (Terry Malloy), Karl Malden (Father Barry), Eva Marie Saint (Edie Doyle), Lee J. Cobb (Johnny Friendly), Rod Steiger (Charley Malloy), Pat Henning (Timothy "Kayo" Dugan), James Westerfield (Big Mac), Tami Mauriello (Tillio), Leif Erickson (Inspector Glover), Tony Galento (Truck), John Hamilton ("Pop" Doyle), John Heldabrand (Mott), Rudy Bond (Moose), Don Blackman (Luke), Arthur Keegan (Jimmy), Abe Simon (Barney), Bary Macollum (J. P. Morgan), Thomas Handley (Tommy), Fred Gwynne (Slim), Mike O'Dowd (Specs), Martin Balsam (Gillette).

Sam Spiegel--Elia Kazan for Horizon Films, U. S. A. 9676 ft., 108 mins.

Terry Malloy, an ex-boxer, hangs aimlessly around New York dockland. A not very bright but basically well-meaning man in his late 20's, he is used as a strong arm boy by the gang controlling the Dockers' Union. Johnny Friendly, the gang's boss, treats him with special affection. Terry's elder brother Charley is a corrupt lawyer in the gang's employ. Terry becomes involved in the murder of a rebellious docker who threatened to speak to the authorities against Friendly. He then meets the dead man's sister Edie, who asks him for help in tracing her brother's murderers. Terry falls in love with the girl and begins to hesitate in his loyalty to the gang; Edie and Father Barry, a dockland Catholic priest, urge him to expose the guilty. When Charley is brutally murdered by the gang, Terry decides to testify before the Crime Commission. He challenges Friendly after the hearing and is badly beaten by his henchmen. But he has broken the gang's hold over the dockland. The workers gather around Terry as he leads them back to work.

On the Waterfront gave rise to an animated controversy concerning the film's message and the moral evaluation of the actions of its protagonist. In his article in "Sight and Sound" (January-

March 1955) Lindsay Anderson described the ending as a "fascist cop-out," while some French critics, notably Coursodon and Boisset in the book "Vingt ans de cinéma américain," called On the Waterfront "an apology for denunciation." Kazan himself said: "It's a film about the necessity in certain situations of speaking out. It shows ... how the attitude of keeping quiet was harmful on the waterfront. It's a true story... It happened like that." One finds it difficult now to understand what all the fuss was about. It appears however that the controversy was the result of some comments about the Union passed by Alvah Bessie, one of the "Hollywood Ten," who was sent to prison for contempt. On his release the Dockers' Union gave Bessie the post of editor on the Union paper, the "Dispatcher." Marxist critics confronted On the Waterfront with Bessie's 1953 interview in which he praised the Union as a powerful force for progress--and accused Kazan, who described the film as very personal, of indulging in reactionary propaganda and attacking the working class and the leftist Union which had been in disfavor with the government for over nine years. Lindsay Anderson particularly objected to Kazan not disclosing the source of the corruption he portrays. Friendly's high-placed protector is shown in a single shot as a silhouette watching the Crime Commission hearings on television.

Time has decided the controversy in Kazan's favor. Now that the emotions of the 50's are behind us, attacks against On the Waterfront seem unjustified to say the least. Terry is seen not as an informer but as a proud and resilient nonconformist, and the picture as a study of a moral awakening. It is also significant that nobody objected to the very similar problem of corruption in a New York City railroad yard and a virtually identical ending in Edge of the City, a film made two years later. There is no question of course that the philosophy of On the Waterfront is very un-Marxist, particularly because of the film's glorification of the individual, while the dockers are shown as a helpless crowd and not as a proletarian force. The film has a distinct Christian complexion, and very interestingly portrays Father Barry: he ardently defends absolute honesty, but believes in standing up for one's rights. He is not just a benign shepherd of souls, but a man who fights when it is necessary, and lets himself be beaten when he has to.

The profuse dialogue scenes in the film are fortunately broken up by action scenes which are well staged and composed. Good narrative pace is also partly due to the expert editing. Low-key camera effects give On the Waterfront pathos and poetry; particularly notable in this context is the sub-plot of Terry keeping pigeons on the roof of a tenement block, and the scene with Terry and Charley in a taxicab. The picture was shot entirely on location in New York, in the starkly realist style similar to that of Kazan's earlier Panic in the Streets. But the greatest strength of this memorable picture is Brando's assured and powerful portrayal as Terry. Gentle and brutal, vulnerable and disgruntled, Terry is one of the most complex and the most accomplished characters in Kazan's cinema.

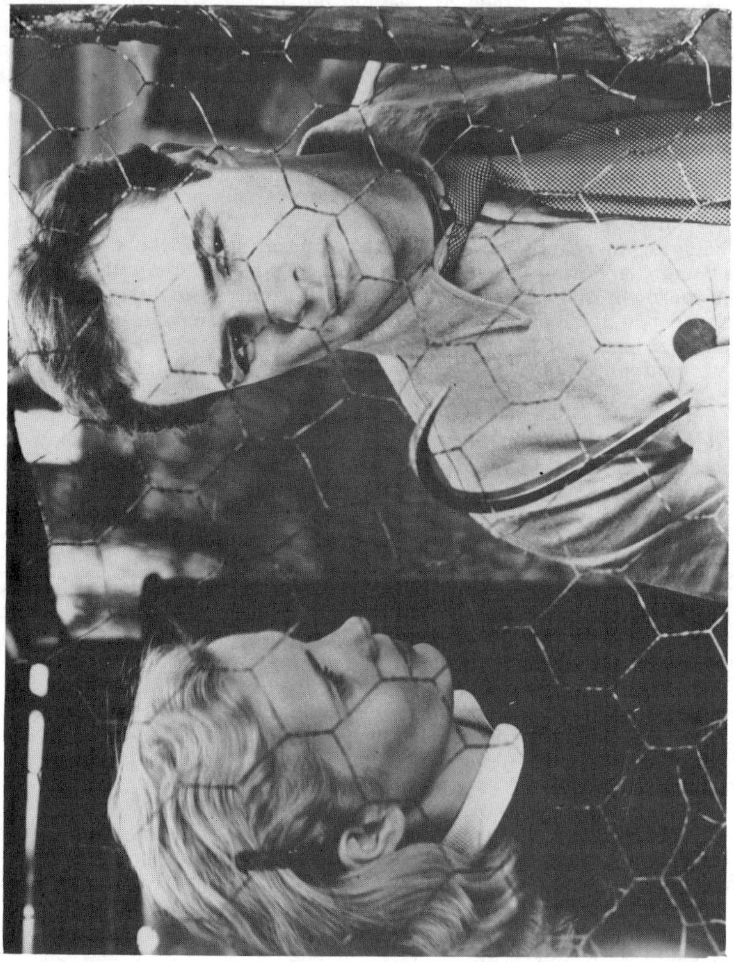

On the Waterfront

ROMEO AND JULIET (Giulietta e Romeo) Renato Castellani

Script: Castellani, from the play by William Shakespeare. Photography: Robert Krasker. Music: Roman Vlad. Costumes: Leonor Fini. Editing: Sydney Hayers. Cast: Laurence Harvey (Romeo), Susan Shentall (Giulietta), Flora Robson (Nurse), Mervyn Johns (Friar Lorenzo), Bill Travers (Benvolio), Enzo Fiermonte (Tybalt), Aldo Zollo (Mercutio), Giovanni Rota (Prince of Verona), Sebastian Cabot (Capulet), Lydia Sherwood (Lady Capulet), Norman Wooland (Paris), Giulio Garbinetti (Montague), Nietta Zocchi (Lady Montague), Dagmar Josipovich (Rosaline), Luciano Bodi (Abraham), Thomas Nicholls (Friar Giovanni).

Sandro Ghenzi--Joseph Janni for Verona Productions, G. B. /Italy. 138 mins. Technicolor.

The ten years which had elapsed since Laurence Olivier's strikingly original screen version of "Henry V" put a seal on the agreement between the cinema and William Shakespeare. His dramas became the starting point of many films, which made good use of Shakespeare's great poetry, the visual potential of his plots and which drew attention to the modern topicality of his message. Yutkevich will soon make Othello and Kurosawa The Throne of Blood, a specifically Japanese version of "Macbeth."

Castellani's Romeo and Juliet remains in the sphere of Olivier's influence. The stress is on the visual aspect with designs referring to the painting of the Renaissance and on the psychological consequences of the events on the heroes (this is the purpose of, for instance, the added episode of the wedding). In both these aspects the maker's intentions were fulfilled: the authentic city walls of medieval Verona, splendid color tonality of visual compositions maintained in the style of the art of the period, scrupulous set and costume designs create a harmonious and enchanting vision. While not actually offering great performances, the actors, fresh and convincing, are still more than mere pawns. Castellani very well handled such episodes as the exchange of glances at the ball, the wedding and the culminating scene in the crypt. Shakespeare's text sounds fine and clear against the ornate background. But this graceful whole is lacking in verve: Castellani is in Romeo and Juliet much closer to the academic calligraphy of his early work than to the Neorealist Two Pennyworth of Hope, full of unbridled movement and sound. As concerns cinematography Romeo and Juliet does not appear to show even a trace of influence of Olivier's Hamlet: it is ascetically theatrical, photographed with a static camera and ponderously edited. While trying to avoid spectacularity (which is evident in the rather cursory treatment of the scenes of fighting) and shunning excessive reliance on the plot for fear of falling into a melodrama, Castellani lost sight of the vivid and fervent heroes of the title. On the other hand, his vision of the Renaissance may have been such a colorful but severe period with people reserved in their reactions towards others. If so, this is not a convincing vision. Zeffirelli's screen version of the drama, made 14 years later, seems incomparably closer to the detail and the spirit of the Renaissance, with the vivid and colorful vision of the period supported by the elemental behavior of the Renaissance characters.

TWENTY-FOUR EYES (Nijūshi-no hitomi) Keisuke Kinoshita

Script: Kinoshita, from the novel by Sakae Tsuboi. Photography: Hiroyuki Kusuda. Music: Chuji Kinoshita. Art Direction: Kimihiko Nakamura. Cast: Hideko Takamine (Hisako Oishi), Eisei Amamoto (Hisako's husband), Shizue Natsukawa (Hisako's mother), Chishu Ryu (Teacher), Toyo Takahashi (Woman teacher), Ushio Akashi (Schoolmaster), Takahiro Tamura (Isokichi Isoda), Hideki Goko (Isokichi in lower class), Hitobumi Goko (Isokichi in upper class), Rei Miura (Takeichi Takeshita), Yukio Watanabe (Takeichi in lower class), Shiro Watanabe (Takeichi in upper class), Yasukuni Toida (Yoshitsugu Tokuda), Makoto Miyagawa (Yoshitsugu in lower class), Jun'ichi Miyagawa (Yoshitusugu in upper class), Giichi Otsuki (Tadashi Morioka), Takero Terashita (Tadashi in lower class), Takaaki Terashita (Tadashi in upper class), Tatsuo Shimizu (Jinta Aizawa), Kunio Sato (Jinta in lower class), Takeshi Sato (Jinta in upper class), Yumeji Tsukioka (Masuno Kagawa), Hiroko Ishii (Masuno in lower class), Shisako Ishii (Masuno in upper class), Toyoko Shinohara (Misako Nishiguchi), Yasuyo Koike (Misako in lower class), Akiko Koike (Misako in upper class), Kuniko Ikawa (Matsue Kawamoto), Setsuko Kusano (Matsue in lower class), Sadako Kusano (Matsue in upper class), Toshiko Kobayashi (Sanae Yamaishi), Kaoko Kase (Sanae in lower class), Kayoko Kase (Sanae in upper class), Yumiko Tanabe (Kotsuru Kabe in lower class), Naoko Tanabe (Kotsuru Kabe in upper class), Ikuko Kambara (Fujiko Yamashita in lower class), Toyoko Ozu (Fujiko Yamashita in upper class), Yoshiko Nagai (Kotoe Katagiri), Hiroko Uehara (Kotoe in lower class), Masako Uehara (Kotoe in upper class).

Shochiku, Japan. 13,901 ft., 154 mins.

When considered in the context of other leading Japanese directors of the 50's, Keisuke Kinoshita, described as one of the best stylists of the national cinema, seems to be closest to Yoshimura. In the first place they share versatility in handling diverse themes and genres. For Kinoshita is good at comedy (take for example Carmen Comes Home (1951), the first Japanese color movie, and Carmen's Pure Love (1952), a well-known satire on the myths of Japanese mass culture); at social drama (A Japanese Tragedy) and at psychological romance. Like Yoshimura, Kinoshita displays considerable ease and skill as a director. However, he shows a typical Japanese delicacy and much more stylistic composure than the maker of The Tale of Genji, but sometimes tends to fall into monotonous sentimentality. Kinoshita began making films in 1943 and after the war concerned himself mainly with chronicles of emotional relationships including in them comedy elements, a rare thing to do in Japan. His interests changed after a six-month stay in France in 1951: he advocated social reform and criticized the relics of feudalism, and before returning to romance and psychological cinema he made a number of pictures in the early 50's which created a considerable impression in Japan. Among them was the already mentioned Carmen's Pure Love (1952), a sociological comedy; A Japanese Tragedy, a story of the sacrifices of a mother struggling for the sake of her children's future, and Twenty-Four Eyes which marks Kinoshita's access to anti-war cinema.

This elegiac film is very different in mood than films on a similar subject made outside Japan: it is a whisper, a calm meditation, a faded diary of tragic events. Made on location on the island of Shodo on the Inland Sea, the film recounts the memories of a woman school teacher who in 1928 started work there in a poor village in a bay. The twenty-four eyes of the title are her 12 pupils, who during the Fascist years experienced poverty, disease, family disasters and the presence of death. That period was also tragic in the life of the heroine: she lost her husband and son and left the school not feeling able to renounce her pacifist convictions. Now, after twenty years, she returns to work in the belief that her new pupils will not share the tragic fate of those previous ones.

Twenty-Four Eyes is one of the most characteristic works of the Japanese cinema: apart from the mood of reflection about the uneasy vicissitudes of fate, sustained in piano and tinged with stoic philosophy, there is the very typical naturalness of imagery, loose time structure subordinated to the inner logic of the intertwined memories, and above all the organic ties of the film with its scenery. If in such genres as the western one can talk about the beauty of the landscape and its relationship to the dramatis personae, in the Japanese cinema landscape is not merely a background of events but an organic whole with the characters and is often used as a natural allegory for their feelings. In Kinoshita's film the camera is never found contemplating the beauty of the seaside scenery of Shodo: the landscape has a spontaneous presence, just as does the elusively present time and the mood. The actors are also used in this fashion. The teacher and her pupils, five boys and seven girls, do not act. They identify themselves with the characters. The secret of Kinoshita's style is that it is imperceptible.

REAR WINDOW Alfred Hitchcock

Script: John Michael Hayes, from the short story by Cornell Woolrich. Photography: Robert Burks. Music: Franz Waxman. Art Direction: Hal Pereira; also Joseph McMillan Johnson, Sam Comer and Ray Mayer. Editing: George Tomasini. Cast: James Stewart (L. B. "Jeff" Jefferies), Grace Kelly (Lisa Fremont), Thelma Ritter (Stella), Wendell Corey (Detective Thomas J. Doyle), Raymond Burr (Lars Thorwald).

Alfred Hitchcock for Patron, U. S. A. 10,094 ft., 112 mins. Technicolor.

A magazine photographer has broken a leg; confined to a wheelchair in his Greenwich Village apartment, he spends most of his time spying on the activities of the neighbors using a telephoto lens. One night he notices a man leaving his flat with a suitcase; the next day the man's nagging wife is no longer in the apartment. Jeff is convinced there has been a murder and with the help of his skeptical girlfriend brings the murderer to justice.

Apart from being a fascinating thriller, *Rear Window* offers a non-banal reflection on man's commitment to an idea, on the relationship of an individual to society. It is also a study of a man of action reduced to the role of passive observer. Hitchcock has always liked such *à rebours* situations; the voyeur motif also constantly recurs in his films. With *Rear Window* he demonstrates that the highly subjective narrative (apart from the final sequence all is seen through Jeff's eyes or rather through his lens) does not have to make a film un-cinematic. In fact it is precisely the spatial limitation of events which generates suspense and concentration. *Rear Window* has very little dialogue and yet it is full of tension and through and through cinematic. The drama is thus built exclusively by way of the (well edited) images. The constant use of the telephoto lens (to an extent unparalleled in feature cinema) is a visual attraction naturally stemming from the hero's profession; another is the interesting color effects in the finale when the immobilized Jeff fends off the murderer who has broken into his apartment by dazzling him with a flashlamp.

SENSO Luchino Visconti

Script: Suso Cecchi D'Amico and Visconti; also Giorgio Prosperi,

Senso

Carlo Alianello and Giorgio Bassani, from the short story "Senso, Scartafaccio segreto della Contessa Livia" (Secret Papers of Countess Livia) in the collection "Senso, nuove storielle vane" (1882) by Camillo Boito. Photography: Aldo Graziati and Robert Krasker; also Giuseppe Rotunno. Music: Anton Bruckner (7th Symphony). Art Direction: Ottavio Scotti and Gino Brosio. Costumes: Marcel Escoffier and Piero Tosi. Editing: Mario Serandrei. Cast: Alida Valli (Countess Livia Serpieri), Farley Granger (Lieutenant Franz Mahler), Massimo Girotti (Marquis Roberto Ussoni), Heinz Moog (Count Serpieri), Rina Morelli (Laura), Marcella Mariani (Prostitute), Christian Marquand (Bohemian officer), Tonio Selwart (Colonel Kleist), Cristoforo de Hartungen (Commander at Venetian Square), Tino Bianchi (Meucci), Sergio Fantoni (Patriot).

Domenico Forges Davanzati for Lux Film, Italy. 115 mins. Technicolor.

The intention of the ironic story of a love affair of an Italian countess and an Austrian army officer (it was to be emphatically entitled "Custozza" after the site of two victories, in 1848 and 1866, of the Austrians over the Italians struggling for their independence) was to demonstrate the guilt of the Italian aristocracy for their country's military defeat. Visconti said he tried to make the film a visual equivalent of Stendhal's novels--fully realistic, touched with the flavor of an Italian melodrama and denouncing the concept of a war conducted only for the benefit of one social class. If Visconti's intentions were realized, the picture would surely amount to the most comprehensive exposition of the philosophy of history in the whole work of this aristocrat-cum-communist. However, the final screen version carries a different title from the story on which it is based, and its emphasis is placed quite differently. This was brought about first by pressure from the producer, and later by a much more drastic intervention of the censor who objected mainly to the political line of the dialogues, especially to the strongly emphasized antagonisms between the patriots led by Giuseppe Garibaldi and the regular armed forces. As a result *Senso* became no more than a romance, set against the epic fresco of the 1866 war and aiming in the direction of opera; a romance which, although given the sarcastic finale of the despair of the renegade countess after the death of her cynical lover, disagrees in tone with the realistic treatment of the epic background. However, one should not blame everything on external circumstances; Visconti passed over the shoddiness of the literary material and committed in his first baroque film all the sins which were later present throughout his work: emphatic treatment on the screen of decadent, self-destructive passion, excessive fatalism of the story line, naturalistic *mise en scène*. All the same, with the help of outstanding photographers (one of whom, Aldo Graziati, known as G. R. Aldo, was killed during the shooting) Visconti made a film which fascinates with its plastic vision pulsating with deep tones of purple and stylized after the art of the period. It exceptionally well combined images and music and very consistently developed (in the Modernist spirit) rationale of the actions of the main characters.

Senso

Special praise is due to Alida Valli who brilliantly conveyed the heroine's possession by a destructive, obsessive passion. While constantly balancing on the verge of kitsch, Senso impresses the viewer with its richness. Such were almost all of Visconti's later films.

A STORY FROM CHIKAMATSU (Chikamatsu Monogatari) Kenji Mizoguchi

---

Script: Yoshikata Yoda, from Matsutaro Kawaguchi's adaptation of the bunraku play "Daikyoji Mukashigoyomi" (The Legend of the Grand Scroll-Maker) by Monzaemon Chikamatsu (1652-1724). Photography: Kazuo Miyagawa. Music: Fumio Hayasaka, Tamezo Mochizuki and Eijiro Toyosawa. Art Direction: Hiroshi Mizutani. Editing: Kanji Sugawara. Cast: Kazuo Hasegawa (Mohei), Kyoko Kagawa (Osan), Yoko Minamida (Otama, a servant girl), Eitaro Shindo (Ishun), Sakae Ozawa (Sukeyemon), Ichiro Sugai (Genbei), Haruo Tanaka (Doki), Chieko Naniwa (Oko), Ishiguro Tatsuya (Isan), Kimiko Tachibana (Ocho), Hisao Toake (Chamberlain Morionkoji), Shinobu Araki (Nobleman's major-domo), Ryunosuke Azuma (Bairyu Akamatsu), Koichi Katsuragi (Priest), Hiroshi Mizuno (Chief State Councillor Kuroki).

Masaichi Nagata for Daiei, Japan. 9144 ft., 102 mins.

A screen version of a tragic 17th-century love story, A Story from Chikamatsu is very typical of Mizoguchi's interest in the wronged and humiliated. As in many of his films, a woman's tragedy is the central motif, and as always it is an accusation of traditional customs and morality in Japan. In fact A Story from Chikamatsu is probably the fullest expression of this attitude of Mizoguchi's: the heroine is here not pitied but deeply respected for her spiritual metamorphosis in the face of adversity, for her dignity in coping with the inhuman requirements of the moral code.

Kyoto, 1683. Osan has been married off to a rich court printer because her family needed money. She bears her lot humbly until her brother contracts debts and pleads with her for help. Osan's husband refuses to lend her the money. Mohei, an employee at the printing shop who has long been secretly in love with her, tries to help her. An unfortunate coincidence not only thwarts their plans but makes the husband suspicious as to the nature of his wife's relationship with his clerk. Osan escapes with Mohei, who confesses his love for her. The laws of the Tokugawa Shogunate prescribe crucifixion for adulterers and property confiscation for cuckolds; the husband hesitates whether to inform the authorities, but Osan rejects the chance to return to him and decides to share the fate of the man who gave her back the will to live. The lovers plan to commit shinjū, the double suicide, which Japanese tradition considers the most exalted form of protest against the limitations of temporal laws and the highest expression of spiritual bondage. However, they are arrested and crucified on the city walls.

A Story from Chikamatsu is one of the most formally perfect of Mizoguchi's films. The chamber character of the story is this time in complete accord with the restraint of the execution, the abandonment of a concrete recreation of the period through the designs, with the near-geometrical composition of the frame and the slowed-down rhythm of the narrative. A Story from Chikamatsu particularly strongly gravitates towards the traditional bunraku theatre: the acting is conventionalized; the actors' gestures, subtle and as if suspended in the air, are meant to convey a wide spectrum of inner feelings. But the specific manner of execution, with dark-grey tonality of the photography and a limited scale of dramatic changes of mood and tension does not lower the inner emotional temperature of the film. Mizoguchi created a ravishing study of the ennobling power of love, dignity in the face of violence--a humanist ballad of protest against the limitation of freedom.

CARMEN JONES Otto Preminger

Script: Harry Kleiner, based on the musical play by Oscar Hammerstein II, taken from the libretto of the opera "Carmen" by Henri Meilhac and Ludovic Halévy, based on the novelette "Carmen" by Prosper Mérimée. Photography: Sam Leavitt. Music: Georges Bizet, arranged by Herschel Burke Gilbert. Lyrics of songs: "Stand Up and Fight," "Beat Out That Rhythm on a Drum," "Dere's a Cafe on de Corner," "Lift 'em Up and Put 'em Down," "Dat's Love," "You Talk Just Like My Maw," "Dis Flower," "De Cards Don't Lie," "My Joe," "Dat's Our Man" and "Whizzin' Away Along de Track": Oscar Hammerstein II. Art Direction: Edward L. Ilou. Set Direction: Claude E. Carpenter. Costumes: Mary Ann Nyberg. Choreography: Herbert Ross. Credit Sequence Design: Saul Bass. Cast: Dorothy Dandridge (Carmen Jones), Harry Belafonte (Joe), Olga James (Cindy Lou), Pearl Bailey (Frankie), Diahann Carroll (Myrt), Roy Glenn (Rum), Nick Stewart (Dink), Joe Adams (Husky Miller), Broc Peters (Sergeant Brown), Sandy Lewis (T-Bone), Mauri Lynn (Sally). Singing Voices: Le Vern Hutcherson (Joe), Marilynn Horne (Carmen Jones), Marvin Hayes (Husky Miller), Bernice Patterson (Myrt), Joe Crawford (Dink), Brock Peters (Rum).

Otto Preminger for 20th Century-Fox, U. S. A. 107 mins. CinemaScope. De Luxe Color.

Taken out of context, the idea of transferring to the screen in 1954, the operatic version of "Carmen" with all its paraphernalia might seem deplorable. One must remember however that ten years earlier the old theme was revived in the form of a musical comedy set in the scenery of the American South and turned out to be a success; Bizet's music found new depth transposed into the syncopes of jazz. When in 1949 Roland Petit added to this an excellent ballet version, the idea of "Carmen" on the screen began to appear as a tempting and viable proposition. So, Preminger once more brought the old weepie to life, making very skillful use of CinemaScope, a technique which was very rapidly gaining popularity, and ended up with a picture dazzling with pace, vigor and movement. However, he made a mistake in being faithful to the original in the melodramatic finale, precisely where he should not have been. Still, in general Carmen Jones fully justifies its existence with its lightness and humor.

The setting turned out to be a very convincing background for the plot, which is mostly due to the skill with which the story was transposed: the setting is the South during the Second World War, Carmen works at a parachute factory near Jacksonville, her beloved trains to be a pilot, and Bizet's toreador has been replaced by a boxer. Admittedly, there is in the film a certain dualism introduced by mixing the authentic and the exotic treatment of the milieu, which was no less irritating to the black people than (for the same reason) the original was to the Spaniards. But one must remember that at the origin of Carmen Jones was an attractive idea and not sociological ambitions. The vocal aspect of the film, entrusted to outstanding black singers, is fine; Dorothy Dandridge displays a splendid screen temperament; and the design of the credit sequence is the first work of Saul Bass, the future master in this field.

LES DIABOLIQUES (The Fiends) Henri-Georges Clouzot

Script: Clouzot and Jérôme Géronimi, from the novel "La Femme qui n'était pas" (published in England as "The Woman Who Never Was") by Pierre Boileau and Thomas Narcejac. Photography: Armand Thirard. Music: Georges Van Parys. Art Direction: Léon Barsacq. Editing: Madeleine Gug. Cast: Simone Signoret (Nicole Horner), Véra Clouzot (Christina Delasalle), Paul Meurisse (Michel Delasalle), Charles Vanel (Inspector Fichet), Pierre Larquey (M. Drain, a teacher), Michel Serrault (M. Raymond, a teacher), Jean Brochard (Plantiveau, the handyman), Thérèse Dorny (Mme. Herboux), Noël Roquevert (M. Herboux), Georges Charamat (Dr. Loisy), Georges Poujouly (Soudieu), Jacques Varennes (M. Bridoux), Roberto Rodrigo (José), Jean-Pierre Bonnefous (De Gascuel), Michel Dumur (Ritberger), Henri Humbert (Patard), Yves-Marie Maurin (Moinet).

Henri-Georges Clouzot for Filmsonor, France. 10,520 ft., 117 mins.

Clouzot followed The Wages of Fear by a no less suspenseful story of "a corpse which would not lie down." With its extremely ingenious story and gruesome mood Les Diaboliques is a supreme film noir. It has few equals when it comes to the ability to frighten the audience.

Michel Delasalle is headmaster of a seedy provincial school. A callous and unpleasant man, he maltreats both his wife Christina, a former South American heiress on whose money he runs the school, and his mistress Nicole, who is on the staff. The two desperate women decide to murder their tormentor. One night they lure Michel to Nicole's house, incapacitate him with whisky laced with a sedative and drown him in the bath. They then throw the body into the school swimming pool. But during the next few days Christina becomes increasingly alarmed by events suggesting that her husband is still alive: the suit he last wore is returned by the cleaners, the pupils insist on having seen him, and when the pool is drained the body is no longer there. In the meantime a retired policeman begins to investigate Michel's disappearance....

But the person who reveals the totally unexpected final twist to someone who has not seen the film deserves a fate worse than murder. For this time Clouzot is not interested in the philosophical implications of crime or the problem of identity (a constant theme for Boileau and Narcejac who later wrote the story for Hitchcock's Vertigo) but primarily in efficient handling of the plot on which the film greatly relies. This he does with mastery, heaping fright upon fright in a true Grand Guignol style. Consider only the celebrated scene of the car journey of the two women with the body in a wicker basket, or the scene when Christina, overcoming terror, creeps down the corridor to Michel's study with a candle in her hand, determined to resolve the mystery. The echoing stone staircases and long corridors, the sound of steps at night, the slowly turning door handle, desolate countryside with leafless trees, a seedy school whose headmaster feeds his pupils on stinking fish, the effects of light and shadow--Clouzot brilliantly creates the atmosphere of decay and menace making use of gruesome naturalistic detail to an even greater extent than in the earlier Manon. On the other hand the director does not fully follow up the film's potential as a study of relationships within a bourgeois ménage à trois. Particularly the two women's uneasy partnership in crime could have been developed more fully. This is not to say that Clouzot was let down by his actors. The leading trio are superb: Paul Meurisse as a sadistic yet attractive headmaster; Véra Clouzot as his frail, tortured and bewildered wife; Simone Signoret as the cool, calculating and diabolically clever Nicole.

Les Diaboliques

20,000 LEAGUES UNDER THE SEA Richard Fleischer

Script: Earl Felton, from the novel "Vingt mille lieues sous les mers" by Jules Verne (1869). Photography: Franz F. Planer; also Ralph Hammeras (Special effects photography) and Till Gabbani (Underwater). Music: Paul J. Smith. Song: "A Whale of a Tale" by Richard and Robert Sherman. Art Direction: John Meehan. Set Decorations: Emile Kuri. Costumes: Norman Martien. Special Processes: Ub Iwerks. Special Effects: John Hench and Joshua Meador. Editing: Elmo Williams. Cast: Kirk Douglas (Ned Land), James Mason (Captain Nemo), Paul Lukas (Professor Pierre Aronnax), Peter Lorre (Conseil, his assistant), Robert J. Wilke (First mate of "Nautilus"), Carleton Young (John Howard), Ted de Corsia (Captain Farragut), Percy Helton (Diver), Ted Cooper (Mate of "Abraham Lincoln"), Edward Marr (Shipping agent), Fred Graham (Casey Moore), J. M. Kerrigan (Billy), Harry Harvey (Shipping clerk), Herb Vigran (Reporter).

Walt Disney Productions, U. S. A. 11,307 ft., 126 mins. CinemaScope. Technicolor.

20,000 Leagues Under the Sea is without a doubt one of the finest achievements of its kind in the cinema. In spite of being almost completely faithful to the plot and the atmosphere of Jules Verne's literary original, the makers succeeded in steering clear of the dangers of falsity and primitivism one has to beware of when transferring the fantastic convention of a science-fiction novel onto the tangible, concrete soil of the cinema. In the movies there is no indefinite article, and while a novelist can say "a car," a filmmaker has to show "the car," be it a Ford or a Rolls-Royce. The same applies of course to submarines. It turned out that the ideas of the 19th-century fantasist feel quite happy on the 20th-century screen. Five million dollars spent on production, the use of CinemaScope and great attention expended on underwater photography and trick effects (in charge of the latter was Ub Iwerks, the creator of Mickey Mouse) and--what is rare in pictures of this type--fully satisfactory performances from all the leading actors, resulted in a fine adventure spectacle for the general audience.

THE ABANDONED (Gli sbandati) Francesco Maselli

Script: Francesco Maselli, Aggeo Savioli and Eriprando Visconti, from a story by the latter. Photography: Gianni Di Venanzo.

Music: Giovanni Fusco. Editing: Antonietta Zita. Cast: Lucia Bosè (Lucia), Jean-Pierre Mocky (Andrea), Isa Miranda (Andrea's mother), Antonio De Teffé, Leonardo Botta, Marco Gugliemi, Giuliano Montaldo, Ivy Nicholson, Iulio Paradisi, Franco Lantieri, Ferdinando Birri, Mario Girotti, Bianca Di Toro, Goliarda Sapienza.

C. V. C. , Italy, 90 mins.

The year 1943, a time of dramatic events in Italy. Twenty-year-old Andrea stays with his mother, the widow of an industrialist, on a country estate near Milan. He pursues a leisurely and safe life; war does not really exist to him until a family of bombed-out refugees are billetted on them. Andrea's interest in the daughter Lucia, a serious and restrained girl, is soon changed into youthful, reciprocated love. After the armistice is announced, the Germans change their attitude to their former allies and begin to transport them en masse to the Reich. One night, a train transporting Italian resistance prisoners stops in the nearby village, and a group of soldiers escape. They decide to join the partisans. Under Lucia's influence Andrea gives them refuge, but a friend of his, afraid of retributions, informs the Nazis. The young man plans to leave home with the girl, but is stopped by his mother's dramatic tirade: she uses emotional blackmail and lectures him on his place in life. Mother and son leave for Switzerland escorted by a German officer; while Lucia, who had waited for Andrea until the last moment, leaves with the refugees and is shot by the pursuing Nazis.

This remarkable feature debut by Antonioni's 24-year-old collaborator triggered off a long sequence of films which followed up the thematic interests of Fellini's I vitelloni and critically examined the consciences of Italian middle-class youngsters, in this case on the background of their parents' callous indifference to the crucial problem of the break-up of Fascism. Maselli for many years remained interested in this theme of inner conflicts between youthful moral sensitivity and the influence of social pressure--but he never managed to match the freshness and subjective tension of The Abandoned. The film is particularly notable for its subtle psychological portrayal, and the dramatic editing which is in sharp contrast to the mood of depression and alienation and is evoked by a fluid use of long takes, grey tones of exterior photography and the melancholy music. The emotional climate of Antonioni's Il grido would be very close to this and not without reason: on that film also the director's collaborators would be Gianni Di Venanzo and Giovanni Fusco.

SABRINA Billy Wilder

Script: Wilder, Samuel Taylor and Ernest Lehman from the play

"Sabrina Fair" by Taylor. Photography: Charles Lang Jr. Music: Frederick Hollander. Art Direction: Hal Pereira and Walter Tyler. Editing: Arthur Schmidt. Cast: Audrey Hepburn (Sabrina Fairchild), Humphrey Bogart (Linus Larrabee), William Holden (David Larrabee), John Williams (Thomas Fairchild), Walter Hampden (Oliver Larrabee), Martha Hyer (Elizabeth Tyson), Joan Vohs (Gretchen van Horn), Marcel Dalio (Baron), Marcel Hillaire (Professor), Nella Walker (Maude Larrabee), Francis X. Bushman (Mr. Tyson), Ellen Corby (Miss McCardle).

Billy Wilder for Paramount, U.S.A. 10,241 ft., 114 mins.

Along with Love in the Afternoon, Sabrina is one of Wilder's romantic comedies illuminated by the charm of Audrey Hepburn.

Sabrina is the escapist story of an American Cinderella. The 19-year-old daughter of a chauffeur working at a Long Island estate has been in love since childhood with the handsome playboy son of her father's employer. David, who has so far taken no interest in Sabrina, finally notices her when she returns from a two year cookery course in Paris; he is even prepared for a misalliance. But the family, anxious to consolidate a business merger by arranging David's marriage to a rich heiress, are not pleased with the situation. Linus, David's solemn and hard-working businessman brother, takes it upon himself to talk Sabrina out of the marriage. This brings rather unexpected results: Linus falls in love with her and Sabrina enters the family after all, but with a different husband.

Billy Wilder, whose brief was to cash in on the popularity of Roman Holiday made by Wyler the previous year, discharged his task well: gave the banal little story charm and pace, made full use of the very good dialogues and thus scored his first success in the comedy field. The mortally ill Humphrey Bogart, cast as the man finally conquered by Sabrina, sends the audience one of his last smiles.

EXECUTIVE SUITE Robert Wise

Script: Ernest Lehman, based on the novel by Cameron Hawley. Photography: George Folsey. Art Direction: Cedric Gibbons and Edward Carfango. Cast: William Holden (McDonald Walling), June Allyson (Mary Blemond Walling), Fredric March (Loren Phineas Shaw), Walter Pidgeon (Frederick Alderson), Barbara Stanwyck (Julia O. Tredway), Shelley Winters (Eva Bardeman), Louis Calhern (George Nyle Caswell), Paul Douglas (Josiah Dudley), Nina Foch (Erica Martin), Dean Jagger (Jesse Grimm), Tim Considine (Mike

Walling), William Phipps (Bill Lundeen), Lucille Knoch (Mrs. Caswell), Edgar Stehli (Julius Steigel), Mary Adams (Sara Grimm), Virginia Brissac (Edith Alderson).

John Houseman for MGM, U. S. A. 9387 ft., 104 mins.

Executive Suite, a psychological drama about a power struggle within the board of a big furniture manufacturing company caused by the sudden death of the president, brought an unexpected success for a theme which so far was not regarded as of interest to a wider audience. This well-cast picture was made with narrative fluency; this and the achievement of sustained tension is owed to the precision with which individual scenes are put together. It is worth noting in this connection that Robert Wise first came to attention as the editor of Welles' Citizen Kane. Executive Suite is for the American cinema the beginning of a new genre--semi-sociological examinations of human actions in the world of business, analyzing the destructive influence of material success and social position on relationships between people. So far, such statements were usually applied to the world of entertainment (as in the case of All About Eve and several anti-Hollywood films) and sometimes to other rather specific milieux, for instance the world of boxing. From the mid-50's onwards barriers between different cinematic genres began to break down and reality came to be penetrated not only within the narrow framework of individual melodramas or character dramas, but on more extensive reaches of daily life.

KNAVE OF HEARTS (Monsieur Ripois) René Clément

Script: Hugh Mills and Clément, from the novel "Monsieur Ripois et la Némésis" by Louis Hémon. Dialogues: Hugh Mills and Raymond Queneau. Photography: Oswald Morris. Music: Roman Vlad. Song: "Song of Margaret" (words by Pierre Mac Orlan, music by V. Marceau), sung by Germaine Montero. Art Direction: Ralph Brinton. Editing: Vera Campbell. Cast: Gérard Philipe (André Ripois), Natasha Parry (Patricia), Germaine Montero (Marcelle), Valerie Hobson (Catherine), Joan Greenwood (Norah), Margaret Johnston (Anne), Diana Decker (Diana), Percy Marmont (Catherine's father), Eric Pohlmann (Boarding house proprietor), Bill Shine (Pub barman), Mai Bacon (Mrs. Rose), Margot Field (Doris Braddock), Julie Anslow (Maisie Smith), Harry Tawb (Stewart), Gerald Campian (Harry), Martin Benson (Art), Beryl Cooke (Kind typist), Arthur Howard (Priest), David Coote (Richard), Richard Hart (Pupil), Eileen Way (First landlady), Judith Nelmes (Second landlady).

Paul Graetz for Transcontinental Film Productions London Ltd. / Transcontinental Films S. A. Paris, G. B. / France. 9286 ft., 103 mins.

Versatile, but also very French in outlook, Clément travels--of all places--to England, to make a film about a compulsive Don Juan, a man incapable of forming a lasting relationship.

The handsome French husband of an upper-class English girl, André Ripois pursues Patricia, his wife's friend. But Patricia receives his attentions with skepticism. To soften her resistance, André tells her the story of his life and loves since his arrival in London: his progress from a humble clerk to marriage with the rich Catherine. He describes his past affairs: with a domineering career woman, with a sweet Kensington girl whom he promised to marry, then with a prostitute. He seduced and abandoned all of them. Finding Patricia unmoved by his story, André threatens to throw himself out of the window. An accident turns a vain threat into reality: he slips and falls. In the last scene of the picture André is seen in a London park, wheeled along in an invalid carriage by his wife and the would-be mistress. He still winks at pretty passers-by.

An elegant comedy of manners, Knave of Hearts is an ironic portrayal of a failed cynic--failed, because he lacked mental stamina and because he was unable to keep a cool head to the end. He was unable to love and unable to hurt those who loved him. A husband of a rich and beautiful wife, he pursues women simply through an uncontrollable addiction. But Clément treats his protagonist very unequivocally: seemingly with cool irony, but with bemused sympathy after André's mishap. It seems however that the deeper reason for this is the director's misogynist attitude: even such a mediocrity as Ripois can operate for years without a hitch because there are always scores of naive women around--and the women in Knave of Hearts are treated with coolness, almost always laced with malice. Anne is a martinet, Catherine--exalted, Norah--silly. On the other hand, the film offers a credible and psychologically very detailed portrayal of the protagonist. Clément cut a dash with the sharp and economical script, and was well served by the great French actor, Gérard Philipe, in the title part. Clément also attached great importance to the accuracy of the description of the background. To achieve authenticity, the scenes in the streets of London were shot with a hidden camera. Paradoxically, Knave of Hearts uses London better and more truthfully than did the abstract and whimsical contemporary British cinema. The score, by Roman Vlad, is very ingenious: each woman is given a musical motif of her own.

A LESSON IN LOVE (En lektion i kärlek) Ingmar Bergman

Script: Bergman. Photography: Martin Bodin. Music: Dag Wirén. Art Direction: P. A. Lundgren. Editing: Oscar Rosander. Cast: Eva Dahlbeck (Marianne Ernéman), Gunnar Björnstrand (Dr. David

Erneman), Yvonne Lombard (Suzanne), Åke Grönberg (Carl-Adam), Harriet Andersson (Nix Erneman), Olof Winnerstrand (Professor Henrik Erneman), Renée Björling (Svea Erneman), John Elfström (Sam), Birgitte Reimer (Lise), Dagmar Ebbesen (Nurse), Sigge Fürst (Clergyman).

Svensk Filmindustri, Sweden. 8550 ft., 95 mins.

The first of Bergman's sweet-and-sour comedies, A Lesson in Love is a story of the maneuvers of a successful gynecologist and his attractive wife, who are on the point of parting after sixteen years of marriage. David is having an affair with a woman patient, and Marianne decides to leave her irritating and disloyal husband and travels to Copenhagen to a sculptor whom she jilted in her youth. The doctor, his pride hurt, hastens to regain his possession, but as it turns out he has little idea about female psychology or the ways of conquering a woman's heart. A series of flashbacks reveal that he was no more skillful in the past either. In the end he wins a tragicomical victory, but in a situation in which his rival is as clumsy as he is. Marianne returns to him from pity rather than love.

One could make a caustic comment and say that Bergman's sense of humor is as refined as is Scandinavian sexuality. But this would be too harsh a criticism, for the director of The Naked Night never makes comedies for mere entertainment; if he temporarily abandons the great problems of his dramas, it is only for the sake of smaller problems in his comedies. A Lesson in Love is rather unkind to the male sex; it has some interesting things to say about Swedish custom and mentality and, although at times a little heavy, is made with charm. The film's complicated time structure and the intelligent editing testify to the quality of Bergman's craft, while symbolic pictorial inserts which exploit the appeal of ornate objects herald the style which was subsequently developed in Smiles of a Summer Night.

SCARLET AND BLACK (Le Rouge et le noir) Claude Autant-Lara

Script: Jean Aurenche, Pierre Bost and Autant-Lara, from the novel by Stendhal. Photography: Michel Kelber. Music: René Cloërec. Art Direction: Max Douy. Costumes: Rosine Delamare. Cast: Gérard Philipe (Julien Sorel), Danielle Darrieux (Madame de Rênal), Antonella Lualdi (Mathilde de la Mole), Jean Martinelli (M. de Rénal), Anna Maria Sandri (Elisa, the maid), Antoine Balpêtré (Abbé Pirard), André Brunot (Abbé Chelan), Jean Mercure (Marquis de la Mole), Mirko Ellis (Norbert de la Mole), Suzette Nivette (Marquise de la Mole), Pierre Jourdan (Count Altamira), Jacques Varennes (President of the court).

Louis Wipf for Franco-London-Film/Documento Film, France/Italy. 146 mins. Wide screen. Eastman Colour.

Scarlet and Black is an extreme example of the literary spirit which dominated the French cinema in the 50's and made it almost completely dependent on the psychological novel. It is a fine screen version of Stendhal's great book, which to a film-maker is as tempting for its richness as it is difficult to make into a movie because of its capricious dramatic structure, the multitude of plots and its introspective character. Autant-Lara and his scriptwriters could not handle the meandering of the plot and the complex references of the story of an impudent plebeian in the world of Restoration saloons: although the titles-quotations (from the novel) are justified by the sheer impossibility of finding a visual equivalent of Stendhal's charming observations, the film contains also internal monologues of the hero which were meant to go some way towards reflecting the complexity of his personality. Also, the novel's very close interweaving of eroticism and social accents (present already in the title) became stratified on the screen into problems of the bedroom and problems of class conflicts. The insistent stressing of the social context (strengthened by the prologue which gives the whole film the frames of a flashback) does not seem to have been an excuse for some other intentions: Autant-Lara was in all his films anti-clerical and anti-bourgeois. All the same, Scarlet and Black is above all else a film about feelings, a film of atmosphere and this is where all its values are found. If one was to forget about Stendhal and treat the film simply as a story of rebellious love bringing about the ruin of a young man who played his part in life like a hand of poker, then (apart from the faults of theatricality and of verbal expression of thoughts) the film contains only credits: precise execution and designs, visual richness, efficient editing, credible characters portrayed by excellent actors. Most praise (and most criticism) has been addressed to Gérard Philipe; he is brilliant and all one can say is that those who criticize his part remember the novel too well. To render the entirety of Julien Sorel's motivation, as portrayed in the book, using the text selected for the screen adaptation would have been an impossible task.

ROOTS (Raices) Benito Alazraki

Script: Carlos Velo and Manuel Barbachano Ponce; also Jomi García Ascot, Fernando Espejo and Mario Lazo, from the short stories "Las Vacas" (The Cows), "Nuestra Señora" (Our Lady), "El Tuerto" (The One-Eyed), and "La Potranca" (The Filly), taken from the book "El Diosero" by Francisco Rojas González. Art Direction: Fernando Gamboa. Editing: Luis Sobreyra and Miguel Campos. Prologue photography: Ramon Muñoz. Prologue music: Silvestre Revueltas.

LAS VACAS: Photography: Walter Reuter. Music: Guillermo Noriega. Cast: Beatriz Flores (Martina), Juan de la Cruz (Esteban), Conchita Montes (Señora), Eduardo Urruchua (Señor), Rafael Ramírez (Cousin), Juan Cano (Don Remigio).

NUESTRA SEÑORA: Photography: Hans Beimler. Music: Rodolfo Halffter. Cast: Olimpia Alazraki (Jane Davis), Miguel González (Doctor González), Angel Lara (Priest), Juan Hernández (Mariano).

EL TUERTO: Photography: Walter Reuter. Music: Blas Galindo. Cast: Miguel Angel Negrón (The one-eyed boy), Antonia Hernández (Mother), Mario Herrera (Friend).

LA POTRANCA: Photography: Walter Reuter. Music: José Pablo Moncayo. Cast: Alicia del Lago (Xanath), Carlos Robles Gil (Eric, the archeologist), Teodulo González (Teodulo, Xanath's father), Laura Holt (Vivian).

Manuel Barbachano Ponce for Teleproducciones, Mexico. 6998 ft., 78 mins.

A Mexican polemic with the films of Fernández: four stories about Mexican-Indian life linked by an intention to convey the authentic spirit of the country and produced by a company which specialized in national Mexican themes. The style of Roots, elemental and dynamic, is alien to the refined visual compositions of Gabriel Figueroa and the melodramatic protests against injustice of Maria Candelaria, Maclovia and Pueblerina. Roots is stylistically closer to ethnographical document, and this is stressed by close-ups of objects of material culture, faces and details of everyday life. Perhaps only the first story--in which a poor Indian sells his wife as a wet nurse--has some thematic links with the films of Fernández, but the intention is different: to show the pride and the inner worth of the original inhabitants of the country, now pushed onto the social margin, but still spiritually sovereign. This message is particularly stressed by the fourth story (of a young Indian who is treated as a sexual object by an archeologist) and the second (which ironically contrasts the aesthetic sensitivity of the peasants with the views of an American ethnographer who believes them to be primitive in this respect). In turn, the third story discovers autonomous national mentality against the exotic background of a Mexican festival. A little boy, blind in one eye, is cruelly treated by other children. During the celebrations a firework accident deprives him of sight in the remaining eye. His mother thinks this to be a miracle. Totally blind, the boy will meet with pity instead of cruelty.

Some situations in the second and third story may be considered a little exaggerated, but each of these screen miniatures has genuine authenticity, and the whole is coherent and stylistically mature. Such a fine debut made many people see Alazraki as the future leader of the Mexican cinema. But the reaction of the director of Roots to his success (confirmed by a prize at Cannes) was rather unexpected: having climbed to the top in the Mexican film industry he never again reached for a serious topic.

THE WOMAN OF RUMOUR (Uwasa-no Onna) Kenji Mizoguchi

Script: Yoshikata Yoda and Masashige Narusawa, based on a treatment by Matsutaro Kawaguchi. Photography: Kazuo Miyagawa. Music: Toshiro Mayazumi. Art Direction: Hiroshi Mizutani. Editing: Kanji Sugawara. Cast: Kinuyo Tanaka (Hatsuko Mabuchi), Yoshiko Kuga (Yukiko, her daughter), Tomoemon Otani (Dr. Kenzo Matoba), Eitaro Shindo (Yasuichi Harada), Bontaro Miyake (Kobayashi), Chieko Naniwa (Osaki), Haruo Tanaka (Kawamoto), Hisao Toake (Yamada), Michiko Ai (Dayu Aioi).

Masaichi Nagata for Daiei, Japan. 7513 ft., 83 mins.

Mizoguchi made this contemporary picture between two period films, Sansho the Bailiff and A Story of Chikamatsu. The setting is a brothel in the notorious Shimabara district of Kyoto, whose middle-aged owner loves a young opportunistic doctor. Anxious to keep him she plans to buy a house to be turned into a private clinic. Having only part of the required 2.5 million yen, she borrows the remainder from a neighbor using the brothel as security. After attempted suicide for love, Madame's daughter Yukiko returns from Tokyo where she was studying at the Conservatory. She is revolted by the idea of having been educated on the proceeds of vice and by the vulgarity of her mother's clients. Yukiko falls in love with the doctor, unaware of her mother's feelings for him; they plan to go to Tokyo together. But when both women realize the doctor's lack of scruples, they reject him. Yukiko becomes reconciled to the situation, and when her mother falls ill, she gradually begins to take over her duties.

As always, Mizoguchi shows himself as a master of atmosphere and an expert at describing the milieu. The highly mobile camera, led by Miyagawa's sure hand, describes the everyday life in the brothel, its topography, personalities of the girls and their clients. The girls are shown as basically honest and hard-working; they are simply victims of poverty and exploitation. The brothel-keeper is also basically decent and vulnerable to the usual human weaknesses. There are no accusations, and everybody is looked at with compassion. But the main interest is characterization rather than moral judgment. The pace is much faster than in Mizoguchi's period films, and editing brisk. The Woman of Rumour relies on team acting effort, but Kinuyo Tanaka still shines. The director's constant actress, she gave outstanding performances in The Lady of Musashino, The Life of Oharu, Ugetsu Monogatari, Sansho the Bailiff, as well as pictures by other Japanese directors, to mention only Gosho's Four Chimneys, Naruse's Mother and Floating Clouds and Kinoshita's The Ballad of Narayama.

A GENERATION (Pokolenie) Andrzej Wajda

Script: Bohdan Czeszko, from his own novel of the same title. Photography: Jerzy Lipman. Music: Andrzej Markowski. Art Direction: Roman Mann. Editing: Czesław Raniszewski. Cast: Tadeusz Łomnicki (Stach), Urszula Modrzyńska (Dorota), Tadeusz Janczar (Jasio Krone), Janusz Paluszkiewicz (Sekuła), Roman Polański (Mundek), Zbigniew Cybulski (Kostek), Ryszard Kotas (Jacek), Ludwik Benoit (Grzesio), Hanna Skarżanka (Stach's mother), Stanisław Milski (Jasio's father), Janusz Ściwiarski (The elder Berg), Zygmunt Zintel (The younger Berg), Jerzy Krasowski, Zofia Czerwińska.

Ignacy Taub for Wytwórnia Filmów Fabularnych Nr 2 we Wrocławiu, Poland. 8148 ft., 91 mins.

A turning point for the Polish cinema: the camera is taken over by the younger generation of film-makers who in the late 50's formed the antiheroic "Polish School." A Generation marks a debut for many of them: for Andrzej Wajda as director, for Kazimierz Kutz as assistant director, for Jerzy Lipman as director of photography and a debut for a number of actors who later became well known. Roman Polański, later a famous director, appears in one of the main parts.

A Generation is set in Warsaw during the Nazi occupation. As the film begins, in 1942, we watch a group of 20-year-olds play a knife game; then they steal coal from a passing German train. One boy is lost and another killed by the train guards. The film follows the life of another boy, Stach. He begins work at a factory which makes equipment for the occupying forces. There he meets a girl who recruits for a Communist Resistance Group; falls in love with her while becoming increasingly involved in their cause. After her arrest, Stach takes over her work of setting up a new Youth Resistance group. He is by now a seasoned fighter.

The story of a wartime urban guerrilla group gave the young team of film-makers an opportunity to proclaim a new cinematic style which questions both the inflexible framework of the Soviet-inspired Socialist Realism and the narrative academicism of Aleksander Ford and Wanda Jakubowska, Poland's first ambitious directors after the war. In A Generation Wajda, himself Ford's pupil, still adheres to the emphatic-romantic tone of the maker of Border Street, but reaches thereby new territories. Labored literary dialogues are replaced by vivid colloquial speech, the film is given intensity by a mixture of lyrical love and death (a quality invariably present in all of Wajda's work for nearly 20 years afterwards), and the inherent expressiveness of objects is given precedence over Ford's stylized visual metaphors. A Generation belongs to the spontaneously emotional cinema which opts for a subjective, ragged narrative line instead of the labored didacticism of heretofore, the cinema which places stress on the painterly quality of the photography rather than on cinematic crusading. Wajda, who came to films from the Fine Arts Academy, displays in A Generation a great pictorial sensitivity as well as other features of his inimitable style, such as a fondness for dynamic contrasts. The whole is not entirely free from a certain coarseness typical of directorial debuts and from traces of Socialist Realist declamation, but wins over the spectator with its freshness--of execution, acting, photography and music. For the first time after the war Polish cinema showed the bravery and courage of ordinary young people, people who are sometimes hesitant and brittle but who reach maturity under the pressure of events--people who are tragic and yet not monumental.

SOUNDS FROM THE MOUNTAINS (Yama-no oto) Mikio Naruse

Script: Yoko Mizuki, from the novel by Yasunari Kawabata. Photography: Masao Tamai. Music: Ichiro Saito. Art Direction: Satoru Chuko. Cast: So Yamamura (Shingo Ogata), Teruko Nagaoka (Yasuko), Ken Uehara (Shuichi), Setsuko Hara (Kikuko), Chieko Nakakita (Fusako Aihara), Fumiko Saito (Fumiko), Yoko Sugi (Eiko Tanizaki), Rieko Sumi (Kinuko), Yatsuko Tanami (Ikeda).

Toho, Japan. 8471 ft., 94 mins.

Naruse's best-known prewar picture Wife, Be Like a Rose was a beautiful tale about the discovery of the wisdom of life by a young girl who lives with her poetess mother. The film was pervaded by the mood known as shikata ga nai--of placid resignation in the face of emotional crisis. The common theme of Repast, Mother, Sounds from the Mountains and Floating Clouds, Naruse's best pictures of the 50's, was the traditional Japanese family system and its effect on women--sometimes a woman who decides to assert her worth and aspirations (as in Repast), but most often a woman unable to break the ties of convention.

So it is in Sounds from the Mountains. The husband no longer loves his wife and has taken a mistress. The wife is pregnant, but wants an abortion, repelled by the idea of bearing a child to a man who does not love her. On the other hand the mistress very much desires a child. The wife develops a mutual understanding with her husband's parents, who feel more attached to her than to their own daughter (the motif which appeared in Ozu's Tokyo Story). It is their kindness, particularly the father's, which makes it possible for her to stay on in the household.

Whatever the outcome of his heroines' plight, Naruse's treatment of them is always sensitive and sympathetic. So it is in Sounds from the Mountains, where the director gives a number of detailed character studies and, using frequent close-ups, conveys people's innermost emotions. It is precisely this ability which made him very highly respected in Japan.

STREET WITHOUT SUN (Taiyō-no-nai machi) Satsuo Yamamoto

Script: Saburo Tatsuno, from the novel by Sunao Tokunaga. Photography: Minoru Maeda. Music: Nobuo Iida. Art Direction: Kazuo Kubo. Cast: Sumiko Hidaka (Takae Haruki), Michiko Katsura (Kayo), Kenji Susukita (Takae's father), Yasumi Hara (Miyaji), Kan Nihonyanagi (Hagimura), Osamu Takizawa (Okawa, president of the company).

Shinsei Eiga, Japan. 12,585 ft., 140 mins.

The year 1928: a great strike of Tokyo printers, one of the final episodes in the tug-of-war between the Japanese left and the big capital; the struggle which ended in the takeover of power by the military. The events, described in a 1930 novel are turned on the screen into an epic social fresco, modeled largely after the Soviet classics by Eisenstein and Pudovkin. The wide panorama of living conditions in the slums, a sober characterization of people on both sides of the barricade, dynamism and emphatic imagery come to a climax in the final scene in which a banner is passed from hand to hand in the crowd and crosses a cordon of police. The execution and acting in Street Without Sun are a little lacking in smoothness, but this fault seems secondary when considered from the perspective of the reliable description and intensive cinematic conveyance, which carry a topical message, sustaining the faith in the rightness of social struggle despite temporary setbacks. Street Without Sun is the last noteworthy product of the independent Japanese cinema which, in the mid-50's, had the ground cut from under its feet. This was brought about by financial difficulties precipitated by the repetitive Socialist Realist themes; by the beginning of the economic boom in Japan which considerably relieved social tensions; and finally by the onset of the domination of the market by six big companies: Shochiku, Toho, Daiei, Shintoho, Toei and Nikkatsu.

STORIES OF POOR LOVERS (Cronache di poveri amanti) Carlo Lizzani

Script: Sergio Amidei, Giuseppe Dagnino, Lizzani and Massimo Mida, based on the novel by Vasco Pratolini. Photography: Gianni Di Venanzo. Music: Mario Zafred. Art Direction: G. Avolio Pek. Cast: Anna Maria Ferrero (Gesuina), Antonella Lualdi (Milena), Cosetta Greco (Elisa), Marcello Mastroianni (Ugo), Giuliano Montaldo (Alfredo), Adolfo Consolini (Maciste), Wanda Capodaglio (Signora), Gabriele Tinti (Mario), Eva Vanicek (Bianca), Bruno Berellini (Carlino), Irene Cefaro (Clara).

Cooperativa Spettatori Produttori Cinematografici, Italy. 102 mins.

Italy in 1925: having consolidated its grip over the country, Fascism ensnares the lower middle classes and the urban proletariat. Stories of Poor Lovers depicts the conflict between Right and Left and reflects the spirit, the uncertainties and social changes of the period in the lives of the inhabitants of Via del Corno, an alley in Florence, with their troubles in love and politics.

This film version of Vasco Pratolini's complex, semi-annalistic novel was made by Lizzani--a critic, film historian and director with consistent views about the social and political importance of the cinema and a close collaborator of Vergano and De Santis. The literary original was very difficult to adapt for the screen not only because of its complexity, but also because of the profusion of dialogues and Pratolini's typically subtle psychological analysis. And yet Lizzani did not resort to cinematic effects as a recompense; as a matter of fact the severity of his film-making at the time would not permit that. Instead he went for precise description of characters and behavior, intimate quality of the acting, functional designs, fidelity of situations, simple film-making relying on long takes and muted photography. The much-stressed greyness of mood, further amplified by the music, finds a lot in common with Zurlini's future Cronaca familiare and helps to convey very faithfully the feel of the period and the character of the prose in the literary original. Although the original's richness of detail is somewhat lost in Lizzani's film, and the dramatic construction may seem a little shapeless against the background of the structure-conscious cinema of the 50's, Stories of Poor Lovers is sociologically the most valuable work of late Neorealism.

THE CAINE MUTINY Edward Dmytryk

Script: Stanely Roberts, based on the novel by Herman Wouk. Additional Dialogues: Michael Blankfort. Photography: Franz F. Planer. Music: Max Steiner. Art Direction: Cary Odell. Editing: William A. Lyon and Henry Batista. Cast: Humphrey Bogart (Captain Queeg), José Ferrer (Lt. Barney Greenwald), Van Johnson (Lt. Steve Maryk), Fred MacMurray (Lt. Tom Keefer), Robert Francis (Ensign Willie Keith), May Wynn (May Wynn), Tom Tully (Captain DeVriess), E. G. Marshall (Lt.-Cdr. Challee), Arthur Franz (Lt. Paynter), Lee Marvin (Meatball), Warner Anderson (Captain Blakely), Claude Akins (Horrible), Katharine Warren (Mrs. Keith), Jerry Paris (Ensign Harding), Steve Brodie (Chief Budge), Todd Karns (Stilwell), Whit Bissell (Lt.-Cdr. Dickson), James Best (Lt. Jorgensen).

Stanley Kramer for Columbia, U.S.A. 11,195 ft., 124 mins. Technicolor.

Ensign Willie Keith, an idealistic young man, joins the crew of a destroyer-minesweeper U.S.S. "Caine." The ship is commanded by a weary Captain DeVriess, who is soon replaced by the disciplinarian Captain Queeg. The officers, including the conscientious Lieutenant Maryk and the intellectual Lieutenant Keefer, who is working on a novel, are disturbed by signs of instability in the captain's behavior. Queeg has a quaint habit of rolling in the palm of his hand a pair of steel balls; he is an eccentric, preoccupied with small details and basically unsure of himself. Worse--during action in the presence of the enemy he shows signs of panic. When some strawberries are missing from the officers' mess, Queeg's reaction is hysterical. Keefer tells Keith and Maryk that he suspects the captain of paranoia. During a typhoon, when Queeg's crazy commands put the ship in danger, Keefer persuades Maryk, the executive officer, to arrest the captain and to take over the bridge. After the storm Maryk has to stand trial as a mutineer. Psychologists pronounce the captain sane, and Keefer refuses to support Maryk from the witness-box. The case for the prosecution seems cast-iron. But during cross-examination the defense counsel manages to break Queeg's crust of normality and exposes him as a neurotic. Maryk is acquitted. Keith is sent to another ship--and finds it to be under the command of Captain DeVriess.

As Dmytryk was embarking on The Caine Mutiny, Wouk's Pulitizer Prize novel had already sold 3.5 million copies, and the play derived from it (concerned exclusively with the court martial) was also doing very well. The Navy objected to the planned film on the grounds that the book portrays the captain of a U.S. vessel as a coward. Scriptwriter Stanley Roberts countered this by suggesting that while Queeg may be sick, he is a good officer who fell victim to combat fatigue. The shifting of the emphasis worked: the project in the end received not only approval, but help from the Navy--just as did Zinnemann's From Here to Eternity from the Army. In both cases at the cost of commercial compromise: The Caine Mutiny is simply a piece of mild criticism of the conditions in the Navy, toned down by blaming much of the trouble squarely on Keefer, a liberal intellectual and latent left-winger.

It is not difficult to guess why the story attracted Dmytryk's attention: it involves a battle of characters, the captain is on the verge of mental illness, there are hints about psychoanalysis. Dmytryk was always keen on these things. The whole trouble is that, despite Kramer's participation as producer, the film is a compromise. Suffice it to say that it has been described as "a recruiting poster for the Navy"--and ends, appropriately, with roistering martial music played by a brass band. It is not that the novel was particularly liberal or even anti-Navy. But it was certainly ambiguous--as concerns motives, feelings, actions. Keefer (in whose part Fred MacMurray is seriously miscast) was in the novel an ambivalent figure; in the film he is a rogue whose obsessive distaste for service life is suggestive of a left-wing threat to American democracy. Dmytryk went for the spectacular element in the story. Civilian emotional complications, Keith's relationship with his domineering mother and girlfriend, the latter conducted in the romantic scenery of California mountains, divert attention from the main story. The direction is steady and conformist; the court's verdict, which was meant to provoke reflection, is overshadowed by the conventional happy end.

On the other hand, action scenes are handled very well. Keith is rather dull (but so he is in the book) and José Ferrer gives a fine performance as the counsel for the defense. Still, the main attraction of The Caine Mutiny is Humphrey Bogart's memorable Queeg--sad, sour, pathetic, a man whose weakness and tension are hidden under the martinet façade. A rather bizarre response to the film was somebody's idea to market sets of "Queeg-balls," advertised as a "suitable gift for your paranoiac friends."

TOUCHEZ PAS AU GRISBI Jacques Becker

Script: Becker, Maurice Griffe and Albert Simonin, from the novel by the latter. Photography: Pierre Montazel. Music: Jean Wiener. Art Direction: Jean d'Eaubonne. Editing: Marguerite Renoir. Cast: Jean Gabin (Max le Menteur), René Dary (Riton), Jeanne Moreau (Josy), Gaby Basset (Marinette), Dora Doll (Lola), Denise Clair (La Mère Bouche), Michel Jourdan (Marco), Daniel Cauchy (Fifi le Dingue), Jean Riveyre (Garçon Moderna), Paul Frankeur (Pierrot), Paul Oettly (Oscar), Delia Scala (Huguette), Marilyn

Bufferd (Betty), Lino Ventura (Angelo), Paul Barge (Eugène), Robert Le Fort (Client), Dominique Davray (Girl).

Del Duca Films (Paris)/Antares Film (Rome), France/Italy. 7740 ft., 86 mins.

After the memorable Casque d'or, a subtle love story set in the milieu of Parisian apaches at the turn of the century, Becker took an interest in a somewhat less stylish crime. A story of ferocious gang warfare related to Rififi and The Asphalt Jungle, Touchez pas au grisbi continues Becker's humanist interests. It is a tale of friendship between men and a reflection on the onset of old age.

The course of events is fairly familiar. Max and Riton, two gangsters, intend to retire. As the last professional project they steal gold bars worth 50 million old francs (then around $90,000) in a daring raid at Orly Airport. Riton inconsiderately confesses to his mistress Josy, who in turn tells her other lover, Angelo, a Montmartre drug dealer. To get hold of the gold Angelo decides to kidnap Riton and Max. While trying to revenge himself on Josy, Riton is indeed captured by the gang who then offer to exchange him for the loot. At the rendezvous outside Paris Angelo still tries to kill the two friends. After a chase and a fierce gun battle he and his gang die as the car with the loot bursts into flames. Empty-handed, Max and Riton flee before the police arrive, but Riton dies from his wounds.

This screen version of a série noire novel contains interesting descriptions of the curious etiquette and the code of honor of the gangster world and uses the underworld argot (already in the title which translates as "lay off the dough"). The gangsters speak quietly and address each other as "monsieur," while friendship is seen to be more important than money (in England the film was released under the title Honour Among Thieves). On the other hand Becker's meticulous description of the milieu makes it appear near-abstract in the final account.

As usual with the director, the film-making is of a high standard: the camerawork imaginative and the dialogues well-written, if a little too profuse. The musical motif, "the Max theme," became very popular. Of the actors, Jean Gabin as Max--avuncular, tough and romantic, with a weary, rugged charm is something of a French equivalent of the Godfather, while Jeanne Moreau, later a famous actress, appears in her first screen part as a treacherous night-club girl.

AN INN AT OSAKA (Osaka-no yado) Heinosuke Gosho

Script: Toshio Yasumi and Gosho, based on the novel by Takitaro Minakami. Script supervision: Mantaro Kubota. Photography: Joji Ohara. Music: Ikuma Dan. Art Direction: Takashi Matsuyama. Cast: Shuji Sano (Kyoichi Mita), Toshio Hosokawa (Tawara), Nobuko Ōtowa (Uwabami), Michiko Megumi (Kimiko Imoto), Mitsuko Mito (Orika), Hiroko Kawasaki (Otsugi), Sachiko Hidari (Oyone), Eiko Miyoshi (Landlady of the inn), Kamatari Fujiwara (Clerk of the inn), Haruo Tanaka (Manager of the branch office).

Shintoho, Japan. 10,935 ft., 122 mins.

Gosho followed Four Chimneys by another film about the small tragedies of ordinary individuals within industrial society. Although for once lacking the director's favorite device--a dominant visual symbol--An Inn at Osaka is a typical example of "Goshoism" with its blend of sentimentality, realism, humor, lyricism and a great feeling for the common man and his problems.

The year 1945: Osaka, the commercial center of Japan. Mita, a young employee of an insurance company, has been transferred from the Tokyo head office and is brought to a small inn at the outskirts of the city by the landlady's permanently drunk brother. The inn employs three maids: Otsugi, a 40-year-old widow who works to bring up her sons; Orika who is supporting her husband; and Oyone, a stray young girl. Mita does not like his work and often discusses things with his friend Tawara, who feels strongly about the ideals of justice and humanity. Mita falls in love with the young daughter of an office colleague, but loses the chance of seeing her when her father kills himself in the wake of a scandal within the company. Orika has descended to prostitution because of financial need; Tawara leaves. Nothing keeps Mita in Osaka any more, and he decides to take up an opportunity to return to Tokyo. He gives a farewell dinner for his friends and leaves in the morning.

As always Gosho impresses with his gift for a precise description of people and their environment, and as usual achieves this via a frequent use of close-ups and a great number (over 1000) of separate shots. Also the atmosphere of post-war Japan, dominated by uncertainty and greed, is suggestively created. The hero himself, the landlady and the employees of the inn, the geisha whom the hero meets at his friend's party and who falls in love with him--although none of them are particularly materialistic, their actions and desires are controlled by money. But it would be unusual for Gosho to offer a remedy in his deeply sad film--he simply describes. When Kinoshita portrayed the destructive effect of the war on society in A Japanese Tragedy, he did it in tones of stringent drama.

"One never knows what the future has in store" Gosho seems to be saying as his hero leaves at the end for a life which might--or might not--be more satisfying. Not a very original conclusion, but a deeply felt one, and conveyed with sincerity and power.

A STAR IS BORN George Cukor

Script: Moss Hart, based on the screenplay for William A. Wellman's film A Star Is Born (1937) by Dorothy Parker, Alan Campbell and Robert Carson, written from a screen story by Wellman and Carson, inspired by Adela Rogers St. John's screen story for Cukor's film What Price Hollywood (1932). Photography: Sam Leavitt. Music: Harold Arlen; also Leonard Gershe (song "Born in a Trunk"). Lyrics: of songs "The Man That Got Away," "Gotta Have Me Go with You," "It's a New World," "Here's What I'm Here For," "Someone at Last" and "Lose That Long Face" by Ira Gershwin; of the song "Born in a Trunk" by Leonard Gershe. Art Direction: Malcolm Bert; also Irene Sharaff ("Born in a Trunk"). Choreography: Richard Barstow. Editing: Folmar Blangsted. Cast: Judy Garland (Esther Blodgett), James Mason (Norman Maine), Charles Bickford (Oliver Niles), Jack Carson (Libby), Tom Noonan (Danny McGuire), Lucy Marlow (Lola Lavery), Amanda Blake (Susan Ettinger), Irving Bacon (Graves), Hazel Shermet (Libby's secretary), James Brown (Glenn Williams), Lotus Robb (Miss Markham).

Sidney Luft--Vern Alves for Transcona Enterprises, U. S. A. 181 mins. CinemaScope. Technicolor.

Hollywood looks at itself: A Star Is Born tells the story of the meteoric movie career of a certain girl singer. Esther Blodgett's run of luck begins when she comes across Norman Maine, a celebrated film actor who is also a hopeless alcoholic. He hears her sing, decides she has star potential, finds her a minor part in a film and marries her. Her first starring part (under the new name of Vicki Lester) proves a sensational success. From then on her career develops at the expense of that of her husband whom she soon overtakes in the popularity stakes. The husband falls into depressive melancholy, drinks more and more, drunkenly interrupts his wife's Oscar-award ceremony with a pathetic, halting speech, and then walks into the sea out of shame and bitterness.

A dramatic landscape of the acting market within a huge film industry, albeit with its sharpest edges smoothed, A Star Is Born tells a lot of truth while containing obvious situational exaggerations. Although in his remake of Wellman's then-courageous 1937 movie (again remade in 1977 with Barbra Streisand and Kris Kristofferson in the main parts) Cukor does not penetrate deeper than did the earlier version, but perfects the theme via highly efficient film-making. This involves brisk camera movement, sharp cutting, impressive lighting effects (a spotlight on a single figure against a dark background) and very good handling of the CinemaScope screen. The great role of Judy Garland, who returned to the movies after several years' absence and appears in a team with James Mason, is a big contribution to the success of the whole.

1955

IL BIDONE Federico Fellini

Script: Fellini, Ennio Flaiano and Tullio Pinelli. Photography: Otello Martelli. Music: Nino Rota. Art Direction: Dario Cecchi. Editing: Mario Serandrei and Giuseppe Vari. Cast: Broderick Crawford (Augusto), Richard Basehart (Picasso), Franco Fabrizi (Roberto), Giulietta Masina (Iris, Picasso's wife), Lorella De Luca (Patrizia, Augusto's daughter), Giacomo Gabrielli (Vargas), Alberto De Amicis (Rinaldo, the drug dealer who hosts the New Year party), Xenia Valderi (Luciana, Rinaldo's girl), Sue Ellen Blake (Susanna, the crippled girl), Irene Cefaro (Marisa, a girl at the party), Mara Werlen (Maggie), Maria Zanolli (Stella Fiorina, a woman who gets swindled), Ettore Bevilaqua (Bevilaqua, man who gets swindled at the housing project).

Goffredo Lombardo for Titanus/S. G. C., Italy/France. 9842 ft., 109 mins.

Fellini continues his meditations about relationships between people: the main theme of La strada was a simple girl's search for the sense of existence; Il bidone (the Italian slang word for "swindler") is a film about mutual understanding. To Fellini people are separated from each other by near-astronomical distances; while living side by side they remain unaware of their own loneliness and do not enter into genuine relationships despite needing each other so much.

Augusto, a weary and cynical crook, has only himself to blame for his loneliness; about to enter the wilderness of old age, he feverishly searches for human warmth. With his two confederates,

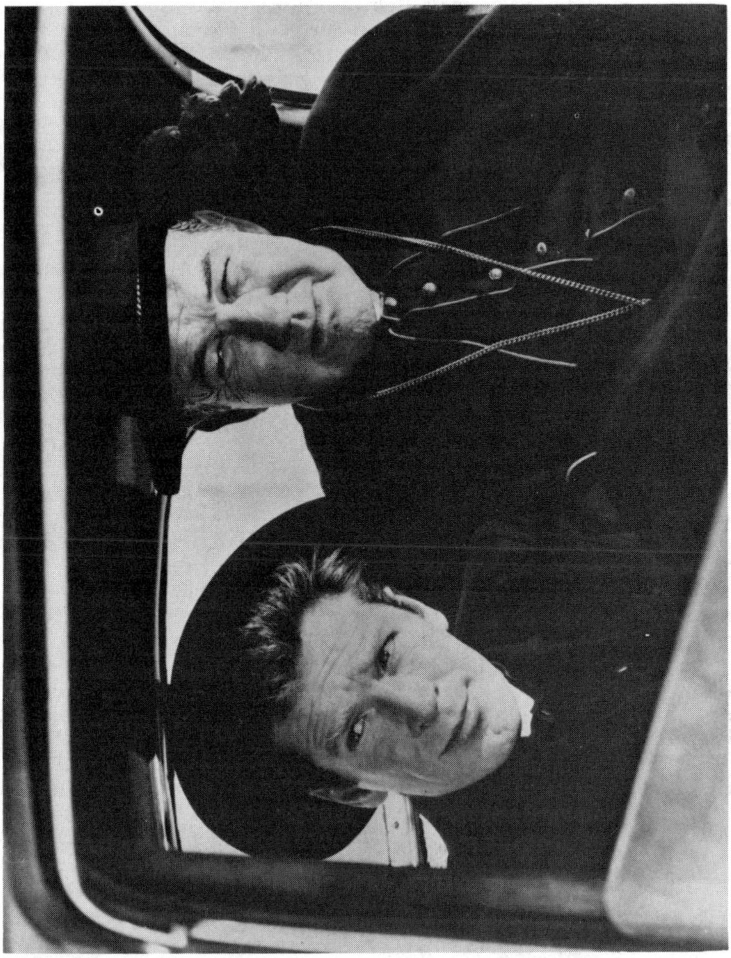

Il bidone

Picasso, a youngster who dreams of being an artist and Roberto, a weak-willed and opportunist con-man, Augusto makes a living by exploiting the poor and gullible. Disguised as priests they trick two peasant women with a story of buried treasure; later they impersonate representatives of a town council and collect deposits on imaginary flats from poor slum-dwellers. Augusto attempts to establish a contact with his teenage daughter Patrizia who intends to be a teacher. When this ends disastrously with his being arrested for some past crime in Patrizia's presence, when both his accomplices quit, Augusto attempts another "buried treasure" fraud with a new gang. Disguised as a priest he is asked to bless a crippled peasant child whose tragedy moves his soul, softened by the anxiety for the future. He tells his accomplices that he refused to take the money from the child's parents (he intends to keep it for Patrizia); they discover Augusto's deception, take the money, stone him and leave him to die on the roadside in the mountains. In agony, he manages to crawl to the road and whispers after a passing group of happy peasants: "Wait, I'm coming with you."

Il bidone is the least coherent internally of Fellini's great films: on the one hand it captivates with its poetry and humanism, on the other it repels with its ration of deplorably literal melodramatic situations and the moral which slips out from under the director's hand despite, as it were, his striving to achieve ambivalence of the situations. This latter circumstance would probably have ended in artistic defeat, were it not for the conceptual indecision, which results precisely in the complexity of the film's ethical context--in the Augusto character and, even more, in Picasso's. Fellini planned a picaresque story much less dramatic in tone than the final result; it appears that during the shooting of the slum episode he met with such depressing cases of human greed and predation that this prompted him to alter the relationship between the crooks and their victims in Il bidone. The picture grew to over 15,000 feet in length and Fellini shortened it very considerably before release--thus the incoherent editing, but also the reflection-inspiring diversity of its meaning, the mixing together of superficial and of brilliant episodes. To the latter belongs the symbolic expedition in cassocks for the "buried treasure"--a scene far from verbatim in its complex overtones. It is thanks to such fragments that Il bidone manages to avoid the dangers of becoming a glib lesson and becomes a moving probe into the motivation of people in search of support and human warmth, a picture which contains more spiritual restlessness and tragic poetry of loneliness than is found elsewhere in Fellini's work.

LES GRANDES MANOEUVRES René Clair

Script: Clair; also Jérôme Gérônimi and Jean Marsan. Photography: Robert Le Fèbvre and Robert Juillard. Music: Georges Van Parys.

Art Direction: Léon Barsacq. Costumes: Rosine Delamare. Editing: Louise Hautecoeur. Cast: Gérard Philipe (Lieutenant Armand de la Verne), Michèle Morgan (Marie-Louise Rivière), Brigitte Bardot (Lucie), Yves Robert (Félix), Jean Desailly (Victor Duverger), Jacqueline Maillan (Juliette Duverger), Pierre Dux (Colonel), Jacques François (Rudolph), Magali Noël (Thérèse), Simone Valère (Gisèle), Catherine Anouilh (Alice), Jacques Fabbri (Armand's batman), Raymond Cordy (Photographer), Oliver Hussenot (Prefect).

Filmsonor/Rizzoli, France/Italy. 9916 ft., 110 mins. Eastman Colour.

Do not play with love: as usual, René Clair returns to this number one theme of the French cinema, but this time approaches it in a serious vein. Of course, one cannot imagine the maker of The Italian Straw Hat as making do without a little humor. But the humor is here subdued, impressionistic, served on the occasion of momentary observations of the background and in the marginal situations--while the tone of the main story is quite serious, similar to the plays of Marivaux. The style of Les Grandes manoeuvres is pervaded by autumnal lyricism, and the finale of this "dramatic comedy" (to use Clair's own words) was even meant to be tragic; it is not such because of its excessive finesse. Exactly: Les Grandes manoeuvres, one of Clair's two last great films, is the first of all works in which the director opted for simplicity. Not simplicity of execution, for the film's dramatic structure and the mise en scène are very elaborate indeed--but the simplicity of human behavior. After the highly refined and structurally most complex (if somewhat abstract) Les Belles de nuit, Clair returns to the psychological naturalness of Quatorze Juillet and Sous les toits de Paris. The scenery is a small garrison town before the First World War. Armand, a handsome cavalry lieutenant and a notorious Don Juan, engages in a bet to seduce, during the month before the regiment leaves on maneuvers, the first woman whose name is drawn out of a hat. At first luck is on his side: the winner is a beautiful divorced Parisienne, Marie-Louise, who runs a millinery shop in the town's main street. But soon Armand becomes victim of his own game: he falls in love with her. Then Marie-Louise learns about the bet. When the whole town watches the dragoons ride out on maneuvers, the windows of her shop remain closed.

Les Grandes manoeuvres, Clair's first color movie, is one of the finest examples of creative use of color in the cinema of the 50's. The color compositions, using one or two clear dominant hues with virtual elimination of others, play an important dramatic role; in perfect agreement with the film's mood, these gentle tones of amber, light-blue, lilac and white are at once poetic and allegorical. The protagonists of Porte des Lilas, Clair's next picture, will once again be ordinary people from the suburbs of Paris. The circle is thus closed, and what might have seemed the beginning of a new period of Clair's work turned out to be nothing of the sort. Porte des Lilas, which followed, was in fact the director's last outstanding film.

Les Grandes manoeuvres

NEW TALES OF THE TAIRA CLAN (Shin Heike Monogatari) Kenji Mizoguchi

---

Script: Yoshikata Yoda, Masashige Narusawa and Kyuichi Tsuji, from the serial published in the magazine "Shukan Asahi" by Eiji Yoshikawa, itself drawn from the 13th-century text "Heike Monogatari." Photography: Kazuo Miyagawa. Music: Fumio Hayasaka and Masaru Sato. Art Direction: Hiroshi Mizutani. Cast: Raizo Ichikawa (Kiyomori Taira), Ichijiro Oya (Tadamori Taira, Kiyomori's father), Michiyo Kogure (Yasuko, Kiyomori's mother), Eijiro Yanagi (Ex-Emperor Shirakawa), Tatsuya Ishiguro (Tokinobu Fujiwara), Yoshiko Kuga (Tokiko, his daughter), Naritoshi Hayashi (Tokitada Fujiwara), Misusaburo Ramon (Ryokan), Eitaro Shindo (Banboku), Ichiro Sugai (Worker), Koreya Senda (Yorinaga), Kunitaro Sawamura (Joku), Shunji Natsumi (Emperor Toba), Tamao Nakamura (Shigeko).

Daiei, Japan. 9669 ft., 107 mins. Eastman Colour.

The 12th century was a time of sharp internal conflict in Japan. Much of the land was then in the hands of nobles and powerful temples and was exempted from tax, while the rising samurai class challenged these privileges and demanded that its own aspirations be satisfied. The Emperor's authority was damaged as a result; anxious to put an end to the turmoil in the country, the ex-Emperor decided to return from retirement and to intervene. There were then two courts in Japan, the second being the ex-Emperor's Cloister Court. This turbulent period is vividly described in Mizoguchi's New Tales of the Taira Clan, an epic story of honor and justice.

The year 1137. Tadamori Taira, the leader of the Taira Clan, and his son, Kiyomori, return victorious from a war against pirates. On the advice of his courtiers who are determined to keep the samurai down, the ex-Emperor does not reward the Tairas for the victory, although they fought at his express orders. Kiyomori learns that his mother was once the favorite of an emperor and that his father was commanded to marry her when she became pregnant. Kiyomori's father might have been the Emperor or an unknown monk seen leaving her room one night. Tadamori dies, humiliated by the courtiers and stripped of his newly-acquired peerage, just as the army of soldier-monks march on Kyoto to force the Emperor to follow their wishes. When his mother finally shows him a definite proof that he is the Emperor's son, Kiyomori, now the head of the Taira clan, rejects the evidence of his high birth and insists on being regarded as Tadamori's son. He decides to fulfill his duty to the clan. The soldier-monks carry holy palanquins (supposed to enshrine the souls of previous emperors) for protection. An arrow from Kiyomori's bow pierces a palanquin and the monks flee in panic. The young man vows on his father's grave to continue

New Tales of the Taira Clan

the fight against the nobility and the clergy and to uphold the rights of his own class. Passing a lord's garden party he comments: "Dance, lords, dance--for your end is near."

Mizoguchi very well balances and blends the film's several interests: the portrayal of a political struggle, the court intrigues and the emergence of the samurai class; Kiyomori's search for his true parentage, the awakening of his class consciousness, the relationship to his parents and the love of the beautiful daughter of a kinsman.

This aesthetically thrilling film is Mizoguchi's second (and last) work in color, following The Empress Yang Kwei-Fei made earlier the same year. Kazuo Miyagawa, the great cameraman (who photographed among others Rashomon, The Tale of Genji, Ugetsu Monogatari and Sansho the Bailiff) uses long, sweeping crane shots and the deep-focus technique to create many splendid images. The scene in which the warriors of the Hiei Temple answer their summons and journey across the forest carrying burning torches is among the most striking. The opening images in the market place, of the Tairas' return from the war and the crowds scattered by a procession of arrogant monks; the sequence of the Spring Festival--instantly and vividly recreate the period and have the feel of the meticulously accurate canvas of a realist painter. Appropriately for the type of story, the colors are warm and dominated by yellow and red; quite different from the rich, saturated compositions of the somber The Empress Yang Kwei-Fei. Mood is created with color, type of movement and quality of sound: the stillness of the court scenes, the bizarre attire of the courtiers are suggestive of treachery and intrigue, while the sensuous sound of rustling silk gowns is associated with Kiyomori's beautiful mother.

It is a pity that Mizoguchi was not to give further expression to his gift as a colorist. He died in 1956 and only completed one further work, Street of Shame, in black-and-white.

RICHARD III Laurence Olivier

Script: Alan Dent, from the play "The Tragedy of King Richard III" by William Shakespeare. Photography: Otto Heller. Music: William Walton. Art Direction: Carmen Dillon. Production Design: Roger Furse. Editing: Helga Cranston. Cast: Laurence Olivier (King Richard III), John Gielgud (Duke of Clarence), Ralph Richardson (Duke of Buckingham), Cedric Hardwicke (King Edward IV), Mary Kerridge (Queen Elizabeth), Claire Bloom (Lady Anne), Pamela Brown (Jane Shore), Alec Clunes (Lord Hastings), Michael Gough (Dighton), Stanley Baker (Henry Tudor, the Earl of Richmond), Norman Woolland (Sir William Catesby), Helen Haye (Duchess of York),

Patrick Troughton (Sir James Tyrrell), Clive Morton (Earl Rivers), Andrew Cruickshank (Sir Robert Brakenbury), Nicholas Hannen (Archbishop of Canterbury), Paul Huson (Prince of Wales).

Laurence Olivier for London Films, G. B. 14,530 ft., 161 mins. VistaVision. Technicolor.

This is Olivier's third screen version of a play by Shakespeare, after Henry V and Hamlet. Let us say at once that Shakespeare's ideas about Richard III are to say the least historically incorrect. The murder of the little princes in the Tower remains the classic unsolved crime of the centuries, and it has been suggested that the crimes were committed at the behest of the Duke of Buckingham.

Richard III, which opens with what is actually the last scene of "Henry VI, Part Three," signifies in a way a return to the formula of Henry V: the film starts from a theatrical convention and departs from it gradually. Only this time there is no return to the theatre at the end. It is a "straight" and very direct adaptation, in sharp contrast to the ostentatiously cinematic Hamlet--and considered by many not only more successful but even the best Shakespearean film up till that time. Yet the adaptation is cinematically no less effective. Richard's soliloquy ("Now is the winter of our discontent ... ") spoken straight into the camera and shot with remarkable agility in a single take, is actually very cinematic--although there is no attempt at all to disguise the theatrical provenience of the monologue, as in Hamlet. On the other hand, the battle of Bosworth is not very imaginatively done and rather insubstantial. But the final slaying of the king is shattering: like an enraged animal, he fights with savage defiance.

The title role is one of only two parts, the other being Archie Rice in The Entertainer (1960), which Olivier played to his satisfaction. Indeed, this adaptation to the screen of his stage performance is probably his finest achievement as an actor: a vision of a tragic monster who speaks in a rasping, halting voice and slinks along like a black spider. Among the fine scenes is Richard's wooing of Lady Anne over the coffin of her husband, which introduces a further dimension, of sexual motivation: Anne is against her will attracted to the man whom she despises, and her attitude within the scene changes from loathing to yielding fascination. There is also the curious moment before the battle as the king bends over the horse, looks straight into the camera and says with a sinister smile: "Richard's himself again"--a chilling interlude added to the text.

A further asset of Richard III is its splendid visuality, with the images stylized after the Gothic. It is the first time such excellent visual balance has been achieved in CinemaScope; East of Eden, made a few months earlier, was an example of a dynamic frame, while the images of Richard III are splendidly static. The color itself is a little uneven, but only the excessively ironic music is a serious fault. William Walton, an outstanding composer, misunderstood the nature of the subject. The music is too enthusiastic--and too literal. As the king writhes in agony, the music is precisely synchronized to his movements.

FLOATING CLOUDS (Ukigumo) Mikio Naruse

Script: Yoko Mizuki, from the novel by Fumiko Hayashi. Photography: Masao Tamai. Music: Ichiro Saito. Art Direction: Satoru Chuko. Cast: Hideko Takamine (Yukiko Koda), Masayuki Mori (Kenkichi Tomioka), Chieko Nakakita (Kuniko Tomioka), Isao Yamagata (Sugio Iba), Daisuke Kato (Sekichi Mukai), Mariko Okada (Osei Mukai), Akira Sera (Kinsaku Ohta).

Toho, Japan. 11,112 ft., 123 mins.

A significant proportion of Japanese critics consider Floating Clouds Naruse's best film. Some go as far as to call it the finest achievement in the whole of the Japanese cinema. Why so much enthusiasm for a psychological love story which, it is true, was made with subtlety and refinement and steeped in melancholy poetry, but which is in the end rather uncomplicated? Floating Clouds seems to condense and reflect exceptionally correctly the traditional Japanese scale of feelings. A young girl and a married man meet in Indonesia during the war; later they continue to meet in the destroyed Tokyo. Alienated from society and living in disregard of accepted norms, they become increasingly engulfed in their own lives. Finally the girl dies on a small island to which they have run away. It is only then that the man realizes the true sense of their relationship--who she was to him and what she was expecting from him with such patience. In one of the most beautiful scenes in the cinema of feelings the hero approaches the bier and very slowly paints the face of his dead mistress--to make her look as young and spring-like as she always wanted to. It is only then that the story of love passes into the past tense, that it acquires full radiance in the eyes of the hero: such is the characteristically Japanese understanding of subtle hues of beauty, made deeper still in the medium of the cinema.

This romantic attitude towards the past is very strong in Japan and stems to a considerable degree from fear of the future and the disasters one will have to accept with stoicism. The very, very long feudal period during which freedom and the dignity of the individual were being oppressed contributed to the philosophy of the Japanese a sense of uncertainty (and also the fear of rebellion born of despair which leads to the madness of fanaticism). In such circumstances the sense of ownership of what was beautiful and has already been experienced was doubly valuable. Hence such wide scope of spiritual life in Japan; hence also the abandonment of the temporal for the sake of dreams--a central emotion of Floating Clouds, and one for which the film is so highly valued at home. As the Japanese see it, this alienation from the present is the prerogative of the poets who abandon the safety of the ordinary for the freedom of inner fantasy, who exchange the restraints of run-of-the-mill existence for poverty and lonely pilgrimage through unknown worlds. Both the hero and the heroine of Floating Clouds exercise this poetic choice, though each does it differently: for the man it means a system of separate spiritual and material domains, the dualism between the memories of the past and the unreal surrogate of the present, between the wife and the mistress; for the girl it means throwing herself into a relationship which is a form of escape from reality, but in which men and women have very different rights, as Naruse so often and so perceptively underlines in his films. Men--capricious, weak-willed and unworthy of the feelings offered to them--are still loved by their women, who serve them, who become sexually attached to them in spite of being aware of their situation. The maker of Mother, whose difficult childhood and youth without a doubt contributed to the pessimism of his philosophy of life, never tried to suggest new solutions to these ever-present dilemmas: his films are simply tragic statements of fact. They are an invaluable testimony to the way these problems are traditionally seen in Japan; enriched by poetic intimacy and an absolute harmony of means of expression, his films can be, as is Floating Clouds, among the most interesting in the Japanese cinema.

THE HEART (Kokoro) Kon Ichikawa

Script: Katsundo Inomata and Keiji Hasebe, from the novel by Soseki Natsume. Photography: Takeo Ito. Music: Yasushi Akutagawa. Art Direction: Kazumi Koike. Cast: Masayuki Mori (Nobuchi), Michiyo Aratama (Nobuchi's wife), Shoji Yasui (Hioki), Tatsuya Mihashi (Kaji), Akiko Tamura (Nobuchi's wife's mother).

Masayuki Takagi for Nikkatsu, Japan. 10,935 ft., 122 mins.

The reign of Emperor Meiji (1868-1912) witnessed the emergence of Japan as a modern industrial nation. The emperor's death was not only the close of an era, but a profound cultural shock comparable to that caused in England by the death of Queen Victoria in 1901. It was the end of a generation.

The Heart opens on April 12, 1912. Nobuchi has been married for many years but has no children. While out swimming he meets and befriends a young student. They go for long walks during which they discuss different things. Nobuchi is deeply affected by the emperor's death the following July and decides to commit suicide. He writes a letter to the student in which he reveals his secret.

When young, he and his friend Kaji lived at the house of the mother of Nobuchi's present wife. Nobuchi destroyed their friendship by proposing to the girl in secret from his friend who was also in love with her. Kaji killed himself in despair and Nobuchi spent the rest of his life in remorse. On receiving the letter the student hurries back to Tokyo but Nobuchi is already dead.

During the 50's Kon Ichikawa emerged as a major Japanese film-maker. Born in 1915, he worked in turn in the four big film companies in Japan. His first film as director, made in 1946, was banned by the occupation forces. Ichikawa works fast (The Heart is his 28th film) and always with excellent cameramen. He is a perceptive observer of the lower registers of human mood and his sensitivity enables him to discover poetry in every situation. He does so in this melancholy story of a man whose life was ruined by a foible of youth, and who finds it impossible to justify his past selfishness. Nobuchi is a typical Ichikawa hero: lonely, thoughtful and contemplative. Such would be the protagonists of The Burmese Harp and Fires on the Plain. But The Heart does not include the horrors of those pictures. The style--subdued, restrained but elegant--is well exemplified in the memorable sequence of the emperor's burial. The elaborate time structure of the picture is based on flashbacks. Nobuchi is played, with distinction, by Masayuki Mori who three years earlier gave a memorable (and spiritually similar) performance as Kameda in Kurosawa's The Idiot. He was also the proud samurai in Rashomon and the potter in Ugetsu Monogatari.

NIGHT OF THE HUNTER Charles Laughton

Script: James Agee, from the novel "The Night of the Hunter" by Davis Grubb. Photography: Stanley Cortez. Music: Walter Schumann. Art Direction: Hilyard Brown. Editing: Robert Golden. Cast: Robert Mitchum (Preacher Harry Powell), Shelley Winters (Willa Harper), Billy Chapin (John Harper), Sally Jane Bruce (Pearl Harper, John's sister), Lillian Gish (Rachel Hooper), Evelyn Varden (Icey Spoon), Peter Graves (Ben Harper), James Gleason (Uncle Birdie), Don Beddoe (Walt Spoon), Gloria Castillo (Ruby), Mary Ellen Clemons (Clary), Cheryl Callaway (Mary).

Paul Gregory, U.S.A. 93 mins.

A certified cult movie, Night of the Hunter is the only film directed by Charles Laughton, the famous actor. Fascinated by the uncanny mood of Davis Grubb's novel, Laughton turned James Agee's last film script into a picture as personal as it is original. Night of the Hunter is simply the cinema's nearest equivalent of an E. T. A. Hoffmann fairytale.

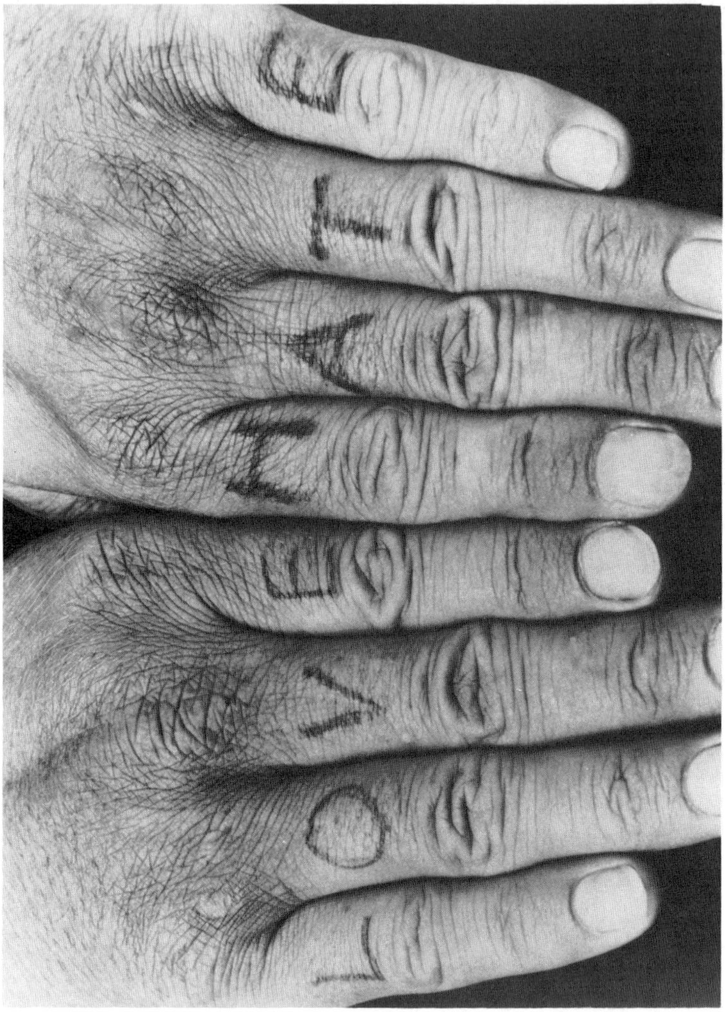

Night of the Hunter

The 30's Depression. Just before the police arrive to arrest him for robbery and murder, Ben Harper tells his two young children, John and Pearl, that he has hidden the stolen $10,000 inside Pearl's doll. While awaiting execution Harper meets Preacher Powell, a psychopath who kills rich women and dedicates the proceeds to furtherance of the Lord's glory. Powell, who is in prison for a minor offense, fails to learn where Harper has hidden the loot. Soon released, he marries Harper's widow, promptly murders her and pleads with the children to tell him the whereabouts of the money, threatening to kill them if they refuse. John and Pearl flee down the river in a boat and find refuge in the house of Miss Rachel, a good old lady who looks after a group of abandoned children. She bravely protects John and Pearl from the Preacher's pursuit. Powell is finally arrested for murder, and the children remain with the good lady.

With the help of the remarkable camerawork by Stanley Cortez (who had photographed, among others, Welles's The Magnificent Ambersons) Laughton created a strange symbolic and timeless parable about the inseparability of the good and evil elements in human nature. The theme is expounded in Powell's remarkable monologue-sermon about the struggle of love and hate. The two words are tattooed on the fingers of either hand and Powell rubs his hands against each other. Sinister and prophetic, the scene evokes, albeit in a diametrically different mood, Chaplin's famous mimed sermon about David and Goliath in The Pilgrim.

To describe Night of the Hunter as an atmospheric picture would be a serious understatement. It is a curious review of moods and cinematic styles: from the Expressionistic imagery of the interior scenes (particularly the scenes in which Powell questions the children, reminiscent of Warning Shadows) which use sharp lighting, unusual camera angles and enormous shadows on the walls; Impressionistic (for instance in the marvellous image of the murdered Willa in a sunken car); idyllic and lyrical (the children's flight down the river); to fable-like (the nursery rhyme told by Miss Rachel). In accordance with the film's title, most scenes are shot at night. Remarkable also is the ease with which Laughton generates the ominous mood of impending horror. Of course, being a distinguished member of the acting profession himself, he knew how to choose and direct the actors. Robert Mitchum, so far considered second-rate, gives in Night of the Hunter his best performance ever. Well-spoken, oddly intense, sinister, his Preacher Powell is identified with the blood-chilling hymn which forms the picture's ironic refrain:

> Leaning, leaning! Safe and secure from all alarms!
> Leaning, leaning! Leaning on the everlasting arms!

Lillian Gish who had appeared in the classic The Birth of a Nation precisely forty years earlier plays the eccentric spinster; Shelley Winters is good as the silly Willa and Evelyn Varden gives a nice character part as an inquisitive neighbor.

RIFIFI (Du Rififi chez les hommes) Jules Dassin

Script: René Wheeler, Dassin and Auguste le Breton, from the novel by the latter. Photography: Philippe Agostini. Music: Georges Auric. Art Direction: Auguste Capelier. Editing: Roger Dwyre. Cast: Jean Servais (Tony le Stéphanois), Karl Möhner (Jo le Suédois), Robert Manuel (Mario), Jules Dassin (César), Magali Noël (Viviane), Marie Sabouret (Mado), Marcel Lupovici (Pierre), Robert Hossein (Remi), Janine Darcy (Louise), Pierre Grasset (Louis), Dominique Maurin (Tonio), Claude Sylvain (Ida).

Indus Films/Pathé/Prima-Film, France. Originally 10,530 ft., 117 mins., after several cuts reduced to 9917 ft., 110 mins.

A brilliantly made and commercially very successful gangster drama, Rififi is in fact the best film of its kind made in the 50's. Four burglars break through the ceiling into an expensive jewelry shop in Rue de Rivoli in Paris, ingeniously immobilize the alarm mechanism, rob the safe and escape with fabulous loot. Their undoing comes not from the police but from the underworld. It is caused by the carelessness of one of the burglars who gave a stolen ring to a girl. He pays with his life for this mistake; death also claims his companions. In an attempt to get hold of the loot, the rival gang kidnap a little boy and plan to hold him for ransom. One of the robbers liquidates the rival gang and frees the child, but is himself mortally wounded.

Thus evil destroys itself; but evil in Rififi is not one-dimensional. Dassin, who as a result of running into trouble with the House Un-American Activities Committee had to leave the U. S. A. for many years, did not leave his social and psychological interests behind. Apart from directing and co-scripting the picture he also appears as César, a traitor, under the assumed name of Perlo Vita. The story develops against the background of a painstakingly shown underworld, whose members are not idols who enjoy an easy and comfortable life, but hard-working professionals.

The highlight of Rififi is the 35-minute-long robbery sequence. An umbrella is pushed through a hole in the ceiling and opened to catch the rubble while the hole is widened; dense liquid is applied from a fire extinguisher to silence the alarm bell; the safe is opened like a tin of sardines. This scene started the long period of the vogue for precise description on the screen of clever super-robberies. Although, chronologically, priority in de-mythologizing the gangster underworld belongs to Huston's The Asphalt Jungle, it was Dassin in Rififi who demonstrated how powerful a tool the screen can be for the meticulous observation of the actions of people who play for very high stakes. The captivating robbery scene is shot in complete silence, with no dialogue and no music. Dassin several times suspends the action thereby increasing the dramatic tension. The sound effects are also brilliantly handled; take for instance the suggestive onomatopoeic sound-track in the remarkable scene preceding the robbery. Worth mentioning also are the energetic editing, the disturbing music and the clever, if rather unexpected, comic interludes. Jean Servais's part is probably the most interesting in this actor's long screen career.

PATHER PANCHALI Satyajit Ray

Script: Ray, based on the novel by Bibhutibhusan Bandopadhaya (1934). Photography: Subrata Mitra. Music: Ravi Shankar. Art Direction: Banshi Chandra Gupta. Cast: Kanu Bannerji (Harihar, the father), Karuna Bannerji (Sarbojaya, the mother), Uma Das Gupta (Durga, the daughter), Subir Bannerji (Apu), Chunibala Devi (Indirtharkun, the old aunt), Runhi Bannerji (Durga as a child), Tulshi Chakravarty (Village teacher).

Hiten Chaudhury/West Bengal Government, India. 10,289 ft., 114 mins. Originally 125 mins.

It is difficult to think of a country whose cinema industry would have reached a deeper abyss of facile commercialism than India. The enormous Indian film production consists mostly of weepy melodramas, whose primitive plots are periodically interrupted by unexplainable dancing interludes. Virtually the sole exception is the work of Satyajit Ray, whose name became synonymous with art cinema in his country. Ray obliquely defines his position vis-à-vis the rest of the Indian cinema in the scene in The World of Apu, in which the protagonist takes his wife to see a ridiculous film, complete with magic and absurd trick effects.

The son of a writer, painter and photographer, Ray is a graduate of Calcutta University. He studied graphic art under Rabindranath Tagore, the Nobel Prize winning Bengali writer and philosopher, to whom he later devoted a documentary. When working for the Calcutta branch of a London advertising agency Ray became fascinated by a book for which he was designing a jacket. It was "Pather Panchali," the starting material for his first film, which caused much stir in the West where Indian cinema was so far completely unknown. Pather Panchali is the first part of what became known as the Apu Trilogy.

Ray's cinema is firmly rooted in the narrative, and this is a simple story of country life. The plot is a succession of ordinary events in a poor village on the verge of the jungle, where a little boy discovers the world as his parents struggle to eke out an existence. Apu's father, Harihar, is a clerk who dreams of becoming a writer. The mother, Sarbojaya, looks after the boy, his elder sister Durga and a wizened old hanger-on known as Auntie. Apu perpetually quarrels with Durga, but is very attached to her. The children play in a field of tall feathery grass. One day they see a play performed in the village by a traveling company. Deeply impressed, Apu puts on a home-made moustache and a crown cut out from silver foil. Another day they go to see a train a few miles away. Harihar goes to town to earn some money. Made irritable by life's worries, Sarbojaya turns out Auntie who goes off to die alone in the forest. After getting soaked in the storm Durga develops pneumonia. She dies before Harihar's return. The family pack up their belongings preparing to leave for Benares. Elders of the village arrive for leave-taking. In the last gesture of loyalty to his dead sister Apu flings in the pond her secret, the necklace she once stole. A snake crawls over the cracked stones of the porch into the deserted house, as an ox-wagon takes the family towards the train. The mother is lost in grief while the father stares blankly.

Ray's cinema has been influenced primarily by Italian Neorealism, Flaherty's documentary films (particularly by Louisiana Story) and by The River (1951) by Renoir whom Ray met during its shooting. As Flaherty did, Ray shows a great talent for observation of nature. He shows long grasses, water-flies stirring up at the surface of the pond, lily leaves curling over in the wind, the play of shadow and sunlight in the forest. He knows how to convey a child's wonderment with the world--for instance in the famous scene in which brother and sister see their first train. Robin Wood remarked in his book about the Trilogy that the "death-in-separation" motif is present in each of the Apu films. In Pather Panchali it is Durga's death while her father is away.

Siegfried Kracauer made a very interesting comment about the time structure of Pather Panchali. He said that the sequence of episodes in the film is such that the viewer is constantly compelled to bear in mind what has happened earlier. One's imagination travels back and forth, weaving the fabric of time as it were, something which has little to do with the actual subject matter of a sequence. Immersed in this internal time, the viewer is no longer able to determine the actual chronology of events. Impossible to apprehend, time flows through a realm of its own, in which past and present become inseparable and mutually complementary.

Thus an Indian film-maker was a pioneer in the process of liberating the cinema from the captivity of the classical time structure. Pather Panchali was shown in France in 1958 and it seems probable that its treatment of cinematic time influenced the work of Alain Resnais. Ray's motivation is of course different than Resnais's: he is interested not so much in the mechanics of the workings of time, as in the mechanics of cinematic description. Pather Panchali develops along a fine curve, as a stream of events and loose observations--now predominantly anecdotal, now symbolic, now narrative. But the development of the story is almost unnoticeable. Slow and contemplative in rhythm, Pather Panchali is also touchingly universal.

MARTY Delbert Mann

Script: Paddy Chayefsky, from his own television play. Photography: Joseph LaShelle. Music: Roy Webb. Art Direction: Edward S. Haworth and Walter Simonds. Editing: Alan Crosland Jr. Cast: Ernest Borgnine (Marty Pilletti), Betsy Blair (Clara Snyder), Esther Minciotti (Mrs. Pilletti), Augusta Ciolli (Catherine), Joe Mantell (Angie), Karen Steele (Virginia), Jerry Paris (Thomas), Frank Sutton (Ralph), Walter Kelley (The Kid), Robin Morse (Joe).

Harold Hecht--Burt Lancaster, U. S. A. 8060 ft., 90 mins.

Marty marks the appearance of a new trend in the American cinema which begins to take an interest in ordinary situations of urban life. The reason for this was the influence of television; the characteristic features were a narrative style based on medium-close-ups, great reliance on the dialogue, a highly mobile camera enclosed within limited space and the intimate quality of the situations. Marty, a feature film debut by a TV director based on his own television play, is descended from the little screen and answers to the above description very well. The television style does not sound a false note in the cinema because it has been assimilated with simplicity and naturalness.

The story concerns a 34-year-old Italian-American who works in a butcher's shop in the Bronx and fears that he will never get married because of his lack of good looks and of success with girls. At a dance hall Marty takes pity on a plain schoolteacher, Clara, as lonely and insecure as himself, who has been deserted by her escort. Marty is attracted to Clara but hesitates when his friends are unimpressed by his choice and his mother jealous, until he suddenly realizes he loves her.

This exceedingly simple plot is cast against a very credibly sketched background of life in the Bronx. Chayefsky and Mann contained in their film a wealth of factual observation and social comment. The characters are treated with humor and a touch of irony, but also with intimacy and understanding; the film is full of sympathy for ordinary people with their small protests against the boring greyness of everyday life and the pressure from the models of behavior promoted by the media. Marty had a sensational box-office success, soon followed by four Oscars (film of the year, script, direction, leading actor--Ernest Borgnine who breaks free for once from a succession of thug parts to give an excellent performance) and then by the Grand Prix at the 1955 Cannes Film Festival. The long-term results of this were on the one hand the invasion of television directors and television topics in Hollywood, and on the other the gradual change of point of view of the whole American cinema, which four years later culminated with Cassavetes' Shadows.

PICNIC Joshua Logan

Script: Daniel Taradash, from the play by William Inge. Photography: James Wong Howe. Music: George Duning. Art Direction: William Flannery and Jo Mielziner. Editing: Charles Nelson and William A. Lyon. Cast: William Holden (Hal Carter), Kim Novak (Madge Owens), Rosalind Russell (Rosemary Sydney), Susan Strasberg (Millie Owens), Cliff Robertson (Alan Benson), Arthur O'Connell (Howard Bevans), Verna Felton (Helen Potts), Betty Field (Flo Owens), Reta Shaw (Linda Sue Breckenridge), Nick Adams (Bomber), Raymond Bailey (Mr. Benson), Elizabeth W. Wilson (Christine Schoenwalder), Phyllis Newman (Juanita Badger).

Fred Kohlmar for Columbia, U. S. A. 10,173 ft., 113 mins. CinemaScope. Technicolor.

A shiftless ex-football star, Hal Carter arrives at a small town in Kansas to visit Alan, a college buddy. He sweeps out the yard of a friendly widow to earn his breakfast and meets her neighbor Madge, who is Alan's girlfriend. Hal and Madge are attracted to each other. In the afternoon Hal, Alan, Madge, her mother and sister, Rosemary the local school mistress, and her suitor go to a town picnic. Madge is elected beauty queen. Rosemary, slightly drunk, makes advances towards Hal and creates a scene which causes Hal to leave the picnic. When Madge joins him, Alan, in a fit of jealousy, tells the police that Hal has stolen his car. Hal avoids arrest and briefly returns to town the next morning to ask Madge to marry him. She agrees, thereby rejecting an excellent match. Hal leaves, as he came, on a goods train. Madge sets off for Tulsa to join him despite her mother's protests. Back in town, Rosemary's suitor is forced into marriage.

American cinema of the 50's suffered from an acute shortage of original screenplays. Directors turned towards television scripts (which brought about Marty, The Bachelor Party, Twelve Angry Men and Middle of the Night), towards literature and theatre. Pictures of theatrical origin include A Streetcar Named Desire from the play by Tennessee Williams and Picnic from the play by William Inge, which Logan had earlier directed on Broadway. Born in 1908, Logan had studied under Stanislavsky at the Moscow Art Theatre, before becoming a stage director, mainly of musicals. He co-directed a film way back in 1938, but ventured to make an independent picture only seventeen years later. One must say at once that apart from Picnic and the subsequent Bus Stop (1956), also from a play by Inge, Logan's work in the cinema brought results of quite outstanding tastelessness. It is he who is responsible for such atrocities as Sayonara (1957) and South Pacific (1958).

Picnic sets out to demonstrate that the contentment of small-town America conceals powerful frustrations and longings. They come to light when a rather dim good-for-nothing brings ferment into the town with his flamboyant sexuality. A nomad who plays havoc with the set relationships within a limited community, he is spiritually related to Alan Ladd's rider-from-nowhere in Shane. Picnic also makes a few comments about the growth of the matriarchal civilization. This dull provincial world was largely implied in the play, as if behind the stage--it even seemed a little abstract. On the other hand the film is full of vigor, vitality, full-blooded observation which gives the theme tangibility even though this is at the expense of the philosophical aspect of the play. Yet the camera did no real harm to Inge's thoughts. Picnic is in fact an example of a successful screen adaptation. This is owed to a considerable extent to the outstanding sets by Jo Mielziner and William Flannery. William Holden and Kim Novak are competent in the leading roles; commendable supporting parts are those of Rosalind Russell as a frustrated schoolmarm and Susan Strasberg as Madge's teenage sister who tells her to follow Hal.

RACE FOR LIFE (Si tous les gars du monde ...) Christian-Jaque

---

Script: Henri-Georges Clouzot, Christian-Jaque and Jean Ferry; also Jérôme Gerônimi and Jacques Rémy, based on the novel by the latter. Photography: Armand Thirard. Music: Georges Van Parys. Art Direction: Robert Gys. Editing: Jacques Desagneaux. Cast: André Valmy (Captain Le Guellec), Jean Gaven (Jos), Doudou Babet (Mohammed), Marc Cassot (Marcel), Georges Poujoly (Benj), Pierre Goutas (Yann), Jean Daurand (Yves), Ebbé Moe (Olaf), Jean-Louis Trintignant (Jean-Louis), Hélène Perdrière (Christine), Mimo Billi (Alberto), Bernardette Lange (Le Guellec's wife), Jacques Donot (Radio announcer), Gilbert Gil (Clerk), Jean Clarieux (Riri), Bernard Dheran (Saint-Savin), Claude Sylvain (Totoche), Gardy Granas (Hertha), Diana Bel (French stewardess), Yves Brainville (Dr. Jegou), Mathias Wiemann (Karl), Peter Walker (Johnny), Colette Ricard (Stewardess at the airport), Margaret Rung (Polish stewardess), Charles Jarrell (Mitch), Andrex (Lajarrigue).

Alexandre Mnouchkine for Ariane/Filmsonor/Francinex, France. 10,080 ft., 110 mins.

Among cinematic appeals for human solidarity one of the most moving was made by the director who since Fanfan-la-Tulipe had gravitated towards popular comedy and whom one would hardly suspect of sentiments of this kind. But Race for Life bears no sign of the glibness of Christian-Jaque's other efforts. It seems that this change of tone was in response to popular demand, a sign of relief at the end of the cold war and the easing of the international situation. This type of reaction was particularly widespread in France; but on the same wave of détente the film found recognition also on the international circuit and won the Grand Prix at the 1956 Karlovy Vary Film Festival.

Almost the entire crew of a French trawler operating in the North Atlantic suddenly fall ill with botulism. The captain's distress signal is picked up by an amateur radio ham in Africa; a chain of radio stations links across Europe in a desperate search for the serum with which the sick have to be injected before morning. Thanks to their help and to the coordinated actions of the military and the air crews of many countries (the serum is taken from Paris to East Berlin and then to Norway on a Soviet aircraft) help reaches the men fighting for their lives in time.

The script of Race for Life has a number of weak points, such as the improbability of some situations and the opportunism of others (a colored man and a racist are the only crew members capable of action; forced to work together in adversity they achieve mutual understanding). The solution leaves one with an uneasy feeling that the director's naivete demonstrates a preassumed thesis. But the film is saved by the manner of execution, full of conviction and commitment. This time Christian-Jaque abandoned refined juggling with images and made the film in a raw, semi-documentary style, expending most of his effort on the precise editing, rhythm and the sustenance of dramatic tension. These narrative virtues, combined with the intrinsic value of the message about the triumph of humanity over red tape and political differences, and the avoidance of easy moralizing, gave the film class. Even if over-optimistic, its fine sentiments are never threatened with loss of topicality.

SMILES OF A SUMMER NIGHT (Sommarnattens leende) Ingmar Bergman

---

Script: Bergman. Photography: Gunnar Fischer. Music: Erik Nordgren. Art Direction: P. A. Lundgren. Editing: Oscar Rosander. Cast: Gunnar Björnstrand (Fredrik Egerman), Ulla Jacobsson (Anne Egerman), Eva Dahlbeck (Desirée Armfeldt), Jarl Kulle (Count Carl-Magnus Malcolm), Björn Bjelvenstam (Henrik Egerman), Margit Carlqvist (Charlotte Malcolm), Harriet Andersson (Petra), Åke Fridell (Frid), Naima Wifstrand (Old Mrs. Armfeldt), Gull Natorp (Malla, Desirée's maid).

Svensk Filmindustri, Sweden. 110 mins.

Midsummer night of the year 1900, spent at a country estate at the invitation of a wise old woman; celebrated with old wine with the milk of a young mother and stallion's sperm, at last properly unites four erotically distressed couples. The daughter of the hostess, 40-year-old actress Desirée, regains her lawyer lover, Egerman, who has been living for two years in an unconsummated marriage with 20-year-old Anne. Anne elopes with her own stepson. Count Malcolm, Desirée's present lover, decides to be faithful to his wife (until the first infidelity); and finally the Egermans' maid forces an engagement on a local servant. People discover their real, deep-seated desires in the closeness of Nature, under the gracious influence of the three smiles of a summer night (the first is for young lovers; the second--at first light--for madmen and paupers; the third--at dawn--for the rest). This is how Bergman sums up the essence of Scandinavian eroticism, which is an extension of a sensual perception of nature, a desire and not a game for its own sake. Paradoxically, all this is done in an erotic comedy whose structure refers to western-European models and which is considered as the closest in the Scandinavian cinema to the rose-and-black classics of French literature. On the other hand a comparison of Smiles of a Summer Night with, say, Clair's Les Grandes manoeuvres makes one realize the difference and see Bergman's picture as a combination of the Scandinavian spirit and the formal convention of the continental tragicomedy of flirtation. For there is here no flirtation as such: no nuances and play on words, no double entendres, furtive glances, allusions, hesitations, anxious uncertainty as to who is in love with whom. The only problem is who desires whom, since it is usually known who sleeps with whom. To Susan Sontag the key to the understanding of the Swedes is pornography, which she considers an expression of their emotional immaturity, a childish escape into their own ego and a complete lack of understanding of eroticism. While trying to keep things in perspective (one is talking only about a brittle comedy, after all) one may say that Smiles of a Summer Night is a good opportunity for reflections of this kind.

The mise en scène is somewhat stiff and theatrical and Bergman's occasional attempts to make cinematic use of situational humor are rather heavy; the irritatingly "humorous" music also does not give the film ease. On the other hand the dialogues are light and sparkling and the charm of the actors plus the lacy texture of Gunnar Fischer's chiaroscuro photography give the film volatility. This time the maker of The Naked Night does not try to philosophize; it is true, he does talk about the foibles of strong men and women who imagine that they are weak and helpless (and thus become such in reality), and he lets into the film a little melancholy. But the dominant note in this, Bergman's most successful comedy, is a mood of serenity and a biological joie de vivre. Smiles of a Summer Night remains one of the most charming screen comedies.

THE GIRL FRIENDS (Le amiche) Michelangelo Antonioni

Script: Antonioni and Suso Cecchi D'Amico; also Alba De Cespedes, from the story "Tre donne sole" (Three Lonely Women) included in the book "La bella estate" (The Beautiful Summer) by Cesare Pavese. Photography: Gianni Di Venanzo. Music: Giovanni Fusco. Art Direction: Gianni Polidori. Editing: Eraldo Da Roma. Cast: Eleonora Rossi Drago (Clelia), Yvonne Furneaux (Momina De Stefani), Valentina Cortese (Nene), Madeleine Fischer (Rosetta Savoni), Gabriele Ferzetti (Lorenzo), Franco Fabrizi (Cesare Pedoni), Ettore Manni (Carlo), Anna Maria Pancani (Mariella), Maria Gambarelli (Clelia's employer).

Giovanni Addessi for Trionfalcine, Italy. 9363 ft., 104 mins.

When considered in the context of the Italian cinema of the 50's, Antonioni, a major director, appears as a completely independent creative personality. Unlike most Italian film-makers at the time, he is not so much concerned with the economic situation of man, as with what goes on in his soul. Antonioni's reality is not a social reality, but a psychological one, and his constant theme is the inability of people to communicate. Born in 1912, he was Carné's assistant on the wartime Les Visiteurs du soir, and later collaborated on the script of De Santis's The Tragic Pursuit. Having been making short films for a couple of years Antonioni turned feature director with Cronaca di un amore (1950), a sombre tale of infidelity and crime whose protagonists foreshadow the future Antonioni characters. I vinti (1953) and La signora senza camelie (1953), both interesting if formally imperfect, were followed by The Girl Friends, his first really notable work.

Clelia, a career woman, returns to her native Turin to set up a branch of a Rome fashion shop. She becomes involved with a circle of society people after Rosetta, an unhappy young woman, attempts suicide in the hotel room next to hers. Rosetta is desperately in love with Lorenzo, a painter jealous about his wife Nene being more successful as an artist. Another member of the group, Momina, bored and abandoned by her husband, takes out her unhappiness on the environment. Clelia falls in love with Carlo, a young architect's assistant, but realizes that marriage to him would put an end to her independence. Tired of her emotional demands Lorenzo rejects Rosetta, who tries suicide again--this time successfully. Clelia accuses Momina of contributing to the tragedy by encouraging the affair between Rosetta and Lorenzo. She causes a scene at her work, thinking she will be dismissed. Instead, her employer sends her back to Rome. Lorenzo and Nene are reconciled.

This bleak tale of emptiness and despair is based on a story by Cesare Pavese, an outstanding writer whose "diffuse" style is very difficult to adapt for the screen. Indeed, the script is rather poor with sentimentality and imperfect dialogues. The film opens with an attempted suicide and ends with a successful one--a somewhat melodramatic device. This is apart from the fact that the plot is trivialized a little: in the story there is no apparent reason for Rosetta's suicide, while in the film she kills herself because she was rejected by her lover. It is interesting to note that Pavese himself committed suicide. Thus thematically The Girl Friends is an average melodrama featuring a rather trite triangle motif between the painter, his wife and an emotional young girl.

It is the narrative style and the perfectly captured atmosphere of Pavese's writing which make the film important. Its semitones of mood combined with an objective narrative foreshadow Antonioni's later psychological analyses. The interaction of characters is handled very subtly, which is his hallmark, and the acting excellent. Weak and undecided, Lorenzo is a typical Antonioni male, a prototype of Sandro in L'avventura. He is even played by the same actor. The "Antonioni narrative" introduced here, based on endless tracking shots had to wait another five years to be appreciated. The film's central interest is in cool and refined observation of the state of loss and emptiness felt by people who lie to each other because they find it impossible to communicate their feelings. Anxiety and emptiness, the characters' inherent lack of a will to live, are well evoked with the aid of steel-grey photography and Fusco's cool score. This study of a world of convulsed littleness is performed through the eyes of a girl who returns to the city after many years' absence. In his later films, such as L'avventura, Antonioni does not use a "medium."

The Girl Friends has good pace and efficient narrative. Particularly fine is the scene of the beach picnic, full of tension and emptiness. Of all Antonioni pictures, these attributes would appear together only in Blow-Up. There is also a great feel for the sad landscapes of northern Italy.

LOLA MONTES Max Ophüls

Script: Ophüls and Annette Wademant (and Franz Geiger for the German version), from the novel "La Vie Extraordinaire de Lola Montès" by Cécil Saint-Laurent. Dialogues: Jacques Natanson. Photography: Christian Matras. Music: Georges Auric. Art Direction: Jean d'Eaubonne; also Willy Schatz. Costumes: Marcel Escoffier and Georges Annenkov. Editing: Madeleine Gug. Cast: Martine Carol (Lola Montès [Maria Dolores Porriz Y Montès, Countess of Lansfeld]), Peter Ustinov (Circus Master), Adolf Wohlbrück [Anton Walbrook] (King Ludwig of Bavaria), Ivan Desny (Lieutenant James), Oscar Werner (The student), Will Quadflieg (Franz [Ferenc] Liszt), Lise

Delamare (Mrs. Craigie), Henri Guisol (Maurice, Lola's coachman), Paulette Dubost (Joséphine, Lola's lady-in-waiting), Willy Eichberger [Carl Esmond] (Lola's doctor), Jacques Fayet (Steward), Daniel Mendaille (Captain), Jean Galland (Baron's secretary), Werner Finck (Painter), Claude Pinoteau (Claudio Pirotto), Héléna Manson (James' sister), Willy Rösner (Minister), Friedrich Domin (Director of the circus), Gustav Waldau (Dr. Jeppner).

Gamma Films/Florida Films/Oska Film/Union-Film, France/West Germany. Originally 12,600 ft., 140 mins., cut to 9900 ft., 110 mins. Second version, drastically re-edited, runs 8100 ft., 90 mins. CinemaScope. Eastman Colour.

Lola Montès is the apogee of the cinema of Max Ophüls: unusual, pervaded by a 19th-century spirit, extremely refined and strikingly original in form and style. Great emotions enclosed within the walls of salons, visions seething with visual splendor, in which dynamic movement with an ever-circling camera is coupled with the static character of the plot--all this combined to produce the extreme example of screen baroque. Lola Montès, or rather Maria Dolores Eliza Rosanna Gilbert, was born in 1818 in Ireland and acquired fame during her travels all over Europe as a "Spanish dancer." When in 1848 she arrived in Munich, the senile love of King Ludwig of Bavaria elevated her to the position of an almost-absolute-ruler of the principality. Not for long though: after the revolution of 1848 she had to take refuge in London. Later still she went to the United States, where she died, in mysterious circumstances, in her 43rd spring.

Ophüls' account of the life of this most famous courtesan of the mid-19th century (Franz Liszt, the composer, was among her lovers) is not in complete agreement with actual facts and is made in a most unusual way for a theme of this kind: eschewing explicit eroticism, in a near-dreamlike portrait drawn with deep hues of pastel, and using a non-chronological order of unhasty scenes, subordinated only to the inner logic of the heroine's memories. The film begins in a circus in New Orleans; the ringmaster introduces Lola and tells the audience they are going to hear her life story; this is then shown in a series of flashbacks. This approach to a spectacular super-production with an international cast and a budget of 650 million old francs quite unsurprisingly brought about a resounding box office failure (in fact one of the most spectacular on record); this was not mended by the massive re-editing involving the cutting and chronological arrangement of the story ordered by the producers despite protests of the director who was to die a few weeks later. All these circumstances did not condemn to oblivion the picture which, for all its extravagance and psychological cheapness, opens new narrative perspectives, impresses with its color CinemaScope compositions and contains several outstanding acting performances (particularly Martine Carol's and Peter Ustinov's).

The storm caused by Lola Montès gives an idea as to the

state of mind prevalent within the French cinema at the time. The film's adherents considered it another Citizen Kane, while its opponents saw it as a mannered, post-Expressionist epigonus. This controversy resulted in a curious written certificate of the picture's avant-garde character signed by Jean Cocteau, Jacques Becker, Jacques Tati, Roberto Rossellini, Christian-Jaque and Pierre Kast: an indeed unusual assembly, but highly symptomatic of how strong and widespread the desire for renewal was becoming. This renaissance soon took place under the name of the Nouvelle Vague--and even though this might at first seem surprising, Lola Montès became one of the films greatly revered in the circle of critics and filmmakers gathered around the journal "Cahiers du Cinéma," the camp of theoreticians of the cinéma d'auteur. It is now a cult movie.

THE MAN FROM LARAMIE Anthony Mann

Script: Philip Yordan and Frank Burt, from the short story by Thomas T. Flynn. Photography: Charles Lang Jr. Music: George Duning. Art Direction: Cary Odell. Editing: William Lyon. Song: "Man from Laramie" by Lester Lee and Ned Washington. Cast: James Stewart (Will Lockhart), Arthur Kennedy (Vic Hansbro), Donald Crisp (Alec Waggoman), Cathy O'Donnell (Barbara Waggoman), Alex Nicol (Dave Waggoman), Aline MacMahon (Kate Canaday), Wallace Ford (Charley O'Leary), Jack Elam (Chris Boldt), John War Eagle (Frank Darrah), James Millican (Tom Quigby).

William Goetz for Columbia, U. S. A. 104 mins. CinemaScope. Technicolor.

The traditional western requires the black characters to perish in the final confrontation with those whose duty or vocation is to uphold moral standards in the West. The superwestern did not renounce this requirement, and the finales of, for instance, High Noon or The Tin Star fully conform with the above description. Anthony Mann's contribution to the development of the genre went not so much towards a moral revaluation of traditional situations, as towards widening the scope of the genre by enriching the western with psychological analyses of characters and their motivation, culled from world literature. Thus Mann described his The Furies (1950) as a film inspired by Dostoyevsky's "The Idiot," and saw parallels between "The Brothers Karamazov" and King Vidor's Duel in the Sun (1946). All this may go some way towards explaining the untypical character of The Man from Laramie.

Will Lockhart, whose brother was killed by the Apaches armed with repeating rifles, arrives in a town in New Mexico to find the man who supplied the weapons to the Indians. He comes across Alec

Waggoman, an aging cattle baron, and his vicious son, Dave, whom a foreman by the name of Hansbro is supposed to keep out of trouble. Lockhart is falsely imprisoned for murder, but freed through the intervention of a woman rancher. After Dave is murdered, Lockhart realizes that he has been killed by Hansbro, his partner in a gun-running enterprise. Hansbro is himself killed by the Apaches and Lockhart can ride back to Laramie.

The complex characters in The Man from Laramie and the complexity of the ethical arguments involved indeed have more to do with Dostoyevsky than with a western movie; the handling of the plot brings to mind a detective novel and the finale, while awarding victory to the obstinate loner, does not bring about a polarization of people's attitudes, but their metamorphosis. Evil destroys itself, as it were, and the hero's composed yet decisive actions not only permit him to accomplish his mission, but also precipitate a moral reform and bring peace to those on the wrong side in the conflict.

It is fortunate that the complicated plot did not lead to a profusion of dialogue and did not detach the film from reality. The Man from Laramie is still a real western not only because it is built on the two classical motifs of vengeance and of conflict concerning the use of land, but also because of its narrative style. It is probably in this picture that Mann best combined dynamic description of wide spaces with the handling of individual characters, it is also here that one finds some of the best examples of sharp description of the hero's dramatic struggles on the way to victory (the prologue, Lockhart's being shot through the hand, the encounter with the blinded and desperate Alec Waggoman). And if some situations seem to have too literary a pedigree, the diversified acting team do their best to make them more concrete.

MAN WITHOUT A STAR King Vidor

Script: Borden Chase and D. D. Beauchamp, based on the novel by Dee Linford. Photography: Russell Metty. Music Supervision: Joseph Gershenson. Songs: "Man Without a Star" by Arnold Hughes and Frederick Herbert; "And the Moon Grew Brighter and Brighter" by Jimmy Kennedy and Lou Singer. Art Direction: Alexander Golitzen and Richard H. Riedel. Editing: Virgil Vogel. Cast: Kirk Douglas (Dempsey Rae), Jeanne Crain (Reed Bowman), Claire Trevor (Idonee), William Campbell (Jeff Jimson), Jay C. Flippen (Strap Davis), Myrna Hansen (Tess Cassidy), Mara Corday (Moccasin Mary), Eddy C. Waller (Tom Cassidy), Richard Boone (Steve Miles), Frank Chase (Little Waco), Roy Barcroft (Sheriff Olson).

Aaron Rosenberg for Universal-International, U. S. A. 89 mins. Technicolor.

Nine years and six (insignificant) films after the unfortunate Duel in the Sun (1946) King Vidor rehabilitates himself in another western, one which became the last classic of the genre in its traditional shape, and is at the same time the last success of its maker.

Man Without a Star tells an episode of the passing of the wide-open Old West. A veteran wanderer, Dempsey Rae has an almost irrational hatred of barbed wire (it emerges later that his brother was killed in a range war); as time passes he keeps moving further and further westward in pursuit of the open range. While traveling on a goods train Rae befriends Jeff Jimson, a youngster keen to become a cowboy. They both find work at the Triangle Ranch, owned by Reed Bowman, an attractive lady who has just arrived from the East. A tough businesswoman, she plans to bring vast herds of cattle; Rae is given the task of fending off the small ranchers in the neighborhood. At first he agrees, but when Reed brings in hired gunmen he leaves the ranch and goes to town to his old girlfriend. After Steve Miles, his successor at the ranch, has him beaten up, Rae takes the side of the local ranchers. There is an impressive scene of a stampede conceived by Miles; but his plans misfire. Jeff, who has fallen in love with the daughter of one of the ranchers, stays behind as Rae moves on in his incessant search of open territory.

Behavioral and situational stereotypes; a traditional generic attitude with slightly overdone humor; a memorable song in the High Noon tradition; the classical motifs of the conflict between free-rangers and ranchers fencing their land with barbed wire and of the friendship of an experienced cow-puncher and a young greenhorn--all these elements were put together by Vidor very traditionally (although highly skillfully), without the tones of dramatic gravity which marred Duel in the Sun (1946). As happened many times previously in the history of the western, the quality of a film stems from a careful balancing of the moral dilemmas of loyalty versus justice--in spite of the lack of psychological refinement and the sometimes irrational behavior of the characters. Kirk Douglas's vigorous performance springs organically from the spirit of the film and remains one of the most colorful in his career. Man Without a Star is a lively and direct western--very appropriate for a director whose autobiography is called simply "A Tree Is a Tree."

THE GRASSHOPPER (Poprigunya) [Featherhead] Samson Samsonov

Script: Samsonov, from the short story by Anton Chekhov. Photography: Fyodor Dobronravov and Vladimir Monakhov. Music: Nikolai Kryukov. Art Direction: Yuri Volchanetsky and L. Chibisov. Cast: Sergei Bondarchuk (Doctor Dymov), Ludmila Tselikovskaya (Olga Ivanovna Dymova), Vladimir Druzhnikov (Ryabovsky), Yevgeni Teterin (Doctor Korostelyov).

Mosfilm, U. S. S. R. 90 mins. Sovcolor.

The Soviet cinema had for many years been in the unfortunate habit of suffocating with great efficiency the vividness and the human traits in the literary works it transformed to the screen. They were lost in the iron cogs of the highly formalistic style of execution, the stifling didacticism with which ideas were being conveyed, the obtrusive acting. The Grasshopper did not turn out to be a signal for change; in fact it is composed of elements genetically similar to those which previously invariably brought about sterility and falsity. And yet this film is one of the finest screen adaptations of Chekhov, and although with its dramatism and social accentation it differs somewhat from the depressed and inertia-bound literary original, at the same time preserves its many subtleties, well captures the period and is piercingly human. Somewhat paradoxically, taking as the starting point the academic scrupulousness of the late 19th-century painting, the mannerisms in acting characteristic for the famous Moscow Art Theatre whereby a line of dialogue is preceded by a gesture, the didactic arrangement of the plot, still allowed for the final effect to achieve sincerity and emotion. The altruistic doctor, who thinks but of his vocation, dotes on his wife and humbly bears her silliness and the arrogance of her parasitic entourage of artists and dilettantes; his thoughtless pleasure-loving wife who realizes his true worth only after he dies of diphtheria after treating a case--are certainly convincing and vivid characters. Credit for achieving this is due equally to the purposely restrained performances from the leading actors, the inspired care of the debuting 28-year-old director who handled the theme using static and craftsman-like means, but who (as it is always most important) felt it very deeply.

REBEL WITHOUT A CAUSE Nicholas Ray

Script: Stewart Stern, from a story by Ray, adapted by Irving Shulman; inspired by the book "Rebels Without a Cause" by Robert Lindner. Photography: Ernest Haller. Music: Leonard Rosenman. Art Direction: Malcolm Bert. Costumes: Moss Mabry. Editing: William Ziegler. Cast: James Dean (Jim Stark), Natalie Wood (Judy), Sal Mineo (John "Plato" Crawford), Jim Backus (Jim's father), Ann Doran (Jim's mother), Corey Allen (Buzz Gunderson), Edward Platt (Ray, a juvenile welfare officer), William Hopper (Judy's father), Rochelle Hudson (Judy's mother), Virginia Brissac (Jim's grandmother), Marietta Canty (Plato's maid), Dennis Hopper (Goon), Nick Adams (Moose), Jack Simmons (Cookie), Frank Mazzola (Crunch), Beverly Long (Helen), Ian Wolfe (Lecturer).

David Weisbart for Warner Bros., U. S. A. 9996 ft., 111 mins. CinemaScope. WarnerColor.

Together with the French Before the Deluge, this is the most famous picture about the conflict of the generations in the 50's. These young people wanted only one thing: to be really loved in a world which is gentle, orderly and honest. Naive and crazy excesses, games which sometimes got out of hand and turned into courting death, ostentatious uniformity of clothes--black jackets, ritualistic blue jeans, switch-blades--all that was only meant to cause their parents' concern, and thereby to force them to give off at last some of the warmth which was so stinted before, as an unnecessary loss of energy in the race after money and social status. Fathers, whose generation was heroic at war, did not want to assume authority even in their own homes and gravitated towards a form of matriarchate. This deepened the disenchantment of the young; futile provocation gave way to immature gestures of despair, but the adult America, trying in vain to find errors in the upbringing of the young, did not reply.

It is difficult to imagine a better messenger for this spiritual state of a generation that James Dean. Nicholas Ray, a friend, understood Dean well. In his opinion, the drama of Dean's life reduces to the conflict which arises again and again between the desire to give and the fear of giving. The roots of this reach childhood--when he was eight, after his mother's death his father gave him to an uncle and aunt to bring up. The struggle inside him was between ebullient vehemence and deep distrust. No wonder then that it was James Dean who took the main part in this story about the young generation--that is to say, if Rebel Without a Cause was meant as a film about a generation and not about Dean himself. The picture is certainly far from perfect: as is usual with Ray, the screen is peopled by somewhat psychoanalytically exaggerated characters; the story can hardly be treated seriously, and the execution obtrusively stresses every element used to construct the thesis. Surprisingly however, despite the tendentious falsity of some situations and psychology, Rebel Without a Cause, while rough in detail, rings true in the most important aspect: in portraying the state of mind of the young and their protest against the existing reality--and for this reason it is a truly moving picture. A great part of the merit for achieving this is owed to Dean--a man with perfect pitch for the cinema and one of the most fascinating film actors ever. This idol of his contemporaries could with one gesture express more than can be described on several pages of a textbook of psychology. Rebel Without a Cause was Dean's last finished film; during the work on Giant (1956) the actor was killed in a road accident in California.

THE MAN WITH THE GOLDEN ARM Otto Preminger

Script: Walter Newman and Lewis Meltzer, from the novel by Nelson Algren. Photography: Sam Leavitt. Music: Elmer Bernstein. Art Direction: Joe Wright. Editing: Louis R. Loeffler. Titles: Saul Bass. Cast: Frank Sinatra (Frankie Machine), Eleanor Parker (Zosh), Kim Novak (Molly), Arnold Stang (Sparrow), Darren McGavin (Louie), Robert Strauss (Schwiefka), John Conte (Drunky), Doro Merande (Vi), George E. Stone (Sam Markette), George Mathews (Williams), Leonid Kinskey (Dr. Dominowski), Emil Meyer (Inspector Bednar).

Otto Preminger, U. S. A. 10,679 ft., 119 mins.

After his release from jail Frankie Machine returns to the Chicago slums supposedly cured from drug addiction. He plans to start a new life as a drummer. But his unsympathetic crippled wife, Zosh, his former employer Schwiefka and a drug pusher Louie induce him to take up his old job as a poker-dealer. Frankie soon reverts to the addiction. Molly, a devoted girlfriend, persuades him to arrange an audition with a band; but Frankie goes to it after an exhausting session of poker and sinks his chances. After a quarrel with Louie who has refused him a shot of dope, Frankie is suspected of murdering the pusher (who was in fact killed by Zosh when he discovered that her inability to walk was only a pretense). He takes refuge in Molly's room and with her help makes a desperate attempt to break with the addiction by "going cold turkey"--total withdrawal from the drug. Zosh kills herself when her guilt is discovered, and Frankie, now cured, is going to rebuild his life in Molly's company.

Nelson Algren's novel captured Preminger's imagination. Fascinated by the problem of addiction, he made it into a powerful movie which offers an unflinching look at one of the most gruesome aspects of urban life. Sinatra, whose "golden arm" for poker has an ironic double meaning, gives a very credible performance and well conveys the hero's torment. Consider, for instance, the harrowing sequence of "cold turkey" cure. The problem with the film's release was that heroin addiction simply was not to be portrayed in films at the time. Despite its Hollywood-style happy ending the picture gave rise to objections from the Motion Pictures Producers' Association of America (and from other quarters) and was indirectly responsible for revisions to the Production Code and ultimately for its abandonment. Apart from objections to some "daring" scenes (such as those showing arm injections) there were complaints that the film does not offer sufficient explanation of why the hero becomes an addict in the first place. Preminger said in reply: "If you study the question, you will find there are many reasons for starting to take dope. Some people start by having an operation, being given it by doctors and then get used to it. One of the most usual excuses is that people started in the war. I deliberately didn't use any of these, because I felt that it was much more realistic to show (and he tells it in the picture in a big scene, if you remember) that he just took it for fun at first, and this is the most dangerous reason."

Very professionally made, The Man with the Golden Arm has

fine photography, a memorable jazz score and an outstanding credit title design by Saul Bass.

SHE WAS LIKE A WILD CHRYSANTHEMUM (Nogiku-no-gotoki kimi nariki) Keisuke Kinoshita

---

Script: Kinoshita, from the novel by Sachio Ito. Photography: Hiroyuki Kusuda. Music: Chuji Kinoshita. Art Direction: Kisaku Ito. Cast: Shinji Tanaka (Masao), Noriko Arita (Tamiko), Haruko Sugimura (Masao's mother), Kazuko Yamamoto (Sada), Chishu Ryu (Masao as an old man), Kappei Matsumoto (Boatman), Takahiro Tamura (Masao's elder brother).

Shochiku, Japan. 8291 ft., 92 mins.

An elegiac film about memory's return to the times of youth, She Was Like a Wild Chrysanthemum is a story of an old man's sentimental journey, after sixty years, to his home town, where he found and lost his first love. The story is told in a series of flashbacks. He loved his cousin, but this love could not survive; he was sent away to study so as to be fit to inherit the family fortune; she was given away in an arranged marriage. She was unhappy and badly treated by her parents-in-law, then suffered a miscarriage and died. Told of the tragedy of his only true love the young man weeps bitterly.

With great insight and subtlety Kinoshita portrays the young people who isolate themselves spiritually from their environment, who idealize their emotions and the rules of the world; this inevitably leads to disappointments, alienation, psychological damage and finally to the destruction of love. She Was Like a Wild Chrysanthemum marks the director's return, after several years of being preoccupied with social problems, to the themes of the films he made immediately after the war, to pastoral lyricism, which is here tinted with distinct tones of melancholy but also nostalgic longing after the past. This is one of the most sincere and purest pictures of this type in the Japanese cinema and Kinoshita has been described as its most delicate miniaturist. Having a great ease of imagery, it fascinates particularly with its manner of achieving the cinematic past tense and with its atmospheric photography using the recurrent images of long grass waving in the wind, twigs and patterns of leaves--expressive, and yet enveloped in the muslin of poetry.

She Was Like a Wild Chrysanthemum

BLACKBOARD JUNGLE Richard Brooks

Script: Brooks, based on the novel "The Blackboard Jungle" by Ed MacBain (written under the pseudonym of Evan Hunter). Photography: Russell Harlan. Music: "Rock Around the Clock" played by Bill Haley and His Comets; "Invention for Guitar and Trumpet" played by Stan Kenton and His Orchestra; "The Jazz Me Blues" played by Bix Beiderbecke and His Gang. Musical Adaptation: Charles Wolcott. Art Direction: Cedric Gibbons and Randall Duell. Editing: Ferris Webster. Cast: Glenn Ford (Richard Dadier), Anne Francis (Anne Dadier), Louis Calhern (Jim Murdock), Margaret Hayes (Lois Judby Hammond), John Hoyt (Warneke), Richard Kiley (Joshua Y. Edwards), Emile Meyer (Halloran), Warner Anderson (Dr. Bradley), Basil Ruysdael (Prof. A. R. Kraal), Sidney Poitier (Gregory Miller), Vic Morrow (Artie West), Dan Terranova (Belazi), Rafael Campos (Pete V. Morales), Paul Mazursky (Emmanuel Stoker), Jameel Farah (Santini), Danny Dennis (De Lica), David Alpert (Lou Savoldi), Christ Randall (Levy), Yoshi Tomita (Tomita), Horace McMahon (Detective).

Pandro S. Berman for MGM, U. S. A. 101 mins.

Born in 1912, for a number of years before his directorial debut in 1950 Richard Brooks worked as a scriptwriter and author. He did his first script in 1944 and soon after one of his novels was filmed by Dmytryk as Crossfire (1947). Brooks' films often seem awkward, even ugly and uninvitingly heavily made, which is primarily caused by his lack of visual inventiveness. But when an expressive script happens to coincide with his predispositions and interests, a good film may result. This happened with Blackboard Jungle, a story of a teacher's harrowing experiences in the New York school system, made from a novel by Ed MacBain.

Richard Dadier, an idealistic young teacher, comes to his first job at a vocational trade school in a slum area. The pupils are tough, rebellious and hostile, ready to resort to verbal and physical abuse. Dadier's class is dominated by West, a vicious and impertinent youth and Miller, a black thug. Dadier is savagely beaten after he saves Lois Hammond, a fellow teacher, from rape by one of the pupils. His wife, Anne, who expects a baby and fears a miscarriage, receives a series of poison pen letters suggesting that her husband is having an affair with Lois. The baby is born prematurely but survives and Anne persuades her husband not to hand in his resignation. When Dadier begins to win the confidence of his pupils, West, who wrote the anonymous letters, attacks him with a knife. Miller, whose sense of decency is awakened, and other boys take the teacher's side and disarm the attacker.

Although very daring for its time (which led to the fuss over its being shown abroad on the grounds that it presents a particularly unflattering image of the United States) Blackboard Jungle does not really point directly to the social background of pupil delinquency and only implies it. Despite its tense, hard-hitting style aimed to shock the viewer (which is achieved through the editing, music and the light contrasts) one feels that the picture does not entirely live up to the ideas inherent in the script. There are a number of powerful sequences and good classroom scenes--but on the other hand Miller's final change of heart and the other pupils' switch to the teacher's side is not entirely plausible. Glenn Ford, an image of tolerance and integrity, is seen here in a part particularly well suiting his acting temperament, and Sidney Poitier is memorable as the black troublemaker. The film was made under the influence of Kazan's On the Waterfront, which is evident from the hesitant delivery of dialogues and from Vic Morrow's acting in which he imitates Marlon Brando.

THE HEROES ARE TIRED (Les Héros sont fatigués) Yves Ciampi

Script: Ciampi and Jacques-Laurent Bost, from the novel by Christine Garnier adapted by Jean-Charles Tacchella. Dialogues: Henri-François Rey. Photography: Henri Alekan. Music: Louiguy. Art Direction: René Moulaert. Editing: Roger Dwyre. Cast: Yves Montand (Michel Rivière), Maria Félix (Manuella Séverin), Jean Servais (François Séverin), Curt Jürgens (Wolf Gerke), Elisabeth Manet (Nina), Gérard Oury (Villeterre), Gert Froebe (Hermann), Gordon Heath (Sidney), Manolo Montez (Pépé), Jean Werner (Olsen), Ruddy Castell (Ruddy).

Julien Rivière for Cila Films (Paris)/Terra Films (Stockholm), France. 108 mins.

The French psychological cinema makes a full circle and returns to the starting point: The Heroes Are Tired is a mirror image of Feyder's Le Grand jeu. That film, set in the exotic scenery of Arab Africa, was a harbinger of Poetic Realism; this one is an echo of the film noir which used and transformed Poetic Realist motifs. The times have changed, though: while Feyder's picture was apolitical and employed the formula of a colonial melodrama for reflections upon human personality, Ciampi's is clearly political in character and uses the same formula to show the people who are the real winners of great wars. This is done in the spirit of Renoir's La Grande illusion, with an adventurous plot à la Huston and to the strains of Beethoven's Fifth Symphony. During the war Ciampi fought in the French Resistance Movement; his tired heroes in the film are two ex-enemy veteran pilots, the Frenchman Rivière and the German

Gerke. Rivière flies for second-rate freight airlines; during one flight his worn-out aircraft crashes; he survives and finds a bag full of diamonds in the wreck. His flights were used for smuggling. Rivière arrives in Free City, the capital of a black African state, intent on selling the gems so as to live in prosperity at long last. There he is traced by Gerke sent by his employer to recover the diamonds. The game of wits between the two finally turns into friendship built on the principle of common experience and the knowledge that the world consists of exploiters and of the exploited. Rivière stays at the hotel run by the drunken Séverin, the Nazi collaborator who hides in Free City from a French death sentence, and falls in love with Séverin's beautiful wife. But the fate of the diamonds with which Rivière and Gerke plan to start an air company of their own is similar to that of gold in Huston's The Treasure of the Sierra Madre. The demented Séverin kills his wife to stop her from escaping with the two pilots and scatters the diamonds over the sea.

Ciampi's film is admittedly very uneven, but its credits outweigh its faults. Among the latter is the extremely stereotyped femme fatale, the excessively repugnant Séverin character, poor dialogues which further compound the already abstract quality of the plot and finally the director's neglect of the atmosphere for the sake of proving his point. The characters are quite clearly not living real lives and have no inner autonomy. On the other hand, the clammy background of Free City (which combines the characteristics of several central African cities) is portrayed with wit and skill; it is possible that this description of the urban background inspired Camus in Black Orpheus. Montand, Jürgens and Froebe give interesting performances; but the main strength of the film is the execution--full of dynamism and tension. Ciampi combined the decorative denseness of dark frames with the allusive and complex mise en scène, modeled on the works of Welles and Wyler.

I LIVE IN FEAR (Ikimono-no kiroku) Akira Kurosawa

Script: Shinobu Hashimoto, Hideo Oguni and Kurosawa. Photography: Asaichi Nakai. Music: Fumio Hayasaka and Masaru Sato. Art Direction: Yoshiro Muraki. Cast: Toshiro Mifune (Kiichi Nakajima), Eiko Miyoshi (Toyo Nakajima), Yutaka Sada (Ichiro Nakajima), Minoru Chiaki (Jiro Nakajima), Haruko Togo (Yoshi Yamazaki), Kyoko Aoyama (Sué Nakajima), Masao Shimizu (Takao Yamazaki), Noriko Sengoku (Kimie Nakajima), Akemi Negishi (Asako Kuribayashi), Kiyomi Mizunoya (Kiichi's first mistress), Saoko Yonemura (Taeko), Kichijiro Ueda (Asako's father), Yoichi Tachikawa (Ryoichi), Takashi Shimura (Harada), Ken Mitsuda (Judge Araki), Toranosuke Ogawa (Hori), Kamatari Fujiwara (Okamoto), Kazuo Kato (Susumu), Nobuo Nakamura (Psychiatrist), Eijiro Tono (Old man from Brazil).

Shojiro Motoki for Toho, Japan. 10,180 ft., 113 mins.

I Live in Fear is a dramatic projection of the nuclear scare which was particularly strong in the late 50's and which found an apocalyptic expression in On the Beach. Nakajima, an elderly owner of a foundry, is scared of the nuclear tests, and has become obsessed by the belief that an atom holocaust will destroy Japan. He first builds a bomb shelter and then decides to close down his business and emigrate to Brazil, where the chances of surviving a nuclear conflict are the highest. He wants to take his entire family with him, but they apply to a court to have him declared insane. When the court decides against him and when all attempts to plead with his family fail, Nakajima is driven to despair. He realizes that the basic source of the conflict is his wealth, and sets fire to his foundry. He ends his days in a mental asylum thinking that he is on another planet and that the earth is burning.

Kurosawa's most unimpressive externally and most static film (despite the director's strenuous attempts to perfect the narrative technique) reveals a mastery in only two scenes: in the tension-filled sequence of the fire and in the final scene in the asylum. The picture did not find approval among the critics and is considered flawed also by Kurosawa himself, who approached the theme with great personal involvement and expended on it an unusual amount of effort. Anderson and Richie have commented in their book on the Japanese cinema: "Kurosawa fails to make the fear of the atom bomb a universal phenomenon by showing it only through the distorted imagination of this crazy old man ... plainly insane from the first sequence on." It is true that I Live in Fear is far from perfect formally and lacks stylistic decisiveness; the conception of the central character and the story itself (quite apart from being wandering and hesitant) are doubtful. On the other hand, the piercing tone of the picture, its despair at the fact that men live in impossible conditions which they have brought upon themselves, its reflection on the contradictions between money and freedom and finally its searching analysis of the behavior of the family first integrated and happy and then divided by greed--all elevated I Live in Fear above average and make it something more than merely a stage in Kurosawa's development.

THE EMPRESS YANG KWEI-FEI (Yōkihi) Kenji Mizoguchi

Script: Yoshikata Yoda and Matsutaro Kawaguchi; also Masashige Narusawa, Kyuichi Tsuji and Shing Tou. Photography: Kohei Sugiyama. Music: Fumio Hayasaka. Art Direction: Hiroshi Mizutani. Cast: Machiko Kyo (Yang Yu-Huan, later Yang Kwei-Fei), Masayuki Mori (Emperor Huan-Tsung), So Yamamura (General An Lu-Shan), Eitaro Shindo (First Eunuch Kao Li-Hsi), Sakae Ozawa (Chao, later Prime Minister Yang Kuo-Chung), Haruko Sugimura (Abbess), Yoko Minamida (Hung Tao), Bontaro Miyake (Commandant of the guard), Tatsuya Ishiguro (Prime Minister Li), Isao Yamagata (Miss Yang Shian), Kinzo Shin, Chieko Murata, Chioko Ai, Noburu Kiritachi, Yukiko Murasae.

Masaichi Nagata--Run Run Shaw for Daiei/Shaw Brothers, Japan/Hong Kong. 8799 ft., 98 mins. Eastman Colour.

The tragic story of Yang Kwei-Fei became part of Chinese folklore and a subject for many legends and literary works. It is therefore not surprising that for a film set in China Mizoguchi based himself on a poem describing the undying love between the emperor and his ill-fated mistress. Made in co-production with a Hong Kong company and filmed mainly in Taiwan, The Empress Yang Kwei-Fei is his first color picture.

Eighth-century China. The Empire is at the summit of prosperity under Emperor Huan-Tsung of the Tang dynasty; the capital Changan, a lively trading center, is the largest city in the world. The Emperor is in great distress after the recent loss of his wife. Anxious to gain influence, the courtiers present various women to him. One of them is Yang Yu-Huan, a kitchen maid whose beauty was discovered by the ambitious General An Lu-Shan, a provincial governor. The Emperor, enchanted by the girl's beauty, sensitivity and artistic talents, makes her his favorite and gives her the name of Yang Kwei-Fei. Common folk strongly resent the favors granted to her relatives and Yang Kwei-Fei asks the Emperor for permission to leave the capital. But she comes to his side in the hour of need, when An Lu-Shan leads a mutiny and proclaims himself the new emperor. Huan's court have to flee the capital. After the angry troops have killed her relations, Yang Kwei-Fei agrees to die to put an end to the mutiny.

The story is told in one long flashback, in the form of memories of the emperor who, having regained power, abdicates in favor of his son and spends the rest of his days in a wing of the Imperial Palace thinking of his dead mistress. Mizoguchi gave this story of a Chinese Cinderella splendid costumes and shot it in a magnificent pastel tonality. Color is used as a visual equivalent of emotion; the palette is dominated by rich hues of deep red and blue which increase in saturation as the story nears its tragic end. The photographer was Sugiyama who worked in Kinugasa's celebrated Gate of Hell (1953). The scene of the heroine's death is marvellous with its subtle understatement, langorous feel and fluent use of the camera; she goes to her death shedding slowly her embroidered jacket, the fur-lined slippers, jewelry, while a white scarf serves as a symbol of lost innocence. The tone of the film is reflexive, elegiac. An intimate drama, The Empress Yang Kwei-Fei develops mainly indoors and was made virtually entirely in the studio (a complete contrast to Mizoguchi's chronologically next New Tales of the Taira Clan, his only other film in color). Still, it does not count among his most successful works. The certain stiffness of some scenes and awkwardness of acting in others is usually explained away by the unfamiliar environment in which the film was made. Lack of familiarity with the Chinese idiom (diametrically different from the Japanese) may also have played a part and some Japanese critics think it was a mistake for Mizoguchi to attempt a "foreign" topic at all.

LADY AND THE TRAMP Hamilton Luske, Clyde Geronimi and Wilfred Jackson

---

Script: Erdman Penner, Joe Rinaldi, Ralph Wright and Donald Da Gradi, from the novel "The Lady and the Tramp" by Ward Greene. Designs and Animation: Milt Kahl, Franklin Thomas, Oliver Johnston Jr., John Lounsbery, Wolfgang Reitherman, Eric Larson, Hal King and Les Clark (Directing animators); George Nicholas, Hal Ambro, Ken O'Brien, Jerry Hathcock, Eric Cleworth, Marvin Woodward, Ed Aardal, John Sibley, Harvey Toombs, Cliff Nordberg, Don Lusk, George Kreisl, Hugh Fraser, John Freeman, Jack Campbell and Bob Carson (Animators); Claude Coats, Dick Anthony, Ralph Hulett, Albert Dempster, Thelma Witmer, Eyvind Earle, Jimi Trout, Ray Huffine and Brice Mack (Backgrounds); Ken Anderson, Tom Codrick, Al Zinnen, A. Kendall O'Connor, Hugh Hennesy, Lance Nolley, Jacques Rupp, McLaren Stewart, Don Griffith, Thor Putnam, Colin Campbell, Victor Haboush and Bill Bosche (Layout); George Rowley and Dan MacManus (Effects animation). Special Processes: Ub Iwerks. Music: Oliver Wallace. Songs: "He's a Tramp," "La La Lu," "Siamese Cat Song," "Peace on Earth" and "Bella Notte" by Sonny Burke and Peggy Lee. Voices: Peggy Lee (Darling/Peg/Si/Am), Barbara Luddy (Lady), Larry Roberts (Tramp), Bill Thompson (Jock/Bull/Dachsie), Bill Baucon (Trusty), Stan Freberg (Beaver), Verna Felton (Aunt Sarah), Alan Reed (Boris), George Givot (Tony), Lee Millar (Jim Dear), Dallas McKennon (Toughy/Professor), The Mello Men.

Walt Disney Productions, U.S.A. 6824 ft., 76 mins. CinemaScope. Technicolor.

The first feature-length cartoon film in CinemaScope: Disney keeps abreast of the times and a mere two years after the introduction of this technique presents in CinemaScope a very time-consuming animated story. This time it is not a screen version of a nursery classic, but a good-humored story about a dog population of a well-to-do neighborhood of an American town in the early 1900's. Lady is a pedigree spaniel puppy owned by a newly married couple; she grows up in company of her friends Jock (a Scottie with a sense of thrift) and Trusty (a bloodhound who has lost his sense of smell). The Tramp is a stray mongrel with whom the heroine has romantic adventures. The dog characters of course lent themselves very well to cartoon witticisms and these potentialities were fully exploited, although Disney's anthropomorphization of animals in this particular film rather irritatingly imitates the Hollywood musical and melodrama. Of course, when considered seriously, certain elements of the script amount to an unbearable apology for suburban conformism with some accents of simulated social criticism; fortunately, however, the film manages to remain on the correct side of the border separating carefree entertainment from moralizing and allows itself to be really liked for its lyricism, good humor, Chaplinesque touches, and if it gravitates towards Hollywood it is only as much as it parodies the narrative style of current film entertainment.

TO CATCH A THIEF Alfred Hitchcock

Script: John Michael Hayes, from the novel by David Dodge. Photography: Robert Burks. Music: Lyn Murray. Art Direction: Hal Pereira and Joseph McMillan Johnson; also Sam Komer and Arthur Krams. Editing: George Tomasini. Cast: Cary Grant (John Robie), Grace Kelly (Frances Stevens), Jessie Royce Landis (Mrs. Stevens), John Williams (H. H. Hughson), Brigitte Auber (Danielle Foussard), Charles Vanel (Bertani), Jean Martinelli (Foussard), René Blancard (Commissioner Lepic), Georgette Anys (Germaine), Roland Lesaffre (Claude), Jean Hebey (Mercier).

Alfred Hitchcock for Paramount, U. S. A. 9601 ft., 107 mins. VistaVision. Technicolor.

A wave of daring robberies spreads through the French Riviera: an exceptionally skillful burglar takes care of the jewelry belonging to rich tourists and locals alike. The thief's technique is highly reminiscent of the methods once used by John Robie, nicknamed "The Cat." An American, Robie used to be an acrobat; when his circus went bankrupt in the 30's he became the most notorious jewel thief in France; during the war he fought in the Resistance Movement and now lives quietly and respectably near Nice. Annoyed at being suspected by the police, Robie decides that he must track down the real thief in order to protect himself.

A number of Hitchcock's pictures contain no riddle at all and To Catch a Thief gravitates towards this category. There is not much mystery here, and if someone wants to unravel what there is, he can do it without much difficulty: already in the early stages of the film it becomes fairly clear where to look for the villain (although the subsequent course of the plot involves a number of inconsistencies, improbabilities and false trails). It is much more fun to treat the film simply as an attractive chase story. Anxious to free himself from suspicion Robie acts with great ingenuity, and while searching for the real thief becomes romantically involved with Grace Kelly, who appears as a bored, rich American girl touring Europe in the company of her jewel-bedecked mother. Among the film credits one must include the light-hearted tone (something rather unusual for Hitchcock) and the quite exceptional lightness of the conduct of the narrative. It is so right from the five shots which open the film: a poster advertising tourist attractions of France, a victim of a robbery calling for help from the balcony, a cat circling on the roof, another victim calling for help, and again a cat walking stealthily in the night. This time psychology is forgotten: the characters are portrayed rather crudely and most of what is untypical in the film is simply the reverse of what would normally be expected. The dialogues are a little too sparkling and too profuse not to impair the dynamism of the film. The Cary Grant-Grace Kelly team are a separate attraction of To Catch a Thief; the latter seemed so well suited to the Côte d'Azur scenery that she soon became the Princess of Monaco.

BEAUTY AND THE DRAGON (Bijo to Kaī-ryū) Kozaburo Yoshimura

Script: Kaneto Shindo, from the kabuki play "Narukami" based on an ancient folk tale. Photography: Yoshio Miyajima. Music: Akira Ifukube. Art Direction: Takashi Marumo. Cast: Chojuro Kawarazaki (Holy Priest Narukami), Nobuko Otowa (Kumo-no-taema Hime), Chiyonosuke Azuma (Toyohide Bunya), Yuriko Tashiro (Nishiki-no-mae), Kunitaro Kawarazaki (Takino), Yoshisaburo Arashi (Mototsune, Emperor's chief adviser).

Toei, Japan. 8944 ft., 99 mins.

Throughout his directorial career Yoshimura specialized in modernizing old Japanese stories, particularly stories of amorous adventures. More correctly, his main concern was to make old texts appear applicable to modern realities. Thus The Tale of Genji was a film version of the world's earliest novel, and Osaka Story (1957), the picture Yoshimura completed after Mizoguchi's death, charted the progress of a poor farmer who through corruption and thrift becomes a wealthy merchant in the Genroku period. Also Beauty and the Dragon, based on the famous kabuki play, demonstrates Yoshimura's feel for the essence of Japanese classical literature.

Nobuko Otowa plays a princess who tempts a self-righteous priest. The film opens in the actual kabuki theatre and only later does the camera move into the open, a device which invites an immediate comparison with Henry V. The style of acting oscillates between the theatrical and the cinematic. Yoshimura set himself a task which is quite difficult to fulfill: to update the contents while preserving the period flavor and the satirical overtones of the original story. The aim was not so much to recreate the past, as to offer a relevant comment on it. Yoshimura does this well. His heroine is spiritually a modern woman.

OTHELLO (Otello) Sergei Yutkevich

Script: Yutkevich, from the play "Othello, the Moor of Venice" by William Shakespeare. Photography: Yevgeni Andrikanis. Music: Aram Khachaturian. Art Direction: A. Vaisfeld, V. Dorrer and M. Karyakin. Costumes: O. Krochinina. Cast: Sergei Bondarchuk (Othello), Irina Skobtseva (Desdemona), Andrei Popov (Iago), Vladimir Soshalsky (Cassio), Yevgeni Vesnik (Roderigo), Yevgeni Teterin (Brabantio), Antonina Maximova (Emilia), M. Troyanovsky (The Doge), A. Kelberer (Montano), P. Brilling (Lodovico).

Mosfilm, U. S. S. R. 9828 ft., 109 mins. Sovcolor.

Following the Russian tradition of the interpretation of "Othello" (Pushkin saw the play as an optimistic tragedy of a lost, but later found, faith in Desdemona) Yutkevich shows it as a double drama--of jealousy and of false accusations. Indirectly, the film was meant as a polemic with Orson Welles' interpretation, which Yutkevich accused of making Othello's anguish too pathological and of playing down the motif of false accusations. However, this is not a fully consistent polemic: Yutkevich's Othello too soon becomes convinced of Desdemona's innocence; both the staging of the culminating scene as that of murder rather than judgment over the unfaithful wife, and also the great prominence given to Othello's final soliloquy, make the spectator search for additional intentions in the so-conceived interpretation. In fact, the idea was to give the drama intelligent and topical political overtones. Othello asks for his deserts to be truthfully handed down to posterity and emphasizes that he was a patriot and never allowed himself to be carried away by passions, until base calumny sowed in his soul a grain of despair and led him to disaster--these words in the U. S. S. R. of 1955 sounded very topical indeed. After the death of Stalin and the fall of Beria the country went through a difficult period and was soon to witness Khrushchev's revision of Stalin's "cult of the individual" during which state administration was almost completely dominated by the intrigues on the part of the security police. Yutkevich's comments indirectly justify such interpretation; according to him "Othello" is a play meant to alert against lies, duplicities and falsehood of all sorts; it is not a tragedy of love, but that of a friend who turns out to be an enemy; it is a protest against the disruption of a peaceful, creative life. Othello's tragedy is his search for peace and harmony of spirit.

This screen version of "Othello" was made against the background of wonderful Crimean locations; the whiteness of the fine and simple designs conjures up a Renaissance scenery which is beautifully shown through the lens of Andrikanis's camera. His clearly composed frames can be matched in the contemporary Soviet cinema only by Urusevsky's color photography for The Forty-First. Unfortunately the remaining aspects of Yutkevich's film are not up to the standard of the photography, staging and the dramatic conception. The scenery is Renaissance all right, but the people are not; the acting team gives a review of different theatrical conventions--cool (Skobtseva), ostentatious (Popov) or bombastically overdone (Bondarchuk), while Bondarchuk's characteristic emotionality is clearly overdosed by the director. For example, when used in the early parts of the film the monumentalizing shots from below seem an appropriate visual comment on Othello's actions and character, but they also appear in many subsequent situations, where the context is quite different. Thus Yutkevich's screen version, apart from a correct understanding and interpretation of Shakespeare, offers not unimportant values of its own; but this is done at the expense of strenuous (and not always successful) efforts to break free of the Soviet cinematic tradition. It is only Kozintsev in Hamlet who broke completely free from those and offered an excellent screen vision of Shakespeare.

KISS ME DEADLY Robert Aldrich

Script: A. I. Bezzerides, from the novel by Mickey Spillane. Photography: Ernest Laszlo. Music: Frank DeVol. Art Direction: William Glasgow. Editing: Mike Luciani. Cast: Ralph Meeker (Mike Hammer), Albert Dekker (Dr. Soberin), Maxine Cooper (Velda), Paul Stewart (Carl Eyello), Gaby Rodgers (Lily Carver), Cloris Leachman (Christina), Juano Hernández (Eddie Yeager), Wesley Addy (Pat), Nick Dennis (Nick), Jack Lambert (Sugar), Marian Carr (Friday), Jack Elam (Charlie Max).

Robert Aldrich for Parklane Pictures, U. S. A. 105 mins.

A stylistically excellent thriller noir and at the same time the last important achievement of the genre in its classical form, in its highly significant finale Kiss Me Deadly explodes the genre's rules. More--it anticipates the course of the evolution of the American underworld, foreshadowing the mood in which it would be shown on the screen after 1968, in the post-Bullitt period. Starting from pulp literature Aldrich had the ambition of expressing his disapproval for its reactionary influence through the way in which the characters are shown. He succeeded completely--one may even say that he turned out to be prophetic.

Mike Hammer, a private eye, gives a lift one night to Christina, a girl who has fled from a mental home. She is very frightened and hints of impending threat, but is killed in a crash before she can explain. Mike follows up a clue she has left (a reference to a poem by Christina Rossetti) and discovers that the girl knew the whereabouts of a case of radioactive material which a gang of spies plan to pass to an unnamed foreign power. The spies kidnap Mike's secretary to stop him in his tracks, but he rescues her from a seaside house where the radioactive substance is hidden just as the house explodes into flames.

The consequence of the treatment of the literary material is that Kiss Me Deadly is not even a mock-up of a thriller noir as The Big Sleep was, but the convention ostentatiously stripped to its bare bones which Aldrich covers up with values of his own: the excellent character description, fine handling of the narrative (which in its fast rhythm differs considerably from the long takes used in American cinema in the period) and a powerful, nightmarish, dreamlike mood obtained with the use of low-key photography, tilted shots and large close-ups. The film is greatly admired in France (where François Truffaut somewhat irresponsibly considered it one of the best American films after the war). Aldrich began his career in the movies as a clerk at RKO, and was later assistant to such famous film-makers as Renoir, Wellman, Zinnemann, Rossen, Milestone, Losey and Chaplin. He worked for TV before his feature film debut in 1953. In the 50's he was interested primarily in revaluing traditional genres in the American cinema. The Big Knife (1955), his next film after Kiss Me Deadly, was an accusation of Hollywood itself; later, in Attack, Aldrich took on the U. S. Army.

JOURNEY INTO AUTUMN (Kvinnodröm) Ingmar Bergman

Script: Bergman. Photography: Hilding Bladh. Art Direction: Gittan Gustafsson. Editing: Carl-Olov Skeppstedt. Cast: Eva Dahlbeck (Susanne), Harriet Andersson (Doris), Gunnar Björnstrand (Consul Sonderby), Ulf Palme (Henrik Lobelius), Inga Landgré (Märta Lobelius), Kerstin Hedeby (Marianne), Sven Lindberg (Palle), Naima Wifstrand (Madame Arén), Ludde Gentzel (Photographer Sundström), Bengt-Åke Benktsson (Director Magnus).

Rune Waldekranz for Sandrew Produktion, Sweden. 7748 ft., 86 mins.

Desires, dreams, disappointments: Journey into Autumn is a psychological study of two women. Susanne is the mature owner of a fashion photography studio; Doris is a young model who works for her. When they go to Göteborg on a business trip (Susanne is to take some fashion photographs of Doris) both hope for a change in their lives. Doris, who has just broken off an engagement to a student, becomes involved with an elderly consul whom she reminds of his insane wife in her youth. She finds in the end that what real life offers is more important and is relieved to find her old boyfriend waiting for her when she returns to Stockholm. Susanne, about to enter a dangerous age, hopes to resume a relationship with a married industrialist, but when she finds that he is dull and undecided, abandons the dreams of a great love affair.

On the threshold of his greatest screen achievements, Bergman displays in Journey into Autumn a fine direction of a somewhat light-weight script. The exposition, built from fast-edited shots of tapping fingers and furtive glances and sustained in the style of the silent cinema, is of particular interest. The actors, belonging to Bergman's usual stable, are very well directed.

INVASION OF THE BODY SNATCHERS Don Siegel

Script: Daniel Mainwaring, from the novel "The Body Snatchers" by Jack Finney, serialized in "Collier's Magazine." Photography: Ellsworth Fredericks. Music: Carmen Dragon. Art Direction: Ted Haworth. Editing: Robert S. Eisen. Cast: Kevin McCarthy (Dr. Miles Bennell), Dana Wynter (Becky Driscoll), Larry Gates (Dr. Danny Kauffman), King Donovan (Jack Belicec), Carolyn Jones (Theodora Belicec), Jean Willes (Sally), Ralph Dumke (Nick), Virginia Christine (Wilma), Sam Peckinpah (Gas man), Kenneth Patterson (Mr. Driscoll), Whit Bissell (Psychiatrist).

Walter Wanger for Allied Artists, U. S. A. 7211 ft., 80 mins. SuperScope.

Dr. Miles Bennell returns to his practice in a small California town after years of absence to notice a strange change of behavior in the inhabitants. Although outwardly unchanged, people seem to have undergone a curious psychological transformation. At the home of their friends, Bennell and his girlfriend discover a partially formed human body which has emerged from a giant pod. Bennell soon finds out what is going on: an invasion from outer space whereby the identity of living people is taken over during sleep by "blanks" deposited by a malignant form of plant life. Before Bennell's friends are able to summon help, they themselves become victims. The lonely and hunted doctor tries to stop passing cars on the highway, but everyone passes him unconcerned....

The deceitfulness of everyday appearances is a constant theme in Don Siegel's films. The story of this one seemed too terrifying to the producers; so the studio imposed on the film a prologue which transfers the events into a flashback, an epilogue in which the hero's life is saved and a commentary explaining how the menace was averted. It is true, this first really successful science-fiction picture, addressing in the subconscious the medieval fears of possession of man by demons, condenses horror very well indeed. The scenery is entirely real, the only fantastic element being the curious giant pods in which doubles are created. In this way, according to classical recipes of the genre, horror is created from the unknown, incomprehensible and intangible. Hitchcock's Psycho was based on the same principle. Invasion of the Body Snatchers without a doubt owes a lot to a high technical efficiency--the narrative coherence, the skillful use of the detail, the dramatic employment of the contrast between dusky interiors and sunlit open spaces. Siegel, who always enjoyed a considerable professional reputation, here proved that it was fully deserved. Recognition and successes as an auteur would come in more than 10 years; thus for almost a quarter of a century after his Oscar-winning debut in a short film Siegel oscillated between B-features and television.

THE LAST ACT (Der letzte Akt) Georg Wilhelm Pabst

Script: Erich Maria Remarque and Fritz Habeck, from the book "Ten Days to Die" by Michael Angelo Musmanno. Photography: Günther Anders. Music: Erwin Halletz. Art Direction: Erner von Schlichting, Otto Pischinger and Wolf Witzemann. Editing: Herbert Taschner. Cast: Albin Skoda (Adolf Hitler), Oskar Werner (Captain Wuest), Lotte Tobisch (Eva Braun), Willy Krause (Dr. Joseph Goebbels), Helga Kennedy-Dohrn (Magda Goebbels), Erik Frey (General Burgdorf), Erich Suckmann (Dr. Heinrich Himmler), Julius Jonak (SS-Obergruppenführer Hermann Fegelein), Kurt Eilers (Martin Bormann), Edmund Erlandsen (Albert Speer), Leopold Heinisch (Field Marshal Wilhelm Keitel), Otto Schmoele (Colonel-General Alfred Jodl), Herbert Herbe (General Krebs), Hannes Schiel (SS-Obersturmführer Gunsche).

Carl Szokoll for Cosmopolfilm, Austria. 113 mins.

G. W. Pabst, whose period of glory ended so abruptly at the beginning of the sound cinema with Don Quixote, subsequently worked in half of Europe and in the United States. However, despite making nearly 20 films (of which only two were in any way ambitious), he never rose above mediocrity. After the outbreak of the Second World War Pabst quite unexpectedly turned up in Berlin, which he had left at the beginning of the Nazi period. His motives for doing so seem to be indirectly explained by The Last Act, a reconstruction of Hitler's last days in the bunker of the Reich Chancellery in Berlin. The film amounts to a judgment on the Nazi leaders passed by a German patriot. It seems that the reasons for Pabst's decision to return to Germany can be summarized by the maxim: "Right or wrong, this is my country." The director was never directly involved with the very extensive Nazi film propaganda machine, probably much to the disappointment of Goebbels, who had been delighted at his return. Still, it seems that Pabst later suffered from a sense of guilt; this is probably why he introduced into The Last Act the fictional character of Captain Wuest, who is used as a commentator and who comments on the ending with the words: "it all started from us obediently saying jawohl [yes, sir]". Also, this is probably the reason why Pabst goes to pains to stress all signs of resistance to Hitler within Germany; as a matter of fact he devoted his next picture, Jackboot Mutiny (1955) to von Stauffenberg's unsuccessful plot to assassinate Hitler.

The originality of The Last Act lies in the fact that its faithful recreation of crucial historical events was not done in the form of a para-chronicle, but as a stifling psychological drama taking stock of the past on many levels. Cinematic reconstruction of important events was previously attempted only in the Soviet Union; the stylistic rule there was that of epic pathos. Pabst on the other hand handles his subject matter with cool firmness and without emotional exaggeration, even though he is talking about the vestibule of hell. Of particular interest is Albin Skoda's Hitler: this is probably the most credible cinematic treatment of the man who is usually portrayed on the screen as a diabolical maniac, though in fact he was no more than a cowardly and hysterical petit bourgeois. The visual aspect of the picture is very appropriate to its theme: basically documentary in character, with its dusky quality reminding one of Pandora's Box, it carries a mood of threat and encirclement in a dimly lit cave of concrete and steel, a sense of the doom awaiting the mass murderers.

THE LADYKILLERS Alexander Mackendrick

Script: William Rose. Photography: Otto Heller. Music: Tristram Cary. Art Direction: Jim Morahan. Editing: Jack Harris. Cast: Alec Guinness (Professor Marcus), Cecil Parker (Major), Herbert Lom (Louis), Peter Sellers ("Harry" Robinson), Danny Green ("One-Round" Lawson), Katie Johnson (Mrs. Wilberforce), Jack Warner (Police Superintendent), Frankie Howerd (Barrow Boy), Fred Griffiths (The Junkman), Philip Stainton (Police Sergeant), Kenneth Connor (Cab driver).

Michael Balcon for Ealing Studios, G. B. 8750 ft., 97 mins. Technicolor.

A worthy elderly landlady does not in her naiveté suspect that her lodger's frequent visitors do not come to practice Boccherini's minuet together; the music she hears comes from a record and the real purpose of the meetings of the five men is to plan a daring robbery of a money-van. Mrs. Wilberforce discovers the truth only after the job has succeeded, when a pile of stolen notes accidentally falls out of a cello case. She threatens to call the police and the robbers decide to get rid of her. But their attempts to do this are so incompetent, that instead of killing the unwanted witness they kill off each other in turn. Finally the whole gang ceases to exist. The police disbelieve the old lady's story and she has no choice but to make use of the £60,000 herself.

This splendid ending worthily rounds off a picture built with much precision, a film in which a paradox chases after a situational irony, horror is intermixed with comic situations and in which the general rule is one of near-Surrealist contrast. The Ladykillers is the last famous comedy of the Ealing Studios which were just being closed down; it claims as its main values the splendid feel for the allusive paradox and the great amplitude of the constantly changing mood. The clever script found an appropriate director in Alexander Mackendrick and a witty musical illustrator in Tristram Cary; but the main credit for the film's success must go to Katie Johnson who plays the apple-cheeked landlady and to Alec Guinness, who as the vampire-like professor of crime once more confirms his astonishing versatility.

LES MAUVAISES RENCONTRES Alexandre Astruc

Script: Astruc and Roland Laudenbach, from the novel "Cette sacrée salade" by Cécil Saint-Laurent. Photography: Robert Le Fèbvre. Music: Maurice Leroux and Henri Crolla. Art Direction: Max Douy. Editing: Maurice Serein. Cast: Anouk Aimée (Cathérine Racan), Gianni Esposito (Pierre Jaeger), Jean-Claude Pascal (Blaise Walter), Philippe Lemaire (Alain Bergère), Claude Dauphin (Dr. Danieli), Yves Robert (Superintendent Forbin), Gaby Sylvia (Hélène).

Les Films Marceau, France. 109 mins.

The origins of the French Nouvelle Vague are usually traced to Alexandre Astruc's celebrated 1948 article in "L'Ecran français." The article introduced the concept of caméra-stylo ("camera-pen") demanding that cinema become a means of expression in its own right, as flexible and subtle as written language. Image should become a completely independent form of expression, formed directly by the camera, instead of being secondary to the verbal ideas of the scriptwriter. Reality should be observed (and not created) on the screen, and shown in its natural form, "in the state of freedom." Astruc put these ideas into practice in his first film, Le Rideau cramoisi (1951), a 45-minute love story set in Napoleonic times, elaborate, stylish--and without a word of dialogue. Les Mauvaises rencontres, his first feature, forshadowed the style and the interests of the Nouvelle Vague, just as did another "Neoromantic" picture--Agnès Varda's La Pointe Courte (1954). Particularly significant in this respect is the theme of search for one's true identity, a quest for authentic values.

Astruc's main interest is in the enigma of woman, and the story of Les Mauvaises rencontres traces the adventures of an ambitious young girl from the provinces in the upper social strata of Paris. Cathérine arrives with her lover Pierre and soon conquers the capital. She becomes involved with a brilliant newspaper editor who makes a known journalist out of her, then with a young photographer. Finally she becomes pregnant. The film begins, and ends, in Quai des Orfèvres, the police headquarters, where Cathérine relives her life as she is questioned about the shady doctor who was to give her an abortion.

The story is told in a series of flashbacks; the constantly circling camera, which seems to be always involved in a search for the best point of view, creates a rhythm of its own--a rhythm which is contrasted with the non-linear, often surprising, development of events on the screen. With its refined effects of shadows, fog, reflections of light, the photography is influenced by the silent German cinema. Aesthetic formal leanings in Les Mauvaises rencontres always have an upper hand over the melodramatic story--but they do not really give the film strength. The atmosphere is monotonous and the story develops accompanied by scraps of sentences on the soundtrack, sometimes even in silence. The script is second-rate and the film's intellectual quality of clear literary origin. But one of the characteristics of the Nouvelle Vague was the ability to override poor, self-conscious literary scripts by way of a convincing and imaginative mise en scène: Resnais's Hiroshima mon amour being the most outstanding example. Astruc meets only with partial success. Intriguing, distant and enigmatic, Anouk Aimée soon found fame in real life, becoming a very well known actress.

A GIRL IN BLACK (To Koritsi me ta mavra) Michael Cacoyannis

Script: Cacoyannis. Photography: Walter Lassally. Music: Argyris Kounadis. Editing: Emile Provelengios. Cast: Elli Lambetti (Marina), Dimitris Horn (Pavlo), Georgios Foundas (Christo), Notis Peryalis (Antonis), Nikos Fermas (Aristides), Anestis Vlachos (Mitsos), Eleni Zafiriou (Froso, Pavlo's mother), Stefanos Stratigos (Panagos).

Hermes Film, Greece. 9438 ft., 105 mins.

The first big success by the most outstanding Greek director and the first Greek film to achieve international reputation, A Girl in Black is the story of the love of Pavlo, a writer from Athens, and Marina, a girl from the island of Hydra off the eastern coast of the Peloponnese. Set entirely in beautifully photographed Mediterranean locations, this picture marks the beginning of Cacoyannis's cooperation with the photographer Walter Lassally, who later in Electra demonstrated even more stunningly his sense for the sharp chiaroscuro of the Greek landscape. Already here, Lassally achieves a fascinating visual appearance. The director's main intention was to give dramatic expression to the conflict between the inhabitants of modern urban Greece (represented by Pavlo) and the harsh, nature-molded customs and ethical norms of the inhabitants of a rocky island--the conflict from which Pavlo emerges more mature and spiritually richer. This is thus the theme which was later fully developed in Zorba the Greek. It seems, however, that the expressive contrasts of characters and situations is not the strongest aspect of A Girl in Black and instead of giving the film a poetic stylization pushes it towards melodrama. Much more valuable is the film's description of the way of life and custom, Neorealist in style and all the more consistent since it was accompanied by pure and sparing narrative, painterly photographic compositions, original guitar music and authentic acting by the non-professionals who appear in the supporting parts.

THE MAN WHO KNEW TOO MUCH Alfred Hitchcock

Script: John Michael Hayes and Angus McPhail, from an original theme by Charles Bennett and D. B. Wyndham-Lewis. Photography: Robert Burks. Music: Bernard Herrmann; "Storm Cloud Cantata" by Arthur Benjamin and D. B. Wyndham-Lewis. Songs: "Que sera sera" and "We'll Love Again" by Jay Livingston and Ray Evans. Art Direction: Hal Pereira, Henry Bumstead; also Sam Comer and Arthur Krams. Costumes: Edith Head. Editing: George Tomasini. Cast: James Stewart (Dr. Ben McKenna), Doris Day (Jo McKenna), Daniel Gélin (Louis Bernard), Brenda de Banzie (Mrs. Drayton), Ralph Truman (Inspector Buchanan), Christopher Olsen (Hank McKenna), Bernard Miles (Mr. Drayton), Mogens Wieth (Ambassador), Alan Mowbray (Val Parnell), Hillary Brooke (Jan Peterson), Reggie Nalder (Rien), Betty Baskcomb (Edna).

Alfred Hitchcock for Filwite Productions, U.S.A. 10,777 ft., 120 mins. VistaVision. Technicolor.

It is difficult to agree with Hitchcock's comment on this remake of his own 1934 picture: "Let's say that the first version is the work of a talented amateur and the second was made by a professional." It is true that the construction and attention to detail are superior to the original and the orchestration better; but it is precisely the excess of smooth professionalism that seems detrimental.

Dr. Ben McKenna, an American on holiday in Morocco with his wife, Jo, and young son (the original opens in St. Moritz, Switzerland) become acquainted with Mr. and Mrs. Drayton, a friendly English couple, and a mysterious Frenchman, Bernard. They witness the assassination of Bernard in the Marrakesh market; before dying he whispers to Ben that he is a French intelligence agent and that a foreign diplomat is to be murdered in London. To ensure the couple's silence the Draytons, who are members of a spy-ring, abduct their son. Ben and Jo travel to London to track down the kidnappers and find them conducting services in a small Bayswater chapel. The assassination is to take place in the Albert Hall during a performance of a cantata; to drown the sound of the shot, the killer is to fire at the precise moment when the score calls for a clash of cymbals. Jo screams at the crucial moment and the bullet misses the ambassador. The couple locate their son at a foreign embassy and rescue him.

One of the main attractions of the 1934 version was a stylish, nostalgic portrayal of London of the past. Here this is missing; although one may say that 1955 is now also firmly in the past, the remake is less atmospheric--and less sinister. Particularly regrettable is the exclusion of the siege scene, the best in the earlier version, which referred to the notorious Sidney Street Siege in 1910 when Winston Churchill was Home Secretary. Also the scene at the dentist's was not used. Instead, Hitchcock considerably expanded the Albert Hall sequence (the new version runs for 120 minutes as opposed to 74), directed the whole with brisk, mellowed efficiency, threw in a song sung by Doris Day--and made an expert thriller based on his favorite principle of innocent passers-by thrown into the midst of sensational events.

MOONFLEET Fritz Lang

Script: Margaret Fitts and Jan Lustig, from the novel by J. Meade Falkner. Photography: Robert Planck. Music: Miklós Rózsa; also Vincente Gómez (Flamenco music). Art Direction: Cedric Gibbons and Hans Peters. Costumes: Walter Plunkett. Editing: Albert Akst. Cast: Stewart Granger (Jeremy Fox), George Sanders (Lord Ashwood), Joan Greenwood (Lady Ashwood), Viveca Lindfors (Mrs. Minton), Jon Whiteley (John Mohune), Liliane Montevecchi (Gypsy), Melville

Cooper (Felix Ratsey), Sean McClory (Elzevir Block), John Hoyt (Magistrate Maskew), Donna Corcoran (Grace), Alan Napier (Parson Glennie), Jack Elam (Damen), Dan Seymour (Hull), Ian Wolfe (Tewkesbury), Lester Matthews (Major Hennishaw).

John Houseman for MGM, U. S. A. 7806 ft., 87 mins. CinemaScope. Eastman Colour.

Encouraged by the financial success of The Big Heat Lang made Moonfleet, his first work in CinemaScope and color. These two films are in fact his only worthwhile works in the 50's. CinemaScope Lang found difficult to handle; appearing in Godard's Le Mépris some years later he commented acidly: "it is not for men, but for snakes and funerals." In Moonfleet, a simple, direct story loosely adapted from a novel written in the 1890's, Lang revises the romantic attitudes of his early films, such as Destiny, Nibelungen and The Spies.

The Dorset coast in the 1770's: John Mohune, a 10-year-old homeless orphan, puts himself into the hands of Jeremy Fox, the man whom his mother had once loved but was not allowed to marry. A suave dandy, Fox is the leader of a smuggling gang. He sends the boy to school but John escapes, finds the smugglers' hiding place and learns of his inheritance, a valuable diamond which is missing. He discovers a clue as to the diamond's whereabouts and enlists Fox's help in finding it. Fox plans to steal the stone in alliance with the sinister Lord and Lady Ashwood, but has a change of heart at the last moment and returns the diamond to the boy.

A coast roamed by smugglers, adventures of a child among criminals and corrupt aristocracy--yes, we recognize these motifs from Hitchcock's Jamaica Inn (1939). But while that picture functioned primarily as a whodunit, Moonfleet is mainly concerned with the atmosphere. Told from the point of view of a young boy with a vivid imagination, it is a Gothic story equipped with the required props: a churchyard, the wind, owls hooting at night, thunderstorms, mystery houses--the mood is there right from the opening sequence and is augmented with some interesting lighting effects. The plot is much less important, and one is therefore inclined to forgive Lang the rather confused narrative (it is not explained, for instance, what happened to Lady Ashwood in the runaway carriage at the end), difficulties with continuity and the implausibility of Fox's final change of heart.

1956

A MAN ESCAPED (Un Condamné à mort s'est échappé ou le vent souffle où il veut) Robert Bresson

Script: Bresson, based on the account by André Devigny, published in "Le Figaro Littéraire" on November 20, 1954. Photography: Léonce-Henry Burel. Music: Wolfgang Amadeus Mozart, Mass in C Minor K. 427. Art Direction: Pierre Charbonnier. Cast: François Leterrier (Lieutenant Fontaine), Charles Le Clainche (François Jost), Maurice Beerblock (Blanchet), Roland Monod (Rev. de Leiris), Jacques Ertaud (Orsini), Jean-Paul Delhumeau (Hébrard), Roger Tréherne (Terry), Jean-Philippe Delamare (Prisoner 110), Jacques Oerlemans (Chief Warder), Klaus Detlef Grevenhorst (German Intelligence officer), Leonhard Schmidt (German escort).

S. N. E. Gaumont/Nouvelles Editions de Films, France. 9162 ft., 102 mins.

In the summer of 1943 a lieutenant in the wartime French Resistance Movement, André Devigny, who had been arrested by the Gestapo and sentenced to death, performed a seemingly impossible feat: he escaped from a solitary cell in the high security prison in the Montluc fortress in Lyon. Devigny's account of his escape, which appeared in the press in 1954, provided inspiration for the greatest of Bresson's films. A Man Escaped is a praise of human intellect transformed into action by way of an indestructible striving for freedom. The picture does not recreate Devigny's story directly; the main character is called Fontaine and remains throughout something of a mysterious stranger, a man without a past. No information is provided about the reasons for his arrest, and even the features of his character are not examined. The subject matter of this film is man's freedom in general terms, and not a praise of some individual hero of the Resistance. This is why, when introducing Fontaine in the prologue, Bresson states that he must not be allowed to die, and yet does not make his character more concrete; only the details of a Nazi prison are precise and meticulous. This is also the reason why the narrative is accompanied by the protagonist's inner monologue, seemingly used clumsily (as it often simply recounts what can be seen on the screen) and not enriching spiritually his character, as Bresson did in Diary of a Country Priest. Still, this monologue is doubly important for the film's message, as it makes the events more intimately felt by the spectator, gives them a general pan-human dimension, adds a touch of warmth to what in purely visual terms is a simple behavioral description, a pedantic registration of gestures and actions, which goes counter to all the accepted practices of screen drama. In this way the internal monologue, old-fashioned in theory, became on the one hand a vital intellectual and formal compliment of the work; on the other, in combination with the ascetic, analytical style of direction (the example of which was Diary of a Country Priest) it opened new, exciting perspectives for cinema aesthetics. A Man Escaped is free of even a trace of visual emphasis and is played throughout on the one string of the indicative mood--and yet it is full of tension. This makes one realize the power of cinema as a precise instrument of detailed observation, a medium capable of conveying things which are the most elusive, but often the most vital. So far, these potentialities of the cinema had been only hinted at by passages from some avant-garde works, fragments of Hitchcock's films, the burglary sequence in Dassin's Rififi; but A Man Escaped sanctions the method. The camera does not for one moment leave Fontaine's immediate vicinity (he is present in almost every frame of the film): it watches his unsuccessful attempt to escape from a moving car, his being recaptured, beaten and placed in solitary confinement, his transfer to a cell, his gradual transition from torpor to concentrated action aimed at establishing acoustic contact with prisoners in neighboring cells, his rare moments outside the cell, his Jobian work on clearing the way towards freedom. Fontaine dismantles the cell door using a metal spoon sharpened on the stone floor; makes ropes from blankets and shirts. Then a 16-year-old boy is put into his cell; Fontaine has to decide whether to kill him or to take him with him. They escape together.

The ascetic purity of this cinematic account is only infrequently accompanied by the equally pure garland of Mozart's music; the remainder of the soundtrack is filled by sounds which the prisoner strains his ears to hear, as they provide him with invaluable information. As the decision to escape begins to take shape, medium long-shots are replaced by mid-shots; during Fontaine's work with the door of the cell the camera moves to close-ups of objects, the prisoner's head, his hands which are becoming more and more adroit. Nothing human is unimportant; neither the protagonist's physical actions nor his contacts with others. The help of the fellow prisoners turns out to be invaluable; the experience gained by one of them who just before death passes on the information on how to get beyond the prison wall is not wasted; also Fontaine's decision to take with him the young deserter sent to his cell at the last minute proves right. The reward waiting in the dark street beyond the outer wall for the man who proved his manhood is freedom.

THE SEVENTH SEAL (Det Sjunde Inseglet) Ingmar Bergman

Script: Bergman, from his own play "Trämålning" (Sculpture in Wood). Photography: Gunnar Fischer. Music: Erik Nordgren. Art Direction: P.-Å. Lundgren. Editing: Lennart Wallén. Cast: Max von Sydow (Antonius Block), Gunnar Björnstrand (Jöns), Nils Poppe (Jof), Bibi Andersson (Mia), Bengt Ekerot (Death), Åke Fridell (Blacksmith Plog), Inga Gill (Lisa, Plog's wife), Maud Hansson (Witch), Gunnel Lindblom (Girl), Inga Landgré (Block's wife), Bertil Anderberg (Raval), Anders Ek (Monk), Gunnar Olsson (Church painter), Erik Strandmark (Skat), Ulf Johansson (Leader of the soldiers), Benkt-Åke Benktsson (Merchant), Lars Lind (Young monk), Gudrun Brost (Woman at inn).

Allan Ekelund for Svensk Filmindustri, Sweden. 8625 ft., 96 mins.

"When the Lamb opened the seventh seal, there was silence in heaven for about half an hour.... Then I saw the seven angels who stand before God, and seven trumpets were given to them.... The first angel blew his trumpet, and there followed hail and fire, mixed with much blood, which fell upon the earth...".

Starting with this symbolic motto from the Revelation of St. John (The Apocalypse) Bergman unwinds the first of his existential dramas about the life of man in a world overcast by the shadow of God. The Seventh Seal was received with much applause at the Cannes Film Festival and strengthened further the director's already high standing in world cinema. This morality play, impressive with its original screen form and the specific gravity of the problems debated seemed to many a conclusive proof of the maturity of the art of the cinema. As it turned out, The Seventh Seal is merely a proof of the academic respectability of the cinema of the 50's. All the same, the certain theatrical quality and the pretentions to philosophical generalization did not seriously detract from its lasting values.

The picture is set in a stylized, epic medieval background and photographed in a magnificently rich scale of black and white. A knight and his squire have just returned from a Crusade. They journey through plague-stricken Sweden towards their castle. The film's opening scene is magnificent: a hostile deserted seashore under overcast skies where an eagle hovers as the narrator's matter-of-fact voice reads the first lines of the Apocalypse; the squire lies exhausted on the beach while the knight challenges Death to a game of chess. The story of this dramatic game forms the framework of The Seventh Seal. The stake is on the one hand the knight's life; on the other the answer to the existential problems which torment him. He knows he must lose, but he is playing for time. Having realized the futility of human life, he wishes to perform one worthwhile deed; also, he does not want to die without first finding an answer to the crucial questions of the existence of God and of life after death--which would give a meaning to the earthly struggles of man. He cannot completely abandon faith, but is besieged by doubts. The country is in the grip of bubonic plague, roads are full of penitents, witches are being burned at the stake, all one can see around is cruelty, suffering and madness. Does all this happen by the Lord's hand? The squire is different: he has lost his faith long ago and seeks no answers. On their way the knight and the squire meet a family of wandering players whom they escort across the forest to avoid the plague.

It turns out that Death does not know the answers either. But he does not have to know, being merely an executor of superior orders. He deceives the knight into disclosing his planned strategy, awaits an opportune moment, makes the mating move and finally takes the knight, his wife, his squire and their companions into the land of darkness. But there are some who escape the dance of death: the pair of wandering players, naive and simple, who despite adversities and hardship enjoy true happiness, love their child, admire the sun in a strawberry clearing. They know not the fear of existence and are not engulfed by the general psychosis. They are spared, because they found the sense of their lives--in simply being together.

The dilemmas of the knight who, despite outward appearances, embodies the problems and aspirations of modern man, parallel the problems which faced Bergman himself. The director was at that time under pressure from the ideals by which he had spent his childhood. The son of a clergyman, he could not, just as the knight could not, liberate himself from the problems of faith, even though the modern world, with its total wars and the nuclear psychosis, seemed to contradict the religious view of things. Bergman said that when his father was preaching in church he himself was always fascinated by "the church's mysterious world of low arches, the smell of eternity, the colored sunlight quivering above the strangest vegetation of medieval paintings and carved figures on ceilings and walls." The idea of The Seventh Seal was indeed drawn from medieval frescoes showing Death playing chess with his victims. A polemic with Christianity and with Kierkegaard's concept of despair as a tragic privilege through which man achieves full awareness, dominated a number of Bergman's subsequent films. Despite variations in the distribution of stress, until Winter Light his solution was to identify God with Love, but he was never able to discard the supernatural completely. It was only The Silence which brought to an end Bergman's "vertical cinema."

The Seventh Seal

The Seventh Seal

THE BURMESE HARP (Biruma-no tategoto) Kon Ichikawa

Script: Natto Wada, from the story by Michio Takeyama. Photography: Minoru Yokoyama. Music: Akira Ifukube. Art Direction: Takashi Matsuyama. Editing: Masanori Tsujii. Cast: Shoji Yasui (Mizushima), Rentaro Mikuni (Captain Inouye), Tatsuya Mihashi (Defence Commander), Taniye Kitabayashi (Old woman), Yunosuke Ito (Village head), Taketoshi Naito (Kobayashi), Yun Hamamura (Ito), Shunji Kasuga (Maki), Akira Nishimura (Baba), Hiroshi Hijikata (Okade).

Masayuki Takagi for Nikkatsu, Japan. 10,479 ft., 116 mins.

July 1945. A unit of the defeated Japanese army struggles over the mountains of Burma towards Thailand. Among them is Private Mizushima, whose tunes played on the Burmese harp give great pleasure to the soldiers. Most of the unit is captured by the British and taken to a P.O.W. camp at Mudon. The war is over. Separated from his comrades, Mizushima is taken care of by a Buddhist monk. Dressed in a monk's robe Mizushima makes his way to Mudon; he is appalled by the sight of the corpses of his countrymen killed in battle. He burns several bodies to drive away the vultures, and soon realizes that his vocation is to honor the dead by burying them. When he accidentally goes past his old unit, other soldiers half-recognize him; he later intimates to them his decision not to return to Japan, and goes back to bury the dead who lie forgotten in the jungle. As the unit sails back home the captain reads aloud to the soldiers a letter from Mizushima.

In a series of flashbacks, Ichikawa's most beautiful picture tells the story of a subtle individual confronted with the gruesome harvest of war. The film's long takes, slow fades and breathtaking vistas of Burma combine to create the effect of noble tranquility. On the intellectual level this story of a soldier who asserts the dignity of mankind faced with catastrophe, upholding the ideas of expiation and hope, is the most perfect reflection in the cinema of the Buddhist philosophy. According to Mahayana (Great Vehicle) Buddhism, the ideal follower of the creed is inspired by great compassion to work for the good of others through perfecting himself in the six virtues of generosity, morality, patience, zeal, concentration and wisdom. Ichikawa contrasts these virtues, as personified in Mizushima, with the cruelty of the Japanese during the war. In the sense of his influence on others, Mizushima interestingly compares with Watanabe, the protagonist of Kurosawa's Ikiru. Takeyama's story, on which the film is based, was originally written to introduce children to basic Buddhist tenets, and this is the reason for the unusual intellectual clarity of the film, for its contemplative character and also for the considerable importance of silence in its formal aspect. Another tenet of the Buddhist philosophy concerns

The Burmese Harp

the interpenetration and identification of all things in universal consciousness. Thus only through understanding and respect for the past can one face the present. The viewer is made acutely aware of the indissoluble links between the dead, the living and the yet unborn. A monk says to Mizushima: "Burma is Burma. Burma is Buddha's country," and Ichikawa creates a coherent vision of a spiritual unity.

And yet The Burmese Harp is basically a simple film. Unfolding at a leisurely pace, it offers visions of forests, skies and symbolic shots of the temples around Mudon. Characters, both Japanese and British, are slightly idealized. When Ichikawa took another look at the war, in Fires on the Plain, it was to be in a completely different mood. Sometimes The Burmese Harp can become simply magical, as in the scene in the village ambush, as the British and the Japanese soldiers break into a song together. This is one of those works of the cinema which are simply impossible to forget.

THE RED BALLOON (Le Ballon rouge) Albert Lamorisse

Script: Lamorisse. Photography: Edmond Séchan. Music: Maurice le Roux. Editing: Pierre Gillette. Cast: Pascal Lamorisse (Boy), Sabine Lamorisse (Girl), Michel Pezin (Teacher). With the children of Menilmontant and all the balloons of Paris.

Les Films Montsouris, France. 3188 ft., 35 mins. Technicolor.

On his way to school a little boy from the Paris suburb of Belleville finds a red balloon hooked on a lamp post. He takes the balloon with him, which leads to all kinds of trouble in the street, at school and at home. But the boy obstinately guards his treasure; after a while the balloon begins to feel an attachment to its owner and does not fly away even when it is no longer restrained by the string. This makes other boys envious: at first they try, unsuccessfully, to take the balloon away, but finally destroy it with a stone thrown from a catapult. And then balloons from all over Paris come to the despairing little boy; carried by them he disappears in the sky.

Lamorisse: "The Red Balloon is the fruit of the child's above-average imagination, a dream seemingly senseless--the wish to own a tame object which would accompany its master everywhere. At the same time this film is even less meant for children than Crin Blanc was." This comment on the cinematic poem which is seemingly so uncomplicated, so obvious in its story line, might be considered superfluous--and yet the full scope of The Red Balloon is seen only when one realizes from the very beginning that this is a picture whose interpretation of events and the philosophical context by far exceeds the perception of a young spectator, although the story was set in the world of the child's emotions and Lamorisse displays a good knowledge of it. Perhaps only the finale does not correspond with the reactions of a child (for him the loss of a beloved toy cannot be compensated even by a thousand other toys; and he can only count on the blessing of forgetfulness)--and this, unfortunately, is a discordant note in the film, since it is easily traced back to the bourgeois belief in achieving happiness through quantity. This is, however, the only weakness of the bitter and lyrical tale about fantasy and friendship as the only refuges from the painful greyness of human existence, from the world motivated by envy, aggression and hostility towards the unusual. Lamorisse's film is formally excellent: ravishing in its mood, lyrical narrative, subtle palette of colors which refers to Impressionist paintings, the background drawn with scattered light in grey and blue hues with strong, pure colors in the foreground. The scarlet stain of the balloon against the greyness of Paris, the awakening of the city in the blue haze--these are marvellous images. Only the culmination of the film takes place in the bright glare of midday, and ends with the scene of the balloon's agony, filled with pregnant silence. This scene is particularly worthy of attention; it is in fact one of the most piercing episodes in all cinema.

LE NOTTI DI CABIRIA (Nights of Cabiria) Federico Fellini

Script: Fellini, Ennio Flaiano and Tullio Pinelli; also Pier Paolo Pasolini. Photography: Aldo Tonti and Otello Martelli. Music: Nino Rota. Art Direction: Piero Gherardi. Editing: Leo Catozzo. Cast: Giulietta Masina (Cabiria), François Périer (Oscar D'Onofrio, the "accountant"), Amedeo Nazzari (Alberto Lazzari, the movie star), Aldo Silvani (Hypnotist), Franca Marzi (Wanda, Cabiria's friend), Dorian Gray (Jessy, Lazzari's girlfriend), Mario Passante (Cripple in the "miracle" sequence), Pina Gualandri (Matilda, prostitute who fights with Cabiria).

Dino De Laurentiis/Les Films Marceau, Italy/France. 9900 ft., 110 mins.

Le notti di Cabiria completes Fellini's trilogy about the human search for values, whose earlier parts were La strada and Il bidone. Compared with those films Le notti di Cabiria offers a transformed, less pessimistic view of the lot of an individual. Fellini abandons the moralizing overtones of the story of the ill-fated confidence trickster and the desperation of the life of Gelsomina. Despite remaining within the same thematic sphere (of the individual's search for warmth, kindness and sublimity) the director changes his tone; among other things he discards the pessimistic attitude to loneliness and the somewhat anachronistic ethical conception of La strada.

Cabiria is a shabby little prostitute who lives on the outskirts of Rome; she skillfully uses her little cunning in everyday life while secretly dreaming of a sudden and wonderful change in her fortunes. Fellini compared her to a lunatic little spider with one eye fixed on the world of dreams and the other on reality. Of course, in Cabiria's station in life one constantly meets with humiliations and disappointments. When she first appears on the screen it is as a disillusioned would-be suicide; in the film's ending she is betrayed, attacked and robbed by a man who pretended he was in love with her. But by then she knows the rules of the game; her experiences were the successive stages of initiation into the selfishness and brutality of other people. Still, she does not abandon hope; one has to accept the world for all its cruelty, as the only alternative is the abyss of loneliness--and to accept means to carry within oneself kindness and openness, as it is only with those that one can hope for happiness. In the last scenes of the film Cabiria wanders alone through the forest; she joins a group of happy people who sing as she walks along with them.

With Le notti di Cabiria Fellini clarifies his attitude to Existentialist philosophy (by bringing Cabiria to choose the attitude of heroic acceptance of her lot) and his attitude to the institutional Roman Catholic Church, of which he is strongly critical in the episode of Cabiria's pilgrimage to a shrine. A man whose mentality is basically Christian (although this is raw, archetypal Christianity rather than its institutional variety), Fellini treated with similar aversion the façade of the Church in his later La dolce vita, an almost apocalyptic, baroque fresco about the modern world. Le notti di Cabiria on the other hand is a modest film, woven from the fabric of commonness. The melodramatic story often verging on the banal with its funny generic episodes, despite being told with narrative skill and with a considerable visual invention, is nonetheless rather second-rate. The picture is not quite redeemed by the moments of fascinating, intellectually rich cinema, such as the Divino Amore sequence, nor by the lyrical interludes; neither is the lack of complexity of characters of help in this respect. Oscar only appears for Fellini to be able to round off his thesis about the inexorable cruelty of the world and one can see through the Cabiria character at one glance. To boot, for most of the film Giulietta Masina with her familiar mannerisms cools the enthusiasm of those who on the strength of La strada proclaimed her an outstanding actress. But as the film reaches its finale, it becomes great cinema whose touching humanist optimism has its source precisely in the leading actress. Fellini is certainly a magician of the screen, but every magician has his medium and his limitations.

TWELVE ANGRY MEN Sidney Lumet

Script: Reginald Rose, from his TV play. Photography: Boris Kaufman. Music: Kenyon Hopkins. Art Direction: Robert Markell. Editing: Carl Lerner. Cast: Henry Fonda (Juror 8), Lee J. Cobb (Juror 3), Ed Begley (Juror 10), E. G. Marshall (Juror 4), Jack Warden (Juror 7), Martin Balsam (Juror 1), John Fiedler (Juror 2), Jack Klugman (Juror 5), Joseph Sweeney (Juror 9), Edward Binns (Juror 6), George Voskovec (Juror 11), Robert Webber (Juror 12), Rudy Bond (Judge), James A. Kelly (Guard), Bill Nelson (Court clerk), John Savoca (Defendant).

Henry Fonda and Reginald Rose (Orion/Nova), U. S. A. 8648 ft., 96 mins.

One of the finest works of the American cinema in the 50's, Twelve Angry Men was widely applauded for its masterly execution. After hearing a murder case about which there seems little doubt, the jury retires to consider its verdict. To everyone's surprise one vote of "not guilty" is entered on the count. Juror No. 8, who casts the dissenting vote, explains that while he is not convinced of the defendant's innocence, he is not certain beyond reasonable doubt of his guilt. Despite general reluctance, the evidence presented at the trial is re-examined and found to be much less conclusive than everybody had thought; one by one the jurors admit to doubts. Finally the Puerto Rican boy from the slums of New York is unanimously found not guilty of murdering his father.

Of the 375 takes of the film almost all were shot in a real jury meeting room and almost all of them from a different camera angle. Before Twelve Angry Men this would have been considered a display of cinematic heresy or deplorable extravagance; in 1956 it was received as a revelation of new narrative possibilities of the cinema. For all the film's simplicity of means of expression, Lumet and the photographer Kaufman (the brother of Dziga Vertov, the Soviet director) achieved dramatic coherence and an intense atmosphere. Subsequent achievements in the cinema and television revealed imperfections in this pioneering concerto for 12 men in an enclosed space and overshadowed its novel transplantation of TV techniques into the cinema. But nothing could take away from the film its tone of authority and human concern: what on the surface seems a praise of American democracy is in fact a warning against the fallibility of the jury system. The eulogy for the just juror No. 8 offers at the same time a bitter and disquieting reflection on the attitudes and mentality of his fellow jury members, on the unreliability of circumstantial evidence, the indifference of the officials in the judicial system. The film's concern is with the independence and objectivity of thought, the qualities of which only one of the twelve

Twelve Angry Men

American citizens present can boast, a veritable rider from nowhere in the world of cheap, ready-to-wear and thereby reactionary attitudes to reality. Juror No. 1 is a glib and pleasant opportunist; juror No. 2--a quiet, 35-year-old bank clerk--is used to not having an opinion of his own; juror No. 3 is a transport executive, peremptory and dogmatic; juror No. 4 considers himself a sharp rationalist, but does not understand that he is dealing with real life and not a detective puzzle; the main desire of juror No. 5 is to forget his childhood spent in a slum; juror No. 6 does not venture beyond the instinctive class sympathies and antipathies; juror No. 7 is a typical customer of the far right, a minor jam manufacturer to whom all evil comes from the Reds; juror No. 9 understands little but comes to hold the balance of the verdict precisely because everyone thought him unimportant; juror No. 10 is a racist and a zealous supporter of authority; juror No. 11, a German-American, has excessive confidence in U. S. justice and combines honesty with snobbery; juror No. 12 is a nobody with an inferiority complex. One may complain that the composition of this assembly of men, well characterized as individuals, is a little too contrived, especially in view of the film's many psychoanalytical references; it is also true to say that despite several outstanding roles the actors are hardly a team, but only a collection of diverse individuals against the background of which juror No. 8 (Henry Fonda) shines with all the more brightness. Finally, the development of the plot itself is too smooth and this harms the credibility of situations. With all that, however, Twelve Angry Men has a much higher specific gravity than most other American social dramas, and the conclusion drawn from the analysis of the group of twelve people (that the unshakeable independence of judgment of one of its members strengthens the independence of judgment of all the others) is correct and important.

THE FORTY-FIRST (Sorok pervyi) Grigori Chukhrai

Script: Grigori Koltunov, from the short story by Boris Lavrenyov. Photography: Sergei Urusevsky. Music: Nikolai Kryukov. Art Direction: V. Kamsky and K. Stepanov. Cast: Izolda Izvitskaya (Mariutka), Oleg Strizhenov (Lieutenant Govorukha-Otrok), Nikolai Kryuchkov (Comissar Yevsukov), G. Shapovalov (Terentyev).

Mosfilm, U. S. S. R. 8322 ft., 92 mins. Sovcolor.

The Forty-First marks the beginning of the series of Soviet films in which the ponderous declamation of the Stalinist period gave way to lyricism and genuine emotion. Protazanov's The Forty-First, made way back in 1927, was a fairly faithful registration of external reality; Chukhrai's version of the same short story by Lavrenyov is a poetic intimation of the spiritual states of the two protagonists--the crack-shot Red Guard girl, Mariutka, and the "White" lieutenant whom the Reds have taken captive. Mariutka has already killed forty enemies in the Civil War; the man whom her bullet missed during a skirmish in the Kara-kum desert surrenders; he turns out to be a White liaison officer carrying particularly important information concerning counter-revolutionary forces in Kazakhstan. The commander orders the girl, a fanatical revolutionary, to take the important prisoner to headquarters; she is told she must not allow him to escape. While crossing the Aral sea the boat is wrecked in a storm; only the girl and her charge manage to reach a deserted, sandy islet. There Mariutka nurses the prisoner who has developed pneumonia. The danger passes, but Mariutka has fallen in love with him. The officer, who has so far kept at an ironic distance from his "primitive" enemies, responds in kind and with boyish openness allows himself to be overcome by the happiness of love. Each of them sees the future differently: the man wants to escape far away from the war, while the girl considers it her duty to fight until victory. But this disagreement is not enough to break their love. In the meantime fighting goes on: when a "White" boat appears off the shore of the islet and the prisoner runs to meet it, Mariutka pulls the trigger in a sudden impulse and this time does not miss. He is her forty-first dead enemy. Only a few moments later does she realize, to her despair, what she has done.

Contrary to the usual interpretation of the film in Russia, it is not a drama of choice, in which the good of society is placed before the personal happiness of individuals, but a tragedy of wartime necessity: the lieutenant must die, because he is in possession of sensitive military information about the deployment of revolutionary forces. It is unfortunate that the imperfect execution of the finale of The Forty-First completely obscures this alternative: in Chukhrai's version of the story Mariutka shoots because she momentarily loses her head. She becomes an instinctive instrument of the revolution; her actions are faster than her emotions and faster still than her analytical thoughts. On the other hand, this necessity to give priority to action over emotions was a genuine attribute of the times; thus if the finale of The Forty-First is not perfect, it is because it departs (as do some scenes in the beginning) from the dominant tonality of the picture. Chukhrai, who goes counter to the established stereotypes in the Soviet cinema, is a lyricist, a humanist who sees renewal as occurring not by way of intellectual polemic and uncompromising realism, but (as the French Nouvelle Vague did a couple of years later) by way of giving proper attention to the interior, the problems and the frailty of man. Socialist Realist cinema was not interested in such things: its protagonists moved along straight lines with unflinching resolve. The Forty-First is the first direct reference in the Soviet cinema to the individual human tragedies along the roadside of history; to the rationale and the personal qualities of the enemies of the revolution--before they were seen simply as monsters. The story of Mariutka and the "White" lieutenant is not free from psychological inconsistencies and formal stumbles (like the ponderous musical background, a remnant of Socialist Realism; or the story of the Man Friday spangled with little stars) but wins over the spectator with its emotionality, honesty, imaginative execution and editing. But even more so with its visual aspect: Urusevsky's photography is a revelation equally in the dramatic scenes of the desert crossing and in the romantic pastel quality of the portrayal of young lovers in a world of water, sand and smooth sky.

THE THRONE OF BLOOD (Kumu-no su-jō) Akira Kurosawa

Script: Shinobu Hashimoto, Ryuzo Kikushima, Hideo Oguni and Kurosawa, based on the play "Macbeth" by William Shakespeare. Photography: Asaichi Nakai. Music: Masaru Sato. Art Direction: Yoshiro Muraki and Kohei Ezaki. Cast: Toshiro Mifune (Taketoki Washizu), Isuzu Yamada (Asaji), Takashi Shimura (Noriyasu Odagura), Minoru Chiaki (Yoshiaki Miki), Akira Kubo (Yoshiteru), Takamaru Sasaki (Kuniharu Tsuzuki), Yoichi Tachikawa (Kunimaru), Chieko Naniwa (Witch).

Shojiro Motoki and Akira Kurosawa for Toho, Japan. 9862 ft., 110 mins.

Seven Samurai was more than a remarkably successful period picture--it revitalized the traditional Japanese jidai-geki genre which had become lost in stylish but insipid tales from the past. Kurosawa gave it immediacy, topicality and power. He continues on this course in The Throne of Blood, a brilliant adaptation of "Macbeth."

Japan in the Middle Ages. Washizu and Miki, two generals who command forts under the authority of Tsuzuki, Lord of Cobweb Castle, are returning from a victorious battle. While riding through the forest they meet an old woman bent over a spinning wheel in a lonely clearing. She prophesies that Washizu will first command the Northern Fort, and later Cobweb Castle itself and that he will be succeeded by Miki's son, not by his own. The first prediction comes true almost immediately. When Washizu tells his wife Asaji about the prophecy, she incites him to murder Tsuzuki--and thus the second prediction is fulfilled. Asaji then tells her husband that she is pregnant and persuades him to murder Miki and his son. But the son escapes and joins the forces of a rival war lord, who is approaching Cobweb Castle. Washizu consults the old woman again. She tells him that he is safe until Cobweb Forest starts to move. It does: the besieging troops cut down the trees for camouflage and march on the castle. Washizu is killed with volleys of arrows by his own men.

The Throne of Blood is among the best cinematic adaptations

of Shakespeare, who is one of Kurosawa's favorite authors. The savage "Macbeth" functions well in medieval Japan. Kurosawa removed most of Shakespeare's minor characters and concentrated on the story of a man being destroyed by ambition. He gave much more attention than the play does to the political aspects of the drama. The story is simply more fully supported by the mechanics of power and by psychological motivations. In the strongly stressed prologue Washizu is introduced as a loyal second-in-command--and history clearly shows what course of action ambitious deputy leaders so often took in Asia. Also different (from "Macbeth") are the arguments used by Asaji: she tells her husband to betray, because otherwise he will be betrayed himself. Thus Washizu's actions are motivated by a kind of self-defense. The resulting chain of "necessary" crimes continues until Miki's death. Washizu goes on killing in order to maintain his power and authority. Demons have been awakened already, and murder is a psychologically inexpensive way of satisfying their demands.

Still, Kurosawa's political philosophy is richly tinted with misogyny: the entire evil is blamed on a woman visited by devils. She does act in accordance with the mechanisms of power, but it is also always she who bears the guilt. At the beginning of The Throne of Blood Washizu had no thought of treason. One may say in Kurosawa's defense that Asaji is the sole female villain in the whole of his cinema.

The film's stylization after the traditional Japanese noh theatre, which had so far very little influence on the cinema, gave most interesting effects. A noh play is performed on a bare stage, traditionally by men only, with carefully measured gestures and utmost restraint. Kurosawa explained: "This is a film in which I borrow most from noh. Shakespeare's dramas invite a comparison with noh and this is where I took the stage design from, characterization, the style of direction. I could even analyze The Throne of Blood shot by shot, by referring to the forms of noh. According to European theatrical conventions, the actor combines the elements of his vision of the character in a uniform acting style. In noh on the other hand, the actor expresses himself through mask-like stylization known as omote to achieve a dramatically expressive result. Omote is the very opposite of acting, and each shot in The Throne of Blood corresponds precisely with one of its forms." This noh stylization is seen in the music, the rhythm of the interior scenes, in the witch character, the use of chorus (as in They Who Step on the Tiger's Tail)--but it is above all associated with the Asaji character. Her face, frighteningly ugly, is a remote, absolutely impassive mask covered by a thick layer of make-up. As she speaks, her eyes are fixed to the floor. This is a most interesting treatment of Lady Macbeth--and a great part by Isuzu Yamada, chilling and brilliant. Macbeth himself, although very well played, is less original and less important--a little, weak man.

The stylization is the main reason for the film's formal restraint. There are almost no close-ups, in which noh gestures would lose their psychological sense. Another reason is that making a film to resemble a play requires the use of a "stage" substitute. There are likewise no fades or dissolves, and scenes are joined with simple cuts or with wipes. Formally this is a very simple film--simple and hard, like the cruel world without hope which it describes.

But this does not stop The Throne of Blood from being visually stunning. Kurosawa reflected the clear-cut photography which recalls Japanese ink drawings. Splendid use is made of such visual effects as fog, rain or shining armor. As in Xanadu in Citizen Kane, the low ceilings of the huge rooms of the castle create a sense of oppression and threat. Everything here is purposeful, functional and effective. As in Rashomon the forest itself is an allegory. In the powerful opening Washizu and Miki are lost in the forest; they are seen to gallop into and out of the fog twelve times, which creates--as Donald Richie remarked--a sense of confusion and futility. The scene of Cobweb Castle moving has the pathos of the inevitable, while the killing of Washizu, who dies in an animal rage, turned into a moving pincushion by the arrows of his men, is almost operatic in its grandiose violence. The Throne of Blood is a superb, gloomy vision of a rain-swept universe of crime and despair.

GERVAISE René Clément

Script: Jean Aurenche and Pierre Bost, from the novel "L'Assomoir" by Emile Zola. Photography: René Juillard. Music: Georges Auric. Art Direction: Paul Bertrand; also Roger Briaucourt. Cast: Maria Schell (Gervaise), François Périer (Coupeau), Suzy Delair (Virginie), Armand Mestral (Lantier), Jacques Harden (Goujet), Mathilde Casadesus (Mme. Boche), Jacques Hilling (M. Boche), Ariane Lancell (Adèle), Jany Holt (Mme. Lorilleux), Hubert Lapparent (M. Lorilleux), Michèle Luccioni (Clémence), Chantal Gozzi (Nana), André Wasley (Père Colombe), Florelle (Maman Coupeau), Pierre Duverger (M. Gaudron), Jacqueline Morane (Mme. Gaudron), Peignot (M. Madinier), Rachel Devirys (Mme. Fauconnier), Max Elbeze (Zidore), Helen Tossy (Mme. Bijard).

Agnès Delahaye/Silver Films/C. L. C. C. , France. 102 mins.

Clément finally proves that he can do everything: after trying his hand at many different cinematic genres he has his last big success with the very authentic film version of Zola's novel. Clément transferred to the screen not only the book's naturalistic style, but the whole atmosphere of the social lows of Paris in the late 19th century. The selection of material from the novel and the condensation of the plots are very well done; the dramatic axis of the film

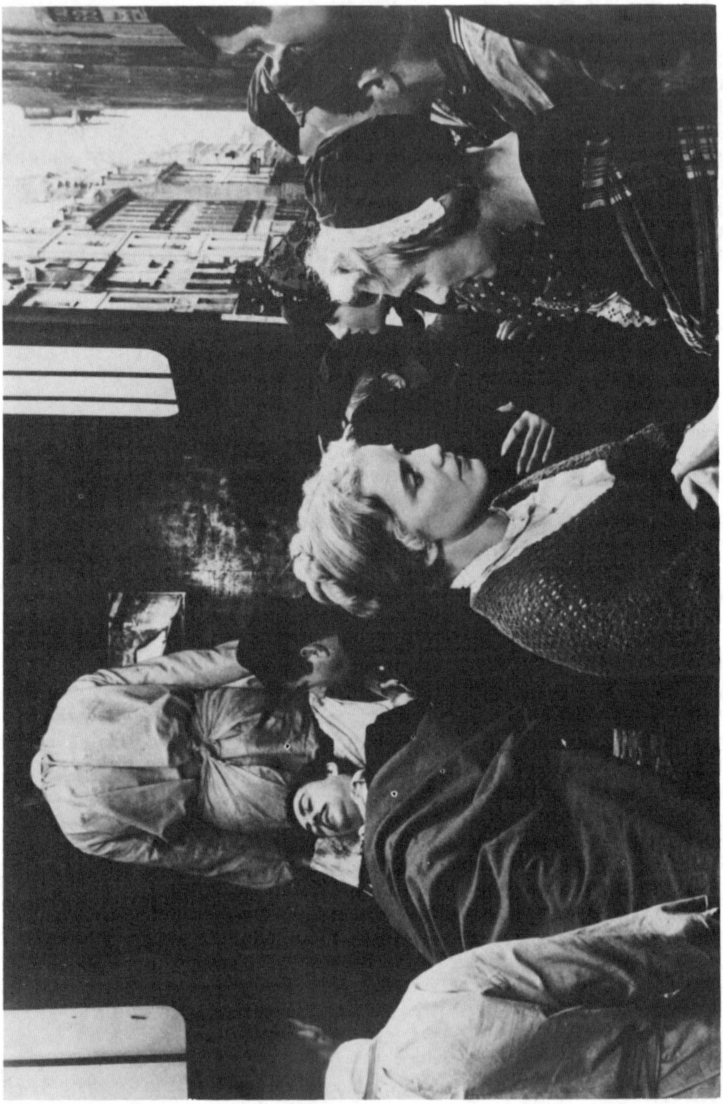

Gervaise

is the life story of a country girl who, having become a Paris washerwoman at the age of ten, and a mother four years later, obstinately fought throughout her youth for a better life, but was ruthlessly pushed into the gutter. It must have been difficult at the time to imagine the delicate Maria Schell in the title part, but in chosing her Clément was as inspired and as right as was later Visconti when he cast Burt Lancaster in the part of a Sicilian aristocrat in The Leopard. The part of the lame washerwoman is the crowning triumph in the career of this Austrian-born Swiss actress, a role which fits perfectly Zola's world of penury and degradation. In Gervaise, Clément once more displays his quite exceptional ability for capturing the character and essence of diverse environments: the film's images, sustained in a uniformly grey tonality, emanate a sense of weariness and hopelessness; one can almost smell the stale dampness of the wash-house, human characters are surrounded by delapidated furniture, peeling walls and muddy streets; the stress given to the detail serves to underline the wretchedness of their existence. Against this background the director sets a number of fine naturalistic scenes, such as the fight in the wash-house, the birthday party, Coupeau's deliric fury--but Clément never chases after a crude effect, and follows Zola with loyalty and consistency both in the way of seeing things and in the film's intellectual conclusions (for instance in treating Nana, Gervaise's third child, as the victim of the parents' hereditary burdens). However, the finest component of Gervaise, a real tour de force, is Clément's narrative precision: the synthetic characterization of characters, the study of their motivation, the intelligent deep-focus staging of the action on the screen, the ability to convey an entire complex situation by concentrating on a mere detail.

BABY DOLL Elia Kazan

Script: Kazan, adapted from an original screenplay by Tennessee Williams based on two of his one-act plays, "Twenty Seven Wagons Full of Cotton" and "The Unsatisfactory Supper." Photography: Boris Kaufman. Music: Kenyon Hopkins. Art Direction: Richard Sylbert. Costumes: Anna Hill Johnstone. Editing: Gene Milford. Cast: Karl Malden (Archie Lee Meighan), Carroll Baker (Baby Doll Meighan), Eli Wallach (Silva Vacarro), Mildred Dunnock (Aunt Rose Comfort), Lonny Chapman (Rock), Eades Hogue (County Sheriff), Noah Williamson (Sheriff's Deputy), Jimmy Williams (Mayor), John Stuart Dudley (Doctor John), Madeleine Sherwood (Nurse), Will Lester (Sheriff), Rip Torn (Dentist).

Elia Kazan for Newtown-Warner Bros., U. S. A. 10,301 ft., 114 mins.

For the theme of his next film after East of Eden Kazan went to two short plays by Tennessee Williams with whom he had cooperated five years before on A Streetcar Named Desire. Baby Doll turned out to be one of Kazan's best works and it is remarkable how well the film succeeds with themes he was unable to handle satisfactorily earlier.

So it's the Deep South again: the story is set in a small town in the Mississippi Delta, and much of the picture was shot in Benoit, near Williams's own birthplace. The teenage bride of middle-aged Archie Lee Meighan, Baby Doll was given away by her father who was anxious for his daughter's future. But the marriage cannot be consummated until her twentieth birthday. On the eve of the day, the frustrated husband, upset by Baby Doll's indifference towards him, burns down the cotton mill belonging to Silva Vacarro, a Sicilian immigrant and a successful business rival. On a hot summer afternoon Vacarro calls on Baby Doll, alone in the rambling house and questions her to find out whether her husband was responsible for starting the fire. He extracts from her an admission of Archie's crime, but also awakens her latent womanhood. When Archie returns they taunt him together. Thinking that Vacarro had seduced Baby Doll, Archie goes berserk and is taken away. His mission fulfilled, Vacarro also leaves. Baby Doll is left alone.

The film made movie history even at the moment of its release. It caused a storm: Cardinal Spellman denounced it from the pulpit of St. Patrick's Cathedral in New York, and it was the first picture made by a major Hollywood studio to be condemned by the Legion of Decency. But fortunately the producers were firm and did not yield to pressure to confine Baby Doll to the shelves. The fuss was caused by the film's atmosphere of sexual innuendo (there is hardly a single shot which could in itself be considered objectionable). A southern Lolita, Baby Doll is a symbol of wanton sexuality and perverse innocence. She lies in the cot sucking her thumb--the epitome of adolescent provocation. It is to Kazan's credit that he succeeded in evoking the mood of ambivalence with such consistency and such a degree of directorial control. A colorful mixture of comedy and passion, Baby Doll is a subtle and mature study of spiritual corruption. Note, for instance, the excellent handling of the disturbing game of hide-and-seek Vacarro and Baby Doll play in the deserted mansion.

Referring to the picture's visual style, Kazan said: "The whole idea was white on white. Bleached out, bleached out--the end of the South." Indeed, the visual contrast between the heroine, all in white, and the confident and aggressive Vacarro, dressed in black, captured in sophisticated high-key photography is symbolic of the decline of the old South, a recurrent motif in Williams's work. The sleazy feel of the Deep South, the aura of decay, with blacks lazing in the sun, is very suggestive on the screen. This is one motif which escaped Kazan in A Streetcar Named Desire. Here he succeeds completely: in creating the atmosphere, conducting the narrative and--very importantly--in directing the actors according to the famous Actors' Studio Method which calls for complete identification of the actor with the role he plays.

YIELD TO THE NIGHT J. Lee Thompson

Script: John Cresswell and Joan Henry, based on the novel by the latter. Photography: Gilbert Taylor. Music: Ray Martin. Art Direction: Robert Jones. Editing: Richard Best. Cast: Diana Dors (Mary Hilton), Yvonne Mitchell (Macfarlane), Michael Craig (Jim Lancaster), Marie Ney (Governor), Geoffrey Keen (Chaplain), Liam Redmond (Doctor), Olga Lindo (Hill), Joan Miller (Barker), Marjorie Rhodes (Brandon), Molly Urquhart (Mason), Mary Mackenzie (Maxwell), Harry Locke (Fred), Athene Seyler (Miss Bligh).

Kenneth Harper for Associated British, G. B. 8994 ft., 100 mins.

In making his passionate pleas for justice and leniency in the courts, André Cayatte employed a lawyer's logic: We Are All Murderers, his protest against capital punishment, considered several individual case histories, but each of them was in some way exceptional. Consequently, a doubt might remain as to the general applicability of the points Cayatte made, and the precision of argument and cinematic excellence could not eliminate the controversial character of his starting point. Lee Thompson, who took up the question of capital punishment in Yield to the Night dispensed with the discussion of facts: the guilt of Mary Hilton is not disputed. Mary has killed the socialite woman who led her lover to suicide; she did it while in a state of exceptional emotional tension, although the law sees the murder as premeditated. It is difficult to find extenuating circumstances in her way of life--she left her husband to live with the lover. Although Lee Thompson with magisterial solemnity explains in a series of flashbacks how hasty and unreliable was the appraisal of the real scale of values of the murderer and her victim, he leaves these questions aside, at a distance, just as they now appear to the heroine.

The main problem of Yield to the Night is that of the moral aspect of the death penalty and is approached by way of a description of Mary Hilton's states of mind during the nerve-racking days of waiting either for the reprieve or the execution. The concentrated observation of the prisoner's behavior, the wardens, the topography of the cell are all done using a wide variety of camera angles (in Lee Thompson's next film, Woman in a Dressing Gown (1957) this unfortunately became a mannerism). This attitude of minute observation, together with the use of the soundtrack are reminiscent of Bresson's A Man Escaped and generate a comparable emotional pressure on the audience, in which the question of the sense and morality of taking life as a punishment acquires a proper specific gravity. One of the most praiseworthy things in the film is Lee Thompson's decision to give the leading part to an actress, who to the British cinema of the 50's was an embodiment of sex appeal. In a part completely different from any she had played before, Diana

Dors turned out to be astonishingly true, direct, dignified and human. Her presence gave this moving drama additional value. Lee Thompson's film assails very effectively the conservative views and way of life of the British, but from quite a different standpoint than did the later films of the Angry Young Men.

GRAND' RUE (Calle Mayor) Juan Antonio Bardem

Script: Bardem, inspired by the comedy "La senorita de Trevelez" by Carlos Arniches. Photography: Michel Kelber. Music: Joseph Kosma; also Isidro B. Maiztegui. Art Direction: Enrique Alarcón. Editing: Marguerite de Ochoa. Cast: Betsy Blair (Isabel Castro), José Suárez (Juan), Yves Massard (Federico Rivas), René Blancard (Don Tomaso), Dora Doll (Tonia), Lila Kedrova (Mme. Pepita), Luis Peña, Matilde Munoz Sampedro, Alfonso Soda, Manuel Alexandre, José Calvo, Maria Gamez.

Manuel J. Goyanes for Suevia/Cesáreo González/Play-Art/Iberia Films, Spain/France. 100 mins.

Grand' Rue, Bardem's attack against selfishness, is in essence a bitter and dramatic accusation of the hypocrisy of provincial Spain, of the whole tangle of reasons, which in the devotional, conservative society, paralyze the influence of every broader, more liberal and civilized outlook and thwart attempts at breaking free of moldy moral tenets. The story of the cruel practical joke which a group of irresponsible young loafers set up to humiliate a 35-year-old spinster is only on the surface a variation on Clair's Les Grandes manoeuvres in a more serious vein. The commentary which opens the film says that the story is set in an undefined place and at an undefined time; but this is only a pretense. It soon becomes abundantly clear that Bardem is talking about Spain in the late autumn of 1955. His intentions are aptly summed up by the following line of dialogue spoken by the only honest man in that hopeless provincial backwater: "Madrid with its neon signs is a mere sham. The real truth about man is to be found here." The deplorable "entertainment" of a group of primitive petty bourgeois, who do not know of more exciting ways to pass the time than to persuade a man recently arrived from Madrid to pretend that he has fallen in love with Isabel and who do not care about the tragedy of their victim who really loves the man, stems partly from selfishness. But this selfishness is only a secondary effect of the suppression of human individuality in the cogs of nightmarish social conventions. Another effect is inertia and irresponsibility: the cowardly "candidate for a husband" cannot summon the courage to tell the woman the truth although his conscience is troubled; the unfortunate victim cannot bring herself to leave the town where she has been wronged. The persuasions of a friend who offers her help in Madrid are in vain: there is no other way of life, there is nowhere else to go, nothing else to do. In the end Isabel isolates herself from the world between the four walls of her flat.

The fine description of characters and psychological situations, supported by sensitive performances from the actors, is achieved in Grand' Rue via the inventive, carefully thought-out narrative structure. In his cinema Bardem does not offer new solutions, but he knows how to make use of the existing ones, appropriately and always with his individual touch. He has made a film which is classical in form and full of vital human problems. There are two basic narrative principles here: the use of the leitmotif and the structure of the musical rondo; the end of the episodes returns to the starting point, while the visual and acoustic elements are repeated. This method creates the sense of isolation, helplessness and futility. Dramatic tension is stepped up by introducing into the frame sharp visual contrasts and by increasing the intensity of the music; the culminations (the proposal made during a religious procession, the evening before the ball, the scene at the railway station) use vehement editing, sharp changes of camera angles, exaggeration and deformation of the sound, and also intensification and condensation of the symbols which Bardem uses often and on many levels throughout the film.

Grand' Rue gave rise to expectations that Bardem would make many more remarkable films. This was not to be. The Spaniard's name came up only twice during the next twenty years--on the occasion of the internally fractured Sonatas (1959) and again after Nothing Ever Happens (1963), a pale repetition of the motifs of Grand' Rue. It was only in 1977 that Bardem found himself in the limelight again.

EARLY SPRING (Sōshun) Yasujiro Ozu

Script: Kogo Noda and Ozu. Photography: Yushun Atsuta. Music: Takanori Saito. Art Direction: Setsutaro Moritani. Editing: Yoshiyasu Hamamuri. Cast: Ryo Ikebe (Sugiyama), Chikage Awashima (Masako Sugiyama), Keiko Kishi ("Goldfish," an office girl), Chishu Ryu (Onodera), So Yamamura (Kawai), Haruko Sugimura (Masako's mother), Kuniko Miyake (Sakae), Eijiro Tono (Hattori).

Shizuo Yamauchi for Shochiku, Japan. 13,363 ft., 149 mins.

Sugiyama, a young white-collar employee of a big Tokyo company is bored with both his job and his wife. He has a fling with a "modern" girl from the office, but this solves nothing. A colleague

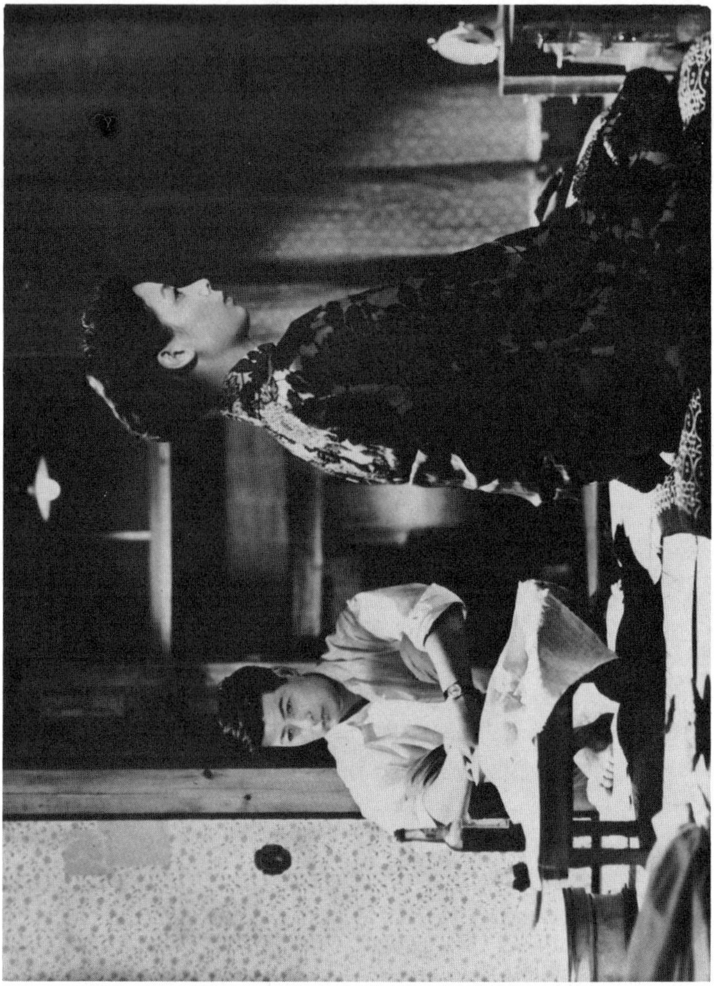

Early Spring

dies. A drink with friends brings back memories of friends killed in the war and ends in sadness. Sugiyama quarrels with his wife. He is transferred to Osaka, to a provincial branch of his firm. He is lonely, but his wife comes from Tokyo to join him. They become reconciled and decide to start all over again.

From this slight plot Ozu made a 149-minute picture, one of his longest. Very little happens in Early Spring: it is a film of subtle observation of ordinary events, of small gestures, insignificant conversations, day-to-day routines at home and at work. Ozu had always been a most perceptive observer. But this time, despite expending an exceptional amount of effort on every aspect of the production (the writing of the script took three months and the shooting three years) he simply was not able to match the excellence of such films as Late Spring or Tokyo Story. Although lacking in cohesion and a little repetitive, Early Spring is a detailed (and, as usual, sympathetic) character study and a social comment about the human price to be paid for industrial progress. Ozu said about the story: "I wanted to show the life of a man with such a job--his happiness over graduating and finally becoming a member of society, his hopes for the future gradually dissolving, his realizing that, even though he had worked for years, he has accomplished nothing." In making the film he used his characteristic style: scenes are introduced by establishing long-shots of buildings or roads. Early Spring opens with a long-shot of the enormous office building accompanied on the soundtrack by the monotonous, incessant rattle of the many typewriters. Thus Ozu makes an instant comment on the boredom and emptiness of office routine which makes people feel like cogs in a machine. There are in the picture a number of well-drawn characters, humor, quiet irony and the particularly successful sequence of an office Sunday excursion. While it is difficult to talk of Ozu ever drawing conclusions, the ending of Early Spring, in which Sugiyama finds refuge in family life, interestingly resonates with the message of Delbert Mann's The Bachelor Party, the film's Western equivalent.

THE BACHELOR PARTY Delbert Mann

Script: Paddy Chayefsky from his TV play. Photography: Joseph La Shelle. Music: Paul Madeira. Art Direction: Edward Haworth. Cast: Don Murray (Charlie Samson), E. G. Marshall (Walter), Jack Warden (Eddie), Philip Abbott (Arnold), Larry Blyden (Kenneth), Patricia Smith (Helen Samson), Carolyn Jones (Existentialist), Nancy Marchand (Julie), Karen Norris (Hostess), Barbara Ames (Girl on stoop), Norma Arden Campbell (Stripteaser).

Harold Hecht for Norma Productions, U. S. A. 93 mins.

A moment of truth about modern loneliness in the crowd. Four New York office workmates give a stag party for the fifth who is about to be married; it is as tawdry as the everyday existence of the participants: under the slight influence of drink Charlie, Walter, Eddie, Kenneth and Arnold travel aimlessly on the subway, watch some blue movies at Eddie's flat, visit a nightclub, then go to a snobbish party in Greenwich Village. They are all too preoccupied with everyday life to be able to relax, too overwhelmed by worries to let go the reins of gaiety, too intimidated by the stresses of civilization to show any inventiveness in enjoying themselves. Walter cannot stop thinking about his son, for whose medical studies he must find money in spite of being in bad health; Charlie is depressed by the thought of the unwanted child his wife is expecting; Arnold, the husband-to-be, is worried about his sexual inexperience. There are also the inexorable deadlines for paying the installments and the evening courses, this nightmarish illusion which consumes every free moment in the name of hope for a salary rise. As the men discover only emptiness and boredom within themselves, they are dazzled by the last glimmer of hope: the family, the thought of being able to communicate with someone really close, of achieving peace and emotional security. This way out of the incapacitating inertia is perhaps as unoriginal as the rest of the situation of the middle-class American male, but it still remains a solution, despite domestic problems, overwork, money worries, the monotony of being always with the same person within the same four walls--for it brings a human element into the world of mechanized uniformity.

Essentially one of the most tragic American films, The Bachelor Party testifies to the further invasion of the TV technique into the cinema: this manifests itself as a profusion of dialogue, the static content of the frame and nervous editing aimed at overcoming the immobility of the camera. The narrative style is not only subordinated to the requirements of the rather intimate type of story, limited to a handful of locations and devoid of situational turns, but is such that the characters are isolated from their background, a device which stresses their loneliness. The photography shuns any decorative leanings. But the whole gives a strong sense of authenticity and generates a suggestive, overpowering mood. This very ordinary drama is one of those which in the 50's discovered new continents in the world of cinema.

KANAL (Kanał) Andrzej Wajda

Script: Jerzy Stefan Stawiński, from his own short story. Photography: Jerzy Lipman. Music: Jan Krenz; also Adam Pawlikowski (Ocarina theme). Art Direction: Roman Mann. Cast: Wieńczysław Gliński (Lieutenant Zadra), Tadeusz Janczar (Korab), Teresa Iżewska (Stokrotka), Emil Karewicz (Mądry), Władysław Sheybal (The musician), Stanisław Mikulski (Smukły), Teresa Berezowska (Halinka), Tadeusz Gwiazdowski (Kula), Adam Pawlikowski (German officer).

Stanisław Adler for ZAF Kadr, Poland. 8569 ft., 95 mins.

Late September 1944, the 56th day of the Warsaw Rising which was to collapse a week later. A decimated Home Army company defends the few streets of the Mokotów district of the city which are still in the insurgents' hands; this area of Warsaw is cut off from the center where their main forces are grouped. The order arrives telling the isolated group of men and women to proceed to the center; the only line of retreat is through the sewers. The film is based on Stawiński's personal experiences and tells about the tragic end of the unit. The prologue tells us this: "These are the last hours of these people's lives. Mark them well!" As we first meet them, they are still together, in the strength-giving daylight; for the passage through the sewers they split into three groups: the wounded Korab ("Brig") assisted by a courier girl Stokrotka ("Daisy") who is in love with him; weakened by alcohol, Mądry ("Wise") is accompanied by his mistress Halinka and a half-mad musician, the main group is led by Zadra ("Splinter"), the commander, with Smukły ("Slender") and Kula ("Ball"). Stokrotka and Korab reach the sewer exit to the river, find it has been blocked by an iron grill by the Germans, and die of exhaustion; the musician goes mad and wanders off into the labyrinth of the sewers playing his ocarina; Halinka commits suicide when her lover confesses to having a wife and children; he himself reaches a manhole and emerges into the street at the place where the Nazis shoot the soldiers of the Rising; Smukły dies while trying to open a mined manhole; Zadra and Kula reach their destination, but when Kula's fraud is revealed (he has maintained throughout that the others are following them, while in fact they have been left behind and are lost in the labyrinth) Zadra shoots him and returns underground to look for his men....

The first film devoted to the hecatomb of the Warsaw Rising in which nearly 200,000 people, mostly civilians, lost their lives, had a rather cool reception in Poland. Instead of making a monument to tragic glory, as was expected, Wajda and Stawiński showed the nightmare of defeat and the exhausted people whose heroism was useless in view of the false political and military strategy of the Home Army Command. It was only after its international success (the Silver Palm at the 1957 Cannes Film Festival) that Kanal was grudgingly given justice at home.

Neither the designs, the topography nor especially the lighting give an authentic replica of the sewers; all the same, Wajda's Expressionist, highly-tensed narrative creates a substitute atmosphere which keeps falsity away. Perhaps only the behavior and reactions of the girl insurgents are untrue; the closing of the Halinka-Mądry sub-plot has clearly more to do with pseudo-Existentialism of the 1957 vintage than with 1944. Overdone are Zadra's sorrow, the emphasis on the tragic irony of fate in all the sub-plots and the protagonists' reaction to it.

Kanal

The release of Kanal was a shock both to home and foreign audiences, although for different reasons. Outside Poland the film was shocking because it revealed something monstrous and unknown; as a result critical commentaries overlooked the faults in the staging of the sewer scenes and the somewhat superficial treatment of the psychology of the protagonists. On the other hand Wajda was justly praised for successfully combining the first, semi-documentary, part of the film with the subsequent apocalyptic account of the insurgents' wanderings through the sewers, this relentless nightmare being described in close shots and from varied camera angles, sharp camera movements in high-contrast lighting and accompanied by the awesome, Expressionist soundtrack. Wajda was also commended for his handling of the ending of the sub-plots--static and still, reflecting the paralysis with the dazzling sunlight, the stifling sensation of realizing that one has been cruelly cheated by a ray of hope. In Poland however, it was the starting premise of Kanal which was in the center of debate. The film's sarcastic attitude to the leaders of the Rising was understood as an attack on heroism, particularly provocative after so many years of official silence about the Rising and discrimination against Home Army members. But Kanal is not anti-heroic; it is only anti-monumental. Wajda would protest against thoughtless heroism in his later Lotna. Kanal shows people as they are determined and molded by events: some persevere bravely while others break under pressure. It is precisely this frank portrayal of all types of human actions which is of the greatest value in Kanal.

Kanal

SEVEN MEN FROM NOW Budd Boetticher

Script: Burt Kennedy. Photography: William H. Clothier. Music: Henry Vars. Art Direction: Leslie Thomas. Editing: Everett Sutherland. Cast: Randolph Scott (Ben Stride), Gail Russell (Annie Greer), Lee Marvin (Big Masters), Walter Reed (John Greer), John Larch (Pate Bodeen), Donald Barry (Clete), Fred Graham (Henchman), John Barradino (Clint), John Phillips (Jed), Chuck Roberson (Mason), Steve Mitchell (Fowler), Stuart Whitman (Cavalry Lieutenant).

Andrew V. McLaglen and Robert E. Morrison for Batjac, U. S. A. 6924 ft., 77 mins. WarnerColor.

The modest and generally undervalued Budd Boetticher was the most interesting superwestern director of the 50's apart from Anthony Mann. One must give him his due mainly in appreciation of the very individual manner in which he treated this national American genre. Boetticher did not aim to discover historical concrete or search for mythology and did not follow the path of revision of the structural canons of the genre. Instead, he used the traditional western locations as a splendid, visually pure backdrop for debating the basic problems of human justice, while being absolutely true to the logic of behavior, of intentions, the logic of the times in which strength triumphs. Greed and vengeance are the motors of human actions in his films; cunning and ruthlessness are the prevalent rules of behavior. Although Boetticher cannot be said to have been a master of staging, often could not give credibility to some aspects of his plots and directed many scenes rather mechanically, he did possess a remarkable narrative terseness and the ability to observe very credibly the nuances of behavior of his uncomplicated protagonists. He had little respect for the rules of dramatic rhythm, allowed himself long pauses in screen tension, but very often conjured up a fascinating climate of authenticity of places and times and filled the empty places in the narrative with a romanticism of open space, the tension of immobility, a reflection on a loner who pursues his great aims. On the one hand Boetticher does not appear to venture beyond the themes of B-movies, but on the other amazes the spectator with the carefully thought-out visual conception of his films and the truth of his coarse and uncompromising vision of people. The superwestern period, i. e. the late 50's when in collaboration with Burt Kennedy and Randolph Scott he made Seven Men from Now, The Tall T (1957), Buchanan Rides Alone (1958) and Ride Lonesome (1959), was in fact only an episode in Boetticher's career. Before that he had been making mostly second-rate sesational pictures, and would later spend almost a decade on a documentary about Arruzzo, the Mexican master of the corrida, which was his passion in his youth. In each of the four films referred to Boetticher had an interesting script at his disposal, but it was only in Seven Men from

Now, a story of a former sheriff's vengeance on the bandits who in the course of a robbery killed his wife, that the script combines with the characteristic features of Boetticher's cinema to result in a lucid and complete film. Still, from the perspective of the years it has become clear that Boetticher must be considered the precursor of Sam Peckinpah and the naturalistic western; it was he who first in the American cinema broke free of the pressure of the stylistic tradition of the genre and showed the man of the West sharply and factually.

ELENA ET LES HOMMES (Paris Does Strange Things) Jean Renoir

Script: Jean Renoir and Jean Serge. Photography: Claude Renoir. Music: Joseph Kosma. Songs: "Méfiez-vous de Paris" by Léo Marjane; "O Nuit" by Juliette Gréco; and songs of the period arranged by Georges Van Parys. Art Direction: Jean André. Costumes: Rosine Delamare and Monique Plotin. Editing: Boris Lewin. Cast: Ingrid Bergman (Princess Eléna Sorokowska), Jean Marais (General François Rollan), Mel Ferrer (Viscount Henri de Chevincourt), Jean Claudio (Lionel Villaret), Jean Richard (Hector, Rollan's batman), Olga Valéry (Aunt Olga), Pierre Bertin (Martin-Michaud), Jean Castanier (Isnard), Dora Doll (Rosa la Rose), Frédéric Duvallès (Gaudin), Mirko Ellis (Marbeau), Juliette Gréco (Miarka), Jacques Hilling (Lisbonne), Jacques Jouanneau (Eugène Godin), Elina Labourdette (Paulette), Gaston Modot (Gypsy), Magali Noël (Lolotte, Eléna's maid), Albert Rémy (Buchez), Renaud Mary (Fleury), Jacques Morel Duchêne), Michèle Nadal (Denise Godin), Léo Marjane (Street singer).

Franco-London Films/Les Films Gibé/Electra Compania Cinematografica, France/Italy. 95 mins. Eastman Colour.

Renoir had always been attracted by the idea of working with outstanding actors. In his time he directed Jean Gabin, Louis Jouvet, Michel Simon, Pierre Fresnay, Erich von Stroheim, Anna Magnani and Jean-Louis Barrault. Eléna et les hommes was likewise made for an actress he very much admires: "For years I have been dying to make something gay with Ingrid Bergman. I wanted to see her laughing and smiling on the screen, to enjoy--and let the audience enjoy--the sort of uncomplicated sensuality which is one of her characteristics. In other words, I was thinking very much of Venus and Olympus ... perhaps a Venus slightly retouched by Offenbach."

Eléna Sorokowska is a Polish princess in exile in Paris (the time is the early days of the Third Republic) whose beauty and charm captivate any man on sight. Impulsive and capricious, she easily becomes enthusiastic about people and causes she thinks noble--

but tires of them quickly. She has aided and inspired the careers of several men, including Villaret, a composer, and Martin-Michaud, the king of footwear. The hero of the moment is General Rollan, a pawn in the hands of his political friends who want to exploit his popularity and stage a coup d'état. Viscount Henri de Chevincourt, Rollan's best friend, who had unwittingly aroused Eléna's interest in the General, and who admires her himself, is dismayed by her desire to become "a power behind the throne." He realizes that the best tactic is to help Rollan to achieve his objectives as soon as possible. When this is done, Eléna, as expected, soon loses interest in Rollan and leaves him to his success. But then she realizes that having spent so much time looking after men who needed her, it is now she who needs Henri--and remains with him.

The film certainly relies on acting very much; although the Rollan character is based on General Georges Boulanger, leader of a right-wing movement in the 1880's--this is not really of importance. There is no "message" to speak of, and this is probably why the whole is as successful as it is. To quote Renoir again: "I devised intricate arabesques of the plot and even got lost in them a little. Some dialogues are there only because I wanted to hear them spoken by my favorite actors". Actors in the plural because Renoir also likes Jean Marais and Mel Ferrer.

Renoir had one more aim in mind--to demonstrate the volatility and transitoriness of all human endeavor, to show ironically that the game of appearances is the true basis of human activity. He tried to do this in the earlier The Golden Coach (1952) and French Cancan (1955), but neither film was completely successful--while Eléna et les hommes has the virtuosity and meringue-cake lightness they were lacking. The adjective "Mozartian," which has been used about the film more than once, renders these qualities very well.

Renoir has a special feeling for the theatre and in Eléna et les hommes he tries several theatrical conventions. Thus the first part of the film is a comedy sustained in the grandiose style of a big spectacle; the second--a satirical vaudeville; the third--a story of confused feelings; and the finale--a dramatic conflict concluded with a song. Not all parts are equally successful: the central passages drag on a little, almost threatening to pull the film apart--but the finale recaptures the incomparable charm of the beginning. Thus Renoir amuses himself, free to apply at will the changes of narrative tone, as was always his favorite occupation. It is interesting that despite all this the film is technically very simple. There are no tracking shots, only few close-ups and the designs are not particularly refined.

BIGGER THAN LIFE Nicholas Ray

Script: Cyril Hume and Richard Maibaum, from the article "Ten Feet Tall" in "The New Yorker" by Berton Roueche, describing a case history. Photography: Joseph MacDonald. Music: David Raksin. Art Direction: Lyle R. Wheeler and Jack Martin Smith. Editing: Louis Loeffler. Cast: James Mason (Ed Avery), Barbara Rush (Lou Avery), Walter Matthau (Wally Gibbs), Robert Simon (Dr. Norton), Christopher Olsen (Richie Avery), Roland Winters (Dr. Ruric), Rusty Lane (La Porte), Rachel Stephens (Nurse), Kipp Hamilton (Pat Wade), Betty Caulfield (Mrs. La Porte), Virginia Carroll (Mrs. Jones), Henry McEvoy (Mr. Jones), Bill Jones (Mr. Byron).

James Mason for 20th Century-Fox, U. S. A. 8553 ft., 95 mins. CinemaScope. Eastman Colour.

Ed Avery, a small-town schoolteacher, suffers from a form of arthritis. He is prescribed cortisone and warned that the drug may affect his mental balance. It does: Ed goes through periods of exaltation alternating with periods of severe depression. He becomes addicted to cortisone, takes to forging doctors' prescriptions, persecutes his family while spinning high-minded plans for reforming the educational system. The situation almost results in tragedy when Ed tries to kill his wife and son. Overpowered by a family friend, he is taken to a hospital and recovers from his previous state.

With this story of a man who tried to overcome his physical limitations through taking excessive doses of a medicine, Ray wanted to appeal to everyone's sense of responsibility, to warn of the madness of consumerism and obsessive preoccupation with the standard of living and also to warn of a temptation to believe in a miraculous turn in one's existence, the illusion that one day one may find an easy solution to problems. To quote Ray's own words: "The film was not a story about cortisone, or any miracle drug. It was a story about a man, or any man, who relied on a miracle of any sort, whether drugs, or the temporary relief of alcohol, or an act of faith, or the money from a rich uncle's will...."

Bigger than Life, another variation on Ray's constant theme of a man devoured by ambition, by overgrowth of personality, is in fact one of his finest achievements. Only the banal optimism of the finale, which fortunately does not cancel out the film's dramatic intensity, can be considered a more serious fault. James Mason and other actors, including Christopher Olsen, deserve praise; fine, compact dialogues well suit the atmosphere not far removed from the hysteria of the plays of Tennessee Williams; the narrative is exceptionally fluid. Ray displays a fully mature style of direction, which attaches importance not only to the individual elements of the *mise en scène*, but also to their mutual interaction. This applies particularly to the use of space in the designs, the detail, the organization of the frame and also the use of color as an instrument of stress--while preserving a fully realistic screen conveyance and binding the whole into a suggestive, kinetic visual form. As an example one may quote the scene in which the hero walks away from the school: the dark colors of the school building give way to a general view of a large parking lot full of yellow cabs, which almost completely fill the screen and create an interesting coloristic comment on Ed's state of mind.

This film alone justifies Ray's being acclaimed by the French critics as one of the most interesting directors in the whole of the cinema.

THE RAILROAD MAN (Il ferroviere) Pietro Germi

Script: Germi, Alfredo Giannetti and Luciano Vincenzoni, from a story by Giannetti. *Photography*: Leonida Barboni. *Music*: Carlo Rustichelli. *Art Direction*: Carlo Egidi. *Editing*: Dolores Tamburini. *Cast*: Pietro Germi (Andrea), Luisa Della Noce (Sara), Sylva Koscina (Giulia), Carlo Giuffrè (Renato), Renato Speziali (Marcello), Edoardo Nevola (Sandro), Sara Urzî (Liverani).

ENIC/Carlo Ponti/Dino De Laurentiis, Italy. 10,440 ft., 116 mins.

The circular path traced by the narrative in many Neorealist films (for instance in *Umberto D.*, where the hero's situation at the end is the same as it was at the beginning) was to be followed by the trend itself: *The Railroad Man* returns in a sense to the starting point of Neorealism, to the generic description and little dramas of *Four Steps in the Clouds.* Germi's film, the best achievement of post-Neorealism, makes no moral appeals or social protests, and is a chronicle of one year's events in the life of the family of a railwayman, as seen through the eyes of a child. Like the narrator, the story is characterized by sharp observation and intimate emotion. The forced marriage of Sandro's sister and its subsequent breakdown, the eldest brother's departure from home, the disastrous error of his engine driver father who drives his express train through a red light and is demoted to driving a goods train, his depression drowned in drink, the joy of reconciliations during the family's Christmas get-together: episodes from life which from the point of view of their dramatic intensity are very ordinary indeed. In the hands of a director of less ability and lesser sense of proportion such material could have easily fallen apart, but Germi handled it very well. He combined the exceptional ease of the narrative with the fine balance of the film's emotions, which are never allowed to turn the picture into a melodrama, even though the situations themselves are potentially very melodramatic. From the crumbs of life Germi built a near-documentary record of the emotions, relationships and the life-style of an Italian family in those years. The actors are chosen and directed very appropriately. As a matter of fact, Germi himself turned out to be the best actor: his acting debut in the title part, the role of the father, full of warmth, energy and directness, reminds one that Germi studied (in the famous Centro Sperimentale) not only film directing. He can in fact easily stake a claim to have been one of the best actors in the Italian cinema of the period.

AN EYE FOR AN EYE (Oeil pour oeil) André Cayatte

Script: Cayatte and Vahé Katcha, from the novel by latter. Dialogues: Pierre Bost. Photography: Christian Matras. Music: Louiguy. Editing: Paul Cayatte. Cast: Curd Jürgens (Dr. Walter), Folco Lulli (Bortak), Lea Padovani (Lola Zordi), Pascale Audret (Bortak's sister-in-law), Dario Moreno (Café owner), Robert Porte (Malic), Paul Frankeur (Surgical case), Héléna Manson (Matron), Marlene Chichportiche (Bortak's daughter), Maria Zanolli (Mother-in-law).

Union Générale Cinématographique/Jolly Film/Galatea, France/Italy. 113 mins. VistaVision. Eastman Colour.

A supplement to Cayatte's series of courtroom dramas: in An Eye for an Eye the point is not the faults of institutional justice, but the imperfections inherent in any sort of justice meted out by one human being to another. The film juxtaposes two emotional attitudes, two mentalities, two cultural backgrounds in order to demonstrate that the pressure from the emotional strata makes it impossible for man to strike a proper balance between the offense and the punishment, that mutual misunderstanding inevitably breeds hatred and inflamed antagonisms bring spiritual destruction upon both the accused and the accuser. Cayatte proceeds to prove this thesis, set in the form of a classical naturalistic tragedy, in an exotic Middle Eastern setting.

After the death, from a misplaced pregnancy, of an Arab woman, Dr. Walter, a European surgeon who treated her with perhaps not enough Schweitzerian self-denial, is blamed by the dead woman's husband for what has happened. The vengeful widower exerts subtle moral pressure on the doctor, who is unquiet and anxious to exonerate himself, and lures him into a trap. Understanding between the two men turns out to be impossible and the conflict, as in von Stroheim's Greed, culminates in a tragic finale in a limitless desert. Why did two honest men deal death to each other?--Cayatte has a ready answer: because they lacked humility and openness. A fine conclusion; it is only that the manner in which it is arrived at gives rise to reservations. Not so much as regards the film's formal aspect, for that is characterized by narrative skill, a tense and mesmerizing dramatic atmosphere and very pure, intentionally gaudy photography. However, the collision of a sensitive European with the taciturn and unyielding Arab is too facile, the presentation of antagonistic cultural references too unbalanced and not objective, the psychological motivation not substantial enough, and finally, some details of the plot are unconvincing. As a result the film now and again falls short of an Evangelical morality play. Yet all this does not mean that An Eye for an Eye can be written off as an artistic failure. Rather, it may serve as an example of a work which is imperfect and yet of grand dimensions, a work which gives rise to reservations but also causes concern and deep reflection in the spectator. Cayatte did not have the good luck to score an equally weighty result in his later didactic jousts against human intolerance: the anti-lynch law The Sword and the Balance (1962) was based on too abstract a story; Mourir d'aimer (1970), an impassioned attack on bourgeois conservatism fell into melodramatic emphasis; while Les Assassins d'ordre (1971), a protest against autocracy and the brutality of the police turned out to be too tendentious in the choice of situations and the way of presenting them on the screen. So, Cayatte's problem was always to be the same one as in An Eye for an Eye: the inability to maintain proportions.

SOMEBODY UP THERE LIKES ME Robert Wise

Script: Ernest Lehman, based on the autobiography of Rocky Graziano, written with Rowland Barber. Photography: Joseph Ruttenberg. Music: Bronislau Kaper. Art Direction: Cedric Gibbons and Malcolm Brown. Editing: Albert Akst. Cast: Paul Newman (Rocky Barbella), Anna Maria Pierangeli (Norma), Everett Sloane (Irving Cohen), Eileen Heckart (Ma Barbella), Sal Mineo (Romolo), Harold J. Stone (Nick Barbella), Joseph Buloff (Benny), Robert Loggia (Frankie Peppo), Donna Jo Gribble (Yolanda Barbella), Sammy White (Whitey Bimstein), Arch Johnson (Heldon), Theodore Newton (Commissioner Eddie Eagan), Robert Easton (Corporal Quinburg), Matt Crowley (Lou Stillman), Judson Pratt (Johnny Hyland).

Charles Schnee for MGM, U. S. A. 9936 ft., 110 mins.

An interest in boxing as a sport which sharply focuses many social and existential problems had already led Wise to making the fine The Set-Up; this time he transfers to the screen the memoirs of Rocky Graziano, once the professional world middle-weight champion. The life story of a man who grew up in the slums of New York and went through the hard school of life before becoming a boxer provides rich material for sociological comment. Although Wise made generalizations which are a little philosophical and a little mystical and took the personal tone of the boxer's reminiscences a little too much to heart with the result that in the film concreteness tends to give way to sentimentality--the realistic texture prevails. Apart from The Set-Up and Huston's much later Fat City, Somebody Up There Likes Me is the best picture on the boxing theme and a fascinating study of the achievement of self-definition by a sovereign personality, whose nonconformity brings many defeats in life in society but also qualities which allow him to break through the corrupt halo of the world of boxing. Wise once more confirmed his directorial skills: unfalteringly maintained the pace of the story, dynamically handled movement within the frame, narrated with economical editing. Also, he well directed the leading actor: Paul Newman, who in the role originally meant for James Dean, gives his first outstanding performance, individual and credible.

APARAJITO (The Unvanquished) Satyajit Ray

Script: Ray, based on the novel by Bibhutibhusan Bandopadhaya. Photography: Subrata Mitra. Music: Ravi Shankar. Art Direction: Banshi Chandra Gupta. Cast: Pinaki Sen Gupta (Apu as a boy), Kanu Bannerji (Harihar, the father), Subodh Ganguly (Headmaster), K. S. Pandey (Pandey), Karuna Bannerji (Sarbojaya, the mother), Ramani Sen Gupta (Old uncle), Kali Charan Ray (Press proprietor), Sudipta Ray (Nirupama), Smaran Ghosal (Apu as an adolescent), Charu Ghosh (Nanda Babu), Santi Gupta (Landlord's wife), Ajay Mitra (Anil, Apu's friend).

Satyajit Ray for Epic Films Private Ltd., India. 10,200 ft., 113 mins.

The winner of the Grand Prix at the 1957 Venice Film Festival, Aparajito is the second part of Ray's Apu Trilogy begun the previous year with Pather Panchali.

Harihar, his wife Sarbojaya and the 10-year-old son Apu arrive in the holy city of Benares. Harihar supports the family as a professional prayer-caller on the banks of the Ganges. He soon dies. Sarbojaya first works at the house of a rich man, later becomes a housekeeper for Apu's grandfather, a priest who lives in the country. The grandfather begins to train the boy for priesthood, but Apu prefers to go to school instead. Several years pass. Now a young man, Apu has done well at school. He wins a scholarship of 10 rupees a month and persuades his mother to send him to the university in Calcutta. He supports himself by working at a printing works at night. The new life, people and interests create a widening gulf between Apu and his mother. Afraid to disturb his preparations for an exam, Sarbojaya does not tell him she is gravely ill. She dies by the time her son reaches home. The grandfather tries to persuade the young man to stay in the village and to become a holy man, like his father, but Apu returns to Calcutta.

Thus the ending of Aparajito, just like that of Pather Panchali, is also a new beginning. While the first part of the Trilogy was primarily a story of a child discovering the secrets of the world, Aparajito shows how a young boy gradually finds his place in society, forms relationships with his environment, forges friendships, crystallizes desires. At first a host of new experiences awaits Apu in the city. He sees fireworks for the first time. To reach the Ganges he has to climb down the stone steps lining the steep bank. To Harihar this is part of daily routine. As Apu climbs the steps when carrying the holy water for his dying father, he is momentarily stopped by the sight of a strong man practicing with a club-shaped weight. Later Apu begins to study and goes beyond mere experience of everyday life. There is a scene in Aparajito in which Ray stresses the role of learning, at the same time making an oblique claim about the universal quality of his cinema. The headmaster, who gives Apu books about Livingstone, Archimedes, Galileo and Newton, says to the boy: "We live in a remote corner of Bengal, but we need not have a narrow outlook."

An important theme of Aparajito is the growing estrangement between Apu and his mother--a painful and prolonged conflict, which Ray observes with sensitivity and subtlety. The inevitable increase of the distance between generations has been a recurrent motif in the work of Ozu, and it is worthwhile to compare Ray's film with Ozu's The Only Son or Tokyo Story.

Aparajito is the least satisfactory part of the Trilogy. Its imperfection can partly be blamed on the changeover of actors as Apu grows up (one does not look much like the other) and partly on the sheer scope of the story which spans many years and on the resulting stylistic indecision on Ray's part. The director continues his experiments with cinematic time. The story itself occasionally returns to Pather Panchali. One of such returns, a kind of childhood revisited, is when Apu goes home to his mother and watches local rural amusements. A man is drumming, a boy walks on his hands. It is only that now Apu is not amazed but bored. As in Pather Panchali, the rhythm of the picture is slow: Ray's objective is not so much to tell a story, as to communicate a complex experience of life.

THE WITCHES OF SALEM (Les Sorcières de Salem) Raymond Rouleau

Script: Jean-Paul Sartre, from the play "The Crucible" by Arthur Miller. Photography: Claude Renoir. Music: Georges Auric. Art Direction: René Moulaert. Editing: Marguerite Renoir. Cast: Yves Montand (John Proctor), Simone Signoret (Elizabeth Proctor), Mylène Demongeot (Abigail), Françoise Lugagne (Jane Putnam), Jean Debucourt (Parris), Pierre Larquey (Francis Nurse), Jeanne Fusier-Gir (Martha Corey), Alfred Adam (Thomas Putnam), Yves Brainville (Hale), Jean Gaven (Peter Corey), Chantal Gozzi (Fancy Proctor), Alexandre Rignault (Willard).

Raymond Borderie/C. I. C. C. /Pathé/DEFA, France/East Germany. 13,005 ft. , 145 mins.

The Witches of Salem is the screen version of the celebrated stage play, whose principal aim--born in the period of McCarthy panic--was to warn of the dangers inherent in entrusting one's philosophy of life to others, of accepting the axiom that conscience is not a personal problem, but a matter subject to the organs of state administration. Of course, while writing his play based on real events in the notorious 17th-century American witch trial, Arthur Miller also had political witch hunts in mind--but in the first place he was interested in the problems of moral responsibility.

Salem, Massachusetts, 1692. John Proctor, a farmer whose puritanical wife refuses to share a bed with him, embarks on an affair with a servant girl, Abigail. When Elizabeth Proctor learns about the two, she sends Abigail away. Later Abigail and other girls are found dabbling in magical rites in a forest; the girls claim they are possessed by the devil and denounce many members of the community as witches. One of them is Elizabeth on whom Abigail wants to take revenge. The Governor orders a trial at which many people are sentenced to death. Anxious to save his wife, Proctor publicly confesses to the adultery and Abigail in turn accuses him of dealings with the devil. He can sign the confession and thus save his life (and is urged to do so by both women) but realizes that only his death can stop the mass hysteria.

Jean-Paul Sartre, the great philosopher who wrote the script, went in a somewhat different direction to Miller. He made the film reflect the results of his deliberations on the problems of social revolt and the freedom of choice, which preoccupied him in that period. He did not do this too adroitly. The main attention was given to two motifs: the conflicts within the marital triangle and the class conflict with the community of Salem being manipulated by the merchants, the clergy and the scheming Governor. As a result

The Witches of Salem

the majority of important problems are enacted within the marital triangle; the background peopled by the inhabitants of Salem and the judges imported from Boston is too black-and-white, too poster-like to serve as a forum for an engrossing dispute on the mechanisms of human actions in the face of terror. What remains is a psychological drama, admittedly of a high standard, which is mainly owing to the excellent performances from the trio Signoret-Montand-Demongeot. The last named, a 20-year-old emerging actress, soon to rival Brigitte Bardot in the popularity stakes in France, never again reached a comparable level of expressiveness and credibility; while Simone Signoret and Yves Montand can count their parts of Elizabeth and John Proctor among the very best in their rich acting careers. Somber defeat for the servant girl, whose intrigues against a rival amid the whirlwind of obscurantist madness bring ruin and death upon the man whom she wanted to win for herself, was presented by Rouleau with considerable pictorial expressiveness, in dense dark frames which refer to Flemish paintings. A lack of finesse in execution and a certain clumsiness in organizing the mass scenes paradoxically gave The Witches of Salem an additional, coarse power. It is decisive for the overall effect, particularly in the final parts of the film: with the increase of emotional tension a drama of characters and passions is transformed into a somewhat Griffith-ian philippic against the destruction of a sovereign human individuality in the name of orthodoxy of any complexion.

THE ROOF (Il tetto) Vittorio De Sica

Script: Cesare Zavattini. Photography: Carlo Montuori. Music: Alessandro Cicognini. Art Direction: Gastone Medin. Editing: Eraldo Da Roma. Cast: Gabriella Pallotta (Luisa), Giorgio Listuzzi (Natale), Gastone Renzelli (Cesare), Maria Di Rollo (Gina), Giuseppe Martini (Luisa's father), Emilia Martini (Luisa's mother), Maria Sittoro (Natale's mother), Angelo Visentin (Natale's father), Maria De Fiori (Cesare's wife), Luisa Alessandri (Signora Bay).

Vittorio De Sica for Titanus, Italy. 8806 ft., 98 mins.

The last chord of Italian Neorealism, The Roof demonstrates that the formula of didacticism and of passive social protest has lost its topicality as the economic situation in Italy improved. After working for four years on the script for which they collected thorough documentation, De Sica and Zavattini presented on the screen one more problem of the underprivileged: the lack of living space. A young married couple are unable to live a normal life in their parents' overcrowded flat, and have no money to rent one of their own. They decide to take advantage of a law which protects houses built on state-owned property as long as they have a door and a roof, and to build a makeshift house under cover of night; the police will not be able to pull it down in the morning. Despite a number of setbacks, they work with their friends throughout the night and succeed in time: the policeman who appears on the scene a little too early shows human understanding and allows the work to be completed.

Thus solidarity triumphs. All the characters in The Roof are positive ones; it is only the social machinery which is faulty, albeit this machinery (like those responsible for it) is not shown in the film. The care of the makers resulted in a picture which is finely constructed, true in details, told with fluency, but as unattractive insofar as the plot goes as it is ideologically superficial--not attempting to penetrate reality or to analyze the personalities of the characters, and not going beyond the dimension of a statement of fact. Thus The Roof could not count as a voice in the debate on the faults of the system; in the first place because even the earlier ambitious Neorealist films never really established contact with the masses, and in the second place because in 1956 the main problem of the Italians was how best to ride on the wave of the speedy economic recovery and not to complain about various shortcomings (which, incidentally, was unpopular with the authorities). Quite apart from that, De Sica who had so far independently produced his films, lost the financial basis for doing this: the costs of making films increased enormously and his earnings as an actor from which he financed his earlier pictures (which usually lost money) were no longer sufficient. Thus Neorealism had to come to a close as a school, although it remained an invaluable creative method.

HE WHO MUST DIE (Celui qui doit mourir) Jules Dassin

Script: Ben Barzman and Dassin, from the novel "O Christos Xanastauronetai" (Christ Recrucified) by Nikos Kazantzakis. Dialogues: André Obey. Photography: Jacques Natteau. Music: Georges Auric. Art Direction: Max Douy. Editing: Pierre Gillette and Roger Dwyre. Cast: Pierre Vaneck (Manolios), Jean Servais (Pope Fotis), Karl Möhner (Lukas), Grégoire Aslan (Agha), Gert Froebe (Patriarcheas), Teddy Bilis (Hadji Nikolis), René Lefèvre (Yannakos), Lucien Raimbourg (Kostandis), Melina Mercouri (Katerina), Roger Hanin (Panayotaros), Dimos Starenios (Ladas), Nicole Berger (Mariori), Maurice Ronet (Michaelis), Fernand Ledoux (Pope Grigoris).

Indusfilms/ Prima-Films/ Cinetel/ Filmsonor/ Da. Ma. Cinematografica, France/Italy. 10,757 ft., 120 mins. CinemaScope.

The year 1921. Lycovrissi in Asia Minor, a Greek village under Turkish domination, prepares for the annual Passion Play which

He Who Must Die

is to take place at Easter. Pope Grigoris has chosen the actors: Manolios, the local shepherd is to play Christ; Katerina the whore is to be Mary Magdalene; Michaelis the patriarch's son--St. John; Yannakos--St. Peter and Kostandis--St. James. Suddenly a horde of refugees from another Greek village, led by Pope Fotis, enter Lycovrissi, their own village having been destroyed by the Turks. It soon turns out that the people given the main parts in the mystery of Christ's Passion come to play these parts in real life. Grigoris is afraid that helping the refugees may anger the Turkish authorities and prevents the villagers from offering assistance. But the sense of justice and solidarity in the face of force prevails: the villagers led by Manolios, Katerina, Michaelis and Kostandis rise in arms hand in hand with the newcomers. Grigoris joins them. The refugees and their allies prepare for the inevitable Turkish attack.

Dassin's most personal film (his first which was made in full agreement with his intentions) is a sort of social morality play, pervaded by conviction in the need to stand up against discrimination, a protest against blind obedience to fate, an accusation of opportunism. Kazantzakis' novel was more leftist in tone; Dassin moves in the sphere of an impassioned humanist protest and treats the theme as an allegorical exponent of the question of man's innate violence, which had always interested him. He does not bother with nuances of psychology--in this drama everything is determined from the outset. The images are epic and emphatic; Cretan exteriors, very rightly filmed in black-and-white and in CinemaScope, are in excellent consonance with the movie's spiritual tonality. The acting team well read Dassin's intentions. The conception according to which He Who Must Die was shot may give rise to reservations, but within its self-imposed framework this is a very homogeneous, thought-out and original work.

MOBY DICK John Huston

Script: Ray Bradbury and Huston, from the novel "Moby-Dick; or, The Whale" (1851) by Herman Melville. Photography: Oswald Morris; also Freddie Francis. Music: Philip Stainton. Art Direction: Ralph Brinton. Editing: Russell Lloyd. Cast: Gregory Peck (Captain Ahab), Richard Basehart (Ishmael), Leo Genn (Starbuck), Harry Andrews (Stubb), Bernard Miles (Man of Man), Orson Welles (Father Mapple), Mervyn Johns (Peleg), Noel Purcell (Carpenter), Friedrich Ledebur (Queequeg), James Robertson Justice (Captain Boomer), Edric Connor (Daggoo), Seamus Kelly (Flask), Philip Stainton (Bildad), Joseph Tomelty (Peter Coffin), Royal Dano (Elijah), Francis De Wolff (Captain Gardiner), Tamba Alleney (Pip), Ted Howard (Blacksmith), Tom Clegg (Tashtego), Iris Tree (Lady with Bibles).

John Huston for Moulin/Warner Bros., U.S.A. 10,346 ft., 115 mins. Technicolor.

One could hardly imagine Huston--glorifier of Adventure as the supreme destiny of man--not crossing paths with Melville's "Moby-Dick." This great allegory of the eternal human aspirations saw the Great Whale as the epitome of the omnipotent forces of Nature; Captain Ahab's struggle against it was equated with the battle of the human will against Destiny, against the might of Nature, against forces man cannot consciously understand--a battle in which man is doomed to failure. While some "shades of meaning" are inevitably lost, Moby Dick is very faithful to the intentions of the original, which was very difficult to achieve in view of the obsolescence of some of Melville's philosophical concepts. And yet the film has an unmistakable feel of authenticity--because the urge to pose a foolhardy challenge to the elements, even if it amounts to madness, is very deeply rooted in man.

The year 1840. Ishmael, a young sailor, arrives at the Spouter Inn in New Bedford. He befriends his chance bedfellow, Queequeg, a harpooner, and despite an ominous prediction both men sign on the "Pequod" skippered by Captain Ahab. A man with a strange reputation, Ahab dedicated his life to the pursuit of Moby Dick, a giant white whale which once took off his leg. He explains this to the crew who, heedless of the advice of mate Starbuck, let themselves be engulfed by their captain's obsession. After a long journey during which they take no notice of the lesser whales and disregard appeals for help from another ship--Moby Dick is sighted. Ahab assaults the whale with rage compounded over the years of fruitless search. He leaps onto the back of the whale which revolves furiously in the sea and while stabbing at it (". . . to the last I grapple with thee; from hell's heart I stab at thee; for hate's sake I spit my last breath at thee") becomes entagled in the lines left there by previous hunters. The whale smashes and sinks the ship. All the crew are lost apart from Ishmael, who narrates the story.

Huston said about the novel: "I always thought that 'Moby-Dick' was a great blasphemy. Here was a man who shook his fist at God. The thematic line in 'Moby-Dick' seemed to me, always, to have been: 'Who's the judge when the judge himself is dragged to the bar? Who's to condemn, but he, Ahab!' This was, to me, the point at which I tried to aim the whole picture, because I think that's what Melville was essentially concerned with, and this is, at the same time, the point which makes 'Moby-Dick' so extremely timely in our age." It is significant in this context how Huston stresses the Starbuck character, a wise and skeptical man who opposes Ahab's obsession and yet is finally overcome by it. Ahab's struggle is in fact a struggle against God and Melville conveys this by making Starbuck a deeply religious Quaker and by placing a great emphasis on the scene of Father Mapple's sermon on the theme "And God had prepared a great fish to swallow up Jonah." In this scene Orson Welles gave a startling and unforgettable appearance preaching in the whaleman's chapel from a pulpit shaped like the bow of a ship: "Shipmates, woe to him who seeks to pour oil on troubled waters when God has brewed them into a gale." It is understandable that it was not possible on the screen to preserve Melville's splendid rhetoric. Still, although it is obvious that Huston felt the essence of Melville's style, he found himself unable to transfer its literary spirit to the screen using the spoken word. Some of the film's dialogues are unacceptable, and Ahab's obsession with which he later infects the crew is not conveyed by the spirit or mood; it is not involving and leaves the spectator cold and detached. Largely to blame for the awkwardness of the entire mystical aspect of the film is Gregory Peck--cheaply demonic, he turns Ahab's profound lust for vengeance into a kind of neurotic rage. The role in Moby Dick is one of the worst in Peck's screen career.

Still, from the powerful opening in which a young boy walking beside a mountain stream turns towards the camera and says, "Call me Ishmael ..." the film's interest rarely fades. The maritime adventure is splendidly cinematic, enthralling with the wide breadth of the open sea, with the romanticism and fascinating spell of a sailor's odyssey. No effort was spared to recreate the conditions of the 19th century; the sea, the whaling village, the ship itself are remarkably well rendered; the human characters from New Bedford and from the whaling ship are convincingly portrayed. Moby Dick was said to contain some of the best sea and ship scenes ever filmed (the whale-hunting scenes were shot off the coast of Madeira and the Canary Islands).

But the thing for which Moby Dick can claim most credit is surely the use of color. Huston and the cameraman Oswald Morris devised a special "desaturation" process which combines monochrome and color photography: three color negatives were superimposed on the low-contrast black-and-white fourth. This produced a realistic, muted type of color, stylized after the golden aquatint tonality meant to imitate old whaling prints--giving the story a unique touch of awesome poetry, suitable for its allegorical content. In general, period stylization is very successful and uniform--literally from the first to the last frame (for even the last title reads "finis" instead of "the end"). This fine achievement confirms Huston's claim to being a brilliant cinema colorist, which he staked with Moulin Rouge.

INVITATION TO THE DANCE Gene Kelly

Script: Kelly. Choreography: Kelly. Editing: Raymond Poulton, Robert Watts and Adrienne Fazan.

CIRCUS: Photography: Frederick A. Young. Music: Jacques Ibert. Art Direction: Alfred Junge. Costumes: Elizabeth Haffenden. Cast: Gene Kelly (Clown), Claire Sombert (Equestrienne), Igor Youskevitch (High-wire walker).

RING AROUND THE ROSY: Photography: Frederick A. Young. Music: André Previn. Art Direction: Alfred Junge. Sets and costumes: Rolf Gerard. Cast: David Paltenghi (Husband), Daphne Dale (Wife), Igor Youskevitch (Artist), Claude Bessy (Model), Tommy Rall (Stage Door Johnny), Belita (Femme Fatale), Irving Davies (Crooner), Diana Adams (Hat-check girl), Gene Kelly (Marine), Tamara Toumanova (Girl on the stairs).

SINBAD THE SAILOR: Photography: Joseph Ruttenberg. Animated part: Fred Quimby, William Hanna and Joseph Barbera. Music: Nikolai Rimsky-Korsakov ("Sinbad" and "Sheherazade" (excerpts); "Nightingale and the Rose," "Dance des Bouffons" from "The Snow Maiden"), adapted by Roger Edens. Art Direction: Cedric Gibbons and Randall Duell. Special cartoon effects: Irving G. Ries. Cast: Gene Kelly (Sinbad), Carol Haney (Sheherazade), David Kasday (Boy Genie).

Arthur Freed for MGM, U. S. A. /G. B. 8388 ft., 93 mins. Technicolor.

Anyone interested in the question of what in the musicals by the Kelly-Donen team is owed to each of the partners should make a study of Invitation to the Dance. Following his artistic predispositions Kelly presents here a feature-length screen ballet, albeit very different in conception from the films he had made in cooperation with Donen, such as On the Town, Singin' in the Rain or It's Always Fair Weather (1955). Instead, Kelly took up and developed Minnelli's philosophy of screen ballet as seen in An American in Paris: expressing the plot through dance instead of merely combining the development of the plot with singing-dancing episodes. The objective of Invitation to the Dance was certainly very ambitious--to give a popular summary of screen ballet in the form of a tripartite film without dialogues. "Circus" is a mimed story referring to the Commedia dell'arte of the tragic love of a clown for an equestrienne who is in turn infatuated with a tightrope walker; "Ring Around the Rosy," a modernistic balletic burlesque, is a story of a bracelet (given by a husband to his wife) which then passes from one lover to another until it returns to the original owner; "Sinbad the Sailor," an Arabian Nights fantasy, combines live action with animation and uses a modern paraphrase of a classical theme.

The outcome is rather controversial. It seems that the reason why the film was only shown to the public four years after it was begun (during which time it was re-cut and re-dubbed a number of times) was the rather uncertain commercial prospects of a 93-minute dance film particularly in view of the sharp decline in motion-picture attendance. But this has nothing to do with the real faults of the work. It is fair to complain that the first part of Invitation to the Dance is pretentious, that the third (and partly the second) part lacks taste, and that the handling of some situations is banal. This sounds rather serious, but dilletantism of the film's references to everything that comes from European culture (like the pantomime of Marcel Marceau and Jean-Louis Barrault or the transposition of symphony music) is unfortunately rather striking. So is the triviality of the stage design in the first and third part. On the other hand, Kelly does very well whenever he is stylistically on home territory. He impressively handles the dramatic line and the choreography in the story of the bracelet and successfully makes up for the weakness of the components used with the witty, choreographic arrangements and their novel combination with animation in "Sinbad the Sailor." In the overall effect Invitation to the Dance is a very interesting, if uneven, attempt at going beyond the confines of the conventions of the musical and screen ballet. This was the reason why the picture was acclaimed by the international critics and won the Grand Prix in the 1956 Berlin Film Festival, thus leaving behind even Olivier's Richard III.

EDGE OF THE CITY (A Man Is Ten Feet Tall) Martin Ritt

Script: Robert Alan Aurthur. Photography: Joseph Brun. Music: Leonard Rosenman. Art Direction: Richard Sylbert. Editing: Sidney Meyers. Cast: Sidney Poitier (Tommy Tyler), John Cassavetes (Axel North), Jack Warden (Charlie Malik), Kathleen Maguire (Ellen Wilson), Ruby Dee (Lucy Tyler), Robert Simon (Mr. Nordmann), Ruth White (Mrs. Nordmann), William A. Lee (Davis), John Kellogg (Detective), Estelle Hemsley (Lucy's mother), Val Avery (Axel's brother), David Clarke (Wallace).

David Susskind for Jonathan Films, U.S.A. 7552 ft., 84 mins. Metroscope.

It was a long time before American cinema got round to adopting what one would call a responsible attitude towards racial minorities. The pioneer in this was Delmer Daves, whose Broken Arrow (1950) gives a sympathetic portrayal of Cochise, leader of the Apache Indians. Still, it was easier to be nice about Indians than blacks. A new attitude towards black Americans began only in the late 50's with Ritt's Edge of the City and Kramer's The Defiant Ones, both with Sidney Poitier. The first picture is the feature debut of a former director of stage and television and Actors' Studio lecturer. It has been pointed out that unlike a number of his contemporaries, Ritt came to films via television rather than from it. His main interest has always been in the socially conscious cinema, and this somber and realistic story is no exception.

A down-and-out army deserter, Axel finds a job in a New York City railroad yard. He had a difficult childhood and suffers from a guilt complex after the death of his brother in a car crash. Axel befriends Tommy, a black freight-handler, who invites him to his home and tries to build up his morale. Axel slowly begins to regain self-confidence. Both men are in conflict with Charlie Malik, a vicious and racially prejudiced union racketeer. When Axel gets involved in a savage fight with freight hooks, Tommy saves his life but is himself killed. Axel is forced to keep quiet about what happened for fear of being exposed as a deserter. He is aware of the contempt Tommy's wife has for him as a weak man. Finally Axel beats up Malik and drags him to justice.

Despite the stereotypes inherent in the script (happy, strong black man versus a white neurotic with an unhappy family background) Edge of the City turned out to be powerful and quite convincing. The black man is not a poster character (by virtue of Poitier's performance), but is uninhibited and relaxed. The character development of Axel, well played by John Cassavetes, the future director, is conducted very well. The film was shot on location in New York using an aggressive narrative style. Considering the similarity of the subject, the visible influence from Kazan's On the Waterfront is not altogether surprising.

ATTACK Robert Aldrich

Script: James Poe, based on the play "The Fragile Fox" by Norman Brooks. Photography: Joseph Biroc. Music: Frank DeVol. Art Direction: William Glasgow. Editing: Michael Luciano. Cast: Jack Palance (Lieutenant Costa), Eddie Albert (Captain Cooney), William Smithers (Lieutenant Woodruff), Lee Marvin (Colonel Bartlett), Robert Strauss (Pfc. Bernstein), Richard Jaeckel (Pfc. Snowden), Buddy Ebsen (Sergeant Tolliver), Jon Shepodd (Corporal Jackson), Peter Van Eyck (German officer), James Goodwin (Pfs. Ricks), Strother Martin (Sergeant Ingersol), Judson Taylor (Pfc. Abramowitz).

The Associates and Aldrich Company, U. S. A. 9415 ft., 106 mins.

The "official" view of the Second World War by Hollywood soon gave way to a less heroic approach. Twelve O'Clock High showed an air squadron suffering from battle fatigue while the characterization of American prisoners of war in Stalag 17 was rather unflattering. The "demythologizing" trend got in full swing in 1953 with Zinnemann's From Here to Eternity. It included Ray's Bitter Victory, Aldrich's Attack, Dmytryk's The Young Lions and culminated in Kubrick's Paths of Glory. All these films saw the war as a catalyst for the worst traits of human character, and drew attention to the arbitrariness of the friend-enemy stereotype, the corruption of the commanders and the wartime bureaucracy. These themes make an appearance in Attack, Aldrich's last really ambitious film. French critic Jean Wagner thus commented on the director's subsequent career: "Whatever happened to Robert Aldrich? To what Baby Jane has he fallen captive?"

Belgium, 1944. The cowardice and weak nerves of Captain Cooney, in command of an American infantry company, has caused heavy casualties among the men. Lt. Costa and Lt. Woodruff bring this to the notice of Colonel Bartlett. But Bartlett relies on Cooney's father for support in making a career in politics after the war ends and dismisses the complaint. Costa is prepared to kill Cooney rather than allow the situation to continue. Costa's platoon is sent to occupy a ruined town; it is crawling with Nazis and they suffer heavy losses after Cooney fails to give them promised fire support. Having lost nearly all his men, Costa knocks out two enemy tanks, staggers into the headquarters in the basement of a ruined house and dies from his wounds before he manages to kill Cooney. When the Captain, almost paralyzed with fear, announces he plans to surrender, he is shot by Woodruff. The men tell the Colonel that Cooney died in battle. But when the Colonel suggests a posthumous decoration for Cooney, Woodruff telephones the divisional commander to tell him the full story.

A doubly false ending. Firstly, the killing of Cooney is theatrical and totally implausible. Secondly, the final optimism of Woodruff's action serves to assure the spectator, rather artifically, that there is still basic justice in the Army and to give a sop to the War Department. While being aggressive and effectively directed, the picture is so glaringly theatrical in structure, with its characters strongly contrasted and given Freudian overtones, and so hysterical in tone, that it is useless as a responsible study of attitudes in combat. It can at the most be considered as a pamphlet against certain elements in the U. S. Army. Such seem to have been the intentions of its director who in pictures as diverse as Apache (1954), Kiss Me Deadly and The Big Knife (1955) registered his personal critical views on different aspects of American life and on current political tendencies. Bartlett is shown as the worst villain, because he is cool and cynical. War to him is only a means of promotion in life, an extension of peacetime policies, as von Clausewitz has said. Cooney is no more than a sycophantic coward. War itself is in Attack something to be taken for granted, and its reasons or morality are not discussed at all. This is very different from the attitude taken by the classical pacifist films.

DREAMS IN THE DRAWER (I sogni nel cassetto) Renato Castellani

---

Script: Castellani and Adriana Chiaramonte. Photography: Leonida Barboni. Music: Roman Vlad. Cast: Lea Massari (Lucia), Enrico Pagani (Mario), Cosetta Greco (Lina), Lilla Brignone (Lucia's mother), Sergio Tofano (Lucia's father), Carlo D'Angelo (Temporary lecturer), Guglielmo Inglese (Professor).

Rizzoli/Francinex, Italy/France. 90 mins.

The story of love and marriage of Mario and Lucia, a young student couple: struggles against serious financial difficulties, objections of parents to the wedding, the torment of exams, Mario's first job as a country doctor. Then, as unexpected as a stroke of lightning on a sunny day--the death of the heroine.

Castellani's film, although seemingly banal (and often superficial) is in fact something more than merely a prototype of Love Story (1970)--and this is not due to the finale (of which there is as a matter of fact a second, conventionally optimistic version), and not the skillful generic and behavioral observation or the dramatic sub-plot of a second pair of lovers: the assistant professor, pushed into cynicism and selfishness by illness and a girl student who is more mature than Lucia, but unable to break out of the tortured relationship. The main value of Dreams in the Drawer is the authentic emotional climate of youthful love. This rare and evasive component, which many similar stories in vain tried to achieve, is present in almost every part of the film--because the actors are natural: naive, awkward and ordinary. Most films of the "rosy Neorealism" (of which Dreams in the Drawer is part even though the hue changes to black in the finale) and of the generic post-Neorealism, the other remnant of the main trend, moved within the same thematic sphere; but this is the only example of a film free of varnish, yet convincing and faithful in its portrayal of the spontaneity and euphoria of youth.

STREET OF SHAME Akasen-Chitai) Kenji Mizoguchi

Script: Masashige Narusawa. Photography: Kazuo Miyagawa. Music: Toshiro Mayazumi. Art Direction: Hiroshi Mizutani. Editing: Keiichi Sakane. Cast: Machiko Kyo (Miki), Aiko Mimasu (Yumeko), Ayako Wakao (Yasumi), Michiyo Kogure (Hanae), Yasuko Kawakami (Shizuko), Eitaro Shindo (Kurazo Tadami), Kenji Sugawara (Yoshikimi), Bontaro Miyake (Patrolman), Toranosuke Ogawa (Miki's father), Daisuke Kato (Policeman Miyazake), Hiroko Machida (Yorie), Yosuke Irie (Yumeko's daughter), Kumeko Urabe (Otane), Jun Tatara (Yumeko's customer), Kuninori Takado (Keisaku Kadowaki).

Masaichi Nagata for Daiei, Japan. 7694 ft., 85 mins.

After two period pictures, in his last completed work Mizoguchi returns to a modern subject. The theme of Street of Shame is very much in accordance with his perennial interest in the life and psychology of women. Reportedly he planned a semi-documentary picture set in a big brothel, but brothel-keepers refused to cooperate for fear of public reaction.

Street of Shame tells the stories of five employees of a fashionable establishment called Dreamland in the notorious Yoshiwara red-light district of Tokyo. Miki comes from a respectable family. She is Americanized, calls herself Mickey and tries to forget her G. I. lover. She bitterly quarrels with her father who is trying to make her return home. Yasumi wants to start a business and extracts money from a man who has fallen in love with her; he nearly kills her on discovering her real feelings. Yorie is saving to be able to marry the man she loves, but returns to the brothel when she realizes that he wants to use her as a servant. Hanae works as a prostitute to be able to support her sick husband and child. Yumeko, a widow, needs money to give her son a decent education. The son is ashamed of his mother's profession and finally rejects her. She loses her mind and is taken to the hospital. As the radio announces that an anti-prostitution law has been defeated in the Diet, a teenage girl timidly enters Dreamland to take Yumeko's place....

Mizoguchi had already made a film, The Woman of Rumour, which was set in a brothel. But while his main interest then was in the personal tragedies of the owner and her daughter, Street of Shame explores the lives of the girls themselves. The theme is treated in a matter-of-fact manner and without even a trace of sensationalism. The brothel is shown as any other place of employment and its employees seen to have similar problems. The finances of the establishment are described and the keeper is not a monster, but a business-like man convinced he is acting in the girls' best interests. As the planned anti-prostitution law is discussed, he tells them about the hypocrisy of the authorities anxious to "liberate" them. In Street of Shame Mizoguchi conducts an examination of motives and social attitudes. The brothel is to him a remnant of the feudal system and he sets out to attack its human consequences. The trouble is that he does it with too great a dose of journalistic fervor--and the Japanese cinematic crusading is very unsubtle. While in the final account the picture is impressive, with its creditable intentions and thematic coherence (despite the variety of problems tackled) and a good, understated ending--it is at the same time very uneven, and relies for its overall impact on several very effective scenes. All this is quite apart from the melodramatic script and fanciful musical effects. Street of Shame is more restrained visually than Mizoguchi's period films. The style is detailed and the narrative clearly divided into episodes. There is good acting, particularly from Machiko Kyo as the ebullient Miki and from Eitaro Shindo as the brothel-keeper.

PUNISHMENT ROOM (Shokei-no heya) Kon Ichikawa

Script: Natto Wada and Keiji Hasebe, from the novel by Shintaro Ishihara. Photography: Yoshihisa Nakagawa. Music: Koji Taku. Art Direction:

Tomoo Shimogawara. Cast: Hiroshi Kawaguchi (Katsumi Shimada), Ayako Wakao (Akiko Aochi), Seiji Miyaguchi (Hanya Shimada), Teruko Kishi (Haru Shimada), Masayoshi Umewaka (Ito), Noburo Nakamura (Professor Motegi), Takashi Kotaka (Ryoji), Keizo Kawasaki (Takeshima).

Hidemasa Nagata for Daiei, Japan. 8609 ft., 96 mins.

The end of the Korean war triggered off an economic boom in Japan. Coming after so many lean years, this brought a sense of prosperity and stability. The effects on Japanese society were twofold: on the one hand it resulted in a decrease of interest in politics among the general public and their turning towards the pursuit of material prosperity and a higher standard of living (exactly the same happened in Italy); on the other hand it gave rise to the disenchantment of the young, a mood of negation and escapism, which paralleled that in the West at about the same time--as expressed on the screen in Before the Deluge, Rebel Without a Cause and The Wild One. In Japan, the epitome of this mood was the novel "Season of the Sun" by Shintaro Ishihara, a sort of a manifesto of a generation, from the title of which the term "sun tribe" (taiyozoku) was derived as a generic name for rebel Japanese youths. The film made from the book by Takumi Furukawa, released on May 17, 1956, was a huge financial success and restored the failing fortunes of Nikkatsu, the company which produced it. Crazed Fruit (1956) directed by Ko Nakahira was another in the series of films sustained in a similar spirit. Other film companies did not allow a chance to pass: a month later Daiei brought out Punishment Room directed by Kon Ichikawa--again from a novel by Ishihara. The finest of many, this film above all left a lasting portrayal of an angry young man in the Japanese cinema.

The hero of Punishment Room, a university student, hates the superficiality of the adult world. His father, a bank manager, works hard and struggles against a stomach disease. Katsumi sees adults as feeble and hates the very idea that he might one day live like his father. He laces the drink of a girl student with sleeping pills and rapes her. The girl falls in love with him, but he rejects her. A bad boy indeed: ruins the life of a young girl, slaps a teacher, betrays his friends. He ends up getting beaten up and crawling up an alley. "Adults are not really alive, it is only me who is"--this is how Katsumi justifies his desperate rebellion. He acts now with child-like naiveté, now with deliberate cruelty.

Thus Ichikawa made Punishment Room riding on the crest of a wave of fashion. But the motif of a desperate, destructive protest is one which interested him deeply at the time. (He returned to it in The Flame of Torment.) He was able to give his film a tone of somber poetry--and, as always, a stylish visual form. Punishment Room, with its unpleasant scenes of violence and deception, sent a wave of indignation across Japan. Needless to say, "sun tribe" was short-lived as a form of social behavior. But some of its ideas and attitudes survived, later to reappear on the screen in the films of Imamura and, in particular, Oshima.

23 PACES TO BAKER STREET Henry Hathaway

Script: Nigel Balchin, from the novel "Warrant for X" by Philip MacDonald. Photography: Milton Krasner. Music: Leigh Harline. Art Direction: Lyle R. Wheeler and Maurice Ransford. Editing: James B. Clark. Cast: Van Johnson (Philip Hannon), Vera Miles (Jean Lennox), Cecil Parker (Bob Matthews), Patricia Laffan (Miss Alice MacDonald), Maurice Denham (Insp. Grovening), Estelle Winwood (Barmaid), Liam Redmond (Mr. Murch), Isobel Elsom (Lady Syrett), Martin Benson (Pilling), Natalie Norwick (Janet Murch), Terence de Marney (Sgt. Luce), Queenie Leonard (Miss Schuyler).

Henry Ephron for 20th Century-Fox, U. S. A. 9250 ft., 103 mins. CinemaScope. De Luxe Color

Philip Hannon, a blind American playwright resident in London, overhears two people, one of them a nursemaid, in a bar discussing plans for murder and kidnapping. Scotland Yard are skeptical, so Hannon helped by his girlfriend Jean and his secretary investigate on their own. The only clue is the scent worn by the woman Hannon overheard. The investigation leads them to a domestic employment agency operated by criminals. They apply for a nursemaid, and are sent Alice MacDonald who is wearing the scent. After another nursemaid is murdered and an attempt made on Hannon's life, the police intervene and arrest several people who have kidnapped a crippled Argentinian heiress. When somebody calls on Hannon, alone in his flat, he turns off the light; after a fierce struggle the intruder falls out of the window. It turns out to be Alice MacDonald in man's disguise.

Ten years after his greatest achievements in "police documentary" Hathaway films a script which again gives him an opportunity for a display of mastery in crime cinema. This time he directs in a style which is at moments reminiscent of Hitchcock: he handles dramatic suspense well, steadily steps up tensions and brings out a human element from the emotions and actions of the blind hero. As a matter of fact, some motifs (a devoted girlfriend, a crippled man struggling against an attacker) are the same as in Hitchcock's Rear Window. The faithful retainer character and, of course, the title, refer to Conan Doyle; if only Hathaway had a better idea of the topography of London! Even though the intrigue, quite original in concept and very rich in detail, is not free from certain naiveté and occasional situational improbabilities, this is compensated for by the intelligent mise en scène and a judicious use of film technique. Hathaway places great stress on the coherence and unity of the soundtrack as the cinematic equivalent of his hero's sensual deprivation. The saturated, moody, low-key photography is the work of Milton Krasner, who photographed Fritz Lang's The Woman in the Window.

THE CAPTAIN FROM KÖPENICK (Der Hauptmann von Köpenick)
Helmut Käutner

Script: Carl Zuckmayer and Käutner, from the play by the former. Photography: Albert Benitz. Music: Bernhard Eichhorn. Art Direction: Herbert Kirchhoff and Albrecht Becker. Editing: Klaus Dudenhofer. Costumes: Erna Sander. Cast: Heinz Rühmann (Wilhelm Voigt), Hannelore Schroth (Mathilde Obermüller), Martin Held (Dr. Obermüller, the mayor), Erich Schellow (Captain von Schlettow), Willy A. Kleinau (Friedrich Hoprecht, Voigt's brother-in-law), Ilse Fürstenberg (Marie Hoprecht, Voigt's sister), Leonard Steckel (Adolph Wormser, a tailor), Walter Giller (Willi Wormser), Maria Sebaldt (Auguste Viktoria Wormser), Wolfgang Neuss (Kallenberg, a prisoner), Josef Offenbach (Wabschke, a cutter), Bum Krüger (Kilian, a policeman), Otto Wernicke (Master cobbler), Friedrich Domin (Prison director).

Gyula Trebitsch for Real-Film, West Germany. 93 mins. Eastman Colour.

The events described by Carl Zuckmayer in his 1931 play had really taken place nineteen years earlier. Shoemaker Wilhelm Voigt, newly released from prison, found it impossible to return to normal life. To find work it was necessary to have a passport, while to obtain a passport one needed a steady job. Voigt decided to emigrate; unfortunately the permission to leave Imperial Prussia could only be sought by passport holders with a job. The only way out for Voigt was to get the necessary document through deception. Accordingly, Voigt bought a second-hand uniform, and impersonating a Captain commandeered a squad of troops, with whom he made an "inspection" of the Köpenick town hall and sent the mayor and the treasurer to Berlin under guard. Alas, it turned out that Köpenick did not have a passport office. Yet he did achieve his aim: Voigt's exploits so delighted the Emperor (and the whole of Germany) that he was graciously pleased to permit his enterprising subject to return to normal "official" existence.

Käutner's screen adaptation gave the play just what it needed after it lost its immediate political topicality--a Chaplinesque touch, owed mainly to the personality of the veteran actor Heinz Rühmann. Stinging satire against the omnipotence of the bureaucrats and the military in Kaiser's Germany, a parody of the cult of the uniform, did not lose its message while avoiding the crude emphasis of Staudte's earlier The Underdog. It is true that while striving to stress the significance of accessories and give a symbolic meaning to the realistic detail and the photographic composition of the frame Käutner neglected a little expressiveness and spontaneity, but he made up for this with his intelligent handling of the narrative. This is in evidence in The Captain from Köpenick right from the opening shot of the marching boots of a military detachment accompanied by the mincing step of Voigt wearing comical old shoes--to the finale which splendidly juxtaposes the happy end with the irony of the reasons for the Emperor's magnanimity.

THE LAST WAGON Delmer Daves

Script: James Edward Grant, Daves and Gwen Bagni Gielgud, from the novel by the latter. Photography: Wilfrid Cline. Music: Lionel Newman. Art Direction: Lyle R. Wheeler and Lewis H. Creber. Editing: Hugh S. Fowler. Cast: Richard Widmark (Comanche Todd), Felicia Farr (Jenny), Tommy Rettig (Billy), Stephanie Griffin (Valinda), Ray Stricklyn (Clint), Nick Adams (Ridge), Carl Benton Reid (General Howard), Susan Kohner (Jolie), Douglas Kennedy (Colonel Normand), George Mathews (Bull Harper), James Drury (Lieutenant Kelly), Ken Clark (Sergeant), Timothy Carey (Cole Harper), George Ross (Sarge), Juney Ellis (Mrs. Clinton), Abel Fernandez (Apache medicine man).

William B. Hawks for 20th Century-Fox, U.S.A. 99 mins. CinemaScope. De Luxe Color.

Arizona, 1873. After four brothers murder the wife and small son of a hunter called Comanche Todd (who had been adopted by the Indians as a child) he seeks them out and kills three one by one, and is arrested by the fourth, now a sheriff. The sheriff and his prisoner join a small wagon train; the train is attacked and destroyed by the Apaches. The survivors reluctantly allow Todd, an experienced and resourceful man, to guide them back to civilization through inhospitable Indian territory, facing the dangers of rattlesnakes, hunger and thirst. When they reach a fort, Todd is charged with murder. However, on hearing his story and the pleas of his companions, the judge sets him free in custody of Jenny, one of the party, with whom Todd has fallen in love.

Thus Richard Widmark (who, although good with knives and axes, is not particularly prepossessing in the film) beats both the Indians and the whites at their own game. Despite its cliché-ridden plot, The Last Wagon functions well as a drama of survival in the desert. Shot almost entirely on location in northern Arizona, in CinemaScope, good color and mostly in long- and medium-long shots, the picture maintains excitement throughout and well conveys the sense of the hostile country and the flavor of the period. Of several interesting action sequences the first occurs even before the credits: Todd in a running battle across a gorge with the four brothers.

Although rather routine by Daves's standards, The Last Wagon is an efficient and muscular action picture. The director's next work is of an entirely different caliber: it is the celebrated 3:10 to Yuma.

WRITTEN ON THE WIND Douglas Sirk

Script: George Zuckerman, based on the novel by Robert Wilder. Photography: Russell Metty. Music: Frank Skinner. Art Direction: Alexander Golitzen and Robert Clatworthy. Editing: Russell F. Schoengarth. Cast: Rock Hudson (Mitch Wayne), Lauren Bacall (Lucy Moore Hadley), Robert Stack (Kyle Hadley), Dorothy Malone (Marylee Hadley), Robert Keith (Jasper Hadley), Grant Williams (Biff Miley), Harry Shannon (Hoak Wayne), Robert J. Wilke (Dan Willis), John Larch (Roy Carter), Edward C. Platt (Dr. Paul Cochrane), Roy Glenn (Sam), Maidie Norman (Bertha).

Albert Zugsmith for Universal-International, U. S. A. 99 mins. Technicolor.

After a whirlwind romance Kyle Hadley, son of a Texan oil tycoon, marries Lucy, a secretary in his father's firm. The father welcomes the marriage, hoping that Lucy will be a steadying influence on his irresponsible son. Kyle's childhood friend Mitch is secretly in love with Lucy and is himself pursued by Marylee, Kyle's nymphomaniac sister who detests Lucy. Having been told that he is sterile, Kyle takes to drink. The father's death exacerbates the conflicts within the family: Marylee leads Kyle to believe that Mitch is having an affair with his wife; on hearing that Lucy is pregnant Kyle, convinced that the child is Mitch's, strikes her and she loses the baby. After a quarrel between the two men Kyle shoots himself. Marylee threatens to accuse Mitch of murder unless he goes away with her, but tells the truth at the trial. She remains alone in the deserted mansion as Mitch and Lucy plan a new life together. Thus Marylee loves Mitch, who loves Lucy, who loves Kyle, who loves only himself.

Throughout his work Sirk was interested in frustrated ambition. Born in 1900 of Danish parents, he was one of a group of directors of European origin who worked in Hollywood, other prominent examples being Wilder, Preminger and Zinnemann. Before the war Sirk worked as director in theatres in Bremen and Leipzig, later as a director for UFA pictures. His first Hollywood movie was Hitler's Madman (1943). Sirk said he wanted Written on the Wind to be a "baroque" film and lavished much attention on the functional use of color. "My ideal was a Greek tragedy enacted within a family.... This family is a reflection of the world, it is a symbol." Condemned worlds always held a fascination for Sirk: in Sign of the Pagan (1954) he studied the fall of the Roman Empire; in Taza, Son of Cochise (1954)--the fall of the Apache nation; in

Time to Live and Time to Die (1958)--the collapse of the Third Reich. His films remind one of Baudelaire, of Scott Fitzgerald and--to find a cinematic analogy--of Orson Welles's The Magnificent Ambersons. The Cain-Abel motif (Mitch-Kyle) is present in the three Sirk films scripted by George Zuckerman.

As a piece of cinema critical of "the rich and the spoilt of the American family," Written on the Wind relates Sirk to Brooks and Ritt. The Hadleys are to him a microcosm of America. "The sense both of failure and being blocked is indeed one of the themes which interest me passionately. Success is not interesting to me. And the end of Written on the Wind is highly significant as far as this is concerned: Malone has lost everything. I have put up a sign there indicating this--Malone, alone, sitting there, hugging that goddamned oil well, having nothing. The oil well which is, I think, a rather frightening symbol of American society."

The strengths of Written on the Wind are the great density of themes, excellent camerawork, lighting and designs. All in all, the picture is much more effective than the thematically related (and much better known) Giant (1956) directed by George Stevens.

MY UNCLE JACINTO (Mio tio Jacinto) Ladislao Vajda

Script: Andres Laszlo, Gian Luigi Rondi, Vajda, José Santugini and Max Korner. Photography: Enrique Guerner. Music: Roman Vlad. Art Direction: José Maria Moreno and Antonio Simont. Cast: Pablo Calvo (Pepote), Antonio Vico (Jacinto), José Marco Davo (Police Inspector), Juan Calvo (Old clothes man), Paolo Stoppa (Antique dealer), Mariano Azana (Watch seller), José Isbert (Sanchez), Julio Sanjuan (Organ grinder), Pastora Pena (Stamp seller), Walter Chiari.

Charmatin/Falco Film/E. N. I. C., Spain/Italy. 8180 ft., 91 mins.

Neorealism in a Spanish variety; of course only in a folkloristic edition. My Uncle Jacinto can be described as a tragicomical remake of Bicycle Thieves. Pepote, a six-year-old boy, lives with his Uncle Jacinto, a drunken old ex-matador, who dreams of a return to the bullring. He is given an unexpected chance to appear in the Plaza de Toros in a comedy sketch involving himself, a harmless young bull and two clowns. Through a stroke of bad luck the occasion is a disaster. Pepote is the witness and active participant of these efforts; he helps his uncle with great earnestness and in the finale saves him from complete humiliation and allows him to preserve his dignity in the world of illusion.

Pablo Calvo plays the boy with talent equal to that of Jackie

Coogan in The Kid. Ladislao Vajda (son of Laidslaus Vajda, a sometime scriptwriter for G. W. Pabst) managed, despite having made the film in the studio, to perfuse it with the specific Spanish character and, while steering clear of melodrama, to move the spectator with its vital human problems. Photography is very good and the relationship between the old man and a little boy well captured. This inconsiderable but likeable picture remains, for all its limitations, one of the more interesting in the Spanish cinema.

1957

WILD STRAWBERRIES (Smultronstället) Ingmar Bergman

Script: Bergman. Photography: Gunnar Fischer. Music: Erik Nordgren. Art Direction: Gittan Gustafsson. Costumes: Millie Ström. Editing: Oscar Rosander. Cast: Victor Sjöström (Professor Isak Borg), Ingrid Thulin (Marianne Borg), Bibi Andersson (Sara), Gunnar Björnstrand (Evald Borg), Folke Sundquist (Anders), Björn Bjelvenstam (Viktor), Naima Wifstrand (Isak Borg's mother), Jullan Kindahl (Agda), Gunnar Sjöberg (Alman), Gunnel Broström (Berit Alman), Gertrud Fridh (Karin Borg), Åke Fridell (Karin's lover), Max von Sydow (Åkerman), Sif Ruud (Aunt), Yngve Nordwall (Uncle Aron), Per Sjöstrand (Sigfrid), Gio Petré (Sigbritt), Gunnel Lindblom (Charlotta), Maud Hansson (Angelica), Anne-Marie Wiman (Mrs. Åkerman), Eva Norée (Anna), Per Skogsberg (Hagbart), Göran Lundquist (Benjamin).

Allan Ekelund for Svensk Filmindustri, Sweden. 8409 ft., 93 mins.

Professor Isak Borg wakes up in the morning after a bad dream. He is 76 and a distinguished Stockholm bacteriologist. He is to travel to Lund that day to receive an honorary doctorate for his services to science. Borg travels by car with his daughter-in-law Marianne. The experiences of the 400-mile journey make him reflect on his life. Marianne feels that her husband, in not wanting to have children, displays the selfish traits of the old man. She tells Borg that underneath the veneer of benevolent tolerance he is cold and arid. They meet three hikers, a girl and two boys and offer to take them to Lund. Later they give a lift to an embittered married couple whose car was involved in an accident. After a visit to Borg's family's former summer house they have lunch beside a lake.

Borg goes back to the past: he remembers the beautiful cousin whom he loved and who married his brother instead; then his failed marriage to a woman who betrayed him. Later in the day Borg calls on his nonagenarian mother. After the degree ceremony he finds that the three young people are really fond of him and he goes to sleep in peace. He dreams of a summer idyll: his father is fishing on a shore, while his mother waves to him. The abandonment of his distant egoism, a gesture of kindness towards his son (as a result of his experiences during the journey he waives a debt of money) will enable the professor to return among the living.

Wild Strawberries opens with one of the most remarkable dream sequences in the whole of cinema. A desolate street in the old quarter of Stockholm. Borg comes to a house with boarded up windows. He sees a clock without hands. An old hearse approaches down the street. One of its wheels catches on a lamp-post and a coffin is spilled out. The outstretched hand of the corpse tries to pull Borg inside.

There are other dream sequences in Bergman's picture. While revisiting the summer house Borg finds himself in a strawberry clearing. He recalls scenes from his childhood, the song sung by twin cousins for a deaf uncle, later his love for a girl, then his tormented relationship with his wife. It is interesting that Borg appears bodily in these flashbacks, as his present self. As he dozes off at his mother's house he has an unpleasant dream. He is being examined before an audience of characters from the film. He is asked to identify a specimen under the microscope, but cannot see anything; then to examine a patient. He declares him dead; at this the patient begins to laugh. The examiner tells Borg that he failed. "What is the penalty?" asks Borg. "The same as always--loneliness." This Expressionistic sequence is richly laced with Freudian symbols (such as an abandoned ladder, or a nail on which Borg tears the palm of his hand).

What is Bergman's film really about? Is it a story of a man whose life was ruined when the girl he loved married his good-for-nothing brother? Or is it a film about a man who became embittered and selfish when he was betrayed by his wife? Not really: the message of Wild Strawberries is that despite life's being cruel, one has to cherish kindness, good-naturedness and openness--because the only alternative is loneliness and stifling emptiness in old age. How close is this to the message of Fellini's Le notti di Cabiria. Some may say that the thought is not particularly original. Maybe so--but as so often happens in art in general and in the cinema in particular, the value of Wild Strawberries is not in the message itself, but in the human climate which surrounds it in a work of art. Bergman offered his thoughts in such a fine artistic form, with such involvement, warmth and emotion, that the result has more impact than many a learned academic dispute about man's condition. Some critics claimed that Wild Strawberries draws its poetry from the plot itself rather than from film technique, the photography or the music. In fact it was drawn from the scenery. Throughout the drive, mostly through the forest, the characters are immersed in peaceful Swedish nature. It is interesting that while some of Bergman's earlier films, most notably The Seventh Seal, were concerned with man's attitude towards God, Wild Strawberries almost gives an impression that the director has thrown God out. During the journey to Lund two of the hitch-hikers, one of whom is an atheist and the other is preparing to become a pastor, are involved in an animated quarrel about religion. Borg's attitude to them is highly significant: a distant half-smile.

The part of Professor Borg is played by Victor Sjöström, the great Swedish director of the silent era who also made several films in America. Wild Strawberries is very much Bergman's homage to his spiritual master who died, aged 80, soon after. Sjöström's performance is one of the classics of the cinema. Bergman recalls the shooting of the final scenes: "Sjöström's face shone, it emanated light--a reflection of a different reality, here absent. His whole appearance was soft and gentle, his glance joyful and tender. It was like a miracle."

PORTE DES LILAS René Clair

Script: Clair, with the collaboration of Jean Aurel, based on the novel "La Grande Ceinture" by René Fallet. Photography: Robert Le Fèbvre. Music: Georges Brassens. Art Direction: Léon Barsacq. Editing: Louisette Hautecoeur. Cast: Pierre Brasseur (Juju), Georges Brassens (The Artist), Henri Vidal (Pierre Barbier), Dany Carrel (Maria), Raymond Bussières (Alphonse), Amédée (Paulo), Alain Bouvette (Paulo's friend), Bugette (Police officer), Gérard Buhr (Inspector), Annette Poivre (Nénette), Gabrielle Fontan (Mme. Sabatier).

Filmsonor/Cinétel/Séca/Rizzoli, France/Italy. 96 mins.

Juju, a kind-hearted idler lives with his friend The Artist in a dilapidated house in Porte des Lilas, a suburb of Paris. When Pierre Barbier, a gangster on the run, takes refuge in the house, Juju offers him help and unselfish friendship. Treated with contempt by everybody, he now finds comfort in feeling useful. The Artist, who plays his guitar at the local bar, is less enthusiastic about harboring the criminal. Maria, the daughter of the owner of the bar, enters the hideout out of curiosity and Barbier decides that he must neutralize the awkward witness by pretending he is in love with her. Juju, who hopelessly admires the girl is even prepared to give her up, if only she was happy. But when he discovers that Barbier has used the girl to provide money for his getaway--he takes justice into his own hands and kills Barbier in a scuffle.

Porte des Lilas

Clair's script removed slang words from Fallet's novel and replaced its rough realism with the poetry of everyday, a melancholy half-smile and subtle bitterness--while abiding with realism even more firmly than ever. Porte des Lilas is a piercing tragedy of betrayed trust and, for all its stylistic simplicity, a masterly exercise in evoking the atmosphere. Pierre Brasseur's incomparable Juju is without a doubt the most human and the most complex character in the whole of Clair's cinema; songs performed by Georges Brassens, the famous poet-singer-composer, are probably the most appropriate musical illustration in any of Clair's populist films, the designs are striking with their credibility and specific charm. No pretentiousness, no obtrusiveness--only a gentle, wistful meditation about feelings.

Unfortunately Porte des Lilas, one of Clair's finest pictures, is also his last outstanding one. The director whose entire life's work was the realization of his beliefs in a cinema for everybody, a good and entertaining popular cinema which is generally understood, was never again able to find within himself his old extraordinary gift for striking the golden mean between art and entertainment. He lamented over the decline of the French cinema (which in the mid-50's was an undisputed fact)--but was not able to see a way out of the situation in which the only alternative was either the multiplication of arid commercial banality or the increasing formal lifelessness of the more serious cinematic projects. A year after Porte des Lilas Clair made the famous (and unfortunate) statement: "Cinema must be for everybody; I oppose with all my heart the aestheticizing cinema which exists solely to project the visions of its maker." Fortunately, history did not decide in Clair's favor. The Nouvelle Vague soon arrived, and with it a radical renaissance of the language of the cinema and the review of the character of a work of the screen. That which in the 50's was cultivated only by the very few, such as Bresson and Antonioni, became in a few years' time, with the coming of the cinéma d'auteur, the ruling principle.

IL GRIDO (The Cry) Michelangelo Antonioni

Script: Antonioni, Ennio De Concini and Elio Bartolini from a story by Antonioni. Photography: Gianni Di Venanzo. Music: Giovanni Fusco. Art Direction: Franco Fontana. Editing: Eraldo Da Roma. Cast: Steve Cochran (Aldo), Alida Valli (Irma), Mirna Girardi (Rosina), Betsy Blair (Elvira), Dorian Gray (Virginia), Gabriella Pallotta (Edera), Lyn Shaw (Andreina), Guerrino Campanili (Virginia's father), Gaetano Matteucci (Edera's fiancé), Pietro Corvelatti (Old fisherman), Pina Boldrini.

Franco Cancellieri for S. P. A. Cinematografica/Robert Alexander Productions, Italy/U. S. A. 116 mins.

A sonata about existence which is fading away, Il grido is one of the most brilliant cinematic evocations of an elegiac atmosphere, built around the story of a journey to nowhere. Antonioni draws a psychological portrait of a man who has been described as a "proletarian Werther." Aldo lost the woman he loved and with whom he had been living for seven years. Irma left him when she found a chance of stability in association with another man. Aldo cannot recover from the blow; he gives up his job at a sugar refinery, takes his six-year-old daughter and for many months wanders through the Po Valley. He meets other women but they cannot bring him consolation. Lost and desolate, he returns to the village from where he started, climbs the high tower of the refinery and before the eyes of his lost mistress throws himself down onto the concrete yard.

Il grido is the first picture in which Antonioni consistently built the narrative according to completely novel principles, which were to exert great influence on the development of the cinema. The dramatic structure is no longer a kinetic carrier of the director's intentions; the decisive role is given to the potential effect of the individual episodes, which convey thoughts, mental states, associations, conclusions. Thus what one sees on the screen is no longer an ordered and improved version of reality, but an aggregate of elements selected with a definite intention in mind. These narrative and structural features of Antonioni's cinema were noticed two years later, in L'avventura, and gave rise to an animated controversy. Il grido, a film less ostentatious in using the "open" narrative structure, still follows the same rules of chaos of events, futility of the protagonist's successive actions, detailed and objective background observation, of conducting the story in the ostinato with the exception of the shattering finale. Antonioni can be accused of occasionally indulging in unnatural symbolism of objects picked out by the camera; this would not be glaring in the contrived La notte or L'eclisse, a film in which the director's style evolved towards precise structures which intellectually transmit mental states. In Il grido, however, the film governed exclusively by the mood, these practices seem alien, but do not rupture the delicate tissue made up of the omnipresent mist which envelops feelings, from the painterly conveyance of the loneliness of a man in a sterile landscape, from the melancholy of the discreet piano music, from the dispassionate description of the background which, for all its precision, reveals nothing but the alienation of the hero. One can say that Il grido combines the film-making craft of the Neorealists with their reliability of looking at things and spontaneous acting; the moods of Poetic Realism; the understated penetrativeness of the American psychological drama. But this does not explain the originality of the film. One can also remark that the tone and the situations of Il grido obviously refer to Visconti's Ossessione--but this does not give justice to Antonioni's achievement either. It seems that the secret of Il grido lies in the clarity of the extremely appropriate means of expression, the mutual contiguity of the story, the mood and the reflection which convey a subjective image of human psyche without resorting to the use of subjective components.

THE CRANES ARE FLYING (Letyat zhuravli) Mikhail Kalatozov

Script: Victor Rozov, from his play "Vyechno zhivye" (The Ever-Living). Photography: Sergei Urusevsky. Music: Moisei Vaynberg. Art Direction: E. Svidetelev. Editing: M. Timofeyeva. Cast: Tatyana Samoilova (Veronika), Aleksei Batalov (Boris), Vasili Merkuryev (Fyodor Ivanovich), A. Shvorin (Mark), S. Kharitonova (Irina), Valentin Zubkov (Stepan), A. Bogdanova (Grandmother), K. Nikitin (Volodya), B. Kokobkin (Tyernov), E. Kupriyanova (Anna Mikhailovna).

Mosfilm, U.S.S.R. 8697 ft., 97 mins.

The Cranes Are Flying brings the explosion of lyricism and the final break, in the wake of The Forty-First, with the formal and psychological stereotypes of the Socialist Realist period regnant in the Soviet cinema for over 20 years. Kalatozov, an ardent believer in the emotional cinema, let himself be known as a talented film-maker with poetic leanings even towards the close of the silent period; later he conformed to the demands and requirements of the authorities. The few pictures he made did not go beyond correctness, and he spent the rest of his time on official functions in the Soviet film industry. The post-1956 political relaxation brought Kalatozov a long-awaited opportunity for expressing freely his creative temperament and his method of influencing the spectator via emotions by using only a few basic twists of the plot and pervading the whole with lyricism to the limits of endurance. On such few twists of plot rests the whole of The Cranes Are Flying, the film version of a (rather substantially transformed) popular stage play.

Veronika is separated from her fiancé Boris when he is called away to the war. A sensitive girl, lost and lonely, she cannot wait as did all her predecessors in Soviet war dramas. Acting on an impulse in a moment of anguish, she gives herself to Mark, the step-brother of her beloved, and later marries him. He soon turns out to be a scoundrel and a coward; the final blow comes when an eye witness conveys the news of the death on the front of Boris, whom Veronika still loves. She refuses to believe and lives in hope until the end of the war. She meets the troop train on Victory Day, carrying a bunch of flowers for Boris. He is not there and Veronika gives the flowers to his fellow soldiers. Only the flock of cranes in the sky is the same as the one they looked at together years before....

The treatment of the heroine on the screen, the presentation of the events on the front and above all the description of the home front during the long months of the mortal struggle of U.S.S.R. against Nazi Germany--in The Cranes Are Flying all this is in complete contrast to the usual practices in a Soviet war film. The heart-rending scene of the farewell of the soldiers departing for the front has nothing to do with the standard blessing of sprightly warriors; the front itself is shown as fear-filled silence brooding over muddy wasteland where death lies in wait; the dominant mood on the home front is one of exhaustion with work for the needs of the war, of depression so far from slogans about optimistic endurance with clenched teeth; there are black marketeers, speculators and shirkers who buy themselves a comfortable life (a pity though, that it is only the middle classes that the film blames for the corruption of war-time). This human landscape is incomparably truer than ever before. Veronika is a character which was earlier impossible to imagine in the Soviet cinema: unfaithful, brittle, very, very deeply absorbed by the problems of personal happiness--and therefore all the more tragic when she loses it irrevocably. Tatyana Samoilova gave her part so much spontaneous expressiveness as to make Veronika one of the most popular Soviet screen heroines; the actress herself gained international reputation with this one role. The certain dualism of the film's unusual visual exuberance comes from the superimposition of the creative temperaments of Kalatozov and the photographer Urusevsky, who were united by their sense for the dynamic, but were very different in aesthetic expression. It would perhaps be over-simplification to say that Kalatozov's contribution to the film is a belated culmination of the pictorial emphasis of the silent Soviet cinema, of post-Expressionism and of the traditional Russian emotional naturalism; while all contributed by Urusevsky is an innovatory demonstration of the capabilities of a liberated, subjective camera--and that therefore the director is responsible for the faults of the film, while the credit for the rest is owed to the photographer. All the same, it is true to say that the borderline between the imageries of the two men is the watershed between the old and the new. The power of The Cranes Are Flying is owed to the fact that Urusevsky's talent captured Kalatozov's imagination, that his dynamic visual inventiveness (the examples are the chase on the staircase shown in one unbroken take, the soldiers' departure for the war, the whirling tree-tops in the moment of Boris's death) gave strength and decisiveness to the material very incoherent in directorial conception, ranging from documentary sharpness to eclectic sensualism. Despite its unevenness, the film they made together amounts to one of the richest and frankest evocations of wartime in the Soviet cinema.

EROICA Andrzej Munk

Script: Jerzy Stefan Stawiński, from his own short stories "Węgrzy" (Hungarians) and "Ucieczka" (Escape). Photography: Jerzy Wójcik. Music: Jan Krenz. Art Direction: Jan Grandys. Editing: Jadwiga Zajiček and Mirosława Garlicka. Cast: SCHERZO ALLA POLACCA: Edward Dziewoński (Dzidziuś Górkiewicz), Barbara Połomska (Zosia

Górkiewicz), Ignacy Machowski (Major Grzmot), Leon Niemczyk (Lt. István Kolya), Kazimierz Opaliński (Mokotów district commander). OSTINATO LUGUBRE: Kazimierz Rudzki (Lt. Turek), Józef Nowak (Lt. Kurzawa), Roman Kłosowski (Lt. Szpakowski), Wojciech Siemion (Lt. Marianek), Józef Kostecki (Lt. Żak), Henryk Bąk (Lt. Krygier), Mariusz Dmochowski (Lt. Korwin-Makowski), Bogumił Kobiela (Lt. Dąbecki), Tadeusz Łomnicki (Lt. Zawistowski).

Stanisław Adler for ZAF Kadr, Poland. 7787 ft., 87 mins.

Poland and the U. S. S. R. were the two Communist countries where the political changes of 1956 had the strongest impact on the cinema. In the U. S. S. R. movies turned towards personal rather than corporate problems, while the Polish cinema embarked on a discussion about the sense of actions and attitudes of individuals in testing historical situations. The principal problem was the role of heroism during and immediately after the war; the dilemmas of choice between cool reason and emotional solidarity presented with the whole complexity of the attendant political pros and cons. Wajda chose an emotional approach to these problems, which was doubtless predetermined by his romantic creative temperament, and by the fact that during the preceding eleven years the contribution of the non-leftist factions in wartime resistance to the liberation of Poland was officially concealed, as were the personal tragedies of many of their members after the war. Andrzej Munk, the most outstanding member of the other wing of what came to be known as the Polish School, gave his films the character of rationalist disputes. This was particularly striking in view of the fact that so far the Polish cinema had approached problems rather superficially, without attempting to offer intellectual support. In this way Munk was responsible for very important progress. In The Man on the Track (1956), the film which foreshadowed the Polish School, he revised the Stalinist view of human attitudes; in Eroica he questioned the problems of wartime heroism, dissecting the conditioning of the national Polish heroic mythology. The film was originally planned to be in three parts: Munk suggested to Stawiński, the scriptwriter, the adding to the two short stories already written a third one dealing with the ordinary, spontaneous heroism of partisans and members of the Underground; it was to open the film. Thus Stawiński wrote "The Nun," the story filmed as "Con bravura," but later personally persuaded Munk to drop it as weaker and very different in spirit from the other two. So, Eroica became a bi-partite film. This added to its quality, but the resulting absence of a counterbalance (to have been provided by "Con bravura") added to the general misunderstanding of the picture in Poland. Eroica was received as an anti-heroic pamphlet, and in the aura of sanctity surrounding Polish armed feats any attempt at looking at them from a different angle was considered inappropriate. Munk was bitter: "We were trying to show a certain, rather sad, combination of events in Polish history and to throw some light on their supposedly shameful and usually discreetly omitted aspects. The anecdotal narrative style was used to help in discharging certain complexes, to demonstrate the irrational component of the traditional

Eroica

Polish heroism. At the root of bravery lies active opposition against evil.... Those who accuse me of anti-heroic views do me a great injustice. Eroica is never unkind to heroes; on the contrary it treats people driven by irrational motives with sympathy and sentiment. All we did was to demonstrate the uselessness of such attitudes."

The main character of "Scherzo alla polacca" is a certain Dzidziuś Górkiewicz, a Warsaw sly-boots and entrepreneur. During the 1944 Warsaw Rising Dzidziuś, who has joined a volunteer group of the resistance but soon tired of the discipline, leaves the burning city and steals through to his wife in the suburbs. He finds her in the company of a Hungarian officer; the Hungarians (allied to the Germans) are prepared to help the insurgents provided certain conditions are met. Dzidziuś sets off to Warsaw to deliver the message and then returns with the reply. The Hungarian offer is refused. It is then that Dzidziuś decides he prefers the dangers of armed struggle to the company of his silly wife and returns once more to Warsaw to join the doomed Rising.

"Ostinato lugubre" is set in a POW camp somewhere in the Alps. A new group of prisoners arrives to join Polish officers who have already spent five years behind barbed wire. The new arrivals are told that only one prisoner ever escaped from the camp. Zawistowski's escape maintains the morale of others and allows them to keep the remains of sanity. But in fact Zawistowski has not escaped; incapacitated by an illness he is hiding from the Germans in a loft above the wash-house. Finally he commits suicide. But his myth does not die; the body is smuggled out in an old boiler. It is a bitter irony that the man who does it is the one most aware in this little world, meant to be the metaphor of Poland. A skeptical rationalist, he justifies his decision with the words: "This has to be done. For himself and for others." The story has a very significant musical background--arid tones of the xylophone. As a matter of fact, Jan Krenz gave a splendid musical illustration also to the first story: the grotesque odyssey of tipsy Dzidziuś is accompanied by the fanfare charge of the trumpet.

The film which so perfectly reflects the Polish way of thinking (not only in the period which it describes) and which so forcefully explains the inevitability of the creation of a heroic mythology in a nation under constant pressure of tragic history, would not reach such near-philosophical dimension were it not for Munk's precise and inventive direction and the inspired acting from Dziewoński and Rudzki. Munk's craft is particularly impressive in the second story, where strikingly true scenery is combined with the authentic behavior of characters, dense and capacious dialogues with terse narrative, precise inter-frame editing with metaphoric quality of contexts, long takes with an overwhelmingly depressing mood of this spiritual trap behind the barbed wire. "Scherzo alla polacca" is more disordered, but has good pace, sharp irony, humor and situational paradoxes. Both parts are excellently photographed by Wójcik; completely in tune with the director's intentions, he nonetheless gives each frame his personal stamp. Particularly striking is his feel for the tangibility of objects. Wójcik's expressive photography finds completely different visual equivalents for the different moods of each of the two parts of Eroica.

3:10 TO YUMA Delmer Daves

Script: Halsted Welles, from a story by Elmore Leonard. Photography: Charles Lawton Jr. Music: George Duning. Song "3:10 to Yuma" by George Duning and Ned Washington. Art Direction: Frank Hotaling. Editing: Al Clark. Cast: Van Heflin (Dan Evans), Glenn Ford (Ben Wade), Felicia Farr (Emmy), Leora Dana (Alice Evans), Henry Jones (Alex Potter), Richard Jaeckel (Charlie Prince), Robert Emhardt (Mr. Butterfield), Sheridan Comerate (Bob Moons), George Mitchell (Bartender), Robert Ellenstein (Ernie Collins), Ford Rainey (Marshal), Barry Curtis (Mathew), Jerry Hartleben (Mark).

David Heilwell for Columbia, U. S. A. 8280 ft., 92 mins.

Of the leading directors of westerns in the 50's Delmer Daves was the one who opposed the traditional mythology of the genre with most vigor. Of course, these were not yet the times when one could afford to adopt the sardonic stand of Arthur Penn in Little Big Man or to pronounce shattering indictments of the colonization of the West, as Nelson did in Soldier Blue. All the same, the fact remains that it was Daves who directed Broken Arrow (1950), the first serious western in which also the Indians are treated seriously; and that it was in his films, such as Jubal (1956) and Cowboy that demythologized pioneers of the West appeared.

Rancher Dan Evans in 3:10 to Yuma, decidedly Daves's best film, is also like them. There is a prolonged drought and the livelihood of the family depends on the supply of water. To build the well would cost $200, as much as the prize offered for the delivery to the state prison at Yuma of Ben Wade, a notorious gunfighter who has just been captured in a posse. There is danger of reprisals from Wade's gang. Evans and Wade wait for the train bound for Yuma in a hotel room. There Wade launches a psychological war of attrition; he does not talk about morality, the defense of the law or the other classical themes from the western code of moral principles--his talk is about money. Finally Evans receives an offer seemingly impossible to reject: $10,000 for a slight negligence of his duties as a guard. Why is it precisely then that he begins to turn into an incorruptible defender of justice ready to die rather than succumb to the temptation? Daves's film leaves the spectator in no doubt as to the reasons: the task undertaken purely for money became a matter of maintaining one's dignity. Thus western abstraction is reduced to a moral proof. All the captivating power of 3:10

to Yuma relies on isolating the factors which develop honesty, inner discipline and strength of character. Apart from the economy of means, high tension and precise description the film can claim no formal qualities--there are here no imposing landscapes, and the struggle of wits and characters in the hotel room takes up a considerable part of the running time of the picture. Only the finale (though not the culmination) is dynamic and traditionally "western": the bandit (in which part Daves perversely cast Glenn Ford, while giving the part of Evans to Van Heflin, who usually appears as a bad guy) jumps into the departing train leaving Evans behind. And when it seems that the farmer's bravery was in vain, Wade stretches his hand and helps him to get onto the fast running train. Why?-- "Well, I owed you that. And I have already escaped from the prison in Yuma before."

PATHS OF GLORY Stanley Kubrick

Script: Kubrick, Calder Willingham and Jim Thompson, based on the novel by Humphrey Cobb. Photography: Georg Krause. Music: Gerald Fried. Art Direction: Ludwig Reiber. Editing: Eva Kroll. Cast: Kirk Douglas (Colonel Dax), Ralph Meeker (Corporal Paris), Adolphe Menjou (General Broulard), George Macready (General Mireau), Wayne Morris (Lieutenant Roget), Richard Anderson (Major Saint-Auban), Joseph Turkel (Private Arnaud), Timothy Carey (Private Ferol), Peter Capell (Colonel Judge), Susanne Christian (German girl), Bert Freed (Sergeant Boulanger), Emile Meyer (Priest), John Stein (Captain Rousseau), Harold Benedict (Captain Nichols).

James B. Harris for Bryna Productions, U. S. A. 7783 ft., 86 mins.

Kubrick's virulent vision is quite simply the best anti-war film of the 50's and one of the best of all. When embarking on writing the script Kubrick planned to set Paths of Glory at an unspecified place and time in order to stress the general applicability of his observations--much as Huston did with The Red Badge of Courage. Finally, afraid of it thus becoming unreal, he set the picture on the Western Front of the First World War. While this circumstance is not actually material for the film's message, which would have been the same in a different setting, it became clear soon after release that the message got home. Paths of Glory caused a diplomatic storm and was banned in France for a whole fifteen years. This is despite the fact that the more sober-minded French critics defended the film from the very beginning.

France in 1916. The French High Command, located a few miles behind the front, decides to mount an attack against a German stronghold nicknamed "Ant Hill." General Mireau orders Colonel Dax to lead it. The reasons for the planned operation are mainly prestige and the chances of success nil. When Dax's exhausted men find it impossible to make any headway, Mireau orders the artillery to fire on them from behind and becomes hysterical when the artillery commander refuses. Later, a believer in setting examples, Mireau persuades General Broulard that there is a need for a court martial. Three arbitrarily chosen men are tried for cowardice. Dax is not allowed to make a fair case for their defense and they are condemned to death. In a last attempt to save their lives Dax tells Broulard that Mireau ordered the artillery to fire on his own troops--but the General takes no action and the three men are executed. It is only then that Broulard tells Mireau that he will have to face an inquiry. He offers the stunned Dax Mireau's job, explaining with an ironic smile that he knew all along that this was what Dax was after.... Dax indignantly refuses and returns to his men.

Karl von Clausewitz, the military theoretician, said: "War is nothing more than the continuation of politics by other means"; while Dr. Samuel Johnson claimed that "patriotism is the last refuge of a scoundrel"--and Paths of Glory is contained in the spiritual framework outlined by these two famous maxims. The military autocrats are less concerned with winning the war than with increasing their own power and influence. The lives of men are insignificant and the picture shows the distance between the commanders and the troops in a series of ironic scenes: a general dispensing platitudinous encouragement to soldiers about to mount an attack; the orchestra playing waltzes for an officers' ball in the elegant rooms of a château. Kubrick's attitude is not emotional, but cold and reasoned. All he does is simply to analyze a certain situation. He clearly demonstrates that treachery and hypocrisy are essential parts of the war machinery. Paths of Glory is biting and ironic--and much more powerful than scores of pacifist movies. Kubrick allows himself only one brief moment of emotion when at the end the soldiers listen to a song about love sung by a German girl prisoner.

Born in 1928, Kubrick for four years worked as a photographer on "Look" magazine. In 1951 he began making short films for the cinema, later for television. His early features, Killer's Kiss (1955) and The Killing (1956) are both most interesting, particularly formally. Paths of Glory, Kubrick's first major film, was made outside the film industry and shot on location in Germany. Its intellectual attitude is matched by the cold, aggressive film technique. The camera now performs sweeping panoramas across trenches, now glides into saloons. Particularly memorable is the scene of the execution. Inspired cutting gave Georg Krause's excellent black-and-white photography a sense of haste and urgency. Kirk Douglas gives one of his finest performances as the honest colonel who opposes corruption, George Macready is effective as a vengeful militarist, as is Adolphe Menjou as a sly, scheming general.

Paths of Glory

A FACE IN THE CROWD Elia Kazan

Script: Budd Schulberg, from his short story "Your Arkansas Traveller" in the book "Some Faces in the Crowd." Photography: Harry Stradling and Gayne Rescher. Music: Tom Glazer. Songs: "A Face in the Crowd," "Free Man in the Morning," "Mama Git-tar" and "Vitajex Jingle" by Tom Glazer and Budd Schulberg. Art Direction: Richard and Paul Sylbert. Editing: Gene Milford. Cast: Andy Griffith (Lonesome Rhodes), Patricia Neal (Marcia Jeffries), Anthony Franciosa (Joey Kieley), Walter Matthau (Mel Miller), Lee Remick (Betty Lou Fleckum), Percy Waram (Colonel Hollister), Rod Brasfield (Beanie), Charles Irving (Mr. Luffler), Howard Smith (J. B. Jeffries), Paul McGrath (Macey), Kay Medford (First Mrs. Rhodes), Marshall Neilan (Senator Fuller), Alexander Kirkland (Jim Collier), Henry Sharp (Abe Steiner), Big Jeff Bess (Sheriff Clyde Hesmer), P. Jay Sidney (Llewellyn), Eva Vaughan (Mrs. Cooley), Burl Ives (Himself), Willie Feibel and Larry Casazza (Printers).

Elia Kazan for Newtown, U. S. A. 126 mins.

Kazan's dynamic tragicomedy is one of the most searching pictures about the mechanism of success. A Face in the Crowd charts the rise and fall of a radio and television superstar. During a visit to a small-town jail in Arkansas, a girl reporter, Marcia, comes across a guitar-twanging tramp. Taken by his ballads and his charm she gets him a spot on the local radio. Lonesome Rhodes sings songs, cracks jokes, chats about this and that, plugs medicine pills; he is so nice, so ordinary and unassuming that one cannot help liking him. Soon the whole town listens to Lonesome's programs; his popularity increases even more rapidly when he goes on television and then moves on to New York to become a national figure. Marcia becomes increasingly alarmed at Lonesome's growing megalomania and his dubious involvement with a somewhat sinister political faction. She realizes it is now her responsibility to destroy the "demagogue in denim" whom she herself started on his vertiginous progress; she does so by turning on the control-room sound switch at the end of one of his shows, just as Lonesome passes contemptuous remarks about his audience thinking that they cannot hear.

It all starts from socially useful actions, from responding to the need for change which is felt by everybody; such is in fact the order of actions of any sensible politician. But Lonesome does not follow a program of action; he is not in control of the situation, but the situation is in control of him. He comes to believe that he is really great, that his powers are limitless: "The whole country's just like my flock of sheep ... hillbillies, hausfraus ... everybody that's got to jump when somebody else blows a whistle ... they're mine."

Schulberg and Kazan trace the degeneration of genuine talent in the maw of the advertising industry although their involvement is not free from exaggeration and they use a rather conformist story outline. The director admits to this: "There was an intention to make that picture larger than life ... on a heightened level.... And I'm criticized often for it. But it's my taste. I don't deal in naturalism anymore."

One may complain that Kazan did not give the personality of the hero sufficient depth, particularly in the second part of the film. Also, the finale is rather doubtful: while castigating Lonesome for his contempt towards the public, Kazan does not seem to have a high opinion of them himself. The television audience rejects Lonesome not because they have seen through his perfidious schemes, but because he has been rude to them. Patricia Neal's brittle gesture plays the role of a security valve. Still, the message is clear and A Face in the Crowd is a warning of demagogy of any kind (something quite relevant coming in the post-McCarthy period); a challenge to society, although one carefully camouflaged under the layers of the plot. All this apart, A Face in the Crowd is an interesting early study of the potentially destructive power of television on the human psyche, and it is illuminating to compare the film with Network made two decades later. It is also a fascinating record of the operation of a television studio in the early days.

WITNESS FOR THE PROSECUTION Billy Wilder

Script: Wilder and Harry Kurnitz, from the play by Agatha Christie. Photography: Russell Harlan. Music: Matty Malneck. Song "I May Never Go Home Anymore" by Ralph Arthur Roberts and Jack Brooks. Art Direction: Alexandre Trauner. Editing: Daniel Mandell. Cast: Charles Laughton (Sir Wilfrid Robarts), Tyrone Power (Leonard Vole), Marlene Dietrich (Christine Vole), Elsa Lanchester (Miss Plimsoll), John Williams (Brogan-Moore), Henry Daniell (Mayhew), Ian Wolfe (Carter), Una O'Connor (Janet McKenzie), Torin Thatcher (Mr. Meyers), Francis Compton (Judge), Norma Varden (Mrs. French), Philip Tonge (Inspector Hearne), Ruta Lee (Diana), Molly Roden (Miss McHugh), Ottola Nesmith (Miss Johnson), Marjorie Eaton (Miss O'Brien), J. Pat O'Malley (Shorts salesman).

Arthur Hornblow Jr. for Theme, U.S.A. 10,436 ft., 116 mins.

The plot of Witness for the Prosecution, the screen version of the classical Agatha Christie stage whodunit, revolves around the trial of a certain handsome gentleman accused of murdering a rich widow. The dead woman left him a considerable sum of money, and the case for the prosecution looks very strong. But Sir Wilfrid

Robarts, a famous barrister, is intrigued by the circumstances and finally accepts the case. When the wife of the accused gives evidence strongly incriminating her husband and reveals that the marriage was in fact bigamous, the "guilty" verdict seems inevitable....

The intrigue is ingenious, very complex, and has a perfidious double twist at the end. But there is no rose without thorns: the film jars with its improbable coincidences, a number of easy effects and the moral opportunism of the ending. It would have been very difficult to use Christie's novel as the basis for a convincing, brutal analysis of characters and indeed the film is more concerned with the mechanics of the plot. Wilder quite rightly did not attempt to make Witness for the Prosecution along the lines of Double Indemnity and The Lost Weekend which brought him fame; instead he transferred the script to the screen abiding by the rules of a murder mystery, and supplemented the text with his fine arrangement of situations, clever climaxing of individual scenes and--above all--with a very precise gradation of suspense obtained mainly through exploiting the verbal encounters in the courtroom. A great asset to the director were the excellent performances from Charles Laughton as the cunning and eccentric lawyer, Marlene Dietrich as the wife of the accused and Una O'Connor as the dead woman's opinionated housekeeper. So, stylized psychology neutralized the logical shoals of situations, comical character observation gave life to the meanders of courtroom proceedings, while Wilder's perverse irony disarmed some overly-serious conclusions which one might have been tempted to draw. Witness for the Prosecution, a sustained and well-built piece of entertainment, became in time one of the classics of the courtroom genre.

THE LOWER DEPTHS (Donzoko) Akira Kurosawa

Script: Hideo Oguni and Kurosawa, based on the play "Na dne" (The Lower Depths) by Maxim Gorky. Photography: Kazuo Yamasaki. Music: Masaru Sato. Art Direction: Yoshiro Muraki. Cast: Toshiro Mifune (Sutekichi), Isuzu Yamada (Osugi), Ganjiro Nakamura (Rokubei), Kyoko Kagawa (Okayo), Bokuzen Hidari (Kahei), Minoru Chiaki (Ex-samurai), Kamatari Fujiwara (Actor), Eijiro Tono (Tomekichi), Eiko Miyoshi (Asa), Akemi Negishi (Osen), Koji Mitsui (Yoshisaburo), Nijiko Kiyokawa (Otaki), Haruo Tanaka (Tatsu), Kichijiro Ueda (Police agent).

Shojiro Motoki--Akira Kurosawa for Toho, Japan. 12,283 ft., 137 mins.

For his second screen adaptation of a classic of Russian literature Kurosawa chose Gorky's famous play, written in 1902 and premiered at the Moscow Art Theatre in the same year. Like The Idiot, The Lower Depths is a very faithful adaptation (apart from changes necessary because of the locality) and is very true in spirit to the original. Renoir's Les Bas-fonds (1936) with Louis Jouvet and Jean Gabin had been a freer treatment.

The story is set in the Tokugawa period in a sordid little flophouse in the slums of Edo (the old name for Tokyo). The lodgers are an odd assortment of people, including an impoverished samurai living on memories of the past, a whore waiting to be saved by Love, a thief, a tinker dreaming of becoming a craftsman, a cynical gambler, an alcoholic actor, and the recent arrival--an itinerant priest. Osugi, the landlady, is a hard and ruthless woman. She loves the thief, Sutekichi, and becomes wild with jealousy when she discovers that he is in love with her sister, Okayo. Incited by the landlady, the thief kills the landlord and is arrested. Okayo loses her mind from grief. The priest, who with determination told everyone of the hopeless down-and-outs the thing that would most comfort them, leaves. The remaining lodgers, having drunk a lot of sake, perform a fantastic, bizarre dance to their own musical accompaniment. Suddenly the news arrives that the actor has hanged himself. The gambler comments: "The fool. Just as the fun was beginning."

It is not difficult to guess why this dark and brooding tale illuminated by momentary flashes of wit, captured Kurosawa's imagination--because of its basic interest in the human condition, the essential affirmation of life and the image of poverty and unhappiness so extreme that it becomes allegorical. The Lower Depths has thus points of contact not only with Kurosawa's thematically similar early films, such as Drunken Angel and Stray Dog, but also with Ikiru and The Idiot. Gorky explained: "The basic question I wanted to pose was: what is better, truth or compassion? What is more necessary? Should compassion be carried to the point where it involves deception as in Luka's (the priest in the film) case? This is not a subjective matter but a question of universal philosophy." The conflict between truth and compassion, between harsh facts and the beautiful lie seems to reflect Gorky's own state of mind at the time; in his subsequent works he resolved it by embracing Marxist ideology. It is to the play's credit that it rejects didacticism, and offers no fixed answers leaving the story ambiguous and inconclusive. The nearest to a recognizable "message" is the cardsharper's famous monologue in Act Four.

Kurosawa showed himself an equal master of confined space as he was of open vistas in Seven Samurai. He conducted The Lower Depths like a performance in a traditional Japanese theatre--even to the point of opening and ending the film with a single stroke of the kabuki clapper. The sequence of 22 scenes was rehearsed with lights and costumes for 40 days before the shooting, done almost entirely on a single set with three cameras working simultaneously. There are no leading characters in the normal sense of the term: The Lower Depths is, like Seven Samurai, an example of team acting. But Mifune, Kurosawa's favorite actor, still manages to shine. While the film has its own style and a coherent cinematic formal conception, it still reflects to a considerable extent the strengths and weaknesses of the play. Chekhov's comments in a letter to Gorky are illuminating in this respect: "Act Two is especially fine--the best, the strongest.... You have left the most interesting characters out of Act Four (apart from the Actor) and you would do well to consider what you lose by that." He then adds: "The Actor's death is terrifying. You hit the spectator in the face without warning." So it is in the film: the middle section, full of tumult and violence and shot in very long takes is best; the last 20 minutes are less well handled (and, incidentally, most theatrical). Another inheritance of the theatre is the profusion of dialogue; a sin of which Kurosawa was guilty again in the thematically similar Dodes'ka-den. There are very few close-ups; Kurosawa used mostly mid-shots and very imaginative lighting. The entire soundtrack is filled by the actors themselves with their canting, humming and banging. The Lower Depths is an engrossing study of a world of delirium and illusion.

THE TIN STAR Anthony Mann

Script: Dudley Nichols, from a story by Barney Slater and Joel Kane. Photography: Loyal Griggs. Music: Elmer Bernstein. Art Direction: Hal Pereira and Joseph MacMillan Johnson. Editing: Alma Macrorie. Cast: Henry Fonda (Morg Hickman), Anthony Perkins (Ben Owens), Betsy Palmer (Nona Mayfield), Michel Ray (Kip Mayfield), Neville Brand (Bart Bogardus), John McIntyre (Doc McCord), Mary Webster (Millie Parker), Peter Baldwin (Zeke McGaffey), Lee Van Cleef (Ed McGaffey), Richard Shannon (Buck Henderson), James Bell (Judge Thatcher), Howard Petrie (Harvey King), Russell Simpson (Clem Hall), Hal K. Dawson (Andy Miller), Jack Kenney (Sam Hodges), Mickey Finn (McCall).

William Perlberg--George Seaton (Pearlsea), U.S.A. 8375 ft., 93 mins. VistaVision.

Morg Hickman, one-time sheriff who is now a bounty hunter, arrives in a small town to witness the difficulties of Ben Owens, a young and inexperienced sheriff, with a gang of outlaws. Morg helps Ben with his experience and advice, and later joins a posse taken out by Ben after a stage had been held up and the local doctor murdered. The bandits are apprehended and a lynching prevented, and Morg leaves the town with Nona, the woman who has been ostracized on account of her half-Indian son.

The Tin Star is a story of an encounter between Experience and Youth not pitted against each other but forming a common front against the forces of Evil. Formally, victory is won by Experience, but the moral triumph surely rests with Youth. In this stylish western, which has a few new comments to make around the classical dramatic structure of a story told with a classical simplicity of style, Mann, one of the masters of the genre, achieves perfection. The Tin Star, a dignified and nostalgic western, contains reflections of other famous westerns of the 50's: the starting situation is a variation on the story of Shane, while the message is the same as that of High Noon--law, made and professed by society can be upheld only by individuals who often act in defiance of orthodox theories of law enforcement, and are nearly always alone.

THE HOUSE WHERE I LIVE (Dom, v kotorom ya zhivu) Lev Kulidzhanov and Yakov Segel

---

Script: Yosif Olshansky. Photography: Vyacheslav Shumsky. Music: Yuri Biryukov. Art Direction: Vladimir Bogomolov. Cast: Viktor Zemlyanikin (Seryozha Davydov), Zhanna Bolotova (Galya Volynskaya), Valentina Telegina (Klavdya Kondratyevna Davydova), Nelly Myshkova (Lida Kashirina), Mikhail Ulyanov (Dmitri Kashirin), Yevgeni Matveyev (Konstantin Davydov), Ksenya Elanskaya (Ksenya Nikolayevna), Nikolai Elizarov (Pavel Konstantinovich Davydov), Pavel Shalnov (Nikolai), Rimma Shorokhova (Katya), Kleopatra Alperova (Galya's mother), Lev Kulidzhanov (Galya's father), Zoya Danilina (Galya in childhood), Yuri Myasnikov (Seryozha in childhood).

Moskovskaya Kinostudia Khudozhestvennykh Filmov im. Gor'kogo, U. S. S. R. 9003 ft., 100 mins.

The tragedy of the Second World War seen from the vantage point of four flats in a Moscow apartment block built in the mid-30's. The family of Davydov, a master craftsman, the scientist Volynsky with his wife and daughter, the young geologist Kashirin and his wife, a distinguished actress who is living on her own. These four flats are treated by the makers of the film as the microcosm of the urban population of the entire Soviet Union; in the life stories of the occupants there are contained observations on social integration in the country in the second decade of Communist rule, on the war years which took away so many from among the living and finally on the life after the war. The well-conceived script, which uses events synthetically and brings out intimate reflection on crucial moments in life and an emotional response in the viewer to the truthful treatment to tragedies experienced by so many, is supported on the screen by straightforward narrative, lyrical sincerity, true situations and behavior. These qualities put The House Where I Live among the best works of the new Soviet cinema. The film lies on the boundary of two cinematic styles: the "cross-section" quality of characters and situations dates back to the Socialist Realism period--but this characteristic synthetic style takes on the screen a tonality of a Neorealist stream of life; and while the picture does not revise the traditional political attitudes, it equally lacks emphasis or excessive didacticism. Even the shortcomings in the execution (such as the insufficient inventiveness on the part of the director, occasional awkwardness in the mise en scène and the chaotic narrative) generate a sense of authenticity and freshness, of being close to the feelings and problems of real people. It was precisely this latter quality which was the greatest strength of the Soviet cinema in the late 50's.

GUNFIGHT AT THE O. K. CORRAL John Sturges

Script: Leon Uris, based on the article "The Killer" by George Scullin. Photography: Charles Lang Jr. Music: Dimitri Tiomkin. Song "Gunfight at the O. K. Corral" by Dimitri Tiomkin and Ned Washington. Art Direction: Hal Pereira and Walter Tyler. Costumes: Edith Head. Editing: Warren Low. Cast: Burt Lancaster (Wyatt Earp), Kirk Douglas (John H. "Doc" Holliday), Rhonda Fleming (Laura Denbow), Jo Van Fleet (Kate Fisher), John Ireland (Johnny Ringo), Frank Faylen (Cotton Wilson), George Mathews (John Shanssey), Lyle Bettger (Ike Clanton), Earl Holliman (Charles Bassett), Ted De Corsia (Shanghai Pierce), Dennis Hopper (Billy Clanton), Kenneth Tobey (Bat Masterson), Whit Bissell (John P. Clum), John Hudson (Virgil Earp), DeForest Kelley (Morgan Earp), Martin Milner (James Earp), Joan Camden (Betty Earp), Brian Hutton (Rick), Nelson Leigh (Mayor Kelley), Olive Carey (Mrs. Clanton), Tony Merrill (Barber), Jack Elam (Tom McLowery), Charles Herbert (Tommy Earp), Lee Van Cleef (Ed Bailey).

Hal B. Wallis, U. S. A. 11,042 ft., 123 mins. VistaVision. Technicolor.

At dawn on October 26, 1881, in the town in Arizona appropriately named Tombstone, one of the most famous episodes in the history of the West took place. In less than a minute 34 shots were fired and six men killed. Sturges's film takes its title from the site of the event, whose participants were U. S. Marshal Wyatt Earp of Dodge City, his brothers Morgan and Virgil and Doc Holliday on the side of the law and the Clanton gang on the other. The episode and its participants became part of western folklore; the gunfight, now re-staged in Tombstone each year for the benefit of tourists, was portrayed on the screen many times--among others by Ford in My Darling Clementine. In Sturges's treatment the gunfight itself takes more than five minutes of running time (it took 44 hours to film), and the picture does not limit itself to straight re-counting of the story or trying to disentangle fact from legend, but aims to convey the many tales and anecdotes which have accumulated about Earp and the colorful Holliday.

Gunfight at the O. K. Corral

Fort Griffith. Doc Holliday, a dentist turned gunman and professional card-sharp, is warned by his former girlfriend Kate and by Wyatt Earp that an outlaw, Bailey, whose brother Doc had killed in the past, is coming to town to seek revenge. In the event it is Doc who shoots Bailey. Wyatt then saves Doc from a lynch-mob and leaves with him and Kate for Dodge City. Doc reciprocates by helping Wyatt in a fight against a gang of bank robbers. A strong bond of friendship develops between the two men. Wyatt falls in love with a woman gambler and decides to settle down when his brother Virgil, Marshal of Tombstone, arrives with an urgent request for help in fighting the Clanton gang which terrorizes the town. With Doc's assistance the Earps challenge the Clantons to a showdown at the O. K. Corral and wipe them out after a fierce gun-battle.

Gunfight at the O. K. Corral is a vigorous classical western with tense action sequences. It is a pity though that the sung ballad pre-states the events. The characterization of the protagonists is accomplished and sympathetic: Kirk Douglas as a gentleman gone to seed, Burt Lancaster as a civilized Marshal who speaks good English, Jo Van Fleet as Doc's tarnished lady. Sturges's treatment of the wide screen is nearly choreographic and the picture has many fine and stylish visual compositions. The final walk to the show-down has a measured, determined solemnity, while the gun-battle itself is handled with power and assurance.

THE BRIDGE ON THE RIVER KWAI David Lean

Script: Pierre Boulle, Carl Foreman and Michael Wilson, from the novel "Le pont sur la rivière Kwaï" by Boulle. Photography: Jack Hildyard. Music: Malcom Arnold; "Colonel Bogey March" by Kenneth J. Alford. Art Direction: Donald M. Ashton. Editing: Peter Taylor. Cast: William Holden (Shears), Alec Guinness (Colonel Nicholson), Jack Hawkins (Major Warden), Sessue Hayakawa (Colonel Saito), James Donald (Major Clipton), Geoffrey Horne (Lieutenant Joyce), André Morell (Colonel Green), Peter Williams (Capt. Reeves), John Boxer (Major Hughes), Percy Herbert (Grogan), Harold Goodwin (Baker), Ann Sears (Nurse), Henry Okawa (Captain Kanematsu), Keiichiro Katsumoto (Lieutenant Miura), M. R. B. Chakrabandhu (Yai).

Sam Spiegel for Horizon Pictures, G. B. 14,506 ft., 161 mins. CinemaScope. Technicolor.

The year 1957 opened a period of world cinema's increased interest in assessing the moral and psychological damage caused by the war. Directors working in countries as diverse as the U. S. A., the Soviet Union, England and Japan looked at the global cataclysm

The Bridge on the River Kwai

as reflected in experiences of individuals thrown into the vortex of history, examining the moral conflicts of these people and the difficult decisions they had to make. The Bridge on the River Kwai, the most sumptuous and most famous of these pictures, sums up as it were, the diverse attitudes of those whose tasks was to fight.

Siam, 1943. Colonel Nicholson and his battalion are captured by the Japanese and employed on the notorious "death railway" which is to link Siam with Burma. Their task is to build a vital bridge on the river Kwai. Nicholson, quoting the Geneva Convention, refuses to permit his officers to do manual work alongside the men. Colonel Saito is determined to break his determination, but finally Nicholson wins a moral victory despite torture and degradation. He then takes charge of the construction, determined to improve the morale of the men and to demonstrate by building a splendid bridge (which he hopes grandiosely will last 600 years) that the British are superior to their captors. He is oblivious to the fact that he is helping the enemy. In the meantime, a British commando force which includes Shears, an American who had earlier escaped from the camp, is making its way towards the bridge with orders to destroy it. Just as the first train is about to cross, Nicholson, fanatically proud of his achievement, notices the fuse and alerts the Japanese. In the ensuing fight Shears, Saito and Nicholson are killed, but the charge is detonated and the bridge destroyed. "Madness, madness"--is the final comment from a British doctor as he looks at the debris of the bridge float downstream the river.

The message of the novel, whose author was himself a prisoner of the Japanese, is that in war nobody wins. It is not a straight pacifist story, but one whose ironic ambiguity is open to different interpretations. One does not find in it ready-made evaluations of characters leading to their being approved of or condemned, but merely a review of four typical wartime attitudes. Colonel Nicholson is a man faithful to principles and to the code of honor--but also a man who allows these to interfere with his judgment of wartime realities. The viewer is made aware of the essential absurdity of his obsession with the bridge--but also of his bravery. What was the best thing to do in Nicholson's position? One feels that the film's sympathies are excessively biased towards the central character--very well played by Alec Guinness, who was given an Oscar for the part--Colonel Nicholson is the epitome of a stiff-upper-lip British officer. The character of Colonel Saito, a cruel disciplinarian, is less ambiguous--even though the picture stresses that the two officers are living according to the same set of principles. This conclusion echoes Renoir's La Grande illusion. To make the point even more forcefully, Saito studied at a polytechnic in London before the war. Now, as an enemy, he invites nothing but condemnation. But, from a purely practical point of view, what action should he have taken in the circumstances shown in the film? Then there is Major Warden, who leads the raid, a soldier of cool common sense whose mission is to destroy--and Shears, who symbolizes moral duty. The last two are more familiar characters in war movies.

The Bridge on the River Kwai, a British picture made on American money, is a supreme example of the efforts of the 50's film industry to retain the declining audiences. Lean, a veteran British director whose career had been sagging for several years, was given a large budget and an international cast. The shooting was done on location in Ceylon. It is a pity though that Lean's newly-found gusto for the spectacular (the Oscar for directing The Bridge on the River Kwai was followed a few years later by one for Lawrence of Arabia) overshadowed in the fleeting memory of the public his subtle psychological dramas of the previous decade.

BITTER VICTORY (Amère victoire) Nicholas Ray

Script: René Hardy, Ray and Gavin Lambert, from the novel "Amère victoire" by Hardy (1956). Additional dialogues: Paul Gallico. French dialogues: Raymond Queneau. Photography: Michel Kelber. Music: Maurice le Roux. Art Direction: Jean d'Eaubonne. Editing: Léonide Azar. Cast: Richard Burton (Captain Leith), Curd Jürgens (Major Brand), Ruth Roman (Jane Brand), Raymond Pellegrin (Mokrane), Sean Kelly (Second Lieutenant Barton), Anthony Bushell (General Patterson), Andrew Crawford (Private Roberts), Nigel Green (Wilkins), Sumner Williams (Anderson), Ronan O'Casey (Sergeant Dunnigan), Christopher Lee (Sergeant Barney), Harry Landis (Browning), Joe Davray (Spicer), Christian Melson (Perkins), Alfred Burke (Major Callander), Fred Matter (Lutze), Raoul Delfosse (Kassel).

Paul Graetz for Transcontinental Films S. A. / Robert Laffont Productions, France. 97 mins. CinemaScope.

Nicholas Ray joins the many film-makers who studied human attitudes and reactions in wartime. In Bitter Victory the typical Ray hero is placed on the African front in 1942. To be more precise, Major Brand is not a hero but an anti-hero who has no right to claim the sympathy of the audience: in fact the picture sets out to compromise him and his type mercilessly, the usurpers of war glory. Brand is in command of a special document raid on German H. Q. in Benghazi. Aware that he had shown himself to be a coward in front of a colleague, Captain Leith, a non-professional soldier whom he also suspects of having had an affair with his wife, Brand is anxious to see Leith dead. This wish is fulfilled when Brand allows a scorpion to bite Leith in the leg. After return to base the major is decorated for bravery in combat. But his subordinates have discovered during the march across the desert that their commander is a coward and a murderer. Brand himself is conscious of that by now; his nerves fail and he confesses to his wife. But there is no forgiveness: his wife leaves him in contempt; he can see contempt in the faces of his men. In a gesture of despair Brand pins his medal on the chest of a practice dummy.

An acknowledgment of total defeat or another show-off? In any case, there is no guarantee that Brand will change his ways. Quite so: for it is precisely people like him, the hard janizaries of the god of war, that survive. The psychological and moral situations of Bitter Victory are all-too-typical of the anti-heroic current in contemporary American literature and cinema: professional officers are shown in dark colors and find their gruesome usefulness only in conditions of wartime necessity; the non-professional officers contribute intellect and humanism to the army. Conflicts between these two groups increase the losses suffered in the actual struggle against the enemy. However, it would be unjust to accuse Ray's film of being derivative in its ideas: the characters are too convincing and autonomous for that, the narrative style too individual in its nervous expressiveness, the culmination too thought-out in its use of the metaphor and formal means of expression (the exposition, which very precisely defines the situation, mood and scenery is equally fine). With the help of Curd Jürgens and Richard Burton, well cast as Brand and Leigh, Ray transformed the well-known novel into one of the most inquisitive and convincing pictures about people under extreme stress.

LIFT TO THE SCAFFOLD (Ascenseur pour l'échafaud) Louis Malle

Script: Roger Nimier and Malle, from the novel by Noël Calef. Photography: Henri Decaë. Music: Miles Davis, played by himself, Barney Wilen, René Urtreger, Pierre Michelot and Kenny Clarke. Art Direction: Rino Mondellini and Jean Mandaroux. Editing: Léonide Azar. Cast: Maurice Ronet (Julien Tavernier), Jeanne Moreau (Florence Carala), Georges Poujoly (Louis), Lino Ventura (Inspector Chérier), Yori Bertin (Véronique), Ivan Petrovich (Horst Bencker), Elga Andersen (Frieda Bencker), Félix Marten (Subervie), Jean Wall (Simon Carala), Charles Denner (Inspector), Micheline Bona (Geneviève), Jacques Hilling (Garage owner), Gérard Darrieu (Maurice), Jean-Claude Brialy (Customer in bar), Sylviane Aisenstein (Barmaid), Gisèle Grandpré, Hubert Deschamps.

Jean Thuillier for Nouvelles Editions de Films, France. 92 mins.

A brilliant debut by Louis Malle, a 25-year-old director whose name would soon be linked--under the banner headline of the Nouvelle Vague--with the names of a group of film-makers of similar age who took a stand against the fossilized traditional French cinema. The mood of change was in the air: the compromised Fourth Republic was on the threshold of collapse and May 1958 saw the takeover of power by De Gaulle supported by big capital. Malle came from an affluent background and certain things in his film, namely its analysis of the process of the whole of society's infection with the moral gangrene of the privileged, were interpreted as expressions of support for the factions which were getting ready to take over power. But Lift to the Scaffold offered no political or aesthetic program, and it later turned out that the anti-bourgeois stand was an organic element of the whole of Malle's work. The fine film-making craft, which was one of his main ambitions, had from the beginning a classical tone: it was not by accident that Malle did his apprenticeship with Bresson on A Man Escaped. This does come to one's mind while watching on the screen Julien's desperate attempts to get out of a lift immobilized in an office block after the current has been turned off for the weekend. This ruins his carefully planned perfect murder of the industrialist husband of his mistress, Florence (in this part Jeanne Moreau first attracted attention to her great acting talent). Julien made Carala's death in the office to appear as a suicide. He still has a chance to sneak out of the building on Monday morning; but in the meantime things become very complicated by the unfortunate theft of his car by a couple of teenagers who later kill two people with Julien's gun. Florence tries desperately to save her lover who cannot produce an alibi for one murder without thereby admitting the second. But fate continually thwarts the lovers' plans.

Malle handles the clever intrigue of the film with great narrative talent, well copes with the dramatic line, character description, interaction of sub-plots and the cinematic rhythm. But he achieves his best results on the soundtrack and within individual frames of the film: makes use of the dramatic value of silence, employs acoustic "deep focus" within the frame and anxious sounds of percussion and trumpet in Miles Davis's jazz improvisations, and thereby achieves an unusually wide range of tension--if one is to consider that the director limits himself to intimate and dynamically moderate mise en scène. A similar function of widening the scale of moods is performed by the inventive use of light, darkness and the silhouettes of characters. This virtuoso stylistic quality makes Lift to the Scaffold a very fine visual poem, quite apart from its status within the cinema of sensation.

THE HOUSE OF THE ANGEL (La casa del angel) Leopoldo Torre Nilsson

---

Script: Beatriz Guido, Torre Nilsson and Martín Rodríguez Mentasti, from the novel by Guido. Photography: Aníbal González Paz. Music: Juan Carlos Paz. Art Direction: Emilio Rodríguez Mentasti. Editing: Jorge Garate. Cast: Elsa Daniel (Ana), Lautaro Murua (Pablo), Guillermo Battaglia (Señor Castro), Jordana Fain (Naná), Berta Ortegosa (Señora Castro), Bárbara Mujica (Vicenta), Alejandro Rey (Julián), Lilí Gacel (Julieta).

Leopoldo Torre Nilsson for Argentina Sono Film S. A., Argentina.
78 mins.

Until The House of the Angel was applauded at the 1957 Cannes Film Festival, Latin American cinema was identified with Mexico, and internationally known only through the works of Fernández, Alazraki's Roots and the works of Buñuel, a Spaniard in self-imposed exile in Mexico. More than twenty years later Torre Nilsson is still the only worthwhile Argentinean director. Born in 1924 as a son of a film-maker, Nilsson made his first film in 1954 from a short story by Borges, then unknown outside his home country. However, the turning point in his career was the beginning of a cooperation with Beatriz Guido, his future wife, who wrote the scripts for all his films from 1957 onwards. The House of the Angel, Nilsson's sixth film, is an adaptation of her bestselling first novel.

The young daughter of a wealthy politician, Ana lives in the house of the Angel. Her puritanical mother and a superstitious nanny protect her from as much as an awareness of the existence of sin. The sexually and emotionally frustrated girl throws herself into the arms of Pablo, an aspiring politician who is going to fight a duel in the house. But Pablo does not marry her. After her mother dies and sisters move away Ana, obsessed by the taboos instilled in her since childhood and half-deranged with shame, remains in the house with her father. Pablo continues dining with them once a week...

Nilsson's cinema is very specific in character. His primary interest is in the peculiar relationships between the sexes in Argentinean society, where anachronistic conventions lead to a lack of understanding between men and women. Throughout his work Nilsson strove to find ways in which the spell can be broken. There is also the influence of old-fashioned Catholic morality, which according to Mario Trajtenberg amounts to "almost a disease of the imagination." In The House of the Angel Nilsson, whose films are usually about women and always champion the feminine point of view, creates a suffocating, sultry atmosphere of tension and claustrophobia, of guilt and oppressive convention. Both Ana and Pablo are victims: Ana--of her mother, Pablo--of Ana's father's political schemes and improprieties. One detects influences of Bergman (the motif of obsession with sin), of Buñuel's Mexican films and of Orson Welles's The Magnificent Ambersons.

Visually the film is very impressive. The subtle camerawork of Aníbal González Paz carries Expressionist reminiscences, creating an eerie mood and a sense of mystery. This is appropriately accompanied by dodecaphonic music on the soundtrack.

BROTHERS BORN OF DIFFERENT MOTHERS (Ibo kyōdai) Miyoji Ieki

Script: Yoshikata Yoda and Nobuyoshi Terada, from the novel by Torahiko Tamiya. Photography: Yoshio Miyajima. Music: Yasushi Akutagawa. Art Direction: Totetsu Hirakawa. Cast: Rentaro Mikuni (Hantaro Kido), Kinuyo Tanaka (Toshie Kido), Akiichi Nishida (Ichiroji), Hiroshi Kondo (Gojiro), Shinji Nambara (Yoshitoshi), Katsuo Nakamura (Tomohide), Hizuru Takachiho (Haru, maid), Yaeko Toyoshima (Tsuta), Masayuki Endo (Ichiroji in boyhood), Yoshio Otomo (Gojiro in boyhood), Koji Namie (Ichiroji in childhood), Hiroyuki Kasugai (Gojiro in childhood), Akio Sugano (Tomohide in childhood).

Dokuritsu Eiga, Japan. 9931 ft., 110 mins.

Miyoji Ieki, who in the 50's worked for independent film companies, is among those Japanese directors who were taking a sustained interest in the life of the working classes and the conflicts of Japan's Fascist past. Brothers Born of Different Mothers, his best-known picture, has a firm place among the leading pacifist movies. The film traces the rise and fall of the family of a professional officer in the Imperial Army in the years 1921-1946, and revolves around the story of an illegitimate son victimized by his legitimate brothers. The household is run in the spirit of the dreariest barracks by the martinet husband who terrorizes his wretched wife and trains his sons from early childhood to become obedient and unquestioning warriors. The highest principles in the household are Honor, the Emperor and the Country, while the main rules of conduct are the suppression of feelings and military service. Thinking is forbidden. The feudal hierarchy of the household is destroyed only by the military defeat of Japan. Such is the functioning of an individual cell in the structure which kept Japan going while the military spun grandiose dreams of subordinating a quarter of the world.

It is easy to stray into journalistic exaggeration and propagandist high contrasts when dealing with such topics. But, for all the forcefulness of his conclusions, Ieki remained concrete and objective. The fact that he did not resort to attractive cinematic style and did not evade a certain dramatic abeyance, but immersed the film in the mood of a nightmare not only does not detract from the work but gives it additional strength by placing extra stress on the content. Brothers Born of Different Mothers is primarily concerned with the content and the message; Ieki meant to portray the social situation of Japan in the 20's and 30's, to expose the militaristic mentality of those years, to trace the origins of Japanese Fascism--the system which by combining the spirit of Prussian militarism with the more infamous elements of Japan's feudal past gave rise to a universe of hatred.

GUENDALINA Alberto Lattuada

Script: Leo Benvenuti, Piero De Bernardi and Lattuada, from a story by Valerio Zurlini. Photography: Otello Martelli. Music: Piero Morgan. Cast: Jacqueline Sassard (Guendalina Redaelli), Rafaele Mattioli (Oberdan Pancani), Sylva Koscina (Francesca Redaelli, Guendalina's mother), Raf Vallone (Guido Redaelli, Guendalina's father), Leda Gloria (Oberdan's mother), Patrizia Ralli (Attilia), Lilli Cerasoli (Bianchina Norman), Flavia Solivani, Fanny Landini, Loretta Capitoli, Decimo Cristiani, Tonino Cianci, Geronimo De Meynier, Piero Malò, Emanuele Pantanella, Fiorella Lavelli, Fiametta Lovatelli, Titti Fabiani, Patrizia Tosi, Nadia Scarpitta, Leonardo Botta.

Carlo Ponti Cinematografica/Les Films Marceau, Italy/France. 95 mins.

In Guendalina Lattuada adheres to his avowed belief that simplicity is the surest way towards art: the ordinary, rather banal theme of the first love and the melodramatic script did not prevent him from making a modest, but sincere and subtle film. This was made possible precisely by the simplicity, the natural mise en scène, the intelligent observation of the personality of the 16-year-old beginner actress in the title role. The rest is unimportant: she had been ill and did not go on holiday, he has trouble with school and an exam to re-sit in the autumn. They meet by accident and begin to take interest in each other, go for walks, study together. Everything would be fine if Guendalina's father did not neglect his wife for other women; one must try to save the family, one must go away. Such is life. Guendalina parts from Oberdan, although her drama will not help very much in repairing the relationship of her parents.

So, a stereotype--by all means--but one on which Lattuada erected a delicate structure made up of genuine emotion and truth about an idealistic outburst of young love--seemingly self-evident and yet so difficult to achieve. Other film-makers very rarely succeeded in doing this, but then they did not have Jacqueline Sassard who irradiated Guendalina with her extraordinary, cyclamen charm.

WHITE NIGHTS (Le notti bianche) Luchino Visconti

Script: Suso Cecchi D'Amico and Visconti, based on the short novel "Belye nochi" by Fyodor Dostoyevsky. Photography: Giuseppe

Rotunno. Music: Nino Rota. Art Direction: Mario Chiari and Mario Garbuglia. Costumes: Piero Tosi. Choreography: Dick Sanders. Editing: Mario Serandrei. Cast: Maria Schell (Natalia), Marcello Mastroianni (Mario), Jean Marais (Lodger), Clara Calamai (Prostitute), Giorgio Listuzzi (Policeman), Marcella Rovena (Housewife), Dick Sanders (Dancer), Elena Fancora (Cashier), Alberto Carloni (Bar proprietor), Maria Zanolli (Housekeeper); The Family Who Are Friendly With Mario: Ferdinando Gera (Father), Leonida Montesi (Mother), Anna Filippini (Daughter).

Franco Cristaldi for Cinematografica Associata/Vides (Rome)/Intermondia Film (Paris), Italy/France. 9567 ft., 106 mins.

Very versatile as regards the use of different media, Visconti has always worked simultaneously in the theatre, the cinema and the opera. In White Nights he abandons the directness of his Neorealist films and the fever and fatalism of Senso in favor of a deliberately theatrical and artificial style. Stylistically this screen adaptation of the famous short novel by Dostoyevsky recalls the pictures of Carné and Prévert. Visconti himself described White Nights as "Neoromanticism."

Mario, a shy young clerk, is a stranger to the town. One night he meets a girl on a canal bridge; she is crying and Mario asks whether he can help. When they meet the following night, Natalia tells him she is in love with a man who had been a lodger at her grandmother's house. He departed promising to return a year later; the appointed time has come, but he is not back. Natalia thinks he may be staying at a nearby hotel and asks Mario to deliver a letter to him. But Mario, who has fallen in love with the girl, tears it up in anguish. The following evening they meet again and go to a dance; Mario confesses his love and Natalia runs away. The next evening they make plans for a life together. Mario thinks the girl is his, when Natalia suddenly runs towards a canal bridge: her man has returned. Mario goes away, forlorn and lost. A stray dog is his only companion.

The making of White Nights was a very difficult undertaking. The story is in effect the very essence of Dostoyevsky's writing with its mood of St. Petersburg spleen and the inimitable dialogues. Visconti shot the picture almost entirely in the studio and does not try to disguise the fact. For one thing, the time of year did not permit him to work on location, for another--he thought that the mood would be easier to obtain in the studio, despite the fact that the same year Antonioni demonstrated in Il grido what atmospheric effects can be achieved on location. Visconti always had a tendency to use too much dialogue (the most extreme example of this being Bellissima, 1951), and although the story is not told, as in Dostoyevsky, in first-person monologue, the dialogues are a little too profuse. It was extremely difficult to transform the story of a daydreamer and a naive girl, set in the St. Petersburg of a century ago to the busy present-day Livorno. It is highly significant that the finest scene of White Nights, that of the wild rock'n'roll at the dance-hall to which Mario takes Natalia, the scene which is to this day the best visual representation of rock music in the cinema, is so unlike anything in Dostoyevsky. Incidentally, the scene is also without any dialogue. The point is that while the mood, decidedly the greatest value of the picture, is not necessarily an equivalent of that in the literary original, it is still powerful and striking. Alongside Dreyer's Vampyr and Ophüls's Liebelei, White Nights rates as one of the principal "dreamlike" films in the cinema.

The film expounds Visconti's constant theme of an individual who turns towards his interior and not towards others, of an escape from reality into the world of illusion. The director's comment on this attitude is contained in the ironic treatment of his protagonist. The motif of an illusion, of a destructive spell which overcomes the protagonist and brings defeat, appeared in each Visconti picture from Ossessione onwards. The French critic-director Jacques Doniol-Valcroze calls it "the theme of a charlatan" because the scene in Bellissima (1951) in which Anna Magnani succumbs to it in the film studio is accompanied on the soundtrack by the "charlatan" theme from Donizetti's opera "L'elisir d'amore" (The Elixir of Love).

On his part, Visconti made White Nights while obviously under the spell of Maria Schell. Fey and innocent, she gives a very unusual performance. Her Natalia is capable of changing her mood instantly from laughter to tears, a butterfly temperament which gives her an aura of mystery. It is striking how Slavonic she is! Marcello Mastroianni is also very good as a bewildered young man. The fine camerawork makes good use of chiaroscuro effects of shadowy streets and canals at night. The juxtaposition of the world of dreams and the actual, trivial, reality with its pop music, prostitutes and youths on motor-bikes creates the mood of decadence and nostalgia. Very skillful is the use of flashbacks, as Natalia tells about her meeting with her grandmother's lodger and about their night at the opera. The scene of a boat trip on the canals in the falling snow is very memorable.

A fascinating episode in Visconti's work, White Nights is an atmospheric film par excellence. It seems to have influenced the cinema of Alain Resnais. Fourteen years later Dostoyevsky's story was filmed again, by Robert Bresson, as Four Nights of a Dreamer.

SAINT JOAN Otto Preminger

Script: Graham Greene, from the play by George Bernard Shaw. Photography: Georges Périnal. Music: Mischa Spoliansky. Art Direction: Raymond Simm. Editing: Helga Cranston. Cast: Jean Seberg (Joan), Richard Widmark (Charles VII of France), John Gielgud

(Earl of Warwick), Richard Todd (Dunois), Adolf Wohlbrück [Anton Walbrook] (Cauchon, Bishop of Beauvais), Felix Aylmer (Inquisitor), Harry Andrews (John de Stogumber), Barry Jones (de Courcelles), Finlay Currie (Archbishop of Reims), Bernard Miles (Master Executioner), Patrick Barr (Captain la Hire), Kenneth Haigh (Brother Martin), Archie Duncan (de Baudricourt), Margot Grahame (Duchess de la Trémouille), Francis De Wolff (Duke de la Trémouille), Victor Maddern (English soldier), David Oxley (Gilles de Rais, "Bluebeard"), Sydney Bromley (Baudricourt's steward), David Langton (Captain of Warwick's Guard).

Otto Preminger, U. S. A. 110 mins.

Preminger says that he had been planning to make a screen version of Shaw's play from the moment he first read it in 1921. Both he and Graham Greene, the distinguished novelist who wrote the script, consider "Saint Joan" one of the greatest plays ever written. However, since Gabriel Pascal, the director of Major Barbara, had exclusive film rights to the plays by GBS for life, Preminger had to wait for over thirty years (Pascal died in 1955).

Shaw described Joan of Arc as "the most notable warrior saint in the Christian calendar, and queerest fish among the eccentric worthies of the Middle Ages." The play was not intended as a mere chronicle of events, but a study of an individual in the cogs of a social system; to Shaw, a man who had ideas of his own about social philosophy, St. Joan was not so much a martyr, as a challenge to the orderly, bureaucratized feudal system.

Fifteenth-century France. Much of the country is ruled by the Burgundians and the English. Joan, a simple peasant girl arrives at the Dauphin's palace with a letter from Captain de Baudricourt. She has heard the voices of St. Catherine, St. Margaret and Michael the Archangel telling her to bring peace to France by having Dauphin Charles, heir to the throne, crowned king. The Dauphin makes her commander of his army. After the victorious battle against the English at Orléans, the Dauphin is crowned as Charles VI, King of France. Joan continues to fight, but now without his support; French troops begin to suffer losses. She is captured by the Burgundians and sold to the Earl of Warwick, the English commander, who turns her over to the church authorities to be tried. After the trial at Rouen Joan is burned, aged 19, at the market place as a heretic. The date is May 30, 1431.

Preminger says he wanted the film to be sober, even austere, in appearance, and at the same time fresh and innocent--and this defines his approach to the play. His all-star cast was built around an unknown young actress in the title role. Jean Seberg, whose only previous acting experience was in the amateur theatre, was given the part after a world-wide search. Preminger did not indulge in the spectacular (for instance, he added no battle scenes to the play) and deliberately shot the film in black-and-white and in the normal aspect ratio "because I want to put the emphasis on people, on characterizations, on emotions, on the words of Bernard Shaw." The order of some scenes was changed and some arguments shortened, but otherwise the film closely sticks to the text; the play's epilogue is used as a frame for the story, told in two long flashbacks as King Charles' dream.

In his preface to the play Shaw says about the heroine: "Everything she did was thoroughly calculated; and though the process was so rapid that she was hardly conscious of it, and ascribed it to her voices, she was a woman of policy and not of blind impulse. In war she was as much a realist as Napoleon: she had his eye for artillery and his knowledge of what it could do." The most interesting aspect of the play is the conflict between reason (or calculation) and vision, and the main problem with the film is that Jean Seberg could not convey this dualism fully: she is not commanding, but merely innocent and childish. This is partly to be blamed on the director who saw her not so much as a fervent heroine, but a pawn in the hands of politicians around her. Richard Widmark is eccentric and whimsical (perhaps excessively so) as the Dauphin and John Gielgud icy and sinister as Warwick. Despite the publicity which preceded the film's release, Saint Joan was one of the all-time commercial flops.

LOVE IN THE AFTERNOON Billy Wilder

Script: Wilder and I. A. L. Diamond, based on the novel "Ariane" by Claude Anet. Photography: William Mellor. Musical adaptation: Franz Waxman. Songs: "Fascination" by F. D. Marchetti and Maurice de Féraudy; "L'Âme des poëtes" by Charles Trenet; "C'est si bon" by Henri Betti and André Hornez; "Love in the Afternoon," "Ariane" and "Hot Paprika" by Matty Malneck. Art Direction: Alexandre Trauner. Editing: Léonide Azar. Cast: Audrey Hepburn (Ariane Chavasse), Gary Cooper (Frank Flannagan), Maurice Chevalier (Claude Chavasse), Van Doude (Michel), John McGiver (Monsieur X), Lise Bourdin (Madame X), Bonifas (Commissioner of Police), Audrey Wilder (Brunette), Olga Valéry (Lady with dog), François Moustache (Butcher), Charles Bouillard (Valet at the Ritz), Gregory Gromoff (Doorman at the Ritz), Jean Sylvain (Baker).

Billy Wilder for Allied Artists, U. S. A. 125 mins.

Ariane, a young music student at the Paris Conservatoire warns Frank Flannagan, a rich American playboy on his annual visit to the French capital, that one of the local cuckolds intends to shoot him. The girl learned about the threat when she overheard a conversation in the office of her private detective father. Ariane's help is received with gratitude and Flannagan is intrigued by the girl's refusal to reveal her identity and her insistence that they can meet only in the afternoon. The romantic girl, whose interest in Flannagan developed through close study of her father's files, falls in love head over heels, but the romance is soon interrupted by the millionaire's departure for America. When they meet again a year later, Ariane tries to seduce him with stories of her imaginary amorous adventures. Finally, his pride piqued, Flannagan hires a private detective to check the facts. This turns out to be Ariane's father, who asks the playboy not to ruin the girl's life. Flannagan retracts and prepares to leave Paris, but at the last moment realizes he loves Ariane and takes her away with him.

This story could have easily been turned into a film as dreadful as its literary original if it were not for the fact that the director was Billy Wilder. Love in the Afternoon is the second project, after Sabrina, in which his energetic hand, his ability to keep reins on the grotesque and the extravagant, his intensive treatment of comedy situations easily averted the dangers inherent in the theme. Love in the Afternoon is constantly threatened with becoming distasteful; but Wilder, who was well aware of this when he took the project on, unceremoniously got rid of the erotic thrills and unrestrained passions thought out by the author of the novel, and steered clear of token social criticism which in the future was to ruin many films and lead astray even such fine directors as Stanley Kubrick in Lolita (1962). Instead of all this there is in Love in the Afternoon a recurrent tune of a grotesquely functional gypsy band, the permanently bewildered Maurice Chevalier and Gary Cooper with a smile which is apologetic rather than seductive, a good pace with a profusion of gags--and even something faintly reminiscent of René Clair's films. And of course, there is something else, as indispensable here as it was in Sabrina--what would become of Love in the Afternoon without Audrey Hepburn? That which rounds off the picture as a charming sentimental comedy, Wilder owes in the final effect to the talents of his leading lady.

COWBOY Delmer Daves

Script: Edmund H. North, from the autobiographical book "On the Trail; My Reminiscences as a Cowboy" by Frank Harris. Photography: Charles Lawton Jr. Music: George Duning. Art Direction: Cary Odell. Editing: William A. Lyon and Al Clark. Cast: Glenn Ford (Tom Reece), Jack Lemmon (Frank Harris), Anna Kashfi (Maria Vidal), Brian Donlevy (Doc Bender), Dick York (Charlie), Victor Manuel Mendoza (Mendoza), Richard Jaeckel (Paul Curtis), King Donovan (Joe Capper), Vaughn Taylor (Mr. Fowler), Donald Randolph (Señor Vidal), James Westerfield (Mick Adams), Eugene Iglesias (Manuel Arriega), Buzz Henry (Slim Barrett), Frank de Kova (Alcaide), William Leslie (Tucker), Guy Wilkerson (Peggy).

Julian Blaustein for Phoenix, U. S. A. 92 mins. Technicolor.

The superwestern re-examined the tenets of the traditional genre, but also brought its ennoblement. 3:10 to Yuma did both these things, but with Cowboy it becomes evident that Daves's aim is to reconstruct the bygone realities of the West and not to debate the moral-psychological aspects of the old myth. This follows from the fact that Cowboy is the screen version of one of the most famous autobiographies in American literature--the memoirs of a man who, in the last quarter of the 19th century worked for many years as a cowboy, herding cattle mainly on the trail from Wichita to Chicago. Characteristically, Harris himself (the book was published in the 20's) tended to oppose the literary-cinematic western myth. He made it clear that to be a cowboy meant hard work in constant fear of a stampede (which could be caused by the mere howl of a coyote and meant a great loss of weight in the charging cattle); that no more than 10 miles were covered per day; that there were no impressive raids across the prairie, and the cowboys had no time for antagonisms and romantic fantasies; and that an arrival at a town was almost a red-letter day. The most important qualities required for this work were not so much courage and fast shooting as tolerance, self-sufficiency and comradeship and also the sense of humor which played the role of a psychological safety valve but which the western usually simply explained as an expression of spontaneity and which Hawks identified (for example in El Dorado) with western mythology.

The picture is set in the 1870's and traces the progress of a former hotel clerk on a 2000-mile cattle drive from Chicago to the Rio Grande. Daves is faithful to the intentions of the book and concentrates mainly on realism, "the saddlesore truth," on humanizing the characters and honest portrayal of the way they lived--while not neglecting the spectacular and generic color, as is seen in the scenes in the hotel, the saloon and the opera. It is true to say that while seeming almost to shun attractive scenery and fast narrative rhythm Daves was at the same time unable to offer any new visual concepts--but in the end it is not the photography that matters in Cowboy. Emphasis is placed on the study of the two leading characters: an apprentice cowboy (played by Jack Lemmon) and a tough, hard-bitten cattle man (Glenn Ford). Both actors are very good; it is particularly interesting to watch Lemmon in a part so different from his hitherto comedy emploi.

AT NIGHT, WHEN THE DEVIL COMES (Nachts, wenn der Teufel kam) Robert Siodmak

---

Script: Werner Jörg Lüddecke, based on Will Berthold's true account in "Die Münchner Illustrierte." Photography: Georg Krause. Music: Siegfried Franz. Art Direction: Rolf Zehetbauer. Editing: Walter Boos. Cast: Claus Holm (Commissioner Axel Kersten), Mario Adorf (Bruno Lüdke), Peter Carsten (Mollwitz), Hannes Messemer (SS-Gruppenführer Rossdorf), Werner Peters (Willi Keun), Annemarie Düringer (Helga Hornung), Carl Lange (Major Wollenberg), Monika John (Lucy Hansen), Christa Nielsen (A tart), Rose Schäfer (Anna Hohmann).

Robert Siodmak for Divina, West Germany. 104 mins.

In the years 1946-1949 Siodmak made several fine thrillers with psychological undertones in the U. S. A. But after that successful run he cannot, with one exception, claim remarkable achievements. The exception is At Night, When the Devil Comes, and the credit for this goes not so much to Siodmak's skillful direction as to the story itself. The film recounts real events of the police investigation into the notorious Lüdke case which had been kept in deep secrecy until revealed by the Munich newspaper "Die Münchner Illustrierte" in 1956, many years afterwards.

In the years 1924-1943 a psychopath murdered around 80 women in Germany. Nazi propaganda, which liked to publicize crime in other countries as proof of the moral collapse of the enemies of Germany, was naturally keen to keep the whole affair secret. During the war, when the murders which had so far been investigated by the ordinary police continued, the government ordered the Gestapo to take over the case. Axel Kersten, one of the ablest Berlin detectives who was also enlisted, caught the track of the murderer, a certain Lüdke, and unmasked him using a clever trick during the visit to the scene of the crime. But by that time the authorities had sacrificed someone else, a high Nazi dignitary who used to be the lover of one of the victims and was known to threaten her. When Hitler heard that Lüdke was an Arian, he personally ordered his liquidation and a complete cover-up. Kersten, who protested against such practices, was sent to the Eastern front where he was killed a few months later. But his secretary was able to preserve the documents of the investigation. These formed the basis of the newspaper report which aroused Siodmak's interest. Siodmak had reasons of his own for being interested in this denunciation of the Nazi state machinery: in 1933, when he was already a noted documentary filmmaker, an attack from Dr. Goebbels, the Minister of Propaganda, forced him to leave his native country. Only in the mid-50's did Siodmak return to Germany. He thus not only took care of the dramatic structure and style of the film (Expressionist in manner particularly as concerns the high-contrast photography) but also tried to give a faithful reconstruction of conditions in a Nazi-run society. This succeeded very well, and although the reconstruction applies only to a narrow section of reality, it gives special value to the film made at the time when the political situation in Germany still laid obstacles to a no-holds-barred reckoning with the black shirt past.

MAIGRET SETS A TRAP (Maigret tend un piège) Jean Delannoy

Script: Michel Audiard, from the novel by Georges Simenon, adapted by R. M. Arlaud, Audiard and Delannoy. Photography: Louis Page. Music: Paul Misraki. Art Direction: René Renoux. Editing: Henri Taverna. Cast: Jean Gabin (Inspector Maigret), Annie Girardot (Yvonne Maurin), Jean Desailly (Marcel Maurin), Olivier Hussenot (Lagrume), Lucienne Bogaert (Mme. Maurin), Jeanne Boitel (Mme. Maigret), Alfred Adam (Barberot), Paulette Dubost (Mme. Barberot), Gérard Séty (Jojo), Lino Ventura (Inspector Torrence), Jean Tissier (Elderly reporter), Guy Decomble (The suspect).

Intermondia/J. P. Guibert/Jolly Film, France/Italy. 10,742 ft., 119 mins.

The area of Paris around the Place des Vosges is terrorized by a psychopathic killer, who has already claimed four women victims. The last time he struck he left a clue: a butcher's knife. Inspector Maigret sets a trap for the murderer: he arrests a stooge and sends out policewomen as decoys. But the man again escapes. Maigret then turns his attention to Marcel Maurin, a prosperous architect who lives with his wife Yvonne in a fashionable suburb. But his mother owns a house in the district where the murders took place. Maurin is arrested and questioned; but just as Maigret feels he is ready to confess, the news comes of another knife murder. Exhausted, Maigret makes one more desperate effort. He succeeds--but it turns out to be a bitter victory.

Already in the 30's crime ceased to be looked upon as a vile challenge to society, to be unreservedly condemned. The detective no longer represented traditional moral virtues, as Sherlock Holmes once did. Criminal behavior began to be treated as a reaction to the pressures of society; very often this new point of view gave rise to stories where criminals were equated with the police. The Belgian-born Georges Simenon on whose novel the film is based, is the most eminent detective story writer in French. He introduced an entirely new point of view to the detective novel. While Sherlock Holmes, for instance, operated on the principle of deduction and solved his mysteries by examining the evidence, Maigret relies on psychological analysis. He tries to recreate the criminal's way of thinking, his idiosyncrasies and mental defects; like a psychoanalyst he diagnoses the deviations of contemporary society. The Maigret novels are psychological vivisections of characters based on sensational motifs and characterized by a subtlety and an attitude of tolerant skepticism towards human foibles. To this Simenon added precise description of a milieu and an ability to evoke a grim but fascinating world. In his novels crime is not committed for reasons such as jealousy and greed. In "Maigret Sets a Trap" the murderer comes from a "good family" and is a child at heart, spoilt by his wife and the admiring mother.

Jean Delannoy, who since Les Jeux sont faits had mostly been making very bad films for the whole ten years, became interested in the novel which contains one of the best Simenon plots and a good sample of Simenon's world: grim, degenerate, ridden by anomalies and complexes, steeped in an aura of tiredness. Maigret, always on the verge of retirement, is repelled and exhausted by all this. In the finale, having finished with the case, he exposes his face to the rain: what a relief. Relief is the only positive feeling in Maigret Sets a Trap; the rest is gloomy and dusky--and this is well rendered by the photography and the music. The picture has a good pace and realistic character description well supported by the acting from Jean Desailly as Maurin and Annie Girardot as his wife.

1958

ASHES AND DIAMONDS (Popiół i diament) Andrzej Wajda

Script: Jerzy Andrzejewski and Wajda, based on the novel by the former. Photography: Jerzy Wójcik. Music: Filip Nowak and Michał Kleofas Ogiński (Polonaise "Farewell My Homeland"). Music for the credit sequence: Adam Pawlikowski. Art Direction: Roman Mann. Editing: Halina Nawrocka. Cast: Zbigniew Cybulski (Maciek Chełmicki), Ewa Krzyżewska (Krystyna), Adam Pawlikowski (Andrzej), Wacław Zastrzeżyński (Szczuka), Bogumił Kobiela (Drewnowski), Jan Ciecierski (Porter), Stanisław Milski (Pieniążek), Artur Młodnicki (Kotowicz), Zbigniew Skowroński (Słomka), Jerzy Jogałła (Szczuka's son), Halina Kwiatkowska (Mrs. Staniewicz), Ignacy Machowski (Major Waga), Barbara Krafftówna (Stefka), Aleksander Sewruk (Swięcki).

Stanisław Adler for ZAF Kadr, Poland. 9639 ft., 107 mins.

The key work of the Polish School, Ashes and Diamonds is not principally concerned with the question of heroism (as were A Generation and Eroica) but performs a wider task of summing-up the affairs of a nation at the crossroads. The making of the film was prompted by the urgent need to end the conspiracy of silence about the contribution of non-left factions to the wartime struggle against Nazi Germany. The film is based on an outstanding novel written in 1947 which, after the political upheavals of 1956, came to be interpreted in the spirit of the moment--in the mood of consolidating a nation divided by conflicts brought about by the complete change of the political system at the end of the war.

Ashes and Diamonds is set in a provincial Polish town on May 9 and 10, 1945. The protagonist is Maciek

Ashes and Diamonds

Chełmicki, a young soldier in the right-wing faction of the London-run Home Army. He fought in the Warsaw Rising and after the liberation continues to fight, this time against the new Communist authorities; he remains in the underground more out of loyalty to his superiors than from conviction. Maciek is ordered to kill Szczuka, the newly arrived District Secretary of the Party. The assassination attempt, which opens the film, fails and two innocent people are killed instead. This, and his emotional involvement with the local barmaid, increase Maciek's doubts as to the rightness of the renewed order to kill Szczuka. Thrown into the impossible dilemma of having to choose between the demands of conscience and loyalty, Maciek is a doomed, tragic character. He tries to run away from his inner anxieties, from the new post-war realities--and this is why he dies. He decides to leave the underground, but after fulfilling the order first. At the hotel Szczuka stays in the next room to where Maciek meets Krystyna; the girl awakens in him desires for a normal, peaceful life. Meanwhile a victory banquet is being held downstairs. The polonaise called "Farewell, My Homeland" is for some the end of their political careers, while others prepare to leave for government posts in Warsaw. In the evening, in a deserted street, Maciek kills Szczuka (who, ironically, was on his way to see his son, arrested as a member of an underground group), and the next morning is himself accidentally shot when trying to run away from a passing military patrol.

Zbigniew Cybulski, for whom Ashes and Diamonds brought instantaneous international fame, gave the Maciek character much more than what simply followed from the literary original--perhaps because as a contemporary of the hero, he wanted to start a myth. His Maciek is not only a full, complex personality, but a character close to every Pole, a man whose curse, whose sense of being lost they well understood. Apart from that, Cybulski gave expression to the dilemmas and frustrations of young people in the late 50's, the contemporaries of James Dean. Cybulski was to a certain

Ashes and Diamonds

extent a European equivalent of Dean, and it is interesting to note that Maciek's external appearance is applicable simultaneously to 1945 and 1958. The protagonist overshadows other characters, which is as a matter of fact fortunate as not all that is seen in the background measures up to the standard of the foreground. For instance, the Szczuka character is over-retouched and given rather artificial lines; also some episodic parts are stiff and exaggerated.

There is no doubt that Ashes and Diamonds was stylistically inspired by the early Neorealism of De Santis and Rossellini, by Eisenstein's Ivan the Terrible and by Expressionist art. Of the stylistic tools in Wajda's picture the most striking is the use of visual metaphors and the montage of antitheses, both most often used in the dramatic scenes (such as the killing of Szczuka; the glasses full of burning vodka pushed along the bar counter in memory of dead friends; Maciek and Krystyna's visit to a ruined church with Christ on the cross hanging head down; the questioning by the police of Szczuka's son; the end of the banquet). Particularly the scene of the shooting of the Party Secretary provides a good sample of Wajda's directorial style: Maciek and Szczuka symbolically fall into each other's arms in an absurd embrace seconds after the assassination, at the precise moment when the fireworks announce the end of the war. This is a scene of contrasts and juxtapositions: of silence and the sound of shots, darkness of the street and the light of fireworks, the drama of death and the euphoria of the end of the war. The cool finesse of Jerzy Wójcik's plastic vision gave these contrasts added expressiveness. The work of this great cinematographer combines here raw rendering of the texture of objects with warm and incisive observation of human characters. But it was not the inventive mise en scène nor the baroque quality of the images that were decisive in giving Ashes and Diamonds brilliance and power--but Wajda's romantic, stormy, very personal vision. The film is so great because it is organically linked with the entire national tradition of the country in which it was made--emotional and cultural.

A striking example of this is the end of the banquet, the scene which is a metaphor for the attitudes and the state of mind of the Poles in the tradition of the national drama, with its dream-like dance and the entrancing music, like in the works of Mickiewicz, Słowacki and Wyspiański. Thus Wajda, who returned to these motifs later in Landscape After the Battle and The Wedding, refers to Poland's romantic poetry. It was in fact from the poem by Cyprian Kamil Norwid, the 19th-century visionary, that the title of the novel was taken:

> Now and again burning rags
> Fly away from you like sparks from a resinous chip
> Burning, you know not if you shall be free
> Or will all that is yours perish?
> Or will only ashes remain and chaos
> That follow the storm into the abyss?
> Or will there remain among
> The ashes a star-like diamond,
> The dawn of eternal victory....

NAZARIN (Nazarín) Luis Buñuel

Script: Buñuel and Julio Alejandro, from the novel by Benito Pérez Galdós. Photography: Gabriel Figueroa. Art Direction: Edward Fitzgerald. Dialogues: Emilio Carballido. Editing: Carlos Savage. Cast: Francisco Rabal (Don Nazario), Marga López (Beatriz), Rita Macedo (Andara), Noé Murayama (El Pinto), Jesús Fernández (Ujo), Ignacio López Tarso (Lean thief), Ofelia Guilmain (Chanfa), Luis Aceves Castañeda (Murderer), Rosenda Monteros (La Prieta).

Manuel Barbachano Ponce, Mexico. 8460 ft., 94 mins.

The period of Buñuel's splendid maturity is opened with the film which is the richest in reflections about the motivation of human action of all his works, while being the least obvious as to its conclusions. Don Nazario is a Catholic priest in Mexico at the turn of the century who tries to follow literally the teaching of Christ. His unshakeable faith and his absolute self-denial make him a saint from the point of view of Christian ethics, while condemning him to be misunderstood and ostracized by the world, to suffer disapproval on the part of the Church hierarchy and repressions from the civilian authorities.

When Don Nazario allows Andara, prostitute wanted for murder, to take refuge in his room, the Church authorities censure him assuming he has been living with her. The priest decides to beg his way as Christ did and is followed by Andara and by Beatriz, a beautiful woman whom he helped when she tried to commit suicide on being abandoned by her lover. Nazario teaches humility and poverty. Living off alms, he asks a foreman for work on the railway in exchange for a piece of bread; in so doing he undercuts other workers' wages and causes a riot. Later, he administers the last rites to a plague victim only to discover that she prefers to spend her last moments with her lover rather than with a priest. He also discovers that the two women follow him because they love him as a man. When Andara is arrested, Nazario is accused of being her accomplice. In the last scene of the film we see him alone, walking in the sun with his guard. An old woman approaches and, taking pity on him, offers him a pineapple. His first reaction is to refuse; but after a moment's hesitation he accepts it with gratitude. This scene is accompanied on the soundtrack by a deafening roll of the drums of Calanda, Buñuel's native village.

In contrast to Viridiana, which was made three years later and demonstrated the total failure of Christian charity in the modern world and was because of this condemned by the Vatican, Nazarin gained the support of the guardians of Catholic ideology although in fact it offers a very similar proof of the practical uselessness of Christian principles. The simplest explanation is that Nazarin was interpreted, wrongly, as the message of a proselyte. Indeed, this complex film perplexed even the surrealists and atheists who were ideologically close to Buñuel; it seems that their accusations of treason piqued the director to make Viridiana, a much more forceful statement, even if a little less perfect. The point is, however, that there are vital differences between the two films. Viridiana forsakes the path of Christian virtue, while Father Nazario remains faithful to his ideals; Viridiana's activities benefit nobody and her defeat is a moral defeat, while Nazario loses only on a physical scale and his altruism cannot be said to have been completely useless; finally Viridiana is merely a pathetic product of devotional upbringing while Nazario is an enlightened and intelligent man. He prays for the life of a dying child, but insists that the doctor's instructions be followed. When the little girl unexpectedly recovers he attributes this to God's will and not to his intercession. He tries to avoid the company of the two women who worship him as a saint. Church officials describe his nature as rebellious, although Buñuel's modest hero does not in fact rebel against anything; but his uncompromising actions in the name of Christian love are quite sufficient to expose the moral bankruptcy of the institutionalized Church. For example, the main concern of the Church authorities is that the acceptance of alms supposedly brings discredit to the dignity of a priest. In giving refuge to the wounded prostitute Nazario challenges also the legal order of the State. Does he not realize that his actions precipitate conflict between the ideals of goodness and the rules of real life; between the ideals of forgiveness and the earthly need for self-respect, social order and redress for wrong? He is indeed fully aware of all that. But, as every idealist, he follows the voice of hope. He believes that in man's dualist nature the element of good is capable of breaking through the crust of evil which is mainly acquired under social pressure. Institutions and ordinary people do not accept his actions,

Nazarin

preferring sensual experience to spiritual purity, profit to the joy of giving--and do not understand that the two women traveling with the priest do not have to be his mistresses. Unfortunately, Nazario will not admit to himself that the sense of his actions is in conflict with the popular mentality; he refuses to understand that his experience disqualifies Nazarethan Christianity in its confrontation with the rules of the struggle for survival.

This latter concept dominated the works of Benito Pérez Galdós (1843-1920), the great Spanish writer. Buñuel explained that his own intention was simply to repeat after the author of the film's literary original that we all live in a society which makes love of one's neighbor impossible, quite independently of whether the church exists or not. The picture fulfils this promise with the reservation that the title character tends to get out of the director's hand: Father Nazario is too engaging in his nobleness of spirit, his moral strength well defends him against critical vivisection, and he seems as if subconsciously treated with deep respect by Buñuel himself. The ambiguity of the film's message comes from these very facts and not from any imperfection of cinematic craft. For Nazarin is stylistically very coherent and balanced, especially by Buñuel's standards who as a matter of principle did not cherish the content of the frame, particularly in the 50's when his mise en scène was still a little stiff. This was to change only with Belle de Jour (1967) and Tristana.

Nazarin is Buñuel's twenty-second picture; one must remember however that this figure includes a lot of commercial rubbish (particularly among his Mexican undertakings of the 40's) which the director never treated seriously himself and at the most used as an opportunity for an odd free-thinking jest to upset the bourgeoisie; only occasionally in works such as Adventures of Robinson Crusoe, El (1952), The Criminal Life of Archibaldo de la Cruz (1955) and particularly in Los olvidados was he able to create a more comprehensive conception of reality, to convey his thoughts on the human being. On these occasions poetic Surrealist reminiscences, a nonconformist view of reality and vitriolic sense of humor were not merely ornaments of the plot and the narrative was conducted with care. So it is in Nazarin, where the few subjective images and ironic metaphors (a picture-like Christ in a crown of thorns made to laugh by a prostitute's attempts to expiate) perform a functional psychological role, while the whole is subordinated to a concentrated summation of meanings. Buñuel was particularly anxious to see that the film does not appeal to the audience via its external appearance. This brought about his many arguments with the photographer Figueroa who found it difficult to accept the ancilliary role of the photography; this also caused the renouncement of music (apart from the roll of the drums in the final scene) and the discreet quality of other formal elements. The effect is remarkable: there is greatness in this simplicity and as a matter of fact Figueroa contributed considerably to achieving this. Contrary to his natural inclinations he was able to create photography which is toned down and yet extraordinary.

Neither the fact that in the final result the distribution of stress in Nazarin turned out to be different from which the director intended, nor the resultant ambiguity detract from Buñuel's greatest film. On the contrary, they give it splendor--as always happens when an ethical dispute is conducted on the screen unobtrusively but with the aid of powerful, many-sided argumentation. While confronting Don Nazario's Nazarethan principles with the hard realities of life Buñuel perceives the essence of Christianity in striving to reform man's selfish passion into self-denying love for the community. The human character by its very nature dooms these idealistic intentions to failure: Beatriz and the plague-stricken girl discard spiritual love for the sake of sexual love and eternal happiness for the sake of temporal experiences; the ecstasy of the peasant women who invoke God at the bed of a sick child has an obvious erotic basis; Beatriz's worshipping of Nazario originates from her admiration for him as a miracle-worker and from her unfulfilled desire after the departure of her lover and is no more than a subconscious substitute for passion; the dream of the dwarf Ujo is to possess the prostitute who treats him with scorn (and kicks him in the stomach); the hurt male pride of El Pinto prompts him to renew his relationship with Beatriz.

With all that Nazarin is not an intentional polemic with Christianity if only because Buñuel completely disregards the social problems of the Christian movement, equally those which brought about its birth and those which apply to the present. A Buñuel is not interested in pre-conceived and universal ideals, but only in individual and spontaneous ones, in accordance with his philosophy which he himself described as simple and very flexible: it consists of searching for God inside the human being. Nazarin on the one hand communicates a bitter truth about the failure of altruism, but on the other is a superb homage to the goodness of man. But the film's very essence is somewhere else still: Nazarin is an exponent of Buñuel's message about the need for loyalty to one's impulses, to every man's need to discover and fulfill his own vision of happiness.

INVENTION OF DESTRUCTION (Vynález zkázy) Karel Zeman

Script: Zeman and František Hrubin, based on the novel "Face au drapeau" and motifs from other novels by Jules Verne. Commentary: Jiří Brdečka. Photography: Jiří Tarantik. Music: Zdeněk Liška. Art Direction: Zdeněk Rozkopal. Special effects: Karel Zeman. Cast: Arnošt Navrátil (Professor Thomas Roch), Lubor Tokoš (Engineer Simon Hart), Miroslav Holub (Artigas), Jana Zatloukalová (Jeanne), František Šlégr (Artigas's ship captain), Václav Kyzlink (Engineer Serke).

Československý statni film, Studio dětského filmů, Gottwaldov, Czechoslovakia. 7710 ft., 86 mins. Prints tinted sepia.

After the Second World War animated features became the main speciality of the Czechoslovak film industry. In particular puppet film where the most outstanding creative individuality was that of Jiří Trnka. As a matter of fact, puppet theatre has been a favorite with the Czechs for centuries. Thus Karel Zeman, a Paris-trained expert in advertising and since 1943 a film-maker, mastered his craft in a country with good traditions. After some ten years he had to his name films made using different techniques; among other things he combined puppets with animated drawings. In the projects that followed, of which Journey into the Past (1954) was the first, he combined live actors with animation. As such experiments were already done much earlier in the U. S. A. the idea was not new, but nobody so far undertook a project on the scale of Invention of Destruction, where the human figure becomes an integral part of the picture--and nobody achieved a result which can as much as be compared with this film.

The co-author of this success on par with Zeman is Jules Verne, the French fantasist, and this in a rather unusual way. It was not at all that the stunning imagination of the 19th-century writer would provide locomotion for any such project. Granted, the plot based on one of the lesser known Verne novels is quite neat, but it is entirely contained in the classical stereotypes of the genre: a great inventor who works on tapping enormous new sources of energy for the benefit of mankind is deluded by an evil Count who plans to dominate the world and for the time being occupies himself with pirate attacks on ships. The fabulously equipped laboratory which the Count has built in his headquarters inside an extinct volcano is an extra incentive for the professor. Only the professor's assistant realizes what is going on; but he succeeds in carrying out his escape plan only when the professor finally grasps the truth, comes to his senses and--sacrificing his own life--blows up the lair of the pirates. The whole is thus made complete by a happy end according to the "noble sacrifice" variety and the story offers no departures from the stereotype. The revelation rests elsewhere--in the fact that Zeman with remarkable intuition expressed on the screen the moods dominant at the time when the novel was written. This was his only concern and he resisted the temptation to wink his eye at the audience or to modernize the story or its message. By maintaining the designs in the style of the etchings of the period, and referring to the works of the cinema pioneer Georges Méliès, by using a very appropriate acting convention (or, rather, an appropriate way of directing the figures of the actors) Zeman made a film which may be described as 19th-century screen apocrypha, a film which with full respect and charm recreates the imaginary world of Verne and his readers. This is to the credit of the author of the novel: it turned out that his fantasies, which after 100 years of technological progress necessarily faded and became somewhat infantile, remain extremely interesting while in the context of their natural chronological environment. Invention of Destruction is not an imitation, and even the term "transposition" can be applied only to those episodes in which Zeman gently draws attention to the arch-serious 19th-century pedantry.

Invention of Destruction

These were probably the reasons why a film which became a veritable time machine (a feat which the director never managed to repeat) makes one discover that Verne contained in his stories many non-trivial universal reflections. In this case--about the responsibility of scientists who wield the power to destroy. This sounded particularly topical in the period of nuclear scare (which by 1958 was fortunately drawing to a close) and explains why the film was officially delegated to represent Czechoslovakia at the 1958 Brussels Film Festival organized on the occasion of the World Exhibition. It was awarded the Grand Prix. Thus a refined poetic vision of a fantastic world was also a pacifist political statement.

LA TETE CONTRE LES MURS Georges Franju

Script: Jean-Pierre Mocky, from the novel by Hervé Bazin. Dialogues: Jean-Charles Pichon. Photography: Eugen Schüfftan. Music: Maurice Jarre. Art Direction: Louis le Barbenchon. Editing: Suzanne Sandberg. Cast: Jean-Pierre Mocky (François Gérane), Pierre Brasseur (Dr. Varmont), Paul Meurisse (Dr. Émery), Charles Aznavour (Heurtevent), Anouk Aimée (Stéphanie), Jean Galland (François's father), Jean Ozenne, Thomy Bourdelle, Roger Legris.

Sirius/Atica/Elpénor, France. 8820 ft., 98 mins.

Georges Franju, a lonely but sovereign island in the archipelago of the French film industry, was 46 at the time of his debut in feature cinema. He had earlier co-founded (in 1936) the Cinémathèque française (French National Film Archive) and was the most outstanding documentary film-maker in France. He became well-known mainly through two brilliant documentaries: Le Sang des bêtes (1949) about the La Villette slaughterhouse in Paris, and Hôtel des Invalides (1951) about the institution for the crippled veterans of the First World War. Both films had a striking and unusual atmosphere obtained through original use of the soundtrack and unique combination of shocking objects with an unreal, visionary manner in which they were shown on the screen. These three components: the dreamlike ("onirique," in French) sound, the immanent poetry of unusual objects or their poetic vision on the screen, and finally the cruelty of the topics discussed--dominate Franju's whole work which lies on the crossroads of Surrealism, Kafkaesque allegory and a horror story. This description well applies to La Tête contre les murs, his impressively lucid first feature.

François Gérane, an upper middle-class dropout, is committed by his lawyer father to a mental hospital after he stole some money from him and burned an important document. François is too defensive to live an independent life, too cool emotionally to build his life on love and too little enterprising to gain lasting liberty from his escape from the hospital. He leaves the flat of the girl who loves him, is recaptured and separated from the world forever: the director of the hospital likes permanent solutions and does not believe in curable cases.

While being faithful to reality in portraying everyday life and describing the psychiatric hospital, Franju gives to every situation and almost to every frame of the film a metaphorical meaning; while describing the situation of François he talks about the loneliness of an individual in modern civilization, his alienation and his subjugation by those in power. His protest against the latter is perhaps not as vehement as in Forman's future One Flew Over the Cuckoo's Nest--but seems even more piercing. This is characteristic of Franju, who in this film revealed himself as not only a humanist non-conformist, but also as anticleric and an uncompromising enemy of the bourgeoisie. Yet the principal value of La Tête contre les murs is not social criticism of the content but the mastery of form which gave its message exceptional suggestiveness: the fusion of the music and the hallucinatory photography mostly bathed in greyness only sometimes accentuated with expressive lighting; the subtle but dense symbolism for the hero's states of mind; the choice of the specific scenery; the direction of actors (of whom Pierre Brasseur is particularly remarkable) and the unerring instinct for the rhythm of editing. Both here and in his latter films Franju resorts to traditional means of expression--and yet creates with them a new imagery, which resonates with the tendencies which at the close of the 50's brought about revolutionary changes in the French cinema.

VERTIGO Alfred Hitchcock

Script: Alec Coppel and Samuel Taylor, from the novel "D'entre les morts" by Pierre Boileau and Thomas Narcejac. Photography: Robert Burks. Music: Bernard Herrmann. Art Direction: Hal Pereira and Henry Bumstead. Costumes: Edith Head. Special Sequence: John Ferren. Editing: George Tomasini. Cast: James Stewart (John "Scottie" Ferguson), Kim Novak (Madeleine Elster/ Judy Barton), Barbara Bel Geddes (Midge), Tom Helmore (Gavin Elster), Henry Jones (Coroner), Raymond Bailey (Doctor), Ellen Corby (Manageress), Konstantin Shayne (Pop Leibel), Lee Patrick (Mistaken identity).

Alfred J. Hitchcock Productions, U.S.A. 11,511 ft., 128 mins. VistaVision. Technicolor.

Boileau and Narcejac: crime writers whose extraordinarily ingenious plots (they scripted Les Diaboliques) often contain near-philosophical observations, usually concerned with the question of identity. To the two Frenchmen the problem is not who done it, but what was really done. Boileau and Narcejac wrote the novel on which Vertigo is based with Hitchcock in mind, aware that his interests coincide with theirs. What gives a human being a unique identity?--Hitchcock, fascinated by the obsession of the novel's protagonist with recreating the image of a dead girl through another, made a truly Pirandellian picture with the texture of a dream, a film which no doubt influenced the style of the Nouvelle Vague. Vertigo was greatly admired, particularly in France, and has since become a myth, especially since it seems almost impossible in recent years to get a viewing of it--apparently on Hitchcock's express orders. Brian De Palma's Obsession is a homage to Vertigo.

"Scottie" Ferguson, whose fear of heights once caused the death of a colleague and led to his subsequent resignation from the police force, is asked by an old college friend to shadow his wife, Madeleine, described as a suicidal neurotic. The girl is beautiful and strangely remote and Scottie soon falls in love with her. He saves her when she attempts to drown herself but, because of acrophobia, cannot prevent her death when she throws herself from the church steeple. A few months later Scottie meets another girl, Judy, who is the image of Madeleine, but says she has never met Scottie before. The detective becomes obsessed with the uncanny resemblance and refuses to believe Madeleine was really killed. He is right: when Judy puts on a locket Madeleine used to wear, Scottie begins to guess what has really happened....

The reviewer Leonard Maltin said about Vertigo that it defies rational description, and there is more in this comment than meets the eye. For instance, it is almost impossible to locate the source of the film's strange fascination. Is it the story itself that does it, or is it the handling of it? The visual style or the acting? It is difficult to answer, especially since Hitchcock uses the usual elements of his craft side by side with new and unexpected stylistic devices. He has repeatedly shown himself to be more interested in suspense than in solving a mystery (and often there even isn't one) and in Vertigo he reveals Judy's identity, although only to the viewer, thus characteristically opting for suspense rather than surprise. On the other hand, the unhurried pace of the editing and the deliberate narrative rhythm are a far cry from Hitchcock's other films which mostly rely on sharp motion. The aim was to give a formal equivalent to the dreamlike, mysterious story. Herrmann's excellent music, well suited to the mood, serves the same purpose. The film's subtle, implied eroticism is fascinating. Scottie's obsessive attempts to make Judy like Madeleine have an almost mesmerizing quality. The photography is likewise most impressive. Note, for instance, the vertiginous shot looking down the church steeple with Madeleine's body lying on the roof and Scottie walking out of the church. Some shots from the tower were filmed using a clever technical device: a track-out combined with a forward zoom.

Vertigo

THE BALLAD OF NARAYAMA (Nara-yama bushi-kō) Keisuke Kinoshita

Script: Kinoshita, from the short story by Shichiro Fukuzawa. Photography: Hiroyuki Kusuda. Music: Rokuzaemon Kineya and Matsunosuke Nozawa. Art Direction: Kisaku Ito. Editing: Yoshi Sugiwara. Cast: Kinuyo Tanaka (Orin), Teiji Takahashi (Tatsuhei), Yuko Mochizuki (Tama-Yan), Danko Ichikawa (Kesakichi), Keiko Ogasawara (Matsu-Yan), Seiji Miyaguchi (Mata-Yan), Yunosuke Ito (Mata-Yan's son), Ken Mitsuda (Teru-Yan).

Masaharu Kokaji for Shochiku, Japan. 8733 ft., 98 mins. Tohoscope. Fujicolor

The Ballad of Narayama is the number one picture of Kinoshita, the director who always strove towards formal perfection; it was chosen in Japan as film of the year and is almost unanimously considered the height of visual mastery.

The film is based on a folk (or pseudo-folk) tale about an ancient custom in the poor villages of the Shinawa country, where old people were traditionally abandoned on the slopes of the holy mountain Nara. In a mountain village there lives an old woman whose days are numbered; but she is extraordinarily lively and wants to depart on her last journey conscious that she spared no effort to safeguard peace and prosperity for her family. She finds her widowed son a new wife in the remote countryside and only when she has ensured that the couple are happy does she decide to depart. It is before New Year when the first snows come; in accordance with tradition, she is taken to the mountain by her beloved son. On his way back the son sees how another villager throws his father into the precipice. Outraged, he punishes the villain in the same way; then, on a sudden impulse, he returns to his mother. But she is already still and cold. It is snowing.

At the roots of the film's achievement is without a doubt the fact that Kinoshita reached into the magnificent heritage of Japanese culture. The character of the story inclined the director to use stylization based on the convention of the kabuki theatre; the film refers to it with its narrative frame, the use of the commentator's voice, the use of a prologue, the theatrical lighting. Such methods always carry a threat of stiffness and artificiality even in the cases when unity of form and content has been achieved. But The Ballad of Narayama avoids such trouble; this happens not merely because Kinoshita's style, described in Japan as soft and feminine, is a complete contradiction of the vehemence and sharpness of kabuki. What was decisive was mainly his deeply human treatment of the characters, his poetic feel for the scenery and the rhythm. From the very first frames of the film Kinoshita builds up a captivating mood evoked with the powerful images and well-integrated music based on old folkloristic motifs. With the progress of the story the magic of this majestically developed tale becomes stronger and stronger to reach its climax in the piercing finale. Even if not everything in the film is based on authentic tradition, its great harmony makes one forget additions or retouchings. As always in outstanding achievements of the screen, the director's power and autonomy of expression is decisive, making The Ballad of Narayama one of the finest manifestations of national character in the cinema.

ROOM AT THE TOP Jack Clayton

Script: Neil Paterson, from the novel by John Braine. Photography: Freddie Francis. Music: Mario Nascimbene. Art Direction: Ralph Brinton. Editing: Ralph Kemplen. Cast: Laurence Harvey (Joe Lampton), Simone Signoret (Alice Aisgill), Heather Sears (Susan Brown), Donald Wolfit (Mr. Brown), Ambrosine Phillpotts (Mrs. Brown), Donald Houston (Charles Soames), Raymond Huntley (Mr. Hoylake), John Westbrook (Jack Wales), Allan Cuthbertson (George Aisgill), Mary Peach (June Samson), Hermione Baddeley (Elspeth).

John and James Wolf for Remus, G. B. 10,553 ft., 117 mins.

For many years an associate producer, Clayton was not connected with the Free Cinema movement which triggered off important changes in the British cinema in the late 50's. But he chose as starting material for his first film the best-selling book by a certified "angry young man." The film exerted considerable influence and was also an important breakthrough for British cinema on the U. S. market. The social problems Clayton touched upon were promptly taken up by other directors.

Set in a sad and ugly northern English industrial town, Room at the Top is the story of an insignificant clerk who is determined to make good in life. Anxious to find the "room at the top" for himself in society, Joe Lampton begins to court the daughter of a local industrialist. When Susan's father promptly sends her abroad, Joe becomes involved with Alice, a mature French teacher who loves him with a strong and true love. Joe seduces Susan after she returns and is forced to marry her when she becomes pregnant. Alice takes to drink and soon after dies in a car accident. Joe disappears, gets drunk and is beaten up by hooligans. But he is found in time for his own wedding.

Room at the Top is quite traditional as concerns the film-making. From the formal point of view, its main strength is clarity, the main weakness--melodramatic leanings (Alice's death). But it is surely the film's moral problem which is of greatest interest. Room at the Top offers bitter comment on the English class structure, a disenchanted view of provincial England with its boredom and its municipal corruption. The film also contains an uninhibited (by contemporary standards) view of sex. The stable British hierarchy is shown with all its unpleasantness and the town photographed in such a way as always to include in the frame the symbolic chimneys of the factory belonging to Susan's father, the chimneys which bear down on ordinary people. While not being particularly "angry" (certainly less abrasive than was Braine in his book), Clayton is surely "young" in his attitude. He reveals himself as a talented director.

Of the acting, the most notable is Simone Signoret's sensitive Oscar-winning performance as Alice. Clayton was not to cultivate his social interests: his next project, The Innocents (1961) is a smooth screen version of a Henry James ghost story.

BLACK ORPHEUS (Orfeu Negro) Marcel Camus

Script: Jacques Viot, Camus and Vinicius de Moraês, based on the play "Orfeu da Conceição" by the latter. Photography: Jean Bourgoin. Music: Antonio Carlos Jobim and Luiz Bonfá. Songs: "Felicidade" (music by Jobim, lyrics by de Moraês), "O Nosso Amor" (music and lyrics by Jobim), "Manhã de Carnaval" and "Samba de Orfeu" (music by Bonfá, lyrics by Antonio Maria). Editing: Andrée Feix. Cast: Marpessa Dawn (Euridice), Breno Mello (Orfeu), Léa Garcia (Serafina), Adhemar da Silva (Death), Lourdes de Oliveira (Mira), Alexandro Constantino (Hermes), Waldetar de Souza (Chico Boto), Jorge dos Santos (Benedito), Aurino Cassanio (Zeca).

Sacha Gordine for Tupan/Dispatfilm/Gemma Cinematografica, Brazil/France/Italy. 9540 ft., 106 mins. Eastman Colour.

Black Orpheus transplants the ancient Greek myth of Orpheus and Euridice onto the soil of contemporary Latin America, to the suburbs and carnival streets of Rio de Janeiro.

Euridice, a village girl arrives at the former Brazilian capital the day before the Carnival to visit a cousin. She meets a handsome tram-conductor who is also a guitar-player, singer and dance leader at one of the schools of samba in the Negro quarter. Love at first sight, passion and intoxication amid carnival crowd during the night; after that a tragic tangle of human envy and ruthless fate. Euridice is pursued by the jealous Mira, Orpheus's partner, and takes refuge in a tram depot; Orpheus switches on the current to find her in the dark and accidentally causes her death. Later he dies himself, thrown over the cliff. At dawn, the hero's young followers summon the sun singing his song accompanied by the strains of his guitar.

It may well be that the circumstances which led to the making of Black Orpheus were more down-to-earth than the film itself. It may also be that Viot and Camus were attracted by the thought of resurrecting once again, in highly exotic scenery, the world of the films of Marcel Carné, the world of destiny and hopeless love. All this is possible, and one is permitted to speculate: after all, the director of Black Orpheus spent half his life traveling around the world making films in most attractive places, even though he never developed an individual style and his films were never much above average. Never that is, with this single stunning exception, a film made with great intuition born of a fascination with the Rio Carnival, a work touchingly fresh and beautiful. All this does not alter the fact that the whole second part of Black Orpheus balances on the verge of disastrous falsity. But melodrama flees here constantly under the pressure of naturalness: the obtrusive symbolism is redeemed equally by the wit and lightness of generic observation and by the spontaneous behavior of non-professional actors. The scenes of carnival festivities, threatened with ethnographic postcard style, gave the rhythm and the mood of the film incomparable intensity; the beautiful scenery inspired the images with lyricism and poetry; the exceptionally good music did the rest. It seems therefore that in the case of Black Orpheus the genius loci was crucial.

Preparations for the making of the film were very careful. Local authorities helped Camus during the filming of the 1958 Rio Carnival. The production lasted more than a year. This concentration of efforts was undoubtedly vital: Black Orpheus does not even have a hint of being a look from the outside, it is a Brazilian tale par excellence. This manifests itself as the authentic expression of a specific cultural milieu, a unique amalgam of joy, eroticism, belief in magic, madness and death--but is also evident in every detail of the images, such as the magnificent rainbow coloristic scale. Europe, where in the 50's the cinema was congealed into academic shapes, got acquainted with Black Orpheus at the 1959 Cannes Film Festival and, delighted, awarded it the Grand Prix. On a larger time scale, the film helped considerably to bring about a return to originality and spontaneity in the cinema, particularly in France where a great upheaval was in the offing. It was in fact those days of May 1959, the days of the triumph of Black Orpheus, that witnessed also the proclamation of the Manifesto of the Nouvelle Vague.

THE MUSIC ROOM (Jalsaghar) Satyajit Ray

Script: Ray, from the story by Tarashankar Bannerji. Photography:

Subrata Mitra. Music Direction: Ustad Vilayat Khan. Instrumental Music: Dakhin Mohan Takhur, Asis Kumar and Robin Majumder. Art Direction: Banshi Chandra Gupta and R. R. Sinde. Editing: Dulal Dutta. Cast: Chabi Biswas (Huzur Biswambhar Roy), Pinaki Sen Gupta (Khoka, his son), Padma Devi (His wife), Tulsi Lahari (Estate manager), Kali Sarkar (Servant), Ganga Pada Basu (Mahim Ganguly), Pratap Mukhopdhya, Tarapadada Nandy. Musicians: Akhtari Bai (First singer), Ustad Waheed Khan (Second singer), Roshan Kumari (Kathak dancer), Bismilla & Company.

Satyajit Ray, India. 100 mins.

Between Aparajito and The World of Apu Ray made two films unconnected with the Apu Trilogy. The first, The Philosopher's Stone (1958), is a marginal comedy, while the second, The Music Room, belongs to his finest works.

The story of The Music Room is set in the early 30's. Huzur (Lord) Biswambhar Roy is the last in a long line of noblemen. His fortunes are low and the prospect of bankruptcy approaches fast. The sole remaining witness of past affluence is a moldering palace in the middle of arid flats bounded by the sea, with the jalsaghar (music room) hung with paintings of the present owner's illustrious ancestors. Roy also has an elephant, a magnificent horse and two remaining servants. His sole passion is music and he ruins himself to recruit more and more famous performers to his musical soirées. While so preoccupied, he allows the activities of an ambitious and ostentatious money-lender neighbor to remain unchecked. As one of the musical evenings is in progress, the nobleman hears that his wife and son have been drowned. He closes the jalsaghar and says he will never listen to music again. He changes his mind, annoyed by his upstart neighbor who inaugurates his own music room, so far Roy's privilege. The old man goes grandiosely insane: spends his last rupee to pay for a blow-out of song and dance with the participation of a great visiting dancer. Then he orders Tufan, his one horse, to be saddled, goes for a wild drunken gallop across the sands, is thrown and killed.

A greatly accomplished picture, The Music Room is Ray's most romantic work to the present day. The mood is one of contemplation and nostalgia--not placid, as in Ozu's films, but wistful and languid as in the plays by Chekhov. People devoured by passion, be it for music, chess or for learning, belong to stock Ray characters. As his protagonist roams over the crumbling estate, Ray leaves us in no doubt that he is portraying a world which irrevocably belongs to the past, and stresses this by the use of symbols. Thus a spider crosses a painting as the nobleman toasts "his noble self." Yet Ray does not use malice while characterizing his protagonist, a man for whom aesthetic enjoyment is both a refuge and a form of protest against the onset of a world of shallowness and greed. Ray's cinema often moves on the boundary of two civilizations: the native Indian culture and the influences brought by the British. Thus

Apu in Aparajito works at a printing house called "The Royal Press" and the story of the later Kanchenjunga has something of both the Orient and the West. In The Music Room Ray makes a very interesting observation about the linguistic status of educated Indians, and a wry comment about the British influence: when at his maddest, the protagonist speaks English.

Formally The Music Room is a highly assured picture, masterly paced, excellently edited and beautifully photographed by Subrata Mitra. The way in which his camera explores the moldering palace is very impressive. The music, based on the Indian modal system, is of interest in itself.

DAY SHALL DAWN (Jago hua savera) Aaejay Kardar

Script: Kardar. Dialogues: Faiz Ahmed Faiz. Photography: Walter Lassally and Sadhan Roy. Music: Timir Bahan Rahat and Nauman Taseer. Editing: Bill Bovet. Cast: Zurain Rakshi (Mian), Anis Ama (Kassim), Tripti Mitra (Mala), Shemsun Nihar (Fatima, Mian's wife), Kazi Khaliq (Lal Nian), Maina Latif (Ganju).

Nauman Taseer for Century Films, Pakistan. 8200 ft., 91 mins.

A remarkable cinematic impression about the life of a group of Bengali fishermen from a village on the banks of the treacherous River Meghna in East Pakistan (now Bangladesh). Poverty, perseverance, dignity and mutual good will, hard work and silent stoicism. The time of action is the early 20th century--but in fact neither chronology nor the development of the plot (which can be summarized as the story of the villagers' efforts to materialize their greatest dream, the purchase of a boat which would make them independent of the machinations of a rich merchant) are really of importance. Day Shall Dawn is a registration of a world which exists in symbiosis with nature, in social stagnation subject only to the lingering pulse of existence. The camera registers loose everyday episodes, only occasionally exceptional events, but even these are only latently tragic and the film contains no stylistic culminations while the dialogue is extremely sparse. The Island, the Japanese masterpiece made two years later, had a similar structure--but Kaneto Shindo based himself on a complex dramatic structure and elaborate rhythm, while Kardar and Lassally invested the entire strength of their film in the images with their exquisite chiaroscuro. This, plus the primeval quality of the narrative, very appropriate for the theme, gave Day Shall Dawn its appeal. The picture has something of an ethnographic document in its precise registration of details, perceptive portrayal of people and objects and reference to social structures. It seems that the creative temperaments of the director and the cinematographer were in very good resonance: the former gave the film the authentic national color, while the latter contributed a deep awareness of the camera as a creative tool, based on the knowledge of the achievements of Robert Flaherty and the founders of the British Documentary School, later adopted by the young film-makers of the "Free Cinema" to which Lassally himself belonged. This is clearly seen in the mature, formally excellent handling of many scenes in the most touching of which a fisherman dies just as the new boat is delivered and the purpose of his entire life thus fulfilled.

RIO BRAVO Howard Hawks

Script: Jules Furthman and Leigh Brackett, from the story by B. H. McCampbell. Photography: Russell Harlan. Music: Dimitri Tiomkin. Songs "My Rifle, My Pony and Me," "Cindy" and "Deguello" by Tiomkin and Paul Francis Webster. Art Direction: Leo K. Kuter. Costumes: Marjorie Best. Editing: Folmar Blangsted. Sets: Ralph S. Hurst. Cast: John Wayne (John T. Chance), Dean Martin (Dude), Ricky Nelson (Colorado Ryan), Angie Dickinson (Feathers), Walter Brennan (Stumpy), Ward Bond (Pat Wheeler), John Russell (Nathan Burdette), Pedro Gonzalez-Gonzalez (Carlos), Estelita Rodriguez (Consuela), Claude Akins (Joe Burdette), Malcom Atterbury (Jake).

Howard Hawks for Armada, U. S. A. 12,677 ft., 141 mins. Technicolor.

Fashions changed, many cinematic genres passed into oblivion, but the western remained basically unperturbed. This permanence alone testifies to the rich potentialities of the western formula. Successive periods in the cinema brought with them fundamental changes of attitude towards the West and its inhabitants, but all these new ideas generally did not detract from the value of older films. The reason for this lies in the realities of life in the West--in the unruly, extremely varied and classically polarized human attitudes and conflicts. Another reason is the folk quality of the films about the West, permitting (or rather, inviting) the spectator to identify with the screen characters in order to put his own reactions to a test.

Such reflections naturally come to mind in connection with the cinema of Howard Hawks, particularly Rio Bravo, which is without a doubt one of the most famous and most popular works of the genre. With this story of five people united in action against a mercenary gang which comes to the rescue of the arrested brutal murderer, Hawks seems to return to the traditional way of looking at the affairs of the West: he finds no use for philosophical abstractions, debating ethical conflicts or on extra-temporal generalizations.

What counts here is professionalism and efficiency reached through experience. The dividing line between good and bad is clear and is left to the spectator: one does not discuss morality, one carries it within oneself. Rio Bravo is thus very different from the haughty High Noon. In fact, many things are different--the fluent and colorful narrative, familiar sense of humor, inventive and well-staged situations (the famous scene of the blood of a wounded criminal hiding on the gallery in the saloon dripping into the glass in the bar below; a flower pot being thrown through the window to avert attention; shooting at sticks of dynamite thrown towards the bandits in order to blast them into surrender). Finally, one of the main differences with High Noon is the stressing of the sense of common action, solidarity and comradeship. None of the five principal characters of Rio Bravo is perfect: Dude, the sheriff's friend, is a delinquent and a drunkard; old Stumpy is lame and terribly obstinate; Colorado is a greenhorn; Feathers can hardly be called a lady; and the sheriff himself is--shall we say--of limited intelligence, very conservative and says that he accepted the office out of laziness. But strength is to be found in unity. Bad men are defeated, Dude reforms his drinking habits, Colorado becomes a man, Feathers turns into an exemplary member of the community and sheriff John T. finds a wife.

Is Rio Bravo therefore a traditional, superficial and sweetly optimistic story about the good old West? It is good-humored and optimistic--but certainly not superficial. For all its classical character Rio Bravo undoubtedly belongs to the series of psychological westerns of the 50's. Nothing in this film comes about mechanically and nothing is merely passive registration: Hawks painstakingly characterizes people and traces motives of their actions, sources of antagonisms, mechanisms of the formation of human worth; he observes people during trials of resistance, dignity, will-power, in triumph and in failure. Also the scenery is more than a mere ornament; to Hawks it is a complement to the human being. In El Dorado and Rio Lobo, the remaining parts of his unofficial trilogy about partnership of men of good will, generic attractions and noisy humor were taken too far and allowed to trivialize the outcome. Rio Bravo is related to other outstanding contemporary westerns through the intimate quality of the plot: everything here happens in one place and wide landscapes are only seen in the far background. Thus the spectators' attention naturally concentrates on the protagonists and their problems. John Wayne and his partners build their roles with expressive, thick lines and give justice to such distribution of accents. Rio Bravo has all the attributes of a popular great western.

I WANT TO LIVE Robert Wise

Script: Nelson Gidding and Don Mankiewicz, based on newspaper articles by Ed Montgomery and letters of Barbara Graham. Photography: Lionel Lindon. Music: John Mandel. Art Direction: Edward Haworth. Editing: William Hornbeck. Cast: Susan Hayward (Barbara Graham), Simon Oakland (Ed Montgomery), Virginia Vincent (Peg), Theodore Bikel (Carl Palmberg), Lou Krugman (Jack Santo), Philip Coolidge (Emmett Perkins), Wesley Lau (Henry Graham), James Philbrook (Bruce King), Bartlett Robinson (District Attorney), Gage Clark (Richard G. Tibrow), Joe De Santis (Al Matthews), John Marley (Father Devers), Alice Backes (San Quentin nurse), Raymond Bailey (San Quentin warden).

Walter Wanger for Figaro, U. S. A. 120 mins.

An eloquent plea against capital punishment, I Want to Live is based on a real episode in recent judicial history. On June 5, 1955, a 32-year-old woman died in the gas chamber at San Quentin, having been found guilty of murdering Mrs. Mabel Monahan, an elderly widow, two years previously. Barbara Graham insisted to the last that she was innocent, and there is doubt as to her guilt to this day.

Victim of a broken home, prostitute, forger and convicted perjurer, Graham has already served three years in jail when she starts work for two crooks, Santo and Perkins. She tries to go straight, gets married and gives birth to a child. But money difficulties and her husband's drug addiction make normal life impossible. She is arrested for the murder committed (in the film) by her two gambler associates. When their accomplice turns state's evidence and accuses her of the killing, she desperately tries to buy a false alibi which is exposed in court and results in her being sentenced to death. She bitterly blames Edward J. Montgomery, the reporter who led a press campaign against her, for the verdict, and invites him to the execution. Montgomery has a sudden hunch that something was not right with the trial and sentence. In a series of articles in the "San Francisco Examiner" he starts to inquire into the case and, together with the noted criminal psychologist Carl Palmberg, launches a campaign to save the convicted woman. The various appeals for clemency and for a fresh trial fail; Graham is taken to the death cell and executed after three last-minute postponements to enable the court to consider the submissions of the defense.

Montgomery was awarded the Pulitzer Prize for the defense of Bloody Barbara, although he failed to save her. He later devoted himself to the cause of reforming the American judicial system. The script of I Want to Live was based on his unpublished notes, the transcript of the trial and on Graham's letters. The film is openly crusading in character. Wise is less interested in Graham's guilt or innocence, and the viewer is not really given sufficient evidence to decide for himself whether or not she was guilty. But the picture's emotional pitch and the use of Susan Hayward in the main part create a presumption of innocence. This looks like loading the issue. Is capital punishment wrong because of the possibility of judicial error; or because of the brutality of the police and their use of informers; or because of the past weighing heavily against the accused ("people are judged by who their friends are"); or because of the bias of the media? Wise failed to make his argument clear. The film would have been intellectually more effective if Graham was guilty beyond doubt. Cayatte presented a more reasoned and convincing argument in We Are All Murderers by doing just that. It is also a pity that Wise is not more concerned with the characters' motivation.

Yet I Want to Live is a very powerful picture, particularly in the second part. Wise steers clear of literary poses and ornamentation, stages scenes sharply and tersely and obtains the tense climate purely through cinematic means. The documentary description of the "technology of death" in the gas chamber is fascinating. After three years' absence from cinema, Susan Hayward gives an excellent performance. Being a Hollywood star, she could hardly afford too realistic a portrayal of the red-haired prostitute, but she is still unforgettable. She was rewarded with the Oscar which had eluded her three times in the past.

THE FLAME OF TORMENT (Enjō) Kon Ichikawa

Script: Natto Wada and Keiji Hasebe, from the novel "Kinkakuji" (The Temple of the Golden Pavilion) by Yukio Mishima. Photography: Kazuo Miyagawa. Music: Toshiro Mayuzumi. Art Direction: Yoshinobu Nishioka. Editing: Shiego Nishida. Cast: Raizo Ichikawa (Goichi Mizoguchi), Tatsuya Nakadai (Togari), Ganjiro Nakamura (Dosen Tayama), Yoko Uraji (Young woman), Michiyo Aratama (Teacher of flower arrangement), Tamao Nakamura (Prostitute), Yoichi Funaki (Tsurukawa), Kinzo Shin (Assistant to Superior of Temple), Tanie Kitabayashi (Aki Mizoguchi).

Masaichi Nagata for Daiei, Japan. 8629 ft., 96 mins. Daieiscope.

The Flame of Torment thematically resembles Ichikawa's previous Punishment Room It is also a dark story of protest--but this time set against the background of Japanese history and cultural tradition. The film is as cold and clinical as Yukio Mishima's novel, a fictional account of the events leading to the destruction of the famous Golden Pavilion at Kyoto.

Goichi's father has been ill for a long time; he dies humiliated by his wife's adultery. A shy young man with a speech impediment, Goichi remembers how his father used to say: "The Golden Pavilion in the Shukaku Temple is the most beautiful thing in the world." The young man's admiration for it borders on worship. He becomes an acolyte of Dosen, the head priest at the temple and his father's friend. Dosen helps him to enter a university. It is then that disenchantment sets in: Goichi finds his crippled friend made evil by his deformity, and beautiful girls to be vulgar and cruel. When the war ends, the priests exploit the pavilion as a tourist attraction. American soldiers bring local prostitutes to see it. When Goichi discovers that his worshipped master is a hypocrite and secretly keeps a mistress, his disillusionment is complete. He sets fire to the Golden Pavilion--it is too beautiful for this world of impurity and evil. Then he escapes into the mountains from where he watches the conflagration. He is arrested, but throws himself from a moving train on the way to prison.

It seems that the idea of crime as a way of giving vent to frustrations reflected Mishima's own state of mind at the time. Having turned towards Fascist ideology, the author ended his life in suicide. The Flame of Torment caused a stir in Japan, making Ichikawa, an experienced director, instantly famous. Dusky youth without love, a speech defect, the shattered dreams--Goichi's desperate search for an absolute of some kind is an expression of the Weltschmertz of the age. His protest is not only against social conventions--it is also a moral and political protest. With his purity, sense of justice, his lack of involvement in the hierarchy, Goichi instantly sees through corruption and hypocrisy. The Flame of Torment is only seemingly a study of pathology; in reality it is a study of the destruction of youthful idealism. The drama is enacted mostly in the mind of the young hero, excellently played by Raizo Ichikawa. The main obstacle the film came across was that it is virtually impossible to communicate visually Goichi's feelings towards the Pavilion. Even the great Miyagawa, who had photographed Rashomon and Sansho the Bailiff, could not be expected to make the rather modest wooden 14th-century building appear delightful enough to evoke the idea of pure beauty necessary to give plausibility to the protagonist's deed. All the same, Miyagawa used the black-and-white, widescreen technique with consummate brilliance. He makes good use of architectural objects and gives his images the appearance of relief. The narrative is conducted in a series of assured flashbacks.

THE LEFT HANDED GUN Arthur Penn

Script: Leslie Stevens, based on the TV play "The Death of Billy the Kid" by Gore Vidal. Photography: J. Peverell Marley. Music: Alexander Courage. Art Direction: Art Loel. Editing: Folmar Blangsted. Cast: Paul Newman (Billy Bonney), John Dehner (Pat Garrett), Lita Milan (Celsa), Hurd Hatfield (Moultrie), James Congdon (Charlie Boudre), James Best (Tom Folliard), Colin Keith-Johnston (Tunstall), John Dierkes (McSween), Bob Anderson (Hill), Wally Brown (Moon), Ainslie Pryor (Joe Grant), Denver Pyle (Ollinger), Martin Garralaga (Saval), Nestor Paiva (Maxwell), Paul Smith (Bell), Jo Summers (Mrs. Garrett), Robert Foulk (Brady).

Fred Coe for Haroll, U. S. A. 102 mins.

The Left Handed Gun opens the final stage in the development of the western: the legend which was created by the early silent pictures, formulated in Stagecoach, recast and made intellectually respectable by High Noon and Shane is now destroyed. Two legends are destroyed in fact: that surrounding the genre itself and that of Billy the Kid, one of the mythical western characters. All this was done by a newcomer to feature cinema, a man who later became a major director. Born in 1922, Penn joined Joshua Logan's theatre company towards the end of the war. He later studied in Italy, then at the Actors' Studio. From 1951 he worked as director for stage and television (where he directed "The Miracle Worker," a production he repeated in 1959 on Broadway and three years later turned into a feature film). The part of Billy the Kid (who in fact was not left-handed) had been James Dean's cherished project, unfulfilled because of the actor's death. Penn used Paul Newman, a rising star, who three years earlier appeared in a TV production of Gore Vidal's "The Death of Billy the Kid."

Billy Bonney befriends a mild-mannered cattle owner Tunstall. After Tunstall is killed by four cowpokes Billy vows to revenge his death. The sheriff is corrupt and there is thus no hope in official justice; Billy has to take the law into his own hands. A posse is mounted against him after he kills two of the murderers. The house in which he has been hiding is burned down; Billy, believed dead, escapes with severe burns. He kills the third murderer and finally, at the wedding of his friend Pat Garrett, the fourth. Garrett, who has earlier refused to become sheriff now takes the office and organizes the posse in which Billy is captured. He is tried and sentenced to death, but escapes from prison. Pat finally tracks Billy down and shoots him dead. He finds that Billy's hands as well as his holster were empty.

In this disenchanted vision of the West worthy citizens abandon themselves to an orgy of destruction as soon as an occasion presents itself. The posse is ostensibly in Billy's pursuit, but is in fact only an excuse for giving vent to aggression. The pursuers are not interested in the fact that other people, sometimes completely innocent, are killed. Penn later developed the theme of the spontaneous violence of the establishment in The Chase.

There has never been any doubt that Billy the Kid was a dangerous criminal. He was an illiterate accustomed to violence literally since childhood: at the age of eleven he killed a drunk who insulted his mother. While deglamorizing the West Penn also cuts the Billy myth down to size. It is a pity though that towards the end of the film, when he shows the loneliness and isolation of a man who was simply uncompromisingly honest, the director finds himself unable to steer completely clear of melodrama. But before Penn destroys a myth he demonstrates how it was born. This is done through the Moultrie character, a hack who glorifies Billy's exploits in pulp fiction stories--motivated by gratitude for the help Billy has given him in the past. The myth grows virtually independently of real events. Penn sees Billy as an illiterate outlaw who is unable to match his legend, much as was the protagonist of The Gunfighter: "You are not him" shouts the man who betrays him.

While Billy may be simple and violent, he is always honest. He becomes an outlaw when he takes revenge for Tunstall's killing. Tunstall did not carry a gun; he taught Billy to read and Billy partly identified him with his mother. The illiterate protagonist can express himself only through violence; using a gun is his only ability. When, having been injured in the fire, he is after a while again able to use a gun, he describes the feeling as like coming alive again. He is certainly ruthless: he kills a sheriff which will in the end cost him his life, despite being asked by the bridegroom to restrain his instincts; he kills a murderer at Pat Garrett's wedding, which loses him a friend. But morally he is always right. Penn sees Billy as a rebel of the generation of the 1880's and it would have been marvellous if he could have had James Dean for the part. Still, Paul Newman, who has become almost a professional substitute for Dean (having stood in for him two years earlier on Somebody Up There Likes Me) gave an excellent performance.

Among a number of touching moments in The Left Handed Gun are the scenes following Billy's escape from a burning house, as he roams half-dead in the prairie. The style is fine and dynamic, the characters and situations very true; for instance the youthful prankishness of Billy and his associates is very convincingly conveyed. Were it not for the certain melodramatic gloss of the second part of the picture which follows the rapacious romanticism of the first part--this could have been a great film. The music, an exercise in Hollywood confectionery, is another weakness. The high-contrast black-and-white photography is very good indeed. Its texture and tonal contrasts are well suited to the dynamic character of the movie.

LE BEAU SERGE Claude Chabrol

Script: Chabrol. Photography: Henri Decaë. Music: Emile Delpierre. Editing: Jacques Gaillard. Cast: Gérard Blain (Serge), Jean-Claude Brialy (François), Bernadette Lafont (Marie), Michèle Meritz (Yvonne), Claude Cerval (Priest), Jeanne Perez (Mme. Chaunier), Edmond Beauchamp (Glomaud), André Dino (Michel, the doctor), Claude Chabrol (La Truffe), Philippe de Broca (Jacques Rivette de la Chassoule), Michel Creuse (Baker).

AJYM-Films, France. 8868 ft., 99 mins.

As soon as they realized the exceptional importance of the 1959 Cannes Film Festival for the cinema, young French film-makers gathered, on May 11, 1959, at La Napoule to compose the text of the Manifesto of the Nouvelle Vague. This was done "in total agreement as to the principle of unrestrained making of films rather than making a career, and in total disagreement as to the details." Those present stressed their indebtedness to Claude Chabrol and his Le Beau Serge, the picture which he had the courage to make outside the French film industry. The signatories of the Manifesto were listed in alphabetical order, except for Chabrol who was given the honorary first place. Born in 1930, Chabrol was one of the intellectuals associated with "Cahiers du Cinéma." In 1956 his own production company AJYM produced Rivette's first short and later features by other young film-makers. In 1957 Chabrol co-wrote, with Eric Rohmer, a book about Hitchcock. Le Beau Serge, his first feature, was financed by the 37 million old francs inherited by Chabrol's first wife. The film was shot mostly in 1957 and completed the following year. Chabrol's film-making talent is evident right in the first sequence. A bus arrives at a village square and the two protagonists look at each other. Nothing is said, very little happens, but the whole situation is instantly intimated to the viewer. This may be because Chabrol shot the film at a place he knew well--in the village of Sardent (Creuse) in the Massif Central where he spent his childhood.

François, an intellectual recovering from tuberculosis returns to his native village after many years' absence. His childhood friend Serge, who had wanted to go away to study, was forced to marry a girl he made pregnant. He has taken to drink after she gave birth to a mongoloid child which died. Yvonne is expecting another baby and Serge fears that the same can happen again. Anxious to save his friend, François resolves that Serge's plight is caused by Yvonne and that he must leave her. He himself becomes involved with Yvonne's attractive sister Marie. It is partly the fault of François when Marie is raped by a half-crazy vagrant. Finally François begins to realize that his judgment of the situation was wrong, his attempts to intervene useless and his motivation questionable. When Yvonne's labor begins, François, who has suffered a relapse of his illness, risks his life when he wades through the snow to fetch the doctor. He then drags the drunken Serge to his wife's bedside. As François collapses on the floor a baby is born. It is normal.

The Zola-esque naturalism of the film's narrative seems somewhat clumsy with its gloomy atmosphere of xenophobia, primitivism and aggression. Serge is a delinquent and his wife a whore. The narrative relies for elasticity on the camera movement and the fast editing. Yet the images are simple. However, the dialogues of Le Beau Serge are decidedly stiff and the psychological motivation of the characters ambiguous. It is conceivable that the latter was at least partly intentional on Chabrol's part--his is a cinema of human obsession in which the viewer extrapolates his own experience of life disregarding psychological implausibility.

The finale of Le Beau Serge is beautiful, even if its optimism may seem a little doubtful, especially when considered in the light of Chabrol's later pictures. It is interesting that as soon afterwards as 1962 the director described Le Beau Serge as "unbearable" because of the film's Christian references and its "overloading with idiotic symbolism." François sacrifices his health, and possibly his life, for his friend. Robin Wood and Michael Walker described this obvious Christian symbol as "exchange of salvation" and traced it to Hitchcock's constant motif of "exchange of guilt," quoting Strangers on a Train as an example: a very interesting observation The point here is that each of the two protagonists could have been the other. The idea finds further support in Les Cousins, Chabrol's second feature, in which the parts played by the two actors are as if it were reversed.

It is evident that Chabrol has an extraordinary gift for the cinema. Trained as a pharmacist, he never went to a film school and never even worked as an assistant director. And yet his first film, which he made at the age of 27, testifies to a technical skill which puts to shame many a seasoned professional. The release of Le Beau Serge made a considerable impact in France. It was felt that the picture really marked the beginning of a new cinema; not only because of its style, but also because of the subject. For once rural France appears on the screen instead of the plush and glitter of Paris, as was usual in the contemporary cinéma de papa. For once an intellectual arrives in a village instead of a provincial in the capital. Surprisingly, even in his second picture Chabrol changed his bearings. Refined and stylized, his subsequent work tore to shreads the notion that the Nouvelle Vague was synonymous with socially-conscious cinema.

THE HIDDEN FORTRESS (Kakushi toride-no san-akunin) Akira Kurosawa

---

Script: Shinobu Hashimoto, Ryuzo Kikushima, Hideo Oguni and Kurosawa. Photography: Ichio Yamazaki. Music: Masaru Sato. Art Direction: Yoshiro Muraki and Kohei Ezaki. Cast: Toshiro Mifune (General Rokurota Makabe), Misa Uehara (Princess Yukihime), Minoru Chiaki (Tahei), Kamatari Fujiwara (Matakishi), Susumu Fujita (General Hyoe Tadokoro), Toshiko Higuchi (Girl), Eiko Miyoshi (Old lady-in-waiting), Takashi Shimura (General Izumi Nagakura), Kichijiro Ueda (Slaver), Koji Mitsui (Soldier).

Masumi Fujimoto--Akira Kurosawa for Toho, Japan. Originally 12,474 ft., 139 mins, reduced to 11,329 ft., 126 mins. Tohoscope.

After a run of several tragic and violent films Kurosawa takes

The Hidden Fortress

a freer breath. This does not necessarily mean that The Hidden Fortress is merely a "one hundred per cent entertainment picture, but not without suspense and humor" as the director himself described it. True, there is here plenty of suspense and humor, starting from the almost Eisensteinian beginning (the prisoners' mutiny), through the burlesque wheelings and dealings of two crafty peasants, to the heroic samurai adventure in the jidai-geki convention.

The Hidden Fortress is in many ways related to Kurosawa's earlier They Who Step on the Tiger's Tail. Sixteenth-century Japan, the period of civil wars. Princess Yukihime survives the defeat of Lord Akizuki, to whom she is heiress, and hides in a fortress guarded by one of her generals. They want to escape with a treasure of gold bars into a friendly province. Two oafish farmers whom the general has captured join the party. After many adventures involving coincidence, honor, cunning (the princess is disguised as a peasant girl), loyalty and sheer luck the destination is reached.

The Hidden Fortress is a rare example of a virtuoso use of wide screen (Tohoscope) technique. Encouraged by this successful debut in wide screen, Kurosawa will use it in all his future films. There are also in the film interesting experiments with sound and rhythm (which is connected with Kurosawa's continued employment of the elements of the noh theatre--note the scene of the duel with spears and the Princess's gestures) and a number of other experiments with the narrative. Is therefore The Hidden Fortress merely a series of variations in cinematic craft on the canvas of a colorful adventure story? Kurosawa is too inventive to be satisfied with that. He makes frequent moral reflections, studies of attitudes and custom; as he did in his two subsequent, related films of which one, Tsubaki Sanjuro (1961) fell into naiveté, but the other, Yojimbo, was a work of considerable class. The Hidden Fortress does not quite match that, perhaps because Kurosawa expended more effort on experiments with various elements of style and content than on harmonizing them together. Yet the values of the film are quite clear; to mention the editing, the ease with which the director varies the pace and is able to achieve an instant increase in tension. The main characters are described with unfailing expressiveness: the general is cunning, gallant and ruthless (he sacrifices his own sister for the sake of the Princess), the two peasants are ludicrous blundering cowards, while the Princess (a character untypical for Kurosawa) combines girlish charm with wisdom, dignity and will-power. The moral commentary on the price and sense of loyalty and sacrifice begins right in the film's title (in the original: "Three Bad Men in a Hidden Fortress") challenging the spectator to decide who is the third villain and why.

THE YOUNG LIONS Edward Dmytryk

Script: Edward Anhalt, from the novel by Irwin Shaw. Photography: Joseph MacDonald. Music: Hugo Friedhofer. Art Direction: Lyle R. Wheeler and Addison Hehr. Editing: Dorothy Spencer. Cast: Marlon Brando (Lt. Christian Diestl), Montgomery Clift (Noah Ackerman), Dean Martin (Michael Whiteacre), Hope Lange (Hope Plowman), Barbara Rush (Margaret Freemantle), Maximilian Schell (Capt. Hardenberg), May Britt (Gretchen Hardenberg), Dora Doll (Simone), Lee Van Cleef (Sgt. Rickett), Liliane Montevecchi (Françoise), Parley Baer (Brant), Arthur Franz (Lt. Green), Hal Taylor (Pvt. Burnecker), Richard Gardner (Pvt. Cowley), Herbert Rudley (Capt. Colclough), John Alderson (Corp. Kraus), Sam Gilman (Pvt. Faber), L. Q. Jones (Pvt. Donnelly), Julian Burton (Pvt. Brailsford), Robert Burton (Colonel Mead), Harvey Stephens (Gen. Rockland), Ashley Cowan (Maier), Gene Roth (Café manager).

Al Lichtman for 20th Century-Fox, U. S. A. 14,987 ft., 167 mins. CinemaScope.

Twentieth-century American literature traditionally dealt with war topics using the impressionistic style best exemplified in the novels of Hemingway, which considered not so much the sense of events as the emotions of individuals involved in them. Irwin Shaw's epic novel and Norman Mailer's "The Naked and the Dead," another bestseller, introduced a new approach to the war. Shaw looks at the war via the experiences of typical characters; he is not concerned with creating a social fresco, as John Dos Passos did, but with demonstrating the validity of a selected didactic point. He portrays the moral bankruptcy of Nazism and the triumph of a modest humanist, exemplified by the Noah character. Very complex structurally, the story is divided into two parallel narrative streams involving three main characters living on two continents who meet accidentally at the end: a Jew persecuted by fellow soldiers, a cynical entertainer whose fiancée shames him into going to war, and a Nazi who finds he can neither kill ruthlessly nor escape the consequences of being a German.

As the United States enters the war, Michael Whiteacre becomes friendly with Noah Ackerman, whom he met when they were both reporting for call-up. Noah marries a girl he has met through Michael. At the barracks, Noah is persecuted because he is a Jew; after he is savagely beaten in a series of fights, Michael reports the matter, but the sadistic captain gets rid of him by finding him a favorable posting. Noah deserts, is caught and imprisoned, but regains courage on hearing that his wife is expecting a baby. He chooses to rejoin his old unit where he is given a friendly welcome.

In Germany, Christian Diestl, an admirer of Hitler, has become a lieutenant in the Wehrmacht and is among the Germans marching on Paris. Shocked by the brutal methods used by the Gestapo, he obtains leave promising to deliver a shawl to the wife of his C.O., Captain Hardenberg, in Berlin. After a brief affair with her, Christian is posted to Rommel's Afrika Korps and finds he is unable to kill as ruthlessly as Hardenberg. During a retreat across the desert Hardenberg receives terrible facial burns and commits suicide in a hospital. Disgusted by Frau Hardenberg's indifference to the news, Christian returns to the front near the German frontier. Michael and Noah are also there; the war is almost over. Christian, by now a gaunt remnant of a lost cause, finds himself in a concentration camp, which makes him sick with shame. He smashes his gun in the surrounding forest and comes across Michael and Noah who have just looked at the horror of the camp. They shoot Christian dead.

It is interesting to consider the changes Dmytryk's film made to the story. One is the playing down of the Michael character, who is in the novel an archetypal disenchanted egghead, but here a little more than a background for Noah. Another is a complete shift of emphasis in dealing with the Christian character, who in the novel is made _more_ brutal by the war. In the novel he was a declared Nazi, here he is shown as a "good German" who comes to detest Nazi ideology while not actively opposing it--basically a victim of the war, who learns of the existence of concentration camps only at the end. A curious change of emphasis, if one considers that at the same time Dmytryk exposes racism within the U.S. Army. Still, Christian's story is the most interesting of the three, those of Noah and Michael being fairly conventional. Further, it is interesting how the makers of _The Young Lions_ try to adapt themselves to the current political thinking. Consider only Michael's line "I do not want to fight the people who in ten years' time will be our friends." It is hard to imagine a U.S. soldier saying this in 1944.

Together with _Paths of Glory_ and a few other films, _The Young Lions_ belongs to the most important works of the anti-heroic trend in the American cinema, which saw war as polarizing human attitudes, but also as a force which liberates the lowest instincts in people, reducing them to their lowest common denominator. _The Young Lions_ does make certain commercial concessions; the wartime situations are rather familiar and the moral attitudes somewhat mechanically juxtaposed. The consequence of the wide treatment of the topic is a lack of a central point of reference. Still, this is a competent and exciting picture: effectively photographed, with a fine musical score and good acting. Marlon Brando, taciturn and enigmatic, gives a particularly good performance. Of the several powerful sequences the most memorable is that of Hardenberg's unit ambushing and slaughtering a British patrol in the desert.

THE DEFIANT ONES Stanley Kramer

Script: Nedrick Young and Harold Jacob Smith. Photography: Sam Leavitt. Music: Ernest Gold. Song "Long Gone" by William C. Handy and Chris Smith. Art Direction: Fernando Carrere. Editing: Frederic Knudtson. Cast: Tony Curtis (John "Joker" Jackson), Sidney Poitier (Noah Cullen), Theodore Bikel (Sheriff Max Muller), Charles McGraw (Captain Frank Gibbons), Lon Chaney Jr. (Big Sam), Cara Williams (Woman), King Donovan (Solly), Claude Akins (Mac), Lawrence Dobkin (Editor), Kevin Coughlin (Woman's son), Whit Bissell (Lou Gans), Carl Switzer Angus), Boyd Morgan (Joe).

Stanely Kramer, U. S. A. 8673 ft., 96 mins.

During the 22-year period before taking the director's chair in 1955, Stanley Kramer tried his hand at most Hollywood jobs and finally became one of the most ambitious American producers. Champion, The Men, High Noon, Death of a Salesman, The Wild One, The Caine Mutiny--this impressive list clearly defines what Kramer's interests were. With the exception of the first two films, Kramer did not abandon these interests after becoming a director and continued making socially critical, sometimes outright crusading pictures about topical problems of America and the world at large.

While the results of these efforts were rather varied in quality, intolerance was always the main object of attack. So it is in The Defiant Ones, Kramer's first well-known picture as director, an exploration of the color problem set in the American South. Two prisoners, an aggressive white youth called Jackson and a proud Negro, Cullen, who have been shackled together by a "humorous" guard, escape when the truck carrying the chain-gang overturns. The two have a twelve-hour start on the sheriff and the posse sent after them. They may hate each other as much as they like, but until they cut the chain (which the film uses as a meaningful symbol) they are condemned to be together and every weakness of either damages the chances of escape for both. They dive into a clay pit, cross a river, break into a small-town store hoping to find food and a chisel, are nearly lynched by the crowd, but set free by a man whose wrists betray the scars of manacles. They are helped and unshackled by a farm-woman. Attracted to Jackson and planning to run away with him, she gives Cullen directions to the railway which, if followed, would mean his sure death in the swamp. Jackson runs after Cullen to warn him, but is wounded by the woman's son. As the posse approaches, they find Cullen waiting with the white man cradled in his arms.

The peculiar combination of opposing elements: sensational plot plus discursive contents, exterior scenery plus conclusions reached almost entirely via the dialogues, brought very interesting results. In The Defiant Ones reliable and tangible images are in complete union with a passionate, aggressive message. Yet the film has almost as many faults as it can claim merits. The faults have nothing to do with the staging, which is dramatically perfect, but come from the weakness in the starting premises. Even if one was to skim over the film's incompetent description of the realities of the South, one must complain about excessive emphasis on certain dialogue lines, the demagogy of the development of the plot, relying on coincidences regardless of whether they are credible or not, and rather forced emotionality. True, all this is done with consistency and supported by fine acting--but it is precisely this consistency which weakens the authenticity of the metamorphosis of the characters, which is crucial for the effectiveness of the film's argument. It is indeed typical of Kramer to start from a general assumption instead of from observation, and to transform intellectual structures into concrete events; this is responsible for the insufficient differentiation of the social background and situational artificiality which is not redeemed by the overall correctness of the message. Time amplified these characteristics: Kramer, a well-meaning liberal who believed in the brotherhood of man as the foundation of democracy, did not notice that the hands of people on the opposing sides in the racial conflict were clenching into fists. This was way back in 1958; what was then an ardent appeal for mutual understanding, remained after the passage of years only a noble, deeply humanist witness to American ideals and became part of the American myth. When the rapprochement of races began in reality--it happened in a different way and in a different situation.

ORDERS TO KILL Anthony Asquith

Script: Paul Dehn, from the story by Donald C. Downes, adapted by George St. George. Photography: Desmond Dickinson. Music: Benjamin Frankel. Art Direction: John Howell. Editing: Gordon Hales. Cast: Paul Massie (Gene Summers), Eddie Albert (Major MacMahon), Leslie French (Marcel Lafitte), Irene Worth (Léonie), James Robertson Justice (Naval commander), Lillian Gish (Mrs. Summers), John Crawford (Kimball), Anne Blake (Mme. Lafitte), Lillie Bea Gifford (Mauricette), Jacques Brunius (Commandant Morand), Lionel Jeffries (Interrogator), Sandra Dorne (Blonde), Nicholas Phipps (Lecturer lieutenant), Miki Iveria (Louise).

Anthony Asquith and Anthony Havelock-Allan for Lynx Films, G. B. 10,046 ft., 112 mins.

There were two thematic phases in the films concerned with the post-war stock-taking undertaken by the cinema in all the leading film-producing countries. In the first, attention was focused on the events in the army and on the front; the second, which came generally later and was earliest and fullest in the Soviet cinema, talks about people who did not wear a uniform but who were sometimes even more painfully experienced by the years of fear. In Orders to Kill Anthony Asquith, whose first notable pacifist drama, Tell England, was made way back in 1931, combined as it were these two tendencies in anti-war cinema.

The year 1944: Gene Summers, a U. S. airman who was born and brought up in France, is sent by the American Intelligence on a special mission in occupied Paris. There he is to liquidate Marcel Lafitte, an allied agent suspected of betraying the Free French to the Gestapo. Summers undergoes special commando training. But when the crucial moment comes he is almost completely convinced of Lafitte's innocence. He is coldly rebuked by Léonie, an experienced agent: the order to kill must not be disputed but carried out without delay. After the Liberation another U. S. Intelligence officer finds Gene in a hospital suffering from alcoholism. Gene discovers that the man he had killed was in fact innocent. This completes his ruin. Overcome by remorse and sense of guilt he becomes a delinquent and finishes as one of the war's tragic victims.

Asquith's entire effort is concentrated on the humanist and moral aspects of a debate on the effects of war on the individual. Thoughtful, mature direction eschews visual effects for the sake of the matter-of-fact narrative and psychological vividness. This is the reason why the Gene Summers character makes such a strong impression on the spectator. The story is firmly rooted in reality (note the scenes of the training of agents) which strengthens the film's conclusion. There are reservations however: even if one is to overlook the fact that the French Resistance would hardly approve of the practice of wheeling in a foreign specialist to liquidate a traitor, the motivation of the plot seems logically weak when seen in the hard light of wartime contingencies. It is simply that the need to eliminate real and suspected traitors was (with all the tragic nature of making such decisions) an indisputable wartime necessity. This was piercingly demonstrated in Melville's L'Armée des ombres. Also, the practice of making the prospective victim kind and gentle as a psychological basis for doubts whether he is in fact a traitor is questionable. After all, in a family circle Nazis themselves could be sentimental bourgeois pet-lovers. Finally, it seems highly unlikely that someone as indispensable in wartime as a bomber pilot would be sent on a mission like this. This last improbability must not be held too strongly against Asquith, especially since it gave rise to a very interesting moral point. The things criticized above were used to support Asquith's intellectual protest against war, a protest abstract in its total pacifism and naively appealing, in a manner similar to that in The Browning Version, to a subtle humanist. But the dramatic comparison of the two reactions of the same man who when a pilot indifferently causes the death of thousands of civilians in Hamburg or Le Havre, but when faced eye to eye with a single victim undergoes a traumatic shock, is in the final account the most important problem posed by the film. How far does moral hypocrisy relax the sense of responsibility for death dealt from afar to others in wartime? This problem retained its topicality for a long time after the making of the film.

LES COUSINS Claude Chabrol

Script: Chabrol. Dialogues: Paul Gégauff. Photography: Henri Decaë. Music: Paul Misraki, Wolfgang Amadeus Mozart and Richard Wagner. Art Direction: Jacques Saulnier and Bernard Evein. Editing: Jacques Gaillard. Cast: Gérard Blain (Charles), Jean-Claude Brialy (Paul), Juliette Mayniel (Florence), Claude Cerval (Clovis), Corrado Guarducchi (Italian count), Geneviève Cluny (Geneviève), Michèle Meritz (Vonvon), Guy Decomble (Bookseller), Stéphane Audran (Françoise), Françoise Vatel (Ernestine), Paul Bisciglia (Marc), Jean-Pierre Moulin, Jean-Louis Maury, Jeanne Perez, André Jocelyn.

AJYM-Films/Société Français du Cinéma pour la Jeunesse, France. 9718 ft., 108 mins.

Le Beau Serge, the brilliant debut of the 27-year-old Chabrol, attracted so much attention and gave him so much credit of confidence that Chabrol for the next five years moved along with the original impetus, towing along his Nouvelle Vague colleagues rather than personally capitalizing on his reputation. The quality of Chabrol's subsequent pictures is very uneven and they are not always sufficiently conceptually thought-out. But one cannot deny him film-making talent. The dilletante who had gone through no more than a self-education course in cinema theatres showing film classics moved on the set with assurance and skill greater than that of many seasoned professionals, exploded with ideas, made films in no time at all. He assembled around himself a fine collective of people, discussed things with them on an equal footing, put into practice the ideas of others, won people over with his easy manner and sense of humor. These things were so far lacking in the French cinema, and the need for them was clearly felt.

Les Cousins puts a seal on the success of Le Beau Serge. Set in the milieu of Paris students, it is thus close to the interests of the young people who mold fashions and aesthetic trends. Charles Thomas, a poor young man from the provinces, arrives in Paris to study at the University and to stay with his rich cousin. With a typically Nouvelle Vague flair for juggling with themes and styles Chabrol reversed the situations and personalities from Le Beau Serge: this time it is Gérard Blain who is sensitive, defensive and straightforward, and Jean-Claude Brialy--provocative and extravagant. Charles is appalled by Paul's parasitic style of life, his cynicism and preoccupation with organizing wild parties rather than work. Paul steals his girl and later unexplainably passes the university exams, while Charles fails. The polarization and later open conflict of the protagonists is among Chabrol's basic motifs; others are evil victorious in the struggle with good, the fluidity of equilibrium in interhuman contacts and the ill-fitting of appearances and reality, the idea which probably originated in Hitchcock's influence. In the finale of Les Cousins Chabrol in turn makes a bow towards Germaine Dulac, the avant-gardist of the 20's and her La Souriante Madame Beudet (1922): embittered and discouraged, Charles loads a gun and tries to shoot his diabolical cousin. The gun does not go off. The following morning Paul accidentally kills Charles while playing with the gun which he believed to be unloaded. How profound the shock of killing his cousin is going to be--Chabrol does not say. This is one reason why the message of Les Cousins appears ambiguous--is this film a pessimistic reflection on the degeneration of young middle-class mandarins, or does it suggest that a return to moral order is the inevitable reaction to an irresponsible transgression of the limits of libertinism? There seems to be more support for the latter eventuality: Chabrol is a good observer and a keen painter of detail but in his early films he also has evident ambitions as a social moralist. This follows from the treatment of the main characters, the rather unusual arrangement of situations and, for all their ambivalence, from the polarization of the attitudes. This would probably be unconvincing if, with all his youthful contempt for aristocratic hedonism, Chabrol was not so forthright in his intellectual views, if he did not make use of what may be termed as the magic of psychological pathology--and if he did not cement the loose, capricious structure of Les Cousins with his suggestive craft: lapidary albeit incisive, based on resolute editing of short glimpses by a fluently led camera.

THE LAST TRAIN FROM GUN HILL John Sturges

Script: James Poe, from the screen story "Showdown" by Les Crutchfield. Photography: Charles Lang Jr. Music: Dimitri Tiomkin. Art Direction: Hal Pereira and Walter Tyler. Editing: Warren Low. Cast: Kirk Douglas (Marshal Matt Morgan), Anthony Quinn (Craig Belden), Carolyn Jones (Linda), Earl Holliman (Rick Belden), Brian Hutton (Lee Smithers), Ziva Rodann (Catherine Morgan), Lars Henderson (Petey), Brad Dexter (Beero, Belden's foreman), Bing Russell (Skag), Val Avery (Bartender), Walter Sande (Sheriff Bartlett).

Hal B. Wallis/Bryna Productions, U. S. A. 8413 ft., 93 mins. VistaVision. Technicolor.

In The Last Train from Gun Hill Sturges and Poe demonstrate the isolation of the just man with no less force than did Zinnemann and Foreman in their celebrated High Noon. Of course, the situation is central for the mythology of the West, but Sturges is motivated not only by the rules and traditions of the genre. After all, it was he who in Bad Day at Black Rock (1954) transplanted western stereotypes into modern drama. The Last Train from Gun Hill places even more stress than did High Noon on the refusal of the population of a town to declare themselves on the side of the law.

The beautiful Cherokee Indian wife of Marshal Mat Morgan is raped and murdered by two young thugs while out riding. Her husband recognizes the handsome saddle left behind by the killers as belonging to Craig Belden, an old friend who has once saved Matt's life. Belden is now a cattle king and a virtual ruler of the town of Gun Hill. His son Rick was one of the killers. But family ties are more important to the imperious father than loyalty towards an old friend. When lies and persuasions ("you owe me a debt--I once saved your life") fail, the father resorts to force. The entire town aids him in one way or another, including the local sheriff who refuses to intervene saying: "All right, I'm a coward. But in forty years' time, when grass grows over us, nobody will remember either that or that you let yourself be killed like a fool." But Matt is determined to bring the criminal to justice. He captures Rick in a saloon and barricades himself with the prisoner in a hotel room. He has to wait six hours for the return train. A siege begins; Matt is surrounded by people whose actions are motivated by fear and by awareness of strength. A woman who loves Craig but feels sympathy for the Marshal brings Matt a shotgun.

Although, in accordance with the convention, Matt scores a moral victory thanks to some rather extraordinary situations (which are not among the strongest points of the script)--the value of The Last Train from Gun Hill rests in the analysis of the behavior of a community which joins forces against the law (a reference, it seems, to the McCarthy era), and not in the plot itself, or the (clear and energetic) narrative or the expressive roles of the four main actors. Sturges is fully aware of the structural conventionality of a western and knows very well why he himself cultivates this type of morality play ("Actually the West wasn't really as we show it at all. Everybody in the West was young, a man of 30 was an oddity, and most of them were foreigners--Swedes, French, and so on. We age the town, too. I'll never forget a reviewer who wrote that the town looked so new it was pathetic. But all western towns were brand new, some only six months old. Dodge City was put up in three months"). This is why it is not the film-making skill, although considerable, but the message that is most important in The Last Train from Gun Hill: the indictment of racialism, the debate on the meaning of responsibility, the warning before xenophobia, arrogance and abuse of power, before a tacit approval of the breaking of the law by others for the sake of one's own peaceful existence.

BRINK OF LIFE (Nära livet) [So Close to Life] Ingmar Bergman

Script: Ulla Isaksson, from her short story "Det vänliga, värdiga" (Of Friendship and Dignity) in her book "Dödens faster" (Register of Death). Photography: Max Wilén. Art Direction: Bibi Lindström. Editing: Carl-Olov Skeppstedt. Cast: Ingrid Thulin (Cecilia Ellius), Eva Dahlbeck (Stina Andersson), Bibi Andersson (Hjördis Pettersson), Barbro Hiort af Ornäs (Sister Brita), Max von Sydow (Harry Andersson), Erland Josephson (Anders Ellius), Anne-Marie Gyllenspetz (Social worker), Gunnar Sjöberg (Dr. Nordlander), Margareta Krook (Dr. Larsson), Inga Landgré (Greta Ellius), Lars Lind (Dr. Thylenius), Sissi Kaiser (Sister Marit), Monica Ekberg (Hjördis's friend), Gun Jönsson (Night nurse), Inga Gill (A mother).

Nordisk Tonefilm, Sweden. 7470 ft., 83 mins.

Three women in a ward of a maternity clinic: Cecilia's marriage is unhappy and she fears that motherhood will increase further the distance between her and her husband; Stina, who loves and is loved, is enraptured by the idea of a child as a longed-for fulfillment of happiness; while the 18-year-old Hjördis is expecting an illegitimate child and has attempted an abortion. One might say that the outcome of this tangle of three dramas is along traditional lines: Cecilia suffers a miscarriage in the third month of pregnancy, Stina's baby is born dead while Hjördis changes her mind and decides to have her child. Possibly such dramatic structure is the main reason why Brink of Life became, with the passage of time, treated very reluctantly by Bergman himself. Still, the defects of the film do not invalidate either its originality or its indisputable merits, such as excellent character description, narrative mastery, profound analysis of the influence of love on the psychology of a future mother. This latter element links Brink of Life with Bergman's much later films: it lacks metaphysics, so typical for his work of the 50's, to mention only The Seventh Seal, made the previous year. Instead, it has much to say about love as a superior influence (and, incidentally, as something much more important than the perfect state of social services in Sweden). Also the style is quite different than in other films of the period: Brink of Life is in tone not far from a report at times verging on naturalism, rich in detail and using mainly close shots. The film called for good acting, but then Bergman had Ingrid Thulin, Eva Dahlbeck and Bibi Andersson, members of his regular team. The three actresses give really magnificent psychological portrayals of three expectant mothers--and it is their roles which are in the final reckoning the greatest value of the film. All the more since with their spontaneity, the quiet frankness of their description of women who are not of exceptional intelligence or social status but still command the spectator's respect, they break through the somewhat cold climate of vivisection performed on very intimate human problems.

THE DIARY OF ANNE FRANK George Stevens

Script: Frances Goodrich and Albert Hackett, from their play, based on Anne Frank's Diary. Photography: William C. Mellor. Music: Alfred Newman. Art Direction: Lyle R. Wheeler and George W. Davis. Editing: David Bretherton, Robert Swink and and William Mace. Cast: Millie Perkins (Anne Frank), Joseph Schildkraut (Otto Frank), Richard Beymer (Peter Van Daan), Shelley Winters (Mrs. Van Daan), Gusti Huber (Mrs. Frank), Lou Jacobi (Mr. Van Daan), Diane Baker (Margot Frank), Douglas Spencer (Kraler), Ed Wynn (Mr. Dussel), Dody Heath (Miep).

George Stevens for 20th Century-Fox, U.S.A. 15,361 ft., 171 mins. CinemaScope.

A painstaking screen version of one of the most famous documents of the Nazi era--the diary of a 13-year-old Jewish girl from occupied Holland. Anne Frank, her parents and five other people, all Jews, were for over two years hiding from the Nazis in an attic of an Amsterdam warehouse. Food was brought to them by their industrialist protector and his secretary. They were arrested in August 1944, just before the liberation of Holland and taken to a concentration camp. After the war Otto Frank, the only survivor, returned to the warehouse and in a bundle of papers found his daughter's diary. One passage in it reads: "In spite of everything, I still believe that people are really good at heart...."

The principle of fidelity to the literary original which Stevens adopted carried with it limitations which were in this case very difficult to overcome. The story relies entirely on the limited number of events and the drama hinges on the mood of hope and fearful expectation, on tensions between people condemned to be with each other; the events took place in three small rooms; objective assessment of situations and artistic generalizations had to be abandoned when dealing with a subjective account of a young girl--which in turn had to bring about exaggeration of everyday conflicts and a tone of exaltation, especially in view of the sentimental picture of Anne Frank in the minds of most people. Stevens did not deny being emotionally involved in the theme, but on the other hand was confident that the method of screen adaptation which absolutely respects the mood and the details of the original was bound to bring the desired result. On the whole he was right; perhaps there is too much symbolism in the film, perhaps the young Millie Perkins could not always cope with such an exceedingly difficult part, perhaps the rhythm is somewhat too heavy (a common occurrence, incidentally, in Stevens's cinema)--but if one is to bear in mind all the a priori limitations and the very specific point of view of The Diary of Anne Frank, one must give the picture justice not so much even as a penetrating protest against the inhumanity of man to man, but as a document of a state of mind of a real young girl in real historical circumstances. It is precisely the ease with which the film is understood, the shock at its combination of the ordinariness of life in the attic with the monstrosity of what was going on outside that made so many Americans realize what Nazism really meant.

MON ONCLE Jacques Tati

Script: Tati; also Jacques Legrange and Jean L'Hote. Photography: Jean Bourgoin. Music: Alain Romans and Frank Barcellini. Art Direction: Henri Schmitt and Pierre Etaix. Editing: Suzanne Baron. Cast: Jacques Tati (Monsieur Hulot), Jean-Pierre Zola (M. Arpel), Adrienne Servantie (Mme. Arpel), Alain Bécourt (Gérard Arpel), Lucien Frégis (Richard), Dominique Marie (Neighbor), Betty Schneider (Concierge's daughter), J.-F. Martial (Walter), André Dino (Sweep), Yvonne Arnaud (Georgette), Claude Badolle (Rag picker), Nicolas Bataille (Worker), Régis Fontenay (Suspenders seller), Adélaide Danielli (Mme. Pichard), Denise Péronne (Mlle. Février), Michel Goyot (Car seller), Dominique Derly (Arpel's secretary).

Louis Dolivet for Specta-Films/Gray-Film/Alter-Film/Film del Centauro, France/Italy. 10,440 ft., 116 mins. Eastman Colour.

Mon oncle is the continuation of the adventures of Monsieur Hulot; this time not in a specific situation of a man on a seaside vacation as in *Mr. Hulot's Holiday* but amid everyday urban life. One does not say "ordinary life" because Tati perceives very extraordinary things in the modern urban landscape. *Mr. Hulot's Holiday* ridiculed the bourgeois by placing them side by side with the maladjusted protagonist; *Mon oncle* continues and intensifies this caricature by throwing the worthy and old-fashioned Monsieur Hulot into the nightmarish household of crazy snobs of modern inventions.

Monsieur Arpel, a plastics manufacturer, lives with his wife and little son Gérard in a pretentious, gadget-filled, fully automated, ultra-modern house. The little boy feels oppressed by these impersonal surroundings and very much enjoys visiting his uncle Hulot in his old house in an ordinary back street. The Arpels, displeased about little Gérard's admiration for his uncle, find Hulot a job, then a wife, and finally take him into their business. All these attempts finish, how else, with disaster. The film ends with Hulot's departure to a post as Arpel's representative abroad.

The inhabitants of the old quarter are treated with warmth and sympathy; so are the children who dislike automated life, and so are dogs. The contrast of scenery has a parallel on the soundtrack: the gentle tones associated with the homely and lively back street collide with the deformed sounds of the electro-mechanical circus of the Arpels. This amounts to a successful continuation of Tati's ingenious satirical treatment of the stereotypes of sound cinema in Mr. Hulot's Holiday--but formal originality of Mon oncle is limited to the soundtrack. The camera is static and the takes monotonous. The mood is created almost entirely by the light-hearted and sentimental Monsieur Hulot and his friends--while other characters are subjected to ridicule which is wonderfully inventive but too cold and clinical. Or is it only the film's characters that are such? Apart from the pseudo-functional house there is the automated factory of plastic tubes, which is of course as ideal a target for satire as was the memorable assembly line in Chaplin's Modern Times. On the other hand, it gives rise to doubts as to what is more important in this parody: to ridicule the dull bourgeois who feels compelled to continue the ritual of impressing his neighbors while being too stupid to draw real benefit from the blessings of modern technology--or to protest against the mechanization of man's environment. These doubts are entirely the fault of Tati who sets the targets so that he can hit them at will, and produces laughter which is often facile. To put it shortly, Tati's treatment of modern technology in Mon oncle reminds one of some people's laughter at Picasso and modern art. The fact that Tati partly identifies himself with the protagonist adds a further ambiguity--for it is precisely Hulot who causes the breakdown of those gadgets which have logic and potential use in them (the rest are simply badly designed and do not work anyway). It is only Tati's subsequent explanations and his later films, Playtime (1967) and Trafic (1970) which made it clear that he did not attack modern inventions as such, but the people who let themselves become captives of the world of gadgetry, fashion, uniform behavior and who let themselves be involved in the absurd spiral of progress for its own sake. The trouble is that the two subsequent films mentioned above are not very good. Tati is quite clearly a gagman with an episodic imagination; Mon oncle, like his previous films, is a mosaic of rather loosely connected comical scenes--while Playtime (1967) where the director clearly tried to give the plot fluency and continuity, got lost in the monotonous slow narrative and the antiseptic, clinical quality of the film-making.

LES AMANTS Louis Malle

Script: Malle, freely adapted from the story "Point de Lendemain" by Dominique-Vivant Denon (1777). Dialogues: Louise de Vilmorin. Photography: Henri Decaë. Music: Johannes Brahms, fragments of the first and second movement from the Sextet No. 1 for strings, op. 18. Art Direction: Bernard Evein and Jacques Saulnier. Costumes: Renée Pellemoine. Editing: Léonide Azar. Cast: Jeanne Moreau (Jeanne Tournier), Jean-Mare Bory (Bernard Dubois-Lambert), Alain Cuny (Henri Tournier), José Louis de Villalonga (Raoul Florès), Judith Magre (Maggy Thiébaut-Leroy), Gaston Modot (Coudray, a manservant), Michèle Girardon (Hélène, Henri Tournier's secretary), Claude Mansart (Marcelot), Georgette Lobbe (Marthe), Patricia Garcin (Catherine), L. Hamon (Chantal).

Nouvelles Editions de Films, France. 7974 ft., 89 mins. Dyali-Scope.

Les Amants, Malle's second feature after Lift to the Scaffold, is a story of an awakening to love of a woman of thirty. Jeanne has been married for eight years to Henri Tournier, a rich newspaper proprietor. A busy man, he does not give her the attention she needs. They live near Dijon, and Jeanne's only distraction is a weekly visit to her friend Maggy in Paris. There she has acquired a lover, Raoul, a well-bred athletic bachelor. But Jeanne is as bored with him as she is with her husband. One day she tells Henri to invite her friends to stay with them in Dijon. She arranges for Raoul to pose as Maggy's lover. As she returns home from Paris, her car breaks down and a young archeologist passing by offers her a lift in his modest car. Henri politely invites Bernard to join their party and to stay the night. During the dinner Jeanne and Bernard discover mutual attraction. Late in the evening, when everyone has gone to bed, they meet accidentally in the garden and wander in the moonlight towards the river nearby. They realize that they are in love and spend a night of passion in Jeanne's bedroom. Life as she knew it is at an end for Jeanne: in the morning the lovers drive off to a new life in Bernard's car.

It seems amazing today that not only Le Beau Serge and Les Quatre cents coups, but even Les Amants once gave rise to hopes for a renaissance of socially-conscious cinema in France. Such hopes soon turned out to be a complete misunderstanding. While it is true that in Les Amants Malle criticizes the French upper classes, this is a libertine criticism, entirely on the level of social behavior: the young generation of the bourgeoisie is looking coldly at the older generation, with its evasions, lies and absurd house party conversations. On the other hand, stylistically Les Amants is a typical Nouvelle Vague picture with everything this description entails. It makes a distinct, if still a little clumsy, attempt at using an "open" dramatic structure; it has the inimitable poetic mood and the characterization of the protagonists--and the very symptomatic literary leanings of the script which make the film approach at moments a women's magazine love story. Consider for instance the commentary read on the soundtrack: "Jeanne this.... Jeanne that.... Love can be born at any moment.... She felt that the fetters of shame and convention were falling off her...." The outcome of Les Amants being so typical of the Nouvelle Vague cinema was that the picture was very overrated on its release (and won the Silver Lion at the 1958 Venice Film Festival). This is not to say that it is not interesting and emotionally very true. Malle said he wanted Les Amants to invoke the analytical French novel, particularly the writings of Flaubert with their splendid psychological portrayals of women. This he certainly achieved: Les Amants returns to the moods and attitudes of not only Flaubert, but also Stendhal, Pierre Choderlos de Laclos and the Marquis de Sade. It is all the more remarkable that this new anti-morality is advocated by a director of 26.

Quite apart from that the film functions well as a story of Tristan and Isolde in which passion is the only reality--with a fine extended love scene and the mood evoked through Decaë's sensual, impressionistic photography of the misty landscape and the beautiful music by Brahms. These aspects of Les Amants which were received at the time as boldly radical (particularly the film's eroticism, as explicit as never before in the cinema; the heroine's defiance of the moral imperatives in force within her social class, her abandonment of her husband, child and lover in favor of sensual experience and an uncertain future) were in fact an attack against the traditional, saucy-cum-frivolous treatment of marital infidelity by the boulevard comedy. This is epitomized in the triangle Jeanne-Henri-Raoul. Jeanne Moreau gives a very fine performance as the heroine and Malle was right to say that she is at her best in bed. Alain Cuny is also good as her betrayed husband.

SLEEPING BEAUTY Clyde Geronimi

Sequence Directors: Eric Larson, Wolfgang Reitherman and Les Clark. Script: Erdman Penner, from the fairy tale "La Belle au bois dormant" in the collection "Histoires ou Contes du temps passé" (alternative title: "Contes de ma mère l'Oye") by Charles Perrault (1697). Additional Story: Joe Rinaldi, Bill Peet, Winston Hibler, Ted Sears, Ralph Wright and Milt Banta. Designs and Animation: Milt Kahl, Franklin Thomas, Marc Davis, Oliver Johnston Jr. and John Lounsbery (Directing animators); Donald Da Gradi and Ken Anderson (Production design); Frank Armitage, Thelma Witmer, Albert Dempster, Walt Peregoy, Bill Layne, Ralph Hulett, Dick Anthony, Fil Mottola, Richard H. Thomas and Anthony Rizzo (Backgrounds); McLaren Stewart, Tom Codrick, Don Griffith, Erni Nordli, Basil Davidovich, Victor Haboush, Joe Hale, Homer Jonas, Jack Huber and Ray Aragon (Layout); Eyvind Earle (Color styling); Tom Oreb (Character styling); Hal King, Hal Ambro, Don Lusk, Blaine Gibson, John Sibley, Bob Carson, Ken Hultgren, Harvey Toombs, Fred Kopietz, George Nicholas, Bob Youngquist, Eric Cleworth, Henry Tanous, John Kennedy and Ken O'Brien (Character animation); Dan MacManus, Joshua Meador, Jack Boyd and Jack Buckley (Effects animation). Special Processes: Ub Iwerks. Music: George Bruns, adapted from the ballet suite "Spyushchaya krasavitsa" (Sleeping Beauty) by Pyotr Tchaikovsky. Songs: "Once Upon a Dream" by Sammy Fain and Jack Lawrence; "Hail the Princess Aurora" and "The Sleeping Beauty Song" by Tom Adair and George Bruns; "I Wonder" by Winston Hibler, Ted Sears and George Bruns; "The Skump Song" by Tom Adair, Erdman Penner and George Bruns. Voices: Mary Costa (Princess Aurora), Bill Shirley (Prince Phillip),

Eleanor Audley (Maleficent), Verna Felton (Flora), Barbara Jo Allen (Fauna), Barbara Luddy (Merryweather), Taylor Holmes (King Stefan), Bill Thompson (King Hubert), Candy Candido (Goons).

Walt Disney Productions, U. S. A. 6750 ft., 75 mins. Technirama 70. Technicolor.

Disney makes further technical progress in animated cinema: having used a wide screen technique in Lady and the Tramp he now introduces further innovations, in the first place stereophonic sound. Sleeping Beauty, which took six years and cost six million dollars to make, is a real animated superproduction. Thus probably the abandonment of the jaunty humor of Lady and the Tramp; the tone is now more serious and even contains a touch of horror, something Disney seemed to steer clear of since the 30's. This probably has to do with Disney's new plans of making a picture whose visual aspect would be more than merely subservient to the story line. Accordingly he further develops his designs, bases the background on medieval illuminations and chooses a rather more ambitious story than in his earlier productions. Unlike Fantasia, a film not necessarily made for children, and unlike most Disney films, the images in Sleeping Beauty are an independent and dominant element, while earlier they were subordinate to music or were simply the visual accompaniment of music. Sleeping Beauty is without a doubt a step forward in the development of animated feature cinema, but Disney was to abandon eventually this way of ennobling his productions. His future undertakings used a less realistic graphical style and were simply screen versions of stories for young children.

TOUCH OF EVIL Orson Welles

Script: Welles, freely adapted from the novel "Badge of Evil" by Whit Masterson. Photography: Russell Metty. Music: Henry Mancini. Art Direction: Alexander Golitzen and Robert Clatworthy. Editing: Virgil W. Vogel and Aaron Stell. Cast: Orson Welles (Hank Quinlan), Charlton Heston (Ramon Miguel "Mike" Vargas), Janet Leigh (Susan Vargas), Akim Tamiroff ("Uncle" Joe Grandi), Joseph Calleia (Pete Menzies), Ray Collins (District Attorney Adair), Valentin De Vargas (Pancho), Joanna Moore (Marcia Linnekar), Dennis Weaver (Motel Clerk), Mort Mills (Schwartz), Marlene Dietrich (Tanya), Victor Millan (Manolo Sanchez), Lalo Rios (Risto), Michael Sargent (Pretty Boy), Mercedes McCambridge (Gang leader), Joseph Cotten (Detective), Zsa Zsa Gabor (Owner of strip joint), Phil Harvey (Blaine), Harry Shannon (Gould).

Albert Zugsmith for Universal-International, U. S. A. 8388 ft., 93 mins.

After Mr. Arkadin (1955), probably his least satisfactory work, Welles was given the task, although largely through a misunderstanding, of directing his first Hollywood picture in almost ten years. Shot in Venice, a suburb of Los Angeles, Touch of Evil is a fascinating study of the limits and the abuses of power, of the conflict between morality and justice, a demonstration of the price which has to be paid for power, irrespective of whether one's ends and one's motivation are justifiable or not.

Already the film's prologue is striking: the camera shows, in a close-up, a time-bomb being planted in a car, then swings into an unbroken traveling shot to follow the car through the dilapidated streets of Los Robles, a town on the Mexican-American border, and then across the border itself. On the soundtrack we hear the ticking of the timing mechanism. The car finally explodes, after the whole credit sequence has been shown and at the precise moment in which Welles's name appears on the screen.

Vargas, a narcotics investigator for the Mexican government, is on his honeymoon when a bomb planted in the car belonging to the boss of Los Robles explodes on the American side of the frontier. The oversize Hank Quinlan, a police captain in charge of the case is ordered to cooperate with Vargas, but is reluctant to comply. Vargas later catches him planting dynamite on Sanchez, a man engaged to the victim's daughter, and realizes that Quinlan's extraordinary "intuition" really consisted of framing his victims. Quinlan becomes involved in the kidnapping of Vargas's wife, who is drugged and left in a room with fabricated evidence of a narcotics orgy; he then strangles Grandi, an underworld boss, and calls in the police. Mrs. Vargas is accused of murder. But Vargas manages to convince Quinlan's assistant, Menzies, that his boss is corrupt, and Menzies provokes Quinlan's confession, which Vargas tapes. Quinlan shoots Menzies and is himself killed. But then the news comes through that Sanchez has confessed--it was he who planted the bomb after all. Quinlan's intuition was right; he was "a great detective but a lousy cop."

Touch of Evil is a film of the extremes--and, typically for Welles, attracted extreme adjectives. Its formal aspect has been called luxuriant, opulent, extravagant, nightmarish, ominous, baroque. The remarkable night-time photography makes use of wild, heavy shadows, tilted angles and sharp movements of the camera. The frame is almost always very dark. Almost the entire film was shot through a short-focus 18. 5 mm lens which gives great focal depth of image (as in Citizen Kane and The Magnificent Ambersons) but which also purposely deforms the perspective. The effect resembles Lang's Expressionism--it seems something straight from his films about Dr. Mabuse. Optical deformation is the visual key to the Quinlan character; it is never used on others.

Welles plays a man who became obsessed with the idea of the inefficiency of the law after his wife was murdered and the culprit got off--and who took to planting evidence on suspects. Gross, seedy, rheumy-eyed, tragic yet terribly true--this is a fascinating, almost Shakespearean performance. Quinlan is a man who soils everything around him, and Welles almost always shows him on the screen in association with dirt: in dirty streets, wallowing in his death-throes in oil in a disused canal.

Welles: "In the Quinlan character I contained everything I hate. He is the sum of my idiosyncrasies. I loathe excesses of the police." But in fact Quinlan is more complex than that. Take the theme of the psychological duel between him and Vargas. We have here an alternative between a policeman who is sincere and incorruptible (if self-righteous) and a bad policeman, a contrast between an open man and a racist who hates Mexicans. Further, the concept of taking liberties with the law for justifiable means ("the Raskolnikov motif") is very interestingly treated in Touch of Evil. The point is that Welles does not load the issue by making the man on whom Quinlan planted incriminating evidence innocent: it is most significant that Sanchez was in fact guilty of the crime. But other characters in the film are hardly better than Quinlan and Sanchez: thus in Welles's treatment Los Robles became a vortex of corruption, a visionary town devoured by wickedness.

The theme of man's deception has a narrative accompaniment in a consciously winding development of the story, with three separate sub-plots handled in parallel. The episodes flash past in fast succession and only in the last two reels do they coalesce to leave the viewer with the impression of a suspenseful, fascinating story. Cinema was to get accustomed to this narrative style only much later. On its release Touch of Evil was ignored by American critics, thus finally ruining Welles's chances for a Hollywood comeback. But it has always been highly valued in continental Europe.

Welles left the production before the final cutting. However, his complaints about "the wholesale re-editing of the film by the executive producers" and the "several scenes which I did not write and was not intended to direct" cannot be treated seriously. The additional scenes, credited to Harry Keller, apparently took less than half a day to shoot, and it seems that the final result is very close to what Welles originally intended.

THE FACE (Ansiktet) Ingmar Bergman

Script: Bergman. Photography: Gunnar Fischer. Music: Erik Nordgren. Art Direction: P.-A. Lundgren. Costumes: Manne Lindholm and Greta Johansson. Editing: Oscar Rosander. Cast: Max von Sydow (Albert Emanuel Vogler), Ingrid Thulin (Manda Vogler), Gunnar Björnstrand (Dr. Vergérus), Naima Wifstrand (Vogler's grandmother), Åke Fridell (Tubal), Lars Ekborg (Simson), Toivo Pawlo (Chief Constable Starbeck), Erland Josephson (Consul Egerman), Gertrud Fridh (Ottilia Egerman), Bibi Andersson (Sara Lindqvist), Sif Ruud (Sofia Garp, Egerman's housekeeper), Ulla Sjöblom (Henrietta Starbeck), Oscar Ljung (Antonsson), Axel Düberg (Rustan), Birgitta Pettersson (Sanna).

Allan Ekelund for Svensk Filmindustri, Sweden. 101 mins.

Sweden in 1846. The era of "rationalist" science is at its height. But many people are aware that authoritarian science is not capable of explaining everything, and feel that it attempts to restrain human imagination. Magnetism, mesmerism and other psychic theories are spreading rapidly, trying to reclaim at least part of the human psyche which science has taken over.

Dr. Vogler, an itinerant mesmerist and hypnotist, travels from town to town with a troupe including a grandmother-witch, a mysterious boy assistant (who is in fact his wife in disguise) and a sly impresario. While traveling to Stockholm they are stopped at a customs post in a provincial town and brought before an investigating committee of local officials--the Consul, the Chief of Police and a Medical Officer named Vergérus. The committee are almost certain that Vogler is a charlatan, and although he pretends to be dumb subject him to a harsh investigation. The party are forced to stay overnight at the Consul's house. The next morning Vogler is ordered to give a performance during which the officials expose some of his tricks. But Vergérus, although a dry skeptic, is disturbed and fascinated by Vogler's personality. Vogler revenges himself for the humiliation by frightening Vergérus almost to death after an autopsy in the attic. The troupe are about to face further inquiry--when a message arrives from the King summoning Vogler to present his turns at the palace. The magician and his troupe ride away in triumph.

It is striking how reminiscent The Face with its mixture of genuineness and hoax, of real human concern and lucrative tricks, is of the history of the study of psychic phenomena. Such is Vogler with his face of a suffering Christ--outwardly composed, mysterious and dignified, but anxious and insecure underneath. The film offers a comment on the conflict between the world of rationalism and the world of the occult, or more precisely between their adherents. By escaping from fear of existence into metaphysics, Vogler attempts to compensate his complexes; while Vergérus, treated with very little sympathy, epitomizes the superficiality and blind indifference of those who, afraid of the unknown, tenaciously persevere in the "certainty" of their minds. Thus, unlike in his finest works of the 50's, Bergman probes here human personality rather than the sense of existence: The Face anticipates in a way the period in his work which followed The Silence.

The style is suited to the theme, and The Face is a mixture of comedy, suspense story and horror richly laced with symbols.

A witch searching for herbs, a half-way house, a woman disguised as a man, corpses rising, a dumb man speaking, the macabre masquerade in the attic--things treated by Bergman perhaps not completely seriously, but always with wit. Some interludes in the narrative are indeed Shakespearean--vehement and coarsely humorous. The photography is excellent right from the opening, as Vogler's troupe are traveling through the forest. When the magician says "Haven't I done everything to give you a sensation" this feels like a wry comment on the film director's art. Bergman certainly has done everything in that province. But this does not excuse, and perhaps contributes to, the main fault of The Face--its excessive, irritating theatricality.

THE BIG COUNTRY William Wyler

Script: James R. Webb, Sy Bartlett and Robert Wilder, from a Saturday Evening Post serial "Ambush at Blanco Canyon" (later published in book form as "The Big Country") by Donald Hamilton, adapted by Jessamyn West and Robert Wyler. Photography: Franz F. Planer. Music: Jerome Moross. Art Direction: Frank Hotaling. Costumes: Emile Santiago and Yvonne Wood. Editing: Robert Swink, Robert Belcher and John Faure. Cast: Gregory Peck (James McKay), Jean Simmons (Julie Maragon), Carroll Baker (Patricia Terrill), Charlton Heston (Steve Leech), Burl Ives (Rufus Hannassey), Charles Bickford (Major Henry Terrill), Alfonso Bedoya (Ramon), Chuck Connors (Buck Hannassey), Jim Burk (Cracker), Dorothy Adams (Hannassey woman), Buff Brady (Dude Hannassey).

William Wyler--Gregory Peck--Robert Wyler for Anthony-Worldwide Productions, U. S. A. 14,978 ft., 166 mins. Technirama. Technicolor.

Is The Big Country a polemic with the West's myth of force? This seems to be suggested by the story, in which a Baltimore dandy who does not carry a gun is seen to bring law and order to a town where so far guns took care of all problems. But nobody can ignore the hard laws of the West, and although the newcomer may have little idea about horse-riding, he must acquire authority by another kind of physical skill. It is only then that he can be accepted as mediator by the warring clans, and can begin to rely on his cunning instead of on his gun. There will have to be a shoot-out, to be sure, but only between people whose posturing conceals stupidity, selfishness and cowardice. Such people must lose everywhere so they lose in the West to give way to the more intelligent.

The final conclusion is thus the same as in one of the classical varieties of western: the new generation of responsible settlers replaces the socially undisciplined cattle-breeders. In the 50's the American cinema still awaited the arrival of the protagonist who loses and thus defies the dogma of success. For the time being therefore a spokesman for peace must base his courage on the awareness of strength: Russell Rouse expressed this thought well in The Fastest Gun Alive (1956), a film which does not otherwise go beyond correctness. What is it then in The Big Country that departs radically from the traditional? Only the message that in the West also real strength is strength supported by wisdom--but this truth, derived from the classical Jewish maxims, is in the end nothing extraordinary. The Big Country offers a few moments of reflection jotted down on the margin of the epic spectacular which well conveys the feel of vast lands and their beauty. This time Wyler did not make the error of heaviness of his previous film, Friendly Persuasion (1956) and included in the expansive narrative rhythm a number of dynamic, well-staged scenes. He made good use of irony, well directed the actors and supplemented the images with an attractive musical motif. In fact The Big Country is faultless within its self-imposed limits. It evokes the past of these lands but in a much more sophisticated way than the older westerns--thanks to the skillful and witty observation of detail and the purposeful use of color and the wide screen.

ASSAULT IN BROAD DAYLIGHT (Es geschah am hellichten Tage)
Ladislao Vajda

Script: Friedrich Dürrenmatt, Hans Jacoby and Vajda, based on the novel "Das Versprechen" (The Pledge) by Dürrenmatt (1958). Photography: Heinrich Gaertner. Music: Bruno Canfone. Art Direction: Max Röthlisberger. Editing: Hermann Haller. Cast: Heinz Rühmann (Lieutenant Matthäi), Gert Froebe (Mr. Schrott), Michel Simon (Mr. Jacquier), Robert Liesey (Professor Manz), Anita von Ow (Annemarie), Berta Drews (Mrs. Schrott), Maria Rosa Salgado (Mrs. Heller), Albert Lieven (Police Commissioner), Evald Balser (Doctor), Emil Hegetschweiler (Mayor), Hans Gaugler (Mr. Moser), Margit Winter (Mrs. Moser), Siegried Lowitz (Lieutenant Henzi), Sigfrit Steiner (Detective Feller), René Magron (Officer Weber), Annelise Setschart (Schoolteacher), Max Werner Lenz (Schoolmaster), Ettore Cella (Garage owner).

Lazar Wechsler for Praesens-Film CCC, Switzerland/West Germany. 9130 ft., 101 mins.

Fear grips the Swiss countryside near Berne after an elusive psychopath murders several local children with a razor. When a nine-year-old girl is murdered in a forest the police arrest the man who found the body--an itinerant pedlar with a rather complicated past. He first denies the charge, but placed under duress confesses to the crime and then commits suicide. The police close the file on the case. But Inspector Matthäi does not believe in his guilt and is convinced that the real murderer will strike again. Since nobody shares his conviction, Matthäi decides to solve the case alone. His only clue is a child's drawing found at the site of the crime showing a man, a black car and a mysterious worm. The Inspector concludes, with a psychiatrist's assistance, that the murderer probably lives in the Canton of Grisons (having identified the worm as the unicorn in the canton's coat of arms), travels to eastern Switzerland and sets a risky trap using a little girl as a bait for the criminal. His reasoning was right: the killer falls into the trap and is arrested just as he is about to kill the child.

In Dürrenmatt's novel this very interesting crime story is psychologically much more complex than in the film which focuses on the fascinating process of disentangling a mystery and on situational tension. But the film is none the worse for that; it is in fact among the better works of the genre in the late 50's. Vajda contributed comparatively little to what was in the script: skillful filmmaking, a choice of suggestive scenery of rain-soaked Swiss villages, the ability to make good use of the actors, of whom Heinz Rühmann, the memorable Captain from Köpenick, gives a particularly sensitive performance. But the most remarkable thing in Assault in Broad Daylight is Vajda's firm departure from the half-serious stereotype of a detective novel puzzle; instead, he gives attention to the details of a crime investigation and the gruesome realities of police work.

ME AND THE COLONEL Peter Glenville

Script: S. N. Behrman and George Froeschel, from the play "Jakobowsky und der Oberst. Komödie einer Tragikomödie" by Franz Werfel. Photography: Burnett Guffey. Music: George Duning. Art Direction: George Wakevich and Walter Holscher. Editing: William A. Lyon and Charles Nelson. Cast: Danny Kaye (S. L. Jacobowsky), Curd Jürgens (Colonel Prokoszny), Nicole Maurey (Suzanne Roualet), Françoise Rosay (Mme. Bouffier), Akim Tamiroff (Szabuniewicz), Martita Hunt (Mother Superior), Alexander Scourby (Major von Bergen), Liliane Montevecchi (Cosette), Ludwig Stossel (Dr. Szicki), Gerard Buhr (German captain), Franz Roehn (M. Girardin), Celia Lovsky (Mme. Arle), Clement Harari (Gestapo man), Alain Bouvette (Rothschild's chauffeur), Albert Godderis (M. Gravat), Karen Lenay (Denise), Eugène Bordet (Pierre Michel), Maurice Marsac (French lieutenant).

William Goetz/Court Enterprises, U. S. A. 9865 ft., 110 mins.

The deserved success of Werfel's stage play about the adventures of a mild-mannered Jewish tailor and an arrogant Polish colonel who escape together from the Nazi forces advancing into France in 1940 probably had to be followed, sooner or later, by a screen version. At the same time, one would expect the film to be far inferior to the stage original with its verbal finesse, sophisticated humor and philosophical undertones. Not so: Glenville abandoned psychological nuances consistently replacing them by situational (which is not to say primitive) humor, threw in vigorous execution and very good casting of the actors. A surprise here was Curd Jürgens, seemingly an actor of monotonously cheerless emploi (compare An Eye for an Eye) who in Me and the Colonel is often splendidly funny--although there are also moments when he merely clowns. His Colonel Prokoszny, a character expertly equipped by Werfel with a Sarmatian mixture of swaggering, irresponsibility, gallantry and drunkenness--is a fine satirical take-off of a pre-war Polish officer. Similarly, Danny Kaye gives a splendid cheerful parody of a crafty Jew from Horodenka. Still, the principal aim of both the play and the film was not to ridicule a Polish swaggerer and his industrious companion (who from his mother took the belief in the principle that "there are always two possibilities") but to offer a reflection about human fellowship in the face of danger. Me and the Colonel, "a comedy of a certain tragedy" as the subtitle of the literary original has it, treats its protagonists with great warmth and sympathy. It is only the spectre of Nazism which is dismal and alien--and all people of good will have to combine their forces against it, even people who are as different from each other as fire and water, as S. L. Jacobowsky and Colonel Prokoszny.

THE GODDESS John Cromwell

Script: Paddy Chayefsky. Photography: Arthur J. Ornitz. Music: Virgil Thompson. Art Direction: Edward Haworth. Editing: Carl Lerner. Cast: Kim Stanley (Emily Ann Faulkner), Lloyd Bridges (Dutch Seymour), Steve Hill (John Tower), Betty Lou Holland (Emily Ann's mother), Elizabeth Wilson (Secretary), Patty Duke (Emily Ann, age 8), Joan Copeland (Aunt), Gerald Hiken (Uncle), Burt Brinckerhoff (Boy), Bert Freed (Lester Brackman), Donald McKee (R. M. Lucas), Werner Klemperer (Mr. Woolsy), Margaret Brayton (Mrs. Woolsy), Gerald Petrarca (The Minister), Joan Linville (Joanna).

Milton Perlman for Columbia, U. S. A. 9445 ft., 105 mins.

Before embarking on a Hollywood career in the early days of the sound cinema, John Cromwell had for many years been working in the theatre as an actor and director. This is probably the reason why in his work for the cinema he specialized in using renowned actors in unobtrusive and firmly outlined psychological dramas. Cromwell's greatest success came towards the close of his career in films. The Goddess was scripted by Paddy Chayefsky, a man with whom Cromwell had one thing in common--they both knew the Hollywood scene very well. Their combined experience made this story of a film star--from the unhappy childhood in a provincial Minnesota town to the brink of nervous collapse brought about by her being a Hollywood idol, an incisive reflection of situations and relationships in the factory of dreams. Cromwell remained as if in the shade and transferred the fine script to the screen with restraint, but also with great conviction. His contribution includes the excellent directing of the debuting Kim Stanley in the title role. The Goddess is a penetrating examination of a career in the American style, whose traps are most glaring in the celluloid world, where everything is on display. David O. Selznick missed the point when he described the heroine as "an idol of the world who is completely impossible and who cannot be wife, mother or human being, and who is completely worthless to be anything but a movie star." The key to the whole film is to be found in its first two parts: the third part, "Portrait of a Goddess," describing the heroine at the height of fame in the years 1952-57, is basically a repetition of the accusations of Hollywood to be found in several earlier pictures--while "Portrait of a Girl" (1930) and "Portrait of a Young Woman" (1942-47) reveal the reason for the present state of things: the conditions in which the heroine grew up. The stagnation of a small town, the longing for something out of the ordinary, the total hypocrisy, the ease with which myths form--all this is much more revealing than the subsequent spiritual vivisection of the heroine when already on the pedestal of a movie idol. A storm of speculations started after The Goddess was released: whom did Chayefsky have in mind? Marilyn Monroe? Judy Garland? Ava Gardner? But it was all a misunderstanding. He had in mind any potential goddess of the American screen.

THE NUN'S STORY Fred Zinnemann

Script: Robert Anderson, from the book by Kathryn C. Hulme. Photography: Franz F. Planer. Music: Franz Waxman. Art Direction: Alexandre Trauner. Editing: Walter Thompson. Cast: Audrey Hepburn (Sister Luke), Peter Finch (Dr. Fortunati), Edith Evans (Mother Emmanuel), Peggy Ashcroft (Mother Mathilde), Dean Jagger (Dr. Van der Mal), Mildred Dunnock (Sister Margharita), Beatrice Straight (Mother Christophe), Patricia Collinge (Sister William), Eva Kotthaus (Sister Marie), Ruth White (Mother Marcella), Niall McGinnis (Father Vermeuhlen), Patricia Bosworth (Simone), Barbara O'Neill (Mother Katherine), Lionel Jeffries (Dr. Goovaerts), Margaret Phillips (Sister Pauline), Rosalie Crutchley (Sister Eleanor), Dorothy Alison (Sister Aurelie), Molly Urquhart (Sister Augustine), Colleen Dewhurst (Archangel), Stephen Murray (Chaplain), Orlando

Martins (Kalulu), Errol John (Illunga), Jeannette Sterke (Louise), Richard O'Sullivan (Pierre), Diana Lambert (Lisa), Marina Wolkonsky (Marie), Penelope Horner (Jeannette Milonet), Ave Ninchi (Sister Bernard), Charles Lamb (Pascin), Ludovice Bonhomme (Bishop), Dara Gavin (Sister Ellen), Elfrida Simbari (Sister Timothy).

Henry Blanke--Fred Zinnemann for Warner Bros., U.S.A. 13,656 ft., 152 mins. Technicolor.

Belgium a few years before the Second World War. Gabrielle Van der Mal, daughter of a famous surgeon, enters a convent and is given the name of Sister Luke. She hopes to be sent to the Congo as a nursing nun. The period of initial training at the Mother House is very trying; a proud and intelligent girl, Sister Luke finds the principle of unquestioning obedience difficult to accept. She cannot bring herself to obey the order to fail deliberately, as a proof of humility, an exam in tropical medicine of which she is a brilliant student. She is sent to do extremely difficult work at a mental hospital near Brussels. She eventually does go to the Congo--to work as an assistant of Dr. Fortunati, a brilliant and handsome hospital surgeon, whose atheism is a further challenge to her beliefs. She is sent back to Belgium with a delicate patient. After the news comes of her father's death at the hands of the Nazis, who are in the meantime occupying the country, she decides to give help to the resistance movement. Finally realizing that she will never be able to accept the discipline and fulfill the extreme spiritual demands required of a nun, she obtains release from her vows and leaves the convent.

Zinnemann started with a bestseller, and ended with an honest and straightforward film--despite the fact that some of the novel's contrived literary devices remained. Technically The Nun's Story is almost trivial, and its visual style, with the camerawork dominated by huge close-ups and prominently using the human head, can be traced back to the silent cinema. At the same time, the handling of many scenes (such as the ceremony of the novitiate) is nearly perfect. The almost documentary sequences of Sister Luke's training at the Mother House and her work at the mental hospital are very fine, while the closing image of her walking out the back door of the convent into the world has rare poetry and power. The aesthetic key to the film is the classical purity of construction, composition of the frame, color, acting--all used with strict consistency. Only Franz Waxman's overly emotional music is an unfortunate exception. There is also Audrey Hepburn's pure personality in her Oscar-winning performance as Sister Luke. She is accompanied by Peter Finch and a whole group of outstanding actresses in the supporting parts, to mention only Peggy Ashcroft and Edith Evans. Zinnemann was intelligent enough not to go in the direction of portraying visually "a battle raging in the nun's soul," and this rather unexpectedly parallels Bresson's approach in Diary of a Country Priest. The critic Albert Johnson commented in "Film Quarterly" (Winter 1958): "Not only is this film a major directorial achievement in the career of Fred Zinnemann, but The Nun's Story is the best study of religious life ever made in the American cinema." This still holds true. Finally, one must mention an aspect which is very interesting although not given much prominence: The Nun's Story as a description of the courageous stand of an individual in a repressive environment.

THE HOUSE UNDER THE ROCKS (Ház a sziklák alatt) Károly Makk

Script: Sándor Tatay. Photography: György Illés. Music: István Sárközy. Art Direction: László Duba. Editing: Sándor Boronkay. Cast: János Görbe (Ferenc Kós), Irén Psota (Tera), Margit Bara (Zsuzsa), József Bihary (Old Kós), Ádám Szirtes (Sándor), Viola Orbán (Mrs. Kós), Sándor Deák (Firedi), György Bárdi (Forester), Béla Barsi (Brother-in-law), Mária Sivó (The wife), Erzsi Máthé (Stall-keeper).

Hunnia Filmstúdió, Hungary. 8957 ft., 100 mins.

A variation of the classical motif of a marital triangle: Ferenc comes back from the war harrowed and ill; his wife died while he was away and his little son was brought up by his crippled sister-in-law, Tera. Tera is secretly in love with Ferenc and expresses her feelings by the unusual care with which she looks after him and his son; but this does not bring for her the desired result. Ferenc marries the beautiful Zsuzsa and Tera, tormented by near-pathological jealousy, refuses to leave the household. Relations between husband and wife gradually deteriorate and disaster hangs in the air. In despair Ferenc pushes Tera over the precipice; Zsuzsa becomes alienated from her husband when she finds out the truth and Ferenc gives himself up to the police.

The story of The House Under the Rocks is good material for an intense chamber psychological drama; but Makk's inventive direction allowed him to achieve even more than what was inherent in the theme. He gave the film conviction, strength and clarity, strikingly described the characters, conferred a functional role to both the interiors and the severe landscapes, well handled the key scenes, particularly the scene of Tera's death and created suggestive atmosphere with the same skill which later brought such fine results in Love and Catsplay. Makk did not limit himself to registering dramatic events but contained in the fabric of the story a moral anxiety and a reflection on one's responsibility for the growth of conflicts. This bitter film, very Hungarian in character, foreshadowed the successes of the Hungarian cinema in the 60's in handling dramas of similar type.

DESIRE (Touha) Vojtěch Jasný

Script: Jasný and Vladimír Valenta. Photography: Jaroslav Kučera. Music: Svatopluk Havelka. Art Direction: Karel Lier. Editing: Jan Chaloupek. Cast: THE BOY WHO SOUGHT THE END OF THE WORLD (O chlapci, který hledal konec světa): Jan Jakěs (Joska), Václav Babka (Father), Věra Bublíková (Mother), Jan Chremčík (Grandfather), Vlastimil Brodský (Uncle Novosad). PEOPLE ON EARTH AND STARS IN THE SKY (Lide na zemi a hvězdy na nebi): Jana Brejchová (Lenka), Jiří Vala (Jan), František Vnouček (Lenka's father), Oto Simánek (Brother-in-law), Eva Blažková (Tonča). ANDELA: Věra Tichánková (Anděla), Václav Lohninský (Michal), Zdeněk Kutil (Pavelka), František Mušánek (Father), Vladimír Menšik (Tractor driver). MUM (Maminka): Anna Melíšková (Mother), Jiří Pick (Václav), Ilja Racek (František).

Film Studio Barrandov, Czechoslovakia. 8527 ft., 95 mins.

Desire brings the first full manifestation of the creative interests of a director who later became one of the leaders of the new Czechoslovak cinema in the 60's. In all his work Jasný, the son of a small-town teacher, is faithful to the principles of his home background: his films tell about the hopes and desires of sensitive people in search of happiness, and sharply oppose intolerance, selfishness, abuse of democracy, the ignoring of man's attachment to custom and tradition. On paper this creative program (especially since Jasný's pictures are often set on the outskirts of cities, in small towns and villages) may seem rather limited and banal--but it acquires a completely different dimension on the screen, where it is supported by a very powerful poetic vision.

Desire is a panorama across generations in which Jasný concentrates his attention on lonely dreamers who have rejected material values and the thrifty urge towards the good life, and search for the ideal of feeling, question the spiritual essence of events and contemplate man's links with nature. The protagonists are in turn a young boy inquiring into the secrets of the world, a 30-year-old amateur astronomer searching for the princess of his dreams, a 40-year-old peasant woman frustrated in her exacting aspirations, and a retired woman teacher living in a town very like herself--silenced and eroded by time. Neither the story content nor the dramatic structure is the strong point of this cinematic calendar of the seasons in human life; its essence lies precisely in the melodramatics of the whole film, in the subtle sketching with the camera. The occasional narrative flaws, not without reason, occur where the tissue of the story is disrupted by a more forceful and literal statement or by a poem read on the soundtrack. All that is best in Desire is achieved through the images of a human figure surrounded by nature, brought out by the rhythm or by the scenery--it relies on the volatility of the mood, although it is rooted in a concrete, realistic observation. As promised by the title, the final effect of the film is determined by the wistful longing for the unusual, dreamlike and unattainable.

MAN OF THE WEST Anthony Mann

Script: Reginald Rose, from the novel "The Border Jumpers" by C. Scott Boyles Jr. Photography: Ernest Haller. Music: Leigh Harline. Art Direction: Hilyard Brown. Editing: Richard Heermance. Cast: Gary Cooper (Link Jones), Julie London (Billie Ellis), Lee J. Cobb (Dock Tobin), Arthur O'Connell (Sam Beasley), Jack Lord (Coaley), John Dehner (Claude), Royal Dano (Trout), Robert J. Wilke (Ponch), Jack Williams (Alcutt), Guy Wilkerson (Conductor), Chuck Robertson (Rifleman), Frank Ferguson (Marshal).

Walter A. Mirisch for Ashton, U. S. A. 8648 ft., 96 mins. CinemaScope. De Luxe Color.

Arizona in 1874. The alternatives for an ex-bandit: to return to crime or to engage in an uneven struggle against five outlaws. Link Jones is on his way to Fort Worth when the train in which he travels is ambushed; he faces the train-robbers in their hideout in an old shack; it turns out he is the nephew (and a former right-hand-man) of their half-deranged leader. The attempt to maintain the countenance of a respectable family man and citizen (who was on his way to hire a school-teacher for his local community) fail. One has to fight; Link pretends he is willing to cooperate in their future criminal ventures only to shoot them one by one.

The last of Mann's outstanding westerns, Man of the West is also the most advanced stage of the evolution of the genre in his work; the most dramatic vision of man in the realm of lawlessness--as violent in the final parts as it is thoughtful and unhasty in the earlier ones. The film's mixture of desperate fighting and idyllic landscapes, with meadows in flower as a metaphorical expression of protest against violence, brings to mind the future cinema of Sam Peckinpah. But the principal tonality of Man of the West is different; one can find in it Germanic traits (Mann often said that he was most impressed by the work of F. W. Murnau), manifested as the economy of dialogue for the sake of powerful but not vehement expressiveness of human gestures and the scenery.

THE QUIET DON (Tikhyi Don) Sergei Gerasimov

Script: Gerasimov, from the novel by Mikhail Sholokhov. Photography: Vladimir Rapoport. Music: Yuri Levitin. Art Direction: Boris Dulenkov. Cast: Pyotr Glebov (Grigori Melekhov), Elina Bystritskaya (Aksinya), Zinaida Kirienko (Natalyia), Danilo Ilchenko (Pantelei Melekhov), A. Filippova (Iliinichna), Lyudmila Khityayeva (Darya), Natalya Arkhangelskaya (Dunyasha), Nikolai Smirnov (Pyotr), G. Karyakin (Mikhail Koshevoi), Aleksandr Blagovestov (Stepan Astakhov), A. Zhukov (Miron Korshunov), Igor Dmitriev (Yevgeni Listnitsky), A. Denisova (Lukinichna), B. Novikov (Mitka), A. Karpov (Grandpa Grishaka), Yelena Maksimova (Koshevaya), V. Khmara (Mashutka Koshevaya), A. Shatov (General Listnitsky), Dmitri Kapka (Grandpa Sashko), V. Shatunovsky (Shtokman).

Tsentralnaya Kinostudyia Detskikh i Yunosheskikh Filmov im. M. Gor'kogo, U. S. S. R. Part I (1957): 9925 ft., 110 mins.; Part II (1957): 10,512 ft., 117 mins.; Part III (1958): 11,095 ft., 123 mins. Sovcolor.

This screen version of the most outstanding epic novel in Soviet literature, telling a story of a Don Valley Cossack against the background of the 1914 war and the Revolution, was made by the man who is probably the most typical of the older generation of Soviet directors. Gerasimov's vast, tripartite screen fresco generally does not venture beyond illustrating the novel with dynamic images, and when it does--it is via very traditional and aesthetically doubtful effects, such as stormy feelings being banally symbolized by landscapes. The film rests mainly on the acting and the dialogue; the trouble is that the actors exaggerated somewhat in their naturalistic manner, while the profusion of words weakened the drama of the protagonists' experiences and the painful national tragedy of those years. Bearing in mind however the enormous material with which Gerasimov had to cope and that the presentation of the whole saga on the screen necessitated academic treatment of the literary material, The Quiet Don appears as a fairly successful undertaking which preserves the main features of Sholokhov's prose. The Russian spirit which pervades the whole is quite convincing; so is the sense of an individual being immersed in, and determined by, history, the attention to detail and the expressively photographed scenery.

Of the three parts the first is the least pungent, weighed down by the multitude of sub-plots and generic observation; the second can be described as a hasty summation of complex events; while the third, the most dynamic, narratively uniform and deeply tragic--closes the cycle on the note which is decisive for the overall effect.

THE SNOWY HERON (Shirasagi) Teinosuke Kinugasa

Script: Kinugasa and Jun Sagara, based on the novel by Kyoka Izumi. Photography: Kimio Watanabe. Music: Ichiro Saito. Cast: Fujiko Yamamoto (Oshino), Keizo Kawasaki (Junichi Inaki), Yosuke Irie (Takashi Inaki), Shuji Sano (Kumajiro Gosaka), Hitomi Nozoe (Nanae Date), Natsuko Kahara (Otori), Hideo Takamatsu (Yokichi).

Masaichi Nagata for Daiei, Japan. 8694 ft., 97 mins. Daieiscope. Agfacolor.

For the second time, after Gate of Hell (1953), Teinosuke Kinugasa displays his mastery as a refined colorist of the screen--but this time the content is worthy of the form. The Snowy Heron is a tragic story of a geisha who is in love with a subtle painter and plans life together with him, but only after serving off the debt she had to incur in order to buy out her criminal brother. The waiting turns out to be too protracted: the girl, unwilling to submit herself to a repulsive protector, commits suicide.

Although the outline of the story is melodramatic, Kinugasa conducted the narrative with a delicate hand and did not harm the fine visual aspect of the film. The predominantly static takes, the designs and the composition of the frame in The Snowy Heron all refer to the traditional Japanese miniature; Kinugasa also makes use of the potentialities of the wide screen, manipulating the planes of light and darkness. Still, it is with the color that he achieved the most ravishing effects: while Gate of Hell (1953) used strong, unexpected contrasts and the predominantly dark scale, here Kinugasa relied on light and delicate pastel tonality--willow-green, turquoise, grey, light violet. It is only against this background that sharp accents of red and black appear. The Snowy Heron was awarded many prizes for its visual beauty and is one of the most often quoted examples of the coloristic sensitivity of the Japanese cinema.

LES TRICHEURS Marcel Carné

Script: Carné and Charles Spaak. Dialogues: Jacques Sigurd, Roland Armontel and Roland Lesaffre. Photography: Claude Renoir. Music: Maxime Saury, Ray Brown, Roy Eldridge, Herb Ellis, Stan Getz, Dizzy Gillespie, Coleman Hawkins, Gus Johnson, Oscar Peterson, Sonny Stitt and Norman Grant. Art Direction: Paul Bertrand. Editing: Albert Jurgenson. Cast: Jacques Charrier (Bob Letellier),

Laurent Terzieff (Alain), Pascale Petit (Michèle), Andréa Parisy (Clo), Roland Lesaffre (Roger), Dany Saval (Nicole), Jacques Portet (Guy), Pierre Brice (Bernard), Alfunso Mathis (Peter), Jean-Paul Belmondo (Lou), Denise Vernac (Michèle's mother).

Robert Dorfmann for Silver Films/Cinétel/Zebra Films, France. 125 mins.

It is difficult to think of another picture which would be such a great misunderstanding from the social point of view and which would at the same time offer such an accurate perspective of the problem it aims to present--which would be at once so anachronistic and so difficult to accept by traditionalists. Disturbed by the attitudes of the young generation of urban bourgeoisie, Carné struck the tone of a moralist: it is the society, passive and stagnant, which is responsible for the nihilism of the young. But instead of shaking up consciences, Carné caused general displeasure: the older generation accused the picture of immorality and pessimism, while the young turned their backs on the man who--they felt--was completely unable to understand them.

Les Tricheurs portrays the way of life of a group of Paris teenagers. Bob makes the acquaintance of Alain by surprising him in the middle of stealing a record from a shop. A properly brought-up son of an industrialist, Bob is overwhelmed and fascinated by his friend's scorn for all conventions. At the Café Bonaparte in the St. Germain-des-Près district, he meets Alain's "crowd." He is asked by a girl, Clo, to a party during which they become lovers. The same evening he meets another girl, Michèle, who makes a deep impression on him. Bob soon becomes part of the student scene. Reluctantly, he becomes involved in blackmail which is to provide funds for a car for Michèle. When he delivers the money, however, he finds her in bed with Alain. He throws the money in her face and leaves. At another party Alain subjects them to the cross-examination of the "truth game." But they are both too involved in their poses for the truth to come out. Bob asks Clo (who needs a father for a child she is expecting) to marry him. Michèle drives off. Bob is unable to overtake her and she dies in an accident.

Carné's melodrama is the last ambitious achievement of the old cinéma de qualité, a species soon to be made extinct by the arrival of the Nouvelle Vague. The Fourth Republic for which Les Tricheurs sounded a death knell was also soon brought to an end. One may say that Carné performed an unusual feat: using the stereotyped formulae which had become completely worn out in the course of the preceding twenty years, he built a totally artifical cinematic construction--but he filled it with authentic behavioral and social observation and in the final effect he achieved the impression of truth, a curious imitation of life. Some scenes, such as Alain's vertiginous rescue of a kitten from a high-storey window ledge or the climactic car chase, are very good. Only the unsubtle ending is indefensible--the rest has the value of a document, also of a document of the mentality of the French upper middle-class under the Fourth Republic. The irony is that while portraying the mythology and the poses of his protagonists (something which Wajda soon rendered much better in Innocent Sorcerers) Carné surrendered to it himself. The antidote he has to offer does not go beyond the most superficial, threadbare 19th-century sentimentality. It is hardly surprising that the Nouvelle Vague directors received Les Tricheurs with such fury. As if by irony, it is this Carné picture which saw the debut of a group of young actors who later appeared in many Nouvelle Vague films: Petit, Charrier, Terzieff, Parisy....

GIRLS IN UNIFORMS (Mädchen in Uniform) Geza Radványi

Script: Franz Höllering and F. D. Andam, from the play "Gestern und Heute" (Yesterday and Today) by Christa Winsloe. Photography: Werner Krien. Music: Peter Sandloff. Art Direction: Emil Hasler and Walter Kutz. Editing: Ira Oberberg. Cast: Romy Schneider (Manuela von Meinhardis), Lilli Palmer (Fräulein von Bernburg), Therese Giehse (Headmistress), Christine Kaufmann (Mia), Danik Patisson (Edelgard), Blandine Ebinger, Gina Albert, Sabine Sinjen, Marthe Mercadier, Paulette Dubost, Ginette Pigeon, Adelheid Seeck.

CCC-Farbfilm/ Films Modernes/ S. N. C. , West Berlin/ France. 95 mins.

One should beware of remaking films whose appeal relies mainly on a resonance with topical events and current problems. Leontine Sagan's Girls in Uniforms, made way back in 1931, fits this description very well and it might seem that Radványi was ill-advised in deciding to make, 27 years later, a new screen version of Christa Winsloe's play about a militaristic atmosphere in a school for young ladies of good families--especially since he did this without changing the period and without trying to relate the story to the problems facing Germany some ten years after a shattering military defeat. Why is thus Girls in Uniforms an exception from the rule? Perhaps because the director of the memorable Somewhere in Europe handled this remake not only with great care but with obvious emotional involvement. It is true that the critical accents of this story of young women caught in the cogs of a severe para-military machinery did not come through. Also, the new film lacks the suggestive chiaroscuro of the 1931 black-and-white version. But on the other hand Radványi knew how to enrich the psychological description of the heroine and her emotional links with a woman teacher (even if he did this with a certain German forcefulness) and well illustrated the moods of the film with color compositions in which the luminous pastel portraits of the young girls are contrasted with the black dominant associated with the dry and cold headmistress. The actresses

ses in the three main parts contributed considerably: the warmly feminine Lilli Palmer, Therese Giehse as the headmistress and the girlishly sensual Romy Schneider in her first notable role.

ICE COLD IN ALEX J. Lee Thompson

Script: T. J. Morrison and Christopher Landon, from the novel by the latter. Photography: Gilbert Taylor. Music: Leighton Lucas. Art Direction: Robert Jones. Editing: Richard Best. Cast: John Mills (Captain Anson), Sylvia Syms (Sister Diana Murdoch), Anthony Quayle (Captain Van der Poel), Harry Andrews (M. S. M. Pugh), Diane Clare (Sister Denise Norton), Richard Leech (Captain Crosbie), Liam Redmond (Brigadier), Walter Gotell (German officer).

W. A. Whittaker for A. B. P. C., G. B. 11,894 ft., 132 mins.

The Libyan front in 1942. As Tobruk is about to fall to the Nazis, Captain Anson, commander of a motor ambulance brigade, is ordered to conduct two young nurses to Alexandria in an old ambulance. Anson is disintegrating under the stress of battle fatigue and an increasing reliance on booze. When the last bridge not yet in German hands is blown up, Anson decides that the only way is to brave a vast minefield; then meets a South African soldier's request for a lift only because the man has three bottles of gin. One nurse dies in an encounter with a German convoy, but the South African persuades the Germans to let them pass. When he does it again, Anson begins to realize that he is a Nazi spy. In the meantime the surviving nurse has fallen in love with the Captain and gives him strength to carry on. When they finally reach Alex they have to solve one more problem: what to do with the spy, for whom they have developed genuine respect. Anson decides to treat him as a brave comrade rather than an enemy. Over the ice-cold beer which Anson had long been promising himself, they strike a compromise which satisfies both duty and honor--and then go their separate ways.

Some dismissed Ice Cold in Alex as no more than a variation on the motifs of The Wages of Fear. Granted: it is clear that Lee Thompson had seen Clouzot's picture. But if one looks beyond the basic situation, one finds that the film does have values of its own to offer: a first-class script; very good acting; concentrated film-making; a vigorously treated humanist theme (which at the 1958 Berlin Film Festival earned the director the Fipresci Prize of the International Federation of Film Critics). Ice Cold in Alex succeeded in achieving suspense without resorting to the spectacular, something which became Lee Thompson's habit in the 60's. This is not a great film, of course--but a reliable and honest one.

1959

PICKPOCKET Robert Bresson

Script: Bresson, inspired by the novel "Prestupleniye i nakazaniye" (Crime and Punishment) by Fyodor Dostoyevsky. Photography: Léonce-Henry Burel. Music: Jean-Baptiste Lully. Art Direction: Pierre Charbonnier. Editing: Raymond Lamy. Cast: Martin Lassalle (Michel), Marika Green (Jeanne), Pierre Leymarie (Jacques), Jean Pelegri (Police Inspector), Kassagi (Master pickpocket), Pierre Etaix (Pickpocket), Dolly Scal (Michel's mother).

Angès Delahaie, France. 6750 ft., 75 mins.

Pickpocket is a near-philosophical treatise about the individual's striving towards perfection, pure and moving with its faith in man. Bresson uses motifs taken from the writings of Dostoyevsky, returns to the fascination with sleight of hand he discovered in himself during the shooting of A Man Escaped and creates a parable about man's search for self-realization inscribed into the scenery of contemporary Paris.

Michel, a sensitive and solitary young man, who lives apart from his sick mother, decides to become a pickpocket. After an unsuccessful theft he is briefly arrested but later released. The police inspector with whom Michel enters into intellectual discussions about the rights and wrongs of crime keeps him under observation, while his self-righteous friend Jacques in vain tries to help him. When his mother, who has been looked after by a neighbor Jeanne, dies, Michel briefly reflects but then joins a gang of pickpockets. The inspector does not arrest him partly because of lack of sufficient evidence, and partly because of his interest in Michel's ideas.

When his accomplices are arrested, Michel hurriedly leaves France. He returns some years later and finds Jeanne abandoned with a child by Jacques. He returns to stealing only to be caught and imprisoned. Jeanne visits him in prison and Michel realizes that his entire life was only a path leading up to their being in love.

For the sensitive protagonist of Pickpocket self-fulfilment is a necessity; people like him cannot remain passive and are unable to bear loneliness. For them, the only alternative to finding peace within themselves is a head-on collision with society. In the closing scene of the film Michel does achieve such inner harmony in the realization of his love for Jeanne (their relationship is a variation on the motif of Raskolnikov and Sonia from "Crime and Punishment") but before this happens he comes near the abyss of total frustration, of complete negation of the moral order of the world. He has lived in semi-poverty, on the margin of life and this he felt as doubly painful--as an insult to his above-average ambition, and as a refusal of a chance for above-average achievements. He rejected the bourgeois philosophy of life and his friend's lectures about the need for patient summation of life's achievements. To Michel, the escape into the security of stabilized life is a refuge for mediocrity--while he himself searches for a form of existence which would reflect his ability, his intelligence, his spiritual concentration, his whole personality. He finds his chance in picking pockets--not primarily in the financial gain, but in surmounting fear, in achieving a near-hypnotic control over his victims, in perfecting his manual and tactical skill. It would have been too perverse of Bresson if this fascinating psychological gamble was shown in objective narrative; in any case he always shows spiritual tensions in man from the inside, a device which produces extraordinary urgency and intensity of the narrative. So it is in Pickpocket, where the story is told in the form of Michel's diary (as in Diary of a Country Priest); and the narrative structure of the film is subordinate to the inner logic of his feelings and his perception of the world, and not to the logic of story-telling. Although in 1959 this could not yet have led to a space-time mosaic quality of the narrative, it certainly resulted in Bresson's further departure from the current stylistic rules of the cinema: he uses exclusively mid-shots and medium-long shots, uses only a simple frieze of classical music, closes scenes with fade-outs, eliminates camera movements and formal exertions and permits himself only one, but very impressive, editing etude, which describes the methods of operation of a pickpocket gang on a train. This sequence is a clear proof of Bresson's fascination with the subject. Joining the gang, finding accomplices is in Michel's life like signing a Faustian pact with the Devil: it means breaking through the complex of marginality by choosing the way of personal fulfillment, and breaking through the complex of loneliness. It also provides some compensation for the lack of sexual contacts--by the almost sexual contact with the victims and through the intellectual friendship with an accomplice. After that, Michel's salvation for society, involving his acceptance of the generally accepted hierarchy of values, can take place only by way of a moral, not physical, defeat. It comes, when after the arrest of his accomplices and a prolonged period of renewed loneliness Michel is defeated by the clever provocation of a police inspector. Prison is for him tantamount to spiritual death, again in a double sense: firstly, the loss of contact with the world means inaction and thus takes away the meaning of existence; secondly, it is an unacceptable humiliation. In this situation the love for Jeanne, someone in equal need of warmth and help, is a desperate act of hope--and thus the credibility of the finale is difficult to fault. Especially since Bresson skillfully steps up the emotional intensity of the film--with the mode of narration and with the contents. It might seem that the close-ups of pages in Michel's diary accompanied on the soundtrack by a voice reading from them is excessive and incompetent from the point of view of narrative efficiency. Not so: perhaps because Martin Lassalle, lean, haunted and fanatical, imparted to the film so much of his magnetic personality: maybe because all the other actors also expressed manifest human truth; but most probably because Pickpocket is a masterpiece of tensions, rhythm, of visual conveyance of man's tangible relationship with matter--a masterpiece directed by a man to whom cinema is at once a carrier of ideas and the idea itself. Pickpocket is without a doubt one of the most convincing proofs of the autonomous greatness of cinema as a medium and art form.

BALLAD OF A SOLDIER (Ballada o soldatye) Grigori Chukhrai

Script: Valentin Yezhov and Chukhrai. Photography: Vladimir Nikolayev and Era Savelyeva. Music: Mikhail Ziv. Art Direction: B. Nemechek. Editing: M. Timofeieva. Cast: Vladimir Ivashov (Alyosha Skvortsov), Zhanna Prokhorenko (Shura), Antonina Maksimova (Alosha's mother), Nikolai Kryuchkov (General), Yevgeni Urbansky (Invalid soldier), Ella Lezhdyei (Invalid soldier's wife).

Mosfilm, U. S. S. R. 8045 ft., 89 mins.

The year 1942; Soviet forces are still retreating before the onslaught of the Nazi armies; the struggle is unyielding and desperate. The opening scene of Ballad of a Soldier is firmly rooted in the realities of the front: a young soldier, the last survivor of his platoon, finds himself eye to eye with five enemy tanks. He starts to run. One of the tanks gives chase trying to crush him with the caterpillars. But then the pursued soldier finds an abandoned bazooka in a trench, turns it on the tank and fires. A second shot destroys another tank, the rest retreat. His conduct in battle is commended as heroic; instead of a decoration he is given a few days' leave to see his mother. The village where he comes from is 24 hours away in peacetime; in wartime chaos the journey takes much longer. Almost the entire film is an account of this journey home. Although the young soldier is in a great hurry, he does not refuse help to those in need; he is a boy of sterling character, sensitive and honest and not yet eroded by life. He gives comfort to an embittered, legless veteran afraid to return to his wife in his present state, delivers two cakes of soap, a precious wartime gift from a fellow soldier to his wife (only to find her living with another man), shares his property with others. He makes up for the lost time by his ingenuity in finding means of transport. He reaches home just in time to say hello and goodbye to his mother. But before that he finds on his journey one thing of his own: an awkward, shy and unfulfilled love to a girl, a fellow stowaway on the freight train. They never meet again--the soldier is killed on the front. So many of them died--fine young men who were only beginning to live. Chukhrai shows only one of them, but the enormity of the loss is acutely conveyed and constantly felt in the film.

Ballad of a Soldier, the most celebrated and structurally pure picture of the new Soviet cinema, appeals principally with its lyrical power. Chukhrai does not curb emotional tension and tenderness towards his protagonist--and is entitled to that by the assumed stylistic form of a ballad. On the other hand, he is true in details and moods and does not resort to stilted symbols (faults which mar The Forty-First and Clear Skies); with concentrated frankness builds a cinematic reminiscence about someone of his own generation. There are here no intrusive overstatements or pompous phraseology which earlier did so much harm to Soviet cinema, there is no obsession with the protagonist being representative of the whole of society. The abandonment of the latter feature was as a matter of fact one of the main strengths of new Soviet films. Chukhrai does not start from general truths; instead, like a reporter, he jots down attitudes and actions of individual people on the home front. It is only by summing up the many episodes strewn along the dramatic axis of the soldier's journey home, that he creates a vision of a country in crisis. Despite its poetic character, this is a much more authentic vision than anything achieved in U. S. S. R. cinema for a very long time. Instead of showing a monolithic social organism absolutely subordinated to the single idea of defeating the enemy, Chukhrai shows genuine, un-retouched people, varied in their reactions and attitudes (in one scene, for instance, we see a soldier accepting a bribe). However Ballad of a Soldier is not a reckoning with the past (as Chukhrai's later Clear Skies is): it is a debate about basic human values which are tested in the crucible of war. The fact that the director strives to achieve faithful vision and spontaneous emotional judgment does not mean that he renounces the metaphor, the subjective narrative and the semantic shortcuts. It is only that the use of these stylistic means matches precisely the character of the story. The frame of the film, the mother walking along a country road, sounds a very clear tone; very suggestive are the slanted shots in the opening sequence which well render the fear of the single soldier running away from the tanks. Despite the balladic tonality and the very simple structure, Ballad of a Soldier is a picture of considerable sophistication--in editing, the choice of camera angles, the manner of describing objects; the episode with the soldier stopping a truck to ask for a lift is an example of how much can be expressed with the "thinking camera." But formal exertions are almost unnoticeable in this fine picture--its dominant feature is simplicity, the main attribute of all real art.

DESTINY OF A MAN (Sud'ba cheloveka) Sergei Bondarchuk

Script: Y. Lukin and F. Shakhmagonov, from the story by Mikhail Sholokhov. Photography: Vladimir Monakhov. Music: Venyamin Basner. Art Direction: A. Golovanov, I. Novodereshkin and S. Voronkov. Editing: V. Leonov. Cast: Sergei Bondarchuk (Andrei Sokolov), Pavel Boriskin (Vanya), Zinaida Kirienko (Irina Sokolova), Pavel Volkov (Ivan Timofeyevich), Y. Averin (Müller), K. Alekseyev (German major).

Mosfilm, U.S.S.R. 9209 ft., 102 mins.

The two most outstanding works of the new Soviet cinema in the late 50's are poles apart in their mood and emotional attitude: Ballad of a Soldier is calm and tender, Destiny of a Man is forceful and peremptory. Both films are profoundly Russian in character; but Destiny of a Man is sustained in a more traditional spirit of emotional ostentation and handles many episodes as do the classics of emphatic imagery. What is quite novel is the distribution of accents: this is not a film of painful and optimistic heroism, but of bitter tones of tragic humanism.

During the Second World War Andrei Sokolov experiences virtually everything except death itself. Before the outbreak of the war he had been a carpenter in a village near Voronezh and led a peaceful life with his family. Well, perhaps he liked to drink a bit too much and did not treat his wife with enough respect--but on the whole was quite unexceptional. On the front he drives a munition truck, suffers a concussion in an attack by an enemy plane and is captured by the Germans. This is equivalent to civil death: wartime Soviet propanganda considered those who allowed themselves to be captured as traitors. Sokolov escapes from a POW camp, is recaptured and sent deeper into Germany to work in a stone quarry. Sentenced to death by the camp commandant he saves his life by impressing the Nazi officers with his unusual resistance to liquor. He manages to survive until 1944 when he becomes a chauffeur to a German staff major. By that time the tide of war has turned and Soviet forces are advancing into Germany. Sokolov waits for a suitable moment and escapes again; only this time he kidnaps the major--it is only a brave deed like this that can rehabilitate him in the eyes of the Soviet authorities. He returns home only to find a bomb crater where his house had once been. All his family are dead apart from his son, an exceptionally gifted mathematician, at present an artillery captain decorated for bravery. But on Victory Day he is told of his son's death. Four years of war have made a human rag out of Sokolov; he has no one in the world and the end of the war seems to him something a little abstract. That which to others was an excruciating but well-rewarded effort, was to him merely a Calvary of humiliation and suffering ending in loneliness. He settles in Uryupinsk, a town not far from home, to embark on what seems an aimless existence. But then he comes across a small orphaned boy who imagines Sokolov is his lost father. In a most touching scene Sokolov says it is really so. So, there is after all someone for whom to live. But he fears the day, close he thinks, when he will die of a heart attack; the boy will be frightened....

The film was made from fine literary material and this is partly responsible for its high quality. Sholokhov's story was written in 1957, soon after political changes in the Soviet Union. Previously any reference to Soviet prisoners of war was taboo; Sholokhov told the story with great emotional power, in the form of a direct account by the hero. It is strikingly credible and direct. The characterization of Sokolov on the few pages of the book is remarkably full-blooded and complete: this literary miniature is probably the best work of the genre in the whole of the Soviet literature. In his film Bondarchuk retained the form of dependent narrative, but gave it a completely different scope: he replaced the book's tone of painful confession with the tone of monumental epic, Eisensteinian in spirit and in parts reminiscent of Dovzhenko and Donskoy. Stylistically Destiny of a Man is not uniform and can be accused of a number of formal errors; certain details are doubtful or incomplete--but the whole film is held together by its passionate narrative; at times sounding like an organ, at times like a cello. The epic symbolic scenes, the many monumental culminations might have finally torn the structure of the film apart were it not for the fact that Bondarchuk had living man very much in mind and always referred the naturalistic nightmare of the described events to the inner world of the protagonist. This time the aim was not so much to give testimony to the times, to offer a heartening generalization or social comment--but to convey a dusky and intimate truth. Thus the worn-out imagery of the Soviet cinema was filled with new powerful spirit.

LA DOLCE VITA Federico Fellini

Script: Fellini, Tullio Pinelli, Ennio Flaiano and Brunello Rondi. Photography: Otello Martelli. Music: Nino Rota. Art Direction: Piero Gherardi. Editing: Leo Cattozzo. Cast: Marcello Mastroianni (Marcello Rubini), Yvonne Furneaux (Emma), Anouk Aimée (Maddalena), Anita Ekberg (Sylvia), Alain Cuny (Steiner), Annibale Ninchi (Marcello's father), Magali Noël (Fanny), Lex Barker (Robert), Nadia Gray (Nadia), Jacques Sernas (Film star), Walter Santesso

La dolce vita

(Scandalist photo-reporter), Valeria Ciangottini (Paola), Mino Doro (Nadia's lover), Riccardo Garrone (Riccardo), Harriet White (Edna), Alain Dijon (Frankie Stout), Giulio Girola (Police Inspector), Nico Otzak (Sophisticated blonde), Audrey McDonald (Sonia), Renée Longarini (Mrs. Steiner), Carlo Di Maggio (Totò Scalise), Adriana Moneta (Prostitute), Sandra Lee (Ballerina), Gloria Jones (Gloria), Lilli Granado (Lucy), Laura Betti (Laura), Iris Tree (Poetess).

Giuseppe Amato for Riama/Pathé, Italy/France. 15,805 ft., 176 mins. Totalscope.

Fellini's devastating social canvas opens with a stunning image: the enormous marble statue of Christ the Worker is flown by helicopter over the Holy City to St. Peter's Square. With this ironic symbol the director introduces a film which is a continuation of his survey of contemporary man, of which the earlier parts were I vitelloni, La strada, Il bidone and Le notti di Cabiria. With its constantly changing field of vision, La dolce vita is a generalized study of the fears and frustrations which rend the affluent society, expressing the contemporary Angst with a force so far unencountered.

Our guide to the modern Babylon is Marcello, a third-rate reporter who spends his time hunting for scandal and gossip among the Roman plutocracy. The same day on which he accompanied Christ's figure on its flight, Marcello meets Maddalena, the bored daughter of a millionaire, and spends the night with her. He arrives home the next morning just in time to prevent his jealous mistress from committing suicide. He then dashes off to the airport to cover the arrival of Sylvia, a Hollywood star. He accompanies her, dressed as a priest, to the dome of St. Peter's. After a press conference and a visit to a night club Marcello drives Sylvia off in his car. He wades after her into the Trevi fountain. The episode ends in an encounter with Sylvia's husband. Next, Marcello spins off a sensational report about two children who claim to have had a vision of the Madonna; later still meets his father who has arrived from the provinces. He finds they have nothing to say to each other. After a civilized discussion at the literary salon of Steiner, a rich intellectual, Marcello thinks he has found a firm point of reference--he then hears that Steiner has killed his children and committed suicide. Having come to the conclusion that life has no meaning or purpose, Marcello abandons himself to wild parties.

La dolce vita is the first of Fellini's apocalyptic visions of civilization. It is "moral and social" in tone; the later $8\frac{1}{2}$ was "psychological" while Fellini Satyricon (1969) and Fellini's Casanova were "caricatural." It is also the first of his two frescoes of Rome. During the shooting Fellini said: "My aim is to create a fresco of Rome at a definite moment of its history, in the summer of 1958. My protagonist is no more than a tourist in a world of passions--of others and of his own. He is a kind of a continuation of Moraldo from I vitelloni." Again, after the release of La dolce vita: "I presented the problem forcefully. But am I to be expected to offer remedies? Am I a saint, or the Pope or a head of state? Let spiritual shepherds and social reformers take care of that. I have merely recorded my views. Besides, this was not meant to be a socially didactic picture, but a kind of fairytale à propos of a social phenomenon."

A forceful fairytale indeed. Fellini composed his contemporary apocalypse with a passion equal to von Stroheim's in Foolish Wives and The Wedding March. He portrays the moral bankruptcy of the aristocracy and the bourgeoisie and demonstrates that the national Italian attitudes are closely related to, and molded by, the Catholic Church. Most important of all--he portrays the bankruptcy and decay of modern civilization: both of the Western world (where everyone from high society down to a little journalist participate in nihilist orgies) and of the contemplative Eastern world which is supposed to be searching for the sense of existence (a reference to the Church and also to the evening at Steiner's). Journalists are merely the scavengers of urban civilization. The Steiner character epitomizes the spiritual impasse of the intellectuals, their sense of nothingness and futility, their desire to escape from the oppressive nightmare of reality into refined dreams. Steiner compromises himself by murdering his children. Fellini's message is that alienated intellectuals, broken and sick, will not become a force for spiritual renewal. This is a very significant conclusion in the Italian context, comparable with Pasolini's attitude in the period immediately preceding his death, and related to the message of Visconti's Conversation Piece and also to certain aspects of Antonioni's cinema--through the Marcello character Fellini concludes that sex has become the last remaining means of human communication.

It is remarkable how forthright and unorthodox (by Italian standards) is Fellini's attitude to religion in La dolce vita. Antonio Gramsci, the Marxist philosopher, pointed out that the religious element is so deeply ingrained in Italian culture, that even the antagonists of the Roman church succumb to its influence. Fellini clearly does not: he portrays faith as powerless and completely marginal. The prologue shows Christ as an empty sign of something nobody believes in any more; Christ's spread arms are an ironic, useless gesture. The ecclesiastical authorities understood the message and attacked Fellini with fury. So did the Roman nobility, one of whose members challenged him to a duel.

Yet Fellini the moralist is always kept in check by Fellini the artist. La dolce vita is a panopticon of rich, brilliant, suggestive, fluidly edited images. Some of them are unforgettable: the allegorical prologue, the scene at the Trevi fountain, but particularly the nostalgic ending. An orgy breaks at dawn and the participants file through the pine trees down to the sea. The fishermen are just pulling in a strange, ominous-looking marine monster. Marcello sees across the stream a girl, beautiful and innocent, a messenger from a different world. She--who knows--could perhaps save him. The girl calls to Marcello, but her voice is carried away by the wind. He turns back and joins the others.

HIROSHIMA MON AMOUR Alain Resnais

Script: Marguerite Duras, from her short story. Photography: Sacha Vierny and Michio Takahashi. Music: Giovanni Fusco; also Georges Delerue. Editing: Henri Colpi, Jasmine Chasney and Anne Sarraute. Cast: Emmanuele Riva (She), Eiji Okada (He), Bernard Fresson (German soldier), Stella Dassas (Mother), Pierre Barbaud (Father).

Argos/Como/Pathé/Daiei, France/Japan. 8190 ft., 91 mins.

Hiroshima mon amour is without doubt one of the most influential pictures in the history of cinema, and the most intellectually respectable of the films made in the momentous late 50's. Resnais does not consider himself a Nouvelle Vague director, and was not among the signatories of its Manifesto. He explained that he simply allowed himself to be carried along by the tide which swept French cinema at that time, but made the picture within the traditional framework of the film industry. Born in 1922, he attended a film course at IDHEC, but did not complete it. Soon after the war he established himself as an outstanding documentary film-maker. His 16mm film Van Gogh (1948) blown up to 35mm brought him an Oscar the following year. His other famous shorts included Night and Fog (1955), a vision of the Auschwitz concentration camp, and the dazzling Toute la mémoire du monde (1956) about the National Library in Paris, shown in an endless series of tracking shots. Hiroshima mon amour, Resnais's first feature, opened before the cinema the perspectives of subjective narrative, of projecting a personal vision of the world. Resnais tells the story in a manner which imitates the mechanism of the thought process.

A 34-year-old French actress has played a nurse in an anti-war film about Hiroshima. She has a husband and children in Paris. On the eve of her return to France she meets a young Japanese architect and spends the night with him. Her lover tries to persuade her to stay with him in Japan. The experience revives in the mind of the heroine memories of her first love--for a German soldier during the war, in her home town of Nevers. He was killed on the day of the town's liberation and she had her head shaved as a punishment for associating with an enemy. Her parents kept her shut up in a cellar to hide her humiliation. Later she was quietly sent to Paris, where she arrived on the day the news of Hiroshima appeared in the newspapers. Past and present merge in the heroine's mind; her personal tragedy with that of a city; Nevers in France with Hiroshima in Japan. But she refuses to subject herself to feelings. Forgetfulness is a more powerful force than love, and she will forget the Japanese as she has forgotten the German soldier--just as the people of Hiroshima will eventually forget the tragedy of their city. But the similarities and contrasts between Nevers in 1944 and Hiroshima in 1958 have given her a new awareness of the past.

Resnais: "I never attached the slightest importance to memory as such. I am not interested in memory, but in interpreting reality." It is important to note that in Hiroshima mon amour Resnais does not reconstruct memory, but the past consciousness of the heroine. The director again: "A film about love which accuses war? No. This would be too simple. My aim was to make a film about love which encompasses the most contradictory feelings, and which would arouse the most contradictory feelings in the viewer. A film about contemporary love ... I wanted to show a love story in the context of a tragedy of others, to juxtapose the human search for personal happiness, and the constant awareness of collective tragedy and threat." Thus, typically for his art, Resnais throws bridges between the past and the present. While memory may not be the film's subject, it is certainly a medium through which the past is reconstructed. Hiroshima mon amour negates the traditional treatment of the past in the cinema. Instead of using the conventional extended flashbacks, Resnais relies on fast cuts between present and past events without resorting to dissolves and fades, uses jump-cuts and associative editing in which the images of Hiroshima and Nevers are in constant counterpoint. The story is not told chronologically, but recorded as the heroine painfully summons the events from her subconscious mind.

Hiroshima mon amour makes use of two main stylistic components: (1) fast editing in the early parts; (2) long takes, for instance in the final sequence where the heroine and her lover wander through the streets of Hiroshima. There are two reasons for this apparent stylistic dichotomy. In the first part of the film Resnais is anxious to impress on the viewer that he is looking at a record of human consciousness rather than at a record of actual reality. Once this has been communicated via the editing, Resnais quiets the narrative down considerably, and shifts his emphasis to the mood--although this is a psychological mood rather than a sensual one. Another reason for the use of the two styles is that Resnais aims to show the heroine's anxiety early on in the film giving way to calm reflection later. Thus the narrative style of Hiroshima mon amour is totally different from that advocated by the film-makers of the Nouvelle Vague and by André Bazin, their theoretician, mainly as concerns the use of editing (which according to Bazin "damages reality"). Hiroshima mon amour gives back to the editing, of sound and of images, the creative function it had earlier in the history of the cinema. This was partly inspired by Agnès Varda's La Pointe Courte (1954) one of the precursors of the Nouvelle Vague, on which Resnais had been editor. The difference is that the subject matter of Varda's film was not time but, as in "The Wild Palms/The Old Man," Faulkner's simultaneous novels whose chapters alternate in one volume, the parallelism of two motifs--the personal and the social. All the same, Hiroshima mon amour formally resembles Faulkner's book. It seems that Resnais has also been inspired, this time as concerns his picture's temporal structure, by Satyajit Ray's Pather Panchali which was being shown in France in 1958.

To summarize, the amorphous quality of the dramatic structure of Hiroshima mon amour contradicts the traditional "functionality" of feature cinema narrative. What Resnais achieved is not merely an "open" dramatic structure--this is a narrative of feelings rather than of facts. This is the reason why the importance of Hiroshima mon amour for the cinema is greater than that of any other contemporary picture, including the work of Antonioni. Resnais developed the themes present here in the subsequent Last Year in Marienbad.

The main weakness of the film is its literary quality and Marguerite Duras's "sophisticated" dialogues. This is despite her overall ability to convey the psychology of the characters. Both these faults plagued the entire post-Nouvelle Vague French cinema. But Resnais was largely able to overcome this by suspending the very authentic emotional reactions of his protagonists in a very suggestive space-time structure. As a result, while the film's references and clues may be literary and artificial, the images never lie. Significantly, the first impression is created by the image of the lovers' embrace in the opening sequence. Their bodies seem at first made of concrete, then of a silvery metal, then as if drenched in mud, then like bronze. The image and Resnais's revolutionary ideas always win. He follows the mechanism of consciousness and remembrance--and this amounts to a breakthrough in the cinema. If the picture may seem over-insistent about the "equivalence" of the tragedy of a girl from Nevers with the tragedy of a big city--this apparent parallel is not more than a means of expression, and never enters the picture's philosophical, emotional or semantic message. The outstanding performance from Emanuelle Riva, who perfectly conveys the complex and subtle directorial intentions, and Fusco's extraordinarily fine music made a great contribution to the final harmony of the means of expression. Henri Colpi, the film's editor, wrote a whole discourse about the music, isolating motifs and discussing their complex associative functions, the music being often asynchronous with respect to the image. For instance, Nevers sequences use Japanese sound. Resnais described the role of music as purely lyrical, but it also permits subtle changes of mood which together with the image create a unique reality of feelings.

Hiroshima mon amour is a film about the magnificence of tragic love and the need to forget the cruel in order to be able to remember the beautiful.

FLOATING WEEDS (Ukikusa) Yasujiro Ozu

Script: Ozu and Kogo Noda, based on Tadao Ikeda's script for Ozu's film Ukikusa Monogatari (1934). Photography: Kazuo Miyagawa. Music: Takanori Saito. Art Direction: Tomo Shimogawara. Cast: Ganjiro Nakamura (Komajiro Arashi), Machiko Kyo (Sumiko), Haruko Sugimura (Oyoshi), Hiroshi Kawaguchi (Kiyoshi), Ayako Wakao (Kayo), Mantaro Ushio (Sentaro), Haruo Tanaka (Yatazo), Koji Mitsui (Kikinosuke), Tadashi Date (Sensho), Chishu Ryu (Owner of the theatre).

Masaichi Nagata for Daiei, Japan. 10,679 ft., 119 mins. Daieicolor.

It is a great pity that the most outstanding Japanese directors of the 50's began working in color so late in their careers: Mizoguchi two years before his death, Ozu--four, while Kurosawa made his first color film in the 60's. Ozu's first was Equinox Flower (1958), followed by Good Morning! (1959), a remake of the comedy I Was Born, but... . Then came Floating Weeds--again a remake, of his silent Story of Floating Weeds (1934). An elegiac, truly universal work, the new version is among his finest achievements.

On a hot summer day, a traveling troupe of actors arrive in a small harbor town in the Wakayama peninsula. They offer a historical kabuki performance, bloody and dramatic. Arashi, the boss, has special reasons for coming to this remote place: his former mistress Oyoshi and his son Kiyoshi live in the town. Arashi hides his true identity from the boy, pretending to be his uncle. At the same time he is anxious to conceal the whole situation from his present mistress Sumiko, who is a member of the troupe. But Sumiko finds out and calls at Oyoshi's house when Arashi and Kiyoshi are there. Her lover throws her out before she has time to reveal the truth to the boy. Instead, she pays Kayo, another actress, to seduce the boy as a revenge. But the affair soon becomes real for Kayo. A catastrophe befalls the troupe when a member runs off with the cash register. They have to break up and to sell their costumes to pay the owner of the theatre. Oyoshi wants Arashi to stay behind with her and their son; the arrival of the boy with Kayo forces a confrontation. Kiyoshi at last hears the truth and is angered by the comedy his parents have been playing. He wants to lead his own life with Kayo. Arashi leaves; at the station he meets a lonely and disheartened Sumiko. Their life of love and quarrels will continue.

Ozu has, of course, long abandoned camera movement and the use of optical devices such as zooms, fades, dissolves and wipes. While the film's silent predecessor, set in the mountainous north of

Japan, did use some camera movement, the style of Ozu's late work has been abstemious and severe. Surprisingly, the story of Floating Weeds is out of character: fairly dramatic, it relies on action and emotion, things which do not usually come to the surface in his cinema. Note in this context the scene of the fight in the rain between Arashi and Sumiko. But Ozu's philosophy remains intact: the circular structure and formal symmetry (arrival-departure) of the picture stresses the constant renewal of life. People are drifting like the floating weeds of the title and life eventually always returns to the starting point. Kiyoshi will have to face the same problems as his father when he grows up. The abandoned mistress says that Arashi left her like that before, promising to come back and remain with her. The same situations recur over and over again and action cannot change the inevitable in life. Ozu contemplates this with melancholy: an example of the mono-no aware mood, the film is permeated by a sense of loss, nostalgia for things which were beautiful but are no more. In the finale Floating Weeds finds an unexpected parallel with Bergman's cinema. The estranged lovers meet again and acknowledge that togetherness is always better than loneliness, just as Albert and Anne did in The Naked Night. Man can find solace only in another human being--the message recalls another European picture, Fellini's La strada.

"Color makes my composition more interesting" said Ozu simply, and Floating Weeds is stunningly photographed by Miyagawa, who usually worked with Mizoguchi, Ichikawa, Kurosawa and Yoshimura, but only this once with him. Lively colors underline the theatrical and the melodramatic, bringing out the splendid badness of the troupe's performances. Ganjiro Nakamura and Machiko Kyo are very good as the boss of the company and his young mistress. It is interesting how Ozu alternates members of his stock company between big and small parts in different films. For instance, Chishu Ryu, who has appeared in almost all of his films, most often in leading parts, is seen here in the small part of the owner of the theatre. Koji Mitsui, who played the son in the silent version, now plays one of the actors in the troupe.

THE GREAT WAR (La grande guerra) Mario Monicelli

Script: Agenore Incrocci, Furio Scarpelli, Luciano Vincenzoni and Monicelli. Photography: Giuseppe Rotunno and Roberto Gerardi. Music: Nino Rota. Art Direction: Mario Garbuglia. Costumes: Danilo Donati. Cast: Vittorio Gassman (Giovanni Busacca), Alberto Sordi (Oreste Jacovacci), Silvana Mangano (Costantina), Folco Lulli (Bordin), Romolo Valli (Lieutenant Gallina), Bernard Blier (Captain Castelli), Mario Valdemarin (2nd Lieutenant Loquenzi), Livio Lorenzon (Sergeant Battiferri), Gerard Herter (Austrian captain), Vittorio Sanipoli (Major Venturi), Carlo D'Angelo (Captain Ferri), Ferruccio

Amendola (De Concini), Elsa Vazzoler (Bordin's wife), Luigi Fainelli (Giacomazzi), Tiberio Mitri (Mandich), Guido Celano (Italian major).

Dino De Laurentiis/Gray Film, Italy/France. 113 mins. CinemaScope.

The Great War is the last in the series of pacifist pictures which saw war as cruel absurdity, whatever the color of one's banner. The scenery is certainly not unusual: once again this is the First World War, or to be more precise, the fighting on the Austrian-Italian front in the Julian Alps in 1917. Although it might seem that the totally critical approach to the Great War has been used to the full before in the cinema and, more importantly, that it became anachronistic after what had happened in the world some 25 years later--Monicelli made a remarkable tragicomedy which is a summary of the contribution to the theme by its literary and cinematic predecessors; but he gave this complex fresco a new, plebeian, general angle. The combination of the tones of gravity and derision brought a result incomparably superior to Dalton Trumbo's Johnny Got His Gun (1971), probably the last, and the most drastic, accusation of the Great War. Monicelli and his scriptwriters had a much better, near-Chaplinesque in fact, instinct for combining contrasting elements. Only in the finale does the film turn into a tragedy with sarcastic overtones; earlier the spirit of the Good Soldier Schweik dominates, and is generated by the behavior of the two protagonists. One of them, a professional thief coming from Milan considers himself an anarchist and likes to rely on his intelligence. Vittorio Gassman is good in this role, although he tends to overdo the mime. More convincing still is Alberto Sordi's barber's assistant from the Rome district of Trastevere--a little slyboots with a heart of gold, and an enormous coward. These typical screen anti-heroes are used to convey the plebeian common-sense (and very Italian in character) condemnation of war as an irrational mixture of logic and chance, confusing all the norms evolved by civilization, belittling human experience, making it impossible to comprehend things big and small, to distinguish between an honorable man and a scoundrel. But The Great War would only be a fraction of what it is were it not for the irony of the peripheral social accents (like the soldier who undertakes acts of extraordinary courage to ensure the survival of his starving family)--and were it not for the final twist in which the couple of shirkers nerve themselves to die a heroic death not for reasons of patriotism but out of solidarity with their comrades. The ending puts a big question-mark over the film's earlier univocal intellectual evaluation of an imperialist war--it demonstrates that the war can bring out greatness of soul where normally it could not be expected. Thus the ending introduces a bitter and intriguing ambiguity into the film.

A director with a gift for effective narrative, Monicelli spent most of his career on trivial comedies. In The Great War (and again in I compagni) he not only tackled an uncommon theme, but displayed real directorial mastery. He resisted the temptation to use the wide screen for a battalistic spectacular. The value of the film rests in its well-proportioned representation of the rich context of the front and the home-front, a fresco which is never naive. Fine is not only the forefront, but also the background, the very functional use of sound, the carefully thought-out dialectics of the situational contrasts. Thus the many stereotypes within the tissue of the film, far from weakening it, take on a new dimension. Skeptical and free-thinking, fluid in momentary moods but moving as a whole, The Great War is the best achievement of the Italian populist cinema in the post-Neorealist period.

ANATOMY OF A MURDER Otto Preminger

Script: Wendell Mayes, based on the novel by John D. Voelker. Photography: Sam Leavitt. Music: Duke Ellington. Editing: Louis R. Loeffler Titles: Saul Bass. Cast: James Stewart (Paul Biegler), Lee Remick (Laura Manion), Ben Gazzara (Frederick Manion), Arthur O'Connell (Parnell McCarthy), Eve Arden (Maida), Kathryn Grant (Mary Pilant), Joseph N. Welch (Judge Weaver), Brooks West (Mitch Lodwick), George C. Scott (Claude Dancer), Orson Bean (Dr. Smith), Russ Brown (Mr. Lemon), Murray Hamilton (Alphonse Paquette), Alexander Campbell (Dr. Harcourt), Howard McNear (Dr. Dompierre), Ken Lynch (Sgt. Durgo), Don Ross (Duane Miller), John Qualen (Sulo), Jimmy Conlin (Clarence Madigan), Ned Weaver (Dr. Roschid), Duke Ellington (Pie-Eye).

Otto Preminger for Carlyle Productions, U. S. A. 14,440 ft., 160 mins.

Preminger has always been attracted by the workings of the law, particularly by courtroom proceedings--as seen in Laura, Fallen Angel (1945), The Court Martial of Billy Mitchell (1955), Saint Joan and Advise and Consent (1962). Anatomy of a Murder was taken from a bestseller by a United States Justice, and was shot entirely in the town where the book had been written.

In a small town in Michigan, Frederick Manion, an army lieutenant, is accused of the murder of a local bar proprietor who had allegedly beaten and raped his wife Laura. Although the woman supports her husband's account, the police surgeon finds no physical evidence of rape. Manion is defended by Paul Biegler, a small-town lawyer who has lost the job of Public Prosecutor and taken the case because he needs money. Biegler discovers that Manion is violently possessive towards his wife who has a reputation for giving her favors to other men. He realizes that the prosecution will claim that Laura has been the mistress of the bar owner, and that the husband killed her lover and then beat her up. The lawyer enters a plea of not guilty on the grounds of "temporary insanity" on Manion's behalf. Knowing that his case is weak and relies largely on a single precedent, he sends his secretary and a mildly alcoholic colleague to find a witness who would save the accused. Eventually the dead man's daughter makes a last-minute appearance in court and Manion is found not guilty. Discharged, he disappears without paying the lawyer's fee.

Preminger's picture is not so much an anatomy of a murder, as an anatomy of a trial. We are never told what really happened to Laura and whether or not Manion was in the grip of "irresistible impulse." The verdict is left in doubt, and the film demonstrates how the jury are being confused. This is a perverse examination of the jury system, perhaps less direct than Cayatte's Let Justice Be Done, where the problem was not guilt or innocence but the influence of external factors on the jury's decision--but perhaps even more effective. People are shown as unfathomable and contradictory, their motives as highly ambivalent, and the mood is one of disenchantment and equivocation. Moral ambiguity in itself is hardly a novelty if one considers the film noir of the 40's. The point is that in Anatomy of a Murder ambiguity is institutional.

The picture takes up the polemic with the American judicial system with no less intelligence, but in a more commercial vein than did the earlier Twelve Angry Men and I Want to Live. Preminger is very attentive to detail; from the opening scenes the camera observes trifles, things which are seemingly marginal; from the beginning it watches the tricks of the lawyer who undertook the defense for a living, the schemes of an old man who is anxious to prove that he is still needed (N. B. the character is copied from Dude, the self-pitying drunk in Hawks's Rio Bravo, which was released a few months before). There are also the tricks of Lieutenant Manion who is anxious to save his skin, and the tricks of his intriguing wife. Thus Anatomy of a Murder is also an anatomy of a social situation.

Ellington's dramatic jazz score seems at first not to fit Preminger's narrative--sharp, provocative, cold, ironic, distant. The point is that the key to the role of the music is its relationship to Laura Manion. The music contains the film's comment on her role in the events: Laura's sexuality plays havoc with the ordered world of masculine calculations.

In the final effect the strength of Anatomy of a Murder rests on the dialogues--precise and witty, if somewhat ostentatious; on the very skillful film-making (the $1\frac{1}{2}$-hour-long trial scene is gripping, the camerawork twisting and suggestive, the credit titles striking), and finally on the acting. Joseph N. Welch, the Boston attorney who rose to national fame during the McCarthy hearings (he uttered the condemnation of the late senator) plays the wise old judge. The publicity resulting from this helped to promote the film. James Stewart is good as a lawyer with a passion for fishing, and George C. Scott memorable as the slick and arrogant prosecutor.

SOME LIKE IT HOT Billy Wilder

Script: Wilder and I. A. L. Diamond, suggested by Robert Thoeren and M. Logan's scenario for the film Fanfaren der Liebe (1951) directed by Kurt Hoffmann. Photography: Charles Lang Jr. Music: Adolph Deutsch. Songs Supervision: Matty Malneck. Songs: "Running Wild" by A. H. Gibbs and Leo Wood; "I Want to Be Loved by You" by Herbert Stothart and Bert Kalmar; "I'm Through with Love" by Matty Malneck and Gus Kahn. Art Direction: Ted Haworth; also Edward G. Boyle. Editing: Arthur Schmidt. Cast: Jack Lemmon (Jerry alias Daphne), Tony Curtis (Joe alias Josephine), Marilyn Monroe ("Sugar Kane" Kowalczyk), George Raft ("Spats" Colombo), Joe E. Brown (Osgood Fielding III), Pat O'Brien (Inspector Mulligan), Nehemiah Persoff (Bonaparte), Joan Shawlee (Sweet Sue), Billy Gray (Sig Poliakoff), George E. Stone ("Toothpick" Charlie), Dave Barry (Beinstock), Edward G. Robinson Jr. (Johnny Paradise), Barbara Drew (Nellie), Beverly Wills (Dolores), Helen Perry (Rosella), Laurie Mitchell (Mary Lou), Sandy Warner (Emily), Tito Voula (Mozarella), John Indrisano (Waiter), Tom Kennedy (Bouncer).

Billy Wilder for Mirisch Company, U. S. A. 10,930 ft., 121 mins.

Some Like It Hot is without a doubt Wilder's most successful comedy. Fifteen years later it would be described as "retro" and its stylish appeal explained as due to the public's fascination with the past. In 1959 it was received simply as the best clownery to be had on the screen, and the setting of the story needed no explaining. What other period provides such a splendid backdrop for comedy romps as Chicago in the Roaring Twenties, during Prohibition thirst, gangster warfare, the last carnival before the Depression, the beginning of the Swing Era?

February 14, 1929. Joe (Tony Curtis) and Jerry (Jack Lemmon), two unemployed musicians are accidental witnesses of the St. Valentine's Day Massacre. To avoid being caught by the henchmen of Spats Colombo (who has just liquidated the rival gang of Toothpick Charlie) Joe and Jerry dress as women and join an all-girl band headed for Miami. Joe falls in love with Sugar Kane (Marilyn Monroe) and woos her disguised as an indolent rich playboy, while Jerry, still in female attire, is pursued by an elderly albeit eager millionaire. Alas, it turns out that their Miami hotel is the scene of a gangland meeting. Joe and Jerry are recognized, and they have to use their wits and go through many adventures before they escape from the gangsters and the police, to the millionaire's yacht; they take Sugar with them. In the last scene Jack Lemmon decides to confess that he will not be able to meet the millionaire's expectations. "I cannot have children." "We can adopt some." Then he says in desperation: "But I am a man." To this he receives an answer generally considered to be one of the funniest lines in cinema history: "Nobody's perfect."

It is true that many situations in Some Like It Hot are easily recognizable as excuses for well-known, facile quips. Wilder was never afraid to handle third-rate material or to risk occasional unsavory double entendres, and generally avoided the attendant traps with a whole skin. This he managed also in Some Like It Hot, where some episodes are really rather doubtful to say the least (like Sugar's erotic maneuvers during her visit to the yacht), a fault to be blamed entirely on the director. However, this is compensated for by so many splendid situations and brilliant dialogue lines, so many multi-storey comical scenes (illicit whisky being transported in a hearse, the tango, Lemmon's desperate strip) that one is inclined to lower the curtain of mercy on the errors. To the film's credit are its brisk pace, the bravura editing, the skill with which Wilder scatters gangsters' corpses all over the screen and his ease in switching over from macabre grotesque to carefree fun. The picture contains four first-class comedy performances: Wilder said it was "sheer happiness" to work with Jack Lemmon; Tony Curtis was never in such good form; Joe E. Brown is unforgettable as an eccentric millionaire temporarily between the wives; while Marilyn Monroe in her speciality of a dumb blonde reaches perfection which can be compared only with her appearance in Let's Make Love (1960). The fact that it is most difficult to play a fool is confirmed by the authority of Laurence Olivier, who from among his many screen parts favors that of Archie Rice in The Entertainer (1960). Despite everything one feels Marilyn Monroe is still not sufficiently recognized as an actress, and the lack of recognition of a talent imprisoned inside a beautiful body was the main reason for the depression which finally claimed her life. Some Like It Hot is one of the last manifestations on the screen of the fascinating personality of the actress who only after her death in 1962 became one of the great myths of the cinema. Lee Strasberg, Marilyn's teacher from the Actors' Studio so rightly said over her grave:

> Others were as physically beautiful as she was, but there was obviously something more in her, something that people saw and recognized in her performances and with which they identified. She had a luminous quality--a combination of wistfulness, radiance, yearning--that set her apart and yet made everyone wish to be part of it, to share in the childish naïveté which was at once so shy and yet so vibrant.

LE TROU (The Hole) Jacques Becker

Script: José Giovanni, Becker and Jean Aurel from the novel by Giovanni. Photography: Ghislain Cloquet. Editing: Marguerite Renoir, Geneviève Vaury. Cast: Philippe Leroy (Manu), Marc Michel (Gaspard), Jean Kéraudy (Roland Darban), Raymond Meunier ("Monseigneur"), Michel Constantin (Jo), André Bervil (Prison Governor), Jean-Paul Coquelin (Grinval), Eddy Rasimi (Bouboule, the guard), Catherine Spaak (Nicole).

Serge Silberman for Play-Art/Filmsonor/Titanus, France/Italy. Originally 140 mins., reduced to 11,049 ft., 123 mins.

After he made Touchez pas au grisbi Becker's career flagged for several years. He made a film about Ali-Baba, then one about Arsène Lupin, the arch-detective. Later still, following the death of Max Ophüls, Becker rewrote the script and took over the direction of Montparnasse 19 (1958), a film about the painter Modigliani. But then came Le Trou, Becker's finest work. Peter Cowie, the critic, commented on this superb picture: "It is a compelling comment on humanity in harness as well as a work of suspense, and consequently it is among the finest escape films of all time." Becker drafted the script of Le Trou in 1947, eleven years before he made the film, after the press had reported an attempted escape by five prisoners from the Santé prison. The decision to go ahead with the project was taken after Becker read the novel by José Giovanni, one of the participants. He met Giovanni and through him three of the others. One of the men, Jean Kéraudy, plays a part which closely corresponds with his own story.

Four long-term convicts occupy Cell 6, Division II of the Santé prison in Paris: Manu, the murderer and leader of the group; Monseigneur, an old crook; Roland, who was a thief during the Occupation and who has made repeated attempts to escape; and Jo, a deserter turned criminal. Gaspard, a younger prisoner accused of attempting to shoot his wife, is transferred from another cell. They decide to let him into their confidence: they are planning to escape. A splinter of looking-glass tied to a toothbrush and thrust through the spy-hole serves as a periscope to warn them if the guards approach. They start to dig, file through iron, smash a mass of concrete, reach the vaults, then the sewers. Two of them have a glimpse of the outside world through a street manhole before returning to the cell to make the final arrangements. Then Gaspard is summoned before the Governor: his wife has withdrawn the charges, and he will soon be free. He betrays the plan to the guards who pounce on the would-be escapers.

Le Trou is spiritually and formally contained between La

Grande illusion on which Becker was an assistant to his mentor Renoir, and Bresson's A Man Escaped. As were those pictures, whose attitudes Becker combines, it is a story about man's invincible striving for freedom. It is interesting that Becker tried very hard to get away from the influence of A Man Escaped, wanting his film to be "human and warm," as was Renoir, instead of "human and impersonal" as was Bresson. In the event his creative method is basically the same as Bresson's; it is only that instead of objects the camera scrutinizes faces. Equally fine is his film technique, the editing and the photography, equally intense the film's realism. The effect is similarly fascinating. The main difference is that, apart from the last seconds of the film, Becker uses natural sound effects in place of music.

Becker: "I was fascinated by a purely psychological problem--the communal existence of individuals of different temperaments and different attitudes, who are condemned to be continually in each other's company." Rather than portraying the milieu, as in Casque d'or and Touchez pas au grisbi, Becker portrays here human characters within a milieu. In this idealistic picture he treats his protagonists with enormous sympathy. They have staked everything on their freedom, and are working towards it as systematically as they fold cardboard boxes in the prison workshop. As in Bresson, the backgrounds of the men remain obscure. It is not important who they were before they found themselves in prison. But while they are confined cooperation means all and Becker sums it up in succinct shots. One of them shows Roland's hand groping for Jo's who is buried in a cave-in. This is a story of the struggle of man against matter. Although the protagonists fail to escape in the end, they win a moral victory. The only real loser is the man who betrayed them--because his defeat is a moral one.

After the short burst of violence at the end of Le Trou, the image fades away and Rubinstein's "Melodie" is heard over the credits. This is the end of Becker's cinema. The director died prematurely, aged 54, on February 21, 1960.

FIRES ON THE PLAIN (Nobi) Kon Ichikawa

Script: Natto Wada, from the novel by Shohei Ooka. Photography: Setsuo Kobayashi. Music: Yasushi Akutagawa. Art Direction: Tokuji Shibata. Editing: Kon Ichikawa. Cast: Eiji Funakoshi (Tamura), Osamu Takizawa (Yasuda), Micky Curtis (Nagamatsu), Mantaro Ushio (Sergeant), Yoshihiro Hamaguchi (Officer), Kyu Sazanka (Army surgeon), Masaya Tsukida and Yasushi Sugita (Soldiers).

Masaichi Nagata for Daiei, Japan. 9700 ft., 108 mins. Daieiscope.

Winter 1945, the last stages of the war in the Philippines. The Japanese army is collapsing under the attack of the American forces and harried by the Filipino guerrillas who burn huge fires for the purpose of communication on the extensive central plains. Told they must never surrender, the soldiers can either run or commit suicide. Private Tamura, a sensitive man, suffers from tuberculosis. Having been rejected by a hospital, he takes to the hills. In a deserted village he comes upon the corpses of massacred Japanese troops; he tries to be friendly with two young Filipino lovers, but shoots the girl in panic when she begins to scream. Tamura returns to the jungle and throws away his gun. Meeting three Japanese soldiers he is horrified to hear that they have lived on human flesh during the New Guinea campaign. They set off for the coast but are shelled by American tanks while trying to cross a highway. Tamura hides in the hills, delirious with hunger and thirst; he comes across Nagamatsu, a soldier he met outside the hospital, and his companion Yasuda who live on what they say is monkey meat. Truth dawns on Tamura when he discovers a severed human hand. Nagamatsu shoots Yasuda and gorges on his flesh; Tamura, sickened by the spectacle, kills Nagamatsu and staggers towards the fires on the plain. Half-demented, he wants to surrender, but is shot down by a guerrilla soldier. He falls, his hands raised as if in protest.

Tamura's Calvary is shown in tones of gruesome poetry in a picture which thematically, if not stylistically, parallels The Burmese Harp. The central character has only sensitivity in common with Mizushima, the protagonist of that film, and lacks his mystic sense of purpose. Ichikawa is no longer interested in the ideas of expiation and hope: hope is abandoned, catharsis impossible and the film studies man's essential need to survive juxtaposed to his attempts to maintain at least a vestige of human dignity. In the film which is one of the most desperate cries of protest against war in the cinema, Ichikawa does not explain or analyse. He shows people as mere insects caught up in a situation beyond their control. War is condemned because it brutalizes people and makes impossible the ideal of beauty and harmony which he, an aesthete, pursued all his life. Ichikawa is not interested in motivation, as was Masaki Kobayashi in The Human Condition, made at the same time, nor in the historical reconstruction of events, but in stark facts of despair and hunger. A man invites Tamura to eat his arm when he is dead; a tear rolls down the cheek of a young soldier as he tastes salt again.... In this fatalistic vision of a holocaust the enemies are the guerrillas, the Americans, even the sly and treacherous fellow countrymen--and nature which always follows its inexorable course.

While Fires on the Plain is one of the most horrifying portrayals of war ever seen on the screen, it is also a film of an almost hypnotic fascination. The narrative is slow and contemplative and includes enclaves of sudden violence. The film has great inner discipline, and over half of it is without dialogue. Ichikawa has always been able to discover poetry even in the most unexpected situations, and so he does here. Fire is one of his favorite images (note in this context The Flame of Torment) and is used here both as a symbol of purification and as that of fast vanishing hope. Setsuo Kobayashi's photography is reminiscent of an etching.

LOOK BACK IN ANGER Tony Richardson

Script: Nigel Kneale, from the play by John Osborne. Dialogues: Osborne. Photography: Oswald Morris. Music: Chris Barber. Art Direction: Peter Glazier. Editing: Richard Best. Cast: Richard Burton (Jimmy Porter), Mary Ure (Alison Porter), Claire Bloom (Helena Charles), Edith Evans (Mrs. Tanner), Gary Raymond (Cliff Lewis), Glen Byam Shaw (Colonel Redfern), Phyllis Neilson-Terry (Mrs. Redfern), Donald Pleasence (Hurst), Jordan Lawrence (Producer), George Devine (Doctor), Benice Swanson (Sally), Jane Eccles (Miss Drury), Walter Hudd (Actor).

Woodfall, G. B. 9014 ft., 100 mins.

On May 8, 1956, the Royal Court Theatre in London premiered John Osborne's play "Look Back in Anger," and that day is considered the beginning of the Angry Young Men movement in British arts, particularly the cinema and the theatre. Angry Young Men protested against the dullness and philistinism of British society in general and against the lethargy of the cultural establishment in particular. They demanded a cinema with a new sphere of interest and a new aesthetic program, a cinema which would reflect real life and not merely middle-class fancies. It is significant in this context that the members of the movement had a background of making documentary films. Some of these demands had been met already, by Clayton's Room at the Top, but the clearest exposition of the Angry Young Men is to be found in Richardson's Look Back in Anger.

A disgruntled intellectual, Jimmy Porter runs a sweet-stall at the street market in a dull English town. His easy-going partner Cliff shares a small attic flat with Jimmy and Jimmy's wife Alison. Jimmy hates the smug middle-class values, and expresses this in aggression towards Alison of whose family background he disapproves. She married him for love despite the wishes of her parents, but still keeps in contact with them. Alison is now expecting a baby, but dares not tell her husband about it. The situation becomes more complicated when Alison's friend Helena, a young actress, comes to stay at the flat. She is appalled by Jimmy's attitudes and by the way he treats his wife. When Jimmy returns from a visit in hospital to the dying Ma Tanner, the woman trader who set him up in the stall, he finds Alison gone. Jimmy and Helena become lovers; Cliff leaves. When the news comes that Alison has lost her baby, Helena also decides to go. Alison returns to a difficult reconciliation with her husband; both are aware of how much separates them.

As Osborne's play took by storm the ossified and bourgeois British theatre, Richardson's first feature film took by storm the similarly ossified British cinema. Look Back in Anger relies for its impact mainly on the actors' gestures. It is a provocation, a cry of protest, and not a constructive proposal for social changes. Born in 1928 and educated in Oxford, Richardson worked at first as a repertory theatre director. Together with Lindsay Anderson and Karel Reisz he originated the influential Free Cinema programs at the National Film Theatre in London. They included his first short, Momma Don't Allow (1955) made in collaboration with Reisz. Members of Free Cinema set out to make committed films which took interest in the individual and, referring to the traditions of the British documentary, stressed the significance of everyday life. Lindsay Anderson said in a 1970 interview: "The movement of the Angry Young Men was never a social movement. In any case it did not have political character. Journalists badly misrepresented these things. In fact it was a ferment among intellectuals, related to the symptoms of cultural renewal in evidence throughout Europe, and to criticism of some British institutions. An Act of Parliament passed in 1956 opened the door to further education for the working class, and hopes for regenerating British culture and intellectual life were aroused. It was thus a movement of young liberal intellectuals motivated by an aversion to outdated social conventions. The only battle they finally won was the battle against censorship. The movement was in fact an association of individuals, each of whom acted for the good of his own career in the cinema."

The story of the frustration of an idealist, Look Back in Anger is a rather faithful adaptation of the play which Richardson also directed at the Royal Court. Only Jimmy's long speeches are cut from the text. The power of the protagonist's anger is conveyed through the very expressive film-making and the excellent acting. The impact of the narrative is strengthened through the use of contrasts in the image and on the soundtrack: between silence and loud trumpet solos and violent quarrels; between dark interiors and the oppressive, bright outdoor compositions. Human silhouettes in semi-darkness appear very white; there is also frequent use of close-ups. This rather un-English expressiveness is a characteristic feature of Richardson's style. In Look Back in Anger it is very effective. The actors were obviously personally sympathetic towards the spirit, emotions and the message of the picture. Fine performances are given by Richard Burton, Mary Ure (the only one in the cast who appeared in the original stage production) and by Edith Evans as the old cockney Ma Tanner (who is only spoken of in the play). Richardson, who always showed a remarkable sense for the authenticity of the dialogue, was able to overcome the stage provenance of the story. He made a film which is a vivid and genuine document of its time.

THE WORLD OF APU (Apur Sansar) Satyajit Ray

Script: Ray, based on the novel by Bibhutibhusan Bandopadhaya. Photography: Subrata Mitra. Music: Ravi Shankar. Art Direction: Banshi Chandra Gupta. Editing: Dulal Dutta. Cast: Soumitra Chatterji (Apurba Kumar Roy), Sharmila Tagore (Aparna), Shapan Mukerji (Pulu), S. Aloke Chakravarty (Kajal).

Satyajit Ray, India. 9540 ft., 106 mins.

It appears that when making Aparajito Ray had not yet decided whether or not to make a third Apu picture. He went on to make two films on other subjects. It was only after the passage of two years that he directed The World of Apu, which turned out to be the best part of the Trilogy.

Apu has left university and is trying to make his way as a writer. His friend Pulu takes him to the wedding of his cousin Aparna in the country, but the ceremony does not take place because the bridegroom is mad. Tradition requires that the bride be married all the same and Pulu, acting on behalf of the family, asks Apu to marry the girl. Apu agrees. The couple spend a few happy months in Calcutta--until Aparna returns to her family to have a baby and dies in childbirth. Apu desperately grieves after her death and even refuses to see his son. Having destroyed his unfinished novel he leaves Calcutta and works in a coal-mine in Central India. Five years later, Pulu returns from abroad to find Apu's son Kajal a savage. He tries to persuade Apu to take care of the child. Apu sees the boy, wins his affection and finally accepts him with joy. Father and son leave for Calcutta together.

Throughout the film Ray registers, with great sensitivity and remarkable economy the emotions of a young man in the seething world. Note, for instance, how he describes, with a few touches of the camera, the changes Aparna brings into Apu's bachelor flat. But he does more than that--he intimates feelings by pictorial means, and this is the thing most difficult to achieve in the film director's art. The growth of love between the young couple after their improvised wedding is shown with rare finesse. Apu's suffering and prostration after Aparna's death, his attempted suicide are extraordinarily communicated in what are now classical sequences of modern cinema. In a series of haunting images accompanied by the sitar music of the famous virtuoso Ravi Shankar, Ray creates a mood of profound melancholy. It is true that apart from poetry and beauty there is also some melodrama in The World of Apu--but it redeems itself by simply being an organic part of a fine film.

As in previous parts, the end of the picture offers a new beginning; thus the Trilogy closes on the note of natural continuity and perpetual rebirth. In the end of The World of Apu Kajal is very much as Apu was at the beginning of Pather Panchali. The film's last scene is marvellous: the small figure of a child way behind his father walking along the river bank. And yet, the protagonist of the Trilogy, as Robin Wood observed, is something of the Everyman character. This juxtaposition of intimacy and general applicability makes Ray's cinema truly universal. Thus Ray emerged from a backward country with a third-rate film industry to become a major contemporary artist. Soumitra Chatterji and Sharmila Tagore later became his constant actors.

LES QUATRE CENTS COUPS (The 400 Blows) François Truffaut

Script: Truffaut. Dialogues: Marcel Moussy. Photography: Henri Decaë. Music: Jean Constantin. Art Direction: Bernard Evein. Editing: Marie-Josèphe Yoyotte. Cast: Jean-Pierre Léaud (Antoine Doinel), Claire Maurier (Antoine's mother), Albert Rémy (Antoine's father), Guy Decomble (Schoolmaster), Patrick Auffay (René Bigey), Georges Flamant (M. Bigey), Yvonne Claudie (Mme. Bigey), François Truffaut (Roundabout man), Jeanne Moreau (Woman in street with dog), Jacques Démy (Policeman).

Les Films du Carosse/SEDIF, France. Originally 98 mins., reduced to 8460 ft., 94 mins. DyaliScope.

One of the leaders of the Nouvelle Vague, François Truffaut belongs to the group of directors who came into the cinema from film criticism. His colleagues were Chabrol, Godard, Rivette and Rohmer. Born in 1932, Truffaut had been something of a delinquent as a child. His escape from a summer holiday camp probably inspired the final scene in Les Quatre cents coups. During the final years of the war Truffaut became a committed film buff. The friendship with André Bazin, whom he met through his interest in cinema, had a formative influence on Truffaut's life. When he was imprisoned for deserting from the army, it was Bazin who obtained his release. In 1953 Truffaut was introduced to "Cahiers du Cinéma," then in its third year of publication, and rapidly established himself as an influential and severe critic. He wrote around 75 major articles and many reviews for the Cahiers, virulently attacking the old cinéma de qualité opposing it to the new cinéma d'auteur. He announced that the time of "directors" is over and the time of "authors" has come. People would write their own scripts and then make them into films themselves. Despite some minor theoretical differences (mainly as concerns the role of the film-maker's personality in the cinema) Truffaut accepted the main principles of Bazin's theory, which are as follows:

(1) Unlike the aesthetics of a painting, the aesthetics of a photographic image are determined by visual resemblance. In consequence, the relationship to reality is the main artistic criterion in the cinema. This divides directors into those who primarily believe in reality and those who believe in the image;

(2) The aesthetic quality of cinematic image is determined by the way it is presented on the screen. This divides film-makers into those who rely on editing (Bazin considered this incorrect, claiming it "damages reality") and those who rely on the actual content of the frame. Cinema should portray undeformed reality, authentically and realistically; it should strive to capture the ambiguity and multiple levels of meaning. Thus Bazin's enthusiasm for long takes and deep-focus photography.

The Nouvelle Vague developed much according to this prescription. Truffaut himself lived up to what he preached. After making three shorts, he entered feature cinema, aged 27, with the film which won first prize for direction at the momentous 1959 Cannes Film Festival. Les Quatre cents coups appeared directly after Chabrol's first two films and just before Godard's A bout de souffle. The cost was 37 million old francs, exactly the same as that of Chabrol's Le Beau Serge, and a quarter of the cost of an average commercial production. The film is dedicated to the memory of Bazin, who died six months too soon to witness his protégé's triumph.

Thirteen-year-old Antoine Doinel is the son of middle class parents living in a glum inner Paris suburb. The father is weak and henpecked by his wife; his only interest is in cars. The mother has a lover. The parents often quarrel. But in fact the father is basically a good sort, while the mother loves her son in her own way. On the whole Antoine's home life is not exceptionally unhappy. At school, teachers administer old-fashioned punishments in the old classroom. One day Antoine explains his absence from school the previous day by claiming that his mother just died. She confounds the excuse somewhat by suddenly appearing at school in person. As a result Antoine and his friend René are forbidden to come to school for a week. Antoine sleeps in hiding in René's house; they are planning a trip to the seaside which Antoine has never seen. The boys steal a typewriter from an office, find it impossible to sell and are caught as they try to return it. Antoine is sent to an institution for juvenile delinquents. His mother tells him that his father is no longer interested in him. The last scene is famous: Antoine escapes from the reform school, and after a run across the countryside which lasts 90 seconds on the screen, reaches the sea. As he turns the camera stops--on a frame which is reminiscent of an identity-card photography.

Humanism has always been at the center of Truffaut's interests, and Les Quatre cents coups is a tender and sensitive chronicle of the thirteenth year of life, a lyrical document of adolescence with its naiveté, ideals and dreams--gently humorous and very personal. While there is no doubt that the film does contain autobiographical elements (for instance, the René character is based on the director's friend, Robert Lachenay) this is not very prominent. Truffaut does not lament over his difficult youth. He said: "I am more familiar with the world of children than with the world of adults. I decided to give a study of this particular period in life, as faithfully as possible, because it is not well known to parents." The film has the open, restrained tone of a report, and indeed a feel of Balzac, whom Truffaut and his protagonist so much admire. The director succeeded in avoiding the usual problems of such a story: while being firmly based on reliable observation of facts, Les Quatre cents coups is neither a dissection of a single isolated case, nor a general social thesis. It is rich in social observation--about the decomposition of the middle-class family, the omnipresent deceit in human relationships. But his attitude is emotional rather than social. Truffaut shows that the borderline between "normal" and "abnormal" social behavior, once clearly and unambiguously defined by stiff moral norms, has become at best unclear and at worst fictitious. Social machinery is much too crude and too summary to deal with an exceptional case. Anyone who is different is promptly consigned to the social margin. Truffaut sees Antoine's behavior as a kind of self-defense.

Les Quatre cents coups puts into practice Bazin's beliefs in observing the changing forms and structures of reality. Long takes are separated by short ones; static and dynamic takes, objective and subjective takes alternate. The basic attitude of the camera can be described as "a glance of an eye": a long-held take with one or more short pans within it, as the camera transfers its attention, in steps, from one object to another. Formally the film is very simple and direct, and much of it is improvised. Its rhythm is one of collisions, conflicts, antagonisms. Description (for instance of Antoine's home or the home of his friend) is precise and interesting. At last the true Paris appears on the screen--grey, ordinary and beautifully photographed by Decaë, one of the leading cameramen of the Nouvelle Vague.

Truffaut talking about Léaud (who is excellent and later became Truffaut's constant actor): "I encouraged him to play by ear. He performed freely, reacting in his own manner and responding in his own words." Particularly fascinating in this context is the scene of Antoine's interview with an unseen psychologist. A work of considerable influence, Les Quatre cents coups is one of the most touching and understanding portrayals of childhood in the cinema.

THE GENERAL DELLA ROVERE (Il generale della Rovere) Roberto Rossellini

Script: Sergio Amidei, Diego Fabbri, Indro Montanelli and Rossellini, from the short story by Montanelli. Photography: Carlo Carlini. Music: Renzo Rossellini. Art Direction: Piero Zuffi. Editing: Cesare Cavagna. Cast: Vittorio De Sica (Emanuele Bardone), Hannes Messemer (Colonel Mueller), Vittorio Caprioli (Banchelli), Giovanna Ralli (Valeria), Sandra Milo (Olga), Anne Vernon (Chiara Fassio), Giuseppe Rossetti (Fabrizio), Baroness Barzani (Countess della Rovere), Kurt Polter (German officer), Kurt Selge (Schrantz), Mary Greco (Madame in a brothel), Lucia Modugno (Prostitute), Linda Veras (German secretary).

Zebra Film/S. N. E. Gaumont, Italy/France. Originally 137 mins., reduced to 11,830 ft., 131 mins.

It might have been a coincidence that The General della Rovere shared the Grand Prix at the 1959 Venice Film Festival with Monicelli's The Great War--but these two pictures have more in common than might appear at first. It is not only that they both describe human tragedies brought about by the World Wars (Monicelli's by the First, Rossellini's by the Second) and that they are both manifestations of independent, not to say controversial, attitudes, free from the usual moralizing. Another important similarity is their aim to demonstrate how wartime chaos polarizes and unexpectedly revalues human attitudes. The thought is not in itself something extraordinarily inventive and this is why The Great War wins in a direct confrontation between the two films. The pacifist Monicelli turned out to be much more original than the anti-Fascist Rossellini; his film is much richer in contexts, while the main message of The General della Rovere, a picture more chamber in character, is that a small-time rascal had to become a hero when he could not become a big-time scoundrel.

The story is set in Genoa during the German occupation, in the winter of 1943-44. The Americans are near Rome, at Anzio. This causes increased activity from the underground organizations, and in turn increased terror from the Nazis and their Italian supporters. A certain Bardone is making a living out of the situation by pretending he has influence with the Gestapo and extracting bribes from the families of imprisoned partisans. He is uncovered by the local Nazi Commandant who then decides to make use of him. In exchange for forgiveness of his past sins Bardone, disguised as the Italian General della Rovere, is to find out the identity of a partisan leader, Fabrizio. The General has in fact been killed in an attempt to contact Fabrizio, but only the Germans know about it. They are confident that Fabrizio is among the prisoners in the San Vittore jail in Milan. Bardone agrees at first, but is deeply shocked by the brutal treatment of prisoners, especially after he contributed to the death of one of them. Gradually, impressed by the behavior of the partisans and full of moral scruples, Bardone comes to believe in his new identity. He chooses to be shot rather than reveal the secret he has discovered.

Rossellini's film was favorably received and considered a proof of the master's return to his old excellence--a return to the Neorealist severity of expression, to important problems, to authenticity. But the applause was exaggerated, and Rossellini himself described The General della Rovere as a step backwards, a pointless continuation of old forms of narrative cinema, smooth and balanced structures, undertaken only to enable the director to do the one thing which really interested him--to study the psychology of the protagonist. Indeed, the best scenes of the film are the chamber ones with the participation of the main characters, where acting is of decisive importance. De Sica himself gives a splendid performance, while Hannes Messemer is very good as the very objectively portrayed colonel of the Nazi security force. Similarly, the second part of the film, showing Bardone's metamorphosis in the grey prison scenery, is much more convincing than the first. In the overall effect however only some dynamic scenes in the film's final sequences (the bomb raid, the prisoners' protest at the shooting of the supposed General) are really great, while those which do not resort to pathos are stiffly staged and sketchy in their development of the plot. In the first part of the film there is even more to complain about: the description of the milieu in which the swindler Bardone operates lacks authenticity, even the outside scenery looks theatrical, and Rossellini cannot handle his extras (just think, the man who was the father of Neorealism!). It seems that the director made an error in using what can be described as "painstaking negligence"--the deliberate disorder on the set, intended to have the effect of authenticity but instead resulting in redoubled artificiality. This well exemplifies the anachronism of the Neorealist method: in 1959 the spirit and scenery of 1944 had to be recreated and not filmed directly. Rossellini returned once more to a para-documentary treatment of a wartime story in Era notte a Roma (1960); when the film disappointed his expectations he embarked on a consistent search for authenticity of people and objects not on the basis of the old Neorealist method, but by reconstructing hypothetical human behavior in definite historical periods. This is how he made the magnificent The Sun-King, or the Assumption of Power by Louis XIV.

ON THE BEACH Stanley Kramer

Script: John Paxton and James Lee Barrett, from the novel by Nevil Shute. Photography: Giuseppe Rotunno. Music: Ernest Gold.

Art Direction: Fernando Carrere. Editing: Frederic Knudtson. Song "Waltzing Matilda" by Marie Cowan and A. B. Patterson. Cast: Gregory Peck (Dwight Towers), Ava Gardner (Moira Davidson), Fred Astaire (Julian Osborn), Anthony Perkins (Peter Holmes), Donna Anderson (Mary Holmes), John Tate (Admiral Bridie), Lola Brooks (Lt. Hosgood), John Meillon (Swain), Lou Vernon (Davidson), Guy Doleman (Farrel), Ken Wayne (Benson), Richard Meikle (Davis), Harp McGuire (Sundstrom), Jim Barrett (Chrysler), Basil Buller Murphy (Sir Douglas Froude), Keith Eden (Dr. Fletcher), John Royle (Senior Officer), Frank Gatcliff (Radio officer), Paddy Moran (Port man), John Casson (Salvation Army captain), Kevin Brennan (Dr. King), C. Harding Brown (Dykers), Grant Taylor (Morgan), Peter Williams (Professor Jorgenson), Harvey Adams (Sykes), Stuart Finch (Jones), Joe McCormick (Ackerman), Audine Leith (Betty), Jerry Ian Seals (Fogarty), Carey Paul Peck (Boy), Katherine Hill (Jennifer Holmes), Peter O'Shaughnessy (Jorgenson associate).

Stanley Kramer for Lomitas, U. S. A. 12,088 ft., 134 mins.

Kramer, who has repeatedly shown himself to be a socially well-intentioned director and producer, followed The Defiant Ones, a study of the color problem, by On the Beach, a vision of a nuclear disaster which he sees as a logical result of the death wish which fuels the arms race. It is one of the series of responsible apocalyptic pictures about the end of the world, of which another eminent work was Lumet's Fail-Safe (1964).

April 1964. The Northern Hemisphere has been destroyed by a nuclear war, and radioactive fallout is expected to reach Australia in about five months. The government distributes suicide pills for which queues form in the streets. Dwight Towers, captain of the U. S. submarine "Sawfish" which put into Melbourne, is sent on a voyage north to investigate. Julian Osborn, a nuclear physicist, and Peter Holmes, an Australian liaison officer, also take part in the cruise. There are reports of garbled radio signals from the San Diego area. The submarine reaches San Francisco, now a deserted town. The radio signal was sent by a soft drink bottle caught in a blind cord tapping on a Morse key. After the return to Australia, Julian wins a Grand Prix car race (in which many drivers literally seek death) and then kills himself; Peter, his wife and baby take the alleviating pill. The submarine crew, some of whom begin to be affected by radioactivity, demand that the ship returns to America. Dwight, who has in the meantime fallen in love with a hard-drinking Australian girl, decides to take "Sawfish" home. The ship submerges for the last time....

Kramer took his warning to the world very seriously indeed, and the film had simultaneous premieres in eighteen important cities around the globe. Some thought that he exaggerated a bit in his naive good will--but then Nevil Shute, the author of the novel, exaggerated the facts. It is simply that by 1959 mankind did not yet wield the power for world destruction nor could it make possible the events shown in the film. More pertinent than that is Penelope Houston's criticism that the leading actors (Gregory Peck + Ava Gardner + Fred Astaire + Anthony Perkins) are quite unnecessarily international stars: "Kramer is unlikely to convince anyone that this quartet is in imminent danger of any kind of extinction." True--but then the effect of this commercial compromise was largely counter-balanced by two circumstances. Firstly, the acting is in itself very good and the casting rather unusual. Secondly, Giuseppe Rotunno, the Italian Neorealist cameraman, gave his sharp, grainy and austere photography a certain documentary texture, which makes the stars appear simply as human beings.

There is a remarkable scene in the picture: the submarine emerges in San Francisco Bay to a fascinating vision of empty, silent streets. For all its faults, this is certainly a well-made film. Even though 1964 is safely past, it retains much of its original power, which at the time was of considerable political importance.

TIGER BAY J. Lee Thompson

Script: John Hawkesworth and Shelley Smith, from the short story "Rudolphe et le revolver" by Noël Calef. Photography: Eric Cross. Music: Laurie Johnson. Art Direction: Edward Carrick. Editing: Sidney Hayers. Cast: Horst Buchholz (Bronek Korczyński), Hayley Mills (Gillie), John Mills (Police Superintendent Graham), Megs Jenkins (Mrs. Philips), Yvonne Mitchell (Ania), Anthony Dawson (Barclay), George Selway (Det. Sgt. Harvey), George Pastell (Captain of the "Paloma"), Marne Maitland (Dr. Das).

John Hawkesworth for Julian Wintle/Leslie Parkyn, G. B. 9450 ft., 105 mins.

Gillie, the lonely 11-year-old girl is a chance witness of a quarrel between a Polish sailor and his girl who during his absence found another man. During the scuffle the girl dies from a shot from a gun which she drew herself. Young Gillie steals the gun to impress her friends who think her childish and then lies to the police about the murder. The sailor decides to leave Great Britain surreptitiously and to protect himself makes the girl hide with him until the ship sails. A warm mutual attachment develops between the two. Gillie is delighted by such a turn of things: she is friendly with an outlaw, lives through great adventure, spins dreams of a sea voyage. When the sailor leaves, a police superintendent finds the girl and takes her aboard the ship, which is still within British territorial waters, to identify the killer. She refuses and it seems that he will go free when she falls overboard; but the fugitive dives to save her at the price of his freedom.

After the interesting The Yellow Balloon (1952) Lee Thompson again returns to the behavior of a child in the presence of crime. Tiger Bay is a success not only because the director had the good luck to find the 13-year-old Hayley Mills, a girl with an extraordinary acting intuition, a daughter worthy of the reputation of her father John Mills. It is quite another thing that Hayley Mills would never again be given a better opportunity to use her talent. An equally important reason for the film's success is the use of a correct proportion of sensation, sense of humor, lyricism, behavioral observation and the mood. Disturbing this proportion could very easily have turned the picture into a conventional melodrama (and this danger was inherent in the script), into maudlin, "poetic" nonsense or a story of violence. In the already mentioned The Yellow Balloon (1952) Lee Thompson opted for cold drama of atmosphere; while the moods dominant in Tiger Bay are those of optimism and warmth. It is true that he could have shown more insight in portraying the two main characters united in their sense of isolation (Horst Buchholz, a not always convincing actor, is here very good)--but even in this less ambitious dimension the picture can never be accused of superficiality. This is mainly due to narrative fluency and inventive handling of decisive scenes. Lee Thompson once more impressed with his film-making craft in The Guns of Navarone. Unfortunately, this was his only successful undertaking after he abandoned intimate dramas for the sake of giant spectaculars.

MIDDLE OF THE NIGHT Delbert Mann

Script: Paddy Chayefsky, from his own TV play, later directed on Broadway by Joshua Logan. Photography: Joseph Brun. Music: George Bassman. Art Direction: Edward S. Haworth. Editing: Carl Lerner. Cast: Fredric March (Jerry Kingsley), Kim Novak (Betty Preisser), Glenda Farrell (Mrs. Mueller), Albert Dekker (Walter Lockman), Martin Balsam (Jack), Joan Copeland (Lillian), Jan Norris (Alice, Betty's sister), Lee Grant (Marilyn), Effie Afton (Mrs. Carrol, a neighbor), Lee Philips (George), Edith Meiser (Evelyn Kingsley), Betty Walker (Rosalind Neiman), Audrey Peters (Elizabeth Kingsley), David Ford (Paul Kingsley), Rudy Bond (Gould), Lou Gilbert (Sherman), Anna Berger (Caroline).

George Justin for Sudan Productions, U. S. A. 10,553 ft., 118 mins.

Middle of the Night was scripted by Paddy Chayefsky from a television, later a theatre play presented on Broadway by Joshua Logan (himself director of Picnic, a spiritually related film): the scriptwriter's name alone gives one an idea of the picture's sentiments.

Jerry Kingsley, a 56-year-old widower, is a co-owner of a clothing factory. His sister keeps house for him. Jerry meets Betty Preisser, a divorcee half his age who works at the factory, falls in love with her, and she agrees to marry him. Both families, particularly Jerry's married daughter, oppose the marriage; Jerry goes through much suffering and quarrels with Betty. When her ex-husband unexpectedly comes back and she turns to him for help, Jerry vows not to see her again. He changes his mind after the suicide of his partner, and decides that he and Betty need each other.

Family life as a refuge from frustration and loneliness is Chayefsky's theme familiar from Delbert Mann's Marty and The Bachelor Party. The new motifs are the preoccupation with old age and the Jewish-gentile angle (Jerry is Jewish but Betty is not). The ending leaves some doubts as to the stability of the future marriage--but the point was simply that being together is always better than loneliness, the conclusion of Bergman's films repeatedly reached in the 50's in a quite different environment. One might complain that the alternative between Jerry and Lockman, his salacious business partner, is a bit too easy. Fredric March's performance is largely responsible for the film's impact. Kim Novak, inexperienced and vulnerable as Betty, is not really able to help the hero (unlike in The Man with the Golden Arm where she is a great support for Sinatra).

What is supposed to be a universal problem of loneliness and the difficulty of communication between people belonging to different generations in fact has a distinct American ring around it: in the land of the cult of success people struggle desperately against being pushed onto the social margin. Middle of the Night is an essentially American mid-20th century expression of the belief in the need for activity in life, a protest against the emptiness of an automated existence. Consider how differently this problem would have been treated in a different country and in a different period--for instance in Chekhov's Russia.

NORTH BY NORTHWEST Alfred Hitchcock

Script: Ernest Lehman. Photography: Robert Burks. Music: Bernard Herrmann. Art Direction: Robert Boyle, William A. Horning, Merrill Pye, Henry Grace and Frank McKelvey. Editing: George Tomasini. Cast: Cary Grant (Roger O. Thornhill), Eva Marie Saint (Eve Kendall), James Mason (Philip Vandamm), Jessie Royce Landis (Clara Thornhill), Leo G. Carroll (Professor), Philip Ober (Lester Townsend), Josephine Hutchinson ("Mrs. Townsend", the housekeeper), Martin Landau (Leonard), Adam Williams (Valerian), Edward Platt (Victor Larrabee), Robert Ellenstein (Licht), Les Tremayne (Auctioneer), Philip Coolidge (Dr. Cross).

North by Northwest

Alfred Hitchcock for MGM, U.S.A. 12,256 ft., 136 mins. VistaVision. Technicolor.

Hitchcock returns once more to his favorite motifs of mistaken identity, of the deceptive outward appearances of things and of sudden danger lurking for every ordinary citizen. A respectable advertising executive (Cary Grant) becomes accidentally involved in a struggle between American Intelligence with a foreign spy network. Mistaken for a Mr. Caplan, a non-existent CIA agent, he is kidnapped by the spies, framed for a murder committed in the UN Building, and finds himself a fugitive from both the law and the spies. In the course of his fantastic adventures which take him from New York, through the sights of America and end in South Dakota, he several times narrowly escapes death and becomes involved with the spies' beautiful accomplice.

Hitchcock has always maintained that the introduction of even a most ingeniously devised scene must be motivated by the events of the film; but here he clearly does not take this rule too seriously himself. Stylistically probably the most typical of his American films, North by Northwest does not hold water from the point of view of the contents, even if treated as an intentional spoof of a spy movie. Hitchcock cracks a double-edged joke about the character of the story in the film's title, taken from Act II, Scene 2 of "Hamlet." In that scene Hamlet hints to Rosenkrantz and Guildenstern that he is not really mad: "I am but mad north-north-west: when the wind is southerly I know a hawk from a handsaw." North by Northwest is a series of brilliantly staged episodes propelled by a logically disjointed and outright nonsensical plot, and the witty interludes hinting at the absurdity of many details cannot really justify inconsistencies typical of stereotyped sensational productions. The difference lies in quality: North by Northwest is far superior to run-of-the-mill entertainment movies (for instance to the James Bond series which it resembles) with its inventive building of situations, the ease of the ironic humor, the skillful visual effects and the excellent use of the scenery. The 7-minute sequence, entirely devoid of dialogue or action in which Cary Grant waits for a car among the fields and is then attacked by a crop-dusting plane, the final scramble on the gigantic stone heads of the most famous American presidents hewn in the rocks of Mount Rushmore, are the best testimony for the style and the film-making craft of North by Northwest, and find a permanent place among screen classics.

WARLOCK Edward Dmytryk

Script: Robert Alan Aurthur, based on the novel by Oakley Hall. Photography: Joseph MacDonald. Music: Leigh Harline. Art

Direction: Lyle R. Wheeler and Herman A. Blumenthal. Editing: Jack W. Holmes. Cast: Henry Fonda (Clay Blaisdell), Richard Widmark (Johnny Gannon), Anthony Quinn (Tom Morgan), Dorothy Malone (Lily Dollar), Dolores Michaels (Jessie Marlow), Wallace Ford (Judge Holloway), Tom Drake (Abe McQuown), Richard Arlen (Bacon), DeForest Kelley (Curley Burne), Regis Toomey (Skinner), Vaughn Taylor (Richardson), Don Beddoe (Dr. Wagner), Whit Bissell (Petrix), Bartlett Robinson (Slavin), J. Anthony Hughes (Shaw), Donald Barry (Calhoun), Frank Gorshin (Billy Gannon), Ian MacDonald (MacDonald), L. Q. Jones (Jiggs).

Edward Dmytryk for 20th Century-Fox, U. S. A. 10,980 ft., 122 mins. CinemaScope. De Luxe Color.

Warlock can be described as the psychoanalytical variety of the superwestern. Dmytryk, who from the anti-racialist Crossfire (1947) to the Machiavellian Mirage (1965) constantly showed an inclination to describe deviations of human characters in different situations and different historical periods, this time chooses a shanty town in the 19th-century West as the background for his Freudian analyses. As a matter of fact this is his second effort of this kind; but while Broken Lance (1954) was a striking example of a pretentious psychological speculation, Warlock amounts to one of the best achievements of the genre.

The citizens of the small town of Warlock hire Clay Blaisdell, a professional gunman, to bring order to the community. They consider this a necessary evil: Blaisdell and his club-footed gambler friend Morgan are still not as bad as the degenerate San Pablo cowboys who terrorize the town. Order is introduced, but not for long. Women become involved in the conflict. While the townsfolk plan to rid themselves of the troublesome Blaisdell-Morgan team--after Blaisdell did what he was hired for--and give sheriff's job to a local candidate, a violent conflict breaks out in which Morgan forces Blaisdell to shoot him. This temporarily unhinges Blaisdell's reason. In the morning however he realizes that his day is over, throws down his gun and leaves the town. The period of pioneers and chaos is finished; normal law takes over in Warlock.

Dmytryk directed the film with a sure hand, expressively staged the numerous dramatic conflicts, stressing them still further by condensing the atmosphere, which even created a somewhat hysterical effect (rather common as a matter of fact in the American cinema of the period, and always caused by the same thing--the combination of great ambition and lack of a sense of humor). But the picture's main strength is in the script by Robert Alan Aurthur, who had earlier similarly contributed to the drama Edge of the City. Richness of situations and observation ranging in character from Freud to ancient tragedy seems even to exceed the capacity of the film and puts strain on the dramatic structure of Warlock. Some of these elements get lost on the roadside in the course of the complex narrative, but those which remain open new perspective for the western. The study of the relationship between the two comrades who need each other, which dominates the film is less relevant here than the very interesting description of the relationship between professional gunmen and the whole of the community, and the redefining of the man who is instrumental in introducing order. How different is Blaisdell from the traditional hero of the West! He is not concerned with abstract moral imperatives but with the more tangible financial gain, not with peace as a social necessity but with efficient countering of violence by violence, not with romantic gratitude but with rational acquisition of a social position. In the final effect the film compromises the cult of strength and gives support to one of the classical tenets of the western (that only a man with clean hands can be the instrument of the law)--but this finale is arrived at via an absolutely un-traditional, but very credible, development of situations. In the overall effect Warlock occupies a special place among westerns, in that it makes a step towards de-mythologizing of the genre not in the direction in which further polemic with tradition will go. There is in the film too much disproportion, nervous narrative, alien thematic inserts, such as bookish symbolism--which could have ruined the structure of the drama were it not for the actors, whom Dmytryk knew how to appreciate and use properly. Anthony Quinn and especially Henry Fonda with great involvement portray the crashed anarchists of the West and give the cold solemnity of the film a tone of moving thoughtfulness.

BALTIC EXPRESS (Pociąg) [Night Train] Jerzy Kawalerowicz

Script: Jerzy Lutowski and Kawalerowicz. Photography: Jan Laskowski. Music: Andrzej Trzaskowski. Art Direction: Ryszard Potocki. Cast: Lucyna Winnicka (Marta), Leon Niemczyk (Jerzy), Teresa Szmigielówna (Blondie), Zbigniew Cybulski (Staszek), Ignacy Machowski (Canon), Roland Głowacki (Murderer), Zygmunt Zintel (Man who suffers from insomnia), Helena Dąbrowska (Conductress).

Jerzy Rutowicz for ZAF Kadr, Poland. 9043 ft., 100 mins.

Four important directors emerged in Poland during the 50's: Wajda, Kutz, Munk and Kawalerowicz. Kawalerowicz made his first independent film in 1954, two years before the rise of the "Polish School." Baltic Express is a reflection of the changes which had taken place in the national cinema since his debut: its mood of sadness is a reaction to the previously mandatory Socialist Realist optimism.

Marta buys a sleeping car ticket to the Baltic coast from a stranger. The compartment turns out to be for men only, and Jerzy, who was hoping to have it for himself, is forced to share. During the journey an uneasy relationship develops between the two. Marta is running away from a lover (who is also on the train pleading with her to return); Jerzy is a doctor whose patient has just died after an operation. Police board the train looking for a murderer who holds berth no. 16 and Jerzy is arrested. But Marta, who has exchanged berths with Jerzy, recognizes the man who sold her the ticket hidden behind an overcoat in another compartment. The murderer jumps off the train and is caught by the passengers. On arrival at the coast Jerzy is met by his wife. Marta remains alone.

The picture has been superficially compared with Hitchcock's The Lady Vanishes. But its true allegiances are in the contemporary cinema in Western Europe. Kawalerowicz said he had been influenced by Antonioni's Il grido, and his film is concerned with the loneliness and emotional starvation of people who pass each other as ships in the night, with the need for, and impossibility of, love. The intrigue and the "problem" are consciously almost eliminated, in favor of expanded generic and psychological observation. The whole of Baltic Express is sustained in the tone of an understated reflection--refined in rhythm, very inventive in staging, while on the intellectual level the story of a sleeping carriage where no one sleeps strikes with its melodramatic banality. The literary and pretentious script, poor in situations and conflicts and telling the spectator little about the characters, is in fact the main weakness of Baltic Express.

Still, as if to spite the script, Kawalerowicz made a very interesting picture. He was fascinated by people who cannot achieve things they aim for, by the sense of unfulfillment, a longing for change and adventure--and conveyed this feeling via the film's very precise execution. Wójcik's excellent photography performs the task of psychological analysis, bringing out poetry in many situations. The image of the passengers returning at dawn to a brightly-lit train instantly conveys the sense of dew, cold, tiredness and embarrassment. Often the style is similar to Antonioni's, even though Baltic Express does occasionally use cinematic effects which are too subtle to be sincere. Kawalerowicz brilliantly stages individual scenes in-depth along the axis of the corridor of a carriage--with the passing landscape, very well caught in movement, as a continual counterpoint for the static scenes inside the crowded train. He builds an inner logic of encounters, glances and conflicts. The rhythm is precise and sharp, punctuated by the opening-closing of carriage doors. This accuracy of dramatic construction creates an increasing sense of anxiety and expectation.

The stylized unnaturalness of the pair of main characters is surprising in Kawalerowicz, who in his early Cellulose (1954) showed that he knew how to make a realistic picture. Unfortunately, this later became a lasting feature of his style--bringing coolness to Mother Joan of the Angels and Pharaoh, and leading to total disaster in The Game (1969).

ODD OBSESSIONS (Kagi) Kon Ichikawa

Script: Natto Wada, Keiji Hasebe and Ichikawa, from the novel by Jun'ichiro Tanizaki. Photography: Kazuo Miyagawa. Music: Yasushi Akutagawa. Art Direction: Tomowo Shimogawara. Editing: Kon Ichikawa. Cast: Ganjiro Nakamura (Kenji Kenmochi), Machiko Kyo (Ikuko Kenmochi), Tatsuya Nakadai (Kimura), Junko Kato (Toshiko Kenmochi), Tanie Kitabayashi (Hana), Ichiro Sugai (Masseur), Jun Hamamura (Dr. Soma), Mantaro Ushio (Dr. Kodama), Kyu Sazanka (Curio dealer).

Hiroaki Fujii for Daiei, Japan. 9630 ft., 107 mins. Daieiscope. Daieicolor.

The production of Odd Obsessions was undertaken by Daiei for obvious commercial reasons. Sex was something bound to attract the interest of the public, the company had the blessing of Tanizaki, the well-known author of the popular novel--and a director of the standard of Ichikawa, who had recently made The Flame of Torment and Fires on the Plain. The project had a certain attraction for Ichikawa, who planned to make yet another study of an abnormal state of mind. It did not quite work out that way: in the first place because of the basic incompatibility of the novel with any dramatic convention known to cinema at the time, and secondly because of commercial pressures. Odd Obsessions is no more than a formal exercise, a sophisticated portrayal of sexual torment.

An aging Kyoto art historian married to a young woman is anxious to rekindle his failing sexual passion. When the effects of hormonal injections wear off, Kenmochi finds stimulation in taking nude pictures of his wife Ikuko. Later he drives Kimura, the avaricious fiancé of his daughter, into Ikuko's arms to add jealousy as a further stimulant. He dies in her bed while watching her undress. The three remaining characters die from insecticide in the salad served by an old color-blind maidservant. She confesses to the police but is not taken seriously. The authorities found Ikuko's diary which made them believe that she killed herself from grief after her husband's death, and that her daughter and Kimura committed suicide in sympathy.

An odd film indeed. Clinical study of despairing masculinity is soon replaced by maverick melodrama and then by black comedy. With its cryptic and flippant story, visual (mainly sexual) symbolism and occasional signs of Western influence, Odd Obsessions can claim to be a description of the vagaries of hypertrophic sexuality--but not really its study. But from the formal point of view the film is almost perfect. Miyagawa's splendid Scope photography, dominated by tones of brown, bluish green and yellow and completely dispensing with coloristic accents, is as suitable to the mood of the film as the camera movements, furtive and sensuous, are suitable to its theme of sickness and perversion. Ganjiro Nakamura as the lecherous and pathetic husband and Machiko Kyo as his entrancing and ambiguous wife, give excellent performances. The same year they appeared, with equally commendable results, as a director of a traveling theatre and his mistress in Ozu's Floating Weeds.

THE VIRGIN SPRING (Jungfrukällan) Ingmar Bergman

Script: Ulla Isaksson, based on the 14th-century ballad "Töres dotter i Vänge." Photography: Sven Nykvist. Music: Erik Nordgren. Art Direction: P.-A. Lundgren. Costumes: Marik Vos. Editing: Oscar Rosander. Cast: Max von Sydow (Töre), Birgitta Pettersson (Karin), Birgitta Valberg (Märeta Töre), Gunnel Lindblom (Ingeri), Axel Düberg (Thin herdsman), Tor Isedal (Mute herdsman), Ove Porath (Boy), Allan Edwall (Beggar), Gudrun Brost (Frida), Oscar Ljung (Simon), Axel Slangus (Old man at river ford).

Carl Anders Dymling for Svensk Filmindustri, Sweden. 87 mins.

The Virgin Spring is a screen version of a medieval ballad about the wickedness of man, told with narrative mastery, but also with brutal naturalism. This time the story is for Bergman a starting point not for a debate about major problems of existence, but for comments about the fragility of moral principles of man who so easily allows himself to be dominated by cruelty, and for reflection on the changeability of religious norms in various historical periods. Also the simplicity of the story is something unusual for the director.

Fourteenth-century Sweden. Three itinerant shepherds rape and murder the daughter of a rich landowner while she rides on a beautiful horse through the forest. Later they seek shelter for the night at the house of the girl's father. When they try to sell to him some of the fine clothes they have stolen from the victim, he guesses what has happened and metes out terrible punishment; he later regrets having killed the herdsmen and promises to build a chapel at the site of the crime; when his daughter's body is lifted off the ground a spring rises at the spot where she was murdered.

The aim of The Virgin Spring was to illustrate the legend literally; this is clearly seen in the painstaking Gothic designs and also in the meticulous fidelity to historical detail and the presumed behavior, custom and the way of thinking of people at the time. Thus the symbols which refer to primitive folk fancies: the envious servant girl conceals a toad in bread her mistress is to take, a raven on a branch as the parents set out to search for their daughter. But even if one is to acknowledge the somber beauty of the film and disregard the one-dimensional character of its message--even then the transposition to the screen of a medieval ballad with all its paraphernalia and in consequence with its drastic violence which becomes extreme in the scene of rape and murder, does not appear convincing. For all its uncommonness one must count The Virgin Spring, together with Bergman's next picture, The Devil's Eye (1960), as one of the least successful efforts in his best period which extended from Summer with Monika to The Silence.

A BOUT DE SOUFFLE (Breathless) Jean-Luc Godard

Script: Godard, based on the idea by François Truffaut. Photography: Raoul Coutard. Music: Martial Solal. Editing: Godard. Cast: Jean-Paul Belmondo (Michel Poiccard), Jean Seberg (Patricia Franchini), Henri-Jacques Huet (Antonio Berrutti), Van Doude (Editor), Daniel Boulanger (Police Inspector), Jean-Pierre Melville (Parvulesco), Claude Mansard (Claudius Mansard), Jean-Luc Godard (Informer), Liliane Robin (Minouche).

Georges de Beauregard/Société Nouvelle de Cinéma, France. 8104 ft., 90 mins.

This is without a doubt the most momentous film for the Nouvelle Vague and a landmark in the development of the cinema. Together with Resnais's Hiroshima mon amour and Antonioni's L'avventura, Godard's film was decisive for the course of the cinema of 60's, but in a different way--not by creating new values, but by destroying the old cinema aesthetics. Twenty-nine-year-old Godard's first film is formally far from perfect and rather trivial in content--but it has the great importance of a manifesto, an inspiration for progress along new paths. It was planned as a film noir about people obsessed with the idea of death (among the editors of "Cahiers du Cinéma," of whom Godard was one, there was much sympathy for this particular genre) but in the course of the four-week shooting the strong personality of Godard, who wanted to use the film as a vehicle for his own ideas about the cinema, made the actual story something of secondary importance. The dominants of A bout de souffle are the narrative style, the implications of situations, the description of the consciousness of the main characters--although the whole is contained within the standard framework of a sensational movie.

Michel, a young loafer steels a car in Marseilles, finds a gun in the glove compartment and kills a policeman who stops him as he drives towards Paris. In the Champs Elysées he seeks out

A bout de souffle

his American girl friend, Patricia, who sells "The Herald Tribune" while studying in Paris. He takes over her flat (or, more correctly, her bed), robs a man to have money for an evening with Patricia whom he tries to persuade to go to Italy with him, and does not seem to be greatly disturbed by the hunt mounted for him by the police. The girl, a rationalist with her head full of fashionable bookish ideas about emotional independence, is fascinated by Michel but afraid of deeper involvement with him. When Patricia denounces him to the police, Michel defiantly rejects a chance to escape and provokes death. Mortally wounded in a street of Montparnasse, he makes funny faces at her and affectionately calls her dégueulasse ("little bitch"). As Patricia asks a policeman what the slang word means, Michel dies.

The structure of the plot alone makes it clear that Godard disagreed with the current ideas about what cinema should be like: the characters do not act according to the classical logic of motivation, which before was a fundamental requirement from the script. This applies even to Patricia, a girl set on making a patient career in life--never mind Michel, who rejects accepted values of society and behaves with unrestrained spontaneity. Michel's independence is nihilistic, not merely anarchistic. He gives expression to the new mythology of freedom understood as boundless authenticity. Destruction of old practices is even more evident in the dialogue, unforgivably marginal from the point of view of traditional dramatic scriptwriting, and not very functional as regards the progress of the plot. At the same time the dialogue describes the psychology of the characters extremely well. Finally the technical aspect. The film is shot almost entirely with a hand-held, highly mobile camera, in the natural scenery of streets and apartments of Paris--and thus opens a new era in cinematography. Some shots are badly exposed, hazy, extravagantly imperfect. Instead of editing with straight cuts (which according to André Bazin, the theoretician of the Nouvelle Vague, destroys the order of reality) Godard joins individual scenes with rapid jump-cuts. Also in other aspects of the narrative he is very individual. This became even more evident in some of his later films, which resemble essays rather than screen dramas.

But the disjointed A bout de souffle is uniform in one aspect: the character of the screen material corresponds to Michel's actions, and the whole picture is a visual equivalent of his way of thinking. This was the whole point: the integration of the modes of cinematic expression, behavior of the actors and, most importantly, the philosophy of the director who wants to express himself, his aesthetic autonomy and his outlook on life. Godard did not intervene into what was recorded by the camera; it is the very heart-beat of life that was to be transferred to the screen. The script of A bout de souffle was very fragmentary and the dialogue is said to have been improvised. Thus the principal ideas of the candid cinéma d'auteur were expressed, common to all films embraced by the term "Nouvelle Vague."

CROSS-EYED LUCK (Zezowate szczęście) Andrzej Munk

Script: Jerzy Stefan Stawiński, from his short story "Sześć wcieleń Jana Piszczyka" (The Six Incarnations of Jan Piszczyk). Photography: Jerzy Lipman and Krzysztof Winiewicz. Music: Jan Krenz. Song "Kriegsgefangenenpost" by Andrzej Markowski and Andrzej Nowicki. Art Direction: Jan Grandys. Editing: Jadwiga Zajiček. Cast: Bogumił Kobiela (Jan Piszczyk), Barbara Kwiatkowska (Jola), Maria Ciesielska (Basia), Aleksander Dzwonkowski (Jan's father), Edward Dziewoński (Jelonek), Tadeusz Bartosik (Wąsik), Krystyna Karkowska (Jola's mother), Jerzy Pichelski (Major), Jan Stanisławski (Scout squad leader), Wojciech Siemion (Personnel manager), Henryk Bąk (Director), Tadeusz Janczar (Sawicki), Kazimierz Opaliński (Prison governor), Irena Stalończyk (Mrs. Kropaczyńska), Wiesław Gołas (State security officer), Wojciech Wityński (Piszczyk as a boy).

ZRF Kamera, Poland. 10,857 ft., 120 mins.

Munk continues his re-examination of the attitudes of his compatriots in a theme much wider than before--and perhaps even too wide for the capacity of a single picture. The background of Cross-Eyed Luck is the panorama of events in Poland starting in the 20's and running until shortly after 1956; the film is a story of the failed life of a certain cross-eyed opportunist. The aim was to make a pamphlet about people who amid changing currents of history always try to find for themselves the safest and the most convenient current. In order for the film not to be poster-like, or a banal satire but a stimulus for reflection, Munk gave his protagonist a number of positive characteristics which were stressed further by Kobiela's brilliant performance. Not without importance is the fact that the narrative was conducted in a flashback, in the form of a confession by the ill-starred Piszczyk (a surname derived from the Polish word for "squeak"). However, these measures turned out to have a double edge: in the final effect unfortunate coincidences play too great a part in Piszczyk's biography. Also, in Munk and Stawiński's vision the interaction of history with a less resistant individual looms too large for the film to be a rationalist tragicomedy with legitimate ethical diagnosis--particularly since the makers treated Piszczyk's triumphs in the post-war Stalinist administration much too emotionally. Further, the grotesque interludes with speeded-up motion and caricatured characters do not add to the film's dramatic coherence. As a consequence Cross-Eyed Luck caused even more controversy in Poland than Munk's earlier Eroica, and the film's meaning was variously interpreted. Munk and Stawiński were criticized, for instance, for attacking short-sighted activity rather than lackey-like opportunism. Outside Poland this picture, filled with references to complex internal social and political events in the course of 25 years, remained almost totally obscure.

SHADOWS John Cassavetes

Photography: Erich Kollmar. Music: Charles Mingus. Editing: Len Appelson and Maurice McEndree. Cast: Lelia Goldoni (Lelia), Ben Carruthers (Ben), Hugh Hurd (Hugh), Anthony Ray (Tony), Rupert Crosse (Rupe), Tom Allen (Tom), Dennis Sallas (Dennis), David Pokitellow (David), Davey Jones (Davey).

John Cassavetes/Maurice McEndree/Seymour Cassel/Nico Papatakis, U. S. A. 87 mins.

Shadows started as a series of improvisations by members of the Variety Arts Studio in New York. Much in the spirit of Stanislavsky's method, Cassavetes, the Studio's director, devised a dramatic situation with the aim of involving a group of white and colored students. It went very well and it was decided to record it on film. The project attracted public subscriptions after it was mentioned on television. The film was made over a long period of time on a very modest budget of $30,000; it was shot with a 16mm camera, then filled out and blown up to 35mm. Shadows was improvised without a proper script. There are no script credits--there was only a story outline which was discussed by the actors before each scene was shot. As the makers could not afford to buy the permission to film in the streets, they had to do such filming furtively. The result is that the picture is not always technically flawless. Cassavetes, until then known only as an actor, had to go to Europe to find a distributor. The British firm, Lion International of London, brought Shadows to the U. S. A. in 1961 where it did quite well commercially. Eventually Cassavetes found the doors of Hollywood open.

Lelia, a girl who can pass for white, moves in artistic-literary circles of New York. She falls in love with Tony, a handsome white boy. When Tony discovers that Lelia's brothers are black and that she is in fact a mulatto, he begins to hesitate and finally leaves her. Lelia shares a Manhattan flat with her brothers Hugh and Ben. Hugh is a night-club entertainer who finds the world of tarts and strippers disgusting and dreams of something better in life. Ben passes the time searching for his identity: a would-be musician, he drifts around in the company of his friends Tom and Dennis. They are beaten by a rival group. Tom and Dennis decide to change their way of life and leave. Ben remains alone.

On its release Shadows was received as a revelation and praised for its fresh and direct portrayal of the New York of would-be intellectuals, musicians and drifters. When viewed now it seems a badly edited, lengthy melodrama. How quickly one forgets that Shadows discarded contemporary convention and was fresh and original in comparison with the hopeless "socially-conscious" Hollywood productions. But some of the original value is retained: one can still sense the spontaneity and authenticity of an improvisation. Shadows is a personal film, very much dominated by Cassavetes's personality. Among the several memorable, complex passages are the scenes of Hugh throwing Tony out of the flat; and Lelia humiliating the black boy with whom she has agreed to go out. A sense of racial tension and of urban loneliness and insecurity are well conveyed with an urgency augmented by grainy photography. Ben is movingly played by Ben Carruthers.

YESTERDAY'S ENEMY Val Guest

Script: Peter R. Newman, from his TV play. Photography: Arthur Grant. Art Direction: Bernard Robinson and Don Mingaye. Editing: James Needs and Alfred Cox. Cast: Stanley Baker (Captain Langford), Guy Rolfe (Padre), Leo McKern (Max), Gordon Jackson (Sgt. McKenzie), David Oxley (Doctor), Richard Pasco (2nd Lt. Hastings), Russell Waters (Brigadier), Philip Ahn (Yamazaki), Bryan Forbes (Dawson), Wolf Morris (Informer), David Lodge (Perkins), Percy Herbert (Wilson), Edwina Carroll (Suni), Barry Lowe (Turner), Alan Keith (Bendish), Howard Williams (Davies), Timothy Bateson (Simpson), Arthur Lovegrove (Patrick), Donald Churchill (Elliott), Nicholas Brady (Orderly), Barry Steele (Brown).

Hammer, G. B. 8581 ft., 95 mins. MegaScope.

Yesterday's Enemy is the most poignant in the series of films about the necessities of wartime and an unofficial summing-up of the polemic on the problem which continued in the world cinema throughout the 50's.

Burma in 1942. Japanese offensive has destroyed a British brigade; a remnant led by Captain Langford is cut off in the jungle. While trying to join up with the core of the force they enter a peaceful-looking village and surprise in it a small enemy detachment. After a violent struggle all the Japanese are killed, among them a colonel with a map onto which the strategy of future actions against the British is coded. A Burmese agent of the Japanese refuses to disclose the key to the code. Langford forces him to do so by making good his threat to shoot two villagers. Having obtained the information which could decide the outcome of the whole campaign, Langford tries to relay it to the headquarters. But his detachment is captured by an enemy patrol, and the Japanese commander uses the same means of repression towards the British which Langford had used towards the Japanese.

In vain cruelty, in vain sacrifice in the name of superior necessity: the finale in which a glib commentary praising the bravery of a British soldier completes the conclusion about the senselessness of the imperial struggles in South-east Asia, sound a note of derision. No less deplorable seems the rationale of the civilians, a chaplain and a journalist, who accompanied the detachment and protested against Langford's actions, measuring the situations of military necessity with a fine yardstick of peacetime ethics. The principal objective of Yesterday's Enemy does not therefore seem to be to weigh out of the rights and wrongs of individual decisions, but to impeach the sense of all wartime attitudes (apart from separately condemning the escalation of violence necessitated by the military way of thinking). This sounds far more bitter than in the anti-heroic films of the Polish School and much more aggressive than in other British and American anti-military productions--but does not rely on cold negation as did many third-rate pictures of the period, but on painful and thorough analysis. This without a doubt gives a convincing tone to a film whose archetypal situations are clearly of stage origin. Of equal importance to the film's impact is Guest's arresting style of direction, frames thick with detail, energetic use of the camera, and high pitch of dramatic tension.

WE DON'T BURY ON SUNDAYS (On n'enterre pas le dimanche)
Michel Drach

Script: Drach, based on the novel by Fred Kassak. Photography: Jean Tournier. Music: Eric Dixon and Kenny Clarke. Editing: Geneviève Winding. Cast: Philippe Mory (Philippe Valence), Christina Bendz (Margaretha Lundahl), Albert Gilou (Courtalès), Hella Pétri (Mme. Courtalès), Marcel Cuvelier (Police commissioner), Robert Lolliot (Police inspector), Frédéric O'Brady (Editor).

Port Royal Films, France. 95 mins.

Philippe, a black student from Martinique and Margaretha, a blond Swede meet at the Grévin Museum in Paris where Philippe works as a guide. When Margaretha returns to France to study at the university, Philippe finds her work as an au pair girl with the family of a certain Courtalès who is interested in publishing his book "We Don't Bury on Sundays." But the love of the young people soon turns into tragedy: first Courtalès seduces Margaretha, then his wife replies in kind with Philippe whom she tells about the situation. When in turn Courtalès hears of his wife's infidelity, he tries to kill Philippe, but instead himself dies in the scuffle; the body is found by the police only eight months later. Margaretha guesses the truth and breaks with Philippe. The police know nothing of his relationship with Mme. Courtalès; the man who interrogates him awaits news from a maternity clinic. Philippe hopes that this will be about Mme. Courtalès and that the child will not be black. But it is Margaretha who gives birth to a white child.

Drach's first film is all told in a flashback and its very structure reflects its personal character, the principal feature of the best works of the Nouvelle Vague. It gained acclaim in the form of the Prix Delluc at the time of the greatest interest in the work of young film-makers. A deserved recognition, although the inner imbalance of this crime drama is beyond question. Drach said that he made the film because he was fascinated by the psychological content of Kassak's novel, a year earlier awarded the Grand Prix for the best French crime novel. Still, the film's melodramatic intrigue, skillful as it is, seems a bow towards commercial cinema and seems but a supplement to what is more interesting in the picture--the impression of loneliness. It is true that this study of loneliness would not alone be sufficient material for a feature and in fact comes to the forefront only in the early sequences--but it is directed very well indeed. Drach later turned into an adherent of poetic half-tone, but got lost in sentimentality and monotonous nuances; here he is expressive and moving. The way of conducting the camera which now hovers above the hero, now looks at the world through his eyes (as in the scenes of his peregrinations around Paris inside a bottle-advertisement), creates a suggestive mood of alienation. A fine complement is the soundtrack--modern jazz and percussion syncopations of Afro-Cuban music; also the manner in which objective soundtrack and internal monologue are juxtaposed. The middle part of the film is less original. Drach copes much worse with the description of feeling, although he communicates well with the non-professional actors and in the end overcomes narrative problems (despite a few errors) even in the difficult latter part of the picture, where it is a sensational drama of action. As marked in the film are the semi-amateur circumstances of production (it was made in 5 weeks for around $55,000) as is the skillful and suggestive film-making by the 29-year-old Drach--an apparent paradox, encountered often in Nouvelle Vague films. But only apparent--the pictures of the young French film-makers were so convincing precisely because they did not use cumbersome professional methods but an intimate style based on personal experience. Directness was thus shown to be as fruitful as the experience of many years.

EYES WITHOUT A FACE (Les Yeux sans visage) Georges Franju

Script: Jean Redon from his novel, adapted by Franju, Redon, Claude Sautet, Pierre Boileau and Thomas Narcejac. Photography: Eugen Schüfftan. Music: Maurice Jarre. Art Direction: Auguste Capelier. Editing: Gilbert Natot. Cast: Pierre Brasseur (Professor Génessier), Alida Valli (Louise), Edith Scob (Christiane Génessier), François Guérin (Jacques), Juliette Mayniel (Edna Gruber),

Béatrice Altariba (Paulette), Alexandre Rignault (Inspector Parot), René Genin (Bereaved father), Claude Brasseur (Policeman).

Jules Borkon for Champs-Elysées Productions/Lux, France/Italy. 90 mins.

Franju followed his startling first feature, La Tête contre les murs, a Kafkaesque drama about the isolation of an individual inside the impassive social machinery, by Eyes Without a Face--an excursion into pure horror.

Professor Génessier, an eminent surgeon, is determined to repair the face of his daughter Christiane, badly disfigured in a car accident for which he feels himself responsible. He does it by abducting, with the help of his assistant Louise, a young girl and grafting her living tissue onto Christiane's face. He fails, although he has already succeeded with a similar operation on Louise. The young victim is thrown in the river, and the professor later identifies the body as that of his daughter. Louise finds a second victim, but the operation again fails--the transplant is immunologically rejected. As a result of the suspicions of Christiane's fiancé, the police plant a decoy as another would-be victim. As the operation is about to begin, the police summon the professor to the adjoining hospital where he is a consultant. Christiane frees the patient, stabs Louise with a scalpel, and releases dogs and birds from their cages in the cellar. The dogs lacerate Génessier's own face and tear him to pieces.

Franju has always been fascinated by strangeness and in Eyes Without a Face he gave full vent to his Gothic imagination. He himself described the film as "a poetic fantasy" and treated the story mainly as an exercise in style, without worrying much about philosophical or social implications. An old desolate mansion, a dark park of leafless trees, hounds baying in the cellar--the film's quaint poetic feel, amplified by Schüfftan's evocative camerawork, makes it an inevitable inclusion in all "Surrealism in Cinema" programs in art theatres. Particularly memorable is the final image of demented Christiane walking into the night with a white bird perching on her outstretched arm. A bird is Franju's favorite symbol of unattainable freedom, one which he uses repeatedly in his work.

It is interesting to see the names of Boileau and Narcejac in the credits. One who is familiar with the idiosyncrasies of these two crime writers, would expect that Eyes Without a Face would be concerned with the problem of identity. Indeed, the exchange of faces and the motif of the living girl being supposedly dead, bring to mind faint echoes of Hitchcock's Vertigo, which was based on their novel. But Franju merely signals these motifs without developing them fully--neither does he enlarge on Génessier's obsession. Eyes Without a Face should not be treated as more than a film of atmosphere--and as such it works very well right from the first scene of Louise's drive, at night, with the body of a hapless victim. Edith Scob gives a haunting performance as Christiane; frail and subtle, she wanders around the big house with covered windows, making furtive phone calls to her fiancé during which she says nothing more than his name. Pierre Brasseur is good as the mad professor. Only Alida Valli is not satisfactory. One is not convinced by her devotion to Génessier, and her acting contains a certain false intensity which entirely spoils her last line of dialogue ("Why did you do it, Christiane").

THE REST IS SILENCE (Der Rest ist Schweigen) Helmut Käutner

Script: Käutner, based on the play "Hamlet, Prince of Denmark" by William Shakespeare. Photography: Igor Oberberg. Music: Bernhard Eichhorn. Art Direction: Herbert Kirchhoff and Albrecht Becker. Editing: Claus Dudenhöfer. Cast: Hardy Krüger (John H. Claudius), Peter van Eyck (Paul Claudius), Ingrid Andree (Fee von Pohl), Adelheid Seeck (Gertrud Claudius), Rudolf Forster (Dr. von Pohl), Boy Gobert (Mike R. Krantz), Rainer Penkert (Major Horace), Heinz Drache (Herbert von Pohl), Charles Regnier (Detective Superintendent Fortner), Richard Allan (Stanley Goulden), Robert Meyn (Dr. Voltmann), Reinhold Nietschmann (Cornelius), Josef Sieber (Factory porter), Werner Schumacher (Factory driver), Joachim Wolff (Cemetery gardener), Erich Weiher (His assistant), Gustl Busch (Innkeeper).

Freie Filmproduktion GmbH., West Germany. 9313 ft., 103 mins.

The post-war period was decidedly lean for the German cinema. For all the unevenness of his work, Helmut Käutner emerged as the principal German director during the last two years of the war and for some fifteen years afterwards. All this on the strength of virtually four films: Romance in the Minor Key (1943), The Last Bridge, The Captain from Köpenick and The Rest Is Silence, a picture which uses the Hamlet allegory to come to terms with the German past. Käutner directed it after returning home from Hollywood where he made two films. The story of Shakespeare's "Hamlet" has been transferred to the screen many times before. The Rest Is Silence, together with Chabrol's Ophelia, made three years later in France, is the most successful attempt to "modernize" the tragedy.

John H. Claudius (the middle initial presumably stands for "Hamlet") spent the war in the United States where he had been sent to pursue his studies by his industrialist father. He is now teaching philosophy at Harvard and has come to Düsseldorf summoned by his uncle to settle details of the will left by his father who died during the war, supposedly killed in an air raid. John's mother Gertrud had soon afterwards married her husband's brother, Paul. John suspects that his father was in fact murdered. With the help of his friend Horace he accumulates circumstantial evidence pointing to Uncle

Paul's guilt. The murder scene is reenacted during the performance of an American ballet company, while John studies the reactions of his mother and uncle. Conclusive proof, in the form of his father's diary, cannot be found--but in the course of a final confrontation Gertrud admits Paul's guilt and shoots him dead.

In his powerful and very well done adaptation Käutner brought out the psychological conflicts of the play very clearly, while not losing any of its brooding quality. An important part in the enjoyment of such films is always in recognizing the familiar characters from the play. In this case this is not very difficult: Laertes is an ex-Nazi; Ophelia does not drown but is confined to a mental asylum as a schizophrenic; the murdered king is a captain of industry; and his ghost contacts Hamlet by telephone. All this is not only perfectly credible but positively compelling. Käutner turns the story into a fascinating, economically staged thriller. There are no forced points to be made--we are given very few facts about the family and invited to draw our own conclusions. Parallels between the past and the present are drawn subtly and Käutner, while not avoiding the subject, steers clear of the temptation of basing the drama solely on the antagonism of people with different attitudes to the Nazi past. Ophelia is charming and Uncle Paul, played by Peter van Eyck in his usual style, is appropriately sinister and malevolent. The sensitive camerawork is a great help in achieving the mood of menace and desolation.

PLEIN SOLEIL (Blazing Sun) René Clément

Script: Clément and Paul Gégauff, based on the novel "The Talented Mr. Ripley" by Patricia Highsmith. Photography: Henri Decaë. Music: Nino Rota. Art Direction: Paul Bertrand. Editing: Françoise Javet. Cast: Alain Delon (Tom Ripley), Marie Laforêt (Marge), Maurice Ronet (Philip Greenleaf), Elvire Popesco (Mme. Popova), Erno Crisa (Inspector Riccordi), Frank Latimore (O'Brien), Bill Kearns (Freddy), Ave Ninchi (Signora Gianna).

Robert and Raymond Hakim for Paris Film Production/Panitalia, France/Italy. 10,817 ft., 120 mins. Eastman Colour.

Clément's technical skill guaranteed success in handling various cinematic genres and convincing imitations of different styles. Plein soleil seems related to the director's favorite psychological dramas, but it is difficult to resist the impression that his other aim was to show ironically to the young film-makers of the Nouvelle Vague how close to the tree of the traditional sensational cinema fall the un-ripe apples of their films. The Nouvelle Vague accused Clément of eclectism and sterility; but French critics rightly pointed out that Plein soleil was precisely the kind of picture that could have been made by Vadim, Chabrol or Molinaro. The recipe was simple enough: assimilate the style of Hitchcock (this Clément did very well in both scenes of murder), set the plot among middle-class young people, preferably during holiday time. Following this recipe Clément quite skillfully did what had been done by many directors of the Nouvelle Vague, more interested in taking over the brushed-up commercial cinema than in new contents. At the same time Clément chose a plot which enabled him to distribute stress quite differently than in the Nouvelle Vague films--to offer a negative image of the whole of the young generation, instead of its individual groups. Philip Greenleaf, an American idler who wastes his time on the Mediterranean coast, is almost as unpleasant as the envious Tom Ripley despatched after him by his rich parents to bring him back to the world of affairs. Ripley finally murders his charge for the sake of money and a girl and begins to impersonate him. Practically everybody in this film is repulsive with the exception of the beautiful Marge who feels most and is the most tragic.

The aggressiveness of this vision would not have been so controversial if Clément was able to support his dislike towards the supposedly totally opportunistic and cynical generation with a reliable distribution of moral judgment. He did not. In his first outstanding part Alain Delon gives the main character a most prepossessing appearance; his Tom Ripley, in contrast to Monsieur Ripois in Clément's Knave of Hearts, fails in the end only because of an unfortunate accident--indeed elsewhere in the picture his cynicism brings nothing but success. A further extenuating circumstance in Ripley's favor is his love of a beautiful girl (Marie Laforêt in her first movie part). It seems therefore that this time the provocative director was seduced by a provocative screen character and his study of a disturbing milieu resulted in a rather disturbing message. The fact that the dramatic structure, mood, the use of scenery and color are all excellent and the only fault of the film craft is its psychologically unconvincing description of the Greenleaf-Ripley relationship, cannot change the final judgment--this film of Clément's has a deceptive and repulsive opalescence.

THE LETTER THAT WAS NOT SENT (Neotpravlennoe pismo) Mikhail Kalatozov

---

Script: Grigori Koltunov, Valery Osipov and Viktor Rozov, from the short story by Osipov. Photography: Sergei Urusevsky. Music: Nikolai Kryukov. Editing: N. Anikina. Cast: Tatiana Samoilova (Tanya), Innokenti Smoktunovsky (Konstantin Sabinin), Vasili Livanov (Andrei), Yevgeni Urbansky (Sergei).

Mosfilm, U.S.S.R. 7920 ft., 88 mins.

This picture sees the team Kalatozov-Urusevsky in pursuit of their creative program outlined by The Cranes Are Flying. The tasks are divided as before: Kalatozov conducts the emotion while Urusevsky visually records dynamic action. In The Letter That Was Not Sent both film-makers found themselves even closer than before to their favorite interests: dramatic struggles of people in critical situations (Kalatozov) and the visual beauty of wild landscapes (Urusevsky). One can say that the film provided an unusual opportunity for them to follow the impulse of their creative temperaments. For it is based on events which took place in Siberian Yakutia during the prospecting for diamond-bearing kimberlite rocks: on the one hand formidable and menacing nature, constantly threatening the lives of the members of a small party; on the other--the passion of the explorers of virgin territories, aware of the great importance of their work. The script combines these violently opposed elements: the party of three geologists and a guide, including a girl, die one by one, but manage to deliver the charts of a discovery.

This was a chance for making a great film. It was not taken up; not only because Kalatozov, bewitched by Urusevsky's talent, allowed him, as once Fernández allowed Figueroa, to dominate the film with photography. Another reason was that the director dismissed psychological portrayal of the characters with a handful of stereotypes, did not put enough work into the dialogues, recklessly segmented the story into loosely joined episodes, and pervaded the whole with excessive emphasis (particularly noticeable, and redundant, in the music which is in fact often creative and modern, but in culminations banally intensifies the "heroism" of the mood). It was not an error to reduce the film's dramatic structure to the conflict between the human being and the elements, to integrate the attitudes of the members of the party and to eliminate conflicts between their sense of duty and the need to survive--after all the protagonists belong to a specific profession, which relies on vocation and on the awareness of risks. But it was surely a mistake not to describe the details of behavior and actions of the members of the expedition. For instance, not enough attention is given to the methodical scientific routine of specimens, maps and tools. Thus human warmth vanished from the film which became a fervent praise of heroism in the name of ideals--especially since although Urusevsky used a subjective visual style, conducting the camera with daredevil bravura and intercutting close-ups of faces with dizzy, trembling visions of the surroundings, all he achieved thereby was an atmosphere of terrifying fever, of hypnotic execution of an order. The intensity and visual beauty of this vision are impressive, but emotion and lyricism are lost in it. Thus, paradoxically, despite being a vehement aesthetic protest against the former stiff and impersonal character of the Soviet cinema, The Letter That Was Not Sent did not achieve its aim of reversing the hierarchy of seeing men and ideas. The film is merely a belated explosion of old passions in a director who had worked in the cinema since the early days of sound. Harmonious association by human intimacy with background events had to be brought by those Soviet film-makers who started without the ballast of the past.

THE LADY WITH THE LITTLE DOG (Dama s sobachkoi) Yosif Kheifits

---

Script: Kheifits, from the short story by Anton Chekhov. Photography: Andrei Moskvin and D. Meskhiev. Music: Nadezhda Simonian. Art Direction: Berta Manevich and Isaak Kaplan. Editing: S. Dereviansky. Cast: Aleksei Batalov (Dmitri Gurov), Iya Savvina (Anna Sergeyevna), Nina Alisova (Gurov's wife), Yuri Medvedev.

Lenfilm, U. S. S. R. 8099 ft., 90 mins.

An adaptation of Chekhov's short story, by a veteran of the Soviet cinema who directed his first film way back in 1928. On the whole Kheifits cannot be described as distinguished; this is not only his best picture, but quite simply the finest screen version of any work by Chekhov until the 70's. The Lady with the Little Dog, a faithful, almost literal treatment of the story, offers an excellent period reconstruction of life in Russia at the turn of the century and faultlessly recreates the mood of the original: a mixture of nostalgia, paralyzing indecision and latent tragedy. The reason for this success was probably the political neutrality of the subject which accorded the director freedom from ideological restrictions and an opportunity for personal expression.

The Crimean resort of Yalta--a favorite with the aristocracy and the professional classes. Dmitri Gurov meets Anna Sergeyevna, who is on holiday accompanied only by her small dog. She is married to an official and lives in a distant provincial town. Dmitri and Anna become lovers, but have to part at the end of the holiday. Dmitri returns to Moscow to his dull wife and suddenly realizes that he is desperately in love with Anna. He travels to her home town and sees her during a concert. They begin to meet secretly in Moscow. "We must, we must find a way" says Anna forlornly; the film ends with her watching from a high window as Gurov leaves her hotel, while a street musician offers his sad pipings.

Chekhov firmly believed that it is not up to the author to provide conclusions. Nothing is ever resolved in his books and neither is it in this dreamy story of impossible love. This is a simple and clear film--elegant and restrained. The film technique is virtually unnoticeable. Good atmospheric photography (by Moskvin who worked on Eisenstein's Ivan the Terrible) contrasts the vistas of snow-bound Moscow overlooked by the onion-bulb roofs of the Orthodox churches with the bare streets of Anna's home town. Aleksei Batalov, one of the most outstanding Soviet actors, is passive and likeable, and Iya Savvina--fragile and charming. Both very well render the desolation of being "like birds of passage caught in separate cages." The Lady with the Little Dog is a film which lingers in one's memory.

STARS (Zvezdi) [German title: STERNE] Konrad Wolf

Script: Angel Vagenshtayn. Photography: Werner Bergmann. Music: Simeon Pironkov. Art Direction: José Sancha. Editing: Christa Wernicke. Cast: Sasha Krusharska (Ruth), Jürgen Frohriep (Walter), Erik S. Klein (Kurt), Stefan Peytchev (Bai Petko), Georgi Naumov (Blashe), Ivan Kondov (Ruth's father), Milka Tuykova (Partisan girl), Stilyan Kunev ("Doctor"), Naitcho Petrov (Police chief), Elena Khranova (Old Jewess), Hannjo Hasse (Hauptmann), Albert Zahn (Sentry).

Studya za igralni filmy (Sofia)/DEFA, Bulgaria/East Germany. 8245 ft., 92 mins.

Autumn of 1943 in a little town in Bulgaria under Nazi occupation. Sergeant Walter, formerly a fine art student, is in charge of the civilian workers in a car-repair workshop. Compared with the life of his friends on the front he is on holiday. But even he has to go through a wartime soul-searching, when a transport of Greek Jews on the way to the Auschwitz concentration camp is provisionally housed at the local school. Ruth, a young teacher who acts as a nurse for the transport, asks him to call a doctor to a woman in labor. At first he refuses, but then, his conscience uneasy, changes his mind; later still he gives further help to the prisoners. But exceptions do not change the course of history: Walter does not succeed in arranging for the beautiful Ruth to escape. Left with the awareness of his own and his compatriots' guilt towards other nations, he decides to help the local Resistance by supplying them with German arms.

The Bulgarian scriptwriter and the German director of Stars met while studying at the Moscow Film School and decided there and then to make the film. Vagenshtayn had been active in the wartime guerrilla movement, while the recurrent motif in Wolf's work is the analysis of the actions of lone individuals at a time of terror and oppression, most often during the Nazi period. This able director never did better than in this first East German/Bulgarian coproduction--owing to simple directorial candor, the serious tone of calm reflection, despite the ornamental exertions of the script, visual symbolism and the Expressionist stylistic elements. Stars is in fact the first picture to give objective and dignified account of the dilemma of honest and sensitive citizens of Nazi Germany, to tell that their awareness could not bring much tangible result at the time but still placed the onus of terrible responsibility on the consciences of those who did not close their eyes to reality.

LE DEJEUNER SUR L'HERBE (Lunch on the Grass) Jean Renoir

Script: Renoir. Photography: Georges Leclerc. Music: Joseph Kosma. Art Direction: Marcel-Louis Dieulot. Editing: Renée Lichtig. Cast: Paul Meurisse (Professor Etienne Alexis), Catherine Rouvel (Nénette), Fernand Sardou (Nino, her father), Jacqueline Morane (Titine, Nénette's sister), Jean-Pierre Granval (Ritou, Titine's husband), Ingrid Nordine (Countess Marie-Charlotte), Robert Chandeau (Laurent), Micheline Gary (Madeleine, his wife), Frédéric O'Brady (Rudolf), Ghislaine Dumont (Magda, his wife), Charles Blavette (Gaspard, the old shepherd), André Brunot (Old curate), Hélène Duc (Isabelle, the secretary), Jacques Dannoville (M. Paignant), Marguerite Cassan (Mme. Paignant), Jean Claudio (Rousseau, the majordomo).

Compagnie Jean Renoir, France. 92 mins. Eastman Colour.

Professor Alexis, the illustrious biologist, is a front-runner for the office of President of a United Europe. He plans to use his research on artificial insemination as a tool in engineering a new responsible society. Alexis is related to major chemical fortunes in France and Germany, and plans to marry the beautiful Countess Marie-Charlotte, head of the international Girl Guide movement. The engagement ceremony takes place in Provence. But the rustic site of the celebration is close to a ruined temple of Diana. A shepherd with his flute sits quietly in the ruins. Suddenly the pipes of Pan sound, a gale blows and the dignified luncheon party is dispersed in chaos. Entranced by the sight of a new maid, Nénette, bathing in the river, the professor drives off with her. It occurs to him for once that happiness may be achieved by submitting oneself to the laws of nature, instead of manipulating them. He likes the life on Nénette's family farm, but is soon found by the authorities and taken back to civilization, science--and to his fiancée. But as he prepares for the wedding he meets Nénette again, learns that she is expecting his child--and decides to marry her instead.

Le Déjeuner sur l'herbe opened to some of the worst reviews ever received by a Renoir picture. The intrigue, superficially referring to topical issues of the time such as artificial insemination and the Common Market, is certainly silly and the conclusion that procreation is more pleasant without the aid of a test tube is unoriginal to say the least. Further, Renoir naively attacks the dictatorship of scientists (*what* dictatorship??) and also includes the theme of conflict between nature and learning--setting easy targets for himself and getting poor marks as a result.

The less said about the picture's intellectual aspect the better. The point is that Renoir used the plot merely as an excuse for playing self-indulgently with the cinema, much as he did earlier in Eléna et les hommes. First and foremost, this is a picture made by a man who loves life. The title is taken from the famous painting by Manet, and the film is clearly intended as a homage to Impressionism. The setting is Les Collettes, the villa where Auguste Renoir lived. Thus Le Déjeuner sur l'herbe continues the themes of Partie de campagne. The tangibility and authenticity of the portrayal of nature on the screen is really splendid. All this seems even more remarkable if one considers that Renoir, who was then experimenting with television techniques, made the film very rapidly, using up to five cameras simultaneously. Rarely before has there been on the screen such pure and sensuous color photography, which makes full use of shimmering lights and half- and quarter-tones, and there has never been such sheer depth of air, a sense of space. This is instinctive cinema which often, by purely visual means, achieves moments of pure lyricism. Catherine Rouvel as Nénette is actually very like the girls in Auguste Renoir's paintings. The freshness and human warmth of Le Déjeuner sur l'herbe, its gentle landscapes of Provence, drowsy summer heat, light-blue skies, are in a pleasant contrast to the sad eroticism of the Nouvelle Vague.

LE SIGNE DU LION (The Sign of Leo) Eric Rohmer

Script: Rohmer. Dialogues: Paul Gégauff. Photography: Nicolas Hayer. Music: Louis Saguer. Editing: Anne-Marie Cotret and Marie-Josèphe Yoyotte. Cast: Jess Hahn (Pierre Wesselrin), Van Doude (Jean-François Santeuil), Michèle Girardon (Dominique), Jean Le Poulain (Clochard), Stéphane Audran (Concierge at Hôtel de Seine), Gilbert Edard (Photographer), Christian Alers (Paul), Françoise Prévost (Hélène), Jill Olivier (Pierre's girl), Jean-Luc Godard (Man listening to gramophone at party).

Roland Nonin for AJYM-Films, France. 90 mins.

A member of the group of intellectuals associated with the "Cahiers du Cinéma," and the journal's former joint editor-in-chief, Rohmer is one of the most interesting directors of the Nouvelle Vague. Born in 1920, he worked as a critic, made short films and wrote a book on Hitchcock in co-authorship with Claude Chabrol. It was Chabrol's company which produced Le Signe du lion, Rohmer's first feature. Made on a small budget of around $84,000, the film was improvised during the shooting. These circumstances remind one of Godard's A bout de souffle, as does the effect of Rohmer's picture.

Pierre Wesselrin, a 40-year-old penniless musician living in Paris, learns that he has inherited a fortune from an aunt. He throws a celebration party on borrowed money and then learns that the inheritance went to a cousin. It is August, Paris is full of tourists and all his friends are gone. Pierre cannot get in touch with his journalist friend, Jean-François, who has been sent abroad. Unable to pay the rent, he has to leave his apartment. He tries to make do by selling some books, but soon runs out of money completely, finally becoming a clochard. Meanwhile, Jean-François and his girl return to Paris and try to get in touch with Pierre. Eventually they find him begging in the street and are able to break the news: his cousin has died in an accident and Pierre has inherited a fortune after all.

Thus Rohmer ends his film on a note of an ironic joke which echoes the finale of Murnau's The Last Laugh. His dominant interest has always been in moral and psychological analysis, and Le Signe du lion is a study of a man's growing isolation from society, of a gradual slide into spiritual disintegration. It is interesting, says Rohmer, how relative are the demarcation lines of respectability, and how easy it is to shed the values instilled by society. Buñuel demonstrated a similar process, albeit in a quite different environment, in Adventures of Robinson Crusoe.

Le Signe du lion offers a precise record of Paris in the summer. The mood of oppression is very well conveyed through impassive observation of ordinary things as they happen. Rohmer has a gift for bestowing a certain special interest on a seemingly marginal observation. This picture is in great part simply a study of boredom. Pierre, a fat, weak-willed but ultimately amiable drifter well played by Jess Hahn, sleeps on park benches, thinks idle thoughts, tries to steal a roll or to fish out a packet of potato crisps from the river--and the camera makes it all appear interesting.

With time Rohmer became one of the leading French filmmakers--a long-term investment of the Nouvelle Vague which paid dividends long after most of its other directors were overtaken by commercialism or fell into obscurity.

THE CROSS OF VALOUR (Krzyż walecznych) Kazimierz Kutz

Script: Józef Hen and Kutz, from the short stories "Krzyż walecznych" (The Cross of Valour), "Pies" (A Dog) and Wdowa po Joczysie" (Joczys's Widow) by Hen. Photography: Jerzy Wójcik. Music: Andrzej Markowski. Art Direction: Roman Mann. Editing: Halina Nawrocka and K. Komosińska. Cast: KRZYŻ (The Cross): Jerzy Turek (Corp. Franciszek Socha), Stanisław Milski (Bartłomiej). PIES (A Dog): Andrzej May (Sypniewski), Aleksander Fogiel (Buśko), Bronisław Pawlik (Florczak). WDOWA (The Widow): Grażyna Staniszewska (Małgorzata), Zbigniew Cybulski (Więcek), Adolf Chronicki

(Ołdak), Jadwiga Hańska (Malgorzata's mother), Zenon Burzyński (Priest).

Tadeusz Karwański for ZAF Kadr, Poland. 7757 ft., 86 mins.

Prior to The Cross of Valour the Polish School concentrated its attention on showing the contribution of non-leftist factions to the liberation of Poland during the war. Such were Kanal and Ashes and Diamonds. The main preoccupation was to devalue false and futile bravery and to explode national heroic myths. The picture of 29-year-old Kazimierz Kutz, who had been Wajda's assistant on A Generation and Kanal, does not conform to the above program and thus opens a new chapter in the Polish cinema: grandiose gestures are confronted with real bravery and justice is given to all who acted out of a sense of conviction and necessity. One might say that the individual parts of The Cross of Valour outline the thematic frames of a series of films to be made by Kutz, Lesiewicz and Różewicz: all three stories deal with heroism as an individual or social imperative, while in each the inspirations and worth of heroism are different. The first story deals with a spontaneous hero and the authority he thereby achieves in a plebeian mentality; the second part refers to the permanent heroism of the sappers, continuous, undervalued and often unnoticed; while the theme of the last story is the agony of model heroism. The film's intention is in fact not only to register a new voice in a continuing dispute on the subject of wartime heroism, but to express the rationale and the way of thinking of the Polish peasant soldiers who fought with the Soviet armies. Kutz follows these people from the meadows on the Bug River in the summer of 1944 to western Poland where, some 18 months later, they somewhat awkwardly embark on a new life. The film begins on a tragic note and ends on the ironic, but always looks at its protagonists with sympathy. Kutz's directorial debut is marred by poor organization of the frame, faults in directing the actors, a certain roughness of cinematic craft and the dialogue which rather obtrusively seeks to promote the director's intellectual concepts. On the other hand the excellent script is developed with considerable invention, with realistic observation and good characterization. But in the final account the most important is the director's personal involvement with the theme, his warm treatment of people and their problems. These things were always of greatest interest to Kutz.

KIKU AND ISAMU (Kiku to Isamu) Tadashi Imai

Script: Yoko Mizuki. Photography: Shunichiro Nakao. Music: Masao Oki. Art Direction: Junji Eguchi. Cast: Emiko Takahashi (Kiku Kawata), George Okunoyama (Isamu, her younger brother), Tanie Kitabayashi (Shigeko, their grandmother), Koji Kiyomura

(Seijiro, a neighbor), Aiko Asahina (Kimie, his wife), Michiko Araki (Miss Matsuda), Masao Oda (Mr. Onodera), Teruko Kishi (Katsu), Seiji Miyaguchi (Doctor), Osamu Takizawa (Man with a camera), Eijiro Tono (Policeman), Rentaro Mikuni (Reporter), Masao Mishima (Chief of touring theatre company).

Daito Eiga, Japan. 10,556 ft., 117 mins. Ultrascope.

After the success of And Yet We Live Imai, the pillar of the socially-conscious trend of the Japanese cinema, made several pictures of local importance such as the anti-militarist The Tower of Lilies (1953) about the tragic life and the death of schoolgirls from Okinawa during the war; Muddy Waters (1953), a social protest in the name of the improvement of the situation of women; Rice (1957) showing the poverty of peasants; and Darkness at Noon (1956), a violent attack on the police and the judiciary system. Mindful of the Neorealist principle that the director's intentions should reach every spectator, Imai fell into melodramatics and aesthetic commonness and never showed original style--but was always highly respected for the effective execution of his films.

The American occupation of Japan lasted until 1952 and left in its trail many half-cast children. Kiku and Isamu is a story of two such children, an 11-year-old girl and her 6-year-old brother. They do not even know whether they had the same father. After their mother dies, the brother and sister are raised by their grandmother in a village in northeastern Japan. The villagers, unaccustomed to half-breeds, treat them with mistrust. The boy is adopted by a family in America, and the girl is left to face life alone. Kiku and Isamu belongs to Imai's best pictures precisely because it does not try to put across fundamental social statements. The camera does not register any particularly important events, and concentrates on the description of a community polarized by the presence of people of a different color of skin. This does not mean that this is a predominantly generic story. Kiku and Isamu does contain a social message, in fact one typical for Neorealism--it promotes solidarity and comradeship without barriers of race or nationality. This time Imai avoids forcefulness in the story and in the execution; it has certainly been made much easier by the dramatically very carefully polished script.

THE MOUSE THAT ROARED Jack Arnold

Script: Roger McDougall and Stanley Mann, from the novel by Leonard Wibberley. Photography: John Wilcox. Music: Edwin Astley. Art Direction: Geoffrey Drake. Editing: Raymond Poulton. Cast: Peter Sellers (Tully/Gloriana XII/Mountjoy), Jean Seberg (Helen),

David Kossoff (Kokintz), William Hartnell (Will), Timothy Bateson (Roger), Macdonald Parke (Snippet), Monty Landis (Cobbley), Leo McKern (Benter), Harold Krasker (Pedro), Colin Gordon (BBC announcer), George Margo (O'Hara), Richard Gatehouse (Mulligan), Jacques Cey (Ticket collector), Stuart Sanders (Cunard Captain), Ken Stanley (Cunard 2nd Officer), Bill Nagy (U. S. policeman), Mavis Villiers (Telephone operator), Charles Clay (British Ambassador), Harry de Bray (French Ambassador), Bill Edwards (Army Captain), Austin Willis (U. S. Secretary of Defense), Guy Deghy (Soviet Ambassador), Robert O'Neill (Reporter).

Carl Foreman for Open Road, G. B. 7459 ft., 83 mins. Technicolor.

The ice of the "cold war" has partly melted, and although some still refer to the nuclear threat in an alarmist mood (as in On the Beach), others resort to satire which previously might have sounded inappropriate. Jack Arnold, hitherto well known as director of terrifying sci-fi visions struck the satirical note with evident pleasure. He had before him a script which without prejudice combined mischievous allegory about the current state of international affairs with Surrealist fantasy in the spirit of Lewis Carroll and the typically British situational humor.

A cheap Californian imitation of its national wine has brought the Duchy of Grand Fenwick to the verge of bankruptcy. The prime minister persuades the Grand Duchess Gloriana XII that the best course is to declare war on the United States, lose it promptly and benefit from an economic miracle as did Germany, Italy and Japan after the Second World War. Accordingly a field marshal is sent to America with a twenty-man army clad in chain-mail. They find New York deserted during an air-raid drill, capture the destructive Q-bomb, its inventor and his beautiful daughter and win the war. America sends an ambassador to the Duchy to negotiate an honorable surrender and undertakes to pull the Californian wine off the market. The bomb is found to be a fake.

For the director this story was a good opportunity for fun-making especially since he had at his disposal Peter Sellers in the triple role of Duchess/Field Marshal/Prime Minister. Whether or not this particular idea was inspired by Alec Guinness's famous multiple appearance in Kind Hearts and Coronets, is not clear; but the fact remains that the results are comparable. The part of Duchess Gloriana emitting her lines in a melancholy contralto would alone suffice to ensure one of the early successes for Sellers. As a whole, The Mouse That Roared is only partially successful; the seams in the story are all too clearly visible, as are the studio designs. On the other hand there are in the film many original ideas, amusing observations--and a lot of unassuming optimism.

THE TESTAMENT OF DR. CORDELIER (Le Testament du Docteur Cordelier) Jean Renoir

Script: Renoir, based on the novel "The Strange Case of Dr. Jekyll and Mr. Hyde" (1886) by Robert Louis Stevenson. Photography: Georges Leclerc. Music: Joseph Kosma. Art Direction: Marcel-Louis Dieulot. Editing: Renée Lichtig. Cast: Jean-Louis Barrault (Dr. Cordelier/Opale), Teddy Billis (Maître Joly), Michel Vitold (Dr. Séverin), Jean Topart (Désiré, the majordomo), Micheline Gary (Marguerite), Jacques Dannoville (Commisaire Lardout), André Certes (Inspector Salbris), Jean-Pierre Granval (Hotel owner), Jacqueline Morane (Alberte), Ghislaine Dumont (Suzy), Madeleine Marion (Juliette), Didier d'Yd (Georges), Primerose Perret (Mary), Gaston Modot (Blaise, the gardener), Raymond Jourdan (Cripple), Sylvianne Margolle (Little girl), Jaque Catelain (Ambassador), Régine Blaess (His wife).

R. T. F. / Sofirad/ Compagnie Jean Renoir, France. Originally 100 mins., cut to 95 mins.

The novel by Robert Louis Stevenson always held a great fascination for film-makers. The materialization of two sides of human personality is an idea which seems written especially for the cinema. Films based on the novel include John S. Robertson's with John Barrymore in the title parts (1920), Rouben Mamoulian's (1932) and Victor Fleming's (1941); among later treatments were Jerry Lewis's *The Nutty Professor* (1963) and Roy Ward Baker's *Dr. Jekyll and Sister Hyde* (1971). The story attracted also Renoir, interested in the conflict between nature and learning (the subject of his chronologically next *Le Déjeuner sur l'herbe*), and in the rivalry between impulse and intellect in man's psyche.

Dr. Cordelier, a Paris physician, has developed a drug which can transform him into his evil alter ego. After a series of vicious attacks on women and children which appear to be linked to a certain evasive Opale, Maître Joly, Cordelier's lawyer, is alarmed to discover that his client has made a new will which names Opale as the sole beneficiary. Opale is in fact Cordelier's evil *Doppelgänger*. But Cordelier finds it increasingly difficult to revert to his normal self when Opale, as it requires steadily increasing doses of the drug. Finally he needs a dose which proves fatal. In death he becomes Cordelier again.

In the late 50's Renoir began to dabble in television: "I want to build a new cinema, brick after brick. I am now moving to TV; my cinema is very intimate and comes out badly in big theatres, but well on the little screen. By shooting with a hidden camera I want to achieve authenticity, the main value of a live-action TV spectacle." Although made for French television, The Testament of Dr. Cordelier was filmed in such a way that it can be shown in cinemas as well. The shooting method was similar to that used by Kurosawa on The Lower Depths: before the cameras began to roll actors were rehearsed, as in the theatre, for 15 days; the actual filming took only 10 days and was broken into scenes rather than shots which is the usual practice. Up to eight cameras placed at different angles and as many microphones were simultaneously used. The sound was recorded directly. The total cost of the picture was only $76,000. To achieve the desired authenticity, Renoir shot much of the film on location in the streets of Paris, which gave these scenes a strange, frightening quality--the effect first discovered by Murnau in Nosferatu. Reportedly the scene in which Opale snatches a baby from the pram was improvised and the camera recorded the real reactions of passers-by. To avoid discovery, only one take of each location scene was made.

While the result is not always technically perfect, it certainly has the immediacy Renoir was so concerned about. He always liked to work with outstanding actors, the most recent example of this being Eléna et les hommes with Ingrid Bergman. Here he uses Jean-Louis Barrault, the famous French actor who mostly appears on the stage, and whose best cinema work was in the films of Marcel Carné. Barrault's performance as Cordelier/Opale is the main value of the picture. At last the tragic dimension of Cordelier is given us on the screen. Like the tragic genius whom he portrays, the actor undergoes a total transformation as soon as he partakes of the wondrous draught. Dr. Cordelier is noble, restrained and distinguished; Opale--blood-curdling and sinister with his oddly gleeful gait and bizarre prancings. In building this character Barrault relies rather on his mime powers than on heavy make-up as is usual. It is largely to his credit that Renoir was able to communicate his ideas.

APPASSIONATA (Taková láska) Jiři Weiss

Script: Pavel Kohout and Weiss, from the play by the former. Photography: Václav Hanuš. Music: Ludwig van Beethoven (sonata "Appassionata"). Art Direction: Oto Janeček and Karel Skvor. Cast: Marie Tomášová (Lída Matysová), Miloš Nedbal (Man in the Gown), Svatopluk Matyáš (Milan Stibor), Vladimír Ráž (Petr Petrus), Marie Vášová (Milan's mother), Jarmila Smejkalová (Dr. Petrusová), Jiřina Seibalová (Lída's mother), Felix le Breux (Tenor), František Vnouček (Drvota), Bedřich Karen (Dean), Taťana Vavřincová (Clerk), Alena Kreuzmannová (Majka).

Filmove Studio Barrandov, Czechoslovakia. 80 mins.

An examination of consciences conducted by an advocate of universal justice, a symbolic man in a lawyer's gown, on the people involved in a tragic love affair which ended in the suicide of a girl student. The aim of Appassionata is to determine who was guilty. Was it the girl herself, when one day before marrying the man who loved her she followed the memories of a love of five years previously, without regard to the fact that she was destroying a family? Was it the girl's mother who was too insistent in persuading her to make "a good match" and who turned her daughter out of the house when she became involved with a married man? Or was it the fault of the two undecided men: the would-be husband and the lover submissive to the pressures of the environment? The deceived wife who seemed to place her dignity above everything else? Or finally perhaps the entire middle-class environment which constantly usurps the right to moralize and unceremoniously intrudes in one's private life? The verdict of the man in a gown is that everybody was guilty.

The original formula of moral examination of people involved in a tragedy allowed Weiss's film to avoid the dangers of a melodrama. In fact there was a more serious potential danger stemming from the theatrical pedigree of the script, particularly as concerns the gowned man character, whose stage origin is quite evident. Still, it would have been hard to do without it. Weiss had thus the task of combining fire and water and making up for the use of a theatrical character by unusual narrative effects. The experiment was only a partial success: the Expressionist lighting and slanted frames seem outdated; even Beethoven does not accord full support. On the other hand, the ease with which the complicated narrative structure is handled, the energetic editing and the very suggestive mood are to the film's credit. The good points prevail, making Appassionata one of the most interesting psychological dramas of the late 50's. Despite the gowned man's final verdict this is a film of open questions. Still, for all the makers' belief in the primary character of love (when allowed to make a choice again, the heroine does the same although now she knows the consequences) they wanted not only to praise a feeling, but also to attack obscurantist ideas on morality, the institution of marriage, and the distinction between public and private life. It is worth noting that Weiss's previous picture, Wolf Trap (1957) which brought him international recognition and the Fipresci Prize at the Venice Film Festival, already showed him as a critic of bourgeois mentality. The author of the play said he addressed it to all those who claim the right to treat the lives of others as a spectacle. They are shaken by a tragedy--but forget about it overnight. This aspect quite unexpectedly links the seemingly anachronistic picture of the 46-year-old Weiss with the program of the French Nouvelle Vague, and partly with the new Czechoslovak cinema of a few years later. They have in common the criticism of the middle class intelligentsia and a praise of great and independent love.

THE BRIDGE (Die Brücke) Bernhard Wicki

Script: Michael Mansfeld and Karl-Wilhelm Vivier, from the novel by Manfred Gregor. Photography: Gerd von Bonin. Music: Hans-Martin Majewski. Art Direction: Peter Scharff and Heinrich Graf Brühl. Editing: C. O. Bartning. Cast: Fritz Wepper (Albert Mutz), Michael Hinz (Walter Forst), Frank Glaubrecht (Jürgen Borchert), Karl Michael Balzer (Karl Horber), Günther Hoffmann (Sigi Bernhard), Volker Lechtenbrink (Klaus Hager), Volker Bohnet (Hans Scholten), Cordula Trantow (Franziska), Wolfgang Stumpf (Stern), Günter Pfitzmann (Cpl. Heilmann), Siegfried Schürenberg (Lt.-Colonel), Heinz Spitzner (Cpt. Fröhlich), Ruth Hausmeister (Mrs. Mutz), Eva Vaitl (Mrs. Borchert), Edith Schulze-Westrum (Mrs. Bernhard), Hans Elvenspoeck (Mr. Forst), Trude Breitschopf (Mrs. Forst), Klaus Hellmold (Mr. Horber), Edeltraut Elsner (Barbara), Inge Benz (Sigrun).

Hermann Schwerin for Fono-Film/Jochen Severin, West Germany. 106 mins.

April 1945, the agony of Hitler's Reich. As German armies are collapsing, younger and younger recruits are drafted. Seven 16-year-old schoolboys in a small town receive their call-up papers; having been indoctrinated for years by Nazi propaganda, they are overjoyed and look forward to the army as an exciting change from dull provincial routine. Barely trained, they are assigned to the comparatively easy task of defending the town's bridge; but their commander is killed and they are left alone. When American tanks unexpectedly appear, they knock out two of them at first, but when the Americans attack, five boys are killed. As German sappers prepare to blow up the bridge, one of the two remaining schoolboys, seeing that their bravery was in vain, shoots a German soldier and is himself killed. The only survivor, shaken and bewildered, returns to the town as white flags of surrender begin to appear.

The third picture of Käutner's former assistant does not examine the reasons for the war or the motivation of the fighting sides. It accuses war, perhaps conventionally, but nonetheless with considerable force, by showing it to be senseless. The first part of the picture, portraying the demoralized and corrupt population of the town is stereotyped and of little interest; the film's main value lies in the forceful scenes of the carnage on the bridge. While earlier in the film Wicki included a suggestion of the "good German" versus "bad German" stereotype, he does not load the main issue: we are not expected to sympathize with the boys, the committed Nazis, but to reflect on the painful central situation--the death of six misguided youngsters, which is clearly pointless and absurd.

LOTNA Andrzej Wajda

Script: Wojciech Zukrowski and Wajda, from the short story by the former. Photography: Jerzy Lipman. Music: Tadeusz Baird. Art Direction: Roman Wołyniec. Editing: Janina Niedźwiedzka and Lena Deptuła. Cast: Jerzy Pichelski (Captain Chodakiewicz), Adam Pawlikowski (Lieutenant Wodnicki), Jerzy Moes (Ensign Grabowski), Mieczysław Łoza (Sergeant-Major Latoń), Bożena Kurowska (Ewa).

Stanisław Adler for ZAF Kadr, Poland. 8010 ft., 89 mins. Agfacolor.

Wajda falls off a high horse: Lotna is one of cinema's most remarkable would-be masterpieces. September 1939; Poland is fighting a losing battle against the invading Nazi armies; infantry and detachments of the proud Polish cavalry are despatched to fight against advancing tanks. The film tells a story of a cavalry squadron, whose commander is given a beautiful mare called Lotna ("volatile") by a bed-ridden, solitary aristocrat, owner of a country estate. The horse, a symbol of fate which awaits the men, changes owners as the squadron melts in the fighting. At the end of the film the decimated squadron disbands; Lotna breaks a leg and has to be shot. The last two men to ride her abandon their dead and their country to head towards the frontier.

If told directly, Lotna would have been, like its literary original, no more than an anecdote from a world which vanished forever in 1939. But Wajda intended the picture to be a complex tangle of allusions and metaphors about Poland after the collapse of the prewar order. Certain fragments of his vision have great power and splendid accuracy of aim (for instance the scene in which a soldier of low birth accepts Lotna as a sign of leadership from the hands of a better born) while other fragments are not sufficiently thought-out and sometimes do not correspond with the actual events of the September Campaign. That part of the picture which amounts to the most radical statement in the anti-heroic trend of the Polish School--completely misfires. On the one hand Lotna is a ravishing film to watch, with its pastel tonality of the photography, its golden autumnal landscapes, limpid skies, sepia night sequences--it is in fact Wajda's visually most refined work before the much later Birch Wood and The Shadow Line. On the other hand, it contains a number of provocative images of extravagant Surrealist imagery whose aesthetics jar badly, apart from being in conflict with the film's overall pictorial style. Lotna is full of obsessively recurring images of death of men and animals: the Captain's body is carried past the butcher hacking with a cleaver at a meat carcass; the scene, clearly inspired by Greed, in which a bride's veil catches on a funeral bier; a fallen horse being run over by a tank; throbbing silvery fishes lying on a kitchen table; a coffin full of apples. On the one hand Lotna fascinates

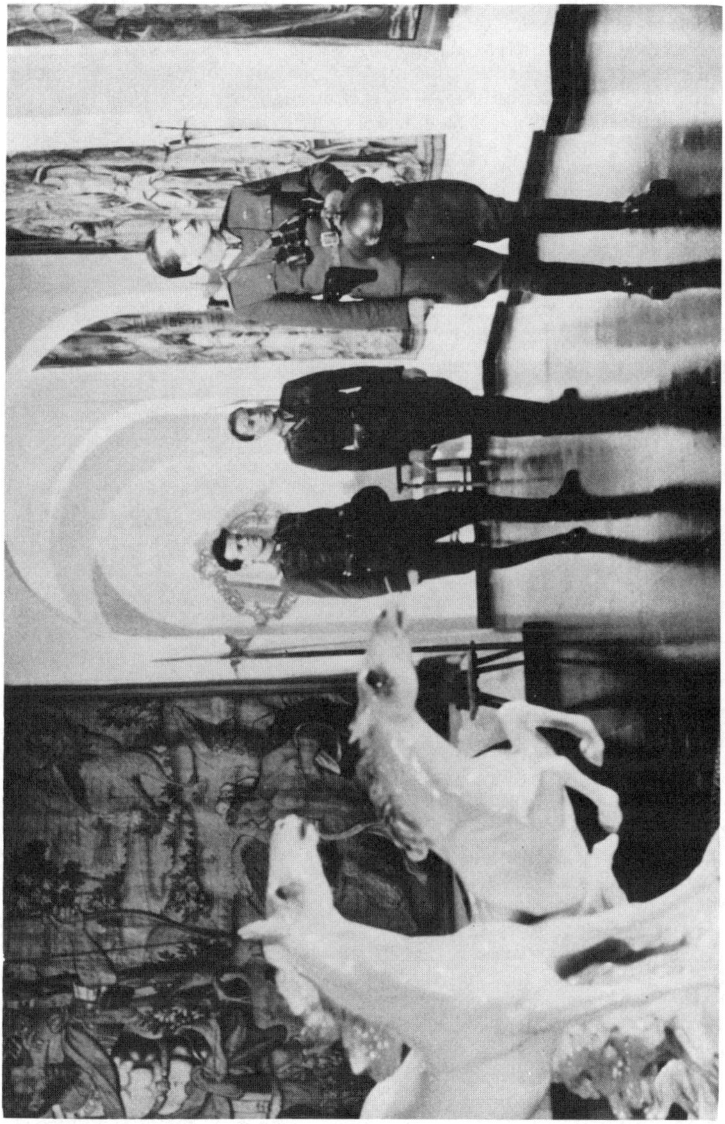

Lotna

with its poetic, dreamlike atmosphere, but on the other suffers occasionally from incompetent staging, wooden acting and the tendency to abortive symbolism, often verging on the ridiculous, a quality characteristic of the first decade of Wajda's work. Take the shot of a burning stuffed eagle, the significance of which escapes those who do not know that an eagle is the emblem of Poland. It is indeed difficult to find a picture which would give rise to as many contradictory feelings as Lotna.

LOS GOLFOS (The Delinquents) Carlos Saura

Script: Mario Camus, Saura and Daniel Sueiro. Photography: Juan Julio Baena. Music: "Petenera" played on the guitar by Perico el del Lunar; also Ramirez Angel and J. Pagán. Art Direction: Enrique Alarcón. Editing: Pedro del Rey. Cast: Manuel Zarzó (Julián), José Luis Marín (Ramón), Oscar Cruz (Juan), Juanjo Losada ("El Chato"), Ramón Rubio (Paco), Rafael Vargas (Manolo), Maria Mayer (Visi), Arturo Ors, Teresa González, Lola García, Angel Calero, Miguel Merino, Carmen Sánchez, Maruja Lázaro, Abelardo Díaz Caneja, Francisco Vernal, Antonio Belices.

Pedro Portabella for Films 59, Spain. 8100 ft., 90 mins. Wide screen.

In Buñuel's Los olvidados there was a scene in which a group of boys play at bull-fighting. The theme of Los golfos recalls this moment. But the tone is different: Los golfos is not an apocalyptic vision of hell as was Los olvidados, but an ironic drama of dashed aspirations.

A group of delinquents live in the slums of Madrid: some are sons of poor families, some immigrants from sun-drenched villages of Andalusia. They receive no attention from anybody except the police. They decide to help their friend Juan, who has so far worked as a laborer at the market, to fulfill his ambition to become a bull-fighter. To collect the money for his debut they commit a series of thefts. On the eve of the fight Paco is recognized by a truck driver they once robbed and is drowned in a sewer while trying to escape. Shocked by their friend's death the rest go to the arena where Juan awaits his triumph. But the fight is a disaster: Juan is jeered by the crowd. It is only with great difficulty that he succeeds in killing the bull. "It is hard to become somebody here," one of the protagonists remarked wistfully. Nothing has changed in their lives, and the bull's squalid death is a wry comment on their future prospects.

Throughout the 50's Spanish art cinema was identified with

the names of Bardem and Berlanga. There was also Buñuel, who for many years worked abroad, and only briefly returned to Spain at the beginning of the 60's to make Viridiana. Then the next generation makes its presence felt: Saura, born in 1932, a film school graduate, with Los golfos, and the Italian-born Marco Ferreri with The Wheel-Chair. Los golfos, a modest but ambitious picture, strikes with its directness and lack of pretension. It was made in a semi-documentary style, entirely on location and with a mostly non-professional cast. Saura displays a talent for observing the background and gives his film assurance and vigor, punctuated by occasional touches of poetry. He is at once objective and sympathetic towards his protagonists. Note in this respect the cross-cut scenes of Juan training at the bull-ring while his friends raise money for his dream to come true. The final sequence is powerful and excellent. The exalted rite of bull-fighting, a sacred, quasi-religious national tradition, has never before been shown with such disillusioned irreverence.

1949

SUPPLEMENT

CINDERELLA Wilfred Jackson, Hamilton Luske and Clyde Geronimi

---

Script: Kenneth Anderson, Ted Sears, Homer Brightman, Joe Rinaldi, Bill Peet, Harry Reeves, Winston Hibler and Erdman Penner, from the fairy tale "Cendrillon ou la Petite Pantoufle de verre" in the collection "Histoires ou Contes du temps passé" (alternative title: "Contes de ma mère l'Oye") by Charles Perrault (1697). Designs and Animation: Eric Larson, Ward Kimball, Norman Ferguson, Marc Davis, John Lounsbery, Milt Kahl, Wolfgang Reitherman, Les Clark, Oliver Johnston Jr. and Franklin Thomas (Directing animators); Marvin Woodward, Hal Ambro, George Nicholas, Hal King, Judge Whitaker, Fred Moore, Hugh Fraser, Phil Duncan, Cliff Nordberg, Ken O'Brien, Harvey Toombs and Don Lusk (Character animators); Dick Anthony, Merle Cox, Ralph Hulett, Brice Mack, Ray Huffine, Art Riley and Thelma Witmer (Backgrounds); A. Kendall O'Connor, Thor Putnam, Charles Philippi, Tom Codrick, Don Griffith, McLaren Stewart, Lance Nolley and Hugh Hennesy (Layout); George Rowley, Joshua Meador and Jack Boyd (Effects animation); Claude Coats, Mary Blair, Donald Da Gradi and John Hench (Color and styling). Special Processes: Ub Iwerks. Music: Oliver Wallace and Paul J. Smith. Songs: "Bibbidi Bobbidi Boo," "So This Is Love," "A Dream Is a Wish Your Heart Makes," "Cinderella," "The Work Song" and "Sing, Sweet Nightingale" by Mack David, Jerry Livingston and Al Hoffman. Voices: Ilene Woods (Cinderella), William Phipps (Prince Charming), Eleanor Audley (Stepmother), Rhoda Williams and Lucille Bliss (Stepsisters), Verna Felton (Fairy Godmother), Luis Van Rooten (King/Grand Duke), James Macdonald (Jacques/Gus), Don Barclay, Claire DuBrey.

Walt Disney Productions, U. S. A. 6692 ft., 74 mins. Technicolor.

The period after the making of Snow White and the Seven Dwarfs saw the steady growth of Disney's film company. It was soon to become a real empire. Apart from cartoon films for exhibition in cinemas and on television, Disney began to make features for the young as well as excellent documentaries about the animal world. As far as feature-length cartoons are concerned he undertook several formal experiments: he tried to apply the concept used in Fantasia to popular music; he also attempted to combine live actors with cartoon characters. Yet none of these projects was a complete success--neither were Disney's film versions of fairy-tales: Pinocchio (1940), Dumbo (1941) and Bambi (1942). The last-named is very interesting as a pictorial concept of animal characters, disastrous as far as the story goes. But in 1950 Disney began to transfer to screen, methodically, at great expense and always with reliable results, the best known children's books. In fact he did not allow himself a single sub-standard product. Cinderella, the first in this series is, for all its offenses against good taste, one of the best Disney films. Rather unexpectedly, this is due to the little mice which live in the heroine's house. In the whole of Disney's cinema only the fanciful creatures of Alice in Wonderland and the metamorphoses of Wart in The Sword in the Stone can compete with the rodents which so cleverly help Cinderella make her dreams come true. If only all the characters in Cinderella were designed so dynamically and with such originality! Alas, the heroine herself seems somewhat insipid, the Prince is clearly impossible to fall in love with and the two wicked sisters with their mother are too wicked for anyone to laugh. At most they can give sadistic pleasure. This time even the universal rule that negative characters are easier to portray than positive ones failed, both are here fairly mediocre. Still, the characters without which a Disney movie would not be itself remain: the domestic mice already mentioned and a crowd of other animals. The whole menagerie is set in motion with unfailing precision, kinetically and dramatically. The synchronization of sound and movement, always remarkable in Disney, is particularly impressive. Yet the greatest trumps of the director are--as always--the ability to create mood and bring out emotion, to serve always new and fresh jokes. For all its lack of balance (the palace sequence is particularly objectionable) Cinderella still offers a lot of praiseworthy elements of the craft of the best director in children's cinema.

TWELVE O'CLOCK HIGH Henry King

Script: Sy Bartlett and Beirne Lay Jr., from the novel by Lay and Bartlett. Photography: Leon Shamroy. Music: Alfred Newman. Art Direction: Lyle Wheeler and Maurice Ransford. Cast: Gregory Peck (General Savage), Hugh Marlowe (Lt.-Col. Ben Gately), Gary Merrill (Col. Davenport), Millard Mitchell (General Pritchard), Dean Jagger (Major Stovall), Paul Stewart (Capt. "Doc" Kaiser), Robert

Arthur (Sgt. McIllhenny), John Kellogg (Major Cobb), Robert Patten (Lt. Bishop), Lee MacGregor (Lt. Zimmerman), Don Hicks (Lt. Wilson), Sam Edwards (Birdwell), Roger Anderson (Interrogation Officer), John Zilly (Sgt. Ernie), William Short (Lt. Pettinghill), Richard Anderson (Lt. McKessen), Joyce MacKenzie (Nurse), Lawrence Dobkin (Capt. Twombley), Kenneth Tobey (Sentry).

Darryl F. Zanuck for 20th Century-Fox, U. S. A. 11,914 ft., 132 mins.

During the Second World War, the 918 Bomber Group of the U. S. Air Force, stationed in England, is taking part in daylight bombing raids. The crews are cracking up because of the merciless pressure of missions, heavy losses and also because their commander, Colonel Davenport, "over-identifies" with his men and seems more concerned with the losses than with winning the war. Davenport is relieved of his post and replaced by a martinet General (Gregory Peck) determined to restore the shattered morale. Leave is curtailed, bar closed, discipline enforced rigidly. At first all the pilots apply for a transfer but later realize that their new commander is worth supporting. Savage achieves the desired results but only at the price of his own collapse.

The years 1949-50 brought Henry King's two best films: the war drama Twelve O'Clock High (the title is a description of a plane's position in the sky) and the western The Gunfighter. Both pictures contain very good performances from Gregory Peck. The combination of a concentrated, reliable and un-sentimental script, King's efficient direction and the sense of purpose and conviction permeating Peck's performance and also that of Dean Jagger as his adjutant (who won an Oscar for the part) made Twelve O'Clock High one of the most interesting studies of personal relationships under the strain of combat.

INDEX OF DIRECTORS

This index lists the names of all directors appearing in this volume ("Journey Two," The Fifties) whose films are discussed as separate entries in this or other volumes. Directors whose films are mentioned in passing are not included.

The chronological list of films after the page reference(s) under each director's name contains all relevant films in the period covered by the text. If a film is discussed in the book as a separate entry, it is marked with an asterisk (*) and if the original title of such a film is in a language other than English, it is given in parentheses following the English title.

For a film merely mentioned, only the English title--or the title used in English-speaking countries--is given (without an asterisk). (Note that for some films, e.g. Alexandre Astruc's two, the original, or foreign-language, title is also the one used in English-speaking countries.)

INDEX OF FILMS

This index lists the titles of all films appearing in the text of this volume.

If a film is discussed as an entry of its own in this or other volumes, it is marked with an asterisk (*) and if the original title of such a film is in a language other than English, it is given in parentheses following the entry under the English title; it is also entered in the index under the original title with the English version in parentheses.

For a film merely mentioned in the text, only the one title used in English-speaking countries is given (without an asterisk). (Note that for some films, e.g. A bout de souffle, the original, or foreign-language, title is also the one used in English-speaking countries.)

Alphabetization is without regard to initial definite or indefinite articles in any language.

Pages constituting an entire entry devoted to a particular film are underscored.

Films whose titles are similar to others are further identified by the director's name in brackets.